D0609500

# LOEB CLASSICAL LIBRARY

FOUNDED BY JAMES LOEB 1911

EDITED BY

## JEFFREY HENDERSON

# LIVY

# IX

## LCL 295

# LIVY

## HISTORY OF ROME

### BOOKS 31–34

EDITED AND TRANSLATED BY

### J. C. YARDLEY

INTRODUCTION BY

### DEXTER HOYOS

HARVARD UNIVERSITY PRESS
CAMBRIDGE, MASSACHUSETTS
LONDON, ENGLAND
2017

*First published 2017*

LOEB CLASSICAL LIBRARY® is a registered trademark
of the President and Fellows of Harvard College

Library of Congress Control Number 2016957655
CIP data available from the Library of Congress

ISBN 978-0-674-99705-9

*Composed in ZephGreek and ZephText by
Technologies 'N Typography, Merrimac, Massachusetts.
Printed on acid-free paper and bound by
Maple Press, York, Pennsylvania*

# CONTENTS

# PREFACE

The following three volumes are a replacement of Evan T. Sage's editions of Livy's fourth decade (Books 31–40). Sage's volumes 9, 10, 11, and 12 (the last of which contained his Book 40 and was completed by Alfred C. Schlesinger after Sage's death) appeared between 1935 and 1938. During the nearly eighty years since Sage's editions, much work has gone into reestablishing Livy's text (in particular, there have been Oxford and Teubner texts of the whole decade and Budé editions of individual books), and as a result Sage's text and the accompanying translation are both somewhat dated. A completely new edition was therefore thought to be needed, and not only of Sage's volumes but of the whole of the Loeb Livy, which was the work of four different editors/translators (B. O. Foster, Frank Gardner Moore, Evan T. Sage, and Alfred C. Schlesinger) over a period of forty years (1919–1959). This volume and the two that follow are the start of that process of replacement. It seemed advisable for the fourth decade to appear together in the three volumes, and so Book 40 has been withdrawn from its erstwhile position in volume 12 and now appears in volume 11.

The text used for the three volumes of the fourth decade is that of John Briscoe's two-volume Teubner edition (see bibliography), though there are some variations. In particular, in order to maintain the flow of the narrative, I have in places been somewhat cavalier in the acceptance of readings where Briscoe has shown justifiable caution. The textual notes are, following the Loeb style, limited, and for the most part restricted to where my text deviates from Briscoe's or where a variant reading that must be taken seriously might affect the translation of the Latin. This has meant consulting the Oxford texts of McDonald for Books 31 to 35 and Walsh for Books 36 to 40, Walsh's individual editions of Books 36 to 40, the various Budé editions that have appeared to date for the decade, and, of course, Sage's original Loeb editions (see bibliography). For the most part, the textual notes focus on places where these editions diverge, and where an emendation seems to be generally accepted there may be no note provided. For the sigla I have unashamedly adopted those of Briscoe. (The text of the *Periochae,* which, as in the earlier Loeb editions, follows the text and translation of the relevant book, is that of Paul Jal's Budé edition.)

The translation is a much revised version of that which I provided for the Oxford World's Classics series (see bibliography). It has been adapted to suit what I perceive to be a somewhat different readership from OWC, one that will range from those with only a slight or no grasp of the Latin language to practicing classical scholars and ancient historians, who know it well. I have tried to maintain readability while at the same making the English conform more closely to the Latin than did my OWC. I thank Oxford University Press and Judith Luna, former commissioning editor of the World's Classics series, for not only permitting me to use the translation but even encouraging me to do so.

The notes for the translation presented me with a challenge. They are, of course, intended to help the reader understand what Livy is saying, but a glance at John Briscoe's three superb commentaries on the decade will reveal that there are problems that cannot be adequately dealt with in the small compass of a Loeb note. Where a more detailed explanation is needed for textual, historical, or linguistic problems, I have often referred the interested reader to the relevant section of Briscoe's commentaries (the extent of my indebtedness to them will quickly become clear) and also (for Books 36–40) to those of P. G. Walsh. In the case of some magistrates, usually those most prominent in the narrative, I have followed Broughton's practice in *MRR* of giving in parentheses the number of the article to be found under the family name in *RE*. I have not usually included in my annotation persons who appear only once or twice or do not figure prominently in the work. Given the Loeb policy of ever keeping in view the nonspecialist reader, I have made considerable use of, and reference to, the latest edition of the *Oxford Classical Dictionary* (2012).

I have made extensive use of the *Barrington Atlas of the Greek and Roman World,* assuming that some readers may be as unfamiliar as I was with the geography of Roman campaigns that range from Spain and North Africa through the Mediterranean to the Middle East. Grid references are not given for many places that I assume are well known, nor for a number that have no significant role in the narrative or are not noted by *Barrington* or whose location remains unknown. For ease of reference, I have, for Greece and the East, occasionally added in brackets the Greek form as it appears in the Atlas. For Spain I have also consulted, and referred to, the Union Académique Internationale *TIR* (Tabula Imperii Romani) publications. For the topography of Rome I have used and cited L. Richardson, Jr.'s, *A New Topographical Dictionary of Ancient Rome* (an update of Platner-Ashby's topographical dictionary of the city), which is very useful, but the figures often require a magnifying glass.

In citing other authors for cross-reference, I have used the Loeb texts, where they are available.

I must end with thanks to those who have helped and encouraged me over the past few years, beginning with Richard Thomas and Jeffrey Henderson, who first invited me to take on the project. Jeff, whom I have long been plaguing with incessant questions, has always been immensely helpful and efficient in supplying me with information. Also, I am very thankful to him for suggesting Mike Wheeler, a freshly graduated PhD student in Classics at Boston University, to undertake a thorough check of the text against Briscoe's original. Mike laboriously worked his way through the whole decade and found many malformations resulting from an initial scan of Briscoe that I had missed despite numerous readings of the text. I hope that none have survived and of course I must, as the final arbiter, assume full responsibility for any that may have done.

Aware that the Loeb of Livy's fourth decade would benefit from an introduction by a professional ancient historian, I (with the agreement of Richard and Jeff) invited Dexter Hoyos, with whom I had enjoyed two earlier Livy collaborations, to provide one, and I express my gratitude to Dexter for vastly improving the work by acceding to that request. For help with Spanish and Macedonian matters, I owe a debt of gratitude to two friends: Evan Haley for Spain and Waldemar Heckel for Macedonia. Finally, a warm thank you to two more friends: Christopher Kelk for his help in checking the indices of the three volumes, and Reg Harris for always being ready to assist me with my many computer problems.

J. C. Y.
June 2016

# INTRODUCTION

## OUTLINE

# INTRODUCTION

## 1. *AB URBE CONDITA:* STRUCTURE[1]

"I feel like someone who wades out into the depths after being initially attracted to the water by the shallows of the sea at the shoreline; and I foresee any advance only taking me into even more enormous, indeed bottomless, depths, and that this undertaking of mine, which seemed to be diminishing as I was completing the earliest sections, is now almost increasing in size." So comments a slightly alarmed Livy at the start of the fourth decade of his history (31.1.5), and he was correct about its steady expansion. The next 170 years, down to 30–29 BC with the suicides of Antony and Cleopatra and the reunification of the Roman empire under Caesar Augustus' sole rule, would take another 103 books, and he then wrote 9 more (Books 134–142) to tell the first two decades of the Augustan era.

Although Livy had not foreseen this exponential growth, he remained committed to his "rash promise to cover all Roman history" (31.1.2), fortunately surviving into his late seventies to complete the task. On average each surviving book of *Ab Urbe Condita* consists of fifty-five to sixty "chapters" (in effect, long paragraphs), and the thirty-five books that remain—1 to 10 and 21 to 45—are together nearly as long as Edward Gibbon's *Decline and Fall of the Roman Empire.* Even if the Augustan books were shorter (they narrated chiefly the wars of 29–9 BC, as surviving résumés, called *periochae,* show), the full

[1] All dates are BC unless marked AD.

work will have been four times as long: perhaps the longest sustained oeuvre in Greek and Roman literature.[2]

It is generally accepted that Livy laid out *AUC* in groups of five and ten books (pentads and decades), at any rate after Book 1, which on its own covered the City's era of kings, starting with 753 or 751 (Livy is ambivalent) and ending in 510; then *AUC* 2 to 5 narrated events down to 390. Each pentad and decade aimed to deal with a coherent period of Roman history or at least to end at a notable moment. This coherence was not always achieved: Book 5 does take the early Republic down to the harrowingly memorable sack of Rome by a Gallic army in 390, but Book 10 ends at 293 in the middle of a lengthy sequence of Italian wars. More neatly, the third decade, chapters 21 to 30, narrates the famous Second Punic War from 218 to 201 (the war against Carthage and Hannibal), and its successor, Books 31 to 40, covers the next twenty years, to close with the death of the Macedonian king Philip V—Rome's old antagonist—and the accession of his son Perseus. The years 179 to 167 are the subject of the last extant pentad, 41 to 45, with one of its leading themes the growing hostility between Rome and Perseus that ended in the defeat and partition of Macedon.

[2] Livy was born in 59 and died in AD 17, according to St. Jerome (*Chronicle,* Olympiads 180.2, 199.1); in 64 BC and AD 12, suspects Syme, *Livy and Augustus,* 40–42, 50. Debate continues: Mineo, *A Companion to Livy,* xxxiii; B. Levick, in Mineo, *op. cit.,* 25; L. Bessone, in Mineo, *op. cit.,* 426–27, noting too the occasional view that Livy originally intended a 150-book *AUC,* closing with Augustus' death.

As the history grew, bringing Livy nearer to his own lifetime and multiplying enormously his sources of information, the pentad-decade pattern became harder to maintain, and probably seemed unnecessary too. Thus (for example) Book 70, as its later epitome shows, narrated the years 99 to 91, a period relatively quiet both at home and abroad; but Books 71 to 76 then dealt in detail with the turbulent events of 91 to 89 BC, dominated by the great revolt of Rome's dissatisfied fellow Italians. The destructive civil and foreign wars that ensued from 88 to 80 were covered in Books 77 to 89, again far from any sort of pentadic or decadic schema. In similar fashion, the still greater civil wars of 49 to 44, fought by Julius Caesar, Pompey the Great, and their followers, ran from Books 109 to 116 inclusive. These formed such a unity in themselves that they receive their own headings in the *periochae* (Book 109, "which is the first of the civil war," etc.). It is noteworthy that the second half of *AUC*, Books 72 to 142 as the *periochae* show, dealt with just Rome's most recent eighty or so years, in contrast to the first half's six and a half centuries.

Books 31 to 40 form two recognizable pentads: 31 to 35 narrate the Second Macedonian War of 200–196 and its aftermath (Rome's growing hegemony over Greece and growing tension with the Seleucid ruler of the Near East, Antiochus III, self-styled "the Great"); then 36 to 40 the twelve years from 191 to 180, in which Rome crushed and shrank Antiochus' empire to extend and consolidate her mastery over the eastern Mediterranean's Hellenistic states. There are also detailed narratives of Rome's domestic politics and society and of her western wars.

As is to be expected, some books cover a lengthier period, in rather less detail, than others. Nor does every book close on a completed year. The decade breaks down as follows:

31: 200 BC (with chapters 1–4 rounding off the previous year)
32: 199 to part of 197
33: 197 (remainder) to 195
34: 195 to 193
35: 193 and 192
36: 191
37: 190 and 189
38: 189 to 187
39: 187 to 183
40: 182 to 180

Livy's narrative follows the so-called annalistic format (a modern term) common to many detailed Greek and Latin histories (cf. section 2b). Events of a year are all narrated, before the historian goes on to those of the next. There are exceptions: for instance, 31.22.4–47.3 narrates military operations in Greece from winter 200 to summer 199; then 47.4 returns to finish, briefly, the account of operations in 200 in Cisalpine Gaul that Livy had paused at 22.3. One reason for this unusual arrangement may have been to keep the Eastern narrative coherent. Another, very probably, was that his chief source for Greek affairs, Polybius, used a quite different chronological system—Olympiad years, probably July to July, or August to August (the month of the Olympic Games is debated)—which the Roman historian had to marry with the Roman

format of consular years (at this period, running from
March 15 to March 14, below, section 7). Nevertheless,
the annalistic format is overwhelmingly prevalent, as it
also is in (for instance) Thucydides, Polybius (Olympiad
years, with modifications), Caesar, Tacitus, Cassius Dio,
and Ammianus Marcellinus. Depending on his source materials and his own interest, Livy could vary the amount of
space for different years: Book 31 covers only the year 200
and Book 36 only 191, while in Book 38 the year 188 is
sandwiched, with just seven chapters (38.35.7–42.7), between a long account of the preceding year (38.1.1–35.6)
and that of the first part of 187 (38.42.8–60.10).

Within a given year, Livy usually presents events at
Rome and in different regions in blocks; a year's narrative
can start with events in the City and go on to activities
abroad, or vice versa. Different topics in affairs at Rome
can recur during a year's narrative. That for 191, for example, is laid out in Book 36 thus:

| chaps. 1–4 | Rome, preparations for war with Antio-chus III |
| 5–12 | Antiochus in Greece |
| 13–35 | Roman operations in Greece |
| 36–37 | Rome, religious affairs |
| 38 | northern Italy, operations against the Li-gurians |
| 39–40 | Rome, debated triumph of a consul over the Ligurians |
| 41–45.8 | Eastern Mediterranean, military and na-val operations |
| 45.9 | Rome, elections for 190 |

This topic format is fairly flexible but runs the risk just noted of misplacing events from a Greek source with a Greek chronology, like Polybius, into an otherwise Roman chronological system. At times, too, breaking up events in one area into two or more blocks, for variety's sake, could get him into confusion: T. J. Luce notes how, telling of affairs at Rome in 192, Livy manages to report election matters twice, both before and after a lengthy account of events in Greece, and with contradictory details (35.22–24 and 40–41). The aberration is due, probably, to different sources. Doublets of other, varied types occur too (section 3).[3]

## 2. LIVY'S SOURCES

### a. Polybius

No ancient historian devotes much space to setting out, naming, and discussing the sources that he consults, either literary or documentary. The redoubtable Polybius comes perhaps closest to it, but only to criticize and sometimes lampoon various predecessors (even some who dealt with periods other than his, such as Timaeus and Theopompus). Livy makes immense use of Polybius from Book 21 on, as what survives of the latter's *Histories* shows, yet he

---

[3] On *AUC*'s structure, especially in the books from 31 on, see Luce, *The Composition of His History;* on the slightly nonannalistic layout of 31, ibid., 58–62. On confusions in 35.22–24 and 40–41, ibid., 52–53.

is notorious for actually mentioning his predecessor only six times in the extant *AUC* (four in 31–40).[4]

Polybius, born around 200 and a leading citizen of Megalopolis, the leading city of the Achaean League in Greece, spent sixteen years in Italy and Rome, from 167 to 151, as a (loosely supervised) political detainee, became friends with the family of the Cornelii Scipiones and especially of P. Scipio Aemilianus, adoptive grandson of Scipio Africanus, and witnessed at firsthand how Rome in little more than half a century, between 220 and 167, rocketed from being a western power, at war with her rival Carthage, to becoming hegemon of the Mediterranean world. His enforced stay among the Romans led, rather paradoxically, to admiration for their society, political system, and military practices and prompted a wish to explain how and why Roman hegemony had come to be.

The *Histories'* preface poses Polybius' famous question, "Who is so indifferent or indolent as not to wish to know by what means and under what system of polity the Romans in less than fifty-three years succeeded in subjecting nearly the whole inhabited world to their sole government—a thing unique in history?" (1.1.5, Loeb transla-

---

[4] Luce, *The Composition of His History,* 181n99, points out that some 411 of the 740 chapters in Books 31 to 45 "have a Polybian origin." Livy's references to Polybius: 30.45.5, 33.10.10, 34.50.6, 36.19.11, 39.52.1, 45.44.19. See, e.g., Walsh, *Livy: His Historical Aims and Methods,* 124–33; Luce, *The Composition of His History,* 168–71, 178–81; Tränkle, *Livius und Polybios;* Davidson, *The Cambridge Companion,* 128–29; Briscoe, "Some Misunderstandings of Polybius"; C. B. Champion, "Livy and the Greek Historians," 195–98; Eckstein, "Livy, Polybius, and the Greek East" (all in Select Bibliography, pp. lxxxvii–xcii).

tion). Later, as he explains in Book 3, he revised his terminal date to recount what happened between 167 and 146, to let readers judge what the Romans did with their new mastery of the inhabited world (*Histories* 3.4–5). In practice, Polybius covers an even longer era, for his first two books are an "introduction" (προκατασκευή, 1.3.10), giving the background to the main period: Book 1 on the First Punic War and its aftermath, Book 2 largely on the affairs of Greece and Macedon in the 230s to 220s as well as Rome's progress in those decades. The entire work took forty books, but only 1 to 5 survive complete, along with medieval Byzantine extracts of very varying lengths from most of the others (none from 17, 19, 26, 37, or the index—Book 40). Polybius' rather ungainly literary style may have been partly to blame, but in fact he is the only one of the Hellenistic era's numerous historians—such as Ephorus, Theopompus, Timaeus, and Posidonius—to survive at all. His own sources are not well attested, especially for the decades after 201. There will have been personal interviews with Romans, Greeks, and others (for instance, Masinissa, king of Numidia); he made use of at least some official documents, such as treaty texts; but like most other ancient historians, he is generally reticent about how he knows what he knows.

Polybius describes his work as "practical history" (πραγματικὴ ἱστορία)—history that the reader can use to understand the world. His pursuit of that aim embraces not only narrative and character-portrayals but also admonitions to the reader on what can be learned from particular historical situations, plus geographical digressions (in Book 3 on the Alps, for example, and his devoting Book 34 to the Mediterranean world as a whole), military ones, such as his comparison of the Roman legion with the Macedonian phalanx (18.28–32), the criticisms—often sharp—of past Hellenistic historians (Book 12's extracts are a scathing attack on Timaeus in particular), and in Book 6 a famous description of the Roman political system and the military organization as they existed around 200 BC. His views on historical causes and developments are entirely secular and rationalist; his attitude to religion is that it is an essential method for keeping the masses obedient (6.56.6–12; 16.12.3–9). Yet he also makes regular play with the nonhuman concept of *tyche* ($\tau \acute{v} \chi \eta$), which for him can mean "chance," "fortune," or even "fate": at the very start of his work, he terms Rome's rise to universal hegemony as *tyche*'s "finest and most valuable achievement" (1.4.4).[5]

The first part of Book 6 analyzes Rome's political structures as forming an ideal "mixed polity": a blend of monarchy (the consuls), aristocracy (the senate), and democracy (the People). This Polybius sees as strong enough to avoid the revolving "cycle," $\dot{\alpha} \nu \alpha \kappa \acute{v} \kappa \lambda \omega \sigma \iota s$, of constant transitions—in Greek political theory at any rate—from one form of polity to the next. Yet he avers, pessimistically enough, that even this admirable constitution is fated to fall into dissension one day (*Histories* 6.9.12–13, 6.57). Nor, he makes clear in his later books, does it prevent Romans in his own time from behaving high-handedly, even toward friendly Greek states (for example, the

[5] Discussions of $\tau \acute{v} \chi \eta$: e.g., Walbank, *A Historical Commentary on Polybius,* 1.16–26, *Polybius,* 58–65, and "Fortune (*tyche*) in Polybius"; McGing, *Polybius' Histories,* 195–201.

Achaean League), or avert growing self-indulgence in their private lives—with honorable exceptions, such as his irreproachably moral friend Scipio Aemilianus.

None of these preoccupations and idiosyncrasies make any appearance in Livy, who does not seek to admonish his readers or digress into theoretical discussions. In the fourth and fifth decades, Polybius is the main source for events east of the Adriatic, while domestic and western affairs are based chiefly on Latin sources. Naturally, though, he often used Eastern details from Latin accounts too and found some reports of domestic items in Polybius (e.g., on the death of Scipio Africanus: 39.52.1 and note). Livy's Polybius-derived material often blends in items from elsewhere: thus into the Polybian account of how the proconsul Flamininus proclaimed freedom for Greece at the Isthmian Games of 196, he inserts an evocative sentence describing the youthfully charismatic proconsul; then for greater literary impact, he transfers to the assembled and astonished Greeks the glowing emotions that Polybius voices as his own (Livy 33.33.2, 4–8; Polyb. 18.46.13–14).

As a result, when Polybius and Livy differ on a matter, the reader has to make a sometimes subjective assessment about whom to believe. This may be straightforward, as in two items about the Roman siege of Ambracia in 189—Polybius has the besieged put thin metal sheets on the ground to listen for enemy tunneling (P. 21.28.8), while Livy simply has them place their ears to the ground (38.7.8–9 and nn.); when clashes break out in the discovered tunnel, Livy's Ambraciots use doors to block their opponents' progress; in Polybius both sides use shields and wickerwork frames for defense (P. 21.28.11). Livy's "doors" may be an amusing mistranslation of Polybius' "shields" (θυρεούς mistaken as θύρας), but his effort at retelling the tunnel episode suffers from other fuzzy understandings of his source.[6]

Similarly, where Livy adds details to a Polybius-based account, the reader has to decide whether they are credible, as in the notorious claim that at Cynoscephalae the Macedonian phalanx men drew their swords for close combat—because he misreads Polybius' report (18.24.9) of the phalanx lowering its spears for the charge as "throwing away" the spears (33.8.13 and n.). Incongruously, the spears reappear later in their defeated hands (33.10.3–5). His version of the Galatian Gauls' treacherous attack on the Roman consul Manlius Vulso in 189 is much more detailed than Polybius' (Livy 38.25; P. 21.39); is this due to Livy adding extra items from another source, to his own imaginative coloring, or possibly to the Polybian version being compressed by the Byzantine excerptor?

Livy also omits Polybian material if he finds it too copious—or embarrassing. Naval activities by the Rhodians in 197 are, he writes, only briefly noted—Polybius' narrative would have been fuller—because his pages are full enough already with Rome's military operations (33.20.13). An

---

[6] Differences from, and additions to, Polybian material by Livy: see, e.g., 31.1.10 n., 33.8.13 n., 35.35.18 n. On θύρας, Briscoe, "Some Misunderstandings of Polybius," 121–22, cites J. Adams' speculation that Livy's text of Polybius itself had the word through miscopying; nonetheless, Briscoe points out several other misunderstandings in Livy's retelling of the episode.

Achaean embassy in 181 and its leader Callicrates' forthright speech to the senate, urging it to use Rome's hegemony in Greece to keep pro-Roman aristocrats (such as himself) in power, was a watershed in Polybius' view, because the senate followed this advice, making Callicrates "the initiator of great calamities for all Greece" (Polyb. 24.8.9–10.8). The episode is not in Livy (Callicrates does not appear until Book 41); the Achaean's and the senate's hardheaded *Realpolitik* may have been a little too raw for him.[7]

The positive values of Livy using Polybius as extensively as he does outweigh these intermittent negatives. The Greek historian, despite his own idiosyncrasies, is very largely reliable so far as can be judged, which in turn benefits Livy's narrative of Rome's interactions with the Hellenistic world. In places where we possess or can infer a Polybian source account along with a Latin one, the contrast is instructive. In the third decade, on the Second Punic War, Livy spurns Polybius' extant Greek translation of the treaty struck in 215 between Philip V of Macedon and Hannibal (P. 7.9) in favor of a manifestly invented and over-the-top version from some pro-Roman source—portraying Philip and Hannibal as, in effect, planning to carve up the Roman and Greek world between them (23.33.10–12). More than once in reporting Roman battles, Livy acknowledges Polybius as his source, then notes with scorn the divergent and dubious versions of Valerius Antias

---

[7] Eckstein, "Livy, Polybius, and the Greek East," 410, charitably but unpersuasively suggests that Livy omitted Callicrates' embassy and speech only to avoid slowing down his narrative.

or Claudius Quadrigarius (e.g., 33.10.7–10, 36.19.10–12, 38.23.8). For most domestic and western events, Livy had to draw on other predecessors, but Polybius is the only one he praises—and not once but twice (30.45.5; 33.10.10, "no unreliable authority on Roman history in general, and particularly on events in Greece").

## b. Others

Romans writing history went back only to the start of the second century BC, with Q. Fabius Pictor and L. Cincius Alimentus, senators and contemporaries of Hannibal. They and several ensuing writers composed their works in Greek, which enabled them to address a Greek readership as well as educated Romans. Reacting against this, M. Porcius Cato (the Censor) around 160 wrote his own seven-book history of Rome, *Origines,* in Latin. Latin historiography thereafter became the norm, with a range of authors—often but not invariably senators—adding to the growing corpus of Roman histories.

In *AUC*'s fourth and fifth decades, only Cato among the earliest historians leaves clear traces in Livy, for example in the detailed account of his campaigning in Spain as consul in 195 (34.8.4–21.8; with a dry comment on Cato as "certainly not one to underestimate his own achievements," 34.15.9). The speeches of his mentioned in later Books (38.54.11; 39.42.6–7, 43.1; 45.25.2; cf. *Periochae* 41, 49), Livy probably or certainly (see 45.25.2) found in the *Origines.* Similarly, of known Roman historians of the later second century, Livy cites only P. Rutilius Rufus, and him only once (rejecting his and Polybius' date for the death of Scipio Africanus: 39.52.1); he may of course have made more use of him in books now lost.[8]

Two other early historians, Cassius Hemina and Calpurnius Piso, were possibly consulted by Livy in composing Books 31 to 40, without naming them: both, as well as Valerius Antias, recounted the discovery in 181, by farm workers on the Janiculum hill, of buried ancient books of lore (supposedly written by Rome's second king, Numa)— that the senate promptly ordered to be burned (40.29.3–14 and n.). Livy, like Piso, writes that there were seven books each of Latin and Greek, while gently dismissing the notion of all three predecessors that the Greek books were on Pythagorean philosophy. Hemina's and Piso's works were short (five to seven books each), however, and could not have supplied plentiful materials for *AUC*.

Things are very different with two Latin historians of the generation before Livy's: Q. Claudius Quadrigarius and Valerius Antias (*praenomen* unknown). As usual with most early Roman histories, theirs do not survive save for some citations in later writers, Livy in particular. This makes a clear assessment of their histories problematic. What their sources were, apart from the obvious predecessors such as Fabius Pictor, Cassius Hemina, and so on, is unknown, although we may presume they consulted the yearly events list compiled and kept by the *pontifex maxi-*

---

[8] On pre-Livian annalistic historiography: Badian, "The Early Historians"; Cornell, *The Fragments of the Roman Historians*, 1.19–37, 141–281 (including annalists used by Livy), von Ungern-Sternberg, "Livy and the Annalistic Tradition." Rutilius, incidentally, wrote in Greek (Athenaeus, *Deipnosophists* 4.168D).

*mus* and later, perhaps in their time, published as the *Annales Maximi* (below). Livy cites them often, Antias even more than Quadrigarius—but, more often than not, to criticize their version of a matter. Antias had a special fondness for massively exaggerating enemy numbers and casualties, nor was Quadrigarius averse to it (at 38.23.6 Livy is surprised to find him for once outdoing Antias in this). Antias could invent a major battle where, Livy remarks, no other source "whose annals I have read"— Greek or Latin—reported any military activity (32.6.5–7). Both annalists happily and grossly multiplied the size of the war indemnity imposed on Philip V after his defeat (33.30.8, as Livy mentions after relaying Polybius' far more plausible figure).

How far Livy depended on this pair, especially for affairs at Rome and in western theaters, is debated. Perhaps the commonest view is that they, along with Polybius, were his main sources for *AUC* 31 to 45 (and beyond) —sometimes with a further inference that, where he refers to other authors, for instance to Cato and Rutilius, he found their statements cited in Antias' or Quadrigarius' histories. Yet Quadrigarius, who began with the aftermath of the Gallic sack of Rome in 390, reached the year 82 BC in his Book 23—a span of time that in *AUC* runs from Books 6 to 88—and though Antias' history, from the foundation of Rome, like Livy's down to about 91 BC, was a fuller seventy-five books long, an excerpt from it shows that by his twenty-second book he was already at 137 BC; Livy did not get there till *AUC* 55. Other, less obvious sources too must have been used: that Livy rarely mentions any (such as Rutilius Rufus, or one Clodius Licinus: 29.22.10, cf. 39.52.1) cannot *per se* be evidence that he rarely read them. For, as often noted, in his third decade he refers just once, at its very end, to the Greek historian who is his authority for over half of it (30.45.5).[9]

Livy's Latin sources, even those nursing a penchant for inflated or invented enemy defeats, preserved important details of names, places, and events—although modern analysts have to tread carefully (e.g., 33.44.4, 34.41.8–10, 40.16.8, with nn.). Book 40, for example, details the magistrates and armies sent against the intractable Ligurians of northern Italy and over to Spain (1.1–8; 18.3–6; 36.6–14; 44.3–6), the founding of *coloniae* by named commissioners (29.1–2; 34.1–3; 43.1); the arrival in Italy of three thousand migrants from Gaul and their subsequent, peaceful expulsion (53.5–6); as well as plentiful information on religious rites and dedications; and of course the elections of consuls and praetors. Items such as these in AUC appear authentic enough, and scholars generally accept them.

Documentary sources—texts of treaties, senate decrees, public inscriptions, priestly annals, family records—played a smaller role, it seems, in Livy's researches. At some stage in the later Republic, a register of events annually compiled by the *pontifex maximus* and displayed on white boards outside the priestly residence was put together in book form—eighty books, in fact—and called the *annales maximi*. Before this publication they were probably available in storage for historians to consult, and encouraged the year-by-year narrative structure of Vale-

[9] Two-thirds, according to Eckstein, "Livy, Polybius, and the Greek East," 408.

rius, Quadrigarius, and many or most of their predecessors: hence the terms "annalists" and "annalistic history" that, in turn, could equally be applied (but never is) to Livy and other surviving historians. Livy never mentions the *annales maximi,* and if he did directly consult publicly available copies of treaties or senate decrees (for example, Cicero, *ad Atticum* 13.33.3), he never says so.

Livy's account of the senate's decree on the Bacchanalia cult in 186, however, is a reasonable summary of it, as can be seen from the preserved text of the decree itself (Livy 39.18.7–9; *ILS* 18). Again, the text of inscriptions set up in 179 on the Capitoline and in the Campus Martius by the censor M. Aemilius Regillus, to commemorate his son's naval achievements in 190 (40.52.5–7), may derive from personal inspection, but Livy does not claim this. His reports of the peace treaties with Philip V in 196 and Antiochus the Great in 188 follow Polybius—with some rearrangements and a few additions from annalistic accounts (33.30, cf. Polyb. 18.44; 38.38.1–39.2 = P. 21.41–43)— even though inscribed or written copies surely existed, just as the ancient treaties with Carthage still did in Polybius' day.[10]

[10] The peace treaties with Philip and Antiochus: Polybius' report of the treaty itself with Philip does not survive but gives the content in a senate decree. On the terms: Walbank 2.609–12; 3.156–64. Livy's handling of them: Luce, *The Composition of His History,* 219 and n. 51, 210; below, 33.30.1, 38.38.1 nn. The old Roman-Carthaginian treaties: Polybius 3.22–28; "however, he [Livy] did not walk around in Rome, or elsewhere, to discover inscriptions or other new documents" (Ungern-Sternberg, "Livy and the Annalistic Tradition," 169).

## 3. LIVY'S HISTORIOGRAPHICAL METHODS AND DIFFICULTIES

Writing a detailed history in ancient times was never easy. Until the codex, a paginated and bound book, became the norm in the late Roman empire, a work's individual books (*libri*) were written on scrolls (*volumina*), which had to be unrolled and rerolled for reading. Consulting sources was therefore a slow task—preferably also needing daylight for clarity.

How extensive Livy's research was for a given period, book, or topic can only be surmised. It may well be that for a particular episode, for instance the military operations in Greece leading to the battle of Cynoscephalae and its immediate aftermath (33.1–13) or the Trial of the Scipios (38.50.4–60.10), he began by reading a relevant range of sources, perhaps with annotations as guidelines, then composed the relevant chapters. At various points he would pause narration to add comments about discrepancies in his sources (e.g., 33.10.8–10; 38.55.8–57.1), then go back to the story or on to another episode.

Sifting, merging, or compressing sources—always a taxing task—could pose difficulties, as already noted. From time to time the same event is reported twice, usually because two of his authors reported it in slightly differing ways—not only military events but sometimes domestic ones, such as the dedication of a temple to Jupiter in both 194 and 192 (34.53.7, 35.41.8) and two versions of when the new consuls of 191 left Rome (35.40.2 n.)—due to small differences in details, different narrative sequences, or differing chronological systems. Chronology held traps too, since Polybius used Olympiad years for dating, while Roman sources largely operated with consular years. The four-year Olympiads ran from summer to summer (the exact month is debated, as mentioned earlier)—and Polybius might stretch an Olympiad year to cover a complete campaigning season to avoid breaking that up. Consuls, like other magistrates, held office for twelve months, but their entry date changed over time, from around May 1 in the early third century to March 15 by 217, then January 1 from 153 on. As Roman annalists arranged their accounts by consular years, it required some care to fit events into the correct year when drawing on both them and Polybius.

Still other factors could cause trouble. The most striking example in the fourth decade of Livy's difficulties with navigating through a range of sources is his protracted narrative of the corruption trials of Scipio Africanus and his brother Lucius and the aftermath, for he finds himself in intractable confusions about dating, prosecutors, and other details, a skein so tangled that it remains a trouble to moderns (38.50.4–60.10 and nn.). In connection with the trials, too, he assigns the death of Africanus to 187 (38.53.8, 54.1, 55.13), but in the following book he notes—skeptically—the later date, 183, assigned by Polybius and Rutilius, while now wavering in his earlier belief in Antias' 187 (39.52.1–6). A more serious confusion had occurred in Book 21, in his account of the outbreak of the war with Hannibal: after confidently putting all events from the eight-month Punic siege of Saguntum to Hannibal's arrival in Italy into the year 218 (21.6.3), he realized that this was impossi-

ble to fit into one year—but left the discussion at that
(21.15.3–6).[11]

Military details were not a Livian forte: at Cynoscephalae in 197—a battle fought between two separated
Macedonian phalanxes and Flamininus' two equally separated legions—his assumption that armies always deployed into a right wing, left wing, *and* center makes
him posit a stationary Macedonian center "watching the
battle as if they were not involved in it" (33.9.4; he had
done the same at the Metaurus in 207). Geography could
be questionable: he offers a fuzzily impressionistic description of the mountainous terrain of central Greece
(36.15.6–12, and n.), and he transfers the general council
of the Aetolians from its correct meeting place, Thermum
in Aetolia, to Thermopylae (33.35.8, cf. 31.32.3–4 and n.;
cf. P. 18.48.5. For some other geographical oddities:
31.33.6, 36.11.5). Simple misplacement, or misfiling, of
note slips or tablets can perhaps explain why Livy dates
the "Apthir incident," involving Carthage and Numidia, to
193, thirty years earlier than its obviously correct date in
Polybius (34.62.9–10; P. 31.21). It may be a similar error,

---

[11] On the Scipionic trials in Livy: Luce, *The Composition of
His History,* 91–104, 142–44; Briscoe 3.171–208. The false chronology of 21.6.3 was due probably to Roman tradition's unwill-
ingness to admit that Rome had left Saguntum in the lurch
(e.g., Hoyos, *Unplanned Wars,* 202–4). Doublets: e.g., 32.9.4–5,
32.26.1–3; 35.22.3–4, 35.40.1–2 and n.; 36.21.10–11, 36.39.1–2
and n.; 39.29.8–9, 39.41.6–7; 41.36.1–7, 41.48.1–4; 42.3.1,
42.10.5. Polybius' Olympiad-year chronology: Walbank, *Polybius,*
101–3; Feeney, "Time," especially 143–45.

or else an overeager wish to dramatize his narrative, that makes him declare in Book 39, under the year 185, that war with "King Perseus" was imminent (39.23.5). In reality, Perseus' father, Philip V, was still alive, and it was another decade and a half, and another three books, before the Third Macedonian War began.

In common with most ancient historians, Livy includes numerous speeches in his work, to illustrate a speaker's character, heighten the drama of a situation, or make the pros and cons of a debate more vivid by presenting speakers on either side. Speeches, of course, also show off his own rhetorical skills. All these qualities were much admired (Quintilian 10.1.101) and, once at least, got a senator into mortal trouble (Suetonius, *Domitian* 10.3). Some of the speeches are remarkably long: for instance, that of the pro-Roman Achaean leader Aristaenus to his fellow citizens (32.21.1–37), and Cato the Censor's and Valerius Flaccus' elaborate orations against repeal of the Oppian Law in 185 (34.2–4, 5–7, neither of which, in fact, sways the voters: 34.8.1–3). Three-speech sequences occur, notably those of Macedonian, Athenian, and Roman envoys in Aetolia in 199 (31.29.4–31.20; Livy adding a touch of formal variety by making the Athenians alone speak in *oratio obliqua* and fairly succinctly) and of Philip V of Macedon and his feuding sons Perseus and Demetrius in 182 (40.8.7–15.16). Even a long speech may be given in *oratio obliqua,* such as Scipio Nasica's when lauding his kinsmen in the Trials of the Scipios (38.58–59; at one point, 59.4, Livy slips into *oratio recta* for vividness).

Some speeches are based on Polybius, for instance those of Eumenes the Pergamene king and the Rhodian

envoys in 189 (37.53.1–54.28; P. 21.19–23), but Livy can
adapt and sometimes rearrange their content, as in Philip
V's address to the Romans and their allies at a conference
in 198 (32.34.3–13; P. 18.4–6). A good many others are
developed and expanded from material in a source—
Scipio Africanus at his brother's trial (38.51.7–11) speaks
far more grandly than the shorter and pithier remarks in
Antias (quoted by Aulus Gellius 4.11.4)—if not simply
invented to mark a noteworthy occasion. The consul Galba's exasperated exhortation to the reluctant Comitia in
200 for war with Macedon (31.7.2–15), for example, and
the pair given to Manlius Vulso's accusers and Manlius
himself in 187 (38.45.1–49.13) are vigorous productions of
refined Augustan-era rhetoric.

Each pentad opens and closes with significant items:
from the start of the Second Macedonian War (Book 31)
to Antiochus the Great's arrival in Greece to challenge
Rome (Book 35), then from the formal opening of this
new war (Book 36) to the accession of Perseus in Macedon (40)—which would lead in the next pentad to the final Macedonian War. In turn, many individual books
are structured to highlight significant or exciting events.
Thus Book 33 focuses on the Cynoscephalae campaign,
which broke the power of Philip V (chaps. 1–13), the political murder of the pro-Macedonian Boeotarch Brachylles by his enemies and the uproar that ensued (27.5–
29.12 and nn.), Flamininus' proclamation of freedom for
the Greeks (31.7–33.8), and the reforms and exile of
Hannibal at Carthage (45.5–49.7). Book 40, for another
example, highlights the successful machinations of Philip
V's younger son Perseus against his pro-Roman brother

Demetrius (5.1–16.3), the undeserved execution of Demetrius (22.15–24.7), and several major campaigns in
Spain (30.1–34.1, 39.1–40.15, 47.1–50.7).

Overall, Livy succeeds in writing clear and informative
history. He seems to have been the first Roman historian
to appreciate and make extensive use of Polybius (the annalists did not) and his vast array of Roman information
about not just wars and politics but also social, economic,
religious, and administrative life. Given the historical materials existing in his time, Livy's choices were sensible.[12]

## 4. THE EASTERN MEDITERRANEAN
IN *AUC* 31–40

The twenty years after the peace of 201 with Carthage
revolutionized the Mediterranean. In 201 five great powers were coexisting or clashing—the Seleucid empire,
Macedon, Egypt, Carthage, and Rome—with a pool of
smaller states and microstates eddying around them in
both East and West. In 180 Rome was hegemon over them
all. The outcome of the Hannibalic war had been publicly
forecast as early as 217 by a Greek statesman, with fore-
boding: the Aetolian Agelaus told one of Greece's recur-
rent peace conferences that the Greeks and Macedonians
should cease their interminable squabbles and look to the
future, "for if you ever allow the clouds now gathering in
the west to loom over Greece, I deeply fear that all the
games we now play with each other, our truces and our
wars, will be so thoroughly denied us that we shall find

[12] Livy's choice of Polybius: Luce, *The Composition of His
History,* 30–31, 168–71, and passim.

ourselves imploring the gods to grant us this right, to make war and peace with one another as we wish" (P. 5.104.10–11, trans. R. Waterfield). At that stage it probably looked as though Carthage would be the threatening cloud, so Philip V chose to back Hannibal's side. It led to a stalemated conflict with Rome, the First Macedonian War, from 215 to 205, which in turn inclined Rome in 201 to favor appeals from Greek states at odds with Macedon, such as Pergamum, Rhodes, and Athens.

The Second Macedonian War, from 200 to 196, ended Macedon's dominance over Greece, forced its once-ambitious king into humiliating and resented subordination to Rome, and edged the Romans toward a clash with the Seleucid king of the East, Antiochus III (self-styled the Great). The Roman proconsul Flamininus, having shattered Philip's army at Cynoscephalae in 197 and compelled him to accept Rome's terms, proclaimed at Corinth the following year that all Greeks were to be free and independent (with some less-loudly stated exceptions). This more or less inevitably moved Rome toward conflict with Antiochus. His drive to recover cities and lands on the eastern and northern Aegean coasts—he saw them as ancestral possessions—threatened Rome's new Eastern arrangements and again alarmed its friends Pergamum and Rhodes. Abetted by some mainland Greek states, especially the Aetolian League, which felt inadequately rewarded for allying with Rome against Macedon, Antiochus in 192 challenged Rome under the ironic slogan of restoring freedom to the Greeks. To renewed Greek astonishment, the Great King of the East was utterly defeated in a relatively short war (from 191 to 188). His borders were thrust back to the far side of Asia Minor, and a cordon of allied states—Pergamum and Rhodes in particular—rewarded with extra territories as buffers between the Seleucid empire and the Aegean. The Aetolian League paid for its miscalculation by being broken up.

The 180s saw the states and monarchies of the eastern Mediterranean, large and small, seeking to adjust to this unprecedented geopolitical situation. Some stronger states ventured to pursue quarrels of their own as in the old days—most notably Eumenes of Pergamum, who until 167 enjoyed great favor at Rome, and also Polybius' homeland, the Achaean League, in its various Peloponnesian feuds—but even they had to watch for possible Roman intervention. Philip V was free to wrestle with frequent barbarian raids along Macedon's northern frontiers, but activities of his in the Aegean region met with strong disapproval (Livy 39.33–34). Only the Seleucids, henceforth far away in Syria and Mesopotamia, could still act relatively freely—outside Asia Minor.

Meanwhile, numerous Greek embassies to Rome during this decade submitted requests, complaints, and congratulations to the new hegemon: the Achaeans and their neighbors, such as Sparta, constantly seeking Rome's support against each other, Pergamum and Bithynia vying for Rome's favor, Pergamum trying to revive Roman suspicions of Macedon. Roman envoys in turn from time to time crossed the water to one region or another of Greece or Asia Minor to investigate issues, negotiate problems, or announce decisions. Yet Rome's hegemony was still light in the 180s and into the 170s. Eumenes was able to wage one successful war after another against neighbors—not only his inveterate foe Prusias of Bithynia but also the Galatians and the king of Pontus—with minimal regard to

Rome; the Achaeans paid attention only when it suited them to recommendations from Rome on handling their Peloponnesian neighbors. After the Third Macedonian War another decade later, by contrast, the hegemony would become far more imperious.[13]

## 5. HOME AFFAIRS IN *AUC* 31–40

Livy's other principal focus in the fourth decade is, naturally, Rome itself and the affairs of the Roman people. He reports among other things the outcomes of the annual consular and praetorian elections, how the range of new magistrates' tasks (their *provinciae*) were allocated, laws proposed and enacted (or voted down), and how religious matters were administered—most famously, the investigation in 186 into the Bacchanalia cult (39.8–19). Political arguments, rivalries, and controversies (such as the Scipionic trials and, in the same book, the wrangling over whether the proconsul Manlius Vulso should hold a triumph), the founding of Roman or Latin colonies, and even administrative minutiae, such as fines imposed on lawbreaking cattle breeders—probably for encroaching on public land—and actions to repress outbreaks of unrest among rural slaves, all earn mention (fines, 33.42.10–11, 35.10.11–12; outbreaks, 32.26.6–18, 33.36.1–3, 39.29.8–10).

For Livy, Rome of the fourth decade was still overall

---

[13] Detailed studies of Rome and the Hellenistic East in and after the great wars: Gruen, *The Hellenistic World;* Eckstein, *Rome Enters the Greek East,* and "Livy, Polybius, and the Greek East"; Waterfield, *Taken at the Flood.*

the moral society that he had portrayed in the first and third decades, a society led by intelligent, virtuous, and self-sacrificing men imbued with old-style qualities. Rome had leaders such as Cato (praised more than warmly by Livy: 39.40.4–12), Scipio Africanus, Flamininus, and Ti. Gracchus, whose qualities emerge during the Trials of the Scipios and later as praetor in Spain. The Republic, in his view, went to war only to defend friends, like Athens and Pergamum in 200, or because it saw a threat (as from Antiochus the Great), or to restore peace and order in Rome's possessions, as in the reconquest of Cisalpina— Cisalpine Gaul—and the repeated wars in Spain. It liberated the long-harassed states of Greece while treating ex-enemies with (in Roman eyes) moderation. The heartfelt praise of Rome that Livy, adapting Polybius' personal verdict, ascribes to the Greek people after the freedom declaration (p. xxiii above) clearly reads as expressing, too, his own view of early second-century Rome.

Romans' careful devotion to the (proper) gods Livy illustrates, not only in regular notices of rituals, temple foundations, and prodigies but equally in the shocked public reaction to the Bacchanalia in 186 and the decision to burn the just-found ancient "books of Numa" in 181, because these contained "a number of things tending to undermine Roman religion" (40.29.3–14). Following Antias, Livy presents Scipio Africanus availing himself of his fellow citizens' piety to quash his enemies' attacks on his probity (38.51.7–14). Admittedly, in a later book, but equally relevant to the fourth decade, he avows his own sympathy with the beliefs and forms of these older times: "As I write about bygone affairs, my mind in some way takes on an antique cast, and a certain spirit of religious respect prevents me from regarding as unworthy of recording in my history matters that the deeply sagacious men of old deemed meritorious of public attention" (43.13.2).[14]

At the same time Livy is careful not to offer a wholly uncritical portrayal of early second-century Romans (any more than he did in preceding decades). Greed, lack of scruple, personal grudges and rivalries, and immoral indulgence all earn report in the fourth decade. He tells, for example, of Manlius Vulso's loot-hunting campaign against the Galatians, which was bitterly criticized by the eminent Aemilius Paullus among others (38.44–46) and the loot from which was the prime cause of Romans' mounting fondness for luxury (39.6.3–9; Livy ignores his own earlier complaint blaming the loot from Syracuse in 211 for this). There was Cato the Censor's inveterate enmity toward Scipio (38.54.1–2, stating how even in Scipio's lifetime he "made a habit of carping at his eminence"—here Livy uses the disdainful metaphor *adlatrare,* from a dog's barking); the transgressions of cattle breeders in the countryside that led to substantial fines; the alleged lascivious goings-on at Bacchanalian rituals (39.8.1–8 and 13.8–14) that brought down the wrath of the senate and consuls on the cult; and the vicious murder by Flamininus' brother of a Gallic nobleman in Cisalpina to please a prostitute (39.42.6–43.5). Flamininus himself is not entirely free of

[14] On the other hand, for Levene, 113–16, Livy at 43.13.1–6 is more interested in forecasting, via prodigies in 169, the moral decay of his own time than in stating personal religious belief; cf. Chaplin, *Livy: Rome's Mediterranean Empire,* xxi–xxii (with quotation), 336.

criticism, though Livy does his best to deflect it. In an otherwise largely Polybian account, he avoids repeating Polybius' report of how Flamininus tacitly backed the planned assassination of the popular pro-Macedonian Boeotian leader Brachylles in 196 (when approached by the plotters, he "said that he himself would take no part in this deed but would put no obstacles in the way of anyone who wished to do so": P. 18.43.9–10). Yet Livy soon mentions that the outraged Boeotians believed that the assassins "could not have embarked on such a crime without consultation with the Roman commander" (33.29.1)— with no record of Flamininus putting out a refutation.[15]

## 6. CISALPINA, SPAIN, AND THE WESTERN MEDITERRANEAN IN *AUC* 31–40

Even though Livy's narrative of events across the western Mediterranean, northern Italy included, takes up a good deal less space in the fourth decade (and in what survives of the fifth) than do those in Greece and the East, the West was equally if not more important in the eyes of the Senate and People. Praetors governing the Spanish provinces were military commanders as well as peacetime administrators, but, as A. M. Eckstein notes, of the almost two

[15] Crime and immorality in previous decades: inter alia, Manlius' treason, *AUC* 6.11 to 6.20; mass poisonings by wives at Rome, 8.18; unchaste matrons, 10.31; wartime shippers' insurance rackets, 25.3–4; Syracusan loot initiates Romans' unmanly love of art, 25.40; the Pleminius scandal and Scipio's cover-up, 29.16–22.

hundred praetors elected between 200 and 168 none was assigned to Eastern wars. And while thirteen of the period's consuls went east, another fifty-seven down to 166 BC were allocated northern Italy, first against the Cisalpine Gauls and then mainly against the irrepressible Ligurians; from 188 to 172 both consuls every year had these *provinciae*. Another calculation is no less revealing. Even in years without Eastern wars, the numbers of Roman and Italian allied military forces stayed remarkably high: between 187 and 179, for example, there were never fewer than 100,000 soldiers in arms (in 182 perhaps nearly 140,000).[16]

Statistics may not be everything. Eastern commanders brought home often immense quantities of plunder, including slaves, and they earned greater *gloria* and *auctoritas*—coveted attributes for a Roman leader—than any operations in northern Italy or Spain could bestow. Nonetheless, the importance of Rome's western commitments is well shown by these figures. Cisalpine Gaul was both a highly productive land (so Polybius stresses: 2.14.4–15.7) and strategically critical for Rome, as painful experience with Gallic and Hannibalic invasions had made clear. Spain's two provinces, Nearer and Farther, which had been wrested from the Carthaginians, were beginning to yield useful sums in booty (e.g., Livy 31.20.7; 34.10.4 and 7; etc.), and along with Cisalpine Gaul offered plentiful wars for magistrates to win *gloria* for their public careers, even if not on the scale of the rarer Eastern wars.

Romans and other Italians soon began to arrive in these

---

[16] Eckstein, *Rome Enters the Greek East,* 347–48, and "Livy, Polybius, and the Greek East," 416–17. Men in arms: Brunt, *Italian Manpower,* 424–26.

provinces, not simply as merchants but also as settlers.
From the 190s to 170s numerous colonies and smaller
settlements were founded in Cispadane Gaul (Cisalpine
Gaul south of the river Po), either as enlargements to existing towns, Bononia, Mutina, and Parma, for instance, or
on fresh ground; in 173 other public land in the region was
distributed to thousands of individual settlers; and Polybius claims that in his day all of Cisalpina's Gallic inhabitants had been expelled (2.35.4, but exaggerating). In
Spain, establishing towns for loyalist Spaniards, sometimes together with Roman and Italian incomers, was a
fairly regular practice: Tarraco had been a Roman bridge-
head during the Second Punic War, Scipio had settled
wounded veterans at the aptly named Italica (near Se-
ville), and Ti. Gracchus in 179 created Gracchurris on the
middle Ebro river for, it seems, loyalist Spaniards. Roman
soldiers in Spain kept themselves busy in other ways when
not fighting: by 171 there were over four thousand ille-
gitimate adult sons of soldiers and Spanish mothers able
to petition the senate for a town to live in, which they duly
received (43.3.1–4).[17]

In north Africa the defeat of Carthage left Rome's old
rival a virtually disarmed dependency, all the more so after Hannibal's political foes engineered his exile in 195
with Roman support (33.45.5–49.4). Livy's sporadic and
short mentions thereafter of Rome's relations with Carthage and Carthage's immediate and covetous neighbor,
Numidia, are generally read as revealing that Rome was

[17] Livy ignores Italica but the later Greek historian Appian
registers it (*Iberica* 38.153); it was to be the home town of the
families of the emperors Trajan and Hadrian. Gracchurris: Livy,
*Periocha* 41 (the lost beginning of Book 41 probably recorded it).

ineradicably hostile to the Carthaginians in spite of every effort by them to earn favor with gifts and even naval help, and that Rome was invariably benign toward the Numidian king Masinissa's many moves to seize parts of Carthage's remaining territories. In reality, Livy's own text suggests the opposite. Though he misdates to the 190s "the Apthir incident," mentioned above, to give the impression that Rome was already well-disposed to Masinissa, he leaves unclear the outcome of various Carthaginian appeals to Rome over Numidian incursions, and then records a senate decree of 172 that Rome would allow no changes to the Carthaginian borders determined by Scipio Africanus in 201. Soon after, he reports Masinissa calculating in 171, as the Third Macedonian War loomed, that because Rome was continuing to protect Carthage from attack, it would suit his own interests for Macedon—not Rome—to win, for then "all Africa would be his': a remarkable report very unlikely to have been made up by a later historian (or by Livy), because Roman tradition always portrayed the king as Rome's enduringly loyal friend. But no less striking than its effective protectorate over its old enemy as late as this, is that soon after 167 and the end of our extant *Ab Urbe Condita,* Rome's attitude would change for the worse.[18]

Rather like the Romans' attitude to Carthage during the period covered in *AUC* 31 to 45, Livy's view of their greatest enemy, Hannibal, is less hostile than might be

[18] Rome and Carthage after 201: Livy 33.44.5–49.7 (Hannibal's reforms and exile), 33.34.60–62 (in 193), 40.17.1–6, 40.34.14 (181), 42.23–24 (172). Apthir episode: 34.62.9–10; P: 31.21; Walbank 3.489–91; Briscoe 2.143–44; Hoyos, *Mastering the West,* 241–46. Masinissa's calculations in 171: 40.29.8–10.

expected of an author who in Book 21 penned the famously savage addendum to his character portrait (21.4.9–10: "pitiless cruelty, a treachery worse than Punic, . . . no fear of the gods or respect for an oath," etc.). By the closing chapters of Book 30, Hannibal has become an almost avuncular adviser to Scipio Africanus when they confer before the battle of Zama, and, paradoxically, a firm proponent of peace facing down diehard opposition. When Hannibal reappears (33.44–49), it is to reform his corrupt and mismanaged homeland, then to be forced into exile soon afterward by an unsavory (as Livy makes clear) combination of the corrupt defeated faction and their friends at Rome—against the strong objections of Scipio himself. Hannibal's ensuing role as a supposedly honored military adviser to Antiochus the Great is inglorious: his advice on how to defeat the Romans is ignored, he is sidelined to command a small fleet in the southern Aegean and is soon defeated by the outnumbered Rhodians, and he is then forced again to flee after the war to escape Roman vengeance. When finally run to ground in his Bithynian retreat, he takes poison with a bitter speech—a clear Livian composition—denouncing the Romans' persistent rancor and calling on the gods to punish the Bithynian king Prusias, who had betrayed his trust (39.51–52). Instead of a vicious monster, Livy's Hannibal over the course of nineteen books (the fullest account we have of his life) becomes almost Roman in his constancy, candor, resourcefulness, and bravery.[19]

---

[19] In P. Barceló's felicitous phrase, as time passed "Hannibal wurde eingebürgert" by Romans (*Hannibal: Stratege und Staatsmann* [Stuttgart, 2004], 248).

## 7. ROMAN GOVERNANCE

"The Senate and People of Rome," *senatus populusque Romanus,* was the official designation of the Roman Republic; Polybius rather more realistically identified a three-part system (section 2a), adding the consuls to the other two components (*Histories* 6.11.11–18.8).

### a. People

The People meant in fact male citizens sixteen years old and above, provided that they were on the census list. A citizen was registered according to economic status (in effect, property both immovable and movable), which in turn determined his rank in the principal voting assembly, the *Comitia Centuriata* (*AUC* 31.7.1 n.). Unless he was forty-seven years old or more, he could volunteer—or be conscripted—for legionary service; the poorest citizens served as light-armed *velites* (section 8), since a recruit had to equip himself. Every *civis Romanus* had the right to vote, to have recourse to a court when necessary, and to make a valid will. Provided he had enough means to cover expenses of office (magistrates were unpaid) he could seek election to one.

Laws were passed, or repealed, and magistrates elected by various formal assemblies of citizens, meeting in various places in or close to Rome. The senior magistrates—consuls, censors, and praetors—were elected by the *Comitia Centuriata,* meeting on the Campus Martius, located between the Capitoline hill and the Tiber. Another assembly, the *Comitia Tributa,* met in the City; it elected lesser magistrates, such as the quaestors and curule aediles. A third, organized like—and older than—the *Tributa* but limited to plebeian Romans (the great majority of the citizen body), was the *Concilium Plebis*, which elected the plebeian tribunes and plebeian aediles. Rather confusingly to moderns, all three could pass laws as well. Each assembly consisted of voting units: *centuriae* in the *Centuriata* and "tribes" (based on the territorial districts of the Roman state) in the other two. Each unit had one assembly vote, decided by the members who attended the meeting.

The *Comitia Centuriata* had begun in the earliest era of Rome, as the citizenry arrayed for war (hence its meeting place). Since it was the People assembled, it then progressed to making laws, electing magistrates, military tribunes (section 8), and boards of commissioners for specific tasks, for example, founding colonies (e.g., 32.29.4, 33.42.1 and n.), and to judging important trials. In the census registers, senators and the 1,800 formally registered *equites* (cavalrymen) were assigned to the 18 highest ranking of the assembly's 193 *centuriae*. Adjustments to the remaining "centuries" were made before 218 BC but are not entirely clear: the following is perhaps the likeliest outline.

Ranking after the 18 *centuriae* was the *prima classis* (first class) of 70. In these "centuries" the rest of Rome's wealthiest citizens were enrolled. Three further *classes*—their totals much debated—were assigned to Romans on a descending scale of property values. In keeping with the *Centuriata*'s origins, four extra *centuriae* comprised citizens classed as technicians (*fabri*) and military musicians; and a fifth was the *centuria* for the *capite censi:* that is, every Roman censused as nonpropertied. By 200 BC, in each "class" half of the *centuriae* consisted of *iuniores* (men under forty-six), half of *seniores* (those forty-six and above). The total of units remained 193, but the totals of each "class" after the *prima classis* are not precisely known. The adjustments seem to have aimed at aligning the working of the *Centuriata* with that of the *Comitia Tributa*, which consisted of 35 voting "tribes" based on the territorial districts of the Roman state (below). For example, Livy records "all thirty-five tribes" approving peace with Philip V in 196 (33.25.7): making peace, like declaring war, was a centuriate decision.

All the same, a massive majority of unit votes was retained by the wealthier minority of Romans. The 88 top-ranking *centuriae* and the relatively well-off 4 "specialist" ones needed only the second "class" *centuriae,* or some of these, for a numerical majority. How many voters were actually present for a comitial vote did not offset this, for each *centuria* cast a single vote and they voted by rank, starting with the "equestrian" 18 or, later, with a "century" chosen by lot from the *prima classis.* Thus even if 97 *centuriae* of the wealthy levels were attended by (say) 10 members each, and the remaining 96 had 100 voters apiece, the vote would be carried by the 97. In addition, once a majority of *centuriae* was reached for or against a proposal, or for a particular candidate, a result was declared. This meant that some of the lower-ranking "classes" and the single *centuria* of the *capite censi* might rarely— the *capite censi* perhaps never—be asked for their votes.

These were not the only inadequacies. Others applied to all the assemblies: to cast a vote in any of them, a citizen had to attend the relevant meeting place, something virtually impossible for those with limited means and leisure or who lived more than a few hours' travel distance from the City. The numbers able (and willing) to attend meetings no doubt varied depending on the agendas, but only a small percentage of Rome's 250,000 to 300,000 second-century citizens can have come even for major issues such as consular elections. In any case, apart from the *Centuriata,* assemblies met in Rome, usually in the Forum outside the senate house or on the Capitoline hill—fairly cramped spaces for more than a few hundred or a couple of thousand people. At a meeting, only topics or candidates' names approved by the presiding magistrate could be voted on, with any discussion limited to speakers whom he permitted. If a tribune placed a veto on a proposal, the assembly could not proceed with it, nor do so if an ill omen (e.g., a thunderclap) intervened: a frustrating outcome for voters who had taken time from work or had traveled a long way.

The *Comitia Tributa* was organized on the basis of the Roman state's territorial districts: *tribus* (from *tribuere,* "to assign"), a permanent thirty-five in number from 241 BC on. New additions to Roman territory were assigned to one or other of these. Four "tribes" were in the City itself, several more—fairly small because ancient—lay in its neighborhood, and the rest were situated farther afield. Within each tribe the members each had an equal say, then the tribe itself cast a single vote. With thirty-five votes the *Tributa* had a more economical procedure than the *Centuriata*—hence the likely reason why the latter had been adjusted to align with it (above). Nevertheless, the same constraints of time and distance applied to attendance, so that as a rule City residents and men of means were the likeliest participants, and the urban and nearer tribes were better attended.

The plebeian *Concilium,* originally the informal assembly of the oppressed nonpatricians in early Republican times, was also based on the territorial *tribus* (it was probably the model for the *Comitia Tributa,* which developed later). Only plebeians could participate, to elect the officials who represented and defended them, and to pass resolutions, *plebiscita,* put to the gathering by a plebeian official. By the third century the officials—tribunes and plebeian aediles—were de facto magistrates, and *plebiscita* had de facto legal force even if not formally *leges.* While only plebeian citizens could take part in the *Concilium Plebis,* the development of the *Comitia Tributa,* open to patricians and plebeians alike, blurred the distinction in later sources: it is not always possible to tell whether laws carried by tribunes were technically *plebiscita* or *leges,* as they were all impartially reported as these latter (for instance, the *leges Semproniae* carried by the reformer brothers Ti. and C. Gracchus later in the second century).[20]

[20] Roman assemblies: Staveley, *Greek and Roman Voting and Elections,* chaps. 6–11; Lintott, *The Constitution of the Roman Republic,* chap. 5. Still other *comitia* (plural) existed: the very ancient *c. calata,* which the pontiffs held twice-yearly to announce the calendar and other rites, and the *c. curiata* (based on the archaic division of citizens into *curiae*), which formally conferred authority on elected magistrates and priests. Both now required only a token attendance.

## b. Magistrates

The executive element of the *res publica* was a body of elected magistrates in several colleges, most holding office for twelve months—with, typically, a range of starting dates during the year.

The two consuls headed the state: invested with the highest level of authority, *imperium* (apart from that of the dictator, below), they consulted the senate, summoned and put proposals to the *Comitia Centuriata* and *Tributa,* issued orders to lesser magistrates—but not to plebeian tribunes—and commanded the main Roman armies in wartime. In the City they took monthly turns to be attended by twelve *lictores* (31.2.3 n.), who each carried the famous bundle of rods and axes (symbols of coercive power) called the *fasces.* Polybius viewed consuls as the monarchic element in Rome's "mixed polity" and admired how they were sensibly limited by their duality (one consul could veto an act or proposal of the other: a rare event) and their one-year tenure. If a consul died or was slain during the year, a replacement (*consul suffectus*) could be elected.

Praetors began in 367 (a single one), with numbers increasing to two around 242, four a decade and a half later, and six in 197 (Livy 32.27.6); each had six lictors. Holding lesser *imperium* they too could command armies when necessary, normally smaller ones, and serve as governors of the Republic's new provinces. The two oldest praetorships, the *p. urbanus* and *p. peregrinus,* operated at Rome: the first judged lawsuits between Roman citizens, the second those between citizens and foreigners (*peregrini*). Aediles came in two pairs, plebeian and curule, charged with the upkeep of temples, public buildings, and public spaces, including markets, as well as a general duty of maintaining public order and fining transgressors (cf. 31.50.2 n.; 33.42.10–11, 35.10.11–12). The quaestors, created as early as 447 to assist the consuls, grew in numbers and tasks over the centuries, though the totals at given times are unclear. Two were aides to the consuls, two more administered the state treasury (the *aerarium*), others the affairs of provinces as junior colleagues of the governors; four looked after the needs of the *res publica* in various parts of Italy (including one at Ostia to oversee grain supplies to Rome from Sicily and elsewhere).

As consuls and, in major wars, praetors commanded armies, and because wars could last for years and sometimes be fought abroad, a consul's or praetor's *imperium* might be prolonged—the technical word was "prorogued"—beyond his year of office, if the senate saw fit. This practice also became the norm for praetors governing provinces for longer than one year. The prorogued magistrate was viewed as "acting as" a consul or praetor, *pro consule* or *pro praetore;* these phrases later became the single words "proconsul" and "propraetor." An occasional special appointment by order of the People, such as the one for Scipio Africanus' Spanish command in 210, or by the senate (e.g., 35.23.7), also made the holder a promagistrate. The *imperium* of a proconsul was subordinate to that of the current consuls, nor could he go into Rome itself without forfeiting it, except to celebrate a triumph, if he was voted one by the senate. A military commander, meanwhile, could by 200 BC choose one or more fellow senators as his personal deputies, *legati* (e.g., Livy 31.27.1,

35.5.1; *legatus* also meant "ambassador," which can occasionally confuse).

The ten plebeian tribunes began, or so Roman tradition depicted them, as representatives and protectors of the early Republic's *plebs* against patrician exploitation. (They are not to be confused with military tribunes: section 8.) Over time, they also adopted a broader role as watchdogs over public business: it was the two Petillii, tribunes in 187, who prosecuted the Scipio brothers over alleged peculation of state funds (38.50–55), for example. Though only plebeians could be elected and only plebeians could elect them, tribunes acquired through long usage a unique authority. As well as the ability to prosecute alleged offenders before the people, or at any rate the *Concilium Plebis,* and put proposed laws to that body, a tribune could come to the aid of any plebeian (or even patrician) whom he judged to be oppressed: his intervention, *intercessio,* could not be refused. This power evolved into the capacity to veto any proposed measure by any magistrate or any senate resolution, if he judged them improper. A tribune's person was sacrosanct in office, for plebeians were bound by oath to make an end of anyone who struck or harmed him—and the tribune himself could pronounce the offender guilty and throw him to his death from the Tarpeian rock, at the western end of the Capitoline (another practice rarely applied).

Two magistracies had limited but powerful roles in the *res publica,* though only one appears in *AUC* 31 to 40. Every five years two censors were elected, normally ex-consuls, to carry out a census of citizens (this included details of their property and income), update membership of the senate and of the eighteen *centuriae* of *equites,* let out state contracts (*publica*) for collecting taxes, such as customs dues and provincial taxes, and for building or repairing temples, roads, and other public amenities. As overall supervisors of morals, they could remove improperly behaved senators from that body, *equites* from the eighteen *centuriae,* and ordinary citizens from their *tribus* (leaving these voteless). At the close of their eighteen month term, the censors performed the solemn rite of the *lustrum,* a series of processions and sacrifices to purify state and people from past ills and for the coming five years (35.9.1 n., 38.36.10 n.).

The dictator was an emergency magistrate with *imperium* overriding all others, nominated by a consul after consulting the senate. Only an ex-consul could hold the office; he had to abdicate it once the crisis ended or, at longest, after six months, as did the deputy whom he himself nominated, the "master of horse" (*magister equitum:* dictators were forbidden to ride). Apart from military command, the dictator could preside over *comitia* meetings in the absence of the consuls or perform special rites. No dictator, however, was nominated after 202, until the office was reinstated with even wider powers during the first century BC.

Before the *lex Villia* of 180 (40.44.1) there were no prescribed rules on access to magistracies, save that ten years' military service were required (Polyb. 6.19.3). Even so it was a well-established convention to start an intended public career by seeking a lesser magistracy and working up as far as voters allowed. The normal sequence was quaestor, aedile—or alternatively, for plebeians, tribune—then praetor and consul. Competition was fierce and of course ex-praetors, not to mention ex-consuls, were always far fewer than other former magistrates. Exceptions to the convention occurred: in 210 P. Scipio Africanus, a twenty-four-year-old ex-aedile, had been appointed to command in Spain with special consular *imperium,* and on returning home in 205 was elected consul for the following year; Flamininus, an ex-quaestor, was elected for 198 when not yet thirty. The Villian law imposed a minimum age for each senior magistracy (40.44.1 n.), with forty-two the minimum for the consulship. Again exceptions occurred, as when Scipio Africanus' grandson Scipio Aemilianus was elected in 148 for the following year although he was only thirty-six and, like Flamininus, only an ex-quaestor; his brilliant service as military tribune in the operations around Carthage had won the admiration of even the Scipios' old foe Cato.

Early Rome's hereditary aristocracy had been the patricians (*patricii*), families who combined ancient ancestry with economic and religious importance. In the second century BC, surviving patrician families, such as the Aemilii, Claudii, Cornelii, Postumii, and Valerii, enjoyed potent status and eminence—*dignitas* and *auctoritas* are the nearest equivalent Latin terms—enough to attain consulships far out of proportion to their limited numbers. Indeed it was not until 171 that both consuls were plebeians, as the surviving consular lists (*fasti consulares*) show, and this remained unusual. Nevertheless, a large number of plebeian families and individuals had also started to attain the consulship from the late fourth century: in *AUC* 31 to 40 the Cassii, Fulvii, Junii, Popillii, and Sempronii are among the most notable, while newcomers to consular office intermittently arrived to play important roles too— M. Porcius Cato (consul in 195) being the most obvious example. As a result, an informal new term arose for the

Romans of prime political and social eminence: the "notables," *nobiles* (cf. 39.13.14; 39.40.3 and 9; 39.41.1). Originally used, it seems, for families of men who had been "curule" magistrates (those who sat on folding seats of ivory, *sellae curules:* curule aediles, praetors, and consuls), with the growth of empire and the multiplication of aediles and praetors *nobilis* and *nobilitas* eventually were restricted to men of consular ancestry. Newcomers like Cato might be termed "new men," although their descendants too would be *nobiles*—but a family that went too long without fresh consulships would struggle to have its "nobility" recognized, as the aggrieved aspirant L. Sergius Catilina found in Cicero's day.

### c. Senate

The senate of the second century consisted of around three hundred men, ranging (in descending order of *dignitas*) from ex-consuls to junior senators, ex-quaestors, or even men who had not yet held a magistracy. Senators were selected by the censors but kept their membership for life, unless ejected for impropriety by later censors. The body was the Republic's most ancient institution, endowed with religious as well as secular significance. It could meet only in a temple or a consecrated space. It had very limited legal powers: for instance, it nominated an *interrex,* or rather a series of them, to hold fresh elections if both consuls were killed or could not be at Rome (35.6.6), and it supervised the quaestors administering the state treasury and finances. At the same time, it was consulted by consuls and praetors on matters great and small, domestic and foreign; it could also be convened and consulted by tribunes. A magistrate wishing to propose a law to the People had to consult the senate first to receive its imprimatur and might amend or drop the proposal in light of the resulting debate.

In the second century and later, senate meetings can rarely have been full. The *senatus consultum* on the Bacchanalia movement in 186, for example, specified a quorum of at least one hundred senators for decrees on the issue (*ILS* 18), only a third of the putative total. Many senators would be absent as they were ambassadors, provincial governors or their *legati,* or special commissioners; some would be unwell or too old; and magistrates in office did not vote.

The magistrate presiding at a session chose who could speak in the debate and what motions should be put, but immemorial convention dictated that he must give the floor to the senior members—usually the ex-consuls—in order of their seniority. Then he must frame his motion in accord with their majority or unanimous opinion (he was assisted by some of them in drafting it). It was less usual for lesser-ranking senators to be invited to speak. Once a clear majority view had formed in a debate, it was normal for the ensuing vote to be unanimous or near unanimous. A senate decree, *senatus consultum,* was technically advice to the consulting magistrate, but it was a rare magistrate who ignored it (unless a tribune vetoed it).

## 8. ROMAN ARMIES AND FLEETS

During the second century BC, as noted above, the Romans continued to maintain large military forces spread out across numerous regions, provinces, and war theaters—the details of which we owe to Livy above all. In spite of the huge losses suffered in the Second Punic War, adult male citizen numbers grew, as the surviving five-yearly census figures show (most of them from Livy again). By 174 they almost equaled the total returned fifty years earlier: 269,000 compared with the 273,000 reported for 225 by Polybius (2.24); if the *Periocha* of the badly preserved Book 45 is right, at the next census there were nearly 313,000. The Latins and the Italian allies perhaps numbered about twice as many (as in Polybius' figures for 225, which are admittedly much debated). But even a total population of three-quarters of a million adult males—that is, aged sixteen and over—must have been hard put to produce and maintain the tens of thousands of soldiers and some thousands of naval personnel whom the Roman Republic had in arms at any time during the century. At times it was an effort to recruit soldiers: when the consuls and senate wanted to have war declared on Macedon in 200, the voters initially rejected this from simple war-weariness (31.6.3–5). But for a war that promised booty, as those in the east invariably did, the consuls had little trouble gathering volunteers.

One glimpse of a virtual career legionary is offered by Livy rather later, in a speech given to a reenlisting former centurion, Spurius Ligustinus, when this veteran offered himself for the army being recruited in 171 for the Third Macedonian War (42.34.1–35.1). A peasant farmer, Ligustinus had first enrolled in 200 for the Second, then fought in twenty-two annual campaigns including in Spain, become the prime centurion of more than one legion (*primus pilus:* see below), earned numerous decorations—and still found time at home to father two daughters and four sons with his wife (who was also his first cousin), all vigorously alive in 171. Even if a Livian invention, the circumstantial vividness of Ligustinus' speech suggests that it was based on some real evidence.

Polybius regarded Roman military organization as superior to Greek—even to Macedon's, with which Alexander had won his empire. Much of his *Histories* Book 6 offers his detailed and famous description of the Roman system (6.19–42), and after narrating the battle of Cynoscephalae in Book 18, he assesses the relative qualities of the densely packed Macedonian phalanx and the more flexible array of the legion (18.28–32), to the benefit of the latter.[21]

In the third and second centuries, a Roman army commanded by a consul or proconsul normally consisted of two citizen legions and equal or larger contingents, termed *cohortes,* of Latin and Italian allied troops, all similarly equipped and trained. In Eastern wars especially, non-Italian allies often accompanied the army too: thus in the Magnesia campaign against Antiochus, the Romans were

---

[21] Polybius 2.24.14–17 (Roman citizens in 224), cf. Livy, *Periocha* 20 (270,000 in 234); Livy 42.10 (in 174; a slightly different figure in *Per.* 42); *Per.* 45 (169). In the nature of things, census-taking was liable to problems and inaccuracies; if anything, the registered figures are probably too low. On the figures see, e.g., Brunt, *Italian Manpower;* N. Rosenstein, in *A Companion to the Punic Wars,* ed. D. Hoyos (Malden, 2010), 412–29; S. Hin, *The Demography of Roman Italy: Population Dynamics in an Ancient Conquest Society 201 BCE–14 CE* (Cambridge, 2013). Ligustinus' speech: cf. L. Keppie, *The Making of the Roman Army: From Republic to Empire* (London, 1984), 53–54; Hoyos, 39–47. Polybius on phalanx and legion: Walbank 2.585–91.

supported by Pergamene infantry and cavalry under King Eumenes, plus small units of Achaeans, Macedonians, Thracians, and Cretans (Livy 37.39.7–13 and nn.). A praetor's or propraetor's army consisted of one legion with associated Latins and Italian allies, except in the two Spanish provinces, where the military situation usually called for two each; there the praetors' legal authority (*imperium*: section 7) was officially at consular level, a technical but (in Roman eyes) important nicety.

In this period the old formal infantry strength of a legion, 4,200 infantrymen, often rose to 5,000 or more (at Magnesia each was 5,400 strong according to Livy). Although in early times legions were recruited for, and discharged after, a year's campaign, the great wars of the third and second centuries could keep them in service abroad for several years—often to the men's annoyance, especially if there was little plunder to be had. For battle, legionary infantry formed up in three lines, the so-called *triplex acies*, while a looser force of light-armed *velites*, theoretically 1,200 strong, were ranged before or around them. In the older legion 1,200 men formed the first line, the *hastati*; another 1,200 the second, called *principes*; the third comprised 600 seasoned veterans named *triarii*. Larger legions presumably increased their lines more or less proportionally, though the *triarii* may always have remained at 600.

The soldier leading each century was the *centurio*, appointed by the consul or praetor who was levying that army. A hierarchy of centurionships prevailed: the least-ranking centurion was in charge of the "rear" (*posterior*) century of the tenth maniple of the *hastati*, the highest-ranking leader of the "front" (*prior*) century of the first maniple of *triarii.* Termed the *primus pilus,* he was routinely part of the consul's or praetor's war council, along with the army's military tribunes and other senior officers. The *tribuni militum* (not to be confused with plebeian tribunes at Rome) were six to a legion; for the first four legions levied in a year they were elected by their fellow citizens, while those of any further legions were chosen by the recruiting consul or praetor. All were well-to-do, usually young men with senatorial relatives. A commander could also appoint trusted and experienced friends, always senators, as his deputies (*legati*): thus early in Book 31 we find L. Apustius serving as legate with the consul Galba in Greece, C. Claudius Centho another legate with the Roman fleet, and no fewer than five with the other consul Furius Purpurio in Cisalpine Gaul (31.27.1–8; 14.3, etc.; 21.8). In later times, with large armies such as Caesar's ten legions in Gaul, the practice grew of appointing a legate to command each legion, and this was the norm under the emperors.

In each line of the *triplex acies* the men were deployed in ten units, called maniples (*manipuli,* "handfuls"): each consisted of two "centuries" (*centuriae*) drawn up one behind the other. Thus there were notionally 120 men in each maniple of *hastati* and *principes,* and 60 in each of the *triarii*—all notionally, because it was at times difficult to recruit the desired total for a legion, or at other times because a legion was larger; in any case, during a war numbers in the army would inevitably shrink through fighting, disease, or desertion. The Latin and Italian allied cohorts were similarly ranged, with their own *praefecti* commanding them. The cavalry arm of a legion notionally numbered 300, with a larger force of allies, and as a rule were deployed on either side of the infantry when battle approached.

For battle, the maniples took up positions allowing a space between each, to form the maneuverable open deployment that Polybius approved, in contrast to the densely packed array of a phalanx. During battle, standard military doctrine of the period was for the *hastati* and *principes* to engage with the enemy either in turn or with the second line coming up to stiffen the first. They began by hurling their javelins (*pila*) at close range, and then for close combat each man drew his short two-sided sword (*gladius*). The *triarii*, all veterans, remained stationary as a reserve. The *velites* were used both to harass the other side ahead of the close combat and afterward—if victory was won—to harass fleeing enemy troops.

From the late third century another type of deployment appeared, the legionary cohort (the name was borrowed from the allied contingents): this grouped one maniple of *hastati*, *principes*, and *triarii* together, making ten cohorts per legion. Polybius mentions cohorts only occasionally—for instance, at the battle of Ilipa in 206 (11.22.10, 23.1)—but in Livy's fourth decade they appear quite often (31.2.6, 31.37.6, etc.), though it is not always clear whether he intends the term precisely or uses it because this had become the normal term for a legion's subunit (and he applies it at times to Greek units too: 31.24.6, 36.3, etc.). Cohort deployment gave an army further flexibility in maneuvers, but how often it was used in the early second century is not clear. Livy describes the Romans deploying in the *triplex acies* at Magnesia (37.39.8), and it was twenty maniples led by a resourceful military tribune that struck the decisive blow against Philip V's other phalanx at Cynoscephalae (33.9.8, *cum viginti signorum militibus,* following Polybius 18.26.1–2). Even when cohorts became the standard deployment, as seen in Caesar's *Commentaries,* the basic units remained maniples and (increasingly important) the centuries.

Despite ancient sources' proneness to focus on infantry, the cavalry was equally vital. Only well-off Romans could afford the cost of maintaining a cavalry horse and equipment (though the 1,800 mentioned earlier were formally recognized as *equites* by censors and given state assistance), so the cavalry arm of each legion was normally just 300. The bulk of the army's cavalry force came from the Latin and allied contingents and from foreign allies (like Eumenes at Magnesia). Cavalry sometimes decided the outcome of a battle, as at Cannae in 216 and at Magnesia; it always was essential for pursuing defeated enemies and for reconnoitering the terrain as the army marched.

Rome's naval power had debuted relatively recently, in the First Punic War against the sea might of Carthage. The fleets of the first two Punic Wars were larger than those in the second century, when no fleet seems to have been larger than one hundred battleships along with some extra smaller craft (cf. 32.21.27, in a speech by an Achaean leader). On water in the great Eastern wars, Rome again had notable help from allies Pergamum and Rhodes. From the early third century on, the prime warship was the quinquereme, or "fiver," a ship much larger than the trireme of classical Greek times. It seems to have needed three hundred oarsmen, perhaps arranged in groups of five (two on a topmost bench, two below, and one on the lowest bench) but the precise layout is still debated. It had an accompanying force of eighty to one hundred soldiers, as fighting involved ramming and if possible boarding the enemy's ships. Triremes and other smaller craft remained in use as support vessels and for skirmishes. Crews were drawn from Italian coastal allies and poor Romans not qualified to serve as legionaries, for legionaries had to provide their own equipment. As in the Second Punic War, Rome's second-century fleets fought few battles and instead spent their time escorting transport fleets, raiding hostile—and sometimes neutral—coasts, and from time to time attacking enemy cities.[22]

## 9. THE ROMAN CALENDAR

The calendar was an Etruscan-influenced device quite unlike those—for example, Greek, Jewish, Egyptian, and modern calendars—that were organized simply by months and their days. Each Roman month had three fixed reckoning points: the *Kalendae* (1st), *Nonae* (5th, except in March, May, July, and October when the Nones fell on the 7th), and the *Idus* (13th, apart from the months just named; their Ides were the 15th). The four months named had "late" Nones and Ides because they also had thirty-one days; February had twenty-eight when not intercalated (below). The other seven months, until reforms in 46 and 45 BC by Caesar the Dictator, had twenty-nine each.

Other day-dates were counted backward from each of

[22] On the Roman army, see now Erdkamp, *A Companion to the Roman Army;* Campbell and Tritle, *Oxford Handbook of Warfare,* who treat also the armed forces of other states. Hellenistic and contemporary Roman fleets: W. M. Murray, *The Age of Titans: The Rise and Fall of the Great Hellenistic Navies* (Oxford, 2012).

the fixed points, and inclusively too. Thus, while January 12 was called simply "the day before the January Ides" (*pridie Idus Ianuarias*), January 11 was "the third day before" those Ides (the Latin idiom is *ante diem tertium Idus Ianuarias*), and January 21 "the tenth day before the February Kalends," since January had twenty-nine days until Caesar's changes. These rules applied also to March and the other long months: March 14 was *pridie Idus Martias,* March 13 *a. d. tertium Id. Mart.* In a long month like March, March 21 was "the twelfth day before the April Kalends" through counting inclusively again. February was exceptional: not only in having the fewest days, as it still does, but also in losing its last five days every second year, replaced or "intercalated" by an entire extra month— of twenty-three, twenty-four, or twenty-seven days—after February 23 (cf. 37.59.2 n.). This was needed because the twelve-month Roman year was 355 days long: the intercalary month brought the calendar back into line with solar procession over the two-year span.

The task of authorizing the next intercalary month belonged to the College of Pontiffs, but the procedure was not always correctly done. It even seems to have been omitted sometimes: Livy reports a solar eclipse in 190 as occurring on July 11, but in reality the day was March 14 (37.4.4 n.); and he dates a lunar eclipse in 168, on the night before the battle of Pydna, to September 3, when the true astronomical date was June 21 (44.37.8; cf. 40.2.1 n.). Thus the difference between the Roman and solar dates in 190 was close on four months, in 168 two and a half— indicating not a consistent gap but fluctuations due most probably to pontiffs' varying intercalations (or lack of intercalations). As late as 49 BC (the traditional year), Caesar's famous crossing of the Rubicon on the night of January 10–11 actually took place at night on November 23–24 in 50 BC.

A Roman year was named after the two consuls who took office at its start. The start varied over time. Down to about 220, new consulships opened on, most probably, May 1; but by 217 the inaugural day was the Ides of March (Livy 22.1.4)—more or less the start of spring. In 153, to enable an earlier start to campaigning, it was changed to the Kalends of January, where it has remained ever since. As the centuries passed, dating an event to an earlier year required a prodigious memory or access to a detailed list of consuls (*fasti consulares*), such as the one inscribed on marble by the emperor Augustus and now in Rome's Palazzo dei Conservatori. Dating years simply by counting from the founding of Rome was never a common practice, partly no doubt because Rome's foundation year differed in varied strands of Roman tradition (*AUC* 31.1.3 n., 40.2.1 n.).[23]

## 10. THE TRANSMISSION OF THE FOURTH DECADE

For the editorial constitution of the text in this edition, see the Preface, above.

The text of *Ab Urbe Condita* Books 31 to 40 exists, in whole or in part, in several dozen manuscripts, most of

[23] The calendar: A. K. Michels, *The Calendar of the Roman Republic* (Princeton, 1967); D. Feeney, *Caesar's Calendar: Ancient Time and the Beginning of History* (Berkeley, 2007), and Feeney, "Time" (see Select Bibliography).

them late medieval *recentiores* (14th–15th c.) copied from a small number of older manuscripts, most of which are not extant themselves. The *recentiores* omit Book 33 and the last part of 40, showing they descend from an archetype that likewise lacked those sections.

In practice, the principal surviving manuscript is *B* (for Bambergensis), copied in the eleventh century from, it seems, a late Roman predecessor (see below). *B* was discovered at Bamberg in 1615, and Caspar de Lusignan utilized it for his publication of the fourth decade the following year at Rome. Then it disappeared, to reemerge only in 1822. In fact, the fourth decade forms only *B*'s first half and is incomplete at that, ending abruptly at 38.46.4 (the second half contains much of *AUC*'s third decade, from 24.7.8 to the end of Book 30).

Before the discovery of *B*, printed texts of the fourth decade depended on other manuscripts. A century earlier a manuscript probably of the ninth century had been found at Mainz and was used by the early Livian editor Nicholas Carbachius in his 1519 edition, itself published at Mainz, then in turn by Sigmund Gelenius at Basel in 1535. This manuscript is termed *Mg* (for Moguntinus, from the Roman name for Mainz). The use and citations of it by Carbachius and Gelenius were fortunate, for the manuscript itself was later irretrievably lost. *Mg* began at *AUC* 33.17.6 and ended with Book 40, so that *B* and *Mg* cover the complete decade between them. In the usual way of manuscripts, the readings often differ over words and phrases, and both suffer errors through faulty copying by their scribes, so that the textual evidence of other manuscripts, including the *recentiores,* remains important.

Scrappy manuscript evidence dating from earlier than *B* and *Mg* does exist. In 1904 a few fragments from a fifth-

century—thus late Roman—parchment copy of the decade were discovered, again at Bamberg, as parts of the
bindings of much later books. They consist of very brief
and scattered passages, usually only a few lines long, from
Books 33, 34, 35, and 39. The manuscript from which
they came is known to have been brought from Piacenza
in Italy just after the year 1001 and donated to the new
bishopric of Bamberg by the emperor Henry II in 1007—
only to be broken up and used for various purposes, book-
binding included, five hundred years later. The group of
fragments is conventionally termed *F.*

Next, in 1906 a very damaged fragment containing
*AUC* 34.36–40 emerged at Rome in the basilica of St. John
Lateran: it dates from the fifth or even the fourth century,
but in the eighth had been used to wrap up sacred relics.
This fragment, *R* (= Romanus), is full of copying errors
but nonetheless highly important because of its antiquity.
Scholarly consensus now identifies the late Roman *F* as the
immediate ancestor of *B* and *Sp* (below), perhaps also of
*Mg* (but debate on this continues), while *R* stems from a
separate copying tradition close to Livy's original.

Another manuscript no longer extant, *Sp* (Spirensis),
was discovered at Speyer early in the sixteenth century
by the great humanist scholar Beatus Rhenanus and contained most of *AUC* 26 to 40; but from the fourth decade
it omitted Book 33 and the last part of 40, as the *recentiores* do, and thus belongs to the same copying tradition.
As it was later lost, all that is known of *Sp*'s fourth decade
comes in the annotations made by Gelenius. Its recorded
readings and the texts of the *recentiores* nevertheless con-
tribute to establishing the original text of Livy (*Sp*'s chief
importance, however, is for the text of *AUC* 26–30, where
it was used by Rhenanus).

Among the late medieval manuscripts, certain copies have important value for establishing Livy's text. They are conventionally grouped in two families, called $\psi$ and $\phi$ (*psi* and *phi*). The $\psi$ group consists of five fifteenth-century manuscripts termed *N, V, C, L,* and *D,* which generally preserve the same copying errors as *B* (though at times they are influenced by manuscripts in the $\phi$ family). The $\phi$ manuscripts, termed *P, E,* and *A,* offer various errors not in the other family, but both manuscript families descend from a lost predecessor now conventionally called $\chi$ (*chi*). *P* (= Parisinus, early 14th c.) was once owned by Petrarch; another (*A* = *Agennensis,* of the same period but uniquely ending at 38.24.11) was possibly annotated by him, and certainly by Lorenzo Valla later. Another group of manuscripts, denominated $\alpha$ and all copied in 1412/13, show evidence nonetheless that their antecedent was in a continuous script and therefore very old. They are thought to be other descendants of $\chi$, and both $\chi$ itself and *Sp* have been identified as descended from *F*. The $\alpha$ group, therefore, is also an important contributor, especially to the text after *B* breaks off.

Many of the manuscripts—even fragmentary *F*—include corrections and annotations made by their copyists or by subsequent readers (*A* may include corrections by Petrarch, among others). The *recentiores* occasionally preserve text that is missing in *B* or *Mg:* for instance, 32.17.6, *trepidationemque insanam superstantibus armatis praebuerit,* where *B* has a space only about thirty letters long; 34.2.2, *singulas sustinere non potuimus* (*B* omits *sustinere*); 39.30.5, *quieti iis stativis* (omitted by *Mg*). At times too they offer a reading that makes better sense (see, e.g., textual notes to 34.61.2, 37.18.9, 39.21.1). Not all such variants are accepted by every editor: debates often continue over particular readings, as also over discrepancies between *B* and *Mg*. Preference in disputed readings usually remain with the principal manuscripts or the early fragments; but, as this edition's textual apparatus shows, sometimes no manuscript reading is acceptable, and scholarly corrections—also sometimes debated—become necessary.

## 11. FURTHER READING

Briscoe, J. "Praefatio." In *Titi Livi Ab Urbe Condita Libri XXXI–XL.* Vol. 1. Stuttgart, 1991. [in Latin]

de Franchis, Marielle: "Livian Manuscript Tradition." Chap. 1 in *A Companion to Livy,* edited by B. Mineo, 3–23 (with extensive bibliography, 20–23). Malden, MA, 2015).

McDonald, A. H., ed. "Praefatio ad Lectorem." In *Titi Livi Ab Urbe Condita Tomus V: XXXI–XXXV,* v–xlv. Oxford, 1965. [in Latin]

Reeve, M. *Manuscripts and Methods: Essays on Editing and Transmission.* Rome, 2011.

Sage, E. T., ed. and trans. "Translator's Preface." In *Livy: History of Rome.* Vol. 9, bks. 31–34. Loeb Classical Library. Cambridge, MA, 1967 [1935], ix–xvi.

## 12. SIGLA

| | |
|---|---|
| R | Vat. Lat. 10696 (IV–V), fragments |
| F | Bamb. Bibl. Rei Publicae Class. 35a (V), fragments |

| | |
|---|---|
| B | Bamb. Bibl. Rei Publicae Class. 35 (XI) |
| P | Par. Bibl. Nat. 5690 (XIV) |
| A | Lond. Bibl. Brit. Harl. 2493 (XIV) |
| E | Esc. R. I.4 (XIV) |
| N | Oxon. Coll. Novi 279 (ca. 1440) |
| V | Vat. Lat. 3331 (1412/13) |
| C | Flor. Laur. Med. 63.6 (1412/13) |
| L | Flor. Laur. Med. 89 inf. 3 (ca. 1445) |
| D | Cantab. Trin. 637 (XV) |
| Holk. | Bibl. Holkham 344 (XIV) |
| Lips. | Univ. Rep. 1.1 (XIV) |
| Esc. | Esc. G. I.8 (XIV) |
| Voss. | Leid. Voss. Lat. F66 (XIV) |
| Burn. | Lond. Bibl. Brit. Burn. |
| Par. | Bibl. Nat. Lat. |

Codex Moguntinus (IX), lost but which evidently contained Books 33.17.6, *iis partibus*–40.59.8, readings

| | |
|---|---|
| Mg | from libr. 34–40.37.3, *edixerunt* recorded in Mog. |
| Mg* | recorded in Mog. and in the annotations in Carb. |
| Mog. | ed. of N. Carbachus (Moguntiae 1519) |

| | |
|---|---|
| χ | consensus of φ ψ |
| φ | consensus of P A E |
| ψ | consensus of N V |
| α | consensus of Holk. Lips. Par. 5740 Esc. Voss. |
| β | consensus of Burn. and Par. 5741 |
| γ | consensus of Holk. 354 and Ves. |

## 13. WORKS CITED IN THE
## TEXTUAL NOTES

| | |
|---|---|
| Adam | (R.) ed. Budé lib. XXXVIII (Paris, 1982) |
| Ald. | ed. Aldina tom. III (Venice, 1520) |
| Asc. (1510) | ed. Badii Ascensii (Paris, 1510) |
| Asc. | ed. Badii Ascensii (Paris, 1513) |
| Bauer | (C. L.) *Chrestomathia Liviana* (Leipzig, 1770–1824) |
| Bekker | (I.) ed. Berolini (1829–1838) |
| Bessler | (F.) *Quaestionum Livianarum specimen* (Salzwedel, 1847) |
| Briscoe | (J.) *A Commentary on Livy, books XXXI–XXXIII, XXXIV–XXXVII* (Oxford, 1973, 1981); ed. Teubneriana librorum XXXI–XL (Leipzig, 1991) |
| Büttner | (C. F.) *Observationes Livianae* (Primislauiae, 1819) |
| Carb. | N. Carbachius, ed. (Mainz, 1519) |
| Cobet | (C. G.) "De locis nonnullis apud Livium," *Mnem.* (1882): 106–10 |
| Crév. | J. B. L. Crévier, ed. (Paris, 1735–1742) |
| Damsté | (P. H.) "Notae criticae ad T. Livii lib. XXXI–XXXV," "Ad T. Livii lib. XXXVI et XXXVII," "Ad T. Livii lib. XXXVIII–XL," *Mnem.* (1915): 155–69, 446–63; (1916): 396–422 |
| Doering | (F. G.) ed. Gothae (1796–1824) |
| Drak. | A. Drakenborch, ed., vol. IV et V (Leiden, 1741, 1743) |
| Duker | (K. A.) 1670–1752 |
| ed. Rom. | ed. Romae a. 1469 vel 1470 |

| | |
|---|---|
| Engel | (J.-M.) ed. Budé lib. XXXVII (Paris, 1983) |
| Florebellus | A. Florebelli, fl. 1550 |
| Fügner | (F.) *Lexicon Livianum* I (Leipzig, 1889–1897) |
| Gel. S. | Gelenii adnott. in ed. Frobeniana (Basel, 1535) |
| Glar. | H. Glareani adnott. in ed. (Basel, 1540) |
| Goeller | (F.) ed. libri XXXIII (Frankfurt, 1822) |
| Gron. | J. F. Gronov, ed. (Leiden, 1645–1678) |
| Grut. J. | Gruytere, ed. (Frankfurt, 1612–1628) |
| H. J. M. | H. J. Müller, *Wilhelm Weissenborn's erklärende Ausgabe,* VII$^3$, IX$^3$ (Berlin, 1883, 1906–7, 1909) |
| Harant | (A.) *Emendationes et adnotationes ad Titum Livium* (Paris, 1880) |
| Heraeus | (W.) ed. Teubneriana, pars V.1 (lib. XXXIX–XL) (Leipzig, 1908) |
| Hermann | (C. F.) *Disputatio de loco Apollinis in carmine Horatii saeculari* (Göttingen, 1843) |
| Hertz | (M.) ed. Lipsiae, vol. III (1862) |
| Heus. | K. Heusinger, *Livius. Römische Geschichte. Übersetzung mit kritischen und erklärenden Anmerkungen* (Brunswick, 1821) |
| Holleaux | (M.) *Études d' epigraphie et d' histoire grecques* (Paris, 1938–1968) |
| Horrion | (J.) ed. lib. XXXIII (Paderborn, 1617) |
| Hülsen | (C. C. F.) *Dissertazioni della Pontifica Accademia Romana di Archeologia* (1896) |
| Huschke | (P. E.), *Die Verfassung des Königs Servius Tullius* (Heidelberg, 1838) |

| | |
|---|---|
| Jacobs | (F.) ap. Goeller, pp. 385ff. |
| J. Gron. | J. Gronov, ed. (Amsterdam, 1679) |
| Koch | (H. A.) *Emendationum Livianarum pars altera* (Brandenburg, 1861) |
| Kreyssig | (J. T.) edd. Lipsiae (1823–1827, 1828); ed. lib. XXXIII (Misenae, 1839); ap. Goeller, pp. 408ff. |
| Lachmann | (F.) *De fontibus historiarum T. Livii commentatio altera* (Göttingen, 1828) |
| Luchs | (A.) *Emendationum Livianarum particula quarta* (Erlangae, 1889): 4–5 |
| M. Müller | *Beiträge zur Kritik und Erklärung des Livius* (Stendal, 1866, 1871; *NJPhP* 1869: 340–45; *"zu Livius" NJPhP* 1886: 855–63) |
| Madvig | (J. N.) *Emendationes Livianae* (Hauniae, 1860, 1877); ed. Ciceronis *De Finibus* (Hauniae, 1839); ed. Hauniae, vol. III (1863, 1865, pars I² 1884) |
| Mayerhoefer | (A.) *Critika studia Liviana* (Bamberg, 1880) |
| McDonald | (A. H.) ed. lib. XXXI–XXXV (Oxford, 1965) |
| Meibom | (M.) 1630–1710 |
| Merkel | (R.) ed. Ovidii *Fastorum* (Berlin, 1841) |
| Mommsen | (T.) *Römische Forschungen* (Berlin, 1864–1879); *Römisches Staatsrecht* (Leipzig, I–II2, 1887; III, 1888) |
| Muret | (M. A.) 1526–1585 |
| Niese | (B.) *Geschichte der griechischen und makedonischen Staaten seit der Schlacht bei Chaeronea* (Gotha, 1893–1903) |

| | |
|---|---|
| Nitsche | (W.) ap. H. J. M |
| Novák | (R.) in libris XXXI–XXXVIII "Mluvnicko-kritiká studia k Livioci," *Rozpravy Česká Akademia,* roč. 3, tr. 3 (1894); *in libris* XXXIX–XL *adnott. ap.* H. J. M |
| Ogilvie | (R. M.) *Phoenix* (1966): 343–47 |
| Perizonius | J. Voorbroek (1651–1715) |
| Pettersson | (O.) *Commentationes Livianae* (Uppsala, 1930) |
| Pighius | S. V. Wynants (1520–1604) |
| Pluygers | (G. G.) "ἀπομνημονεύματα," *Mnem.* (1881): 15–18 |
| r | G. Lusignanus, ed., princ. lib. XXXIII 1–17.6 (Rome, 1616) |
| Ramsay | (W. M.) *Historical Geography of Asia Minor* (London, 1890); *The Cities and Bishoprics of Phrygia* (Oxford, 1895–1896) |
| Ritschl | (F.) *Parerga zu Plautus und Terenz* (Leipzig, 1845) |
| rmg | F. Bartholini et A. Quaerengi, emendd. in marg. ed. |
| Rossbach | (O.) "Zum 31–35 Buche des Livius," "Zum 36. bis 40. Buche des Livius und zwei noch unbenützte Handschriften dieser Bücher," *WKlPh* (1917): 1128–35; (1918): 280–86, 476–78, 497–501 |
| Rubenius | A. Rubens (1614–1657) |
| Ruperti | (G. A.) ed. Gottingae (1807–1809) |
| Shackleton Bailey | (D. R.) "Liviana," *RFIC* (1986): 320–32 |

| | |
|---|---|
| Siesbye | (O.) ap. Madvig |
| Sig. | C. Sigonius, ed. (Venice, 1555–1572) |
| Smith | apud Walker |
| Tränkle | (H.) *Gnomon* (1967): 365–80; *Livius und Polybios* (Basel-Stuttgart, 1977) |
| Ussing | (J. L.) ap. Madvig |
| Valesius | H. de Valois (1603–1676) |
| Vielhaber | (L.) "Zu Livius," *ZöG* 1868: 405–18 |
| J. H. Voss | *Anmerkungen und Randglossen zu Griechen und Römern* (Leipzig, 1838): 280–88 |
| Walch | (G. L.) *Emendationes Livianae* (Berlin, 1815) |
| Walker | (J.) *Supplementary Annotations on Livy* (London, 1822) |
| Walsh | (P. G.) *CR* (1967): 53–56 |
| Weiss. | W. Weissenborn, *Lectionum Livianarum particula* I (Eisenach, 1833); ed. Teubnerianae partes IV–V (Leipzig, 1851); ed. Weidmann, Bände VII–IX, VII–IX.1 (Berlin, 1860, 1862, 1864, 1867, 1873, 1875); u. etiam H. J. M. |
| Wesenberg | (A. S.) "Emendatiunculae Livianae," *Tidskrift for Philologie og Paedagogik* (1870–71): 1–41, 81–111, 275–302; (1872–73): 205–314 |
| Wulsch | (G.) *De praepositionis "per" usu Liviano* (Halis Saxonum, 1880) |
| Zingerle | (A.) ed. Vindobonae-Lipsiae-Pragae, pars V–VI (1890–1894); "Zur vierten Decade des Livius," *SAWW* (1898) |

# APPENDIX:
## TRÄNKLE'S ANALYSIS OF POLYBIAN MATERIAL IN LIVY

This is a list of H. Tränkle's detailed breakdown of the passages in Books 31 to 40 that he identifies as based on Polybius. Though scholarly opinions may differ in some cases, it is a convenient schema to have in hand.

| Livy | Polybius | |
|---|---|---|
| 31.14.11–15.8 | 16.25.4–26.10 | Attalus I at Athens |
| 16.1 | 28.1–9 | Philip's behavior |
| 17.1–18.8 | 29.3–34.12 | Siege of Abydus |
| 32.32.9–37.6 | 18.1.1–12.5 | Conference of Nicaea |
| 40.10f. | 17.1–5 | Nabis of Sparta |
| 33.2.1 | 17.6 | Attalus I before the Boeotian Council |
| 5.4–10.7 | 18.1–27.6 | Cynoscephalae |
| 11.1f. | 33.1–8 | " |
| 11.4–13.15 | 34.1–39.6 | Peace negotiations |
| 21.1–5 | 41.1–10 | Character of Attalus I |
| 27.5–28.3 | 43.1–12 | Murder of Brachylles of Boeotia |
| 28.10 | 43.13 | " |
| 30.1–35.12 | 44.1–49.10 | Freedom proclamation; end of war |
| 39.1–40.6 | 49.2–52.5 | Negotiations with Antiochus III |
| 35.45.9–46.1 | 20.1 | Antiochus III in Greece |
| 50.5 | 2 | " |

| Livy | Polybius | |
|---|---|---|
| 36.5.1–6.3 | 3.1–7.5 | " |
| 11.1f. | 8.1–5 | " |
| 27.1–29.11 | 9.1–11.8 | Phaeneas and Acilius Glabrio |
| 30.4 | 11.10 | Campaign of Glabrio |
| 33.7 | 11.12 | " |
| 37.6.4–7.7 | 21.4.1–5.13 | Negotiations with the Aetolians |
| 9.1–4 | 6.1–6 | Naval war with Antiochus |
| 9.9 | 6.7 | " |
| 11.13 | 7.1–4 | " |
| 12.9 | 7.5–7 | " |
| 14.5f. | fr. 154(74) | " |
| 18.6–19.8 | 10.1–14 | Antiochus unsuccessfully offers negotiations |
| 20.2 | 9.1–3 | Diophanes the Achaean |
| 25.4–26.2 | 11.1–13 | Prusias' diplomatic efforts |
| 27.5 | 12 | Naval war |
| 33.3–7–36.9 | 13.1–15.13 | Peace efforts of Heracleides |
| 45.3–21 | 16.1–17.12 | Peace negotiations |
| 52.7–56.10 | 18.5–24.15 | Eastern embassies to senate |
| 38.3.1–11 | 25.1–26.6 | Fighting with the Aetolians |
| 5.1–5 | 27.1–6 | Siege of Ambracia |

| Livy | Polybius | |
|---|---|---|
| 5.6–10 | 27.7–9 | " |
| 7.4–8.1 | 28.1–18 | " |
| 9.3–11.9 | 29.1–32.14 | Peace with the Aetolians |
| 12.1 | 33.1 | Manlius Vulso's Galatian campaign |
| 12.7 | 33.2 | |
| 14.3–14 | 34.1–13 | |
| 15.3–6 | 35 | |
| 15.7–11 | 36 | |
| 18.1 and 3 | 37.1–3 | |
| 18.7–10 | 37.4–7 | |
| 18.14f. | 37.8f. | |
| 24.2–11 | 38 | |
| 25.1–10 | 39 | |
| 29.10 | 32b | Capture of Cephallenia |
| 37.1–39.2 | 41.1–44.3 | Roman envoys in Asia Minor conclude peace |
| 39.6 | 45 | " |
| 39.7–40.1 | 46.1–12 | " |
| 39.23.5 | 22.18 | Philip's power politics and Rome's mistrust of him |
| 24.6–13 | 6.1–6 | " |
| 33.1–8 | 11.1–12.10 | " |
| 34.1–35.4 | 13.1–14.12 | " |
| 46.6–48.5 | 23.1.1–4.16 | Demetrius before the senate |

| Livy | Polybius | |
|---|---|---|
| 53.1–14 | 7.1–8.7 | Demetrius' return home |
| 40.2.6–3.2 | 9.1–15 | Philip's brutal behavior |
| 3.3–7 | 10.1–11 | " |
| 5.1 | 10.12–16 | Discord in Macedon's royal family |
| 8.11–16 | 11.1–8 | " |
| 20.1f. | 24.1.1–7 | Embassies before the senate |
| 22.5 | 4 | Philip on Mount Haemus |
| 41.20.1–9 | 26.1.1–11 | Character of Antiochus IV |
| 42.44.1–45.8 | 27.1.1–3.5 | Roman embassies in Greece |
| 46.1–10 | 4.1–5.8 | Perseus' diplomatic activities |
| 48.1–4 | 6.1–4 | " |
| 62.3–63.2 | 8.1–10.5 | Perseus' peace offer after cavalry victory |
| 65.9f. | 11.1–7 | The *cestrosphendone* weapon |
| 43.17.2–9 | 28.3.1–5.6 | Roman embassies in Greece |
| 19.13–20.3 | 8.1–11 | Perseus' negotiations with Genthius |
| 23.8 | 9.1–8 | " |

| Livy | Polybius | |
|------|----------|---|
| 44.7.8f. | 10.1f. | Romans break into Macedon—Perseus reproaches his advisers |
| 9.3–9 | 11.1–3 | " |
| 23.1–24.6 | 29.3.1–4.10 | Perseus' diplomatic activities |
| 24.7–26.2 | 5.1–9.13 | " |
| 29.6f. | 11.1–6 | " |
| 30.4f. | 13.1f. | Genthius murders his brother Plator |
| 35.14 | 14.1–3 | Military operations |
| 35.19 | 14.4 | " |
| 41.4 | 17.2 | Battle of Pydna |
| 42.2 | 17.3f. and 18 | " |
| 45.3.3–8 | 19.1–11 | Rhodian envoys before the senate |
| 7.4 | fr. 74 | Perseus before Aemilius Paullus |
| 8.6f. | 20.1–4 | " |

# ABBREVIATIONS

| | |
|---|---|
| Adam | Richard Adam, *Tite-Live, Histoire Romaine, Livre XXXV* (Paris, 2004). Cited ad loc. |
| *Barr.* | R. J. A. Talbert, ed., *Barrington Atlas of the Greek and Roman World* (Princeton, NJ, 2000). |
| Beard | Mary Beard, *The Roman Triumph.* (Cambridge, MA, 2009). |
| Briscoe 1 | John Briscoe, *A Commentary on Livy: Books XXXI–XXXIII* (Oxford, 1973). Cited by volume and page number or ad loc. |
| Briscoe 2 | John Briscoe, *A Commentary on Livy: Books XXXIV–XXXVII* (Oxford, 1981). Cited by volume and page number or ad loc. |
| Briscoe 3 | John Briscoe, *A Commentary on Livy: Books 38–40* (Oxford, 2008). Cited by volume and page number or ad loc. |
| Engel | Jean-Marie Engel, *Tite-Live, Histoire Romaine, Livre XXXVII* (Paris, 2003). Cited ad loc. |
| Hoyos | Dexter Hoyos, *A Roman Army Reader* (Mundelein, IL, 2013). |

| | |
|---|---|
| *ILS* | H. Dessau, *Inscriptiones Latinae Selectae*, 3 vols. in 5 (Berlin, 1892–1916). |
| Levene | D. S. Levene, *Religion in Livy* (Leiden, 1993). |
| L-S-J | H. G. Liddel, R.Scott, H. S. Jones, *A Greek-English Lexicon*, 9th ed. (Oxford, 1940). |
| McDonald | A. H. McDonald, *Titi Livi ab urbe condita, Tomus V, Libri XXXI–XXXV* (Oxford, 1965). |
| Manuelian | André Manuelian, *Tite-Live, Histoire Romaine, Livre XXXVI* (Paris, 1983. Cited ad loc. |
| Mineo | Bernard Mineo, *Tite-Live, Histoire Romaine, Livre XXXII* (Paris, 2004). Cited ad loc. |
| Mineo *Companion* | Bernard Mineo, ed., *A Companion to Livy*. Blackwell Companions to the Ancient World (Malden, MA, 2015). |
| *MRR* | T. R. S. Broughton, *The Magistrates of the Roman Republic, vol. 1 (509 BC–100BC)*, with the collaboration of Marcia L. Patterson. (Cleveland, OH, 1951, repr. 1968). |
| Oakley | S. P. Oakley, *A Commentary on Livy, Books VI–X*, 4 vols. (Oxford, 1997–2005). Cited by volume and page number. |
| *OCD* | Simon Hornblower, Antony Spawforth, and Esther Eidinow, eds., *The Oxford Classical Dictionary*, 4th ed. (Oxford, 2012). |

| | |
|---|---|
| *OLD* | P. G. W. Glare, ed., *The Oxford Latin Dictionary* (Oxford, 1968–1982). |
| Richardson | L. Richardson, Jr., *A New Topographical Dictionary of Ancient Rome* (Baltimore, 1992). |
| Sage | Evan T. Sage, ed. and trans., *Livy XXXI–XL,* The Loeb Classical Library (Cambridge, MA, 1935–1938). |
| TIR *K-29* | Tabula Imperii Romani Hoja K-29: *Porto. Conimbriga, Bracara, Lucus, Asturica* (Madrid, 1991). |
| TIR *K-30* | Tabula Imperii Romani Hoja K-30: *Madrid. CaesarAugusta, Clunia* (Madrid, 1993). |
| TIR *J-30* | Tabula Imperii Romani Hoja J-30: *Valencia* (Madrid, 2001). |
| TIR *K/J-31* | Tabula Imperii Romani Hoja K/J-31: *Pyrénées Orientales-Baleares. Tarraco, Baleares* (Madrid, 1997). |
| Walbank | F. W. Walbank, *A Historical Commentary on Polybius I–III* (Oxford, 1956, 1967, 1979). Cited by volume and page number. |
| Walsh | P. G. Walsh, *Livy, Books XXXVI, XXXVII, XXXVIII, XXXIX, and XL,* edited with Introduction, Translation and Commentary (Warminster, UK, 1990, 1992, 1993, 1994, 1996). Cited by volume and page number or ad loc. |
| Walsh *OCT* | P. G. Walsh, *Titi Livi ab urbe condita, Tomus VI, Libri XXXVI–XL.* Oxford Classical Texts (Oxford, 1999). |

# SELECT BIBLIOGRAPHY

## [LIVY XXXI–XL]

The bibliography of Livy is vast, and the list here is perforce very selective. Those seeking further bibliographical assistance are advised to consult the bibliographies to be found in S. P. Oakley's four commentaries on Livy, which are indispensable for anyone working on Livy, and in Jane D. Chaplin and Christina S. Kraus's Oxford Readings in Classical Studies, as well as the "Abbreviations" in John Briscoe's commentaries on the fourth decade. These books are listed below.

### Critical Editions

Briscoe, John, ed. *Livius: Ab Urbe Condita, Libri XXXI–XL.* 2 vols. Teubner, 1991.

McDonald, Alexander Hugh, ed. *Titi Livi Ab Urbe Condita, Tomus V, XXXI–XXXV.* Oxford Classical Texts. Oxford, 1965.

Walsh, P. G., ed. *Titi Livi Ab Urbe Condita, Tomus VI, Libri XXXVI–XL.* Oxford Classical Texts. Oxford, 1999.

Weissenborn, W., and H. J. Müller. *Titi Livi ab urbe condita libri.* Berlin, 1880–1911.

## SELECT BIBLIOGRAPHY

### Commentaries

Briscoe, John, ed. *A Commentary on Livy: Books XXXI–XXXIII*. Oxford, 1973.

———. *A Commentary on Livy: Books XXXIV–XXXVII*. Oxford, 1981.

———. *A Commentary on Livy: Books 38–40*. Oxford, 2008.

### Editions with Commentary and Translation

Achard, G. *Tite-Live, Histoire Romaine, Livre XXXIII*. Paris, 2002.

Adam, A-M. *Tite-Live, Histoire Romaine, Livre XXXIX*. Paris, 1994.

Adam, R. *Tite-Live, Histoire Romaine, Livre XXXVIII*. Paris, 1982.

———. *Tite-Live, Histoire Romaine, Livre XXXV*. Paris, 2004.

Engel, J-M. *Tite-Live, Histoire Romaine, Livre XXXVII*. Paris, 1983.

Gouillart, C. *Tite-Live, Histoire Romaine, Livre XL*. Paris, 1986.

Hus, Alain. *Tite-Live, Histoire Romaine, Livre XXXI*. Paris, 1990.

Jal, Paul. *Abrégés des Livres de l'histoire Romaine de Tite-Live: Periochae 1–69*. Paris, 2003.

Manuelian, André. *Tite-Live, Histoire Romaine, Livre XXXVI*. Paris, 1983.

Mineo, Bernard. *Tite-Live, Histoire Romaine, Livre XXXII*. Paris, 2003.

Sage, Evan T. *Livy IX, Books XXXI–XXXIV.* Loeb Classical Library. Cambridge, MA, 1935.

———. *Livy X, Books XXXV–XXXVII.* Loeb Classical Library. Cambridge, MA, 1935.

———. *Livy XI, Books XXXVIII–XXXIX.* Loeb Classical Library. Cambridge, MA, 1936.

Sage, Evan T., and Alfred D. Schlessinger. *Livy XII, Books XL–XLII.* Loeb Classical Library. Cambridge, MA, 1938.

Walsh, P.G. *Livy, Book XXXVI.* Edited with an Introduction, Translation, and Commentary. Warminster, UK, 1990.

———. *Livy, Book XXXVII.* Edited with an Introduction, Translation, and Commentary. Warminster, UK, 1992.

———. *Livy, Book XXXVIII.* Edited with an Introduction, Translation, and Commentary. Warminster, UK, 1993.

———. *Livy, Book XXXIX.* Edited with an Introduction, Translation, and Commentary. Warminster, UK, 1994.

———. *Livy, Book XL.* Edited with an Introduction, Translation, and Commentary. Warminster, UK, 1996.

### *English Translations*

*Livy: Rome and the Mediterranean.* Translated by Henry Bettenson, with an Introduction and Notes by A. H. McDonald. London, 1976.

*Livy: The Dawn of the Roman Empire: Books 31–40.* Translated by J. C. Yardley, with an Introduction and Notes by Waldemar Heckel. Oxford World's Classics. Oxford, 2000.

# SELECT BIBLIOGRAPHY

## *General*

Badian, E. "The Early Historians." In *Latin Historians,* edited by T. A. Dorey, 1–38. London, 1966.

Briscoe, J. "Some Misunderstandings of Polybius in Livy." In *Polybius and His World: Essays in Memory of F. W. Walbank,* edited by B. Gibson and T. Harrison, 117–24. Oxford, 2013.

Brunt, P. A. *Italian Manpower 225 B.C.–A.D. 14.* Oxford, 1971.

Campbell, B., and L. Tritle, L., eds. *The Oxford Handbook of Warfare in the Classical World.* Oxford, 2013.

Champion, C. B. "Livy and the Greek Historians from Herodotus to Dionysius: Some Soundings and Reflections." In Mineo, *A Companion to Livy,* 190–204.

Chaplin, J. D. *Livy's Exemplary History.* Oxford, 2000.

———, trans. *Livy: Rome's Mediterranean Empire: Books 41–45 and the* Periochae. With Introduction and Notes. Oxford, 2007.

Chaplin, Jane D., and Christina S. Kraus, eds. *Oxford Readings in Classical Studies: Livy.* Oxford, 2009.

Cornell, T. J., ed. *The Fragments of the Roman Historians.* 3 vols. Oxford, 2013.

Davidson, J. "Polybius." In *The Cambridge Companion to the Roman Historians,* edited by A. Feldherr, 123–36. Cambridge, 2009.

Dorey, T. A., ed. *Livy.* London, 1971.

Eckstein, A. M. *Rome Enters the Greek East: From Anarchy to Hierarchy in the Hellenistic Mediterranean, 230–170 BC.* Malden, 2012.

———. "Livy, Polybius, and the Greek East (Books 31–45)." In Mineo, *A Companion to Livy,* 407–22.

## SELECT BIBLIOGRAPHY

Erdkamp, P., ed. *A Companion to the Roman Army.* Malden, 2007.

Feeney, D. "Time." In *The Cambridge Companion to the Roman Historians,* edited by A. Feldherr, 139–51. Cambridge, 2009.

Gruen, E. S. *The Hellenistic World and the Coming of Rome.* 2 vols. Berkeley, 1984.

Hoyos, B. D. *Unplanned Wars: The Origins of the First and Second Punic Wars.* Berlin, 1998.

Hoyos, Dexter. *A Roman Army Reader.* Mundelein, IL, 2013.

———. *Mastering the West: Rome and Carthage at War.* Oxford, 2015.

Dessau, H. *Inscriptiones Latinae Selectae.* 3 vols. in 5. Berlin, 1892–1916.

Jaeger, M. *Livy's Written Rome.* Ann Arbor, 1997.

Levene, D. S. *Religion in Livy.* Leiden, 1993.

Lintott, A. *The Constitution of the Roman Republic.* Oxford, 1999.

Luce, T. J. *Livy: The Composition of His History.* Princeton, 1977.

McGing, B. *Polybius' Histories.* Oxford Approaches to Classical Literature. Oxford, 2010.

Mineo, Bernard, ed. *A Companion to Livy.* Blackwell Companions to the Ancient World. (Malden, MA, 2015.

Oakley, S. P. *A Commentary on Livy, Books VI–X.* 4 vols. Oxford, 1997–2005.

Ogilvie, R. M., ed. *A Commentary on Livy, Books 1–5* Oxford, 1965.

Staveley, E. S. *Greek and Roman Voting and Elections.* London, 1972.

Syme, R. "Livy and Augustus." *Harvard Studies in Classical Philology* 64 (1959): 27–87.

Tränkle, H. *Livius und Polybios*. Basel, 1977.

von Ungern-Sternberg, J. "Livy and the Annalistic Tradition." In Mineo, *A Companion to Livy*, 167–77.

Walbank, F. W. "The Fourth and Fifth Decades." In Dorey, *Livy*.

———. *Polybius*. Sather Classical Lectures 42. Berkeley, 1972.

———. "Fortune (*tyche*) in Polybius." In *A Companion to Greek and Roman Historiography*, vol. 2, edited by J. Marincola, 349–55. Oxford, 2007.

Walsh, P. G. *Livy: His Historical Aims and Methods*. Cambridge, 1961.

Waterfield, R. *Taken at the Flood: The Roman Conquest of Greece*. Oxford, 2014.

## Other

Hammond, N. G. L. *Epirus*. Oxford, 1967.

Treggiari, Susan. *Roman Marriage: Iusti Coniuges from the time of Cicero to the time of Ulpian*. Oxford, 1991.

Walbank, F. W. *A Historical Commentary on Polybius*. 3 vols. Oxford, 1957, 1967, 1979.

# HISTORY OF ROME

# LIBER XXXI

1. Me quoque iuvat, velut ipse in parte laboris ac periculi
2 fuerim, ad finem belli Punici pervenisse. nam etsi profiteri
ausum perscripturum res omnes Romanas in partibus sin-
3 gulis tanti operis fatigari minime conveniat, tamen cum in
mentem venit tres et sexaginta annos—tot enim sunt a
primo Punico ad secundum bellum finitum—aeque multa
4 volumina occupasse mihi quam occupaverint quadringenti duodenonaginta[1] anni a condita urbe ad Ap. Clau-
5 dium consulem, qui primum bellum Carthaginiensibus
intulit, iam provideo animo, velut qui proximi litoris[2] vadis
inducti mare pedibus ingrediuntur, quidquid progredior,
in vastiorem me altitudinem ac velut profundum invehi,
et crescere paene opus, quod prima quaeque perficiendo
minui videbatur.
6      Pacem Punicam bellum Macedonicum excepit, peri-

---

[1] lxxxviii *Glar.*: lxxviii $B\chi$ (septuaginta octo $\chi$)
[2] proximi litoris $\chi$: proximi litori $B$: proximis litoris *ed.Rom.*

---

[1] Dates are BC unless marked AD.
[2] Livy's prefaces to this book and to Book 21 (the start of the Hannibalic war) suggest that his history followed a decadal or pentadal structure (see Introduction, xv–xvii).
[3] The first started in 264, and the second ended in 201.

# BOOK XXXI[1]

1. I too am happy to have reached the end of the Punic war, just as if I had myself shared its hardships and dangers![2] While it is most inappropriate for one who has made the rash promise to cover all Roman history to flag in specific sections of such a major work, it does nevertheless occur to me that the sixty-three years from the beginning of the First Punic War to the end of the Second[3] have taken up as many scrolls as did the four hundred and eighty-eight years[4] between the foundation of the city and the consulship of Appius Claudius,[5] who began the first war with Carthage. I feel like those who wade out into the depths after being initially attracted to the water by the shallows of the sea at the shoreline; and I foresee any advance only taking me into even more enormous, indeed bottomless, depths, and that this undertaking of mine, which seemed to be diminishing as I was completing the earliest sections, is now almost increasing in size.

Peace with Carthage was followed by war with Mace-

---

[4] The manuscripts read seventy-eight years, which would give 742/1 as the date for the founding of Rome, whereas Livy elsewhere clearly regards it as 751/0. As numerals are often corrupted in transmission, Glareanus' emendation (see textual note) is to be accepted.

[5] Appius Claudius Caudex (102), consul in 264 (*MRR* 202–3).

culo haudquaquam comparandum aut virtute ducis aut
7 militum robore, claritate regum antiquorum vetustaque
fama gentis et magnitudine imperii, quo multa quondam
Europae maiorem partem Asiae obtinuerant armis, prope
8 nobilius. ceterum coeptum bellum adversus Philippum
decem ferme ante annis triennio prius depositum erat,
9 cum Aetoli et belli et pacis fuissent causa. vacuos deinde
pace Punica iam Romanos, et infensos Philippo cum ob
infidam adversus Aetolos aliosque regionis eiusdem socios
10 pacem, tum ob auxilia cum pecunia nuper in Africam
missa Hannibali Poenisque, preces Atheniensium, quos
agro pervastato in urbem compulerat, excitaverunt ad re-
novandum bellum.

2. Sub idem fere tempus et ab Attalo rege et Rhodiis
legati venerunt, nuntiantes Asiae quoque civitates sollici-
2 tari. his legationibus responsum est curae eam rem senatui
fore; consultatio de Macedonico bello integra ad consules,

---

6 The "enemy commander" is Philip V of Macedon; the "kings
of old" are primarily Philip II (382–336), who established Macedon as a great power, and his even more famous son, Alexander
(to whom Livy devotes an excursus in Book 9 [17–19] on whether
Alexander could have defeated the Romans).

7 This is unfair. The First Macedonian War began in 215,
when Philip made a treaty with Hannibal after the Roman defeat
at Cannae, but the Romans then made an alliance with the Aetolians against Philip in 212 or 211. When, however, they lost interest in Greece later in the Punic War (207/6), the Aetolians, left
isolated, had to make a separate peace with Philip in 206. Preoccupied with Hannibal, the Romans also made a peace treaty with
Philip, at Phoenice in Epirus in 205.

8 Livy often talks of reports brought to the senate of troops
and money having been sent to Africa (30.25.4, 30.33.5, 30.42.4,

don. Though not at all comparable in terms of the threat it posed, the courage of the enemy commander, or the strength of his forces, the Macedonian war was almost more noteworthy because of the fame of Macedon's kings of old, the ancient glory of its people, and the extent of its empire, within which the Macedonians had earlier held much of Europe and most of Asia.[6] The war against Philip had started some ten years before this, but had been discontinued for a three year period when the Aetolians had turned out to be the cause of both the war and peace.[7] But the Romans then found themselves unencumbered as a result of the peace made with Carthage, and they were infuriated with Philip over the treacherous peace that he had concluded with the Aetolians and his other allies in the region, and also over the military and financial assistance that he had recently sent to Africa for Hannibal and the Carthaginians.[8] As a result, entreaties made to them by the Athenians, whom Philip had driven back into their city after pillaging their farmland, prompted them to recommence hostilities against him.[9]

2. At about the same time ambassadors arrived from both King Attalus[10] and the Rhodians, reporting that the city-states of Asia were also being harassed by Philip. The response given to the embassies was that the senate would examine the situation; and the whole question of war with

11.9 below, 34.22.8, 45.22.6). Polybius, however, is silent on this. (For sections of Livy 31–40 that correspond to surviving parts of Polybius, see Introduction, xix–xxvi, lxxviii–lxxxii).

[9] The Athenians had been included in the Peace of Phoenice (29.12.14).    [10] Attalus I of Pergamum (mod. Bergama) in Asia Minor, a Roman ally since 210.

3 qui tunc in provinciis erant, reiecta est. interim ad Ptolomaeum Aegypti regem legati tres missi, C. Claudius Nero
M. Aemilius Lepidus P. Sempronius Tuditanus, ut nuntiarent victum Hannibalem Poenosque, et gratias agerent
regi quod in rebus dubiis, cum finitimi etiam socii Roma-
4 nos desererent, in fide mansisset, et peterent ut si coacti
iniuriis bellum adversus Philippum suscepissent, pristinum animum erga populum Romanum conservaret.

5 Eodem fere tempore P. Aelius consul in Gallia, cum
audisset a Boiis ante suum adventum incursiones in agros
sociorum factas, duabus legionibus subitariis tumultus
6 eius causa scriptis, additisque ad eas quattuor cohortibus
de exercitu suo, C. Ampium praefectum socium hac tu-
multuaria manu per Vmbriam, qua[3] tribum Sapiniam vocant, agrum Boiorum invadere iussit; ipse eodem aperto

---

[3] qua *Madvig*: quam B$\chi$

---

[11] Latin *provincia:* the sphere of authority assigned to a senior
magistrate. Wars were often "spheres of authority," and as these
were often, as here, designated by their territorial name ("Macedonia," "Gaul," etc.), it often refers to a territorial responsibility.
I have usually translated it as "province" but sometimes, where
appropriate, as "area of authority/responsibility." The consuls for
201 were Cn. Cornelius Lentulus (176) and P. Aelius Paetus
(101). Cf. 30.40.5 for their election.

[12] C. Claudius Nero (246): praetor 212, consul 207, censor
204. M. Aemilius Lepidus (68): later curule aedile 193, praetor
191, consul 187 and again in 175, censor 179. P. Sempronius
Tuditanus (96): curule aedile 214, praetor 213, censor 209, consul
204. In 205 he had concluded the Peace of Phoenice (29.12.11–
16).

[13] Ptolemy V Epiphanes (*OCD* sv). A treaty of friendship

Macedon was referred to the consuls, who were at that time involved with their assignments.[11] In the meantime three ambassadors—Gaius Claudius Nero, Marcus Aemilius Lepidus and Publius Sempronius Tuditanus[12]— were sent to King Ptolemy of Egypt[13] to report to the king that Hannibal and the Carthaginians had been defeated, and to thank him for remaining loyal to the Romans at a critical time, when even allies who were their closest neighbors were deserting them. They were also to request of Ptolemy that he maintain his former disposition toward the Roman people should they be forced by Philip's aggression to commence hostilities with him.

At about the same time, in Gaul, the consul Publius Aelius had been told that before his arrival attacks had been made on territory of the allies by the Boii,[14] and he had enrolled two hastily raised legions to meet the crisis, adding to them four cohorts from his own army. He then instructed the allied commander, Gaius Ampius, to invade the territory of the Boii with this makeshift body through Umbria, going by way of what they call the Tribus Sapinia.[15] Aelius himself led his troops to the same area by the

(*amicitia*) existed between Rome and Egypt. Concluded in 273, it had been renewed by Ptolemy IV Philopater in 210 (27.4.10).

[14] A Gallic people, who had helped Hannibal, they lived between the River Po and the Appenines (*Barr.* 40 A3). Their capital was Felsina, later renamed Bononia (mod. Bologna).

[15] The Tribus Sapinia and Mutilum (below) occur elsewhere only at 33.37.1–2. Their location is uncertain, but Sapinia is probably connected with the River Sapis (mod. Savio) near Ravenna, and Mutilum is possibly today's Modigliana, about thirty-one miles southeast of Bologna.

7 itinere per montes duxit. Ampius ingressus hostium fines
primo populationes satis prospere ac tuto fecit. delecto
deinde ad castrum Mutilum satis idoneo loco ad deme-
8 tenda frumenta—iam enim maturae erant segetes—, profectus neque explorato circa nec stationibus satis firmis
quae armatae inermes atque operi intentos tutarentur
positis, improviso impetu Gallorum cum frumentatoribus
9 est circumventus. inde pavor fugaque etiam armatos cepit.
ad septem milia hominum palata per segetes sunt caesa,
inter quos ipse C. Ampius praefectus; ceteri in castra metu
10 compulsi. inde sine certo duce consensu militari proxima
nocte, relicta magna parte rerum suarum, ad consulem
11 per saltus prope invios pervenere. qui nisi quod populatus
est Boiorum fines, et cum Ingaunis Liguribus foedus icit,
nihil quod esset memorabile aliud in provincia cum gessisset, Romam rediit.

3. Cum primum senatum habuit, universis postulantibus ne quam prius rem quam de Philippo ac sociorum
2 querellis ageret, relatum extemplo est; decrevitque frequens senatus ut P. Aelius consul quem videretur ei cum
imperio mitteret, qui, classe accepta quam ex Sicilia Cn.

---

16 *Barr.* 16 F1. They lived close to what is now the French
border and had struck an alliance with Hannibal's brother Mago
when he arrived in Italy in 205 (28.46.11).

17 The power to command in peace and in war, held by dictators, consuls, and praetors, who retained it if their terms were
prorogued. Its holders could impose the death penalty within the
army and had supreme authority over the civilian population,
power that was symbolized by the fasces carried before them by
lictors (see Introduction, lii). It should be noted, however, that no
ancient definition of *imperium* survives.

18 Cn. Octavius (16), praetor in 205, with his office prorogued

8

open road through the mountains. On entering enemy territory, Ampius made a number of relatively successful raids without exposing himself to danger. But then he selected a spot near the fortified town of Mutilum that was convenient for harvesting grain, the crops being already ripe, and set out without reconnoitering the area or establishing armed posts strong enough to protect unarmed men engrossed in their work; and when the Gauls suddenly attacked, he was cut off with his foragers. Even those under arms then fell prey to panic and flight. Some 7,000 men, including the commander Ampius himself, were cut down as they scattered through the fields; and the others were driven in fear back into their camp. The following night the soldiers, left with no recognized leader, made an agreement among themselves, abandoned most of their possessions, and made their way to the consul through mountain ravines that were almost impossible to negotiate. Aelius then returned to Rome, having accomplished nothing of note in his province apart from his raids on the territory of the Boii and a treaty concluded with the Ligurian Ingauni.[16]

3. When Aelius convened the first meeting of the senate, all members requested that no item be considered before that of Philip and the grievances of the allies, and the matter was immediately brought up for discussion. A packed house decided that the consul Publius Aelius should send out a man of his own choice, with *imperium*,[17] to assume control of the fleet that Gnaeus Octavius[18] was

a number of times, became Scipio's legate in Africa in 200. He had been directed to take the fleet to Sicily to be transferred to the consul Gnaeus Cornelius (30.44.13).

9

3 Octavius reduceret, in Macedoniam traiceret. M. Valerius
Laevinus propraetor missus, circa Vibonem duodequadra-
ginta navibus ab Cn. Octavio acceptis, in Macedoniam
4 transmisit. ad quem cum M. Aurelius legatus venisset,
edocuissetque eum quantos exercitus quantum navium
5 numerum comparasset rex, quemadmodum[4] circa omnes
non continentis modo urbes sed etiam insulas partim
ipse adeundo, partim per legatos conciret homines ad
6 arma—maiore conatu Romanis id capessendum bellum
esse, ne cunctantibus iis auderet Philippus quod Pyrrhus
prius ausus ex aliquanto minore regno esset—, haec scribere eadem Aurelium consulibus senatuique placuit.

4. Exitu huius anni cum de agris veterum militum relatum esset qui ductu atque auspicio P. Scipionis in Africa
2 bellum perfecissent, decreverunt patres ut M. Iunius
praetor urbanus, si ei videretur, decemviros agro Samniti
Apuloque, quod eius publicum populi Romani esset, me-
3 tiendo dividendoque crearet. creati P. Servilius, Q. Caecilius Metellus, C. et M. Servilii—Geminis ambobus cognomen erat—, L. et A. Hostilii Catones, P. Villius Tappulus,

---

[4] quemadmodum *B*: et quemadmodum χ

---

[19] M. Valerius Laevinus (211), praetor in 215 and commander
in the First Macedonian War from 215 to 211.

[20] Vibo Valentia, close to the west coast of Italy, about sixty
miles north of Rhegium (Reggio di Calabria): *Barr.* 46 D4.

[21] King of Epirus, he was called to help the Tarentines against
the Romans and conducted campaigns in Italy and Sicily between
280 and 275. Despite successes, his losses in "Pyrrhic" victories
forced him to abandon the effort and return to Greece.

[22] Military campaigns started with the general "taking the

10

bringing back from Sicily, and cross with it to Macedonia. The man sent, with propraetorian authority, was Marcus Valerius Laevinus,[19] who took charge of thirty-eight vessels from Gnaeus Octavius in the vicinity of Vibo,[20] and sailed over to Macedonia with them. Here the legate Marcus Aurelius came to him, briefed him on the size of the armies and the number of ships mobilized by the king, and told him how Philip was rousing men to arms in the islands as well as in all the mainland cities through personal visits or intermediaries. The Romans should prosecute the war with increased vigor, he said, in case their hesitation led Philip to a venture similar to that which Pyrrhus[21] had undertaken from a considerably weaker kingdom. It was then decided that Aurelius should communicate this information by letter to the consuls and the senate.

4. At the end of this year the question was brought up in the senate of land grants for the veterans who had finished off the war in Africa under the leadership and auspices[22] of Publius Scipio. The senators decided that the urban praetor Marcus Iunius should, if he agreed, hold an election to appoint decemvirs for surveying and apportioning Samnite and Apulian land that was public property of the Roman people.[23] The appointees were Publius Servilius, Quintus Caecilius Metellus, Gaius and Marcus Servilius (both with the *cognomen* Geminus), Lucius and Aulus Hostilius Cato, Publius Villius Tappulus, Marcus

auspices," that is, divination of various types (cf. *OLD* sv *auspicium;* Levene 3–4), to ensure that he had the approval of the gods. Often, as here, the word is equivalent to "authority."

[23] Confiscated, presumably because the Samnites and Apulians had defected to Hannibal.

M. Fulvius Flaccus, P. Aelius Paetus, T. Quinctius Flamininus.

4 Per eos dies, P. Aelio consule comitia habente, creati consules P. Sulpicius Galba C. Aurelius Cotta. praetores exinde facti Q. Minucius Rufus, L. Furius Purpureo, Q.
5 Fulvius Gillo, C. Sergius Plautus. ludi Romani scaenici eo anno magnifice apparateque facti ab aedilibus curulibus L. Valerio Flacco et L. Quinctio Flaminino; biduum in-
6 stauratum est; frumentique vim ingentem quod ex Africa P. Scipio miserat quaternis aeris populo cum summa fide
7 et gratia diviserunt. et plebeii ludi ter toti instaurati ab aedilibus plebi L. Apustio Fullone et Q. Minucio Rufo, qui ex aedilitate praetor creatus erat; et Iovis epulum fuit ludorum causa.

5. Anno quingentesimo quinquagesimo[5] primo ab urbe condita, P. Sulpicio Galba C. Aurelio consulibus, bellum cum rege Philippo initum est, paucis mensibus post pacem
2 Carthaginiensibus datam. omnium primum eam rem idi-

---

[5] quinquagesimo *Glar.*: quadragesimo *B*χ

---

[24] The most distinguished is T. Quinctius Flamininus (45), military tribune in 208 and propraetor at Tarentum in 205–4. He would now become the leading figure in the Second Macedonian War and Greek affairs.    [25] P. Sulpicius Galba Maximus (64), earlier consul in 211; C. Aurelius Cotta (95), praetor 202.

[26] Dramatic performances were first put on at the *Ludi Romani* in 240 by Livius Andronicus (see note on 12.10, below).

[27] Celebrated in November. Repetition of Festivals/Games (*Instauratio*) was common, because these were religious ceremonies and correct protocol and procedure were important. A flaw, or incorrect procedure, meant that repetition in part or as a whole was obligatory (cf. *OCD* sv *Instauratio*).

Fulvius Flaccus, Publius Aelius Paetus and Titus Quinctius Flamininus.[24]

In elections that the consul Publius Aelius held at this time Publius Sulpicius Galba and Gaius Aurelius Cotta were chosen as consuls,[25] and then Quintus Minucius Rufus, Lucius Furius Purpureo, Quintus Fulvius Gillo and Gaius Sergius Plautus were made praetors. That year the Roman dramatic festivals[26] were staged in a magnificent and sumptuous manner by the curule aediles Lucius Valerius Flaccus and Lucius Quinctius Flamininus. The performance was repeated for a further two days, and the aediles distributed among the people—at a price of four *asses* per measure, and with consummate impartiality, which earned them the people's gratitude—a large amount of grain sent from Africa by Publius Scipio. The Plebeian Games, too, were three times reproduced in their entirety[27] by the aediles of the plebs, Lucius Apustius Fullo and Quintus Minucius Rufus (who had been elected praetor after his term as aedile). A feast of Jupiter was also put on to celebrate the games.

5. In the five hundred and fifty-first year[28] after the founding of the city, in the consulship of Publius Sulpicius Galba and Gaius Aurelius, the war with King Philip commenced, just a few months after peace had been granted to the Carthaginians. This was the very first item that the consul Publius Sulpicius brought up on the Ides of

---

[28] The manuscripts here read 541st year, which is again ten years out, hence Glareanus' emendation to 551st (see textual note). Since Livy rarely uses *AUC* dating, its appearance here alongside the regular consular dating probably marks an important event, namely the start of a major war.

13

bus Martiis, quo die tum consulatus inibatur, P. Sulpicius
3 consul rettulit, senatusque decrevit uti consules maioribus
hostiis rem divinam facerent quibus dis ipsis videretur
4 cum precatione ea, "quod senatus populusque Romanus
de re publica deque ineundo novo bello in animo haberet,
ea res uti populo Romano sociisque ac nomini Latino bene
ac feliciter eveniret;" secundum rem divinam precatio-
nemque ut de re publica deque provinciis senatum consulerent.
5 Per eos dies opportune inritandis ad bellum animis et
litterae ab M. Aurelio legato et M. Valerio Laevino pro
6 praetore adlatae, et Atheniensium nova legatio venit, quae
regem adpropinquare finibus suis nuntiaret, brevique non
agros modo sed urbem etiam in dicione eius futuram, nisi
7 quid in Romanis auxilii foret. cum renuntiassent consules
rem divinam rite peractam esse, et precationi adnuisse
deos haruspices respondere, laetaque exta fuisse, et pro-
lationem finium victoriamque et triumphum portendi,
tum litterae Valeri Aurelique lectae et legati Athenien-

29 March 15 (the Ides) began the consular year until 153,
when it was fixed at January 1, but there are problems with the
Roman calendar (cf. Introduction, lxv–lxvii; Briscoe 2.17–26).

30 Sacrificial victims were divided by age into "unweaned"
(*lactantes*) and "full-grown" (*maiores*) animals, the latter being
used for the more important thanksgivings/crises.

31 "allies and those with Latin rights" (*socii et nomen Latinum* here, though there are variations throughout Livy) lumps
together two groups with different levels of treaty with Rome.
The Latins had closer ties, including marriage and commercial
rights; the allies' treaties were less favorable. Both were expected
to provide troops, and Livy does not distinguish between them in
military contexts. Cf. Introduction, lviii–lxv.

March—the day of entry into the consulship in those days.[29] He proposed, and the senate decreed, that the consuls should sacrifice to gods of their choice with full-grown victims,[30] using the following prayer: "Whatsoever the senate and People of Rome decide about the welfare of the state and the commencement of a new war, may that turn out successfully and prosperously for the Roman people, and for their allies and those with Latin rights."[31] It was also decided that, after the sacrifice and prayer, the consuls were to consult the senate about the welfare of the state and allocation of the provinces.

At that time, at an opportune moment for inflaming passions for the war, dispatches arrived from the legate Marcus Aurelius and the propraetor Marcus Valerius Laevinus, and a fresh embassy also came from the Athenians to report that the king was approaching Athenian territory and that in a short while their city, and not just their lands, would be in Philip's hands unless assistance were forthcoming from the Romans. Now the consuls had already announced that the sacrifice had been duly performed, that the *haruspices* were declaring that the gods had heard their prayer, that the entrails had been favorable,[32] and that an extension of Roman territory, with victory and a triumph, was predicted. It was after this that the dispatches from Valerius and Aurelius were read out, and the ambassadors from Athens given an audience. There fol-

---

[32] Priests of Etruscan origin concerned with divination, particularly the inspection of the entrails of sacrificial animals. If these manifested certain conditions, a successful outcome of the war at hand would be predicted.

8   sium auditi. senatus inde consultum factum est, ut sociis
gratiae agerentur quod diu sollicitati ne obsidionis quidem
9   metu fide decessissent: de auxilio mittendo tum responderi
placere cum consules provincias sortiti essent, atque is
consul cui Macedonia provincia evenisset ad populum
tulisset ut Philippo regi Macedonum indiceretur bellum.

    6. P. Sulpicio provincia Macedonia sorti evenit, isque
rogationem promulgavit, "vellent iuberent Philippo regi
Macedonibusque qui sub regno eius essent ob iniurias
2   armaque inlata sociis populi Romani bellum indici." alteri
consulum Aurelio Italia provincia obtigit. praetores exinde
sortiti sunt C. Sergius Plautus urbanam, Q. Fulvius Gillo
Siciliam, Q. Minucius Rufus Bruttios, L. Furius Purpureo
Galliam.

3     Rogatio de bello Macedonico primis comitiis ab omnibus ferme centuriis antiquata est. id cum fessi diuturnitate
et gravitate belli sua sponte homines taedio periculorum
4   laborumque fecerant, tum Q. Baebius tribunus plebis,
viam antiquam criminandi patres ingressus, incusaverat

---

33 From Latin *sors* (lot). The most important provinces (which usually meant wars) were reserved for the consuls, who could decide which was whose by mutual agreement or by drawing lots (sortition). The senate decided which provinces should be set aside for the praetors, and these (including the urban and citizen-foreigner jurisdiction) were then assigned by sortition (so "praetorian sortition," below).

34 The basic voting groups of the *Comitia Centuriata* (Centuriate Assembly). The same term (*centuria*) is used for the legionary unit (in theory a hundred men), since the assembly was originally the citizen-soldiery assembled for war. Roman assemblies generally used "block" voting, with each unit (here, the cen-

lowed a senatorial decree that the allies be thanked for not having broken faith despite a long period of harassment and even when they were living in fear of a siege. On the question of sending assistance, however, the senate's decision was that a reply should wait until the consuls had been assigned their provinces and the consul allotted Macedonia as his province had brought before the people a motion that war be declared on King Philip of Macedon.

6. The province of Macedonia came by sortition[33] to Publius Sulpicius, and he promulgated a bill stipulating that the people "wanted and instructed that war be declared on King Philip and the Macedonians under his rule because of his offenses and aggression against allies of the people of Rome." The other consul, Aurelius, was allotted the province of Italy. In the praetorian sortition that followed Sergius Plautus gained the urban jurisdiction, while Quintus Fulvius Gillo drew Sicily, Quintus Minucius Rufus Bruttium and Lucius Furius Purpureo Gaul.

The bill concerning war with Macedon was rejected at the first assembly by nearly all the centuries.[34] This had been the natural reaction of men tired of protracted and relentless warfare—and sick of its dangers and hardships—but the result was also partly due to the tribune of the plebs, Quintus Baebius.[35] He, resorting to the old practice of recriminations against the senate, had accused the body

tury) casting a single vote determined by the majority of votes within the unit. See further Introduction, xlvii–li.

[35] Q. Baebius (20) was a supporter of Scipio Africanus, who disapproved of the proposed war. On the office of plebeian tribune, see Introduction, liv.

bella ex bellis seri, ne pace unquam frui plebs posset.
5 aegre eam rem passi patres, laceratusque probris in senatu
tribunus plebis, et consulem pro se quisque hortari ut de
6 integro comitia rogationi ferendae ediceret, castigaretque
segnitiam populi atque edoceret quanto damno dedeco-
rique dilatio ea belli futura esset.

7. Consul in campo Martio comitiis, priusquam centu-
2 rias in suffragium mitteret contione advocata, "ignorare"
inquit "mihi videmini, Quirites, non utrum bellum an
pacem habeatis vos consuli—neque enim liberum id vobis
Philippus permittet, qui terra marique ingens bellum mo-
litur—, sed utrum in Macedoniam legiones transportetis
3 an hostes in Italiam accipiatis. hoc quantum intersit, si
nunquam ante alias, proximo certe[6] bello experti estis.
quis enim dubitat quin, si Saguntinis obsessis fidemque
nostram implorantibus impigre tulissemus opem, sicut
patres nostri Mamertinis tulerant, totum in Hispaniam
aversuri bellum fuerimus, quod cunctando cum summa
clade nostra in Italiam accepimus?

[6] proximo certe *Madvig*: Punico proximo certe *B*χ

---

36 Between the city and the Tiber and bounded by the Pin-
cian, Quirinal, and Capitoline hills (Richardson 65–67), it was
used for army musters and exercises and also for meetings of the
Centuriate Assembly. On Roman voting assemblies, see Introduction, xlvii–li.   37 The "informal gathering" (*contio*) was an
assembly to hear a magistrate speak on a matter and often preceded the *comitia,* where a vote was taken.

38 Modern Sagunto, about fifteen miles north of Valencia. The
Romans made Hannibal's attack on it in 219 a *casus belli,* claiming
it as an ally, but it lay well south of the River Ebro, established by
the Romans as the northern frontier of Carthaginian expansion in

of tacking one war onto another so that the plebeians could never feel the advantages of peace. The senate was indignant at this, and the tribune of the plebs was subjected to a tongue-lashing on the floor of the house. Every senator then declared that the consul should reconvene the assembly so the proposal could be passed, and to reproach the people for their apathy and make them understand how damaging and humiliating such a deferral of war would be.

7. At the voting assembly in the Campus Martius,[36] the consul called an informal gathering of the people before sending the centuries to vote,[37] and addressed them as follows: "Citizens, I do not think you realize that what you are debating is not whether to have war or peace—Philip, who is mounting a vast land and sea offensive, will not leave you freedom of choice in the matter—but whether you are to transport your legions to Macedonia or else admit your enemy into Italy. The difference between the two, even if you had not learned it earlier, you did at least learn from your experience in the last war. The people of Saguntum[38] were under siege and begging us for protection, and had we been prompt in bringing help to them just as our fathers had been in bringing it to the Mamertines,[39] who can doubt that we would have transferred the entire theater of war to Spain? Instead, by our vacillating, we drew it into Italy, with disastrous consequences for ourselves.

Spain in their treaty with Hasdrubal, Hannibal's predecessor as commander in Spain.

[39] Campanian mercenaries, who seized Messana in 288, expelling its Greek colonists. They then raided Sicily, from which, with Roman aid, they eventually drove out a Carthaginian garrison (which eventually led to the First Punic War).

4    ·"Ne illud quidem dubium est quin hunc ipsum Philippum, pactum iam per legatos litterasque cum Hannibale
ut in Italiam traiceret, misso cum classe Laevino qui ultro
5  ei bellum inferret, in Macedonia continuerimus. et quod
tunc fecimus, cum hostem Hannibalem in Italia haberemus, id nunc, pulso Italia Hannibale, devictis Carthagini-
6  ensibus, cunctamur facere? patiamur expugnandis Athenis, sicut Sagunto expugnando Hannibalem passi sumus,
7  segnitiam nostram experiri regem: non quinto inde mense,
quemadmodum ab Sagunto Hannibal, sed quinto die[7]
8  quam ab Corintho solverit naves, in Italiam perveniet. ne
aequaveritis Hannibali Philippum nec Carthaginiensibus
Macedonas: Pyrrho certe aequabitis. aequabitis[8] dico?
9  quantum vel vir viro vel gens genti praestat! minima acces-
sio semper Epirus regno Macedoniae fuit et hodie est.
Peloponnesum totam in dicione Philippus habet Argosque
ipsos, non vetere fama magis quam morte Pyrrhi nobilita-
tos.
10    "Nostra nunc comparate.[9] quanto magis florentem Italiam, quanto magis integras res, salvis ducibus, salvis tot
exercitibus quos Punicum postea bellum absumpsit, adgressus Pyrrhus tamen concussit et victor prope ad ipsam
11  urbem Romanam venit! nec Tarentini modo oraque illa
Italiae quam maiorem Graeciam vocant, ut linguam ut

[7] quinto die *Madvig*: quinto inde $B\chi$
[8] aequabitis *Smith*: *om.* $B\chi$
[9] comparate $P^x$: compara $B\chi$: comparo *Voss.*

---

[40] Pyrrhus died in Argos in 272 after being struck on the head
by a tile that a woman flung from a rooftop.

"There can be no doubt of another thing either: this same Philip made a pact with Hannibal, through intermediaries and letters, to cross to Italy, and we contained him in Macedonia only by sending Laevinus with a fleet to launch a preemptive strike against him. We did that at a time when we had Hannibal as our enemy in Italy. Are we hesitating to do it now when Hannibal has been driven from Italy and the Carthaginians are defeated? Let us give the king firsthand experience of our lethargy by letting him capture Athens, as we did Hannibal by letting him capture Saguntum! Philip will not be like Hannibal, arriving here from Saguntum after four months—no, he will reach Italy four days after launching his ships from Corinth. Do not compare Philip with Hannibal or the Macedonians with the Carthaginians. You will, of course, compare Philip with Pyrrhus. 'Compare,' do I say? How much greater is the one man than the other, and the one people than the other! Epirus has always been, and remains today, an insignificant annex of the Macedonian kingdom. Philip has the entire Peloponnese under his sway, including Argos itself, not better known these days for its glory of old than it is for Pyrrhus' death.[40]

"And now add our circumstances to the comparison. Pyrrhus attacked an Italy that was so much more prosperous; its resources were so much better preserved, its leaders and its many armies, which the Punic War later wiped out, still intact—and even so he shattered it and came victorious almost to the city of Rome itself. It was not just the people of Tarentum who defected from us, along with that coastline of Italy that they call 'Greater Greece'—so one would assume that their support was for their com-

nomen secutos crederes, sed Lucanus et Bruttius et Sam-
12 nis ab nobis defecerunt. haec vos, si Philippus in Italiam
transmiserit, quietura aut mansura in fide creditis? manserunt enim Punico postea bello. nunquam isti populi, nisi
cum deerit ad quem desciscant, ab nobis non deficient.

13      "Si piguisset vos in Africam traicere, hodie in Italia
Hannibalem et Carthaginienses hostes haberetis. Macedonia potius quam Italia bellum habeat: hostium urbes
14 agrique ferro atque igni vastentur. experti iam sumus foris
nobis quam domi feliciora potentioraque arma esse. ite in
suffragium bene iuvantibus divis, et quae patres censue-
15 runt vos iubete. huius vobis sententiae non consul modo
auctor est sed iam[10] di immortales, qui mihi sacrificanti
precantique ut hoc bellum mihi senatui vobisque, sociis ac
nomini Latino, classibus exercitibusque nostris bene ac
feliciter eveniret, laeta omnia prosperaque portendere."

8. Ab hac oratione in suffragium missi, uti rogaret, bel-
2 lum iusserunt. supplicatio inde a consulibus in triduum
ex senatus consulto indicta est, obsecratique circa omnia
pulvinaria di ut quod bellum cum Philippo populus iussis-
3 set, id bene ac feliciter eveniret; consultique fetiales ab

---

[10] iam $B_a$: etiam $\chi$

---

[41] Sulpicius is, of course, suggesting that since the Greek-
speaking peoples had supported Pyrrhus, they would now also
flock to support Philip, another Greek "compatriot."

[42] Sulpicius is being sarcastic: these peoples did go over to
Hannibal (in 216).      [43] Cf. 5.4 note, above.

[44] The supplication (*supplicatio*) was a period of collective
prayer decreed by the senate in times of crisis or calamity. It could
also be decreed for thanksgiving to the gods, especially for a victory (see Oakley 2.735). Cf. *OCD* sv.      [45] The *fetials* (*fetiales*)

mon language and lineage[41]—but so did the Lucanian, the Bruttian, and the Samnite. Should Philip cross to Italy, do you think these will stay out of the fight or remain loyal to us? For of course they remained loyal in the later stages of the Punic War![42] No, there is no occasion on which these peoples will *fail* to revolt—except when there is no one for them to defect *to!*

"Had you been reluctant to cross to Africa, you would still today have Hannibal and his Carthaginians as your enemies in Italy. Let Macedonia have this war, not Italy. Let the cities and the countryside of our enemies suffer the devastation of sword and fire. We already know from experience that our campaigns are more successful and powerful abroad than they are at home. Go and vote—may the gods help you—and ratify the decision of the senate. It is not just your consul who supports this proposal; so now do the immortal gods. For when I offered sacrifice and prayed that this war should turn out well and successfully for me, for the senate, for you, for the allies and those with Latin rights,[43] and for our fleets and armies, the signs they sent were uniformly promising and favorable."

8. After this address the people were sent to vote, and they called for war. Acting on a decree of the senate, the consuls then ordained a three-day period of supplication, and the gods were importuned at all their couches[44] to vouchsafe a happy and prosperous conclusion to the war that the people had authorized against Philip. The *fetials*[45] were also asked by the consul Sulpicius for their directions

were a college of twenty priests who oversaw and advised the senate on the procedures and laws governing the declaration of wars and making peace. Cf. *OCD* sv *fetiales*.

consule Sulpicio, bellum quod indiceretur regi Philippo utrum ipsi utique nuntiari iuberent, an satis esset in finibus regni quod proximum praesidium esset eo nuntiari. fetiales decreverunt utrum eorum fecisset recte facturum.

4 consuli a patribus permissum ut quem videretur ex iis qui extra senatum essent legatum mitteret ad bellum regi indicendum.

5 Tum de exercitibus consulum praetorumque actum. consules binas legiones scribere iussi, veteres dimittere

6 exercitus. Sulpicio, cui novum ac magni nominis bellum decretum erat, permissum ut de exercitu quem P. Scipio ex Africa deportasset voluntarios, quos posset, duceret:

7 invitum ne quem militem veterem ducendi ius esset. praetoribus L. Furio Purpureoni et Q. Minucio Rufo quina milia socium Latini nominis consules darent, quibus praesidiis alter Galliam, alter Bruttios provinciam obtineret.

8 Q. Fulvius Gillo ipse iussus ex eo exercitu quem P. Aelius[11] habuisset, ut quisque minime multa stipendia haberet, legere, donec et ipse quinque milia socium ac nominis

9 Latini effecisset: id praesidio Siciliae provinciae esset. M. Valerio Faltoni, qui praetor priore anno Campaniam pro-

10 vinciam habuerat, prorogatum in annum imperium est, uti pro praetore in Sardiniam traiceret; is quoque de exercitu qui ibi esset quinque milia socium nominis Latini, qui

11 eorum minime multa stipendia haberent, legeret. et con-

[11] Aelius *McDonald*: Aelius consul Bχ

---

[46] That is, the legions in Gaul, Bruttium, Sicily, Sardinia, Etruria, and Africa.

[47] This is in all likelihood not the consul but P. Aelius Tubero (152), praetor in 201 (see Briscoe 1.78).

on whether the declaration of the war on Philip should go to the king in person or whether it was enough for the announcement to be made at the first fortress within the bounds of his realm. The *fetials* determined that either option would be proper. The consul was granted permission by the senators to send anyone he liked, outside the senate, as an envoy to declare war on the king.

Then the matter of the allocation of armies to the consuls and praetors was discussed. The consuls were instructed to raise two legions each and to demobilize the veteran armies.[46] Supicius, who was officially vested with command in this new and momentous campaign, was allowed to draw all the volunteers he could from the force that Publius Scipio had brought back from Africa, but he did not have the right to take any veteran against his will. To each of the praetors Lucius Furius Purpureo and Quintus Minucius Rufus the consuls were to give 5,000 allies and men with Latin rights whom the praetors were to use to secure their respective provinces, Gaul and Bruttium. Quintus Fulvius Gillo was also instructed to select soldiers from the army that Publius Aelius[47] had formerly commanded, choosing those with the shortest period of active service, until he too had a complement of 5,000 allies and men with Latin rights; this force was to form a garrison for the province of Sicily. Marcus Valerius Falto who had, as praetor, been in charge of Campania the previous year, had his *imperium* prorogued for a year to enable him to cross to Sardinia with propraetorian rank. He, too, was to raise from the army in Sardinia a force of 5,000 allies and men with Latin rights, choosing those with the shortest periods of active service. Furthermore, the consuls were

sules duas urbanas legiones scribere iussi, quae si quo res
posceret, multis in Italia contactis gentibus Punici belli
societate iraque inde tumentibus, mitterentur. sex legionibus Romanis eo anno usura res publica erat.

9. In ipso apparatu belli legati a rege Ptolomaeo venerunt qui nuntiarent Athenienses adversus Philippum pe-
2  tisse ab rege auxilium: ceterum, etsi communes socii sint,
tamen nisi ex auctoritate populi Romani neque classem
neque exercitum defendendi aut oppugnandi cuiusquam
3  causa regem in Graeciam missurum esse; uel quieturum
eum in regno, si populo Romano socios defendere libeat,
vel Romanos quiescere, si malint, passurum, atque ipsum
auxilia, quae facile adversus Philippum tueri Athenas pos-
4  sent, missurum. gratiae regi ab senatu actae, respon-
sumque tutari socios populo Romano in animo esse: si qua
re ad id bellum opus sit, indicaturos regi, regnique eius
opes scire subsidia firma ac fidelia suae rei publicae esse.
5  munera deinde legatis in singulos quinum milium aeris ex
senatus consulto missa.

Cum dilectum consules haberent, pararentque quae ad
bellum opus essent, civitas religiosa in principiis maxime
6  novorum bellorum, supplicationibus habitis iam et ob-
secratione circa omnia pulvinaria facta, ne quid prae-
termitteretur quod aliquando factum esset, ludos Iovi

---

[48] Cf. 8.2 note, above.

directed to enroll two urban legions to be dispatched wherever the circumstances required, for many peoples in Italy had been infected by allegiances with the enemy during the Punic War, and were simmering with animosity toward Rome as a result. The state thus intended to put six Roman legions into service that year.

9. While the Romans were actually involved in preparations for the war, ambassadors arrived from King Ptolemy to report that the Athenians had requested assistance from the king against Philip. Although the Athenians were allies of both the Romans and himself, Ptolemy said, he would nevertheless send neither sea nor land forces to Greece for defensive or offensive operations without the sanction of the Roman people. If the Roman people chose to defend its allies, he would remain inactive in his own kingdom; or, if they preferred, he would let the Romans remain inactive while he himself sent such forces as could easily protect Athens from Philip. The king was thanked by the senate and given the answer that the Roman people intended to defend its allies. They would inform the king of any assistance they needed for the war, and they were aware that the resources of his kingdom represented a secure and loyal support for their Republic. Then gifts of 5,000 *asses* per person were sent to the ambassadors by senatorial decree.

While the consuls were raising their troops and making the necessary preparations for the war, the community was prey to religious fears, as it especially was at the commencement of new wars. Supplications were held, prayers offered at all the couches of the gods[48] and, so that no procedure followed in the past would be omitted on this occasion, orders given that the consul who was allotted

27

donumque vovere consulem cui provincia Macedonia eve-
7 nisset iussit. moram voto publico Licinius pontifex maximus attulit, qui negavit ex incerta pecunia voveri[12] debere,
quia ea pecunia non posset in bellum usui esse, seponique
statim deberet nec cum alia pecunia misceri: quod si fac-
8 tum esset, votum rite solui non posse. quamquam et res et
auctor movebat, tamen ad collegium pontificum referre
consul iussus si posset recte votum incertae pecuniae suscipi. posse rectiusque etiam esse pontifices decreverunt.
9 vovit in eadem verba consul, praeeunte maximo pontifice,
10 quibus antea quinquennalia vota suscipi solita erant, praeterquam quod tanta pecunia quantam tum cum solveretur
senatus censuisset ludos donaque facturum vovit. octiens
ante ludi magni de certa pecunia voti erant, hi primi de
incerta.

10. Omnium animis in bellum Macedonicum versis,

[12] voveri *Crév.*: vovere *B*χ: vovere licere; ex certa voveri debere *Madvig*

---

[49] P. Licinius Crassus Dives (69), who was elected *pontifex
maximus* while curule aedile in 212 (*MRR* 271). The *pontifex
maximus* presided over the college of pontiffs, the most important
of the four main religious colleges, having general oversight of
state religion, including sacrifices, expiation of prodigies, festivals, and other rituals. The other three important colleges were
the augurs, who interpreted divine signs before any major undertaking; the *quindecemviri sacris faciundis,* who had charge of the
Sibylline Books; and the *septemviri epulonum,* a board of seven
who looked after sacrificial banquets.

[50] The *pontifex maximus* could be overruled by his colleagues.

[51] The fulfillment of such vows was contingent on the state
surviving and prospering for a specified period (cf., e.g., 22.10.2,

the province of Macedonia should make a vow promising games and a gift to Jupiter. However, this public votive offering was held up by the *pontifex maximus,* Licinius,[49] who asserted that one must not formulate a vow based on an unspecified sum of money because such money could not be employed for the war; it should be immediately set apart and not lumped together with other monies. In the event of the latter happening, the vow could not be duly discharged, he said. Although the argument and its advocate both carried weight, the consul was nonetheless instructed to refer to the college of pontiffs the question of whether a vow could be correctly formulated with its monetary sum unspecified.[50] The priests determined that it could, and that it was even the more correct procedure. Following the *pontifex maximus'* dictation, the consul formulated the vow using the same phraseology as had been traditionally employed in the past for vows to be discharged after the passage of five years,[51] except that his promise of games and gifts was based on a sum of monies to be determined by the senate at the time when the vow was being discharged.[52] On eight previous occasions vows of the Great Games had been made based upon a specified sum of money; this was the first time a vow was made with the sum unspecified.

10. While everybody's attention was focused on the war with Macedon, word suddenly came of an uprising

"Should the Republic . . . be kept safe for the next five years . . . let the people of Rome offer this gift"; 30.2.8, "Torquatus had made a vow that these games would be celebrated four years later, if the Republic remained in the same condition as it was then").

[52] The games of this vow were held in 194 (cf. 34.44.6)

repente, nihil minus eo tempore timentibus, Gallici tu-
2 multus fama exorta. Insubres Cenomanique et Boii, excitis
Celinibus Iluatibusque et ceteris Ligustinis populis, Hamilcare Poeno duce, qui in iis locis de Hasdrubalis exer-
3 citu substiterat, Placentiam invaserant; et direpta urbe ac
per iram magna ex parte incensa, vix duobus milibus hominum inter incendia ruinasque relictis, traiecto Pado ad
4 Cremonam diripiendam pergunt. vicinae urbis audita
clades spatium colonis dedit ad claudendas portas praesidiaque per muros disponenda, ut obsiderentur tamen
prius quam expugnarentur, nuntiosque mitterent ad praetorem Romanum.
5     L. Furius Purpureo tum provinciae praeerat, cetero ex
senatus consulto exercitu dimisso praeter quinque milia
socium ac Latini nominis; cum iis copiis in proxima regione provinciae circa Ariminum substiterat. is tum sena-
6 tui scripsit quo in tumultu provincia esset: duarum colo-
niarum quae ingentem illam tempestatem Punici belli
subterfugissent alteram captam ac direptam ab hostibus,
7 alteram oppugnari; nec in exercitu suo satis praesidii colonis laborantibus fore, nisi quinque milia socium quadraginta milibus hostium—tot enim in armis esse—truci-

---

53 Cf. *Barr.* 39 D2 (Insubres), F3 (Cenomani), H4 (Boii), but
the identification of the Celines and Ilvates is uncertain.

54 Modern Piacenza. Established as a colony in 218, it was
often under attack from the Gauls. Who this Hamilar was is uncertain, possibly (as Livy says) a member of Hasdrubal's army who
survived the battle of the Metaurus River.

55 Also founded as a colony in 218, it retains its name today.

56 Cf. 8.7, above.

in Gaul, the last thing the Romans feared at this time. The Insubres, the Cenomani, and the Boii had been fomenting discontent among the Celines, the Ilvates,[53] and the other Ligurian tribes. Then, led by the Carthaginian Hamilcar—a former member of Hasdrubal's army who had stayed on in the region—they had overrun Placentia.[54] They had sacked the city, set fire to most of it in their rage, and left behind barely 2,000 men amid the burning ruins. Then, crossing the Po, they headed for Cremona,[55] intending to pillage it. The reports of the destruction of a neighboring city gave the inhabitants of Cremona time to shut their gates and post defensive troops on their walls so they would be able to face a siege rather than be taken by storm, and to send envoys to the Roman praetor.

Lucius Furius Purpureo was governor of the province at that time.[56] In accordance with a decree of the senate, he had demobilized his entire army with the exception of 5,000 allies and men with Latin rights; and with these troops he had taken up a position near Ariminum[57] in the part of his province that was closest to Rome. He then wrote to the senate describing the turmoil in the province. Of the two colonies that had avoided the massive calamity of the Punic War, he said, one had been captured and ransacked by the enemy, and the other was now under attack. In his own army he had not the strength to relieve the colonists' distress—or perhaps the senate wished to expose his 5,000-strong contingent of allies to destruction by the 40,000 enemy troops now under arms, and see the

[57] Modern Rimini. An Umbrian and Gallic settlement, it became a Latin colony in 268, and had remained loyal to Rome during the Hannibalic war.

31

danda obicere velit, et tanta sua clade iam inflatos excidio coloniae Romanae augeri hostium animos.

11. His litteris recitatis decreverunt ut C. Aurelius consul exercitum, cui in Etruriam ad conveniendum diem

2 edixerat, Arimini eadem die adesse iuberet et aut ipse, si per commodum rei publicae posset, ad opprimendum

3 Gallicum tumultum proficisceretur, aut praetori[13] scriberet ut cum ad eum legiones ex Etruria venissent, missis in vicem earum quinque milibus sociorum quae interim Etruriae praesidio essent, proficisceretur ipse ad coloniam liberandam obsidione.

4 Legatos item mittendos in Africam censuerunt, eosdem Carthaginem, eosdem in Numidiam ad Masinissam:

5 Carthaginem ut nuntiarent civem eorum Hamilcarem relictum in Gallia—haud satis scire ex Hasdrubalis prius an ex Magonis postea exercitu—bellum contra foedus fac-

6 ere, exercitus Gallorum Ligurumque excivisse ad arma contra populum Romanum; eum, si pax placeret, revocan-

7 dum illis et dedendum populo Romano esse. simul nuntiare iussi perfugas sibi non omnes redditos esse, ac mag-

---

[13] praetori *M. Müller*: Q. Minucio praetori *Bχ*: L. Furio praetori *ed. Med. 1505*

---

[58] The Numidian king Masinissa had fought for Carthage against Rome in Spain, commanding Numidian cavalry. He defected to the Romans, however, promising to help Scipio if he invaded Africa, and served him well when he arrived there.

[59] Hasdrubal and Mago were Hannibal's younger brothers. Failing to link up with Hannibal in Italy in the spring of 207, Hasdrubal was defeated and killed at the Metaurus River (27.36–49). Mago arrived in Liguria by sea in 205 with some 14,000 men (28.46.7) but was defeated and died while returning to Africa.

confidence of the enemy, already inflated by their annihilation of a Roman colony, further boosted by the massive defeat that he would suffer at their hands!

11. The consul Gaius Aurelius had specified a date for his army to assemble in Etruria; but after Purpureo's letter was read out in the senate, the senators decided that he should issue orders for those troops to muster at Ariminum on that same day. He was then to set off in person, if the interests of the state permitted, to suppress the uprising in Gaul. Otherwise, he was to inform the praetor by letter that, when the legions from Etruria reached him, he should send 5,000 allies to replace them and these would serve temporarily as a garrison for Etruria. Aurelius was then to set out himself to raise the siege of the colony.

The senate also voted to send ambassadors to Africa, both to Carthage and to Masinissa[58] in Numidia. They were to report to Carthage that one of their citizens, Hamilcar, who had been left behind in Gaul—though it was unclear whether he belonged to Hasdrubal's earlier or Mago's later army[59]—was engaging in warfare in contravention of their treaty, and that he had incited Gallic and Ligurian forces to arms against the Roman people. If peace was what the Carthaginians wanted, then they must bring this man home and deliver him to the Roman people. The envoys were also required to report that not all their deserters[60] had been returned to the Romans, and

The uncertainty about Hamilcar probably reflects conflicting evidence in Livy's sources: see Introduction, xix–xxx.

[60] The return of all Roman "deserters, runaway slaves and prisoners of war" was a condition laid down for the Carthaginians at the end of the war (30.37.3; cf. Polyb. 15.18.3).

nam partem eorum palam Carthagini obversari dici; quos comprehendi conquirique debere ut sibi ex foedere resti-
8 tuantur. haec ad Carthaginienses mandata, Masinissae gratulari iussi quod non patrium modo reciperasset regnum, sed parte florentissima Syphacis finium adiecta
9 etiam auxisset. nuntiare praeterea iussi bellum cum rege Philippo susceptum, quod Carthaginienses auxiliis iuvis-
10 set, iniuriasque inferendo sociis populi Romani flagrante bello Italia coegisset classes exercitusque in Graeciam mitti, et distinendo copias causa in primis fuisset serius in Africam traiciendi; peterentque ut ad id bellum mitteret
11 auxilia Numidarum equitum. dona ampla data quae ferrent regi, vasa aurea argenteaque, toga purpurea et palmata tunica cum eburneo scipione et toga praetexta cum
12 curuli sella; iussique polliceri, si quid ei[14] ad firmandum augendumque regnum opus esse indicasset, enixe id populum Romanum merito eius praestaturum.
13 Verminae quoque Syphacis filii legati per eos dies senatum adierunt, excusantes errorem adulescentiamque, et culpam omnem in fraudem Carthaginiensium avertentes:
14 et Masinissam Romanis ex hoste amicum factum, Vermi-

---

[14] ei *Bχ*: sibi *Gron.*: eis *Madvig*: del. *J. H. Voss*

---

[61] Cf. 1.10 and note, above.

[62] The *toga praetexta* (a purple-fringed toga) was worn by holders of the higher (curule) magistracies and religious offices. Accordingly, this, the curule chair, plus a purple toga, a palm-embroidered tunic, and an ivory scepter (the accouterments of a triumphing general) are appropriate status symbols for a king.

[63] The Numidian king Syphax, initially a Roman ally, had defected to Carthage. Defeated by the Romans, he died in prison

that large numbers of them were living openly in Carthage. These had to be arrested and hunted down to be returned to the Roman people in accordance with the treaty. Such were the instructions given to the ambassadors with regard to Carthage. As for Masinissa, the envoys were told to congratulate him not only on recovering the kingdom of his ancestors but also on enlarging it with the addition of the richest part of Syphax's territory. They were also to report that war had been started with King Philip because of the assistance he had given the Carthaginians[61] and his atrocities against allies of the Roman people, which had obliged the Romans to commit sea and land forces to Greece when Italy was aflame with war; by dividing the Roman forces, he had been primarily responsible for their delay in crossing to Africa. The ambassadors were also to request of Masinissa that he send Numidian cavalry to assist their war effort. They were given generous gifts to bear to the king: vessels of gold and silver, a purple toga, a palm-embroidered tunic with an ivory scepter, and a *toga praetexta* with a curule chair.[62] They also had orders to make a pledge to him that the Roman people would, in recognition of his services, take pains to furnish him with whatever he stipulated as necessary to strengthen and extend his kingdom.

At this time the senate was also approached by envoys from Vermina, son of Syphax.[63] They made excuses for Vermina's mistakes, which they attributed to his youth, and laid all the blame on Carthaginian duplicity. Masinissa, too, had become a friend of Rome after being an

in Italy. His son Vermina continued to support Carthage and fought at Zama.

nam quoque adnisurum ne officiis in populum Romanum
aut a Masinissa aut ab ullo alio vincatur; petere ut rex
15 sociusque et amicus ab senatu appellaretur. responsum
legatis est et patrem eius Syphacem sine causa ex socio et
amico hostem repente populi Romani factum, et eum ipsum rudimentum adulescentiae bello lacessentem Roma-
16 nos posuisse; itaque pacem illi prius petendam ab populo
Romano esse quam ut rex sociusque et amicus appelletur:
nominis eius honorem pro magnis erga se regum meritis
17 dare populum Romanum consuesse. legatos Romanos in
Africa fore, quibus mandaturum senatum ut Verminae
pacis dent leges, liberum arbitrium eius populo Romano
permittenti: si quid ad eas addi demi mutarive vellet, rur-
18 sus ab senatu ei postulandum fore. legati cum iis mandatis
in Africam missi C. Terentius Varro Sp. Lucretius Cn.
Octavius, quinqueremes singulis datae.

12. Litterae deinde in senatu recitatae sunt Q. Minuci
praetoris, cui Bruttii provincia erat: pecuniam Locris ex
Proserpinae thesauris nocte clam sublatam nec ad quos
2 pertineat facinus vestigia ulla exstare. indigne passus senatus non cessari ab sacrilegiis, et ne Pleminium quidem,
tam clarum recensque noxae simul ac poenae exemplum,

---

64 C. Terentius Varro (83), consul 216, who suffered the disastrous defeat at Cannae. His career after Cannae (proconsul 215–
213, propraetor 208–7, *legatus* to Philip in 203) suggests that the
sources attributing that defeat to his incompetence and recklessness may not be entirely accurate (so Briscoe 1.86).

65 Epizephyrian Locri on the coast of the toe of Italy (*Barr.*
46 D5). The temple of Proserpina (Persephone) was, according
to Diodorus (27.4.2), the most famous of all of Italy's temples.

66 Quintus Pleminius, propraetorian legate in charge of Locri
after its capture in 205, was notorious for many atrocities, especially his plundering of the temple of Proserpina (29.8–22).

enemy, they said, and Vermina would also make every effort not to fall short of Masinissa or, indeed, of anyone else in his good offices to the people of Rome. They requested, therefore, that the king be given the title "King, Ally, and Friend" by the senate. The reply given to the embassy was that Vermina's father, Syphax, had also suddenly and inexplicably become a foe of the Roman people after being an ally and friend, and that Vermina himself had devoted his early years to harassing the Romans. He should therefore ask for peace from the Roman people before he could be styled "King, Ally, and Friend," a title that was traditionally an honor the Roman people conferred as a reward for important services rendered to them by foreign kings. There was going to be a Roman embassy to Africa, they said, and the senate would dictate to it the terms of the peace treaty for Vermina, who should leave to the Roman people full authority as to its conditions. Any addition, deletion or adjustment that he wanted should be requested in a fresh application to the senate. The envoys sent to Africa with these instructions were Gaius Terentius Varro,[64] Spurius Lucretius, and Gnaeus Octavius, who were each allocated a quinquereme.

12. A letter was then read out in the senate from the praetor Quintus Minucius whose province was Bruttium. Money had been surreptitiously removed from the treasury of Proserpina at Locri[65] under cover of night, said Mincius, and there were no clues as to the guilty party. The senate was exasperated with the ongoing sacrilege and the fact that even the notorious and recent lesson of Pleminius'[66] crime and punishment did not prove a deter-

3 homines deterrere. C. Aurelio consuli negotium datum ut
ad praetorem in Bruttios scriberet: senatui placere quaestionem de expilatis thesauris eodem exemplo haberi quo
M. Pomponius praetor triennio ante habuisset; quae in-
4 venta pecunia esset reponi; si quo minus inventum foret
expleri, ac piacularia, si videretur, sicut ante pontifices
censuissent, fieri.

5 Curam expiandae violationis eius templi prodigia etiam
sub idem tempus pluribus locis nuntiata accenderunt.
in Lucanis caelum arsisse adferebant, Priverni sereno
6 per diem totum rubrum solem fuisse, Lanuvi in[15] templo
Sospitae Iunonis nocte strepitum ingentem exortum. iam
animalium obsceni fetus pluribus locis nuntiabantur: in
Sabinis incertus infans natus, masculus an femina esset,
alter sedecim iam annorum item ambiguo sexu inventus;
7 Frusinone agnus cum suillo capite, Sinuessae porcus cum
capite humano natus, in Lucanis in agro publico eculeus
8 cum quinque pedibus. foeda omnia et deformia erran-
tisque in alienos fetus naturae visa: ante omnia abominati
semimares, iussique in mare extemplo deportari, sicut
proxime C. Claudio M. Liuio consulibus deportatus simi-
9 lis prodigii fetus erat. nihilo minus decemviros adire libros

[15] Lanuvi in *M. Müller*: Lanuvii *B*χ

[67] M. Pomponius Matho (19), propraetorian commander in
Sicily in 203, led the investigation in the Pleminius affair.
[68] On prodigies in Livy, see Levene's Introduction, esp. 4–5,
and, on Books 31 to 40 specifically, 79–103.
[69] Cf. 27.37.6.

38

rent. The consul Gaius Aurelius was assigned the duty of writing to the praetor in Bruttium. He was to inform him that it was the senate's will that investigation of the matter of the purloined treasure follow the same procedure as the praetor Marcus Pomponius[67] had used three years earlier: any monies recovered should be replaced in the treasury, and any shortfall made good; and sacrifices of expiation should be carried out, if the praetor saw fit, in the manner directed by the priests on that former occasion.

The senate's concern to atone for the violation of this temple was intensified by simultaneous reports of prodigies in a number of locations.[68] In Lucania there were claims that the sky had been on fire; in Privernum that the sun had shone red in fine weather throughout an entire day; in Lanuvium that there had been a deafening noise during the night in the temple of Juno Sospita. In several places there were also reports of sinister births of animals. Among the Sabines a child of indeterminate sex was born, and a second was likewise found to be of uncertain sex at the age of sixteen. At Frusino a lamb was born with the head of a pig, at Sinuessa a pig with a human head, and in Lucania, on public land, a foal with five feet. All these appeared to be grotesque and hideous apparitions, indications that nature was running amok and generating monstrosities, but it was the bisexual creatures that most of all aroused revulsion, and orders were issued for them to be immediately taken out to sea, as had been recently done, in the consulship of Gaius Claudius and Marcus Livius, with a similar freak that had been born.[69] Even so, the decemvirs were told to consult the Books regarding

de portento eo iusserunt. decemviri ex libris res divinas
easdem quae proxime secundum id prodigium factae essent imperarunt. carmen praeterea ab ter novenis virgini-
bus cani per urbem iusserunt, donumque Iunoni reginae
10 ferri. ea uti fierent C. Aurelius consul ex decemvirorum
responso curavit. carmen, sicut patrum memoria Liuius,
ita tum condidit P. Licinius Tegula.

13. Expiatis omnibus religionibus—nam etiam Locris
sacrilegium pervestigatum ab Q. Minucio erat, pecuniaque ex bonis noxiorum in thesauros reposita—, cum con-
2 sules in provincias proficisci vellent, privati frequentes,
quibus ex pecunia quam M. Valerio M. Claudio consulibus
mutuam dederant tertia pensio debebatur eo anno, adie-
3 runt senatum, quia consules, cum ad novum bellum quod
magna classe magnisque exercitibus gerendum esset vix
aerarium sufficeret, negaverant esse unde iis in praesentia
4 solveretur. senatus querentes eos non sustinuit: si in Punicum bellum pecunia data in Macedonicum quoque bellum uti res publica vellet, aliis ex aliis orientibus bellis

---

70 The decemvirs for sacrifices (*decemviri sacris faciundi, decemviri sacrororum,* or sometimes, as here, just *decemviri*), were
a priestly college (cf. 9.8 note, above) whose prime function was
guarding and interpreting the Sibylline Books, containing Greek
oracles, supposedly brought to Rome by Tarquinius Superbus,
and consulting them when ordered by the senate.

71 Livius Andronicus (ca. 280–200), brought to Rome as a
captive after the capture of Tarentum in 270, is generally regarded as the founder of Latin literature. He produced a Latin
version of Homer's *Odyssey,* and in 240 he presented a Latin
comedy and/or tragedy at the *Ludi Romani.* Livy's wording here
("within the memory of the senators") suggests that he was dead
by 200. Meager fragments of his work survive. Licinius Tegula is
otherwise unknown.

the portent.[70] After examining the Books, they authorized the same observances as had been held immediately after the earlier prodigy. In addition, they ordered a hymn to be sung throughout the city by three groups of nine young girls and an offering to be made to Queen Juno. The consul Gaius Aurelius saw to the implementation of these rites as prescribed by the decemvirs. The hymn, of the type composed by Livius, within the memory of the senators, was on that occasion composed by Publius Licinius Tegula.[71]

13. Expiatory rites were performed for all these religious phenomena—even the sacrilege at Locri was thoroughly investigated by Quintus Minucius, and the missing monies were expropriated from the guilty parties and restored to the treasury. At this point, when the consuls were wanting to leave for their provinces, the senate was approached by a large number of private citizens who were due to receive that year the third payment of the money that they had put out on loan in the consulship of Marcus Valerius and Marcus Claudius.[72] Since the treasury had insufficient funds for the new war, the prosecution of which required a large fleet and large armies, the consuls had claimed that they were temporarily without resources to repay these people. The senate could not deny the validity of their grievance; if the state also wished to use for the Macedonian war monies loaned for the Punic war, the one conflict following hard on the heels of the other, what else

[72] In 210, when M. Valerius Laevinus (211) and the great general M. Claudius Marcellus (220) were consuls. Laevinus had raised the matter of repayment in 204, and it was decided that it should be made in three installments (29.16.1–3).

quid aliud quam publicatam pro beneficio tamquam ob
noxiam[16] suam pecuniam fore?

5     Cum et privati aequum postularent nec tamen solvendo
aere alieno res publica esset, quod medium inter aequum
6 et utile erat decreverunt, ut quoniam magna pars eorum
agros volgo venales esse diceret et sibimet emptis opus
esse, agri publici qui intra quinquagesimum lapidem esset
7 copia iis fieret: consules agrum aestimaturos et in iugera
asses vectigal testandi causa publicum agrum esse impo-
8 situros, ut si quis, cum solvere posset populus, pecuniam
habere quam agrum mallet, restitueret agrum populo.
9 laeti eam condicionem privati accepere; trientabulumque
is ager, quia pro tertia parte pecuniae datus erat, appella-
tus.

    14. Tum P. Sulpicius secundum vota in Capitolio nun-
cupata paludatis lictoribus profectus ab urbe Brundisium
2 venit, et veteribus militibus voluntariis ex Africano exercitu in legiones discriptis, navibusque ex classe Cn. Corneli electis, altero die quam a Brundisio solvit in Macedo-
3 niam traiecit. ibi ei praesto fuere Atheniensium legati,
orantes ut se obsidione eximeret. missus extemplo Athenas est C. Claudius Centho cum viginti longis navibus et

---

[16] ob noxiam *Bessler*: ob noxam χ: noxiam *B*: obnoxiam *Rossbach*: noxia *Weiss*.

---

[73] A very low rent, equivalent to a few cents in today's terms,
but sufficient to make the point that it was state-owned land. A
Roman "acre" (*iugerum*) was about two-thirds of a modern acre.

[74] From Latin *triens* (a third) and *tabulae* (public records).

[75] The military cloak (*paludamentum*), fastened with a brooch
at the shoulder, was worn by generals on active service. Here it is
the lictors who are *paludati,* but according to Varro (*L.L.* 7.37),

would this be but the money that they had provided as a service being appropriated as if for some wrongdoing on their part?

The request of these individuals being fair, and the state being nonetheless unable to repay the loan, the senate passed a resolution that was a compromise between equity and pragmatism. Since a large number of these citizens observed that there was land for sale in many areas and they needed to buy some, the senate decided that they should be granted the opportunity to use public lands within a fifty-mile radius of Rome. The consuls were to evaluate this land and impose a tax of one *as* per acre[73] to show that it was public land that was involved. The rationale behind this was that, when the public purse was again solvent, anyone preferring cash to land could restore the land to the people. The private citizens were happy to accept the compromise, and the land was given the name *trientabulum*[74] because its granting accounted for one third of the public debt.

14. Then, after making his vows on the Capitoline, Publius Sulpicius set off from the city with his lictors dressed in their military cloaks[75] and came to Brundisium. Here he integrated in his legions a number of volunteers who were veterans of the army in Africa, and made a selection of ships from the fleet of Gnaeus Cornelius. With these he crossed to Macedonia, arriving the day after he cast off from Brundisium. There he was met by a deputation from Athens, who begged him to raise the siege of their city. Gaius Claudius Centho[76] was then immediately

the general is said to be *paludatus* when his lictors put it on (cf. also Livy 41.10.5, 7, 13; 45.39.11).     [76] Probably Sulpicius' legate C. Claudius (cf. also 22.5–8, below).

4 mille militum; neque enim ipse rex Athenas obsidebat: eo
maxime tempore Abydum oppugnabat, iam cum Rhodiis
et Attalo navalibus certaminibus, neutro feliciter proelio,
5 vires expertus; sed animos ei faciebat praeter ferociam
insitam foedus ictum cum Antiocho Syriae rege divisaeque
iam cum eo Aegypti opes, cui morte audita Ptolomaei
regis ambo imminebant.
6    Contraxerant autem sibi cum Philippo bellum Athenienses haudquaquam digna causa, dum ex vetere fortuna
7 nihil praeter animos servant. Acarnanes duo iuvenes per
initiorum dies non initiati templum Cereris imprudentes
8 religionis cum cetera turba ingressi sunt. facile eos sermo
prodidit absurde quaedam percunctantes, deductique ad
antistites templi, cum palam esset per errorem ingressos,
9 tamquam ob infandum scelus interfecti sunt. id tam foede
atque hostiliter gens Acarnanum factum ad Philippum
detulit, impetravitque ab eo ut datis Macedonum auxiliis
10 bellum se inferre Atheniensibus pateretur. hic exercitus
primo terram Atticam ferro ignique depopulatus cum
omnis generis praeda in Acarnaniam rediit. et inritatio
quidem animorum ea prima fuit: postea iustum bellum
decretis civitatis ultro indicendo factum.
11    Attalus enim rex Rhodiique persecuti cedentem in
Macedoniam Philippum cum Aeginam venissent, rex Pi-

---

77 A free city on the coast of the Hellespont (*Barr.* 51 G4).
78 The Eleusinian Mysteries, in honor of Demeter (Ceres),
were held in September and so are an important factor for the
dating of the outbreak of the war.

dispatched to Athens with twenty warships and a thousand men. In fact, the king was not himself present at the siege of Athens; he was at that very time mounting his offensive on Abydus.[77] He had already made trial of his strength in naval battles against the Rhodians and Attalus, achieving little success in either engagement. Even so, in addition to his natural truculence, he was also encouraged by a treaty that he had struck with Antiochus, king of Syria, by which Philip would share with Antiochus the wealth of Egypt, on which both kings had had designs ever since they had heard of King Ptolemy's death.

In fact, the people of Athens had not had a good reason for entering into a war with Philip, preserving as they did nothing of their former condition apart from their pride. In the days devoted to the mysteries,[78] two young Acarnanians, who were not initiated, joined the crowd and entered the temple of Ceres, unaware of the sacrilege involved. Their language easily gave them away when they asked some bizarre questions. They were taken to the priests of the temple and, although it was evident that they had entered by mistake, they were put to death as though guilty of some horrendous crime. The people of Acarnania brought word of this vile and provocative act to Philip, and received his permission to attack Athens, for which they were granted some Macedonian reinforcements. At first the army plundered Attic territory with fire and the sword, and returned to Acarnania laden with all manner of booty. This incursion was the first irritant for the Athenians. Subsequently the war was formalized with an official declaration made by decree of state.

When Philip now began to retire to Macedonia, King Attalus and the Rhodians pursued him and, after they

raeum renovandae confirmandaeque cum Atheniensibus
12 societatis causa traiecit. civitas omnis obviam effusa cum
coniugibus ac liberis, sacerdotes cum[17] insignibus suis
intrantem urbem ac di prope ipsi exciti sedibus suis acceperunt.

15. In contionem extemplo populus vocatus ut rex quae
vellet coram ageret; deinde ex dignitate magis visum scri-
2 bere eum de quibus videretur, quam praesentem aut refe-
rendis suis in civitatem beneficiis erubescere, aut signifi-
cationibus acclamationibusque multitudinis adsentatione
3 immodica pudorem onerantis. in litteris autem, quae missae in contionem recitataeque sunt, commemoratio erat
beneficiorum primum in civitatem suorum, deinde rerum
4 quas adversus Philippum gessisset, ad postremum adhortatio capessendi belli dum se, dum Rhodios, tum quidem
dum etiam Romanos haberent: nequiquam postea, si tum
cessassent, praetermissam occasionem quaesituros.

5 Rhodii deinde legati auditi sunt; quorum recens erat
beneficium, quod naves longas quattuor Atheniensium
captas nuper ab Macedonibus reciperatasque remiserant.
Itaque ingenti consensu bellum adversus Philippum
6 decretum. honores regi primum Attalo immodici, deinde
et Rhodiis habiti: tum primum mentio inlata de tribu
quam Attalida appellarent ad decem veteres tribus ad-

---

[17] cum *ed. Rom.*: *om. Bχ*: in *Weiss.*

---

[79] This scene and the next chapter (to 15.8) closely follow
Polybius' account of Attalus' arrival in Athens (16.25.2–26.10).

reached Aegina, the king crossed to Piraeus to renew and strengthen his alliance with Athens. The entire citizen body along with their wives and children streamed out to meet him; and the priests in all their finery, and one might almost say the gods themselves, summoned forth from their shrines, welcomed him as he came into their city![79]

15. The people were immediately called to a meeting so the king could publicly state his wishes. But then it was deemed more in keeping with his dignity for him to write a letter about any matters of concern to him. Rather this, it was felt, than that he be present in person and be in the embarrassing situation of listing his services to the state of Athens or receiving applause and acclamation from a crowd that would tax his modesty with extravagant flattery. In the letter, which was sent to the assembly and there read out, attention was called first to Attalus' good offices to the Athenian community, and then to his military campaigns against Philip. Finally there came an exhortation to undertake a war against Philip while the Athenians had his support as well as that of the Rhodians and even the Romans. If they hesitated now, they were told, they would in future seek in vain an opportunity that they had let slip.

Next the Rhodian ambassadors were given an audience and their service to the Athenians was of recent date: they had recovered and sent back to them four Athenian warships that had been captured by the Macedonians a little earlier.

So it was that war was declared on Philip by an overwhelming majority. A plethora of honors was showered first on Attalus and then also on the Rhodians; and it was at this time that mention was first made of the addition of a new tribe, to be called "the Attalid," to the ten ancient

7  denda, et Rhodiorum populus corona aurea virtutis ergo
   donatus, civitasque Rhodiis data quemadmodum Rhodii
   prius Atheniensibus dederant. secundum haec rex Attalus
   Aeginam ad classem se recipit; Rhodii Ceam[18] ab Aegina,
8  inde per insulas Rhodum navigarunt, omnibus praeter
   Andrum Parumque et Cythnum, quae praesidiis Macedo-
9  num tenebantur, in societatem acceptis. Attalum Aeginae
   missi in Aetoliam nuntii exspectatique inde legati aliquam-
10 diu nihil agentem tenuere. sed neque illos excire ad arma
   potuit, gaudentes utcumque composita cum Philippo
   pace, et ipse Rhodiique, cum, si institissent Philippo, egregium liberatae per se Graeciae titulum habere potuissent,
11 patiendo rursus eum in Hellespontum traicere, occupan-
   temque Thraciae opportuna loca vires conligere, bellum
   aluere gloriamque eius gesti perfectique Romanis concesserunt.

   16. Philippus magis regio animo est usus; qui cum Attalum Rhodiosque hostes non sustinuisset, ne Romano qui-
2  dem quod imminebat bello territus, Philocle quodam ex
   praefectis suis cum duobus milibus peditum equitibus
3  ducentis ad populandos Atheniensium agros misso, classe

18 Ceam *Gel.*: Ceiam *Bχ*: Ciam *Sig.*

---

80 Cf. Polyb. 16.25.9. The ten tribes were part of Cleisthenes'
reforms in 508/7, but in fact three more had been added by 204.
Two of these, however, were abolished in 201/200. The Attalid
thus became the twelfth tribe of Athens (cf. Walbank 2.534).

81 Not necessarily a real crown. Latin *corona* often refers to a
gift of precious metal (cf. Walbank 3.86, Oakley 2.359–60).

82 The manuscripts are divided over the name, but that Ceos
is meant is clear from Polybius (16.26.10).

83 Like Ceos, all islands in the Cyclades.

tribes.[80] The people of Rhodes were awarded a golden crown[81] for their bravery and all Rhodians were granted Athenian citizenship, just as the Rhodians had earlier granted their citizenship to the Athenians. After this Attalus returned to his fleet at Aegina, while the Rhodians sailed from Aegina to Cea[82] and thence to Rhodes by way of the islands, forming alliances with all of them apart from Andros, Paros, and Cythnos,[83] which were garrisoned by the Macedonians. Attalus was kept inactive for some time in Aegina: he had sent messengers to Aetolia, and was awaiting the return of envoys. He was, however, unable to incite the Aetolians to take up arms, as they were happy to have concluded peace with Philip, whatever its terms. Attalus and the people of Rhodes could have won the remarkable distinction of liberating Greece by their own efforts had they now put pressure on Philip; instead, by allowing him to cross to the Hellespont once more, and to amass his strength by seizing points of strategic importance in Thrace, they merely kept the war alive and left to the Romans the glory of conducting it and bringing it to its conclusion.

16. Philip revealed a spirit more becoming of a king. Though he had been unable to mount effective resistance to Attalus and the Rhodians, he was not frightened even by the impending war with Rome. He sent one of his officers, Philocles,[84] with 2,000 infantry and 200 cavalry to conduct raids on Athenian farmlands, and he assigned a

---

[84] A "friend" (i.e., confidant) of Philip, for whom he conducted numerous military operations, but when he became involved in the dispute between Philip's sons Perseus and Demetrius he was put to death by him (40.55.7).

tradita Heraclidi ut Maroneam peteret, ipse terra eodem
cum expeditis duobus milibus peditum equitibus ducentis
4 pergit. et Maroneam quidem primo impetu expugnavit;
Aenum inde cum magno labore,[19] postremo per prodi-
5 tionem Callimedis praefecti Ptolomaei, cepit. deinceps
alia castella, Cypsela et Doriscon et Serrheum, occupat.
inde progressus ad Chersonesum, Elaevnta et Alopecon-
6 nesum tradentibus ipsis recipit; Callipolis quoque et Madytos deditae, et castella quaedam ignobilia. Abydeni ne
legatis quidem admissis regi portas clauserunt. ea oppugnatio diu Philippum tenuit, eripique ex obsidione, ni
7 cessatum ab Attalo et Rhodiis foret, potuerunt. Attalus
trecentos tantum milites in praesidium, Rhodii quadriremem unam ex classe, cum ad Tenedum staret, miserunt.
8 eodem postea, cum iam vix sustinerent obsidionem, et
ipse Attalus cum traiecisset, spem tantum auxilii ex propinquo ostendit, neque terra neque mari adiutis sociis.

17. Abydeni primo, tormentis per muros dispositis, non
terra modo adeuntes aditu arcebant, sed navium quoque
2 stationem infestam hosti faciebant; postea, cum et muri
pars strata ruinis, et ad interiorem raptim oppositum mu-

---

[19] labore *Bχ*: *post add.* obsedit *Pluygers*, nequiquam op-
pugnasset *M. Müller*

---

[85] Heraclides of Tarentum, one of Philip's principal hench-
men after the Peace of Phoenice.     [86] Modern Maronia, a
port city on the Thracian coast (*Barr.* 51 F3).

[87] Aenus (Ainos), Cypsela, and Doriscus are all in Thrace, east
of Maronea (*Barr.* 51 G3). Serrheum (Serreion?), as-yet unidentified, may be a town in the vicinity of Mt. Serreion and the
promontory of Serreion (*Barr.* 51 F3).

fleet to Heraclides[85] so he could head for Maronea,[86] while the king himself proceeded to the same town overland with 2,000 light-armed infantry and 200 cavalry. In fact, Philip took Maronea at the first assault but subsequently had great trouble with Aenus, which he finally captured only through the treachery of Ptolemy's lieutenant, Callimedes. He then seized other strongholds, Cypsela, Doriscus, and Serrheum.[87] From there he advanced to the Chersonese, where he took Elaeus and Alopeconnesus, whose populations voluntarily submitted to him. Callipolis and Madytos[88] also surrendered, as did some little-known forts. The people of Abydus, however, shut their gates on the king, refusing admission even to his envoys. That particular siege detained Philip for a long time and but for faintheartedness on the part of Attalus and the Rhodians the people of Abydus might have been delivered from the siege. Attalus sent a mere three hundred men to help with the defense, and the Rhodians a single quadrireme from their fleet, even though that fleet was moored at Tenedos. Later, when the people of Abydus were barely able to hold out against the siege, Attalus crossed to the town in person, but only held out some hope of assistance from close at hand without actually helping his allies either by land or by sea.

17. By posting catapults along the walls, the people of Abydus at first succeeded not only in fending off the attacks of those approaching by land but also in putting the enemy fleet at risk as it lay at anchor. Later, when part of the wall had been shattered and the enemy had used tun-

[88] Elaeus, Alopeconnesus, Callipolis, Madytus are all cities in the Thracian Chersonese (*Barr.* 51 G4, H4).

rum cuniculis iam perventum esset, legatos ad regem de
3 condicionibus tradendae urbis miserunt. paciscebantur
autem ut Rhodiam quadriremem cum sociis navalibus
Attalique praesidium emitti liceret, atque ipsis urbe excedere cum singulis vestimentis.
4   Quibus cum Philippus nihil pacati nisi omnia permittentibus respondisset, adeo renuntiata haec legatio ab in-
5 dignatione simul ac desperatione iram accendit ut ad Sa-
guntinam rabiem versi matronas omnes in templo Dianae,
pueros ingenuos virginesque, infantes etiam cum suis
6 nutricibus in gymnasio includi iuberent, aurum et argentum in forum deferri, vestem pretiosam in naves Rhodiam
Cyzicenamque quae in portu erant coici, sacerdotes victi-
7 masque adduci et altaria in medio poni. ibi delecti primum
qui, ubi caesam aciem suorum pro diruto muro pugnantem
8 vidissent, extemplo coniuges liberosque interficerent, aurum argentum uestemque quae in navibus esset in mare
deicerent, tectis publicis privatisque quam plurimis locis
9 possent ignes subicerent: id se facinus perpetraturos prae-
euntibus exsecrabile carmen sacerdotibus iure iurando
adacti; tum militaris aetas iurat neminem vivum nisi vic-
10 torem acie excessurum. hi memores deorum adeo per-

---

89 The expression *socii navales* (naval allies) stems from the
fact that most of the Roman navy was originally raised from Greek
allies in Magna Graecia, but Livy uses it simply to mean sailors.

90 The Saguntum episode (21.6–15) is not exactly parallel and
does not appear in Polybius' account (16.30–34). At Saguntum
there was no premeditated mass suicide (though many did kill
themselves), no order was given to kill women and children in the
event of defeat, and the suicide followed surrender. A number of

nels to reach a hastily erected inner wall, they sent an embassy to the king to discuss terms for the town's surrender. The agreement they were seeking from Philip was that the Rhodian quadrireme with its crew,[89] and the relief force of Attalus, be allowed to depart while they themselves should leave the city with one piece of clothing each.

Philip's reply to them was that no terms were acceptable short of unconditional surrender, and when the results of the delegation were brought back to the people of Abydus indignation and despair roused them to such fury that they resorted to action as insane as that witnessed at Saguntum.[90] They ordered all their married women to be locked in the temple of Diana, and all freeborn boys, girls, and even babies, along with their nurses, in the gymnasium; and they had all their gold and silver brought to the forum, and their expensive clothing loaded onto ships (one from Rhodes and one from Cyzicus) that were in the harbor. Then they had their priests and sacrificial animals brought forth and altars erected in public. There they first selected men who, when they saw their army cut down as it fought before the breached wall, would immediately kill the wives and children, hurl into the sea the gold and silver and the clothing on the ships, and set fire to buildings public and private in as many locations in the city as they could. They bound themselves by oath to carry out this monstrous act, the priests dictating to them the formulas of execration; and the men of military age then swore that none would leave the battle alive unless victorious. These

such mass suicides under siege conditions are reported in the ancient world; Masada is only the best known.

tinaciter pugnaverunt ut, cum proelium nox diremptura esset, rex prior, territus rabie eorum, pugna abstiterit.

11 principes, quibus atrocior pars facinoris delegata erat, cum paucos et confectos volneribus ac lassitudine superesse proelio cernerent, luce prima sacerdotes cum infulis ad urbem dedendam Philippo mittunt.

18. Ante deditionem ex iis legatis[20] qui Alexandream missi erant M. Aemilius trium consensu, minimus natu, 2 audita obsidione Abydenorum ad Philippum venit. qui questus Attalo Rhodiisque arma inlata et quod tum maxime Abydum oppugnaret, cum rex ab Attalo et Rhodiis ultro se bello lacessitum diceret, "num Abydeni quoque" 3 inquit "ultro tibi intulerunt arma?" insueto vera audire ferocior oratio visa est quam quae habenda apud regem esset. "aetas" inquit "et forma et super omnia Romanum 4 nomen te ferociorem facit. ego autem primum velim vos foederum memores servare mecum pacem: sin bello lacessitis, mihi quoque animos facere et regnum et Macedonum nomen haud minus quam Romanum nobile sentietis."

5 Ita dimisso legato, Philippus auro argentoque quae[21] coacervata erant acceptis[22] hominum praedam omnem 6 amisit. tanta enim rabies multitudinem invasit ut prodi-

[20] legatis *B*: legatis Romanis χ

[21] argentoque quae *B*χ: argento quaeque alia *H.J.M*: argento quaeque coacervata alia *M. Müller*: argentoque quae in foro *Damsté* [22] acceptis *Harant*: accepto *B*χ

---

[91] Ribbons or narrow bands of wool worn around the head as symbols of submission.

[92] Marcus Aemilius Lepidus (68): cf. 2.3 and note, above.

men, keeping the gods in mind, fought with such tenacity that when nightfall was about to bring the fighting to an end the king quit the battle before them, terrified by their furious resistance. Those leading citizens who had been charged with the cruelest part of the atrocious deed could now see that few of their men had survived the battle, and that these were incapacitated from wounds and exhaustion; and so at dawn they sent their priests, wearing fillets,[91] to surrender the town to Philip.

18. Before the surrender, Marcus Aemilius,[92] the youngest of the three ambassadors who had been sent to Alexandria, came to Philip, with the agreement of his colleagues, on hearing of the siege of Abydos. Aemilius reproached him for his attack on Attalus and the Rhodians and his offensive against Abydus, which was proceeding at that very time. When the king claimed that it was he who had been the victim of unprovoked aggression on the part of Attalus and the Rhodians, Aemilius replied: "The people of Abydus are not also guilty of unprovoked aggression against you, are they?" Philip, not accustomed to hearing the truth, found his language too insolent to be used before a king. "Your age, your good looks, and above all the name of Rome make you rather insolent," said Philip. "My own first choice would be for you to observe our treaties and remain at peace with me; but if you attack me, you will realize that the kingdom and name of Macedon—as noble as those of Rome—give me courage, too."

With that Philip dismissed the ambassador. He then seized the gold and silver that had been amassed, but all human booty he lost. Such fury gripped the population of Abydus that, thinking the men who had fallen in battle had

tos[23] rati qui pugnantes mortem occubuissent, periuri-
umque alius alii exprobrantes et sacerdotibus maxime, qui
quos ad mortem devovissent, eorum deditionem vivorum
7 hosti fecissent, repente omnes ad caedem coniugum libe-
rorumque discurrerent seque ipsi per omnes vias leti
interficerent. obstupefactus eo furore rex suppressit impetum militum, et triduum se ad moriendum Abydenis dare
8 dixit. quo spatio plura facinora in se victi ediderunt quam
infesti edidissent victores, nec, nisi quem vincula aut alia
necessitas mori prohibuit, quisquam vivus in potestatem
venit. Philippus, imposito Abydi praesidio, in regnum re-
9 diit. cum velut Sagunti excidium Hannibali, sic Philippo
Abydenorum clades ad Romanum bellum animos fecisset,
nuntii occurrerunt consulem iam in Epiro esse, et Apolloniam terrestres copias navales Corcyram in hiberna de-
duxisse.

19. Inter haec legatis, qui in Africam missi erant, de
Hamilcare Gallici exercitus duce responsum a Carthaginiensibus est nihil ultra se facere posse quam ut exsilio eum
2 multarent bonaque eius publicarent: perfugas et fugitivos
quos inquirendo vestigare potuerint reddidisse, et de ea
re missuros legatos Romam qui senatui satisfacerent. ducenta milia modium tritici Romam, ducenta ad exercitum
in Macedoniam miserunt.

---

[23] ut proditos *Crév.*: ut repente proditos *Bχ*

---

[93] Apollonia in Illyria (*Barr.* 49 B3) and Corcyra (mod. Corfu)
both joined Rome in 229 and became bases respectively for Roman land forces and fleets.     [94] Cf. 11.4–18, above.
[95] "Measure" here translates the Latin *modius,* a dry measure
roughly equivalent to 8.15 liters, or a quarter of a bushel.

been betrayed, they accused each other of perjury, and above all accused the priests, who had delivered alive to the enemy those whom they had by sacred oath marked out for death. They all suddenly ran off to butcher their wives and children and then committed suicide themselves, seeking every possible path to death. Stunned by such murderous insanity, Philip arrested his men's assault and declared that he was giving the people of Abydus three days to complete their deaths. In that space of time the defeated townspeople inflicted more atrocities on themselves than bloodthirsty conquerors would have done, and nobody fell into Philip's power alive apart from those for whom imprisonment or some other form of duress made suicide impossible. Philip established a garrison at Abydus and returned to his kingdom. And just as the destruction of Saguntum had stimulated Hannibal to war with the Romans, so now did the massacre of the people of Abydus stimulate Philip to war with Rome. The news then came that the consul was already in Epirus, and that he had taken his land forces to winter in Apollonia, and his naval forces in Corcyra.[93]

19. In the meantime the deputation sent to Africa[94] had received a reply from the Carthaginians with regard to Hamilcar, commander in chief of the Gallic army. The Carthaginians claimed that they could do no more than punish him with exile and confiscate his property. As for the deserters and fugitives, they said they had restored all they had been able to trace in the course of their investigation, and they would dispatch an embassy to Rome on that matter to give satisfaction to the senate. They sent 200,000 measures[95] of wheat to Rome and 200,000 to the army in Macedonia.

3    Inde in Numidiam ad reges profecti legati. dona data
Masinissae mandataque edita; equites mille Numidae,
4    cum duo milia daret, accepti. ipse in naves imponendos
curavit, et cum ducentis milibus modium tritici ducentis
hordei in Macedoniam misit.

5    Tertia legatio ad Verminam erat. is ad primos fines
regni legatis obviam progressus, ut scriberent ipsi quas
6    vellent pacis condiciones permisit: omnem pacem bonam
iustamque fore sibi cum populo Romano. datae leges pacis, iussusque ad eam confirmandam mittere legatos Romam.

20. Per idem tempus L. Cornelius Lentulus pro consule
2    ex Hispania rediit. qui cum in senatu res ab se per multos
annos fortiter feliciterque gestas exposuisset, postulas-
3    setque ut triumphanti sibi invehi liceret in urbem, res
triumpho dignas esse censebat senatus, sed exemplum a
maioribus non accepisse ut qui neque dictator neque
4    consul neque praetor res gessisset triumpharet: pro consule illum Hispaniam provinciam, non consulem aut prae-
5    torem obtinuisse. decurrebatur tamen eo ut ovans urbem
iniret, intercedente Ti. Sempronio Longo tribuno plebis,
qui nihilo magis id more maiorum aut ullo exemplo futu-

---

96 Cf. 11.16, above.    97 L. Cornelius Lentulus (188),
proconsul in Spain since 206, although, as Livy notes below, he
had not been a consul (his predecessor, Scipio, had been in the
same position in 206 [28.38.1–4]). He was later consul (199), and
proconsul in Gaul (198). Cf. *MRR* 299.

98 According to Valerius Maximus (2.8.1), a body count of five
thousand of the enemy was required (but see Beard, 209ff.)

99 A lesser triumph granted to a man not thought worthy of a
full triumph. He entered Rome on foot or on horseback, not in a

The envoys then set off for the kings' courts in Numidia. Masinissa was given gifts and dispatches from the senate, and the Romans accepted from him a thousand Numidian cavalry of the 2,000 that he offered. The king had the cavalry embarked on vessels and sent them to Macedonia together with 200,000 measures of wheat and 200,000 of barley.

The ambassadors' third call was on Vermina. He came right to the frontier of his realm to meet them and allowed them to formulate themselves whatever peace terms they pleased[96]—any peace with the people of Rome would be good and equitable in his eyes, he said. Terms of the peace were dictated to him, and he was told to send envoys to Rome for its ratification.

20. At this time the proconsul Lucius Cornelius Lentulus[97] returned from Spain. In the senate he gave a detailed account of his achievements and successes over many years and requested permission to enter the city in triumph. The senate voted that Lentulus' record did merit a triumph,[98] but added that they had no precedent from their ancestors for someone celebrating a triumph for exploits performed when he was not a dictator, a consul or a praetor—Lentulus had held command in the province of Spain as a proconsul, not as consul or praetor. Nevertheless they resorted to the compromise of his entering the city with an ovation,[99] although the tribune of the plebs, Tiberius Sempronius Longus, threatened to interpose his veto on the ground that this privilege would be no more in conformity with ancestral practice and would be just

chariot (cf. Beard *passim,* esp. 62–63, and, for Lentulus' case, 206–7).

6  rum diceret. postremo victus consensu patrum tribunus
   cessit, et ex senatus consulto L. Lentulus ovans urbem est
7  ingressus. argenti tulit[24] quadraginta tria milia pondo, auri
   duo milia quadringenta quinquaginta; militibus ex praeda
   centenos vicenos asses divisit.

   21. Iam exercitus consularis ab Arretio Ariminum
   transductus erat, et quinque milia socium Latini nominis
2  ex Gallia in Etruriam transierant. itaque L. Furius magnis
   itineribus ab Arimino adversus Gallos Cremonam tum
   obsidentes profectus, castra mille quingentorum passuum
3  intervallo ab hoste posuit. occasio egregie rei gerendae
   fuit, si protinus de via ad castra oppugnanda duxisset:
4  palati passim vagabantur per agros, nullo satis firmo relicto
   praesidio; lassitudini militum timuit, quod raptim ductum
5  agmen erat. Galli clamore suorum ex agris revocati, omissa
   praeda quae in manibus erat, castra repetivere, et postero
   die in aciem progressi.

6  Nec Romanus moram pugnandi fecit; sed vix spatium
7  instruendi fuit: eo cursu hostes in proelium venerunt. dextra ala—in alas divisum socialem exercitum habebat—in
   prima acie locata est, in subsidiis duae Romanane legiones.
8  M. Furius dextrae alae, legionibus M. Caecilius, equitibus
   L. Valerius Flaccus—legati omnes erant—praepositi.
9  praetor secum duos legatos, C. Laetorium et P. Titinium,

---

[24] tulit *Weiss.*: tulit ex praeda *B*χ

---

[100] Modern Arezzo and Rimini. Arretium had been an ally of
Rome and a base for Roman operations since the third century.
Ariminum had become a Latin colony in 268.

[101] Cf. 5.4 note, above.

[102] The account of the battle is difficult to follow and the details of the army formation obscure. Livy, probably following an
annalistic source, has not worked it into his narrative very well.

as unprecedented. In the end the tribune relented, persuaded by the unanimity of the senators, and by senatorial decree Lucius Lentulus entered the city with an ovation. He brought with him 43,000 pounds of silver and 2,450 pounds of gold, and distributed from his booty 120 *asses* to each of his men.

21. The consular army had by now been transferred from Arretium to Ariminum,[100] and the 5,000 allies and men with Latin rights[101] had marched from Gaul into Etruria. Accordingly, Lucius Furius advanced by forced marches from Ariminum toward the Gauls, who were at that time besieging Cremona, and encamped at a distance of one and a half miles from his enemy. The opportunity for an exceptional feat was within his grasp had he but led his men to attack the enemy's camp immediately after the march: the Gauls were widely scattered and straggling through the fields without having established sufficient protection for themselves. Furius, however, had misgivings about the fatigue of his men, since the column had been taken along at a rapid pace. The Gauls, called back from the fields by the cries of their comrades, dropped the plunder that they had in their hands and headed back to camp. They proceeded to battle stations the following day.[102]

On their side, the Romans did not hold back from the fight, but there was barely enough time to organize the line, so swiftly did the enemy come into battle. Furius had the allied force divided into squadrons, and the right squadron was stationed in the front line, backed up by two Roman legions. Marcus Furius commanded the right squadron, Marcus Caecilius the legions, and Lucius Valerius Flaccus the cavalry, all three as legates. The praetor kept two legates with him, Gaius Laetorius and Publius

habebat, cum quibus circumspicere et obire ad omnes
hostium subitos conatus posset.

10 Primo Galli omni multitudine in unum locum conixi
obruere atque obterere sese dextram alam, quae prima

11 erat, sperarunt posse. ubi id parum procedebat, circuire a
cornibus et amplecti hostium aciem, quod in multitudine

12 adversus paucos facile videbatur, conati sunt. id ubi vidit
praetor, ut et ipse dilataret aciem, duas legiones ex subsidiis dextra laevaque alae quae in prima acie pugnabat circumdat, aedemque Vediovi[25] vovit si eo die hostes fudis-

13 set. L. Valerio imperat ut parte una duarum legionum
equites altera sociorum equitatum in cornua hostium

14 emittat, nec circuire eos aciem patiatur; simul et ipse, ut
extenuatam mediam diductis cornibus aciem Gallorum
vidit, signa inferre confertos milites et perrumpere or-

15 dines iubet. et cornua ab equitibus et medii a pedite pulsi;
ac repente, cum in omni parte caede ingenti sternerentur,

16 Galli terga verterunt fugaque effusa repetunt castra. fugientes persecutus eques; mox et legiones insecutae in
castra impetum fecerunt. minus sex milia hominum inde

17 effugerunt; caesa aut capta supra quinque et triginta milia
cum signis militaribus septuaginta, carpentis Gallicis

---

[25] Vediovi *Merkel*: deo Iovi *B*χ: Diiovi *Valesius*: Iovi *Böttcher*:
Veiovi *Rossbach*

---

[103] The "right squadron" (*dextra ala*) is not difficult: composed of allied troops, which normally accompany the Roman
legions on the two wings, it is referred to a number of times in
this chapter and the next. But there is no mention of the *left*
squadron, which is odd, since Livy seems have given a complete
account of the Roman formation.

Titinius, so that he could survey the battle along with them and counter any unexpected enemy maneuvers.

At the start the Gauls hoped that they could overpower and wipe out the right squadron[103] in the front line by attacking in full force at a single point. Achieving little success with this, they attempted to encircle the wings and outflank their enemy's line, an apparently simple maneuver, since they had large numbers facing a few. The praetor saw this happening, and in order to extend his fighting line he added the two supporting Roman legions to the right and left of the squadron fighting in the front line; and he also vowed a temple to Vediovis[104] should he defeat the enemy that day. He then ordered Lucius Valerius to unleash cavalry (that of the two legions on the one side, that of the allies on the other) against the flanks of the enemy, and not permit them to encircle the line. At the same time, the consul could himself see that the Gauls' center had been weakened by their extending their wings, and he ordered his men to attack en masse and break through their lines. Thus the flanks were driven back by the cavalry and the center by the infantry and, subjected now to massive slaughter everywhere, the Gauls suddenly turned and headed back to camp in a disordered rout. The Roman cavalry chased them as they fled; and soon the legions followed and attacked the camp. Fewer than 6,000 men made good their escape; more than 35,000 were cut down or captured, along with 70 military standards and more than 200 Gallic wagons loaded with ample booty.

---

[104] The reading here, the identity of the god, and the site and date of construction of the temple are a major problem: see Briscoe 1.112–14.

18    multa praeda oneratis plus ducentis. Hamilcar dux Poenus
eo proelio cecidit et tres imperatores nobiles Gallorum.
Placentini captivi ad duo milia liberorum capitum redditi
colonis.

    **22.** Magna victoria laetaque Romae fuit: litteris adlatis
2    supplicatio in triduum decreta est. Romanorum sociorumque ad duo milia eo proelio ceciderunt, plurimi dextrae
alae, in quam primo impetu vis hostium ingens inlata est.
3    quamquam per praetorem prope debellatum erat, consul
quoque C. Aurelius, perfectis quae Romae agenda fuerant, profectus in Galliam victorem exercitum a praetore
accepit.

4    Consul alter cum autumno ferme exacto in provinciam
5    venisset, circa Apolloniam hibernabat. ab classe, quae
Corcyrae subducta erat, C. Claudius triremesque Romanae, sicut ante dictum est, Athenas missae cum Piraeum
pervenissent, despondentibus iam animos sociis spem in-
6    gentem attulerant. nam et terrestres ab Corintho quae per
Megara incursiones in agros fieri solitae erant non fiebant,
7    et praedonum a Chalcide naves, quae non mare solum
infestum sed etiam omnes maritimos agros Atheniensibus
fecerant, non modo Sunium superare sed nec extra fretum
quidem[26] Euripi committere aperto mari se audebant.

---

[26] nec *Asc.*: ne *Bχ*: ne . . . fretum quidem *Novák*: ne . . . Euripi
quidem *Madvig*

---

[105] Hamilcar's death is a problem, as he later appears alive
(32.30.12) and even graces C. Cornelius Cethegus' triumph over
the Gallic Insubres and Cenomani (33.23.5). It seems more likely,
however, that he did die in this battle and that the other version
is embellishment by a Roman source of Livy to bring credit to the
influential Cornelian family.

The Carthaginian commander Hamilcar fell in the battle,[105] as did three Gallic generals of noble birth. As many as 2,000 freeborn captives from Placentia were restored to their colony.

22. It was a great victory, one that brought joy to Rome; and when the dispatch arrived a three-day period of supplication[106] was declared. Up to 2,000 Romans and allies fell in the battle, most of them from the squadron on the right, against which the massive enemy assault had been directed at the start of the engagement. Hostilities had been virtually brought to a conclusion thanks to the praetor; even so, after finishing all the business required of him in Rome, the consul Gaius Aurelius also set out for Gaul and assumed command of the victorious army from the praetor.

The other consul[107] reached his province toward the end of autumn and wintered close to Apollonia. Gaius Claudius and the Roman triremes had been detached from the fleet moored at Corcyra and sent to Athens, as noted above, and their arrival in Piraeus had brought high hopes to the dispirited allies. For one thing, overland raids on Athenian farmlands, which had been made regularly from Corinth by way of Megara, now no longer occurred; and, secondly, pirate ships from Chalcis, formerly a menace to the Athenians not just on the open sea but also in all their coastal farmland, no longer even dared to venture into the open sea beyond the strait of Euripus,[108] and

[106] On *supplicatio,* see 8.2 note, above.

[107] P. Sulpicius Galba (cf. 14.1, above). The Greek narrative, interrupted at 19, now continues.

[108] Between Euboea and the Greek mainland (*Barr.* 55 F4).

8 supervenerunt his tres Rhodiae quadriremes, et erant
Atticae tres apertae naves, ad tuendos maritimos agros
comparatae. hac classe si urbs agrique Atheniensium defenderentur, satis in praesentia existimanti Claudio esse
maioris etiam rei fortuna oblata est.

23. Exsules ab Chalcide regiorum iniuriis pulsi attule-
2 runt occupari Chalcidem sine certamine ullo posse; nam
et Macedonas, quia nullus in propinquo sit hostium metus,
uagari passim, et oppidanos praesidio Macedonum fretos
3 custodiam urbis neglegere. his auctoribus profectus,
quamquam Sunium ita mature pervenerat ut inde provehi
ad primas angustias Euboeae posset, ne superato promunturio conspiceretur, classem in statione usque ad noctem
4 tenuit. primis tenebris movit, et tranquillo pervectus
Chalcidem paulo ante lucem, qua infrequentissima urbis
sunt, paucis militibus turrim proximam murumque circa
scalis cepit, alibi sopitis custodibus alibi nullo custodiente.
5 progressi inde ad frequentia aedificiis loca, custodibus
interfectis refractaque porta ceteram multitudinem armatorum acceperunt.

6 Inde in totam urbem discursum est, aucto etiam tu-
7 multu quod circa forum ignis tectis iniectus erat: confla-
grarunt et horrea regia et armamentarium cum ingenti
apparatu machinarum tormentorumque. caedes inde pas-

---

109 Probably anti-Macedonian activists exiled because they
threatened Philip's control of the city of Chalcis, where Philip II
had installed a garrison in 338. Philip referred to Chalcis as one
of his three "fetters of Greece" (cf. 32.37.4; Polyb. 18.11.5; Strabo
9.4.15), since by holding them he could dominate Greece. Corinth
and Demetrias were the other two.

much less to round Cape Sunium. To supplement these vessels, three quadriremes arrived from Rhodes, and there were also three Attic open-decked ships, furnished for the defense of the coastline. Claudius was thinking that it was enough for the moment if the city and farmland of the Athenians were defended by this fleet, but he was then offered the chance of bringing off something greater.

23. Some exiles from Chalcis, driven from home by atrocities committed by Philip's men,[109] brought word that Chalcis could be taken without a fight. With no fear of an enemy in the vicinity, they said, the Macedonians were drifting aimlessly all over town, while the townspeople were paying no attention to their city's defenses because they relied on the Macedonian garrison. On the basis of their information Claudius set off for Chalcis. Although he reached Sunium early enough to be able to sail on from there to the opening of the straits of Euboea, he nevertheless kept his fleet at anchor until nightfall for fear of being spotted after rounding the promontory. At dusk he moved, and had a smooth crossing to Chalcis, which he reached shortly before dawn. He approached the most sparsely populated area of town where, with a few soldiers, he captured with scaling ladders the closest tower and the wall adjoining it, either finding the guards asleep or no one on guard at all. The Romans then advanced to the built-up areas of the city where they killed the sentries, smashed in the gate, and let in the main body of their force.

They now ran amok throughout the city, the chaos being further intensified because the buildings around the forum were put to the torch. The king's granaries as well as the arsenal, with its huge stock of siege engines and slings, went up in flames. Everywhere fugitives were then

sim fugientium pariter ac repugnantium fieri coepta est;
8 nec ullo iam qui militaris aetatis esset non aut caeso aut
fugato, Sopatro etiam Acarnane praefecto praesidii interfecto, praeda omnis primo in forum conlata, deinde in
9 naves imposita. carcer etiam ab Rhodiis refractus, emis-
sique captivi quos Philippus tamquam in tutissimam cus-
10 todiam condiderat. statuis inde regis deiectis truncatisque,
signo receptui dato conscenderunt naves, et Piraeum,
11 unde profecti erant, redierunt. quod si tantum militum
Romanorum fuisset ut et Chalcis teneri et non deseri
praesidium Athenarum potuisset, magna res principio sta-
12 tim belli, Chalcis et Euripus adempta regi forent; nam ut
terra Thermopylarum angustiae Graeciam, ita mari fretum Euripi claudit.

24. Demetriade tum Philippus erat. quo cum esset
nuntiata clades sociae urbis, quamquam serum auxilium
2 perditis rebus[27] erat, tamen, quae proxima auxilio est, ul-
tionem petens, cum expeditis quinque milibus[28] et trecen-
tis equitibus extemplo profectus cursu prope Chalcidem
contendit, haudquaquam dubius opprimi Romanos posse.
3 a qua destitutus spe, nec quicquam aliud quam ad de-
forme spectaculum semirutae ac fumantis sociae urbis
cum venisset, paucis vix qui sepelirent bello absumptos
relictis, aeque raptim ac venerat transgressus ponte Euri-
pum per Boeotiam Athenas ducit, pari incepto haud dis-

[27] rebus *Luchs: om. B*χ
[28] milibus *B*: milibus (milia *P*) peditum χ

---

[110] Another of Philip's "fetters of Greece." Founded by Demetrius Poliorcetes in 293, it lay in the Gulf of Volos near the
present town of Volos: *Barr.* 55 D2.

indiscriminately massacred along with those offering resistance. When all of military age had either been killed or had taken flight, and when the garrison commander, the Acarnanian Sopater, had also fallen, all the booty was first gathered into the forum and then loaded onto the ships. The prison was also broken open by the Rhodians and its inmates freed, men whom Philip had incarcerated there believing them to be in the most secure confinement. The king's statues were then pulled down and hacked to pieces and when the signal for retreat was sounded the Romans took to their ships and returned to Piraeus, whence they had set out. Had the Roman numbers been sufficient for Chalcis to be held without abandoning the defense of Athens, the king would have been deprived of Chalcis and the *Euripus*—a great success right at the start of the war. For just as the pass of Thermopylae is the gateway to Greece by land, so too is the strait of Euripus by sea.

24. At this time Philip was at Demetrias.[110] Here news was brought to him of the disaster that had befallen his allied city, and although all was lost and it was too late for aid, he wanted the next best thing, revenge. He immediately set off with 5,000 light-armed infantry and 300 cavalry and headed almost at running speed for Chalcis, convinced that the Romans could be caught there. He was frustrated in this hope; all he met on his arrival was the ugly sight of the allied town half demolished and still smoking, with few survivors, barely enough to bury those killed in the battle. He therefore recrossed the Euripus by the bridge as swiftly as he had come and led his troops to Athens through Boeotia in the belief that his initiative would result in a not dissimilar outcome from his

4 parem eventum ratus responsurum. et respondisset, ni
speculator—hemerodromos vocant Graeci, ingens die uno
cursu emetientes spatium—contemplatus regium agmen
ex specula quadam, praegressus nocte media Athenas pervenisset.

5 Idem ibi somnus eademque neglegentia erat quae
6 Chalcidem dies ante paucos prodiderat. excitati nuntio
trepido et praetor Atheniensium et Dioxippus, praefectus
cohortis mercede militantium auxiliorum, convocatis in
forum militibus tuba signum ex arce dari iubent, ut hostes
7 adesse omnes scirent. ita undique ad portas ad muros discurrunt. paucas post horas Philippus, aliquanto tamen
ante lucem, adpropinquans urbi, conspectis luminibus
crebris et fremitu hominum trepidantium, ut in tali tu-
8 multu, exaudito, sustinuit signa et considere ac conquies-
cere agmen iussit, vi aperta propalam usurus quando parum dolus profuerat.

9 Ab Dipylo accessit. porta ea, velut in ore urbis posita,
maior aliquanto patentiorque quam ceterae est, et intra
eam extraque latae viae sunt, ut et oppidani derigere
10 aciem a foro ad portam possent, et extra limes mille ferme

---

111 I.e. he would achieve the same success as the Romans had
at Chalcis.      112 Literally, "Day-runners" ($\dot{\eta}\mu\epsilon\rho o\delta\rho\acute{o}\mu o\iota$). The
word is correct but not its meaning. Livy is clearly explaining what
he found in his Greek source (probably Polybius), but it does not
mean "scouts," which is $\dot{\eta}\mu\epsilon\rho o\sigma\kappa\acute{o}\pi o\iota$ (Day-watchers). He has
mistranscribed or misremembered his source. On Livy's use of
Polybius, see Introduction, xix–xxvi, lxxviii–lxxxii.
113 Livy often uses the Roman term "praetor" for the leading
official, the *strategos* (lit., "general"), in Greek states or sym-
machies. In Athens ten "generals" (*strategoi*) were elected annually to command the city's army and navy, but in the fifth century

enemy's.[111] And indeed it would have, but for a scout—
these men the Greeks call *hemerodromoi*[112] because they
cover huge distances in a day's run—who had spotted the
king's army from a watchtower, set off ahead of Philip and
reached Athens in the middle of the night.

In Athens there reigned the same indolence and the
same negligence that had let down Chalcis a few days
earlier. The Athenian praetor[113] and the commander of
the unit of auxiliary mercenaries, Dioxippus, both of them
galvanized to action by the alarming report, called the
soldiers to the forum and ordered a trumpet signal given
from the citadel to let everyone know that the enemy was
at hand. At all points people ran to the gates and to the
walls. A few hours later, but still some time before dawn,
Philip approached the city, where he saw a large number
of lights and heard the clamor of agitated men, as one
might expect in such an emergency. He halted his troops
and ordered the column to pitch camp and rest. He had
decided to employ force openly now that his stratagem
had not succeeded.

He made his approach from the direction of the Dipy-
lon.[114] This gate, which virtually represents the main entrance to the city,[115] is considerably larger and wider than
the other gates. Wide roads run on the inside and outside
of it, so that the townspeople could draw up a line of
battle from the forum to the gate, while on the outside a

they also came to be the chief political officials. Here "praetor"
probably refers to the chief *strategos*.

[114] On the northwest side of the city, it consisted of two gates,
one behind the other, with a space between them.

[115] Literally, "as if in the mouth of the city."

passus longus, in Academiae gymnasium ferens, pediti
equitique hostium liberum spatium praeberet. eo limite
Athenienses cum Attali praesidio et cohorte Dioxippi, acie
11 intra portam instructa, signa extulerunt. quod ubi Philippus vidit, habere se hostes in potestate ratus et diu optata
caede—neque enim ulli Graecarum civitatium infestior
erat—iram[29] expleturum iri, cohortatus milites ut se in-
12 tuentes pugnarent, scirentque ibi signa ibi aciem esse
debere ubi rex esset, concitat equum non ira tantum sed
13 etiam gloria elatus, quod ingenti turba, completis etiam ad
spectaculum muris, conspici se pugnantem egregium du-
14 cebat. aliquantum ante aciem cum equitibus paucis evec-
tus in medios hostes ingentem cum suis ardorem tum
15 pavorem hostibus iniecit. plurimos manu sua comminus
eminusque volneratos compulsosque in portam consecutus et ipse, cum maiorem in angustiis trepidantium edidis-
set caedem, in temerario incepto tutum tamen receptum
16 habuit, quia qui in turribus portae erant sustinebant tela,
ne in permixtos hostibus suos conicerent.
17 Intra muros deinde tenentibus milites Atheniensibus,
Philippus, signo receptui dato, castra ad Cynosarges—
templum Herculis gymnasiumque et lucus erat circumiec-

---

[29] iram expleturum iri *Weiss. (1860)*: expleturum *Bχ*: exple-
tum iri *Madvig (1884)*

---

[116] Probably a small force left by Attalus on his departure for
Aegina (14.11, above).
[117] An area outside the walls of Athens. Its exact location is
unknown, but it probably lay to the south of the Acropolis.

road about a mile long leading to the gymnasium of the academy offered the enemy's infantry and cavalry space to move freely. The Athenians, along with the garrison of Attalus[116] and Dioxippus' unit, drew up their battle line inside the gate and sallied forth by this road. When Philip saw this he thought he had the advantage of his enemy and that his anger was going to be assuaged by the bloodbath he had long desired (for none of the Greek city-states was more detested by him). He urged his men to look at him as they fought and to be aware that the standards and the battle should be concentrated just where their king was to be found. He then spurred on his horse toward the enemy, impelled not only by anger but also by the promise of glory, because the city walls were already filled with people waiting for the show and he thought he would now be on display putting up a spectacular fight before a huge crowd. He rode with a few of his cavalrymen some distance ahead of his battle line and into the thick of the enemy, and simultaneously inspired great fervor in his own men and great alarm in the foe. In person he followed up large numbers of the enemy whom he had with his own hand wounded at close quarters or at long range, and whom he had driven back to the gate; and, after inflicting yet further slaughter on the panicking Athenians in the narrow gateway, he none the less, in this reckless enterprise, secured a safe retreat because the men on the turrets above the gate held back their missiles for fear of hitting their own comrades who were intermingled with the enemy.

Since the Athenians then kept their men back within their walls, Philip sounded the retreat and encamped at Cynosarges,[117] where there was a temple of Hercules and

18   tus—posuit. sed et Cynosarges et Lycium et quidquid
     sancti amoenive circa urbem erat incensum est, dirutaque
     non tecta solum sed etiam sepulcra, nec divini humanive
     iuris quicquam prae impotenti ira est servatum.

     25. Postero die cum primo clausae fuissent portae, de-
     inde subito apertae quia praesidium Attali ab Aegina
     Romanique ab Piraeo intraverant urbem, castra ab urbe
2    rettulit rex tria ferme milia passuum. inde Eleusinem pro-
     fectus spe improviso templi castellique, quod et imminet
     et circumdatum est templo, capiendi, cum haudquaquam
     neglectas custodias animadvertisset et classem a Piraeo
     subsidio venire, omisso incepto Megara ac protinus Corin-
     thum ducit, et cum Argis Achaeorum concilium esse au-
     disset, inopinantibus Achaeis contioni ipsi supervenit.
3    consultabant de bello adversus Nabim tyrannum Lacedae-
     moniorum, qui tralato imperio a Philopoemene ad Cyclia-

---

118 Levene (80–81) notes Livy's emphasis on Philip's sacrile-
gious behavior here and later in both Books 31 and 32.

119 This must have been Demeter's temple, site of the Eleusinian Mysteries. The fort is problematic (cf. Briscoe 1.121);
Livy probably misunderstood Polybius, whose account of this has
not survived.

120 The "Second Achaean League," territories in the northern
Peloponnese that had formed themselves into a federation in 280,
was anti-Macedonian in the 240s and 230s, but when Arcadian
cities were admitted, especially Megalopolis in 235, Spartan hostility led to reconciliation with Macedon. The League remained
loyal to Macedon in the First Macedonian War and appeared on
Philip's side in the Peace of Phoenice in 205.

121 Nabis is always styled "tyrant" in the sources, which, based
on Polybius, whose father (Lycortas) was a major figure in the

a gymnasium encircled by a wood. In fact, Cynosarges, the Lyceum, and anything else in the vicinity of the city that was of religious importance or aesthetic appeal were put to the torch, and even tombs, not just buildings, were torn down. Nothing within the divine or human compass was protected from the king's uncontrollable rage.[118]

25. The following day the city gates were at first closed, and then suddenly opened again because the garrison of Attalus had arrived in the city from Aegina and the Romans from Piraeus. The king therefore withdrew his camp some three miles from the city. From there he headed for Eleusis, hoping to take the temple, and the fort overlooking and surrounding it,[119] with a surprise assault. However, when he discovered that their defenses had been in no way overlooked and also that a fleet was coming with support from Piraeus, he abandoned the project and led his army to Megara and then straight on to Corinth. On hearing that there was a meeting of the Achaean League[120] at Argos, he surprised the Achaeans by turning up at the actual session. They were debating a war against Nabis, tyrant of Sparta.[121] Nabis had noticed that with the transfer of command from Philopoemen to Cycliadas,[122] who

Achaean League in the 180s, are always hostile to him. Becoming sole king (Sparta traditionally had two) in 207, he introduced some revolutionary left-wing measures.

[122] This is the first mention of Philopoemen, famous *strategos* of the Achaean League and the greatest Greek statesman of his time, much admired by his compatriot Polybius (both being from Megalopolis). Cycliadas, who was pro-Macedonian, was expelled after his year in office and eventually fled to Philip.

dan,[30] nequaquam parem illi ducem, dilapsa cernens
Achaeorum auxilia redintegraverat bellum, agrosque finitimorum vastabat, et iam urbibus quoque erat terribilis.

4 adversus hunc hostem cum quantum ex quaque civitate
militum scriberetur consultarent, Philippus dempturum
se eis curam, quod ad Nabim et Lacedaemonios attineret,

5 est pollicitus,[31] nec tantum agros sociorum populationibus
prohibiturum, sed terrorem omnem belli in ipsam Laco-

6 nicam, ducto eo extemplo exercitu, tralaturum. haec oratio cum ingenti adsensu hominum acciperetur, "ita tamen
aequum est" inquit "me vestra meis armis tutari ne mea

7 interim nudentur praesidiis. itaque, si vobis uidetur, tantum parate militum quantum ad Oreum et Chalcidem et
Corinthum tuenda satis sit, ut meis ab tergo tutis securus
bellum Nabidi inferam et Lacedaemoniis."

8 Non fefellit Achaeos quo spectasset tam benigna polli-
citatio auxiliumque oblatum adversus Lacedaemonios: id
quaeri ut obsidem Achaeorum iuventutem educeret ex

9 Peloponneso ad inligandam Romano bello gentem. et id
quidem coarguere Cycliadas praetor Achaeorum nihil
attinere ratus, id modo cum dixisset, non licere legibus
Achaeorum de aliis rebus referre quam propter quas

10 convocati essent, decreto de exercitu parando adversus
Nabim facto concilium fortiter ac libere habitum dimisit,

---

30 Cycliadan *Drak.*: Cycladem *B*: Cycliadem φ
31 est pollicitus *M. Müller*: pollicitus *B*χ: pollicitus est *Madvig*

---

123 Oreus (formerly Histiaea) lay on the northwest coast of
Euboea (*Barr.* 55 E3).
124 Though pro-Macedonian, he was probably convinced that
he had no chance of winning over the meeting at this time.

was by no means Philopoemen's equal as a leader, the Achaeans' auxiliary forces had dispersed, and he had therefore recommenced hostilities and was now conducting raids on his neighbors' farmlands and even menacing their cities as well. The League was considering the question of each city-state's contribution to a levy of troops to face this enemy, and Philip now undertook to relieve them of all responsibility with respect to Nabis and the Lacedaemonians. He would not only prevent raids on the territory of his allies but would also transfer the entire theater of that frightful war to Laconia itself by immediately taking his forces there. When this speech of his was received with great applause by his audience, he added "It is only fair, however, that my defending *your* territory with my forces should not meanwhile leave *mine* bereft of protection. So, if you agree, just assemble an armed force strong enough to defend Oreus,[123] Chalcis and Corinth, so that I can attack Nabis and the Lacedaemonians feeling sure that my possessions are safe behind me."

The motive behind such a generous commitment and the offer of help against the Spartans did not escape the Achaeans: the object was to take Achaeans of military age away from the Peloponnese as hostages in order to commit their people to a war with Rome. The praetor of the Achaeans, Cycliadas, seeing no point in refuting such a hypothesis,[124] merely observed that Achaean law did not permit discussion of matters other than those for which the meeting had been convened. A decree was then passed concerning mobilization of an army against Nabis, and Cycliadas adjourned a meeting that he had conducted with fortitude and independence of spirit, although until that

11  inter adsentatores regios ante eam diem habitus. Philippus magna spe depulsus, voluntariis paucis militibus con-
scriptis, Corinthum atque in Atticam terram rediit.

26. Per eos ipsos dies quibus Philippus in Achaia fuit
Philocles praefectus regius, ex Euboea profectus cum
duobus milibus Thracum Macedonumque ad depopulandos Atheniensium fines, regione Eleusinis saltum Cithae-
2  ronis transcendit. inde dimidia parte militum ad praedandum passim per agros dimissa, cum parte ipse occultus
3  loco ad insidias opportuno consedit, ut si ex castello ab
Eleusine in praedantes suos impetus fieret, repente hostes
4  effusos ex improviso adoriretur. non fefellere insidiae. itaque revocatis qui discurrerant ad praedandum militibus
instructisque ad oppugnandum castellum Eleusinem profectus, cum multis inde volneribus recessit, Philippoque
5  se venienti ex Achaia coniunxit. temptata et ab ipso rege
oppugnatio eiusdem castelli est; sed naves Romanae a
Piraeo venientes intromissumque praesidium absistere
incepto coegerunt.
6  Diviso deinde exercitu rex cum parte Philoclem Athenas mittit, cum parte Piraeum pergit, ut dum Philocles
subeundo muros comminanda oppugnatione contineret
urbe Athenienses, ipsi Piraeum levi cum praesidio relic-
7  tum expugnandi facultas esset. ceterum nihilo ei Piraei
quam Eleusinis facilior, iisdem fere defendentibus, op-
8  pugnatio fuit. a Piraeo Athenas repente duxit. inde erup-

---

125 Cf. 16.2, above.
126 Mt. Cithaeron separates Attica from Boeotia (*Barr.* 55 E4).

day he had been regarded as one of the king's lackeys. Frustrated in his great hope, Philip enrolled a few volunteers and moved back to Corinth and then into Attic territory.

26. At the very time that Philip was in Achaea, the king's lieutenant Philocles[125] left Euboea with 2,000 Thracians and Macedonians in order to plunder Athenian territory, and crossed the pass of Cithaeron[126] in the vicinity of Elcusis. From here he dispatched half the men to conduct raids at various points in the countryside while he himself covertly encamped with the rest in a location well suited for an ambush in order to make a lightning attack on the enemy while they were dispersed, should a sortie be made on his raiding parties from the fortress at Eleusis. The ambush did not escape detection. Philocles therefore recalled the men who had gone off to plunder, drew them up in battle formation, and set off to assault the fort at Eleusis. Falling back from there with many wounded, he joined up with Philip who was now on his return journey from Achaea. An assault was also made on the same stronghold by the king himself, but some Roman ships arriving from Piraeus and the installation of a garrison in the city forced him to abandon the attempt.

The king then split his forces, sending Philocles to Athens with some and proceeding to Piraeus with the others. His plan was that while Philocles pinned down the Athenians within their city by approaching the walls and threatening to attack, he himself would have an opportunity to take Piraeus, which would be left only lightly guarded. However, he found the attack on Piraeus no easier than the earlier attack on Eleusis since he faced virtually the same defenders. He then abruptly led his force from Pi-

tione subita peditum equitumque inter angustias semiruti
9 muri, qui bracchiis duobus Piraeum Athenis iungit, repul-
sus, omissa oppugnatione urbis, diviso cum Philocle rursus exercitu ad agros vastandos profectus, cum priorem
populationem sepulcris circa urbem diruendis exercuis-
10 set, ne quid inviolatum relinqueret, templa deum quae
11 pagatim sacrata habebant dirui atque incendi iussit. et
ornata eo genere operum eximie terra Attica et copia do-
mestici marmoris et ingeniis artificum praebuit huic furori
12 materiam; neque enim diruere modo ipsa templa ac simulacra evertere satis habuit, sed lapides quoque, ne integri
13 cumularent ruinas, frangi iussit. et postquam non tam ira
satiata[32] quam irae exercendae materia deerat, agro hostium in Boeotiam excessit, nec aliud quicquam dignum
memoria in Graecia egit.

27. Consul Sulpicius eo tempore inter Apolloniam ac
Dyrrachium ad Apsum flumen habebat castra, quo arces-
situm L. Apustium legatum cum parte copiarum ad depo-
2 pulandos hostium fines mittit. Apustius extrema Macedoniae populatus, Corrhago et Gerrunio et Orgesso castellis
primo impetu captis, ad Antipatream, in faucibus angustis

---

[32] satiata *Bχ*: satiata erat *Siesbye*: erat satiata *H.J.M*

---

[127] The Long Walls, linking Athens with Phaleron and Piraeus, were built between 461 and 456. Destroyed by the Spartans in 404, they were rebuilt by Conon in 393, but had by now
evidently fallen into disrepair.

[128] The River Apsus is today the Semeni (*Barr.* 49 B3), and
Dyrrachium (B2) is the Greek Epidamnos.        [129] Antipatrea
lay twenty-two miles east of Apollonia (*Barr.* 49 B3) and the
fortresses were perhaps west of there (cf. Briscoe 1.125).

raeus to Athens. Here the king was repulsed when the Athenian infantry and cavalry made a sudden charge through a narrow defile in the partially demolished walls[127] that link Piraeus to Athens with their two arms, and he abandoned his assault on the city. Dividing his forces with Philocles once more, he set off to plunder the countryside. While Philip had made the destruction of the tombs around the city the object of his earlier marauding expedition, on this occasion—to leave nothing inviolate—he ordered the demolition and burning of the temples of the gods that the people had consecrated in the country villages. And the territory of Attica, richly endowed with monuments of this kind, thanks both to ample resources of local marble and the talent of its craftsmen, provided fuel for Philip's wrath. For he was not satisfied with destroying the temples themselves and toppling the statues, but he even ordered individual stones to be shattered so that they would not add luster to the ruins if left whole. And when, rather than sating his fury, he ran out of material on which to vent it, he left his enemies' territory for Boeotia, and performed no further action in Greece worthy of mention.

27. At this time the consul Sulpicius was encamped on the banks of the River Apsus, between Apollonia and Dyrrachium.[128] Summoning his legate Lucius Apustius to the camp, he dispatched him with a portion of his troops to conduct raids on enemy territory. Apustius ravaged the outlying areas of Macedonia, captured the fortresses of Corrhagus, Gerrunius, and Orgessus with his first assault, and then came to Antipatrea,[129] a town situated in a nar-

3  sitam urbem, venit. ac primo evocatos principes ad conloquium ut fidei Romanorum se committerent perlicere est
conatus; deinde, ubi magnitudine ac moenibus situque
urbis freti dicta aspernabantur, vi atque armis adortus ex-
4  pugnavit, puberibusque interfectis, praeda omni militibus
5  concessa, diruit muros atque urbem incendit. hic metus
Codrionem, satis validum et munitum oppidum, sine cer-
6  tamine ut dederetur Romanis effecit, praesidio ibi relicto,
Cnidus—nomen propter alteram in Asia urbem quam
oppidum notius—vi capitur. revertentem legatum ad consulem cum satis magna praeda Athenagoras quidam, regius praefectus, in transitu fluminis a novissimo agmine
7  adortus postremos turbavit. ad quorum clamorem et trepidationem cum revectus equo propere legatus signa con-
vertisset, et coniectis in medium sarcinis aciem direxisset,
non tulere impetum Romanorum militum regii: multi ex
8  iis occisi, plures capti. legatus, incolumi exercitu reducto
ad consulem, remittitur inde extemplo ad classem.

28. Hac satis felici expeditione bello commisso, reguli
ac principes accolae Macedonum in castra Romana ve-
niunt, Pleuratus Scerdilaedi filius et Amynander Athama-
2  num rex et ex Dardanis Bato Longari filius: bellum suo

---

130 *Barr.* 49 C3.

131 He would be a leading figure in the Second Macedonian
War (cf. below, 35.1, 36.2, 40.8, etc.).

132 The Illyrian king Pleuratus appears as joint ruler with his
father Scerdilaidas in 212/11 (cf. Briscoe 1.127), but as sole king
by 205, suggesting that Scerdilaidas was dead by then.

133 Athamania, in the southeast of Epirus (*Barr.* 55 A2), became independent of Epirus about 230. Its king, Amynander, a
relative of Scerdilaedas, had been instrumental in arranging the

row gorge. He first of all summoned the town's leading citizens to a meeting at which he tried to entice them to put themselves under Roman protection; but when, confident in the size, fortifications, and position of their town, they rejected his overtures, Apustius launched an attack and took the place by armed force. He put to death men of military age and awarded his soldiers all the spoils; then he tore down the walls and burned the town. Fear of similar treatment prompted the strong and well-fortified town of Codrion[130] to surrender to the Romans without a fight. Leaving a garrison there, Apustius went on to storm Cnidus, its name better known—thanks to the other Cnidus in Asia—than the town itself. While the legate was returning to the consul with substantial plunder, an officer of the king, one Athenagoras,[131] attacked him from the rear as he was fording a river, and threw the end of the column into disarray. On hearing the men's cries of alarm, the Roman legate swiftly galloped back, made them wheel round, and then, setting the baggage in the center, deployed the line of battle. The king's troops failed to stem the attack of the Roman soldiers, and many were killed and more taken prisoner. After bringing back the army to the consul unscathed, the legate was immediately sent back to the fleet.

28. The war having begun with this relatively successful expedition, petty kings and leading members of tribes bordering Macedonia came to the Roman camp: Pleuratus, son of Scerdilaedas;[132] King Amynander of the Athamanians;[133] and, from the Dardanians, Bato son of Longa-

Peace of Phoenice in 205 and would play an important part in mediating between Rome and the Aetolians.

nomine Longarus cum Demetrio Philippi patre gesserat.
pollicentibus auxilia respondit consul Dardanorum et
Pleurati opera, cum exercitum in Macedoniam induceret,
3 se usurum; Amynandro Aetolos concitandos ad bellum
attribuit. Attali legatis—nam ii quoque per id tempus venerant—mandat ut Aeginae rex, ubi hibernabat, classem
Romanam opperiretur, qua adiuncta bello maritimo, sicut
4 ante, Philippum urgeret. ad Rhodios quoque missi legati,
ut capesserent partem belli.

Nec Philippus segnius—iam enim in Macedoniam per-
5 venerat—apparabat bellum. filium Persea, puerum admodum, datis ex amicorum numero qui aetatem eius re-
gerent, cum parte copiarum ad obsidendas angustias quae
6 ad Pelagoniam sunt mittit. Sciathum et Peparethum, haud
ignobiles urbes, ne classi hostium praedae ac praemio
essent, diruit. ad Aetolos mittit legatos, ne gens inquieta
adventu Romanorum fidem mutaret.

29. Concilium Aetolorum stata die, quod Panaetolicum
vocant, futurum erat. huic ut occurrerent, et regis legati
iter adcelerarunt et a consule missus L. Furius Purpureo
2 legatus venit; Atheniensium quoque legati ad id concilium

---

134 Demetrius II, son of Antigonus Gonatas. Cf. *OCD* sv Demetrius (6).

135 The Aetolians, living north of the Corinthian Gulf (*Barr.*
55 A3), became very powerful in the third century after defeating
the Gauls under Brennus at Delphi in 279.

136 Literally, "friends" (*amici*): officials in the court of the Hellenistic kings, who served as military officers and as advisors.

137 Situated on two islands of the same name off the coast of
Magnesia (*Barr.* 57 B2).

138 The Aetolian League met twice a year: in the autumn

rus (Longarus had already fought a war of his own against Demetrius,[134] the father of Philip). When these pledged support, the consul replied that he would avail himself of the assistance of the Dardanians and Pleuratus when the time came to lead his army into Macedonia; and to Amynander he assigned the responsibility of inciting the Aetolians[135] to join the war. To ambassadors from Attalus—these had also arrived at this time—he gave the order that their king should await the Roman fleet at Aegina, where he had his winter quarters, and after joining the fleet he was to put pressure on Philip with naval operations, as before. Envoys were also sent to the people of Rhodes asking them to join the war.

Philip, who had now arrived in Macedonia, was no less energetic in his preparations for war. Although his son Perseus was just a boy, he sent him with a portion of his forces to hold the passes into Pelagonia, assigning some of his courtiers[136] to hold his youth in check. Philip demolished Sciathus and Peparethus, towns of some prominence,[137] so they should not become a source of plunder and gain for the enemy fleet; and he sent a deputation to the Aetolians in case this fractious people switched loyalties with the coming of the Romans.

29. The council of the Aetolians, which they call "Panaetolian,"[138] was due to meet on the appointed day. Delegates of the king made special haste to attend the meeting, and the legate Lucius Furius Purpureo came, too, sent by the consul; and a delegation from the Athenians

at Thermus (and thus called "Thermica"), where elections took place; and in the spring (the "Panaetolica") at various other places in confederate territory (this time at Naupactus).

occurrerunt. primi Macedones, cum quibus recentissi-
3 mum foedus erat, auditi sunt. qui in nulla nova re nihil se
novi habere quod adferrent dixerunt: quibus enim de causis experta inutili societate Romana pacem cum Philippo
fecissent, compositam semel pacem servare eos debere.

4     "An imitari" inquit unus ex legatis "Romanorum licentiam, an levitatem dicam, mavoltis? qui cum legatis vestris
Romae responderi ita iussissent: 'quid ad nos venitis, Aetoli, sine quorum auctoritate pacem cum Philippo fecis-
5 tis?' iidem nunc ut bellum secum adversus Philippum
geratis postulant; et antea propter vos et pro vobis arma
sumpta adversus eum simulabant, nunc vos in pace esse
6 cum Philippo prohibent. Messanae ut auxilio essent primo
in Siciliam transcenderunt, iterum ut Syracusas oppressas
7 ab Carthaginiensibus in libertatem eximerent: et Messanam et Syracusas et totam Siciliam ipsi habent vectiga-
8 lemque provinciam securibus et fascibus subiecerunt. scilicet sicut vos Naupacti legibus vestris per magistratus a
vobis creatos concilium habetis, socium hostemque libere
quem velitis lecturi, pacem ac bellum arbitrio habituri
vestro, sic Siculorum civitatibus Syracusas aut Messanam
9 aut Lilybaeum indicitur concilium. praetor Romanus conventus agit: eo imperio evocati conveniunt, excelso in sug-
gestu superba iura reddentem, stipatum lictoribus vident,

---

139 Sicily fell to the Romans as a result of the First Punic War
(264–241), but Syracuse remained a free ally of Rome. However,
its tyrant Hieronymus supported Carthage against Rome in 214
(cf. Book 24.4–7), and it was captured after a lengthy siege in 211.

140 Representing the power to inflict death and corporal punishment, they were the symbols of *imperium* (see Introduction,
lii).

also turned up at this assembly. The Macedonians, with whom the Aetolians had made their most recent treaty, were the first to be heard. They stated that since there had been no fresh developments they had no fresh proposals. The Aetolians, they said, had negotiated a peace with Philip after recognizing the futility of an alliance with Rome, and they had the same reasons for standing by the treaty now that it had been concluded.

"Or do you prefer, to follow the model of Roman highhandedness" asked one of the Macedonian representatives, "or should I call it caprice? The reply they ordered given to your embassy in Rome was 'Aetolians, why bother coming to us now after negotiating peace with Philip without consulting us?' And now those same people are asking you to join them in making war on Philip! Earlier they made out that it was for you and in your interests that they took up arms against him—and now they forbid you to be at peace with Philip! They first crossed to Sicily to help Messana; the second time it was to liberate Syracuse when it was oppressed by Carthage. They themselves are now in possession of Messana, Syracuse, and the whole of Sicily,[139] and they have made them into a tribute-paying province subject to their axes and rods.[140] You are holding this meeting at Naupactus under your own rules and presided over by magistrates whom you have elected; and here you will choose freely whomsoever you wish to have as ally or enemy, and whether you have war or peace will be your decision. And of course it is like that for the city-states of Sicily—for them too a meeting is called, at Syracuse or at Messana or at Lilybaeum. A Roman praetor conducts the proceedings. At his command the people are summoned and assemble; they see him on his raised dais handing

virgae tergo secures cervicibus imminent; et quotannis
10 alium atque alium dominum sortiuntur. nec id mirari de-
bent aut possunt, cum Italiae urbes, Regium Tarentum
Capuam—ne finitimas quarum ruinis crevit urbs Roma
11 nominem, eidem subiectas videant imperio. Capua quidem sepulcrum ac monumentum Campani populi, elato
et extorri eiecto ipso populo, superest, urbs trunca sine
senatu, sine plebe, sine magistratibus, prodigium, relicta
crudelius habitanda quam si deiecta foret.
12 "Furor est, si alienigenae homines plus lingua et moribus et legibus quam maris terrarumque spatio discreti
haec tenuerint, sperare quicquam eodem statu mansu-
13 rum. Philippi regnum officere aliquid uidetur libertati
vestrae; qui, cum merito vestro vobis infensus esset, nihil
a vobis ultra quam pacem petiit fidemque hodie pacis pac-
tae desiderat.
14 Adsuefacite his terris legiones externas et iugum ac-
cipite: sero ac nequiquam, cum dominum Romanum ha-
15 bebitis, socium Philippum quaeretis. Aetolos Acarnanas
Macedonas, eiusdem linguae homines, leves ad tempus
ortae causae diiungunt coniunguntque: cum alienigenis
cum barbaris aeternum omnibus Graecis bellum est erit-
que; natura enim, quae perpetua est, non mutabilibus in
diem causis hostes sunt.
16 Sed unde coepit oratio mea, ibi desinet. hoc eodem

---

141 The status of the three was really very different (Briscoe
1.132), but the Macedonian is striving for effect, not accuracy.

down imperious judgments, his lictors thronging about him; and there are rods threatening backs, and axes threatening necks! And every year they are given by lot a different master. They should not, in fact cannot, be surprised at this, not when they see cities in Italy subjected to the same authority—Rhegium, Tarentum, and Capua,[141] not to mention those neighboring cities on whose ruins Rome grew to greatness. True, Capua has survived, the tomb and funerary monument of the people of Campania, its people buried or driven into exile; it is a crippled city, with no senate, no commoners, no magistrates, a bizarre phenomenon whose continued inhabitation is more cruel than its destruction would have been.

"If foreigners occupy these lands of ours, men separated from us more by language, culture, and legal systems than by mere distance over land and sea, it is folly to expect anything to remain in the same condition. You think Philip's rule some sort of infringement of your liberty; but even when, through your own fault, he was on terms of hostility with you, he asked nothing of you except peace, and today his only wish is that you honor the peace treaty that you concluded with him.

"Make these foreign legions feel at home in these lands and accept their yoke! Too late and to no avail will you want Philip as an ally when you have a Roman overlord. Aetolians, Acarnanians, Macedonians, peoples sharing a common language, are divided and united by trivial and ephemeral issues; but all Greeks are ever, and ever will be, at war with foreigners, with barbarians. For these are our enemies by nature, which is timeless, not because of disputes that change from one day to another.

"But my speech will end where it began. In this very

loco iidem homines de eiusdem Philippi pace triennio
ante decrevistis, iisdem improbantibus eam pacem Romanis, qui nunc pactam et compositam turbare volunt. in qua
consultatione nihil fortuna mutavit, cur vos mutetis non
video."

30. Secundum Macedonas, ipsis Romanis ita con-
cedentibus iubentibusque, Athenienses, qui foeda passi
iustius in crudelitatem saevitiamque regis invehi poterant,
2 introducti sunt. deploraverunt vastationem populatio-
nemque miserabilem agrorum: neque id se queri, quod
hostilia ab hoste passi forent; esse enim quaedam belli
3 iura, quae ut facere ita pati sit fas: sata exuri, dirui tecta,
praedas hominum pecorumque agi misera magis quam
4 indigna patienti esse; verum enim vero id se queri, quod
is qui Romanos alienigenas et barbaros vocet adeo omnia
simul divina humanaque iura polluerit, ut priore popula-
tione cum infernis deis secunda cum superis bellum nefa-
5 rium gesserit. omnia sepulcra monumentaque diruta esse
in finibus suis, omnium nudatos manes, nullius ossa terra
6 tegi. delubra sibi fuisse quae quondam pagatim habitantes
in parvis illis castellis vicisque consecrata ne in unam ur-

same spot, three years ago, the very same men, namely
you, decided on a peace treaty with the very same Philip,
and the people who objected to that treaty were the very
same Romans who now wish to disrupt the peace that we
negotiated and concluded. To the substance of this debate
Fortune has brought about no change, and I do not see
why you should make any change yourselves."

30. After the Macedonians, the Athenians were brought
forward to speak, with the Romans' assent and, in fact,
at their behest—having suffered terrible atrocities at his
hands, the Athenians could more legitimately denounce
the king's cruelty and ruthlessness. They deplored the destruction and pitiful ravaging of their fields, and added
that they were not complaining about having suffered at
the enemy's hands treatment usually meted by an enemy.
There were, they said, certain conventional acts in warfare
that are justifiably imposed and endured by either side:
the burning of crops; the demolition of buildings; plunder
taken in the form of people and animals. All of this constitutes a grim experience for the victim but is not unethical.
No, what they were complaining about was that the man
who was calling the Romans "foreigners" and "barbarians"
had so desecrated all human and divine laws as to wage
an impious war against the gods of the underworld on his
first marauding expedition, and against the gods in heaven
above on his second. All the tombs and funerary monuments in their territory had been torn down, the shades of
all the buried laid bare, the bones of none left with a
covering of earth. They had once had shrines, they said,
which their forefathers had in the past, when they lived in
country demes, consecrated in their little communities
and villages, and which they had not left neglected even

bem quidem contributi maiores sui deserta reliquerint:
7 circa ea omnia templa Philippum infestos circumtulisse
ignes; semusta truncata simulacra deum inter prostratos
iacere postes templorum.
8     Qualem terram Atticam fecerit, exornatam quondam
opulentamque, talem eum, si liceat, Aetoliam Graeciam-
9 que omnem facturum. urbis quoque suae similem defor-
mitatem futuram fuisse, nisi Romani subvenissent. eodem
enim scelere urbem colentes deos praesidemque arcis
Mineruam petitam, eodem Eleusine Cereris templum,
10 eodem Piraei Iovem Mineruamque; sed ab eorum non
templis modo sed etiam moenibus vi atque armis repulsum in ea delubra quae sola religione tuta fuerint saevisse.
11 itaque se orare atque obsecrare Aetolos ut miseriti Atheniensium ducibus dis immortalibus, deinde Romanis, qui
secundum deos plurimum possent, bellum susciperent.
    31. Tum Romanus legatus: "totam orationis meae for-
mam Macedones primum, deinde Athenienses mutarunt.
2 nam et Macedones, cum ad conquerendas Philippi iniurias in tot socias nobis urbes venissem, ultro accusando
Romanos, defensionem ut accusatione potiorem haberem
3 effecerunt, et Athenienses in deos inferos superosque
nefanda atque inhumana scelera eius referendo quid mihi

---

142 The two temples (of Zeus Soter and Athene Soteira) were
close together and known as the Disoterion. Where they were
located in Piraeus is unknown.

when they were incorporated in a single city. Philip had made the rounds of all these temples, attacking them with his fires; and half-burned, dismembered statues of the gods now lay amid temple pillars that had been pulled to the ground.

What Philip had made of Attica, they continued, a land rich in art and affluent in earlier days, he would also make of Aetolia and of the whole of Greece if given the chance. Their *city,* too, would have been in an equally hideous condition had not the Romans come to their aid. The same heinous attacks had been made by him on the city's patron deities and on Minerva, guardian of the acropolis; and likewise on the temple of Ceres in Eleusis and on Jupiter and Minerva in Piraeus.[142] He was, however, driven back by armed might not only from the temples but even from the city walls, and he had then vented his wrath on those shrines whose sole protection lay in the awe they inspired. So, concluded the Athenians, they were begging and pleading with the Aetolians to have pity on the Athenians and undertake a war in which the immortal gods would be their leaders and, after them, the Romans, who were second in power only to the gods.

31. The Roman ambassador then spoke as follows: "The Macedonians in the first place, and then the Athenians, have prompted radical changes in all that I was going to say. The Macedonians first. I had come here to protest against wrongs inflicted by Philip on so many cities allied to us; but by actually denouncing the Romans these men have made me consider defending ourselves more important than accusing him. And then the Athenians. With their account of Philip's nefarious and ruthless crimes against the gods of heaven and the underworld,

4 aut cuiquam reliquerunt quod obicere ultra possim? eadem haec Cianos Abydenos Aenios Maronitas Thasios Parios Samios Larisenses Messenios hinc ex Achaia existimate queri, graviora etiam acerbioraque eos quibus nocendi maiorem facultatem habuit.

5 "Nam quod ad ea attinet quae nobis obiecit, nisi gloria
6 digna sunt, fateor ea defendi non posse. Regium et Capuam et Syracusas nobis obiecit. Regium Pyrrhi bello legio a nobis,[33] Reginis ipsis ut mitteremus orantibus, in praesidium missa urbem ad quam defendendam missa
7 erat per scelus possedit. comprobavimus ergo id facinus? an bello persecuti sceleratam legionem, in potestatem nostram redactam, tergo et cervicibus poenas sociis pendere cum coegissemus, urbem agros suaque omnia cum
8 libertate legibusque Reginis reddidimus? Syracusanis oppressis ab externis tyrannis, quo indignius esset, cum tulissemus opem et fatigati prope per triennium terra marique urbe munitissima oppugnanda essemus, cum iam ipsi Syracusani servire tyrannis quam capi a nobis mallent, captam iisdem armis et liberatam urbem reddidimus.

[33] a nobis χ: om. *B*

---

[143] Messene was the capital of Messenia (*Barr.* 58 B3), and Livy is mistaken in placing it in Achaea (58 B1). It did become a member of the Achaean League, but not until 191.

[144] Allied with Rome against Pyrrhus, the Rhegians asked for a garrison and assistance. Polybius (1.7.6–12) adds that, led by a Campanian, Decius Vibellius, the garrison seized the city, expelling or massacring its Greek citizens. Finally recalled, the offenders were whipped and beheaded in the Roman forum.

[145] Hippocrates and Epicydes, Syracusans by origin but born

what further charge have they left me, or anyone else, to bring against him? Bear in mind that the very same protests are voiced by the peoples of Cios, Abydus, Aenus, Maronea, Thasos, Paros, Samos, Larisa, and—here in Achaea—Messene;[143] and that they are all the more severe and bitter in these cases because there he had wider scope to inflict damage.

"As for the allegations he made against us, I admit there can be no defense—unless the exploits in question actually redound to our credit. Rhegium, Capua, and Syracuse are the basis of his criticisms. In the case of Rhegium, the Rhegians themselves pleaded with us to send them assistance in the war with Pyrrhus, but the legion sent to protect the town illicitly took possession of the city it had been sent to defend.[144] Did we condone this crime? Or did we rather attack the offending legion, bring it back under our control, force it to atone to our allies with floggings and executions, and then restore to the people of Rhegium their city, their lands, and all their possessions along with their independence and legal system? Syracuse suffered under foreign tyrants,[145] so her lot was all the more unbearable. We brought assistance and were well nigh exhausted by a three-year land and sea offensive against the city,[146] which was very well fortified. But though the Syracusans themselves expressed a preference for serving their tyrants to being captured by us, we restored their city to them, captured and liberated by the same armed intervention.

and raised in Carthage, seized power in Syracuse in 214 (cf. Book 24.6–9, 21–32).

[146] Between 214 and 211.

9 "Neque infitias imus Siciliam provinciam nostram esse, et civitates quae in parte Carthaginiensium fuerunt, et uno animo cum illis adversus nos bellum gesserunt, stipendiarias nobis ac vectigales esse: quin contra hoc et vos et omnes gentes scire volumus, pro merito cuique erga nos

10 fortunam esse. an Campanorum poenae, de qua ne ipsi quidem queri possunt, nos paeniteat? hi homines, cum pro iis bellum adversus Samnites per annos prope septua-

11 ginta cum magnis nostris cladibus gessissemus, ipsos foedere primum deinde conubio atque[34] cognationibus, post-

12 remo civitate nobis coniunxissemus, tempore nostro adverso primi omnium Italiae populorum, praesidio nostro foede interfecto, ad Hannibalem defecerunt, deinde, indignati se obsideri a nobis, Hannibalem ad oppugnandam

13 Romam miserunt. horum si neque urbs ipsa neque homo quisquam superesset, quis id durius quam pro merito ip-

14 sorum statutum indignari posset? plures sibimet ipsi conscientia scelerum mortem consciverunt quam ab nobis supplicio adfecti sunt. ceteris ita oppidum ita agros ademimus ut agrum locumque ad habitandum daremus,

15 urbem innoxiam stare incolumem pateremur, ut qui hodie videat eam nullum oppugnatae captaeve ibi vestigium inveniat.

"Sed quid ego Capuam dico, cum Carthagini victae

16 pacem ac libertatem dederimus? magis illud est periculum ne nimis facile victis ignoscendo plures ob id ipsum ad experiendam adversus nos fortunam belli incitemus.

17 "Haec pro nobis dicta sint, haec adversus Philippum, cuius domestica parricidia et cognatorum amicorumque

---

[34] atque *B*: atque inde χ

"We do not deny that Sicily is our province, and that those city-states on it that sided with the Carthaginians and made war on us in sympathy with them now pay tribute and taxes to us. Quite the reverse, in fact; we want you and the whole world to know this, that each people's lot is dependent on its services to us. Are we to feel remorse over our punishment of the Campanians, about which they cannot even complain themselves? We had, on their behalf, been at war with the Samnites for almost seventy years, during which we ourselves suffered heavy casualties; and we had forged links with them first by a treaty, subsequently by intermarriage and family ties, and finally by granting them citizenship. But in our time of difficulty these men became the first of all the Italian peoples to defect to Hannibal, with the foul murder of our garrison, and then, angry at being besieged by us, they sent Hannibal to attack Rome. If their very city no longer survived or not a single one of them, who could complain that the punishment was harsher than they deserved? More actually committed suicide from a guilty conscience than were put to death by us. The rest we deprived of their town and their fields, but granted them some land and a place to live, and left unharmed the city (which was guiltless) so that anyone seeing it today would find no trace there of the assault and capture.

"But why mention Capua when we granted Carthage peace and independence after conquering it? What constitutes a greater danger for us is that by too readily forgiving those we have vanquished we may thereby encourage more people to try the fortunes of war against us!

"Let these points suffice in our defense and in answer to Philip, whose record you, being closer to Macedonia, know better than we: his extermination of family mem-

caedes et libidinem inhumaniorem prope quam crudelitatem vos, quo propiores Macedoniae estis, melius nostis.

18 quod ad vos attinet, Aetoli, nos pro vobis bellum suscepi-
mus adversus Philippum, vos sine nobis cum eo pacem

19 fecistis. et forsitan dicatis bello Punico occupatis nobis
coactos metu vos leges pacis ab eo qui tum plus poterat
accepisse; et nos, cum alia maiora urgerent, depositum a

20 vobis bellum et ipsi omisimus. nunc et nos, deum benigni-
tate Punico perfecto bello, totis viribus nostris in Macedoniam incubuimus, et vobis restituendi vos in amicitiam
societatemque nostram fortuna oblata est, nisi perire cum
Philippo quam uincere cum Romanis mavoltis.”

32. Haec dicta ab Romano cum essent, inclinatis omnium animis ad Romanos Damocritus praetor Aetolorum,
pecunia, ut fama est, ab rege accepta, nihil aut huic aut illi

2 parti adsensus, rem magni discriminis consiliis nullam
esse tam inimicam quam celeritatem dixit: celerem enim
paenitentiam, sed eandem seram atque inutilem sequi,
cum praecipitata raptim consilia neque revocari neque in

3 integrum restitui possint. deliberationis autem[35] eius
cuius ipse maturitatem exspectandam putaret tempus ita
iam nunc statui posse: cum legibus cautum esset ne de
pace belloque nisi in Panaetolico et Pylaico concilio age-

[35] autem χ: *om. B*

---

[147] An apparent reference to Philip's murder of his son Demetrius in 182, and therefore an anachronism.

[148] Praetor = Greek *strategos* (cf. 24.6 and note, above). Damocritus figures prominently in this decade as a misguided fo-
menter of bad relations between the Aetolians and the Romans.

[149] That is, “at Thermopylae,” but Livy has blundered. The

bers, his killing of kinsfolk[147] and friends, and his lechery, which is almost more atrocious than his ruthlessness. As for you, Aetolians, we undertook a war against Philip on your account, and you made peace with him without us. You will perhaps claim that when we were preoccupied with the Punic War you were intimidated into accepting peace terms from him since he was then more powerful; and that we, encumbered with other more urgent matters, also ourselves let drop the war that you had abandoned. Now, however, thanks to heaven's favor, we have concluded the Punic War and brought all our might to bear on Macedonia; and you have been offered the happy opportunity of returning to friendship and alliance with us—unless you prefer perishing with Philip to winning with the Romans."

32. After this speech from the Roman ambassador the feelings of the entire assembly shifted in the Romans' favor. Then the Aetolian praetor, Damocritus,[148] who had, it was rumored, been bribed by the king, stated without expressing agreement with either side that nothing was so inimical to decision-making in important matters as haste. Regret followed quickly, he said, but came too late and to no avail, since decisions hastily and prematurely reached could not be taken back or reversed. However, a date could be fixed even now for discussion of this issue, reflection on which he thought should be allowed time to mature. As their rules stipulated that war and peace could be discussed only in the Panaetolian and Pylaic[149] coun-

---

Aetolian council met in two different sittings: the spring meeting, the Panaetolika, at various sites (see 29.1, above), but the autumn, the Thermaika, at Thermon (*Barr.* 55 B3), which Livy has mistaken for Thermopylae (and does again at 33.35.8).

4   retur, decernerent extemplo ut praetor sine fraude, cum
de bello et pace agere velit, advocet concilium, et quod
tum referatur decernaturque ut perinde ius ratumque sit
5   ac si in Panaetolico aut Pylaico concilio actum esset. dimissis ita suspensa re legatis, egregie consultum genti aiebat:
nam utrius partis melior fortuna belli esset, ad eius societatem inclinaturos. haec in concilio Aetolorum acta.

33. Philippus impigre terra marique parabat bellum.
navales copias Demetriadem in Thessaliam contrahebat;
2   Attalum Romanamque classem principio veris ab Aegina
ratus moturos, navibus maritimaeque orae praefecit Hera-
3   clidam, quem et ante praefecerat; ipse terrestres copias
comparabat, magna se duo auxilia Romanis detraxisse cre-
dens, ex una parte Aetolos, ex altera Dardanos, faucibus
ad Pelagoniam a filio Perseo interclusis.
4   Ab consule non parabatur sed gerebatur iam bellum.
per Dassaretiorum fines exercitum ducebat, frumentum
quod ex hibernis extulerat integrum vehens, quod in usum
5   militi satis esset praebentibus agris. oppida vicique partim
voluntate partim metu se tradebant; quaedam vi expugnata, quaedam deserta, in montes propinquos refugienti-
6   bus barbaris, inveniebantur. ad Lyncum stativa posuit

---

150 Cf. 16.3, above.

151 An Epirote tribe living close to Illyria (*Barr.* 49 C3).

152 A region (*Barr.* 49 D3), not a town, as Livy seems to think.
His geography is certainly suspect here, as the River Bevus is in
Dassaretis (*Barr.* 49 C3), not Lyncus.

cils, they should decree forthwith that their praetor should duly convene a council when he wished to discuss the matter of war and peace, and all proposals and decrees on that occasion should be regarded as legal and binding just as if they had been debated in the Panaetolian or Pylaic council. The delegates were thus dismissed with the issue left up in the air, and Damocritus claimed that their decision was excellent for their people since they would now incline toward a treaty with whichever side had better fortune in the war. Such were the proceedings in the council of the Aetolians.

33. Philip was tireless in preparing for war on land and sea. He brought his naval forces together at Demetrias in Thessaly and, thinking that Attalus and the Roman fleet would move from Aegina at the start of spring, put his fleet and the coastline under the command of Heraclides,[150] whom he had also previously appointed to that post, while he himself proceeded to assemble the land forces. He believed that he had now deprived the Romans of two important sources of assistance, the Aetolians on the one hand, and the Dardanians on the other, since the passes to Pelagonia had been blockaded by his son Perseus.

As for the consul, he was already at war and not just preparing for it: he was leading his army through the territory of the Dassaretii,[151] taking with him the grain that he had brought out of his winter quarters, but leaving it intact since the countryside supplied enough to meet his men's needs. Towns and villages surrendered to him, some voluntarily, others through fear; a number were taken by storm, and some were found deserted, the barbarians seeking refuge in the nearby mountains. At Lyncus[152] Sulpicius established a stationary camp near the River Bevus, prope flumen Bevum; inde frumentatum circa horrea Dassaretiorum mittebat. Philippus consternata quidem omnia circa pavoremque ingentem hominum cernebat, sed parum gnarus quam partem petisset consul, alam equitum ad explorandum quonam hostes iter intendissent

7 misit. idem error apud consulem erat: movisse ex hibernis regem sciebat, quam regionem petisset ignorans. is quoque speculatum miserat equites. hae duae alae ex diverso, cum diu incertis itineribus vagatae per Dassaretios essent,

8 tandem in unum iter convenerunt. neutros fefellit, ut fremitus procul hominum equorumque exauditus est, hostes adpropinquare. itaque priusquam in conspectum venirent, equos armaque expedierant; nec mora, ubi primum hos-

9 tem videre, concurrendi facta est. forte et numero et virtute, utpote lecti utrimque, haud impares aequis viribus per aliquot horas pugnarunt. fatigatio ipsorum equorum-

10 que incerta victoria diremit proelium. Macedonum quadraginta equites Romanorum quinque et triginta ceciderunt. neque eo magis explorati quicquam in qua regione castra hostium essent aut illi ad regem aut hi ad consulem

11 rettulerunt; per transfugas cognitum est, quos levitas ingeniorum ad cognoscendas hostium res in omnibus bellis praebet.

34. Philippus aliquid et ad caritatem suorum et ut promptius pro eo periculum adirent ratus profecturum se,

and from here sent out foraging parties around the granaries of the Dassaretii. Philip could see the general chaos
in the area and the sheer panic of the people but, having
little idea of the direction taken by the consul, he sent out
a squadron of cavalry to seek out where his enemy had
headed. The consul was equally at a loss: he knew the king
had moved from his winter quarters but was unaware of
the region for which he had set his course. He, too, had
sent out some cavalry to reconnoiter. After a long period
of aimless wandering over unfamiliar paths in the territory
of the Dassaretii, these two squadrons, coming from opposite directions, finally converged on the same road. Neither group was unaware that their enemy was approaching
since the commotion of men and horses could be heard in
the distance. They had therefore prepared their mounts
and their weapons before coming into sight of each other,
and at the first glimpse of the foe the charge was immediate. As it happened, they were a match for each other both
in numbers and valor, being the elite of both sides, and
they fought for several hours on even terms. It was the
exhaustion of the men and their horses that broke off the
fight, the victory still undecided. Forty cavalrymen fell on
the Macedonian side, thirty-five on the Roman. And after
that the Macedonians had no more precise information to
report to the king, nor the Romans to the consul, on the
whereabouts of their enemy's camp. This was learned
through deserters who, in all wars, are provided for the
gathering of intelligence on the enemy by their unreliable
character.

34. Philip thought that if he saw to the burial of the
cavalrymen who had fallen in this operation, he would
have greater success in securing his men's affection and

2 si equitum qui ceciderant in expeditione sepeliendorum
curam habuisset, adferri eos in castra iussit, ut conspice-
3 retur ab omnibus funeris honos. nihil tam incertum nec
tam inaestimabile est quam animi multitudinis. quod
promptiores ad subeundam omnem dimicationem videba-
4 tur facturum, id metum pigritiamque incussit; nam qui
hastis sagittisque et rara lanceis facta volnera vidissent,
cum Graecis Illyriisque pugnare adsueti, postquam gladio
Hispaniensi detruncata corpora, bracchiis cum umero
abscisis, aut tota cervice desecta divisa a corpore capita
patentiaque viscera et foeditatem aliam volnerum vide-
5 runt, adversus quae tela quosque viros pugnandum foret
pavidi volgo cernebant. ipsum quoque regem terror cepit
6 nondum iusto proelio cum Romanis congressum. itaque
revocato filio praesidioque quod in faucibus Pelagoniae
erat, ut iis copiis suas augeret, Pleurato Dardanisque iter
7 in Macedoniam patefecit. ipse cum viginti milibus peditum duobus milibus equitum, ducibus transfugis, ad hostem profectus, paulo plus mille passus a castris Romanis
tumulum propinquum Ataeo[36] fossa ac vallo communiuit;
8 ac subiecta cernens Romana castra, admiratus esse dicitur
et universam speciem castrorum et discripta suis quaeque
partibus cum tendentium ordine tum itinerum intervallis,
9 et negasse barbarorum ea castra ulli videri posse. biduum
consul et rex, alter alterius conatus exspectantes, con-

[36] Ataeo ψ: Athaeo φ: *spat. B: nomen incertum*

making them face danger more readily for him; and he therefore ordered the dead to be brought into the camp so that the funeral ceremony could be observed by the whole army. Nothing is so unreliable or unpredictable as the psychology of the crowd. What the king thought would make the men more ready to face any combat instead afflicted them with fear and reluctance. In their frequent clashes with the Greeks and Illyrians they had seen the wounds produced by spears, arrows and, on rare occasions, lances. Now, however, they saw bodies dismembered by the Spanish sword, with arms lopped off complete with the shoulder, heads separated from bodies with the neck sliced right through, intestines laid bare, and other repulsive wounds; and there was widespread consternation as they began to understand the sort of weapons and men they had to face. The king was himself panicstricken, having never yet met the Romans in pitched battle. He therefore recalled his son and the defensive force stationed at the passes into Pelagonia in order to bolster his own forces with those troops, and he thus opened a path into Macedonia for Pleuratus and the Dardanians. With 20,000 infantry and 2,000 cavalry, and using deserters as guides, he set off in person to meet the enemy. He fortified a hillock near Ataeus, not much more than a mile from the Roman camp, with a ditch and a rampart; and it is said that, as he looked down on the Roman camp below, he was amazed at its overall appearance as well as the arrangement of its various units, with rows of men in tents separated by streets at regular intervals. Nobody, he is said to have remarked, could consider that to be a camp belonging to barbarians. Consul and king kept their men within their palisades for two days, each waiting for the

tinuere suos intra vallum; tertio die Romanus omnes in
aciem copias eduxit.

35. Rex, tam[37] celerem aleam universi certaminis timens, quadringentos Trallis—Illyriorum id, sicut alio dixi-
mus loco, est genus—et Cretenses trecentos, addito his
peditibus pari numero equitum, cum duce Athenagora,
uno ex purpuratis, ad lacessendos hostium equites misit.

2 ab Romanis autem—aberat acies eorum paulo plus quingentos passus—velites et equitum duae ferme alae emis-
sae, ut numero quoque eques pedesque hostem aequarent.

3 credere regii genus pugnae quo adsueverant fore, ut
equites in vicem insequentes refugientesque nunc telis
uterentur nunc terga darent, Illyriorum velocitas ad excursiones et impetus subitos usui esset, Cretenses in in-

4 vehentem se effuse hostem sagittas conicerent. turbavit
hunc ordinem pugnandi non acrior quam pertinacior im-

5 petus Romanorum; nam haud secus quam si tota acie di-
micarent et velites emissis hastis comminus gladiis rem
gerebant, et equites, ut semel in hostem evecti sunt, stantibus equis, partim ex ipsis equis partim desilientes immis-

6 centesque se peditibus pugnabant. ita nec eques regius
equiti par erat, insuetus ad stabilem pugnam, nec pedes
concursator et vagus et prope seminudus genere armorum
veliti Romano parmam gladiumque habenti, pariterque et

7 ad se tuendum et ad hostem petendum armato. non tulere

---

[37] tam *ed. Rom.*: non tam *Bχ*

---

[153] 27.32.4 (cf. also 33.4.4, 37.39.10, 38.21.3), but nothing is
known of them. Strabo (14.1.42) refers to "Thracian Trallians" as
founders of the city of Tralles in Asia Minor.

[154] Cf. 27.6, above.

other to make a move; on the third the Roman led out all his troops for combat.

35. Fearing to take a chance on a swift engagement with all his forces, the king sent out 400 Trallians (an Illyrian tribe, as I have noted elsewhere)[153] and 300 Cretans to harass the enemy cavalry, adding to this infantry detachment an equal number of cavalry under the command of one of his courtiers, Athenagoras.[154] The Romans, whose line was little more than half a mile distant, sent forth skirmishers and about two cavalry squadrons so as to have numerical parity with the enemy in cavalry and infantry. The king's men believed the manner of fighting would be that to which they had been accustomed: the cavalry advancing and retreating by turns, at one moment employing their weapons and at the next falling back; the speed of the Illyrians proving effective for sallies and sudden charges; and the Cretans firing arrows on an enemy making a disordered advance. What upset this strategy for the fight was the Roman onslaught, as relentless as it was savage. It was as if they were bringing their entire battle line into the fight: having thrown their javelins, the skirmishers went into close combat with the sword, and the cavalry, after their initial thrust against the enemy, halted their steeds and joined the fray, some from their horses and some dismounting and linking up with the infantry. As a result the king's cavalryman, lacking experience in stationary fighting, proved no match for the Roman cavalryman, nor his foot soldier (a skirmisher who ranged over the battlefield virtually devoid of any kind of armor) for the Roman light-armed man with sword and shield, equally well equipped for defending himself and attacking his

itaque dimicationem, nec alia re quam velocitate tutantes
se in castra refugerunt.

36. Vno deinde intermisso die, cum omnibus copiis
equitum levisque armaturae pugnaturus rex esset, nocte
caetratos, quos peltastas vocant, loco opportuno inter bina
2 castra in insidiis abdiderat, praeceperatque Athenagorae
et equitibus ut si aperto proelio procederet res, uterentur
fortuna, si minus, cedendo sensim ad insidiarum locum
3 hostem pertraherent. et equitatus quidem cessit, duces
caetratae cohortis, non satis exspectato signo ante tempus
excitatis suis, occasionem bene gerendae rei amisere. Romanus et aperto proelio victor et tutus a fraude insidiarum
in castra sese recepit.

4 Postero die consul omnibus copiis in aciem descendit,
ante prima signa locatis elephantis, quo auxilio tum primum Romani, quia captos aliquot bello Punico habebant,
5 usi sunt. ubi latentem intra vallum hostem vidit, in tumulos quoque ac sub ipsum vallum exprobrans metum successit. postquam ne tum quidem potestas pugnandi daba-
tur, quia ex tam propinquis stativis parum tuta frumentatio
erat, dispersos milites per agros equitibus extemplo in-
6 vasuris, octo fere inde milia, intervallo tutiorem frumen-
tationem habiturus, castra ad Otolobum—id est loco
7 nomen—movit. cum in propinquo agro frumentarentur

---

155 The *caetra* was a small round Spanish shield, but Livy also
uses the word of the *pelte* (also a small shield) used by Greek
skirmishers (peltasts).

156 Livy does mention elephants being captured (e.g., 23.46.4,
49.13; 24.42.8), but most were handed over by Carthage by the
peace settlement in 201, and this must have provided the main
supply for the Romans.

enemy. They were thus unable to keep up the fight, and they fled back to their camp with nothing more than their speed to protect them.

36. Then, after one day had passed, the king was ready to enter the fight with all his mounted and light armed forces. During the night he had set in ambush in a suitable location between the two camps some *caetra*-bearing soldiers that they call peltasts,[155] and had given Athenagoras and the cavalry orders to press their advantage if things went well in the pitched battle, but otherwise to retreat little by little and draw the enemy to where the ambush lay. The cavalry did actually retreat, but the commanders of the peltast cohort did not wait long enough for the signal, and by urging their men to premature action they let slip the opportunity of bringing the operation to a successful conclusion. The Roman returned to camp victor in the pitched battle and also unscathed by the ambush.

The following day the consul went into battle formation with all his forces, setting his elephants before the front ranks. This was the first occasion on which the Romans had availed themselves of this type of support—they possessed a number that had been captured during the Punic war.[156] When the consul saw his adversary cowering within his palisade, he advanced into the hills and even up to the palisade itself, taunting him with cowardice. Not even then was he given the opportunity to engage and, since foraging would be dangerous if conducted from a base so close to his enemy (whose cavalry would immediately attack his men while they were dispersed in the fields), he moved his camp some eight miles to a place called Otolobus so he could forage more safely at a distance. While the Romans gathered provisions in a nearby

Romani, primo rex intra vallum suos tenuit, ut cresceret
8 simul et neglegentia cum audacia hosti. ubi effusos vidit,
cum omni equitatu et Cretensium auxiliaribus, quantum
equitem velocissimi pedites cursu aequare poterant, citato
profectus agmine inter castra Romana et frumentatores
9 constituit signa. inde, copiis divisis, partem ad consectan-
dos uagos frumentatores emisit, dato signo ne quem vivum relinquerent, cum parte ipse substitit, itineraque qui-
10 bus ad castra recursuri videbantur hostes obsedit. iam
passim caedes ac fuga erat, necdum quisquam in castra
Romana nuntius cladis pervenerat, quia refugientes in
11 regiam stationem incidebant, et plures ab obsidentibus
vias quam ab emissis ad caedem interficiebantur. tandem
inter medias hostium stationes elapsi quidam trepidi tumultum magis quam certum nuntium intulerunt castris.

37. Consul, equitibus iussis qua quisque posset opem
ferre laborantibus, ipse legiones e castris educit et agmine
2 quadrato ad hostem ducit. dispersi equites per agros quidam aberrarunt decepti clamoribus aliis ex alio exsistenti-
bus loco, pars obvios habuerunt hostes. pluribus locis si-
3 mul pugna coepit. regia statio atrocissimum proelium
edebat; nam et ipsa multitudine equitum peditumque
prope iusta acies erat, et Romanorum, quia medium obse-
4 derat iter, plurimi in eam inferebantur. eo quoque superi-

field, the king at first kept his men within his defense works so that the enemy's carelessness might also increase with their overconfidence. When Philip saw them dispersed, he briskly marched out with all his cavalry and Cretan auxiliaries, at a pace that permitted the swiftest of his infantrymen to keep up with the cavalry, and occupied a position between the Roman camp and the foragers. Then, splitting his troops, he sent one half off to hunt down straggling foragers, with instructions to leave none alive, while he himself remained behind with the rest and blockaded the roads by which he thought his enemy would return to camp. Everywhere now the scene was one of slaughter and flight. No word of the debacle had as yet reached the Roman camp because the fleeing Romans kept running into the king's roadblocks, and more were actually dispatched by the Macedonians blockading the roads than by the soldiers sent out to kill them. Eventually a number did slip between the enemy blockades and in their panic brought alarm rather than reliable news to the camp.

37. Ordering his cavalry to give assistance wherever they could to troops who were under pressure, the consul himself then led his legions from camp and marched them in square formation toward the enemy. Some of the cavalry wandered sporadically through the countryside, misled by cries that arose from different spots, and others met the enemy head-on. Fighting broke out simultaneously at a number of points. It was the king's detachment that put up the most ferocious fight; in sheer numbers of both cavalry and infantry it was close to a regular army and in addition, since it had been blockading the central road, most of the Romans clashed with it. What also gave the

ores Macedones erant, quod et rex ipse hortator aderat, et
Cretensium auxiliares multos ex improviso volnerabant,
conferti praeparatique in dispersos et effusos pugnantes.
5 quod si modum in insequendo habuissent, non in praesentis modo certaminis gloriam sed in summam etiam belli
6 profectum foret: nunc aviditate caedis intemperantius
secuti in praegressas cum tribunis militum cohortes Ro-
7 manas incidere, et fugiens eques, ut primo signa suorum
vidit, convertit in effusum hostem equos, versaque momento temporis fortuna pugnae est, terga dantibus qui
8 modo secuti erant. multi comminus congressi multi fugientes interfecti; nec ferro tantum periere, sed in paludes
quidam coniecti profundo limo cum ipsis equis hausti
9 sunt. rex quoque in periculo fuit; nam ruente saucio equo
praeceps ad terram datus haud multum afuit quin iacens
10 opprimeretur. saluti fuit eques, qui raptim ipse desiluit
pavidumque regem in equum subiecit; ipse, cum pedes
aequare cursu fugientes non posset equites, ab hostibus
11 ad casum regis concitatis confossus perit. rex circumvec-
tus paludes per vias inviaque trepida fuga in castra tandem, iam desperantibus plerisque incolumem evasurum,
12 pervenit. ducenti Macedonum equites eo proelio periere,

Macedonians an advantage was their king being there in person to encourage them, as well as the fact that their Cretan auxiliary troops were inflicting unexpected wounds on many of the Romans because they were fighting as a close-ordered and well-prepared group against a disorganized and scattered enemy. Had they but shown some restraint in their pursuit, their success would have gone beyond a glorious victory in that particular engagement to encompass the entire campaign. As it was, hungry for the kill, they advanced too recklessly and ran up against Roman cohorts that were pushing forward under the command of their tribunes. The moment they saw the standards of their comrades, the retreating Roman cavalry wheeled about their steeds to face a now-disordered foe, and in an instant the fortunes of the battle changed, with the erstwhile pursuers now turning tail. Many fell in the hand-to-hand fighting, many as they fled. Nor did they die by the sword alone—some were thrown into marshes to be swallowed up by the deep mud along with their horses. The king, too, faced danger: he was flung headlong to the ground when his wounded horse stumbled, and was within an inch of being trampled to death where he lay. His salvation was a cavalryman who swiftly dismounted and lifted the terror-stricken king onto his own horse. The man himself, now on foot, was unable to keep up with the retreating cavalry and perished, run through by his enemy's forces that swiftly arrived on the scene when the king fell. The king, fleeing in panic, rode about the marshes, on paths or cross-country, and finally reached his camp, where most had already lost hope of his coming through alive. Two hundred Macedonian horsemen perished in that engagement and about a hundred were captured.

centum ferme capti; octoginta admodum ornati equi, spoliis simul armorum relatis, abducti.

38. Fuere qui hoc die regem temeritatis consulem segnitiae accusarent: nam et Philippo quiescendum fuisse, cum paucis diebus hostes, exhausto circa omni agro, ad
2 ultimum inopiae venturos sciret, et consulem, cum equitatum hostium levemque armaturam fudisset ac prope regem ipsum cepisset, protinus ad castra hostium ducere
3 debuisse; nec enim mansuros ita perculsos hostes fuisse,
4 debellarique momento temporis potuisse. id dictu quam re, ut pleraque, facilius erat. nam si omnibus peditum quoque copiis congressus rex fuisset, forsitan inter tumultum, cum omnes victi metuque perculsi ex proelio intra vallum, protinus inde supervadentem munimenta victo-
5 rem hostem fugerent, exui castris potuerit rex; cum vero integrae copiae peditum in castris mansissent, stationes ante portas praesidiaque disposita essent, quid nisi ut temeritatem regis effuse paulo ante secuti perculsos equites
6 imitaretur profecisset? neque enim ne regis quidem primum consilium, quo impetum in frumentatores palatos per agros fecit, reprehendendum foret, si modum prospe-
7 rae pugnae imposuisset. eo quoque minus est mirum temptasse eum fortunam, quod fama erat Pleuratum Dardanosque ingentibus copiis profectos domo iam in Mace-

Some eighty horses with their trappings were taken, and there were also arms among the captured spoils.

38. There were some people who reproached the king with recklessness and the consul with lack of initiative on that day. Philip, they said, should have remained inactive: with the neighboring countryside entirely depleted he knew that the Romans would face a critical shortage of provisions in just a few days. In the consul's case, he should have led his men to the enemy camp immediately after routing their cavalry and light infantry and almost taking the king himself prisoner—in panic the enemy was unlikely to have stood his ground and could have been finished off in no time. But, as usual, this was a case of something being easier said than done. Had the king engaged with all his infantry as well, then it is possible that in the melee—with his men, beaten and panic-stricken, all seeking refuge within the palisade after the battle, and then immediately running from the camp before an enemy that was clambering over their defense works—he could have been divested of his camp. But since the infantry had remained intact within the camp, and sentinels and pickets were posted at the gates, what could the consul have achieved apart from duplicating the recklessness of the king who, shortly before, had made a disordered pursuit of the panic-stricken Roman cavalry? There could likewise have been no criticism of the king's original strategy of attacking the foragers when they were dispersed through the fields, had he but observed moderation following his success in the battle. Furthermore, his tempting providence also becomes less puzzling in light of the report that was abroad that Pleuratus and the Dardanians had by this time set off from home with enormous forces

8 doniam transcendisse; quibus si undique circumventus
copiis foret, sedentem Romanum debellaturum credi poterat.

9 Itaque secundum duas adversas equestres pugnas
multo minus tutam moram in iisdem stativis fore Philippus ratus, cum abire inde et fallere abiens hostem vellet,
caduceatore sub occasum solis misso ad consulem qui in-
10 dutias ad sepeliendos equites peteret, frustratus hostem
secunda vigilia, multis ignibus per tota castra relictis, si-
lenti agmine abit.

39. Corpus iam curabat consul cum venisse caducea-
2 torem et quid venisset nuntiatum est. responso tantum
dato mane postero die fore copiam conveniendi, id quod
quaesitum erat, nox dieique insequentis pars ad praeci-
piendum iter Philippo data est. montes, quam viam non
3 ingressurum gravi agmine Romanum sciebat, petit. consul, prima luce caduceatore datis indutiis dimisso, haud ita
multo post abisse hostem cum sensisset, ignarus qua se-
queretur, iisdem stativis frumentando dies aliquot con-
4 sumpsit. Stuberram deinde petit atque ex Pelagonia frumentum quod in agris erat conuexit; inde ad Pluinnam
est  rogressus, nondum comperto quam regionem hostes
petissent.

5 Philippus cum primo ad Bruanium stativa habuisset,
profectus inde transversis limitibus terrorem praebuit

---

157 Cf. 34.6, above.      158 A stratagem to make the Romans think his troops were still *in situ*: cf. Frontin. *Str.* 1.1.7,
1.1.9, 1.5.22, 2.12.4.      159 Stuberra and (below) Bruanium
(Bryanion) were towns in Pelagonia (*Barr.* 49 D2), as was, presumably, Pluinna (not mentioned elsewhere). The River Erigon
lies in the same sector, and the Osphagus (below) is presumably
one of its tributaries.

and had invaded Macedonia.[157] If Philip had been cut off
by these forces, one could well have believed that the Roman commander would prevail without taking any action.

And so, after two cavalry engagements had gone
against him, Philip thought that remaining in the same
camp was by far the less safe alternative. Wishing therefore to withdraw and slip away behind his enemy's back,
he sent a herald at sunset to the consul to request a truce
for the burial of his cavalrymen. Then, giving his enemy
the slip, he moved off at the second watch, his column
marching in silence, leaving many fires burning throughout the camp.[158]

39. The consul was taking food and rest when word was
brought of the herald's coming and the reason for it. He
replied only that the herald would be granted an audience
with him the next morning, and this gave Philip just what
he had wanted, namely that night and part of the following day to get a head start on his march. He made for
the mountains, a route he knew the Romans would not
take with their heavily laden column. At dawn the consul
granted the truce, dismissed the herald and shortly afterward realized that the enemy had left. Not knowing where
to direct his pursuit, he passed several days in the same
camp gathering supplies. He then made for Stuberra, and
brought in from Pelagonia the grain that was standing
in the fields.[159] From there he advanced to Pluinna, still
without information on the region for which the enemy
had headed.

Philip had first established his camp near Bruanium;
and setting out from there using byroads he struck sudden

subitum hosti. movere itaque ex Pluinna Romani, et ad
6 Osphagum flumen posuerunt castra. rex haud procul inde
et ipse, vallo super ripam amnis ducto—Erigonum incolae
7 vocant—, consedit. inde satis comperto Eordaeam petitu-
ros Romanos, ad occupandas angustias, ne superare hostes
8 artis faucibus inclusum aditum possent, praecessit. ibi alia
vallo, alia fossa, alia lapidum congerie ut pro muro essent,
alia arboribus obiectis, ut aut locus postulabat aut materia
9 suppeditabat, propere permuniit atque, ut ipse rebatur,
viam suapte natura difficilem obiectis per omnes transitus
operibus inexpugnabilem fecit.
10 Erant pleraque silvestria circa, incommoda phalangi
maxime Macedonum, quae nisi ubi praelongis hastis velut
vallum ante clipeos obiecit, quod ut fiat libero campo opus
11 est, nullius admodum usus est. Thracas quoque rumpiae
ingentis et ipsae longitudinis inter obiectos undique ramos
12 impediebant. Cretensium una cohors non inutilis erat; sed
ea quoque ipsa, ut si quis impetum faceret, in patentem
volneri equum equitemque sagittas conicere poterat, ita
adversus scuta Romana nec ad traiciendum satis magnam
13 vim habebat nec aperti quicquam erat quod peterent. itaque id ut vanum teli genus senserunt esse, saxis passim
tota valle iacentibus incessebant hostem. ea maiore cum
sonitu quam volnere ullo pulsatio scutorum parumper

---

160 Today, Eordaia (*Barr.* 49 D3).

161 Livy here introduces the Greek word without explanation,
while at 32.17.11 he is more descriptive: "the Macedonian wedge,
which Macedonians themselves call a 'phalanx.'" Curtius (3.2.13)
likewise describes it as a "wedge."

162 The famed *sarissa,* the precise length of which is debated,
but probably around fifteen to eighteen feet (cf. M. M. Markle,

panic in his enemy. The Romans therefore moved from Pluinna and pitched camp at the River Osphagus. The king also encamped not far there, constructing a palisade on the banks of a stream that local people call the Erigonus. Then, reliably informed that the Romans would make for Eordaea,[160] he moved forward to seize the pass so as to prevent his enemy from penetrating the narrow gorge that formed the entrance to it. He hurriedly fortified the spot in various ways according to the requirements of the terrain or the availability of materials—a rampart here, a ditch there, a pile of stones to serve as a wall or trees as a barrier—and by blocking off every passage with these contrivances he rendered impassable, so he thought, a road that was already difficult by its very nature.

There was extensive woodland around about, and this particularly bothered the Macedonian phalanx,[161] whose effectiveness depended entirely on the use of very long lances[162] to maintain a kind of barrier before the shields— and that required open ground. The Thracians, too, were disadvantaged by their lances (which were also of great length) among branches that impeded them at every turn. The Cretan division alone retained its capability, but it, too, was handicapped: under attack, it could shoot arrows at horses and riders that were without protection, but faced with Roman shields it lacked the power to penetrate and had no open target at which to aim. And so, when they became aware of the futility of this type of weapon, the Cretans proceeded to pelt the enemy with stones that were lying around throughout the valley. The stones striking the shields (but producing more noise than damage)

"The Macedonian Sarissa, Spear and Related Armor," *AJA* 81 (1977): 323–39.

14 succedentes Romanos tenuit; deinde iis quoque spretis
15 partim testudine facta per adversos vadunt hostes, partim
brevi circumitu cum in iugum collis evasissent, trepidos ex
praesidiis stationibusque Macedonas deturbant et, ut in
locis impeditis difficili fuga, plerosque etiam obtruncant.

40. Ita angustiae minore certamine quam quod animis
proposuerant superatae et in Eordaeam perventum, ubi
pervastatis passim agris in Elimiam consul se recepit. inde
impetum in Orestidem facit, et oppidum Celetrum est
2 adgressus in paeneinsula situm: lacus moenia cingit, an-
3 gustis faucibus unum ex continenti iter est. primo situ ipso
freti clausis portis abnuere imperium; deinde, postquam
signa ferri ac testudine succedi ad portam, obsessasque
fauces agmine hostium viderunt, priusquam experirentur
4 certamen metu in deditionem venerunt. ab Celetro in
Dassaretios processit, urbemque Pelion vi cepit. servitia
inde cum cetera praeda abduxit, libera capita sine pretio
dimisit, oppidumque iis reddidit praesidio valido impo-
5 sito; nam et sita opportune urbs erat ad impetus in Mace-
6 doniam faciendos. ita peragratis hostium agris, consul in
loca pacata ad Apolloniam, unde orsus bellum erat, copias
reduxit.

7 Philippum averterant Aetoli et Athamanes et Dardani
8 et tot bella repente alia ex aliis locis exorta. adversus Dar-

---

163 When attacking under city walls or anywhere where they
faced bombardment from above, Roman soldiers formed the renowned *testudo* ("tortoise shell"), a screen of interlocking shields,
before them and above their heads (cf. Caes. *BGall.* 2.6.3, 5.9.7;
Plut. *Ant.* 45.2; Dio Cass. 49.30).     164 The districts of Eordaia, Elimeia, and Orestis, and the town of Celetrum (Keletron):
*Barr.* 49 D3.     165 *Barr.* 49 C3.

held back the advancing Romans momentarily. Then, disregarding these missiles, too, some made a tortoise formation[163] and attacked the enemy head-on, while others made a short deviation to the hilltop, where they drove the panic-stricken Macedonians from their entrenchments and guard posts and even killed most of them, flight being difficult amid the obstructions of the terrain.

40. The pass was thus taken with less of a struggle than the Romans had expected and they reached Eordaea. After inflicting widespread devastation on the farmland here, the consul withdrew to Elimia. He next attacked Orestis and marched on the town of Celetrum,[164] which is situated on a peninsula; a lake surrounds its walls and access from the mainland is afforded only by a narrow causeway. At first the townspeople, relying on their position, shut their gates and rejected the call to surrender; then, when they saw the standards being brought up, the troops advancing to the gate in tortoise formation and the causeway blocked by the enemy column, they surrendered in alarm rather than risk a battle. From Celetrum the consul advanced against the Dassaretii and took the city of Pelion[165] by storm. He removed the slaves from there, along with the rest of the plunder, but released free persons without ransom and restored the town to them after installing a strong garrison (since the city was also well positioned for conducting incursions into Macedonia). After traversing the countryside of the enemy, the consul led his troops back into pacified territory in Apollonia, whence he had started his campaign.

Philip had been distracted by the Aetolians, the Athamanians, the Dardanians, and all the wars suddenly breaking out in different places. When the Dardanians were

danos, iam recipientes ex Macedonia sese, Athenagoran cum expeditis peditibus ac maiore parte equitatus misit, iussum instare ab tergo abeuntibus, et carpendo postremum agmen segniores eos ad movendos domo exercitus
9 efficere. Aetolos Damocritus praetor, qui morae ad decernendum bellum ad Naupactum auctor fuerat, idem proximo concilio ad arma conciverat post famam equestris ad Otolobum pugnae Dardanorumque et Pleurati cum
10 Illyriis transitum in Macedoniam, ad hoc classis Romanae adventum Oreum et super circumfusas tot Macedoniae gentes maritimam quoque instantem obsidionem.

41. Hae causae Damocritum Aetolosque restituerant Romanis; et Amynandro rege Athamanum adiuncto pro-
2 fecti Cercinium obsedere. clauserant portas, incertum vi
3 an voluntate, quia regium habebant praesidium; ceterum intra paucos dies captum est Cercinium atque incensum; qui superfuerunt e magna clade liberi servique inter cete-
4 ram praedam abducti. is timor omnes qui circumcolunt Boeben paludem relictis urbibus montes coegit petere.
5 Aetoli inopia praedae inde aversi in Perrhaebiam ire pergunt. Chyretias[38] ibi vi capiunt foedeque diripiunt; qui Malloeam incolunt voluntate in deditionem societatemque accepti.

[38] Chyretias *Ogilvie*: Cyretias $B\chi$

---

166 Cf. 32.1 and note, above.

167 Cf. 28.1 note, above.

168 A Magnesian town very close to Lake Boebe ("Marsh of Boebe," below): *Barr.* 55 D1 (Kerkineion).

169 For Perrhaebia, Chyretiae, Malloea, and all other places in the rest of the chapter, cf. *Barr.* 55 B–C 1–2.

already withdrawing from Macedonia he sent Athenagoras against them at the head of some light infantry and most of the cavalry. Athenagoras had orders to put pressure on the tail end of the retreating Dardanians and, by wearing down their rearguard, make them reluctant to move their troops from home in future. As for the Aetolians, the man responsible for the delay in the declaration of war at Naupactus, their praetor Damocritus,[166] had incited them to arms at the next meeting of their council. This followed the news of the cavalry engagement at Otolobus, the invasion of Macedonia by the Dardanians and Pleuratus together with the Illyrians, and especially the arrival at Oreus of the Roman fleet, with the further threat of a naval blockade on Macedonia, which was already surrounded by all these many peoples.

41. Such were the factors that had brought Damocritus and the Aetolians back to the Romans and now, joined by Amynander, king of the Athamanians,[167] they set off and laid siege to Cercinium.[168] The townspeople had shut their gates, though whether under duress or of their own volition is unclear (because they had a garrison of the king in town). At all events, within a few days, Cercinium was taken and burned down; and the survivors of this major catastrophe, free and slave, were hauled off with the rest of the booty. Fear of similar treatment drove all who lived around the Marsh of Boebe to abandon their towns and head for the hills; but, plunder being in short supply, the Aetolians turned aside from the area and proceeded to march on Perrhaebia. Here they stormed and shamefully pillaged Chyretiae, but they accepted the voluntary surrender of the inhabitants of Malloea[169] and made them allies.

123

6    Ex Perrhaebia Gomphos petendi Amynander auctor
erat: et imminet Athamania huic urbi, videbaturque ex-
7  pugnari sine magno certamine posse. Aetoli campos Thessaliae opimos ad praedam petiere, sequente quamquam
non probante Amynandro nec effusas populationes Aetolorum nec castra quo fors tulisset loco sine ullo discrimine
8  aut cura muniendi posita. itaque ne temeritas eorum ne-
glegentiaque sibi ac suis etiam cladis alicuius causa esset,
cum campestribus locis subicientes eos castra Pharcadoni
9  urbi videret, ipse paulo plus mille passuum inde tumulum
10  suis quamuvis levi munimento tutum cepit. cum Aetoli
nisi quod populabantur vix meminisse viderentur se in
hostium agro esse, alii palati semermes uagarentur, alii in
castris sine stationibus per somnum vinumque dies nocti-
bus aequarent, Philippus inopinantibus advenit.
11    Quem cum adesse refugientes ex agris quidam pavidi
nuntiassent, trepidare Damocritus ceterique duces—et
erat forte meridianum tempus, quo plerique graves cibo
12  sopiti iacebant—excitare alii alios, iubere arma capere,
alios dimittere ad revocandos qui palati per agros praeda-
bantur; tantaque trepidatio fuit ut sine gladiis quidam
13  equitum exirent, loricas plerique non induerent. ita raptim educti, cum[39] sescentorum aegre simul equites pedi-
tesque numerum explessent, incidunt in regium equita-

---

[39] cum *B*χ: cum universi *Gel.*

From Perrhaebia Amynander suggested they make for
Gomphi; Athamania lies close to this town and it appeared
that it could be taken without much of a fight. The Aetolians headed for the plains of Thessaly that provided rich
opportunities for plunder, and they were followed by
Amynander, though he did not approve of the Aetolians'
disorganized pillaging or their randomly pitching camp
wherever they happened to be and with no attention paid
to security. He feared that their recklessness and negligence might also bring disaster on himself and his men
and, when he saw them establishing a camp in the open
plains at a point below the city of Pharcadon, he himself
seized a hillock a little more than a mile away that could
be rendered secure with even a slight amount of fortifica-
tion. The Aetolians appeared to be scarcely aware that
they were in enemy territory—apart from the fact that
they were engaged in looting. Some were drifting about
aimlessly and only partially armed, others removing all
distinction between day and night as they slept and drank
in camp, with no sentries on duty, when Philip fell upon
them unawares.

When news of his approach had been brought by men
fleeing in terror from the fields, Damocritus and the other
officers had panicked—it happened to be midday, a time
at which most of the men were lying about heavy and
drowsy from eating. They tried to rouse one another, told
each other to take up their weapons, and sent some of
their number to recall those who were wandering about
pillaging in the fields. So great was the panic that some of
the horsemen left camp without their swords, and most
without putting on their cuirasses. Hurriedly marched out
in this way, they barely totaled six hundred, cavalry and

14 tum numero armis animisque praestantem. itaque primo
impetu fusi, vix temptato certamine, turpi fuga repetunt
castra; caesi captique quos equites ab agmine fugientium
interclusere.

42. Philippus iam suis vallo adpropinquantibus receptui cani iussit; fatigatos enim equos virosque non tam
proelio quam itineris simul longitudine simul praepropera
2 celeritate habebat. itaque turmatim equites in vicem ma-
nipulos levis armaturae aquatum ire et prandere iubet,
3 alios in statione armatos retinet, opperiens agmen pedi-
4 tum tardius ductum propter gravitatem armorum. quod
ubi advenit, et ipsis imperatum ut statutis signis armisque
ante se positis raptim cibum caperent, binis ternisve summum ex manipulis aquandi causa missis; interim eques
cum levi armatura paratus instructusque stetit, si quid
hostis moveret.

5 Aetoli—iam enim et quae per agros sparsa multitudo
fuerat receperant[40] se in castra—ut defensuri munimenta
circa portas vallumque armatos disponunt, dum quietos
6 hostes ipsi feroces ex tuto spectabant. postquam mota
signa Macedonum sunt, et succedere ad vallum parati atque instructi coepere, repente omnes relictis stationibus
per aversam partem castrorum ad tumulum ad castra
Athamanum perfugiunt; multi in hac quoque tam trepida

[40] receperant *ϕNL*: rereperant *B*: receperunt *V*: receperat
*Carb.*

---

[170] Livy applies a Roman term to a Macedonian army. A maniple (see Introduction, lxii) was a division not found in Philip's
army, and it was the lack of flexibility of this kind in the famed
Macedonian phalanx that led to its demise.

infantry together, and they ran into the king's cavalry, which surpassed them in numbers, weaponry, and spirit. Routed with the first charge, they headed back to camp in ignominious flight after barely a taste of battle. Those cut off from the retreating column by the Macedonian cavalry were killed or taken prisoner.

42. As his men were approaching the enemy defense works, Philip ordered the retreat to be sounded since horses and men were both exhausted, not so much by the battle as by the length of the march as well as its rapid pace. He therefore told his men to fetch water and take food, the cavalry by squadron and the light infantry one maniple after the other. Some he kept on sentry duty under arms as he awaited the infantry column, which had been brought along at a slower pace because of the weight of its equipment. When they arrived, the infantry too were ordered to fix their standards in the ground, set down their arms before themselves, and take a hurried meal, a maximum of two or three men per maniple[170] being sent for water. In the meantime, the cavalry and light-armed stood ready and drawn up for action in the event of any movement on the enemy's part.

As for the Actolians—for even the large numbers scattered through the countryside had by this time returned to camp—they now deployed armed men around the camp gates and the rampart to protect their defenses, all the while casting fearless glances at their currently inactive foes from their position of safety. When, however, the Macedonian forces advanced and their men began to approach the rampart prepared and drawn up for battle, they all suddenly quit their posts and fled through the back of the camp toward the Athamanian camp on the hillock.

127

7 fuga capti caesique sunt Aetolorum. Philippus, si satis diei superesset, non dubius quin Athamanes quoque exui castris potuissent, die per proelium deinde per direptionem castrorum absumpto sub tumulo in proxima planitie consedit, prima luce insequentis diei hostem adgressurus.

8 sed Aetoli eodem pavore quo sua castra reliquerant nocte proxima dispersi fugerunt. maximo usui fuit Amynander, quo duce Athamanes itinerum periti summis montibus per calles ignotas sequentibus eos hostibus in Aetoliam

9 perduxerunt. non ita multos in dispersa fuga error intulit in Macedonum equites, quos prima luce Philippus, ut desertum tumulum videt, ad carpendum hostium agmen misit.

43. Per eos dies et Athenagoras regius praefectus Dardanos recipientes se in fines adeptus postremum agmen

2 primo turbavit; dein, postquam Dardani conversis signis direxere aciem, aequa pugna iusto proelio erat. ubi rursus procedere Dardani coepissent, equite et levi armatura regii nullum tale[41] auxilii genus habentes Dardanos oneratosque immobilibus armis uexabant; et loca ipsa adiuvabant. occisi perpauci sunt, plures volnerati, captus nemo,

3 quia non excedunt temere ordinibus suis sed confertim et pugnant et cedunt.

[41] tale χ: om. BPar. 5741 (fort. recte: Briscoe)

Many Aetolians were again captured or cut down in this terror-stricken flight. Had there been sufficient daylight left, Philip had no doubt that he could have taken their camp from the Athamanians; but as it was the day had been used up in combat and then in pillaging the Aetolian camp, and so he took up a position on the level ground closest to him at the foot of the hillock, intending to attack the enemy at first light the following day. The Aetolians, however, prey to the same panic that had made them abandon their camp, scattered and fled that oncoming night. Amynander provided them with the greatest assistance: it was under his leadership that the Athamanians who knew the roads led them back into Aetolia over the mountain tops on tracks unknown to the enemy pursuing them. In the disordered flight some few strayed into the path of the Macedonian cavalry, which Philip sent out at daybreak, when he saw the hillock deserted, to hound the enemy column.

43. During this same period the king's officer Athenagoras had also overtaken the Dardanians as they fell back on their own lands and at first he threw the rear guard into disarray; then, when the Dardanians wheeled round and deployed their battle line, there was a regular but inconclusive pitched battle. When the Dardanians started to advance once more, the king's forces began to harass them with their cavalry and light infantry, the Dardanians having no such auxiliary troops and being also encumbered by unwieldy arms; and the terrain also favored the Macedonians. Very few Dardanians actually lost their lives, more suffered wounds, and none was captured, because Dardanians do not recklessly break formation but close ranks both to fight and to retreat.

LIVY

4    Ita damna Romano accepta bello, duabus per opportunas expeditiones coercitis gentibus, restituerat Philippus
incepto forti, non prospero solum eventu. minuit deinde
5   ei forte oblata res hostium Aetolorum numerum. Scopas
princeps gentis, ab Alexandrea magno cum pondere auri
ab rege Ptolomaeo missus, sex milia peditum et quingen-
6   tos equites mercede conductos Aegyptum uexit; nec ex
iuventute Aetolorum quemquam reliquisset, ni Damocri-
7   tus nunc belli quod instaret, nunc futurae solitudinis admonens, incertum cura gentis an ut adversaretur Scopae
parum donis cultus, partem iuniorum castigando domi
continuisset.

    44 Haec ea aestate ab Romanis Philippoque gesta
terra;[42] classis a Corcyra eiusdem principio aestatis cum L.
Apustio legato profecta Maleo superato circa Scyllaeum
2   agri Hermionici Attalo regi coniuncta est. tum vero Atheniensium civitas, cui odio in Philippum per metum iam diu
moderata erat, id omne in auxilii praesentis spem effundit,
3   nec unquam ibi desunt linguae promptae ad plebem con-
citandam; quod genus cum in omnibus liberis civitatibus
tum praecipue Athenis, ubi oratio plurimum pollet, favore
4   multitudinis alitur. rogationem extemplo tulerunt plebesque scivit ut Philippi statuae imagines omnes nomi-

---

[42] terra *Madvig*: erant *B*χ: *secl. Duker*

171 Scopas had been league *strategos* in 220/19 and again in
212/11, when, together with his kinsman Dorimachus, he engineered the alliance with Rome (26.24.7–15). After a political
setback, however, both men left Aetolia, Scopas going to Alexandria, where, according to Polybius (13.2), he served Ptolemy V,
Epiphanes as a moneygrubbing mercenary.

So it was that Philip, having subdued two nations by timely campaigns, had made good the losses sustained in the war with Rome, and done so with an initiative that was enterprising, not just successful in its result. The number of Aetolian enemies facing him was then reduced by a fortuitous occurrence. A leader of that people, Scopas,[171] sent from Alexandria by King Ptolemy with a large quantity of gold, had hired and transported to Egypt 6,000 infantry and 500 cavalry. (In fact, he would have left behind no Aetolian of military age had not Damocritus cautioned his people both about the imminent war and the depopulation they faced in future, and by his strictures kept some of his younger countrymen at home; but whether he did this from patriotism or to oppose Scopas, from whom he had received insufficient bribes, is debatable.)

44. Such were the land operations conducted that summer by the Romans and Philip. At the start of the same summer the fleet set out from Corcyra commanded by the legate Lucius Apustius, and after rounding Malea it joined King Attalus off Scyllaeum in the territory of Hermione.[172] It was at this point that the city-state of Athens, in anticipation of the forthcoming assistance, fully indulged the hatred for Philip which, out of fear, it had long kept in check, and in Athens rabble-rousing tongues are never in short supply. This is a phenomenon nurtured by the support of the masses in all free city-states, but especially in Athens, where rhetoric is particularly influential. The Athenians immediately formulated a proposal, which the people ratified, that all statues and artistic representations of Philip plus their inscriptions be removed and destroyed,

172 *Barr.* 58 F3.

naque earum, item maiorum eius virile ac muliebre secus
omnium tollerentur delerenturque, diesque festi sacra
sacerdotes, quae ipsius maiorumque eius honoris causa
5   instituta essent, omnia profanarentur; loca quoque in quibus positum aliquid inscriptumve honoris eius causa fuisset detestabilia esse, neque in iis quicquam postea poni
dedicarique placere eorum quae in loco puro poni dedi-
6   carique fas esset; sacerdotes publicos quotienscumque
pro populo Atheniensi sociisque, exercitibus et classibus
eorum precarentur, totiens detestari atque exsecrari Philippum liberos eius regnumque, terrestres navalesque
7   copias, Macedonum genus omne nomenque. additum decreto si quis quid postea quod ad notam ignominiamque
Philippi pertineret ferret, id omne populum Atheniensem
8   iussurum; si quis contra ignominiam prove honore eius
dixisset fecissetue, qui occidisset eum iure caesurum.
postremo inclusum ut omnia quae adversus Pisistratidas
decreta quondam erant eadem in Philippo servarentur.
9   Athenienses quidem litteris verbisque, quibus solis valent,
bellum adversus Philippum gerebant.

45. Attalus Romanique cum Piraeum primo ab Her-
2   mione petissent, paucos ibi morati dies oneratique aeque
immodicis ad honores sociorum atque in iram[43] adversus
hostem fuerant Atheniensium decretis, navigant a Piraeo
3   Andrum. et cum in portu quem Gaurion[44] vocant consti-

[43] iram *B*χ: ira *α*     [44] Gaurion *Hertz*: Caurelon *B*: Gaure-
lon χ: Gaureion *McDonald*

[173] These were Hippias and Hipparchus, the sons of, and successors to, the tyrant Pisistratus. Hipparchus was assassinated in
514, and, after a reign of terror, Hippias was expelled in 510.

together with those of all his ancestors, male and female, and that feast days, religious rites and priesthoods established to honor Philip himself or his ancestors all be deconsecrated; that a curse be put on places in which any monument or inscription had been set up in his honor, and that thereafter no decision be made to erect or dedicate in those places anything that, according to religion, must be erected or dedicated in an unpolluted place; and that whenever the public priests offered prayers for the people of Athens and their allies, armies and fleets, they should on each occasion also curse and execrate Philip, his children, his kingdom, his land and sea forces, and the entire Macedonian race and nation. Added to the decree was a further clause: the Athenian people would ratify in its entirety any proposal apt to bring discredit and dishonor on Philip, while the slaying of any person whose words or deeds worked against Philip's discredit or promoted his reputation would be considered justifiable homicide. A final rider was that all decrees enacted in the past against the Pisistratids[173] should remain in force in Philip's case. Indeed, the Athenians were now waging war against Philip with the weapons of letters and words, wherein lies their only strength.

45. From Hermione Attalus and the Romans had first made for Piraeus. After spending a few days there, during which they were loaded down with decrees of the Athenians as excessive in tributes to the allies as the earlier ones had been in vitriol toward the enemy, they sailed on from Piraeus to Andros. After they came to anchor in the

tissent, missis qui temptarent oppidanorum animos, si
4 voluntate tradere urbem quam vim experiri mallent, postquam praesidio regio arcem teneri nec se potestatis suae
esse respondebant, expositis copiis apparatuque omni
urbium oppugnandarum, diversis partibus rex et legatus
Romanus ad urbem subeunt.

5 Plus aliquanto Graecos Romana arma signaque non
ante visa animique militum tam prompte succedentium
6 muros terruere; itaque fuga extemplo in arcem facta est,
urbe hostes potiti. et in arce cum biduum loci se magis
quam armorum fiducia tenuissent, tertio die pacti ipsi
praesidiumque ut cum singulis vestimentis Delium Boeo-
7 tiae transveherentur, urbem arcemque tradiderunt. ea ab
Romanis regi Attalo concessa: praedam ornamentaque
urbis ipsi avexerunt. Attalus, ne desertam haberet insulam, et Macedonum fere omnibus et quibusdam Andrio-
8 rum ut manerent persuasit. postea et ab Delio qui ex pacto
travecti eo fuerant promissis regis, cum desiderium quoque patriae facilius ad credendum inclinaret animos, revocati.

9 Ab Andro Cythnum traiecerunt; ibi dies aliquot oppugnanda urbe nequiquam absumpti, et quia vix operae
10 pretium erat abscessere. ad Prasias—continentis Atticae

---

174 On the west coast of Andros (*Barr.* 57 C4), which had remained in Philip's hands after the Rhodians' successes in 201/200
(15.8, above).

175 The island of Cythnos (*Barr.* 58 G3) had also remained in
Philip's hands (15.8, above).

176 On the east coast of Attica, south of Brauron: *Barr.* 59 D3.

port they call Gaurion,[174] they sent men off to assess the mood of the townspeople in order to determine whether they would prefer to surrender their city voluntarily rather than face armed force. When the townspeople replied that the citadel was occupied by a garrison of the king and that they had no control over their own fate, King Attalus and the Roman legate set ashore troops and all the equipment for an assault on a city, and moved on the town from opposite directions.

The terror of the Greeks was considerably increased by the sight of Roman weaponry and standards that they had never seen before, and by the spirit of the soldiers who approached their walls with such alacrity. This prompted a sudden flight to the acropolis, and their enemy occupied the town. They held out in the acropolis for two days, more confident in their position than their arms, but on the third the citizens and the garrison reached an agreement that they be transported to Delium in Boeotia, each with one piece of clothing, and they surrendered the city and acropolis. These were awarded to King Attalus by the Romans, who themselves carted off the spoils and the city's ornamental treasures. Not to be in possession of a deserted isle, Attalus persuaded virtually all the Macedonians and a number of the Andrians to remain behind. Subsequently, those who had crossed to Delium under the terms of the treaty were also enticed back by promises made by the king, their yearning for their homeland also making it easier for them to trust him.

From Andros the allies crossed to Cythnus.[175] Here several days were wasted on an assault on the city, and they eventually abandoned the attempt because it was scarcely worth the trouble. At Prasiae[176]—this is a place on the

135

is locus est—Issaeorum viginti lembi classi Romanorum
adiuncti sunt. ii missi ad populandos Carystiorum agros;
cetera classis Geraestum, nobilem Euboeae portum, dum
11  ab Carysto Issaei redirent, tenuit. inde omnes, velis in
altum datis, mari medio praeter Scyrum insulam Icum
12  pervenere. ibi paucos dies saeviente Borea retenti, ubi
prima tranquillitas data est, Sciathum traiecere, vastatam
13  urbem direptamque nuper a Philippo. per agros palati
milites frumentum et si qua alia usui esse ad vescendum
poterant ad naves rettulere; praedae nec erat quicquam,
14  nec meruerant Graeci cur diriperentur. inde Cassandream
petentes primo ad Mendaeum, maritimum civitatis eius
vicum, tenuere. inde cum superato promunturio ad ipsa
moenia urbis circumagere classem vellent, saeva coorta
tempestate prope obruti fluctibus, dispersi, magna ex
parte amissis armamentis, in terram effugerunt.
15  Omen quoque ea maritima tempestas ad rem terra
gerendam fuit. nam conlectis in unum navibus expositisque copiis adgressi urbem, cum multis volneribus repulsi—et erat validum ibi regium praesidium—, inrito
incepto regressi ad Canastraeum Pallenes traiecere. inde
superato Toronae promunturio navigantes Acanthum pe-
16  tiere. ibi primo ager vastatus, deinde ipsa urbs vi capta ac

---

177 A small island off the Dalmatian coast known for the quality of its sailors (*Barr.* 20 D6), today Vis.

178 Carystus and Geraestus: *Barr.* 58 G1 and H2.

179 Scyrus, *Barr.* 55 H3; Icus, F2; Sciathus, E2.

180 Earlier Potidaea (*Barr.* 50 D4), refounded by Cassander
about 316.      181 In Greek, Mende, on the Pallene peninsula
(*Barr.* 51 A5).      182 Canastraeum (Kanastraion), Torona,
Acanthus: *Barr.* 51 B 4–5.

Attic mainland—twenty light craft from Issa[177] joined the
Roman fleet. These were dispatched to conduct raids on
the territory of the people of Carystus, and the rest of the
fleet docked at the famous Euboean port of Geraestus to
await the return of the Issaei from Carystus.[178] Then they
all put out to sea together and, passing in midvoyage the
island of Scyrus, came to Icus. They were detained there
for a few days by a furious north wind, but as soon as good
weather arrived they crossed to Sciathus,[179] where the city
had been recently destroyed and pillaged by Philip. The
soldiers roamed through the fields and brought back to the
ships grain and whatever else might serve for provisions;
but there was no booty, nor had the Greeks here deserved
to suffer depredations. Then, en route for Cassandrea,[180]
they headed first for Mendaeum,[181] a coastal village of that
city. Next, after rounding the headland, they wanted to
bring the fleet right up to the city walls, but a violent storm
arose during which they were almost sunk by the waves.
Scattered, and with most of their tackle lost, they sought
refuge on land.

The storm at sea also served as an omen for their performance on land. After reuniting the ships and setting the
troops ashore, the allies assaulted the town, only to be
driven back with heavy casualties (the king's garrison there
was powerful); and after the failure of the operation they
withdrew and crossed to Canastraeum in Pallene. From
there they rounded the promontory of Torona and set a
course for Acanthus.[182] Here they first raided the countryside, and then took the city by storm and pillaged it. With-

direpta; nec ultra progressi —iam enim et graves praeda
naves habebant—retro unde venerant Sciathum et ab
Sciatho Euboeam repetunt.

46. Ibi relicta classe decem navibus expeditis sinum
Maliacum intravere ad conloquendum cum Aetolis de ra-
2 tione gerendi belli. Pyrrhias Aetolus princeps legationis
eius fuit quae ad communicanda consilia cum rege et cum
3 Romano legato Heracleam[45] venit. petitum ex foedere ab
Attalo est ut mille milites mitteret;[46] tantum enim nume-
4 rum bellum gerentibus adversus Philippum debebat. id
negatum Aetolis, quod illi quoque gravati prius essent ad
populandam Macedoniam exire, quo tempore Philippo
circa Pergamum urente sacra profanaque abstrahere eum
5 inde respectu rerum suarum potuissent. ita Aetoli cum spe
magis, Romanis omnia pollicentibus, quam cum auxilio
dimissi; Apustius cum Attalo ad classem redit.

6 Inde agitari de Oreo oppugnando coeptum. valida ea
civitas et moenibus et, quia ante fuerat temptata, firmo
erat praesidio: coniunxerant se iis post expugnationem
Andri cum praefecto Acesimbroto[47] viginti Rhodiae naves,
7 tectae omnes. eam classem in stationem ad Zelasium mi-

45 Heracleam *hic Pluygers, ante* cum rege *Bχ*

46 mitteret *Weiss.*: *om. Bχ*: *lac. indicat Briscoe*

47 Acesimbroto *Niese*: Hagesimbroto *B*: Hagesimbro *NL*:
Agesimbro *φV*

183 Heraclea (*Barr.* 55 C3) was a Spartan foundation, dating
to 426, sometimes referred to as Heraclea in Trachis, to distinguish it from other towns with the same name.

184 Pyrrhias had played a major part in the Social War (fought
between the Aetolian League and the Hellenic League under

out proceeding further, their ships now being weighed down with booty, they headed back first to Sciathus, their point of departure, and from Sciathus to Euboea.

46. Leaving the fleet there, they entered the Malian gulf with ten light vessels for discussions with the Aetolians about strategy for the war. The head of the delegation that came to Heraclea[183] to formulate plans in concert with the king and the Roman legate was the Aetolian Pyrrhias.[184] Attalus was asked by him to send a thousand soldiers according to the terms of the treaty—this was the number that he had been supposed to furnish to those fighting against Philip. The Aetolians were refused their request on the grounds that they had earlier refused to make a plundering excursion into Macedonia at a moment when they could have distracted Philip (who was then burning places sacred and secular around Pergamum) by causing him concern for his own territory. And so, with the Romans making all manner of promises, the Aetolians were sent off with hopes rather than tangible support, and Apustius returned to the fleet with Attalus.

An assault on Oreus then came under discussion. The city was strong both by virtue of its fortifications and also because, since it had earlier been attacked, it had a powerful garrison.[185] After Andros was taken by storm, the allies had been joined by twenty Rhodian vessels, all with decks, and their admiral Acesimbrotus. This detachment they

Philip [220–217]) and was *strategos* of the Aetolian League in 210/9.

[185] Captured by Attalus and the Romans in 207 when Philip's officer Plator betrayed it to them (28.6.1–6), it was soon retaken by Philip.

serunt—Phthiotidis[48] super Demetriadem promunturium
est peropportune obiectum—, ut si quid inde moverent
8 Macedonum naves, in praesidio essent. Heraclides praefectus regius classem ibi tenebat magis per occasionem, si
quam neglegentia hostium dedisset, quam aperta vi quicquam ausurus.

9 Oreum diversi Romani et rex Attalus oppugnabant,
Romani a maritima arce, regii adversus vallem inter duas
10 iacentem arces, qua et muro intersaepta urbs est. et ut loca
diversa, sic dispari modo etiam oppugnabant: Romanus
testudinibus et vineis et ariete admovendo muris, regii
ballistis catapultisque et alio omni genere tormentorum
tela ingerentes et pondere ingenti saxa; faciebant et cuni-
culos et quidquid aliud priore oppugnatione expertum
11 profuerat. ceterum non plures tantum Macedones quam
ante tuebantur urbem arcesque sed etiam praesentioribus
animis, et castigationis[49] regis in admissa culpa et simul
minarum simul promissorum in futurum memores. itaque
cum praeter spem tempus ibi traheretur plusque in obsidione et in operibus quam in oppugnatione celeri spei
12 esset, interim et aliud agi posse ratus legatus, relictis
quod[50] satis videbatur ad opera perficienda, traicit in proxima continentis, Larisamque—non illam in Thessalia
nobilem urbem, sed alteram quam Cremasten vocant—

---

48 Phthiotidos *Weiss.*: Pthiotidos *Briscoe*: Phthiniae id *B*:
Yshinie (Yschinie A) id χ    49 castigationis *Gron.*: castiga-
tionibus *B*χ    50 relictis quod *B*ψ*a. Fr. 2*: relictis quot φ:
militibus *ante* relictis *suppl. McDonald*

---

186 Cf. 16.3 and note, above.
187 The reference is to Plator's betrayal in 207 (Book 28.6).

140

sent to patrol off Zelasium, a promontory of Phthiotis lying in a key position above Demetrias, to guard against any movement by the Macedonian ships from that quarter. Heraclides, the king's lieutenant,[186] commanded the fleet in the area, and his plan of action was to capitalize on his enemy's negligence rather than risk open force.

The Romans and King Attalus proceeded to assault Oreus from opposite directions, the Romans on the side of the coastal citadel, and the king's forces attacking the valley that lay between the two citadels, where the city was also cut off by a wall. As their points of attack differed, so too did their manner of attack, the Romans bringing up to the walls tortoise formations, siege sheds, and a battering ram, and the king's troops using ballistae, catapults, and all other kinds of artillery to shower bolts and rocks of enormous weight on the enemy. They also dug tunnels and used whatever else had proved effective in the previous assault. However, not only were the Macedonians defending the city and its citadels more numerous than on the former occasion but they also had firmer resolve, remembering, as they did, the king's reprimand for the mistake they had made before,[187] and his threats as well as his promises for the future. As more time was thus being spent there than the legate had anticipated, and more hope now lay in siege works than a swift assault, the legate also felt that some other operation could be attempted in the meantime. He therefore left what he considered a sufficiently large force to complete the siege works, crossed to the part of the mainland closest to him and, with a sudden advance, captured Larisa—not the famous city in Thessaly, but the other one, which they call Cremaste—

13 subito adventu praeter arcem cepit. Attalus quoque Pteleon nihil minus quam tale quicquam in alterius oppugnatione urbis timentibus oppressit.

14 Et iam cum opera in effectu erant circa Oreum, tum
praesidium quod intus erat labore adsiduo vigiliis diurnis
15 pariter nocturnisque et volneribus confectum. muri quoque pars ariete incusso subruta multis iam locis procide-
rat, perque apertum ruina iter nocte Romani in arcem[51]
16 quae super portum est perruperunt. Attalus luce prima,
signo ex arce dato ab Romanis, et ipse urbem invasit stra-
tis magna ex parte muris: praesidium oppidanique in arcem alteram perfugere, unde biduo post deditio facta.
urbs regi, captiva corpora Romanis cessere.

47. Iam autumnale aequinoctium instabat, et est sinus
Euboicus quem Coela vocant suspectus nautis; itaque ante
hiemales motus evadere inde cupientes, Piraeum, unde
2 profecti ad bellum erant, repetunt. Apustius, triginta navibus ibi relictis, super Maleum navigat Corcyram. regem
statum initiorum Cereris ut sacris interesset tenuit; secundum initia et ipse in Asiam se recepit, Acesimbroto et
3 Rhodiis domum remissis. haec ea aestate terra marique
adversus Philippum sociosque eius ab consule et legato
Romanis, adiuvantibus rege Attalo et Rhodiis, gesta.

---

[51] in arcem: *hic Büttner*: *post* portum est *Bχ*: *obelo utitur
Briscoe*

---

[188] Larisa Cremaste (*Barr.* 55 D3) lay about six miles from the
Malian Gulf, and Pteleon some eight miles northeast of it (D2).

[189] Mid-September 199.

[190] The "Hollows of Euboea." For Strabo (10.1.2 [445 C])
these are the waters "between Aulis and the region of Geraestus,"

all except its citadel. In addition Attalus crushed Pteleon[188] whose inhabitants, since an offensive was being mounted on the other city, had no fear of such an attack.

The siege works around Oreus were now nearing completion, and the garrison within was also exhausted because of the unremitting toil, the sleepless days as well as sleepless nights, and wounds. In addition, sections of the wall had collapsed at many points from the pounding of the battering ram, and the Romans, making their way through a breach at night, broke into the citadel that is situated above the harbor. When at dawn a signal was given by the Romans from the citadel, Attalus also burst into the city through the walls that were now mostly in ruins. The garrison and the townspeople sought refuge in the other citadel, and from it surrendered two days later. The city was awarded to the king, the prisoners to the Romans.

47. By now the autumn equinox was drawing near,[189] and sailors are apprehensive about the Euboean gulf known as Coela.[190] Wishing, therefore to quit the area before the onset of the winter storms, the allies headed back to Piraeus, the point from which they had set out for the war. Leaving thirty ships there, Apustius then sailed past Malea to Corcyra. The king was detained until the appointed time of the rites of Ceres, since he wished to take part in the ceremony. After the rites, he too withdrew to Asia, sending home Acesimbrotus and the Rhodians. Such were that summer's operations against Philip and his allies conducted on land and sea by the Roman consul and his legate, assisted by King Attalus and the Rhodians.

but the name perhaps refers to the coast of southern Euboea as a whole (so, tentatively, *Barr.* 58 G1; Briscoe 1.157).

4     Consul alter C. Aurelius ad confectum bellum cum in
provinciam venisset, haud clam tulit iram adversus prae-
5  torem quod absente se rem gessisset. misso igitur eo in
Etruriam, ipse in agrum hostium legiones induxit, popu-
landoque cum praeda maiore quam gloria bellum gessit.
6  L. Furius simul quod in Etruria nihil erat rei quod gereret,
simul Gallico triumpho imminens quem absente consule
irato atque invidente facilius impetrari posse ratus est,[52]
7  Romam inopinato cum venisset, senatum in aede Bellonae
habuit, expositisque rebus gestis ut triumphanti sibi in
urbem invehi liceret petit.

48. Apud magnam partem senatus et magnitudine re-
2  rum gestarum valebat et gratia. maiores natu negabant
triumphum et quod alieno exercitu rem gessisset, et quod
provinciam reliquisset cupiditate rapiendi per occasionem
3  triumphi: id vero eum nullo exemplo fecisse. consulares
praecipue exspectandum fuisse consulem censebant—
4  potuisse enim castris prope urbem positis tutanda colonia
ita ut acie non decerneret in adventum eius rem extrahere—, et[53] quod praetor non fecisset, senatui faciendum

---

[52] est *suppl. M. Müller: om.* Bχ
[53] extrahere et χ: extraheret B: extrahere *Ves.*

---

191 The activities of the consul C. Aurelius Cotta and the praetor L. Furius Purpurio here resume from chapter 22.3.

192 Lying outside the *pomerium,* the city's sacred boundary, its
scant remains have now been identified to the east of the Temple
of Apollo Medicus Sosianus (cf. Richardson 57–58 and fig. 17
[p. 65]). It was frequently used for meetings of the senate to
consider claims for a triumph, as no magistrate could enter the

The other consul, Gaius Aurelius,[191] came to his province to find the war over, and he did not hide his anger with the praetor for having fought the campaign in his absence. He therefore sent him to Etruria while he himself led his legions into enemy territory and waged a war of pillage, which brought him more booty than glory. Lucius Furius had nothing to do in Etruria and he was at the same time intent on gaining a triumph for his Gallic campaign, which he believed could more easily be achieved in the absence of an irate and jealous consul. And so he arrived unexpectedly in Rome, convened the senate in the temple of Bellona[192] and, listing his achievements, requested permission to enter the city in triumph.

48. Furius had the support of a large part of the senate because of his impressive record and also through his personal influence. However, the more senior members opposed the triumph because he had campaigned with an army belonging to another and also because he had left his province when he had the chance from a desire to seize a triumph (an unprecedented action, they said). The consular members in particular opined that Furius should have waited for the consul. By encamping near the town,[193] he could have given protection to the colony without fighting a pitched battle, and thus delayed matters until the consul's arrival. It was incumbent on the senate, they said, to do what the praetor had failed to do, namely wait for

city, i.e., cross the *pomerium,* as triumphator until the triumph had been granted (but see Beard's chapter "Playing by the Rules," esp. 203ff.). Foreign ambassadors were also received here if the senate did not wish to receive them within the *pomerium.*

[193] That is, Cremona (cf. 21.2, above).

5   esse ut consulem exspectaret: ubi coram disceptantes consulem et praetorem audissent, verius de causa existimaturos esse.

6     Magna pars senatus nihil praeter res gestas et an in magistratu suisque[54] auspiciis gessisset censebant spec-

7 tare senatum debere: ex duabus coloniis, quae velut claustra ad cohibendos Gallicos tumultus oppositae fuissent, cum una direpta et incensa esset, traiecturumque id incendium velut ex continentibus tectis in alteram tam propinquam coloniam esset, quid tandem praetori faciendum

8 fuisse? nam si sine consule geri nihil oportuerit, aut senatum peccasse qui exercitum praetori dederit—potuisse enim, sicut non praetoris sed consulis exercitu rem geri voluerit, ita finire senatus consulto ne per praetorem sed

9 per consulem gereretur—, aut consulem qui non, cum exercitum ex Etruria transire in Galliam iussisset, ipse Arimini occurrerit ut bello interesset quod sine eo geri fas

10 non esset. non exspectare belli tempora moras et dilationes imperatorum, et pugnandum esse interdum non

11 quia velis sed quia hostis cogat. pugnam ipsam eventumque pugnae spectari debere: fusos caesosque hostes, castra capta ac direpta, coloniam liberatam obsidione, alterius coloniae captivos reciperatos restitutosque suis,

12 debellatum uno proelio esse. non homines tantum ea victoria laetatos, sed dis quoque immortalibus per triduum

---

[54] suisque *Fr.* 2: magistratus ius quis *B*: suis quis χ: suis quisque *Asc.*

---

[194] On auspices, cf. note on 4.1, above.

the consul; and their judgment of the issue would be more objective after hearing the consul and praetor in open debate before them.

A large part of the senate reckoned that their body should consider nothing other than Furius' accomplishments and whether these fell within his period of office and under his auspices.[194] Two colonies had been established as barriers to curb Gallic uprisings, they said. What on earth was the praetor supposed to have done when one of these had been sacked and put to the torch, and the conflagration was about to cross to the other colony that was so close to it, just as happens with adjoining houses? If no action was permissible without the authority of the consul, then the senate was wrong to assign an army to the praetor; for if it had wanted the operation carried out by the consul's troops and not by the praetor's, it could have defined by senatorial decree that authority lay with the consul and not the praetor. Either that or the consul was culpable for ordering the transfer of the army from Etruria to Gaul but not then joining it in person at Ariminum to take part in a war that could not be legitimately fought without his participation. The critical moments of warfare did not brook delay, they said, or commanders' procrastination; and sometimes one has to fight not because one wants to but under pressure from the enemy. It was the battle itself and its outcome that should be taken into account. The enemy had been routed and massacred, their camp taken and pillaged, a colony relieved of its siege, the prisoners of war from the other colony recovered and returned to their own people, and the war concluded with a single battle. Not only had men been overjoyed with the victory, but a three-day period of supplication to the im-

supplicationes habitas, quod bene ac feliciter, non quod
male ac temere res publica a L. Furio praetore gesta esset.
data fato etiam quodam Furiae genti Gallica bella.

49. Huius generis orationibus ipsius amicorumque
victa est praesentis gratia praetoris absentis consulis
maiestas, triumphumque frequentes L. Furio decreve-
2 runt. triumphavit de Gallis in magistratu L. Furius praetor
et in aerarium tulit trecenta viginti milia aeris, argenti[55]
3 centum septuaginta milia mille quingentos. neque captivi
ulli ante currum ducti neque spolia praelata neque milites
secuti: omnia praeter victoriam penes consulem esse apparebat.

4 Ludi deinde a P. Cornelio Scipione, quos consul in
5 Africa voverat, magno apparatu facti. et de agris militum
eius decretum ut quot quisque eorum annos in Hispania
aut in Africa militasset, in singulos annos bina iugera agri
6 acciperet: eum agrum decemviri adsignarent. triumviri
item creati ad supplendum Venusinis colonorum nume-

---

[55] argenti *B*χ: argenti bigati *Hertz*

---

195 M. Furius Camillus had reputedly defeated the Gauls in
390 (5.49.1–7), and his son L. Furius Camillus defeated them in
349 (7.25–6). P. Furius Philus, consul in 223, who was also involved in a Ligurian war (cf. *MRR* 232), may be a third.

196 The *as* was a copper coin of little value. The silver coins
are not specified in the manuscripts, but usually Livy adds the
word *bigatus* ("stamped with the *biga/bigae,*" the two-horse chariot normally found on the *denarius,* a silver coin originally worth
ten *asses* [*deni* = ten]). *bigati* has possibly here been omitted in
transmission, hence Hertz's supplement (see textual note).

mortal gods had been held on the grounds that the interests of the state had been competently and successfully—not incompetently and imprudently—handled by the praetor Lucius Furius. Moreover, they said, the Gallic wars had been confided to the family of the Furii by some kind of destiny.[195]

49. Thanks to speeches of this nature, delivered by Furius himself and by his friends, the prestige of the absent consul was eclipsed by the personal influence of the praetor who was present, and a crowded senate decreed a triumph for Lucius Furius. The praetor Lucius Furius thus celebrated a triumph over the Gauls during his term of office, and brought to the treasury 320,000 bronze *asses* and 171,500 silver coins.[196] His chariot was not preceded by captives, there was no display of spoils, and his men did not follow behind. Everything clearly belonged to the consul, save the victory.

After this, the games that he had promised in a vow as consul in Africa were celebrated with great pageantry by Publius Cornelius Scipio,[197] and a decree was issued with regard to land distribution to his soldiers—each was to receive two *iugera* for every year of service in Spain[198] or Africa. Decemvirs were to be responsible for the apportionment of the land. A board of three was also established to strengthen the complement of colonists at Venusia after the attrition of that colony's strength during the war with

[197] P. Cornelius Scipio Africanus (336), the renowned conqueror of Hannibal.

[198] Cf. 4.1, above, for distribution to veterans of the African campaign. Now veterans of the Spanish campaigns are added. A *iugerum* was about two-thirds of an acre.

rum, quod bello Hannibalis attenuatae vires eius coloniae erant, C. Terentius Varro T. Quinctius Flamininus P. Cornelius Cn. f. Scipio; hi colonos Venusiam adscripserunt.

7     Eodem anno C. Cornelius Cethegus, qui proconsul Hispaniam obtinebat, magnum hostium exercitum in agro Sedetano fudit. quindecim milia Hispanorum eo proelio dicuntur caesa, signa militaria capta octo et septuaginta.

8     C. Aurelius consul cum ex provincia Romam comitiorum causa venisset, non id quod animis praeceperant 9 questus est, non exspectatum se ab senatu neque disceptandi cum praetore consuli potestatem factam, sed ita triumphum decresse senatum ut nullius, nisi eius qui triumphaturus esset, eorum[56] qui bello interfuissent verba 10 audiret: maiores ideo instituisse ut legati tribuni centuriones milites denique triumpho adessent, ut testes[57] rerum gestarum eius cui tantus honos haberetur populus 11 Romanus videret. ecquem ex eo exercitu qui cum Gallis pugnaverit, si non militem, lixam saltem fuisse quem percunctari posset senatus quid veri praetor vanive adferret? 12 comitiis deinde diem edixit, quibus creati sunt consules L. Cornelius Lentulus P. Villius Tappulus. praetores inde

[56] eorum *Walker*: et eorum $B\chi$: haud eorum *ed. Med. 1505*: et non eorum *Weiss*.

[57] testes *Madvig*: *spat. B*: virtus $\chi$: veritas *L*

---

[199] Venusia (mod. Venosa), on the borders of Lucania and Apulia, was later famous as the birthplace of the poet Horace. It had remained loyal to Rome during the Punic war, when many of its neighbors were under Hannibal's control.

[200] Iberian tribe of Northern Spain: *Barr.* 25 E4; TIR K-30, 206.

Hannibal,[199] and this comprised Gaius Terentius Varro, Titus Quinctius Flamininus and Publius Cornelius Scipio, son of Gnaeus. These then enlisted colonists for Venusia.

In the same year Gaius Cornelius Cethegus, who was proconsular governor of Spain, defeated a large enemy army in the territory of the Sedetani.[200] It is said that 15,000 Spaniards lost their lives in that battle, and 78 military standards were captured.

When the consul Gaius Aurelius came from his province to Rome for the elections, he did not in fact lodge the grievance that had been expected of him, namely that the senate had not waited for him and that he had not, consul though he was, been given the chance to debate the issue with the praetor. Instead he complained that the senate had proclaimed a triumph without hearing the evidence of any who had participated in the war apart from the person who would celebrate the triumph. Their ancestors, said Aurelius, had ordained that legates, tribunes, centurions, and even the common soldiers should participate in a triumph, and their purpose was to let the Roman people see the men who had witnessed the feats of the person to whom that great honor was being accorded. Was there, he asked, any member of the army that had fought the Gauls whom the senate could question about the truth or falsehood of the praetor's version of events—any camp follower even, if not an enlisted man? Aurelius then fixed a date for the elections. In these Lucius Cornelius Lentulus and Publius Villius Tappulus[201] were elected consuls;

[201] L. Cornelius Lentulus (188): proconsul in Spain (206–200), consul this year (199), and proconsul in 198. P. Villius Tappulus (10): praetor in 203.

facti L. Quinctius Flamininus, L. Valerius Flaccus, L. Villius Tappulus, Cn. Baebius Tamphilus.

50. Annona quoque eo anno pervilis fuit; frumenti vim magnam ex Africa advectam aediles curules M. Claudius Marcellus et Sex. Aelius Paetus binis aeris in modios po-
2 pulo diviserunt. et ludos Romanos magno apparatu fecerunt; diem unum instaurarunt: signa aenea quinque ex
3 multaticio argento in aerario posuerunt. plebeii ludi ab aedilibus L. Terentio Massaliota[58] et Cn. Baebio Tam-
4 philo, qui praetor designatus erat, ter toti instaurati. et ludi funebres eo anno per quadriduum in foro mortis causa M.[59] Valeri Laevini a P. et M. filiis eius facti et munus gladiatorium datum ab iis; paria quinque et viginti
5 pugnarunt. M. Aurelius Cotta decemvir sacrorum mortuus: in eius locum M'. Acilius Glabrio suffectus.
6 Comitiis aediles curules creati sunt forte ambo qui statim occipere magistratum non possent. nam C. Cornelius Cethegus absens creatus erat, cum Hispaniam obtineret
7 provinciam; C. Valerius Flaccus, quem praesentem creaverant, quia flamen Dialis erat iurare in leges non poterat;

---

[58] Massaliota *Gel.*: Masiliota ψ: Massioliota *Bφ*: Massiliota *L²*
[59] M. *Mog.*: om. *Bχ*

---

[202] Probably because of that sent from Carthage to Rome and the army in Macedonia by the Roman ambassadors (19.2, above).

[203] The *Ludi Romani,* the earliest Roman games, held in September, originally marked the end of the military season. At first they were apparently devoted to chariot racing and circus games, but Etruscan mimes were added in the fourth century and dramatic performances in 240 (cf. 4.5 note, above). Like all Roman games, they were a religious festival, at first lasting only one day, held in honor of Jupiter. Cf. Oakley 2.770–72.

and Lucius Quinctius Flamininus, Lucius Valerius Flaccus, Lucius Villius Tappulus and Gnaeus Baebius Tamphilus were then made praetors.

50. Grain was particularly cheap that year.[202] The curule aediles Marcus Claudius Marcellus and Sextus Aelius Paetus distributed to the people a large amount of wheat imported from Africa at a price of two *asses* per measure. They also staged the Roman Games[203] with great ceremony, repeating one day,[204] and from money taken in fines they placed in the treasury five bronze statues.[205] The Plebeian Games were three times repeated in their entirety by the aediles Lucius Terentius Massaliota and Gnaeus Baebius Tamphilus, who was praetor designate. In addition, funeral games were that year held in the Forum over a four-day period, put on to commemorate the passing of Marcus Valerius Laevinus by his sons Publius and Marcus. A gladiatorial show was also staged by these men, and there were twenty-five pairs of fighters on the program. Marcus Aurelius Cotta, a decemvir for sacrifices,[206] died this year and was replaced by Manius Acilius Glabrio.

In the elections it turned out that the two curule aediles elected could not serve immediately. Gaius Cornelius Cethegus had been elected in his absence, during his term as governor of the province of Spain; and Gaius Valerius Flaccus, present for his election, could not take the oath to uphold the laws because he was the *flamen Dialis,* and

[204] *Instauratio:* cf. 4.7 and note, above.

[205] For aediles using proceeds from fines for public ornaments/public works, see Oakley 4.259–61.

[206] Cf. 12.9 and note, above.

magistratum autem plus quinque dies, nisi qui iurasset in
8 leges, non licebat gerere. petente Flacco ut legibus solveretur, senatus decrevit ut si aedilis qui pro se iuraret arbitratu consulum daret, consules si iis videretur cum tribu-
9 nis plebis agerent uti ad plebem ferrent. datus qui iuraret
pro fratre L. Valerius Flaccus praetor designatus; tribuni
ad plebem tulerunt plebesque scivit ut perinde esset ac si
10 ipse aedilis iurasset. et de altero aedile scitum plebi est
factum: rogantibus tribunis quos duos in Hispaniam cum
imperio ad exercitus ire iuberent, ut C. Cornelius aedilis
11 curulis ad magistratum gerendum veniret, et L. Manlius
Acidinus decederet de provincia multos post annos, plebes
Cn. Cornelio Lentulo et L. Stertinio pro consulibus imperium esse in Hispania iussit.

---

207 The *flamen Dialis* (priest of Jupiter) was governed by strict
rules (cf. Gell. 10.15), one precluding him from swearing an oath
and another from taking long absences from Rome. Flaccus entered the priesthood unwillingly as such restrictions effectively
debarred him from a political career. He did, however, claim his
right to a seat in the senate and held this aedileship and subsequently (in 183) a praetorship (*MRR* 379).

208 At the *comitia tributa;* cf. Introduction, l–li.

209 Manlius had gone to Spain in 206 and shared his command
as propraetor there with Lucius Lentulus (28.38.1).

only a person swearing to uphold the laws could occupy the office for more than five days.[207] Flaccus requested that the legal obligation be waived in his case, and the senate decreed that if the aedile presented someone who, in the view of the consuls, could take the oath in his stead, then, if the consuls were in agreement, they should discuss with the tribunes of the plebs the possibility of bringing the matter before the plebs. The praetor designate, Lucius Valerius Flaccus, was the man presented to take the oath for his brother. The tribunes then brought the matter before the plebs,[208] and the plebs voted that matters should stand as if the aedile had taken the oath in person. There was also a decree passed in the case of the other aedile. The tribunes canvassed the assembly on which two men they wanted to proceed with *imperium* to the armies in Spain to allow the curule aedile, Gaius Cornelius, to return to enter office and Lucius Manlius Acidinus to leave his province after many years of service,[209] and the plebs directed that Gnaeus Cornelius Lentulus[210] and Lucius Stertinius be invested with proconsular *imperium* in Spain.

[210] Seemingly an error for Cornelius Blasio, mentioned by Livy at 33.27.1 as returning from Spain in 197 and celebrating an ovation, which is confirmed by the *Fasti*.

# LIBRI XXXI PERIOCHA

Belli adversus Philippum, Macedoniae regem, quod intermissum erat, repetiti causae referuntur hae. tempore
initiorum duo iuvenes Acarnanes, qui non erant initiati,
Athenas venerunt et in sacrarium Cereris cum aliis popu-
laribus suis intraverunt. ob hoc, tamquam summum nefas
commisissent, ab Atheniensibus occisi sunt. Acarnanes
mortibus suorum commoti ad vindicandos illos auxilia a
Philippo petierunt et Athenas oppugnaverunt, Athenienses auxilium a Romanis petierunt post pacem Carthaginiensibus datam [quadringentesimo anno ab urbe condita][60]
paucis mensibus. [coeptum est autem anno quingentesimo quinto.][61] cum Atheniensium, qui a Philippo obside-
bantur, legati auxilium a senatu petissent, et id senatus
ferendum censuisset plebe, quod tot bellorum continuus
labor gravis erat, dissentiente, tenuit auctoritas patrum ut
sociae civitati ferri opem populus quoque iuberet. id bellum P. Sulpicio cos. mandatum est qui exercitu in Macedoniam ducto equestribus proeliis prospere cum Philippo
pugnavit. Aboedeni a Philippo obsessi ad exemplum Sa-
guntinorum suos seque occiderunt.

[60] quadringentesimo . . . condita *secl. Rossbach*
[61] coeptum . . . quinto *secl. Jahn*

# SUMMARY OF BOOK XXXI

The causes of the renewal of war with King Philip of Macedon, which had been interrupted, are given as follows. At the time of the Mysteries two Acarnanian youths who had not been initiated came to Athens and entered the sanctuary of Ceres along with some other compatriots of theirs. For this they were killed by the Athenians on the grounds of having committed a most heinous crime. Enraged by the death of their fellow citizens, the Acarnanians sought assistance from Philip to avenge them and attacked Athens, and the Athenians sought assistance from the Romans a few months after the Carthaginians had been granted a peace treaty. When ambassadors of the Athenians, who were under siege from Philip, sought assistance from the senate and the senate voted that this should be given, the plebs remonstrated because the relentless hardship of so many wars was crushing them; but the authority of the senate prevailed, so that the people, too, decreed that help be brought to an allied city-state. The war was assigned to the consul Publius Sulpicius who led his army into Macedonia and successfully engaged Philip in some cavalry battles. The people of Abydus, under siege from Philip, killed their families and themselves following the example of the people of Saguntum.

L. Furius praetor Gallos Insubras rebellantes et Hamilcarem Poenum bellum in ea parte Italiae molientem acie vicit. Hamilcar eo bello occisus est et milia hominum XXXV. praeterea expeditiones Philippi regis et Sulpicii cos. expugnationesque urbium ab utroque factas continet. Sulpicius cos. bellum gerebat adiuvantibus rege Attalo et Rhodiis. triumphavit de Gallis L. Furius praetor.

# SUMMARY OF BOOK XXXI

The praetor Lucius Furius defeated in pitched battle the rebellious Insubrian Gauls as well as the Carthaginian Hamilcar, who was fomenting war in that area of Italy. Hamilcar fell in that battle along with 35,000 men. In addition the book contains military operations conducted by King Philip and the consul Sulpicius, and accounts of cities stormed by each of the two men. The consul Sulpicius fought the war assisted by King Attalus and the Rhodians. The praetor Lucius Furius celebrated a triumph over the Gauls.

# LIBER XXXII

1. Consules praetoresque cum idibus Martiis magistratum
2 inissent provincias sortiti sunt. L. Lentulo Italia, P. Villio
Macedonia, praetoribus L. Quinctio urbana, Cn. Baebio
Ariminum, L. Valerio Sicilia, L. Villio Sardinia evenit.
3 Lentulus consul novas legiones scribere iussus, Villius a P.
Sulpicio exercitum accipere: in supplementum eius quan-
4 tum militum videretur ut scriberet ipsi permissum. praetori Baebio legiones quas C. Aurelius consul habuisset ita
decretae ut retineret eas donec consul novo cum exercitu
5 succederet; in Galliam ubi is venisset, omnes milites
exauctorati domum dimitterentur praeter quinque milia
socium: iis obtineri circa Ariminum provinciam satis esse.
6 prorogata imperia[1] praetoribus prioris anni, C. Sergio ut
militibus qui in Hispania Sicilia Sardinia stipendia per

---

[1] prorogata imperia *Gron.*: prorogato imperio *Bχ*: prorogatum imperium *Holk. 345*

---

[1] On the date of entry into office, see 31.5.2 note.
[2] In fact, as can be seen below, Lentulus was to be assigned
Gaul, sometimes mentioned specifically as a province and sometimes, as here, as part of the province of Italy.
[3] Cn. Baebius Tamphilus (41), praetor for 199 and consul in
182, when he had success in the war with the Ligurians. As Len-

# BOOK XXXII

1. When they entered office on the Ides of March,[1] the consuls and praetors drew lots for their respective provinces. Italy fell to Lucius Lentulus,[2] and Macedonia to Publius Villius, while among the praetors the city prefecture came to Lucius Quinctius, Ariminum to Gnaeus Baebius,[3] Sicily to Lucius Valerius, and Sardinia to Lucius Villius. The consul Lentulus was instructed to enroll fresh legions, and Villius was to take over from Publius Sulpicius command of his army, with permission granted for him to supplement it by enlisting as many men as he thought fit. The legions that the consul Gaius Aurelius had commanded were allocated to the praetor Baebius on the condition that he kept them only until the consul with his new army replaced him. On the consul's arrival in Gaul, all soldiers who had completed their service were to be sent home apart from 5,000 allies—this was a large enough force for securing the province around Ariminum. Gaius Sergius and Quintus Minucius, praetors the previous year, had their terms of office prorogued, Sergius to supervise the distribution of land to soldiers who had served many years in Spain, Sicily, and Sardinia, and Quintus Minucius

tulus has Gaul/Italy, Baebius' sphere is restricted to the area around Ariminum (mod. Rimini).

7　multos annos fecissent agrum adsignandum curaret, Q.
Minucio ut in Bruttiis idem de coniurationibus quaestiones quas praetor cum fide curaque exercuisset perfice-
8　ret, et eos quos sacrilegii compertos in vinculis Romam
misisset Locros mitteret ad supplicium, quaeque sublata
ex delubro Proserpinae essent reponenda cum piaculis
curaret.
9　Feriae Latinae pontificum decreto instauratae sunt,
quod legati ab Ardea questi in senatu erant sibi in monte
Albano Latinis carnem, ut adsolet, datam non esse.
10　Ab Suessa nuntiatum est duas portas quodque inter eas
muri erat de caelo tactum, et Formiani legati aedem Iovis,
item Ostienses aedem Iovis, et Veliterni Apollinis et San-
11　cus[2] aedes, et in Herculis aede capillum enatum; et ex
Bruttiis ab Q. Minucio pro praetore scriptum eculeum
cum quinque pedibus, pullos gallinaceos tres cum ternis
12　pedibus natos esse. a P. Sulpicio pro consule ex Macedonia
litterae allatae, in quibus inter cetera scriptum erat lau-
13　ream in puppi navis longae enatam. priorum prodigiorum

[2] Sancus *McDonald*: Sangus *B*: Saturni χ: Sangi *Gel.*: Sanci *Gron.*

[4] C. Sergius Plautus and Q. Minucius Rufus elected praetors for 200: 31.6.2; investigations into criminality in Bruttium:
31.12.1–5.

[5] Held annually at a date stipulated by the consuls, usually in
the spring. The sacrificial meat was offered to representatives of
the Latin cities and, as usual, any procedural anomaly or omission
in the rite led to repetition of the whole process.

[6] Latin colony south of Rome (*Barr.* 43 C3).

[7] In Latium, southeast of Rome (*Barr.* 43 C2), today Monte
Cavo.

so that the same official could complete the investigations into conspiracies in Bruttium (which he had, as praetor, conducted with commitment and diligence).[4] Minucius was to dispatch to Locri for punishment the men he had sent to Rome in irons after they were convicted of sacrilege, and see to replacing everything that had been misappropriated from the shrine of Proserpina, adding gifts of atonement.

By decree of the pontiffs the Latin Festival[5] was repeated because representatives from Ardea[6] protested in the senate that they had not been given meat on the Alban mount[7] at the time of the festival, as was the custom.

News came from Suessa[8] that two gates and the section of wall between them had been struck by lightning, and representatives from the towns affected reported the same phenomenon occurring at the temple of Jupiter at Formiae, the temple of Jupiter at Ostia, and the temple of Apollo and Sancus at Velitrae,[9] while hair was said to have grown in the temple of Hercules.[10] A dispatch from the propraetor Quintus Minucius in Bruttium recorded the birth of a colt with five feet and of three chicks with three feet each. A dispatch was also brought from the proconsul Publius Sulpicius in Macedonia reporting, among other things, that a laurel tree had grown on the stern of a war-

[8] Suessa Arunca, a Latin colony in Northern Campania (*Barr.* 44 E3), today Sessa Arunca.

[9] Sancus (full name Semo Sancus Dius Fidius): a god of Sabine origin also worshipped in Rome. Velitrae: a Volscian town south of Rome, today Velletri (*Barr.* 44 C2).

[10] Unique among Roman portents. On what the hair supposedly grew is unknown (probably a statue), as is the temple.

causa senatus censuerat ut consules maioribus hostiis qui-
14  bus dis videretur sacrificarent; ob hoc unum prodigium
haruspices in senatum vocati, atque ex responso eorum
supplicatio populo in diem unum edicta[3] et ad omnia pulvinaria res divinae factae.

2. Carthaginienses eo anno argentum in stipendium
2  impositum primum Romam advexerunt. id quia probum
non esse quaestores renuntiaverant, experientibusque
pars quarta decocta erat, pecunia Romae mutua sumpta
3  intertrimentum argenti expleverunt. petentibus deinde ut
si iam videretur senatui, obsides sibi redderentur, centum
redditi obsides; de ceteris, si in fide permanerent, spes
4  facta. petentibus iisdem qui non reddebantur obsides ut
ab Norba, ubi parum commode essent, alio traducerentur,
5  concessum ut Signiam et Ferentinum transirent. Gadita-
nis item petentibus remissum ne praefectus Gades mitteretur, adversus id quod iis in fidem populi Romani venien-
6  tibus cum L. Marcio Septimo convenisset. et Narniensium
legatis querentibus ad numerum sibi colonos non esse et
immixtos quosdam non sui generis pro colonis se gerere,
earum rerum causa tresviros creare L. Cornelius consul

---

[3] edicta χ: dicta *B*: indicta *Weiss*.

---

[11] Full-grown victims: 31.5.3 note; supplication: 31.8.2 note.
[12] By the peace terms of 201, they were to pay ten thousand
talents in equal installments over fifty years, and they had difficulty raising the first payment (30.44.4).     [13] Norba, Signia,
Ferentinum, southeast of Rome: *Barr.* 44 D2.     [14] On the difficulties posed by the treaty with Gades (Cadiz), cf. Briscoe 1.170.
[15] Narnia (mod. Narni, in Umbria): *Barr.* 42 D3. In 209 it was
one of twelve colonies claiming to be unable to provide men and
money for the Roman war effort (27.9.7).

ship. In the case of the former prodigies the senate had voted that the consuls should offer sacrifice with full-grown animals to whatever deities they thought appropriate; in the case of the last one alone the seers were summoned to the senate, and on their recommendation an edict was issued enjoining one day of supplication[11] upon the people, and religious ceremonies were conducted at all the couches of the gods.

2. That year the Carthaginians brought to Rome the first payment in silver of the indemnity imposed on them.[12] Because the quaestors reported that the metal was impure and that a quarter of it had boiled down to dross during the assay, the Carthaginians made good the shortfall of silver by borrowing in Rome. Then when the Carthaginians requested the return of their hostages if the senate so agreed, a hundred hostages were returned; and they were offered hope for the others if they remained loyal. When they further requested that those hostages who were not being returned should be transferred from Norba, where they were not comfortable, to some other location, the hostages were allowed to go instead to Signia and Ferentinum.[13] The people of Gades also had their request granted that a Roman official not be sent to their city; this, they said, contravened the agreement made with Lucius Marcius Septimus when they came under the protection of the Roman people.[14] In addition, when spokesmen from Narnia lodged a complaint that their colonists were not up to the requisite quota, and that certain outsiders not of their race had infiltrated their number and were comporting themselves as colonists,[15] the consul Lucius Cornelius was

7   iussus. creati P. et Sex. Aelii—Paetis fuit ambobus cognomen—et Cn. Cornelius Lentulus. quod Narniensibus
datum,[4] ut colonorum numerus augeretur, id Cosani petentes non impetraverunt.

3. Rebus quae Romae agendae erant perfectis, con-
2   sules in provincias profecti. P. Villius in Macedoniam cum
venisset, atrox seditio militum iam ante inritata nec satis
3   in principio compressa excepit. duo milia ea militum
fuere, quae ex Africa post devictum Hannibalem in Siciliam, inde anno fere post in Macedoniam pro voluntariis
4   transportata erant. id voluntate factum negabant: ab tribunis recusantes in naves impositos. sed utcumque, seu
iniuncta seu suscepta foret militia, et eam exhaustam et
5   finem aliquem militandi fieri aequum esse. multis annis
sese Italiam non vidisse; consenuisse sub armis in Sicilia
Africa Macedonia; confectos iam se labore opere, exsan-
6   gues tot acceptis volneribus esse. consul causam postulan-
dae missionis probabilem, si modeste peteretur, videri
dixit: seditionis nec eam nec ullam aliam satis iustam cau-
7   sam esse. itaque si manere ad signa et dicto parere velint,
se de missione eorum ad senatum scripturum; modestia
facilius quam pertinacia quod velint impetraturos.

---

[4] datum *B*: datum erat χ

---

[16] A Latin colony on the Etrurian coast (*Barr.* 42 A4).

instructed to establish a board of three to investigate the case. Elected to the board were Publius and Sextus Aelius, both bearing the *cognomen* Paetus, and Gnaeus Cornelius Lentulus. When the people of Cosa[16] requested the same concession that had been granted to the people of Narnia, namely an increase in the number of colonists, they were not successful.

3. All essential business finished at Rome, the consuls set off for their provinces. Arriving in Macedonia, Publius Villius faced a horrendous mutiny of the troops that had been fomented some time before but not suppressed with sufficient firmness at the start. It involved 2,000 men who had been transported from Africa after Hannibal's defeat, first to Sicily and from there as volunteers to Macedon about a year later. The men claimed that this had been done against their will and that they had been press-ganged aboard the ships by the tribunes. But whatever the case, they said, whether their service there had been under duress or voluntary, it was now over, and it was only fair that some limit be set to their military service. They had not seen Italy in many a year; they had grown old under arms in Sicily, Africa, and Macedonia; and they were now exhausted from toil and exertion, and drained of blood from all the wounds they had received. The consul admitted that they appeared to have acceptable grounds for seeking demobilization, if these were presented in a reasonable way, but added that neither this nor any other case was sufficiently strong as to warrant mutiny. So if they were prepared to remain at their posts and obey orders, he would write to the senate about their demobilization, and they would more easily gain their end by moderate behavior than by pigheadedness.

4. Thaumacos eo tempore Philippus summa vi oppugnabat aggeribus vineisque, et iam arietem muris
2 admoturus erat. ceterum incepto absistere eum coegit
subitus Aetolorum adventus, qui Archidamo duce inter
custodias Macedonum moenia ingressi nec nocte nec die
finem ullum erumpendi nunc in stationes nunc in opera
3 Macedonum faciebant. et adiuvabat eos natura ipsa loci.
namque Thaumaci a Pylis sinuque Maliaco per Lamiam
eunti loco alto siti sunt in ipsis faucibus, imminentes quam
4 Coelen vocant Thessaliae; quae transeunti confragosa loca
implicatasque flexibus vallium vias ubi ventum ad hanc
urbem est, repente velut maris vasti sic universa panditur
planities ut subiectos campos terminare oculis haud facile
5 queas: ab eo miraculo Thaumaci appellati. nec altitudine
solum tuta urbs, sed quod saxo undique absciso rupibus
6 imposita est. hae difficultates et quod haud satis dignum
tanti laboris periculique pretium erat ut absisteret incepto
7 Philippus effecerunt. hiemps quoque iam instabat, cum
inde abscessit et in Macedoniam in hiberna copias reduxit.

5. Ibi ceteri quidem data quanticumque quiete tempo-
2 ris simul animos corporaque remiserant: Philippum quan-

---

17 Thaumaci (mod. Domokos): *Barr.* 55 C2. As Livy explains
below, it was strategically situated on the route between the Malian Gulf and Thessaly.     18 Latin *vinea*: "A movable pent-
house used to shelter siege-workers" (*OLD* sv), so named probably because it resembled rows of vines (*vineae*).

19 Three times *strategos* of the Aetolian League, he would
lead the Aetolian troops under Flamininus in 197 (Polyb. 18.21.5),
but later he is head of the anti-Roman faction (Book 35.48–49).

20 Livy's derivation from the Greek θαῦμα (marvel) is, like
most ancient place-name etymologies, unconvincing. Another
derives it from a mythological Thaumas, son of Pontos and Ge.

4. At that time Philip was in the process of launching an all-out attack on Thaumaci,[17] using earthworks and mantlets,[18] and was on the point of bringing the battering ram up to the walls. He was, however, forced to abandon the effort by the sudden arrival of the Aetolians who, led by Archidamus,[19] had made their way through the Macedonian guard stations into the city and now, night and day, there was no end to their counterattacks on the Macedonian outposts or their siege works. The very geography of the area also assisted them. Thaumaci is perched high up, right above a gorge, on the road through Lamia as one comes from Pylae and the Malian Gulf, and it overlooks the so-called Hollow Thessaly. One passes through rugged terrain, along roads that wend their way through sinuous valleys, and then, when one reaches the city, suddenly there is the whole plain, stretching out like a vast sea, making it difficult to see where the fields lying below actually come to an end. It is from this marvel of nature that Thaumaci gets its name.[20] The city owes its security not only to its elevation but also to the fact that it sits on a rocky prominence sheer on every side. These difficulties, and the consideration that the town was a prize hardly worth the effort and danger, led Philip to abandon his venture. Winter was also now approaching when he left and took his troops back to winter quarters in Macedonia.

5. There everybody else had used whatever slight repose they were granted for relaxation of mind and body, but in Philip's case the mental release he experienced af-

tum ab adsiduis laboribus itinerum pugnarumque laxave-
rat animum, tanto magis intentum in universum eventum
belli curae angunt, non hostes modo timentem qui terra
3  marique urgebant, sed nunc sociorum nunc etiam popularium animos, ne et illi ad spem amicitiae Romanorum
deficerent, et Macedonas ipsos cupido novandi res cape-
4  ret. itaque et in Achaiam legatos misit, simul qui ius iuran-
dum—ita enim pepigerant quotannis iuraturos in verba
Philippi—exigerent, simul qui redderent Achaeis Orcho-
menon et Heraean et Triphylian Eleis ademptam, Mega-
5  lopolitis[5] Alipheran, contendentibus nunquam eam urbem
fuisse ex Triphylia sed sibi debere restitui, quia una esset
ex iis quae ad condendam Megalen polin ex concilio Arca-
dum contributae forent.
6      Et cum Achaeis quidem per haec societatem firmabat:
7  ad[6] Macedonum animos cum Heracliden amicum maxime
invidiae sibi esse cerneret, multis criminibus oneratum in
8  vincla coniecit, ingenti popularium gaudio. bellum si
quando unquam ante alias, tum magna cura apparavit,
exercuitque in armis et Macedonas et mercennarios mi-
9  lites, principioque veris cum Athenagora omnia externa
auxilia quodque levis armaturae erat in Chaoniam per
Epirum ad occupandas quae ad Antigoneam fauces sunt—
10  Stena vocant Graeci—misit. ipse post paucis diebus gra-

---

[5] Eleis ademptam Megalopolitis *Madvig*: Eleis *Bχ*
[6] ad *Madvig*: om. *Bχ*

---

[21] Orchomenus: *Barr.* 58 C2; Megalopolis: C3; Heraea,
Triphylia, Aliphera: B2. On these places cf. Briscoe 1.174–75.

[22] Cf. 31.16.2, 33.2, 46.8. "Friend," of course, means courtier.

[23] Antigoneia, The Narrows (Stena), Mt. Meropus, Mt. Asnaus, and the River Aous (below): *Barr.* 49 C3. The site of the
battle of the Aous, however, remains unknown.

ter the relentless hardship of marching and fighting only made him all the more focused on the final outcome of the war and racked him with anxiety. His fears were not confined to his enemies, who were applying pressure by land and sea; he now worried, too, about the mood of his allies, and even of his own countrymen. The former, he feared, could abandon him in hopes of gaining an alliance with Rome; and the Macedonians themselves could be overtaken by desire for revolution. He therefore sent a deputation to Achaea to demand an oath of allegiance from the Achaeans—they had undertaken to swear loyalty to him on an annual basis—and also to restore to them Orchomenos and Heraea, along with Triphylia (which he had taken from the people of Elis), as well as to give Aliphera to the people of Megalopolis.[21] The Megalopolitans maintained that this city had never belonged to Triphylia and should be restored to them as being one of the cities granted for the founding of Megalopolis by decision of the Arcadian council.

In fact, Philip did start strengthening his alliance with the Achaeans by these measures. As for the mood of the Macedonians, he could see that what was particularly held against him was having Heraclides as a friend;[22] and so he laid all manner of charges against him and threw him in prison, to the great joy of his compatriots. He then prepared for war more diligently than he had ever done before. There was military training both for Macedonians and for mercenaries, and at the beginning of spring he sent his entire foreign auxiliary force, plus whatever light-armed troops he possessed, all under Athenagoras, through Epirus into Chaonia to seize the gorge at Antigonea, which the Greeks call "The Narrows."[23] A few days later he himself followed with the heavier troops. After a

viore secutus agmine, cum situm omnem regionis adspex-
isset, maxime idoneum ad muniendum locum credidit
11  esse praeter amnem Aoum. is inter montes, quorum alterum Meropum alterum Asnaum incolae vocant, angusta
valle fluit, iter exiguum super ripam praebens. Asnaum
Athenagoram cum levi armatura tenere et communire
12  iubet; ipse in Meropo posuit castra. qua abscisae rupes
erant, statio paucorum armatorum tenebat; qua minus
tuta erant, alia fossis alia vallo alia turribus muniebat.
13  magna tormentorum etiam vis, ut missilibus procul ar-
cerent hostem, idoneis locis disposita est. tabernaculum
regium pro vallo in conspecto maxime tumulo, ut terrorem hostibus suisque spem ex fiducia faceret, positum.

6. Consul, per Charopum Epiroten certior factus quos
saltus cum exercitu insedisset rex, et ipse, cum Corcyrae
hibernasset, vere primo in continentem travectus ad hos-
2  tem ducere pergit. quinque milia ferme ab regiis castris
cum abesset, loco munito relictis legionibus, ipse cum
expeditis progressus ad speculanda loca, postero die con-
3  silium habuit, utrum per insessum ab hoste saltum, quamquam labor ingens periculumque proponeretur, transitum
temptaret, an eodem itinere quo priore anno Sulpicius
4  Macedoniam intraverat circumduceret copias. hoc consilium per multos dies agitanti ei nuntius venit T. Quinctium

thorough inspection of the topography of the region, he concluded that the most opportune spot for a fortified encampment lay beside the River Aous. This flows in a constricted valley between two mountains, called respectively Meropus and Asnaus by the local population, and offers only a narrow pathway along the bank. Philip ordered Athenagoras to hold and fortify Asnaus with his light-armed troops while he himself encamped on Meropus. Where the cliff was sheer units of only a few armed men stood on guard; weaker spots he secured with ditches or a rampart or towers. A large battery of catapults was also deployed at appropriate points to keep the enemy at bay with projectiles. The king's tent was positioned on the most prominent hillock before the rampart so that he could, by his confidence, inspire terror in the enemy and hope in his own men.

6. The consul had been briefed by an Epirote, Charopus, on the passes the king had occupied with his army; and at the start of spring, after passing the winter at Corcyra, he crossed to the mainland and proceeded to march on the enemy. When he was about five miles distant from the king's camp he fortified a position, left his legions behind, and went ahead in person with his light-armed to examine the terrain. The following day he held a meeting to consider whether he should attempt a passage through the gorge held by the enemy despite the enormous hardship and risk to be faced, or alternatively take his troops on the same circuitous route that Sulpicius had used to enter Macedonia the previous year. He had spent many a day considering the problem when news arrived that Titus Quinctius had been elected consul, had been allot-

consulem factum, sortitumque provinciam Macedoniam maturato itinere iam Corcyram traiecisse.

5 Valerius Antias intrasse saltum Villium tradit, quia recto itinere nequiverit omnibus ab rege insessis, secutum
6 vallem per quam mediam fertur Aous amnis, ponte raptim facto in ripam in qua erant castra regia transgressum, acie
7 conflixisse; fusum fugatumque regem, castris exutum; duodecim milia hostium eo proelio caesa, capta duo milia et ducentos et signa militaria centum triginta duo, equos ducentos triginta; aedem etiam Iovi in eo proelio votam,
8 si res prospere gesta esset. ceteri Graeci Latinique auctores, quorum quidem ego legi annales, nihil memorabile a Villio actum, integrumque bellum insequentem consulem T. Quinctium accepisse tradunt.

7. Dum haec in Macedonia geruntur, consul alter L. Lentulus, qui Romae substiterat, comitia censoribus cre-
2 andis habuit. multis claris petentibus viris creati censores
3 P. Cornelius Scipio Africanus et P. Aelius Paetus. ii magna inter se concordia et senatum sine ullius nota legerunt, et[7] venalicium Capuae Puteolisque, item Castris[8] portorium, quo in loco nunc oppidum est, fruendum locarunt, colonosque eo trecentos—is enim numerus finitus ab senatu

----

[7] et *Madvig*: et portoria *Bχ*
[8] Castris *Pettersson*: Castrum *Bχ*: ad Castrum *Madvig*

----

[24] The historian: see Introduction, xxvii–xxviii.

[25] Livy now turns to events in Rome during the year 199, returning to the Macedonian War at 9.6.

[26] Cf. P. Cornelius Scipio Africanus (336) and P. Aelius Paetus (101): *MRR* 327.

[27] On the censors, see Introduction, liv–lv.

ted Macedonia as his province and, accelerating his journey, had already crossed to Corcyra.

Valerius Antias[24] recounts that Villius entered the gorge but because he could not take the direct route since the whole area was in the king's power he followed the valley through which the River Aous flows, hastily constructed a bridge, crossed to the bank on which the king's camp was located, and engaged the enemy in pitched battle. The king was defeated and put to flight, according to Antias, with the loss of his camp; 12,000 of the enemy were killed in the battle and 2,200 were captured, together with 132 military standards and 230 horses. Antias adds that during the battle Villius vowed a temple to Jupiter in the event of a successful outcome. All the other Greek and Roman authors, at least those whose annals I have read, record no exceptional feat on Villius' part and say that the incoming consul, Titus Quinctius, inherited from him a war in which no progress had been made.

7. In the course of these events in Macedonia,[25] the other consul, Lucius Lentulus, who had stayed behind in Rome, held elections for the censorship. From a wide field of distinguished candidates the censors elected were Publius Cornelius Scipio Africanus and Publius Aelius Paetus.[26] In a spirit of close cooperation these two managed to select a list of senators without censuring anyone,[27] as well as to contract out the collection of sales taxes at Capua and Puteoli, and transport taxes at Castra (where there is a town today).[28] They also enrolled for Castra 300 colonists

[28] The difficulties with the taxes involved here and the location of Castra remain unresolved (cf. Briscoe 1.177–78).

erat—adscripserunt, et sub Tifatis Capuae agrum vendi-
derunt.

4  Sub idem tempus L. Manlius Acidinus ex Hispania
decedens, prohibitus a P. Porcio Laeca tribuno plebis ne
ovans rediret, cum ab senatu impetrasset, privatus urbem
ingrediens sex milia[9] pondo argenti, triginta pondo ferme
auri in aerarium tulit.

5  Eodem anno Cn. Baebius Tamphilus, qui ab C. Aurelio
consule anni prioris provinciam Galliam acceperat, temere ingressus Gallorum Insubrum fines prope cum toto
6  exercitu est circumventus; supra sex milia et septingentos
milites amisit: tanta ex eo bello quod iam timeri desierat
7  clades accepta est. ea res L. Lentulum consulem ab urbe
excivit; qui ut in provinciam venit plenam tumultus, trepido exercitu accepto praetorem multis probris increpi-
tum provincia decedere atque abire Romam iussit.

8  Neque ipse consul memorabile quicquam gessit,
comitiorum causa Romam revocatus; quae ipsa per M.
Fulvium et M. Curium tribunos plebis impediebantur,
9  quod T. Quinctium Flamininum consulatum ex quaestura
10  petere non patiebantur: iam aedilitatem praeturamque
fastidiri nec per honorum gradus, documentum sui dantes,

---

[9] sex milia *McDonald*: quinquaginta milia *Luchs*: *lac. indicat*
*Briscoe*

---

[29] On the ovation, cf. 31.20.5 note. Why Manlius was refused
one is not clear (at 31.50.11 Livy refers to his leaving Spain, with
no mention of an ovation). As it was refused, he could not retain
his *imperium* within the *pomerium*.

[30] Cn. Baebius Tamphilus: cf 1.2, above, and note.

[31] T. Quinctius Flamininus (45) had been military tribune in

(the number prescribed by the senate) and sold off land belonging to Capua at the foot of Mount Tifata.

At this time Lucius Manlius Acidinus, on returning from Spain, was refused entry to Rome in ovation by the tribune Publius Porcius Laeca, although Acidinus had been granted his request by the senate. He therefore entered the city as a private citizen[29] and deposited in the treasury six thousand pounds of silver and some thirty pounds of gold.

During the same year Gnaeus Baebius Tamphilus,[30] who had taken charge of the province of Gaul from Gaius Aurelius, consul the previous year, made a reckless incursion into the territory of the Insubrian Gauls and was cut off with practically his entire army. He lost more than 6,700 men, and such a terrible defeat was incurred in a war that by now had ceased to be a concern. The incident brought the consul Lucius Lentulus from Rome. Arriving in a province full of turmoil, and taking charge of a demoralized army, Lentulus gave the praetor a serious reprimand and ordered him to leave the province and return to Rome.

However, the consul achieved no notable success himself since he was recalled to Rome for the elections. These were being held up by the plebeian tribunes Marcus Fulvius and Manius Curius because they refused to allow Titus Quinctius Flamininus[31] to stand for the consulship straight after his quaestorship. The aedileship and the praetorship were now being treated with disdain, they ar-

208 and propraetor at Tarentum in 205–4. He will become the hero of the war with Philip and the champion of "Greek independence."

nobiles homines tendere ad consulatum, sed transcen-
11 dendo media summa imis continuare. res ex campestri
certamine in senatum pervenit. patres censuerunt qui
honorem quem sibi capere per leges liceret peteret, in eo
populo creandi quem velit potestatem fieri aequum esse.
12 in auctoritate patrum fuere tribuni. creati consules Sex.
13 Aelius Paetus et T. Quinctius Flamininus. inde praetorum
comitia habita. creati L. Cornelius Merula, M. Claudius
Marcellus, M. Porcius Cato C. Helvius,[10] qui aediles plebis fuerant. ab iis ludi plebeii . . . [11] instaurati; et epulum
14 Iovis fuit ludorum causa. et ab aedilibus curulibus C. Valerio Flacco, flamine Diali, et C. Cornelio Cethego ludi
15 Romani magno apparatu facti. Ser. et C. Sulpicii Galbae[12]
pontifices eo anno mortui sunt: in eorum locum M. Aemilius Lepidus et Cn. Cornelius Scipio pontifices suffecti
sunt.

8. Sex. Aelius Paetus T. Quinctius Flamininus magistratu[13] inito senatum in Capitolio cum habuissent, de-

[10] C. Helvius *Gel.*: Caelus *B*: Caelius *B¹*: C. Elius *ψ*: Elius *φ*
[11] *lac. ind. Ritschl*
[12] et C. Sulpicii Galbae *Sig.*: Sulpicius et Galba *Bχ*
[13] magistratu *B*: consules magistratu (-us *ψ*) *χ*

---

[32] Not until 180 did the Lex Villia Annalis establish rules for
the various offices in the *cursus honorum* to be held successively,
though an order may earlier have been unofficially recognized.
See Introduction, lv–lvi.

[33] The Campus Martius, where the centuriate assembly met.

[34] Sex. Aelius Paetus (105), aedile in 200 and recently triumvir
for the colonists' quota at Narnia (cf. 2.6–7, above).

gued; nobles now aimed directly at the consulship without climbing the ladder of successive offices and giving evidence of their capabilities in them; by skipping the intermediate stages, were going directly from the bottom to the top.[32] After being debated in the Campus[33] the issue reached the senate. Members there voted that it was right that the people should have the power to elect anyone they pleased, provided that a candidate was standing for an office that the laws permitted him to hold. The tribunes bowed to the authority of the senate, and Sextus Aelius Paetus[34] and Titus Quinctius Flamininus were elected consuls. Then the praetorian elections were held, and the successful candidates were Lucius Cornelius Merula, Marcus Claudius Marcellus, Marcus Porcius Cato and Gaius Helvius, who had been plebeian aediles.[35] The Plebeian Games were repeated[36] by these magistrates, and a feast of Jupiter held to celebrate the games. Furthermore, the Roman Games[37] were celebrated with great ceremony by the curule aediles Gaius Valerius Flaccus, the *flamen Dialis,* and Gaius Cornelius Cethegus. The pontiffs Servius and Gaius Sulpicius Galba died that year, to be replaced by Marcus Aemilius Lepidus and Gnaeus Cornelius Scipio.

8. When, after entering office, Sextus Aelius Paetus and Titus Quinctius Flamininus had convened the senate on the Capitol, the members decided that the two consuls

[35] The reference is only to Cato and Helvius, plebeian aediles in 199 (*MRR* 327).

[36] Cf. 31.50.2 note. Since the length or number of repetitions is usually given, the text may be lacunose here (see textual note).

[37] The earliest games at Rome: cf. 31.50.2 and note.

creverunt patres ut provincias Macedoniam atque Italiam
2 consules compararent inter se sortirenturue: utri eorum
Macedonia evenisset, in supplementum legionum tria milia militum Romanorum scriberet et trecentos equites,
item sociorum Latini nominis quinque milia peditum
quingentos equites; alteri consuli novus omnis exercitus
3 decretus. L. Lentulo prioris anni consuli prorogatum imperium, uetitusque aut ipse provincia decedere prius aut
veterem deducere exercitum quam cum legionibus novis
4 consul venisset. sortiti consules provincias: Aelio Italia
5 Quinctio Macedonia evenit. praetores L. Cornelius Merula urbanam, M. Claudius Siciliam, M. Porcius Sardi-
6 niam, C. Helvius Galliam est sortitus. dilectus inde haberi
est coeptus; nam praeter consulares exercitus praetoribus
7 quoque iussi scribere milites erant, Marcello in Siciliam
quattuor milia peditum socium et Latini nominis et trecentos equites, Catoni in Sardiniam ex eodem genere
8 militum duo milia peditum, ducentos equites, ita ut ii
praetores ambo cum in provincias venissent veteres dimitterent pedites equitesque.
9    Attali deinde regis legatos in senatum consules intro-
duxerunt. ii regem classe sua copiisque omnibus terra
marique rem Romanam iuvare quaeque imperarent Romani consules impigre atque oboedienter ad eam diem
10 fecisse cum exposuissent, vereri dixerunt ne id praestare
ei per Antiochum regem ultra non liceret: vacuum namque praesidiis navalibus terrestribusque regnum Attali
11 Antiochum invasisse. itaque Attalum orare patres conscrip-

---

38 Cf. 31.5.4 note.

should decide between themselves, or by sortition, which should receive Macedonia and which Italy as his province. The one to whom Macedonia came was to enroll, to supplement his legions, a force of 3,000 Roman infantry and 300 cavalry plus 5,000 infantry and 500 cavalry from the allies and those with Latin rights.[38] The other consul, it was decided, would be given an entirely new army. Lucius Lentulus, consul the previous year, had his command prorogued, and was ordered not to leave the province himself or demobilize the veteran force before the consul arrived with the new legions. The consuls drew lots for their provinces, and Italy fell to Aelius and Macedonia to Quinctius. Among the praetors, Lucius Cornelius Merula received the city jurisdiction, Marcus Claudius Sicily, Marcus Porcius Sardinia and Gaius Helvius Gaul. Then began the levy of troops, for, apart from the armies of the consuls, the order was also given for the enlistment of soldiers for the praetors. Marcellus was assigned 4,000 allied and Latin infantry and 300 cavalry for Sicily, and Cato 2,000 infantry and 200 cavalry of the same category for Sardinia. On arrival in their respective provinces, both praetors were to discharge the veteran infantry and cavalry.

The consuls next brought before the senate envoys from King Attalus. These proclaimed that the king was using his fleet and all his land forces to further Roman interests on land and sea, and that he had to that day actively and faithfully carried out all the instructions of the Roman consuls. Now, however, he feared that, because of King Antiochus, he would not be allowed to continue such service, since Antiochus had overrun Attalus' kingdom when it was bereft of naval and land defenses. Attalus was therefore entreating the senate to send a force to

tos, si sua classe suaque opera uti ad Macedonicum bellum vellent, mitterent ipsi praesidium ad regnum eius tutandum; si id nollent, ipsum ad sua defendenda cum classe ac reliquis copiis redire paterentur.

12 Senatus legatis ita responderi iussit: quod rex Attalus classe copiisque aliis duces Romanos iuvisset, id gratum
13 senatui esse; auxilia nec ipsos missuros Attalo adversus Antiochum, socium et amicum populi Romani, nec Attali auxilia retenturos ultra quam regi commodum esset;
14 semper populum Romanum alienis rebus arbitrio alieno usum; et principium et finem in potestate[14] ipsorum qui
15 ope sua velint adiutos Romanos esse; legatos ad Antiochum missuros qui nuntient Attali naviumque eius et militum opera adversus Philippum communem hostem uti
16 populum Romanum: gratum eum facturum senatui si regno Attali abstineat belloque absistat; aequum esse socios et amicos populi Romani reges inter se quoque ipsos pacem servare.

9. Consulem T. Quinctium, ita habito dilectu ut eos fere legeret qui in Hispania aut Africa meruissent spectatae virtutis milites, properantem in provinciam prodigia
2 nuntiata atque eorum procuratio Romae tenuerunt. de caelo tacta erant via publica Veiis, forum et aedes Iovis Lanuvi, Herculis aedes Ardeae, Capuae murus et turres

---

[14] potestate *L*: potestatem *Bχ*

---

[39] "should by rights" because Roman "treaties of friendship" did not bar allies from going to war with other "friends of Rome."

defend his realm if they wished to avail themselves of his fleet and his support for the Macedonian war. If they refused this, they should allow him to withdraw with his fleet and the rest of his forces to defend his own territory.

The senate ordered the following reply to be given to the envoys: The senate was gratified by the support King Attalus had provided by means of his fleet and his other troops. It would not, however, send Attalus assistance against Antiochus, who was an ally and friend of the people of Rome; but no more would it hold on to Attalus' assistance longer than was convenient for the king. The Roman people always employed the resources of others only at the discretion of those others: the people who wished the Romans to enjoy their assistance had it in their power to determine the commencement and termination of that assistance. The senate would, however, send a delegation to Antiochus to report to him that the Roman people were profiting from the assistance of Attalus, his navy and his land forces in the fight against Philip, their common enemy; that he would earn the senate's gratitude if he kept away from Attalus' realm and refrained from war with him; and that monarchs who were allies and friends of Rome should by rights also maintain peace with each other.[39]

9. The consul Titus Quinctius so conducted his levy as to limit his choice almost exclusively to men of proven courage who had served in Spain or Africa. He was in a hurry to reach his province but was delayed in Rome by news of prodigies and by the expiatory rites for them. A public road had been struck by lightning in Veii, as had the forum and the temple of Jupiter in Lanuvium, the temple of Hercules in Ardea, and the wall, towers, and the temple

3   et aedes quae Alba dicitur; caelum ardere visum erat Ar-
reti; terra Velitris trium iugerum spatio caverna ingenti
desederat; Suessae Auruncae nuntiabant agnum cum duobus capitibus natum et Sinuessae porcum cum humano
4   capite. eorum prodigiorum causa supplicatio unum diem
habita, et consules rebus divinis operam dederunt placa-
5   tisque dis in provincias profecti sunt, Aelius cum Helvio
praetore in Galliam; exercitumque ab L. Lentulo acceptum, quem dimittere debebat, praetori tradidit, ipse novis
legionibus quas secum adduxerat bellum gesturus; neque
memorabilis rei quicquam gessit.

6      T.[15] Quinctius alter consul maturius quam priores soliti
erant consules a Brundisio cum tramisisset, Corcyram
tenuit cum octo milibus peditum equitibus quingentis.[16]
7   ab Corcyra in proxima Epiri quinqueremi traiecit et in
8   castra Romana magnis itineribus contendit. inde Villio
dimisso paucos moratus dies, dum se copiae ab Corcyra
adsequerentur, consilium habuit utrum recto itinere per
9   castra hostium vim facere conaretur, an ne temptata quidem re tanti laboris ac periculi per Dassaretios potius
10  Lyncumque tuto circuitu Macedoniam intraret; vicisset-
que ea sententia ni timuisset ne cum a mari longius reces-
sisset emisso e manibus hoste, si, quod antea fecerat, soli-
tudinibus silvisque se tutari rex voluisset, sine ullo effectu
11  aestas extraheretur. utcumque esset igitur, illo ipso tam

[15] T. *Par. 5741*: et T. *Bχ*
[16] quingentis *Bχ*: octingentis *Glar.*

---

[40] On the *supplicatio*, cf. 31.8.2 note.
[41] *Barr.* 49 C–D 3.

called the "White Temple" in Capua. In Arretium the sky appeared to be aflame, and at Velitrae the earth had subsided over an area of three *iugera*, leaving an enormous chasm. There were reports of the birth of a two-headed lamb at Suessa Aurunca and of a pig with a human head at Sinuessa. In view of these prodigies a one-day period of supplication[40] was held, and the consuls devoted themselves to the necessary religious ceremonies and set out for their provinces only after appeasing the gods. Aelius went with the praetor Helvius to Gaul and transferred to the praetor the army that he had taken over from Lentulus and was supposed to disband; his intention was to use the new legions that he had brought with him to conduct the war. In fact, he achieved no notable success.

The other consul, Titus Quinctius, having crossed from Brundisium earlier than had been the practice of former consuls, reached Corcyra with 8,000 infantry and 500 cavalry. He made the passage from Corcyra to the closest part of Epirus by quinquereme and hastened by forced marches to the Roman encampment. After relieving Villius of command, he waited there a few days for his troops to catch up with him from Corcyra and then held a meeting to consider whether to take the direct route and try to force a passage through the enemy camp or, alternatively, without even attempting such a strenuous and risky undertaking, to enter Macedonia by a safe detour through Dassaretis and Lyncus.[41] The second plan would have won the day but for Quinctius' fear that by moving further away from the sea he might let the enemy slip through his fingers—should the king decide to seek protection in the wilds and in the forests as he had done earlier—and the summer would be dragged out fruitlessly. And so, however

iniquo loco adgredi hostem placuit. sed magis fieri id placebat quam quomodo fieret satis expediebant; 10. diesque
quadraginta sine ullo conatu sedentes in conspectu hostium absumpserant.

Inde spes data Philippo est per Epirotarum gentem
2 temptandae pacis; habitoque concilio delecti ad eam rem
agendam Pausanias praetor et Alexander magister equitum consulem et regem, ubi in artissimas ripas Aous cogi-
3 tur amnis, in conloquium adduxerunt. summa postulato-
rum consulis erat: praesidia ex civitatibus rex deduceret;
iis quorum agros urbesque populatus esset redderet res
quae comparerent; ceterorum aequo arbitrio aestimatio
4 fieret. Philippus aliam aliarum civitatium condicionem
esse respondit: quas ipse cepisset, eas liberaturum; quae
sibi traditae a maioribus essent, earum hereditaria ac iusta
5 possessione non excessurum. si quas quererentur belli
clades eae civitates cum quibus bellatum foret, arbitro[17]
quo vellent populorum cum quibus pax utrisque fuisset se
6 usurum. consul nihil ad id quidem arbitro[18] aut iudice
opus esse dicere: cui enim non apparere ab eo qui prior
arma intulisset iniuriam ortam, nec Philippum ab ullis
7 bello lacessitum priorem vim omnibus fecisse? inde cum
ageretur quae civitates liberandae essent, Thessalos pri-

[17] arbitro ψ*Esc.*: arbitrio *B*φ
[18] arbitro *B*ψ*Lips. Esc.*: arbitrio φ

---

[42] Latin *praetor* and *magister equitum,* probably representing
Greek *strategos* (general) and *hipparchos* (cavalry commander).

[43] Rome, it is clear from what follows, is now demanding that
all the Greek states be evacuated by Macedonian forces.

it might turn out, they decided on a direct attack on the enemy despite the difficulty of the position. But the decision to take this action was firmer than their explanation of how to do it was clear; 10. and the Romans had now spent forty days sitting in sight of the enemy without making a move.

By this Philip was given hope that negotiations for peace could be attempted through the agency of the people of Epirus. A meeting was held at which the general Pausanias and cavalry commander Alexander[42] were selected for the task, and they brought consul and king to parley on the banks of the River Aous, where its channel is at its narrowest. The consul's terms were essentially as follows: The king would withdraw his garrisons from the city-states;[43] he was to restore any retrievable assets to those peoples whose land and cities he had pillaged; and an appraisal of the rest was to be made through nonpartisan arbitration. Philip replied that the standing of the various city-states differed from one to another. Those that he had captured himself he would liberate, but he would not relinquish possession of those passed down to him by his ancestors since they were legitimately his by right of inheritance. In the case of grievances lodged by states with which he had been at war over damage suffered during the conflict, he would defer to any arbitrator whom they might choose from among the peoples with whom both parties were at peace. The consul replied that there was no need for an arbiter or judge in the matter since it was clear to anyone that responsibility for injury lay with the aggressor, and Philip had in every case been the first to resort to force without provocation from anyone. Then, when discussion arose of which states were to be liberated,

mos omnium nominavit consul. ad id vero adeo accensus indignatione est rex ut exclamaret "quid victo gravius
8 imperares, T. Quincti?," atque ita se ex conloquio proripuit; et temperatum aegre est quin missilibus, quia dirempti medio amni fuerant, pugnam inter se consererent.
9 Postero die per excursiones ab stationibus primo in planitie satis ad id patenti multa levia commissa proelia
10 sunt; deinde recipientibus se regiis in arta et confragosa loca aviditate accensi certaminis eo quoque Romani pene-
11 travere. pro his ordo et militaris disciplina et genus armorum erat, aptum[19] tegendis corporibus; pro hoste loca et catapultae ballistaeque in omnibus prope rupibus quasi in
12 muro dispositae. multis hinc atque illinc volneribus acceptis cum etiam, ut in proelio iusto, aliquot cecidissent, nox pugnae finem fecit.

11. Cum in hoc statu res esset, pastor quidam a Charopo principe Epirotarum missus deducitur ad consulem.
2 is se, in eo saltu qui regiis tum teneretur castris armentum pascere solitum, ait omnes montium eorum anfractus cal-
3 lesque nosse: si secum aliquos consul mittere velit, se non iniquo nec perdifficili aditu super caput hostium eos educ-
4 turum.[20] haec ubi consul audivit, percunctatum ad Charopum mittit satisne credendum super tanta re agresti censeret: Charopus renuntiari iubet ita crederet ut suae

---

[19] aptum *Gel.*: amplum *Bχ*
[20] educturum *Gron.*: deducturum *Bχ*

---

[44] Cf. 6.1 above.

the consul first of all named the Thessalians. At this the king was so incensed that he cried out: "What heavier condition could you impose on a defeated man, Titus Quinctius?" and with that charged from the meeting. And the two were with difficulty dissuaded from fighting it out with projectiles, separated from each other as they were by the river between them.

The next day, following sallies from the outposts, there were at first numerous skirmishes on the plain, which was broad enough to accommodate them. Then the king's forces fell back on terrain that was constricted and rugged and the Romans, fired with enthusiasm for the fight, followed them into the area. Favoring the Romans were their order, their military discipline, and the nature of their armor, which was fashioned to protect the body; in favor of the enemy were the terrain and the catapults and slings deployed on almost all the cliffs as if on a wall. Many wounds had been dealt on both sides and there had also been some loss of life, as in a regular engagement, when night brought the battle to an end.

11. Such was the situation when a shepherd was brought to the consul, sent to him by Charopus,[44] a leading figure in Epirus. The man claimed that he usually grazed his flock in the valley now occupied by the king's camp and that he knew all the winding tracks and pathways in those mountains. If the consul were prepared to send some men with him, he said, he would lead them by a path that was not hazardous or excessively difficult to a point above the enemy. When the consul heard this, he sent a message to Charopus to inquire whether he thought the peasant could be trusted in a matter of such importance. Charopus had a message sent back that he should trust the man, but

5  potius omnia quam illius potestatis esset. cum magis vellet
credere quam auderet, mixtumque gaudio et metu animum gereret, auctoritate motus Charopi experiri spem
6  oblatam statuit et, ut averteret regem ab suspicione, biduo
insequenti lacessere hostem, dispositis ab omni parte copiis succedentibusque integris in locum defessorum, non
7  destitit. quattuor milia inde lecta peditum et trecentos
equites tribuno militum tradit. equites quoad loca patiantur ducere iubet: ubi ad inuia equiti ventum sit, in planitie
aliqua locari equitatum, pedites qua dux monstraret viam
8  ire; ubi, ut polliceatur, super caput hostium perventum sit,
fumo dare signum, nec antea clamorem tollere quam ab
9  se signo recepto pugnam coeptam arbitrari posset. nocte
itinera fieri iubet—et pernox forte luna erat—: interdiu
cibi quietisque sumeret tempus. ducem promissis ingentibus oneratum, si fides exstet, vinctum tamen tribuno
10  tradit. his copiis ita dimissis eo intentius Romanus undique instat contra[21] stationes.

12. Interim die tertio cum verticem quem petierant
Romani cepisse ac tenere se[22] fumo significarent, tum vero
trifariam divisis copiis consul valle media cum militum

---

[21] contra *Ogilvie*: capit *B*: capi χ: carpit *Harant*: circa
*McDonald*
[22] se χ: *om. B*

---

[45] As a full moon throughout the night occurs only near full
moon, the battle can be placed close to June 25, 198 (Briscoe
1.188).

added the proviso that overall control of the operation should rest in Flamininus' hands, not the shepherd's. It was a case of Flamininus wishing to trust the man rather than his taking a calculated risk, and his feelings were a mixture of elation and apprehension; but, swayed by Charopus' recommendation, he decided to put the prospect set before him to the test. To avert the king's suspicions, he kept up a relentless attack on the enemy during the two days that followed, deploying his forces in every quarter and bringing up fresh troops to relieve the weary. He then assigned 4,000 elite infantry and 300 cavalry to a military tribune. He told him to take the cavalry as far as the terrain permitted and, when they reached an area that a horseman could not negotiate, the cavalry should be left on some level ground while the infantry went ahead following the route indicated by the guide. On reaching the point above the enemy promised by the guide, the tribune was to send up a smoke signal but not raise the shout until, in his judgment, the signal had been received and the battle begun. Flamininus ordered him to make the journey at night—and there happened to be a full moon through the night[45]—and use the daytime for eating and resting. As for the guide, he heaped extravagant promises on him in the event of his proving reliable, but handed him over to the tribune in irons. The troops thus dispatched on their mission, the Roman commander mounted attacks on the king's outposts all the more vigorously from every side.

12. Two days after they set out the Romans were sending up the smoke signal to indicate they had taken, and were holding, the bluff that had been their objective. The consul thereupon split his forces into three parts, made his way up the middle of the valley with the main strength of

robore succedit, cornua dextra laevaque admovet castris;
2 nec segnius hostes obviam eunt. et dum aviditate certaminis provecti extra munitiones pugnant, haud paulo superior est Romanus miles et virtute et scientia et genere
3 armorum: postquam multis volneratis interfectisque recepere se regii in loca aut munimento aut natura tuta, ver-
terat periculum in Romanos temere in loca iniqua nec
4 faciles ad receptum angustias progressos. neque impunita
temeritate inde recepissent sese, ni clamor primum ab
tergo auditus, dein pugna etiam coepta amentes repentino
5 terrore regios fecisset. pars in fugam effusi sunt; pars magis quia locus fugae deerat quam quod animi satis esset ad
pugnam cum substitissent, ab hoste et a fronte et ab tergo
6 urgente circumventi sunt. deleri totus exercitus potuit si
7 fugientes persecuti victores essent; sed equitem angustiae
locorumque asperitas, peditem armorum gravitas impe-
8 diit. rex primo effuse ac sine respectu fugit; dein quinque
milium spatium progressus cum ex iniquitate locorum, id
quod erat, suspicatus esset sequi non posse hostem, substitit in tumulo quodam, dimisitque suos per omnia iuga
9 vallesque qui palatos in unum conligerent. non plus duobus milibus hominum amissis, cetera omnis multitudo,
velut signum aliquod secuta, in unum cum convenisset,
10 frequenti agmine petunt Thessaliam. Romani quoad tu-

his army, and brought the right and left wings to bear
on the king's camp. The enemy showed no less spirit in
confronting him. They surged forward in their eagerness
for combat and fought outside their fortifications, but the
Roman soldiers enjoyed no small advantage in terms of
their courage, expertise, and the nature of their weapons.
When, however, after suffering many wounds and much
loss of life, the king's men withdrew to positions that were
protected by defense works or natural features, the danger
recoiled upon the Romans, who had thoughtlessly advanced into rough terrain and cramped spots that afforded
no easy means of retreat. They would not in fact have
pulled back from that position without paying for their
recklessness had the battle cry not been heard to their
rear, followed by fighting breaking out, which drove the
king's men out of their minds with sudden panic. Some
scattered in flight. Others stood their ground, more from
lack of a place to escape than because they had sufficient
mettle for the fight, and were surrounded by an enemy
bearing down on them front and rear. The entire army
could have been annihilated had the victors pursued the
fleeing Macedonians, but the restricted and rugged terrain hampered the cavalry while the weight of their arms
hampered the infantry. The king first of all took to headlong flight without a backward glance. Then, after five
miles, suspecting that his enemy could not keep up because of the rough ground (which was in fact the case), he
halted on a knoll and sent off some of his men through all
the hills and valleys to gather his scattered troops together
in one spot. No more than 2,000 had been lost; the rest of
the crowd, as if they had been responding to a signal, all
assembled in one spot, and then headed for Thessaly in a

tum fuit insecuti, caedentes spoliantesque caesos, castra
regia, etiam sine defensoribus difficili aditu, diripiunt; atque ea nocte in suis castris manserunt.

13. Postero die consul per ipsas angustias quas inter
2 valle se flumen insinuat hostem sequitur. rex primo die ad
castra Pyrrhi pervenit; locus quem ita vocant est in Triphylia terrae Molottidis. inde postero die—ingens iter agmini,
3 sed metus urgebat—in montes Lyncon perrexit. ipsi Epiri
sunt, interiecti Macedoniae Thessaliaeque: latus, quod
vergit in Thessaliam, oriens spectat, septentrio a Macedonia obicitur. vestiti frequentibus silvis sunt; iuga summa
4 campos patentes aquasque perennes habent. ibi stativis
rex per aliquot dies habitis fluctuatus animo est utrum
protinus in regnum se reciperet, an praeverti in Thessa-
5 liam posset. inclinavit sententia ut in Thessaliam agmen
demitteret, Triccamque proximis limitibus petit; inde ob-
6 vias urbes raptim peragravit. homines qui sequi possent
sedibus excibat, oppida incendebat. rerum suarum quas
possent ferendarum secum dominis ius fiebat, cetera mili-
7 tis praeda erat; nec quod ab hoste crudelius pati possent
reliqui quicquam fuit quam quae ab sociis patiebantur.
8 haec etiam facienti Philippo acerba erant, sed e terra mox
futura hostium corpora saltem eripere sociorum volebat.
9 ita evastata oppida sunt Phacium Piresiae[23] Euhydrium
Eretria Palaepharsalus. Pheras cum peteret exclusus, quia

---

[23] Piresiae *Leake*: Iresiae $B\chi$

---

[46] Not in *Barr.* According to Hammond (*Epirus,* 280–81),
northeast of Konitsa and some thirty-two miles east of the end of
the gorge.    [47] *Barr.* 49 D3    [48] *Barr.* 55 B1(Trikka).
[49] Towns in Phthiotis (*Barr.* 55 C–D2).

dense column. The Romans followed as far as they could in safety, killing stragglers and stripping their bodies. They looted the king's camp, difficult to get at even in the absence of defenders, and then spent that night in their own.

13. The following day the consul tracked his enemy through the gorge through which the river winds down the valley. As for the king, he reached the Camp of Pyrrhus[46] on the first day (the area bearing this name is in Triphylia, in the territory of Molossis), and on the next he made it as far as the Lyncus mountains[47]—an enormous march for an army, but fear was driving them on. These mountains are in Epirus, lying between Macedonia and Thessaly; their Thessalian side faces east, and their northern abuts Macedonia. They are thickly forested and their crests have broad plateaus and year-round springs. Here the king encamped for several days, and debated whether he should immediately retreat into his kingdom or whether he could possibly reach Thessaly before his enemy. Deciding finally to take the army down into Thessaly, he made for Tricca[48] by the shortest routes and from there swiftly marched through the towns on his route. The men who were able to follow him he called from their homes and burned the towns. Homeowners were granted the right to take with them from their houses all the possessions they could, and what remained became the booty of the common soldier. These people suffered everything—no cruel treatment inflicted by an enemy could have surpassed what they endured at the hands of their allies. Philip found these steps repugnant even as he was taking them, but he wanted at least to rescue his allies as living beings from a land that was soon to be his enemies.' As a result the towns of Phacium, Piresiae, Euhydrium, Eretria, and Palaepharsalus[49] were destroyed. When Philip then made for Pherae, he

res egebat mora si expugnare vellet, nec tempus erat,
omisso incepto in Macedoniam transcendit; nam etiam
Aetolos adpropinquare fama erat.

10     Qui audito proelio quod circa amnem Aoum factum
erat, proximis prius evastatis circa Sperchias et Macran
quam vocant Comen, transgressi inde in Thessaliam Cti-
11 menes[24] et Angeias primo impetu potiti sunt. a Metropoli,
dum vastant agros, concursu oppidanorum ad tuenda
moenia facto repulsi sunt. Callithera inde adgressi, similem impetum oppidanorum pertinacius sustinuerunt;
12 compulsisque intra moenia qui eruperant, contenti ea victoria, quia spes nulla admodum expugnandi erat, abces-
serunt. Teuma inde et Celathara vicos expugnant diri-
13 piuntque; Acharras per deditionem receperunt. Xyniae
14 simili metu a cultoribus desertae sunt. hoc sedibus suis
extorre agmen in praesidium incidit quod ad Thaumacos[25]
quo tutior frumentatio esset ducebatur: incondita iner-
misque multitudo, mixta et imbelli turba, ab armatis caesa
15 est; Xyniae desertae diripiuntur. Cyphaera inde Aetoli
capiunt, opportune Dolopiae imminens castellum. haec
raptim intra paucos dies ab Aetolis gesta. nec Amynander

---

[24] Ctimenes *Niese*: Cymenes *B*: Cymines φ: Cimines ψ

[25] ad Thaumacos *Rubenius*: adthaumacum *B*: athaumacum
*AP*: atheumacum ψ

---

[50] *Barr.* 55 C3 (Spercheiai, Makra Kome).

[51] *Barr.* 55 B2 (Ktimene) and B3 (Angeia).

[52] Metropolis and Kallithera: *Barr.* 55 B2.

[53] Acherrae is possibly Ekkara on Lake Xyniae, and Xyniae is
a town on the far side of the lake: *Barr.* 55 C2.

[54] On Thaumaci (Thaumakoi) cf. 4.1, above, and note.

was shut out from the town; and since storming it meant halting and he had not the time, he dropped the idea and crossed into Macedonia, for there was also talk of the approach of the Aetolians.

After hearing of the battle fought at the River Aous, the Aetolians had at first pillaged the areas closest to them, around Sperchiae and Macra (the one called Macra Come),[50] and then, passing into Thessaly, they took Ctimene and Angeia[51] at the first assault. They were driven from Metropolis as they ravaged the fields, when the townspeople hurriedly assembled to defend their walls. Attacking Callithera[52] next, they put up a stouter fight against a similar counterattack from the townspeople; forcing back within their walls those who had made the sortie, they contented themselves with this measure of victory and left because there was simply no hope of taking the town by assault. They went on to storm and pillage the villages of Teuma and Celathara, and accepted the surrender of Acharrae. Xyniae[53] was deserted by its inhabitants from fear of similar treatment. Here, the column of refugees fleeing their homes encountered a contingent of troops being taken to Thaumaci[54] to offer protection for the foraging operations there, and the disorderly, unarmed crowd, including a group of noncombatants, was cut down by armed soldiers. Deserted Xyniae was ransacked. The Aetolians then captured Cyphaera, a fortress that, overlooking Dolopia,[55] was of tactical importance. Such was the swift progress made by the Aetolians in a matter of days. But, after receiving news of the Romans'

55 Dolopia: *Barr.* 55 B2, but site of Cyphaera is uncertain.

atque Athamanes post famam prosperae pugnae Romanorum quieverunt.

14. Ceterum Amynander, quia suo militi parum fidebat petito a consule modico praesidio, cum Gomphos peteret, oppidum protinus nomine Phaecam, situm inter Gomphos faucesque angustas quae ab Athamania Thessaliam

2 dirimunt, vi cepit. inde Gomphos adortus, et[26] per aliquot dies summa vi tuentes urbem, cum iam scalas ad moenia

3 erexisset, eo demum[27] metu perpulit ad deditionem. haec traditio Gomphorum ingentem terrorem Thessalis intulit. dedidere deinceps sese qui Argenta quique Pherinium et Timarum et Ligynas et Strymonem et Lampsum habent, aliaque castella iuxta ignobilia.

4　　Dum Athamanes Aetolique submoto Macedonum metu in aliena victoria suam praedam faciunt, Thessaliaque ab tribus simul exercitibus incerta quem hostem

5 quemve socium crederet vastatur, consul faucibus quas fuga hostium aperuerat in regionem Epiri transgressus, etsi probe scit cui parti Charopo principe excepto Epiro-

6 tae favissent, tamen quia ab satisfaciendi quoque cura imperata enixe facere videt, ex praesenti eos potius quam ex praeterito aestimat habitu, et ea ipsa facilitate veniae

7 animos eorum in posterum conciliat. missis deinde nuntiis Corcyram ut onerariae naves in sinum venirent Ambra-

---

[26] adortus et *B*χ: adortus est et *Weiss.*: adortus est *Madvig*
[27] eo demum *Perizonius*: eodem *B*χ

---

[56] Gomphi: *Barr.* 55 B2; Phaeca B1.
[57] None of these towns is otherwise known.

successful engagement, Amynander and the Athamanians did not remain inactive either.

14. As he had little confidence in his own men, Amynander requested a modest squadron of troops from the consul. He then headed for Gomphi and straightway took by assault a town called Phaeca,[56] which lies between Gomphi and the narrow pass separating Thessaly from Athamania. Next he attacked Gomphi. For several days the inhabitants defended their city with all their might, and it was only by setting up scaling ladders on the walls that he eventually frightened them into capitulation. The surrender of Gomphi struck sheer terror into the Thessalians. After that, the inhabitants of Argenta, Pherinium, Timarus, Ligynae, Strymon, Lampsus,[57] and other fortified towns of little importance close by all surrendered in turn.

Their fear of Macedon removed, the Athamanians and the Aetolians were now making their own the spoils of another's victory, and Thessaly was simultaneously suffering devastation at the hands of three armies without knowing which to believe an enemy or which an ally. In the meantime the consul slipped into the region of Epirus by the pass that his enemy's flight had left open. Although he knew full well which side was favored by the Epirotes (with the sole exception of their leading citizen, Charopus), he could see that, from a desire to gratify him, they were making every effort to carry out his bidding. He therefore set more store by their present than by their past disposition, and simply by his readiness to forgive he won over their support for the future. Then, after sending messengers to Corcyra with orders for cargo vessels to come

cium, ipse progressus modicis itineribus quarto die in
monte Cercetio posuit castra, eodem Amynandro cum suis
8 auxiliis accito, non tam virium eius egens quam ut duces
in Thessaliam haberet. ab eodem consilio et plerique Epirotarum voluntarii inter auxilia accepti.

15. Primam urbem Thessaliae Phaloriam est adgressus. duo milia Macedonum in praesidio habebat, qui
primo summa vi restiterunt, quantum arma quantum
2 moenia tueri poterant; sed oppugnatio continua, non
nocte non die remissa, cum consul in eo verti crederet
ceterorum Thessalorum animos, si primi vim Romanam
3 non sustinuissent, vicit pertinaciam Macedonum. capta
Phaloria legati a Metropoli et a Cierio[28] dedentes urbes
venerunt: venia iis petentibus datur; Phaloria incensa ac
4 direpta est. inde Aeginium petit; quem locum cum vel
modico praesidio tutum ac prope inexpugnabilem vidisset, paucis in stationem proximam telis coniectis ad Gomphorum regionem agmen vertit.
5 Degressusque in campos Thessaliae, cum iam omnia
exercitui deessent, quia Epirotarum pepercerat agris,
explorato ante utrum Leucadem an sinum Ambracium
onerariae tenuissent, frumentatum Ambraciam in vicem
6 cohortes misit; et est iter a Gomphis Ambraciam sicut

---

[28] Cierio *Leake*: Piera *ϕLN*: Pirea *VPar.*: Pierio *McDonald*

---

[58] On the borders of Epirus and Thessaly according to Briscoe
(1.192) and Mineo (Budé n. 127), but not in *Barrington*.

[59] Tentatively identified in *Barrington* (55 B1 Phaloreia).

[60] Metropolis: *Barr.* 55 B2; Cierium: C2 (Kierion).

[61] *Barr.* 54 D2 (Aiginion), but see Briscoe 1.193.

[62] Leucas, Ambracian Gulf, Ambracia: *Barr.* 54 C3–4.

into the Ambracian Gulf, Flamininus himself advanced by short stages and three days later pitched camp on Mount Cercetius.[58] He summoned Amynander with his auxiliaries to this same spot, not because he needed his reinforcement but to have guides for the march into Thessaly. It was from the same motive that several Epirote volunteers were accepted as members of his auxiliary forces.

15. The first city that Flamininus attacked in Thessaly was Phaloria.[59] This had a garrison of 2,000 Macedonians, who at first resisted with all their might, protecting themselves as far as they could with their weapons and defensive walls. However, the continuous assault, night and day without respite, crushed the Macedonians' resolve—the consul believed it crucial for the morale of the other Thessalians if the enemy he first encountered failed to withstand the Roman onslaught. When Phaloria was taken, deputations came from Metropolis and Cierium[60] to surrender their towns; they asked for mercy and were granted it, but Phaloria was burned and pillaged. Flamininus then made for Aeginium,[61] but when he saw the place was secured and rendered virtually impregnable even by its small garrison, he redirected his army toward the region of Gomphi after merely hurling a few projectiles at the closest outpost.

He then went down into the plains of Thessaly, but since by now his army was short of all provisions because he had spared the farmlands of Epirus, he sent ahead to ascertain whether the transport ships had put in at Leucas or the Ambracian Gulf, and then sent his companies out one by one to Ambracia to gather supplies.[62] The road from Gomphi to Ambracia is awkward and difficult, but it

7 impeditum ac difficile, ita spatio perbrevi. intra paucos
itaque dies transvectis a mari commeatibus repleta omni
8 rerum copia sunt castra. inde Atragem est profectus. decem ferme milia ab Larisa abest; ex Perrhaebia oriundi
9 sunt; sita est urbs super Peneum amnem. nihil trepidavere
Thessali ad primum adventum Romanorum; et Philippus
sicut in Thessaliam ipse progredi non audebat, ita intra
Tempe stativis positis, ut quisque locus ab hoste tempta-
batur praesidia per occasiones submittebat.

16. Sub idem fere tempus quo consul adversus Philip-
2 pum primum in Epiri faucibus posuit castra, et L. Quinctius frater consulis, cui classis cura maritimaeque orae
imperium mandatum ab senatu erat, cum duabus quin-
3 queremibus Corcyram travectus, postquam profectam
inde classem audivit nihil morandum ratus, cum ad Samen
insulam adsecutus esset, dimisso C. Livio,[29] cui successe-
4 rat, tarde inde ad Maleum, trahendis plerumque remulco
5 navibus quae cum commeatu sequebantur, pervenit. a
Maleo, iussis ceteris quantum maxime possent maturare
sequi, ipse tribus quinqueremibus expeditis Piraeum
praecedit, accepitque naves relictas ibi ab L. Apustio le-
6 gato ad praesidium Athenarum. Eodem tempore duae ex
Asia classes profectae, una cum Attalo rege—eae quattuor
et viginti quinqueremes erant—, Rhodia altera viginti

---

[29] C. Livio *H.J.M.*: Livio *B*: Libio χ

---

[63] Atrax, Larissa, River Peneios: *Barr.* 55 C1.

[64] Tempe is the continuation of the Peneios valley northeast
of Larisa, between Mt. Olympus and Mt. Ossa (*Barr.* 55 D1).

[65] Strictly, a town on the island of Cephallenia (*Barr.* 54 C5),
but Livy, like Homer (*Od.* 9.24, 16.249), calls the island Same.

is also short. Thus, within a few days, thanks to supplies transported from the coast, the camp was replete with all manner of provisions. From here Flamininus set out for Atrax. This is about ten miles from Larisa, and its people hail originally from Perrhaebia; the city lies above the River Peneus.[63] The Thessalians felt no alarm at the arrival of the Romans; and Philip, while not venturing to advance into Thessaly himself, established a base inside the Vale of Tempe[64] and, as need arose, sent out military assistance to any point under enemy pressure.

16. At about the time that the consul first encamped opposite Philip in the gorge in Epirus, his brother Lucius Quinctius, who had been assigned charge of the fleet and command of the coast by the senate, also crossed to Corcyra with two quinqueremes. When told that the fleet had left Corcyra, Quinctius, thinking he should waste no time, followed it to the island of Same.[65] Here he dismissed Gaius Livius,[66] whom he had succeeded, and came at a slow pace from Same to Maleum,[67] for most of the voyage towing the ships that were following him loaded with supplies. Instructing the rest of his fleet to follow him as speedily as they could, he himself went ahead from Maleum with three light quinqueremes to Piraeus, and assumed command of the ships left there for the defense of Athens by the legate Lucius Apustius. At the same time two fleets set off from Asia, the one, under King Attalus, consisting of twenty-four quinqueremes, and the other a

[66] This is probably C. Livius Salinator (29), curule aedile in 204, praetor in 202 (and later in 191), and consul in 188.

[67] Cape Malea, at the southeastern tip of the Peloponnese.

7 navium tectarum; Acesimbrotus[30] praeerat. hae circa Andrum insulam classes coniunctae Euboeam, inde exiguo
8 distantem freto, traiecerunt. Carystiorum primum agros
vastarunt; deinde, ubi Carystus praesidio a Chalcide rap-
9 tim misso firma visa est, ad Eretriam accesserunt. eodem
et L. Quinctius cum iis navibus quae Piraei fuerant, Attali
regis adventu audito, venit, iussis ut quaeque ex sua classe
venissent naves Euboeam petere.
10     Eretria summa vi oppugnabatur; nam et trium iuncta-
rum classium naves omnis generis tormenta machinasque
ad urbium excidia secum portabant, et agri adfatim mate-
11 riae praebebant ad nova molienda opera. oppidani primo
impigre[31] tuebantur moenia; dein fessi volneratique aliquot, cum et muri partem eversam operibus hostium cer-
12 nerent, ‹. . .›[32] ad deditionem inclinarent. sed praesidium
erat Macedonum, quos non minus quam Romanos metue-
bant, et Philocles regius praefectus a Chalcide nuntios
mittebat se in tempore adfuturum si sustinerent obsidi-
13 onem. haec mixta metu spes ultra quam vellent aut quam
14 possent trahere eos tempus cogebat; deinde, postquam
Philoclen repulsum trepidantemque refugisse Chalcidem

30 Acesimbrotus *Niese*: Hagesimbrotus *B*ψa: Hagessimbrotus
φ

31 impigre *L²*: haud impigre *B*ψ: ut impigre φ: haud pigre
*Whitte*: haud segniter *H.J.M.*

32 *spat. ante* ad deditionem inclinarunt *B*: *sic, sed* inclinarent
*AE*: ‹. . . ut . . .›. . . inclinarent *McDonald*

68 The Rhodian commander; cf. 31.46.6–47.2.
69 Carystus: at the southern tip of Euboea (*Barr.* 57 C3).
70 I.e., of the Rhodians, Attalus, and the Romans.

Rhodian fleet of twenty ships with decks, which Acesim-brotus[68] commanded. These fleets joined up off the island of Andros and crossed to Euboea, which is separated from Andros by a narrow strait. At first they raided the farm-lands of the Carystians;[69] but when it looked as though Carystus was well protected, a relief force having been swiftly dispatched from Chalcis, they moved on to Eretria. After he heard of King Attalus' arrival here, Lucius Quinc-tius also came to Eretria with the ships from Piraeus, hav-ing left orders for each vessel of his fleet to head for Eu-boea on reaching Piraeus.

Eretria was now being subjected to a full-scale attack, as the ships of the three combined fleets[70] were carrying on board all manner of slings and contrivances designed to smash cities, and the countryside provided an abun-dance of wood for building new siege engines. At first the townspeople mounted a vigorous defense of their walls. Later, exhausted and with a number wounded, and also perceiving that a section of their wall had been demol-ished by the enemy's siege engines ‹. . .›[71] they were more disposed to surrender. There was, however, a Macedonian garrison present, which they feared as much as they did the Romans; and the king's prefect, Philocles,[72] kept send-ing them messages from Chalcis to say that he would ar-rive with help at the appropriate moment if they held out against the siege. This mixture of hope and fear prolonged their resistance beyond their wishes or their powers, but then, on receiving the news that Philocles, defeated and in panic, had fled back to Chalcis, they immediately sent

71 There appears to be a lacuna at this point; see textual note.
72 Cf. 31.16.2 and note.

acceperunt, oratores extemplo ad Attalum veniam fidem-
15 que eius petentes miserunt. dum in spem pacis intenti
segnius munera belli obeunt, et ea modo parte qua murus
dirutus erat, ceteris neglectis, stationes armatas opponunt,
Quinctius noctu ab ea parte quae minime suspecta erat
16 impetu facto scalis urbem cepit. oppidanorum omnis multitudo cum coniugibus ac liberis in arcem confugit, deinde
in deditionem venit. pecuniae aurique et argenti haud
17 sane multum fit; signa tabulae priscae artis ornamentaque
eius generis plura quam pro urbis magnitudine aut opibus
ceteris inventa.

17. Carystus inde repetita, unde priusquam e navibus
copiae exponerentur omnis multitudo urbe deserta in ar-
2 cem confugit. inde ad fidem ab Romano petendam oratores mittunt. oppidanis exemplo vita ac libertas concessa
est: Macedonibus nummi treceni in capita statutum pre-
3 tium est et ut armis traditis abirent. hac summa redempti
inermes in Boeotiam traiecti. navales copiae, duabus claris
urbibus Euboeae intra dies paucos captis, circumvectae
Sunium, Atticae terrae promunturium, Cenchreas Corin-
thiorum emporium petierunt.

4 Consul interim omnium spe longiorem Atragis[33] atro-
cioremque oppugnationem habuit, et ea qua minimum
5 credidisset resistebant hostes. nam omnem laborem in

---

[33] Atragis *suppl. McDonald*: Atracis *Heusinger*: *om.* B$\chi$

---

[73] *nummus* (lit. "coin") can refer to various currencies and
values, and here probably to Greek drachmas, which the Romans
would need for supplies.
[74] Corinth had two, Cenchreae on the Saronic Gulf, and
Lechaeum on the Corinthian Gulf. Cf. 23.3–4 below; *Barr.* 58 D2.

spokesmen to Attalus asking for his pardon and protection. Meanwhile, with their attention focused on hopes of peace, they were remiss in the performance of their military duties and, neglecting all other areas, stationed armed patrols only at the spot where the wall lay in ruins. Quinctius therefore made a night attack at a point where it was least expected and took the town by means of scaling ladders. The occupants fled en masse to the citadel with their wives and children and then capitulated. Not much was forthcoming in terms of coined money or gold and silver, but there were more statues, pictures by old masters and artwork of that kind than one might have expected, given the size of the town and its other resources.

17. They then went back to Carystus where, before the troops could be disembarked, the entire population abandoned the town and sought refuge in the citadel. From there they sent spokesmen to ask protection of the Romans. The townspeople were immediately granted their lives and freedom, but a ransom of 300 *nummi*[73] per person was established for the Macedonians, who were also permitted to leave on condition that they surrender their arms. After paying the ransom the Macedonians crossed unarmed to Boeotia. The naval forces, which had now taken two famous Euboean cities in a few days, rounded Sunium, the promontory of Attica, and made for Cenchreae, a commercial port of Corinth.[74]

Meanwhile, the consul's assault on Atrax was turning out to be longer and more ferocious than anyone had anticipated, and the enemy were resisting in a manner he had not at all expected. He had believed that all his efforts

muro crediderat diruendo fore: si aditum armatis in urbem patefecisset, fugam inde caedemque hostium fore,
6 qualis captis urbibus fieri solet; ceterum postquam parte
muri arietibus decussa per ipsas ruinas transcenderunt in
urbem armati, illud principium velut novi atque integri
7 laboris fuit. nam Macedones qui in praesidio erant et multi
et delecti, gloriam etiam egregiam rati si armis potius et
8 virtute quam moenibus urbem tuerentur, conferti pluribus introrsus ordinibus acie firmata, cum transcendere
ruinas sensissent Romanos, per impeditum ac difficilem
ad receptum locum expulerunt.
9    Id consul aegre passus, nec eam ignominiam ad unius
modo oppugnandae moram urbis sed ad summam universi
belli pertinere ratus, quod ex momentis parvarum plerumque rerum penderet, purgato loco qui strage semiruti
10 muri cumulatus erat, turrim ingentis altitudinis, magnam
vim armatorum multiplici tabulato portantem, promovit,
11 et cohortes in vicem sub signis quae cuneum Macedonum—phalangem ipsi vocant—, si possent, vi perrum-
12 perent emittebat. sed ad loci angustias, haud late patente
intervallo diruti muri, genus armorum pugnaeque hosti
13 aptius erat. ubi conferti hastas ingentis longitudinis prae
se Macedones obiecissent, velut in constructam densitate

---

75 Cf. 31.39.10 and note.

would be focused on demolishing the wall, and that if he had opened up a path into the town for his soldiers the enemy would be put to flight and butchered, the usual sequence of events when towns are captured. However, when part of the wall had been shattered by the battering rams and the soldiers had then climbed over the debris into the town, this proved only to be the start of a new effort, in which all was to be done over again. For the Macedonians in the garrison, a large number of elite soldiers, thought it would be a spectacular and glorious feat to defend the town with their weapons and courage rather than by its fortifications. They moved closer together and strengthened their fighting line by introducing more ranks; then, when they realized the Romans were clambering over the ruins of the wall, they drove them back across a space that was obstructed and from which retreat was difficult.

This infuriated the consul. He saw the ignominious setback not only as prolonging the siege of a single city but as affecting the outcome of the entire war, which is very often contingent upon the impact of minor events. He cleared the area that was filled with the rubble of the half-demolished wall and brought forward a tower of enormous height that carried a large number of soldiers on its multiple stories. He also sent out his cohorts one after the other and in regular formation in order to smash, if they could, the Macedonian wedge, which Macedonians themselves call a "phalanx,"[75] by the violence of their charge. But besides the restricted space (the gap where the wall had been broken down was not wide), the type of weapons employed and the nature of the fighting also favored the enemy. The Macedonians, in close order, held out before

209

clipeorum testudinem Romani pilis nequiquam emissis
14 cum strinxissent gladios, neque congredi propius neque
praecidere hastas poterant, et si quam incidissent aut
praefregissent, hastile fragmento ipso acuto inter spicula
15 integrarum hastarum velut vallum explebat. ad hoc et
muri pars utraque integra tuta praestabat latera, nec ex
longo spatio aut cedendum aut impetus faciendus erat,
16 quae res turbare ordines solet. accessit etiam fortuita res
ad animos eorum firmandos; nam cum turris per aggerem
17 parum densati soli ageretur, rota una in altiorem orbitam
depressa ita turrim inclinavit ut speciem ruentis hostibus
trepidationemque insanam[34] superstantibus armatis praebuerit.

18. Cum parum quicquam succederet, consul minime
aequo animo comparationem militum generisque armo-
2 rum fieri patiebatur, simul nec maturam expugnandi spem
nec rationem procul a mari et in evastatis belli cladibus
locis hibernandi ullam cernebat.

3 Itaque relicta obsidione, quia nullus in tota Acarnaniae
atque Aetoliae ora portus erat qui simul et omnes onera-
4 rias quae commeatum exercitui portabant caperet, et tecta
ad hibernandum legionibus praeberet, Anticyra in Phocide in Corinthium versa sinum ad id opportunissime sita

___

[34] insanam χ: *om. B*: ingentem *vel* non vanam *Madvig*: unam
*H.J.M.*: *obelo utitur Briscoe*

___

[76] The sarissas; cf 31.39.10 and note.

[77] The famed *testudo;* cf. 31.39.14 and note.

[78] The comparisons were presumably made by his own soldiers as well as the enemy's.

them lances of extraordinary length,[76] while the Romans hurled their spears to no effect against the solid mass of their shields, built up into what was virtually a tortoise formation.[77] Then, when they drew their swords, they found they could neither engage in hand-to-hand fighting nor lop off the ends of the Macedonian lances (and if they did manage to sever or break the odd one, the broken tip itself was sharp and the shaft, standing amid the heads of the unbroken lances, still played its part alongside them in forming a sort of palisade). Furthermore, the as-yet intact sections of the wall on either side sheltered the Macedonian flanks, and to fall back or make a charge they did not need to cover a lot of ground, something that usually brings disorder to the ranks. In addition, a chance occurrence served to encourage them. When the tower was being maneuvered over a piece of loosely packed soil one of its wheels sank into quite a deep rut, and this made the tower slant at such an angle that it gave the enemy the impression that it was toppling over and also filled the soldiers standing on it with insane panic.

18. Enjoying little success, the consul was not at all happy that he was allowing comparisons to be made between the soldiers of the two sides and the types of weapons involved.[78] At the same time he could see neither any prospect of quickly taking the town nor any means of spending the winter far from the sea in a region laid waste by the ravages of warfare.

He therefore abandoned the siege. There was no port on the entire coastline of Acarnania and Aetolia that could harbor all the cargo vessels carrying supplies for the army and also provide winter accommodation for the legions. Anticyra in Phocis, which faces the Corinthian Gulf,

5 visa, quia nec procul Thessalia hostiumque locis aberat, et
ex adverso Peloponnesum exiguo maris spatio divisam, ab
tergo Aetoliam Acarnaniamque, ab lateribus Locridem ac
6 Boeotiam habebat. Phocidis primo impetu Phanoteam
sine certamine cepit. Anticyra haud multum in oppug-
7 nando[35] morae praebuit. Ambryssus inde Hyampolisque
receptae. Daulis, quia in tumulo excelso sita est, nec scalis
8 nec operibus capi poterat: lacessendo missilibus eos qui in
praesidio erant cum ad excursiones elicuissent, refugi-
endo in vicem insequendoque et levibus sine effectu certaminibus eo neglegentiae et contemptus adduxerunt ut
cum refugientibus in portam permixti impetum Romani
9 facerent. et alia ignobilia castella Phocidis terrore magis
quam armis in potestatem venerunt. Elatia clausit portas,
nec, nisi vi cogerentur, recepturi moenibus videbantur aut
ducem aut exercitum Romanum.

19. Elatiam obsidenti consuli rei maioris spes adfulsit,
Achaeorum gentem ab societate regia in Romanam ami-
2 citiam avertendi. Cycliadan principem factionis ad Philippum trahentium res expulerant; Aristaenus, qui Romanis
3 gentem iungi volebat, praetor erat. classis Romana cum

---

[35] in oppugnando χ: oppugnando B

---

[79] Anticyra is some nine miles southeast of Delphi on the
south coast of Phocis (*Barr.* 55 D4). Aetolia, in fact, is due west
of Phocis, and Acarnania west of Aetolia.

[80] For Phanotea (Phanotis) and the other towns in this chapter, cf. *Barr.* 55 D3–4.

[81] After Delphi, the most important town of Phocis.

[82] Cycliadas had been a pro-Macedonian *strategos* of the

seemed best situated for that: it was not far from Thessaly and the territory of his enemies, and it had the Peloponnese opposite, separated by a narrow stretch of sea, with Aetolia and Acarnania to the rear, and Locris and Boeotia on its flanks.[79] Flamininus captured Phanotea[80] in Phocis with his first assault and without a struggle; the attack on Anticyra did not long delay him; after that Ambrysus and Hyampolis were both taken. Because Daulis occupied a position on a lofty prominence it could be captured neither by scaling ladders nor siege works. Flamininus' men therefore enticed the members of the garrison to make sorties by provoking them with projectiles. Then, alternating retreat and pursuit and engaging the enemy in inconsequential skirmishes, they induced in them such slackness and disdain that the Romans were able to infiltrate their ranks as they withdrew to the city gate and thus make their attack on the town. Other Phocian strongholds of slight importance also came into Flaminus' hands more from fear than as a result of battle. Elatia,[81] however, closed its gates, and it looked as though its inhabitants would receive neither the Roman leader nor his army within their walls unless compelled by force.

19. While he was blockading Elatia, a glimmer of hope of achieving something greater came to the consul, namely turning the Achaean nation from its alliance with the king to a treaty with Rome. The Achaeans had driven out Cycliadas, leader of the faction urging support for Philip, and their praetor was Aristaenus[82] who wanted his people allied to Rome. The Roman fleet, along with Attalus and the

Achaean League (cf. 31.25.3 and note); Aristaenus, a staunch supporter of the Romans, was League *strategos* in 199/8.

Attalo et Rhodiis Cenchreis stabat, parabantque communi
4 omnes consilio Corinthum oppugnare. optimum igitur
ratus est, priusquam eam rem adgrederentur, legatos ad
gentem Achaeorum mitti, pollicentes, si ab rege ad Romanos defecissent, Corinthum contributuros in antiquum
5 gentis concilium. auctore consule legati a fratre eius L.
Quinctio et Attalo et Rhodiis et Atheniensibus ad Achaeos
missi. Sicyone datum est iis concilium.
6    Erat autem non admodum simplex habitus inter
Achaeos animorum: terrebat Nabis Lacedaemonius, gra-
7 vis et adsiduus hostis; horrebant Romana arma; Macedonum beneficiis et veteribus et recentibus obligati erant;
regem ipsum suspectum habebant pro eius crudelitate
8 perfidiaque, neque ex iis quae tum ad tempus faceret aes-
timantes graviorem post bellum dominum futurum cerne-
9 bant. neque solum quid in senatu quisque civitatis suae
aut in communibus conciliis gentis pro sentenda dicerent
10 ignorabant, sed ne ipsis quidem secum cogitantibus quid
vellent aut quid optarent[36] satis constabat. ad homines ita
incertos introductis legatis potestas dicendi facta est.
11    Romanus primum legatus L. Calpurnius, deinde Attali
12 regis legati, post eos Rhodii disseruerunt; Philippi deinde
legatis potestas dicendi facta est; postremi Athenienses, ut

[36] optarent *Bχ*: optimum putarent *M. Müller*

---

[83] That is, the League as it was before Achaea joined Antigonus III Doson's Hellenic League (cf. *OCD* sv Antigonus [3]) in
the late 220s.

Rhodians, was at anchor at Cenchreae where they were all preparing for an assault on Corinth with a joint plan of action. Flamininus therefore thought it best that, before the allies proceeded with the operation, envoys should be sent to the Achaean nation, promising to bring Corinth back into the council of their people (as it was earlier)[83] on condition that they go over from the king to the Romans. At the urging of the consul, envoys were dispatched to the Achaeans by his brother, Lucius Quinctius, and by Attalus, the Rhodians, and the Athenians. They were granted an audience at Sicyon.

However, feelings among the Achaeans were by no means straightforward. The Spartan Nabis, a formidable and relentless foe, frightened them; they were daunted by Roman arms; they felt obligated to the Macedonians for services of old as well as of recent date; the king himself they regarded with suspicion because of his ruthlessness and treachery and, not judging him by his present conduct, which was motivated only by the needs of the moment, they could see that after the war he would be a more severe master. Not only were the Achaeans unaware of what each individual would express as an opinion in the legislative assembly of his own city-state or in the common councils of their nation, but it was not really clear to them, when they reflected on the situation, what their own wishes or aspirations were. It was to men in such a state of uncertainty that the envoys were introduced and given permission to address.

The Roman envoy, Lucius Calpurnius, had the floor first, then the envoys of King Attalus and, after them, the Rhodians. Philip's representatives were permitted to speak after that, and the Athenians were heard at the end,

refellerent Macedonum dicta, auditi sunt. ii fere atrocis-
sime in regem, quia nulli nec plura nec tam acerba passi
13 erant, invecti sunt. et illa quidem contio sub occasum solis,
tot legatorum perpetuis orationibus die absumpto, dimissa
est.

20. Postero die advocatur concilium; ubi cum per praeconem, sicut Graecis mos est, suadendi si quis vellet potestas a magistratibus facta esset, nec quisquam prodiret,
2 diu silentium aliorum alios intuentium fuit. neque mirum
si quibus sua sponte uolutantibus res inter se repugnantes
obtorpuerant quodam modo animi, eos orationes quoque
insuper turbaverant, utrimque quae difficilia essent pro-
mendo admonendoque per totum diem habitae.

3 Tandem Aristaenus praetor Achaeorum, ne tacitum
concilium dimitteret, "ubi" inquit "illa certamina animorum, Achaei, sunt, quibus in conuiviis et circulis, cum de
Philippo et Romanis mentio incidit, vix manibus tempera-
4 tis? nunc in concilio ad eam rem unam indicto, cum legatorum utrimque verba audieritis, cum referant magis-
5 tratus, cum praeco ad suadendum vocet, obmutuistis. si
non cura salutis communis, ne studia quidem, quae in
hanc aut in illam partem animos vestros inclinarunt, vo-
6 cem cuiquam possunt exprimere? cum praesertim nemo
tam hebes sit qui ignorare possit dicendi ac suadendi quod

so that they could rebut the arguments of the Macedonians. Because no people had suffered more or been subjected to as much cruelty as they, the Athenians launched a truly scathing attack on the king. After the day had been consumed by the speeches of all these representatives, delivered one after the other, the meeting was adjourned at sunset.

20. The following day the assembly was reconvened but when, following the Greek practice, the magistrates through a herald gave anyone wishing to make a motion the opportunity to do so, nobody came forward to speak and there was a long silence, with everybody simply looking at each other. In fact, it is not surprising that men whose intellects were somehow befuddled when they merely reflected on conflicting points of view were even more confused by speeches given on both sides over the course of an entire day presenting and supporting claims difficult to assess.

Eventually, in order not to adjourn the meeting with nothing said, the praetor of the Achaeans, Aristaenus, declared: "Men of Achaea, what has become of those clashes of emotions in which you can barely hold back from physical violence in your dinner parties and social gatherings whenever mention is made of Philip and the Romans? Now, in a meeting entirely dedicated to this subject, you have heard speeches from delegates on both sides; the magistrates are laying the matter before you; and the herald is inviting proposals from the floor—and you are mute! If concern for our collective security can elicit no response from any of you, then cannot even those personal feelings that have drawn your support to one side or the other? Especially when none of you is so obtuse as to be unaware

217

quisque aut velit aut optimum putet nunc occasionem
esse, priusquam quicquam decernamus: ubi semel decretum erit, omnibus id, etiam quibus ante displicuerit, pro
bono atque utili fore defendendum."

7      Haec adhortatio praetoris non modo quemquam
unum elicuit ad suadendum, sed ne fremitum quidem aut
murmur contionis tantae ex tot populis congregatae movit.

21. Tum Aristaenus praetor rursus: "non magis consilium vobis, principes Achaeorum, deest quam lingua; sed
suo quisque periculo in commune consultum non volt.
forsitan ego quoque tacerem, si privatus essem: nunc
praetori video aut non dandum concilium legatis fuisse aut
2      non sine responso eos dimittendos[37] esse; respondere autem nisi ex vestro decreto qui possum? et quoniam nemo
vestrum qui in hoc concilium advocati estis pro sententia
quicquam dicere volt aut audet, orationes legatorum hes-
3      terno die dictas ut pro sententiis[38] percenseamus, perinde
ac non postulaverint quae e re sua essent sed suaserint
quae nobis censerent utilia esse.

4      "Romani Rhodiique et Attalus societatem amici-
tiamque nostram petunt, et in bello quod adversus Philip-
5      pum gerunt se a nobis adiuvari aequum censent. Philippus
societatis secum admonet et iuris iurandi, et modo postu-
lat ut secum stemus, modo ne intersimus armis contentum

---

[37] eos dimittendos *Madvig*: eos non dimittendos *B*: eos dimittendos non χ
[38] dictas ut pro sententiis *Briscoe*: pro sententiis dictas *B*χ: ut
pro sententiis dictas *Madvig*

that now is your opportunity to speak and advocate the policy that you as individuals want or consider to be best—now, before we reach any decision. Once that decision is made, it behooves us all, even those earlier opposed to it, to uphold it as being good and expedient."

Such prompting from the magistrate not only failed to elicit a proposal from any individual but even failed to arouse agitation or murmuring from an assembly of such a size and drawn from so many peoples.

21. The praetor Aristaenus then addressed them once again: "Leaders of the Achaeans, you are no more devoid of ideas than you are of the power of speech! Yet, individually, you are reluctant to take a personal risk in offering advice for the common good. Perhaps I, too, would remain silent were I a private citizen. As it is, I can see that, as your praetor, I should either not have granted the deputations an audience in the first place, or having done so, should not now send them off without a reply. But how can I give them a reply without a resolution from you? And since not one of you who have been invited to this meeting has either the wish or the spirit to make any kind of suggestion, let us review the speeches delivered yesterday by the delegates, looking at them as if they were recommendations—just as if the delegates had made to us not appeals that served their own interests, but proposals they deemed profitable for us.

"The Romans, the people of Rhodes and Attalus are asking for an alliance and friendship, and they think it right that we should assist them in the war they are prosecuting against Philip. Philip reminds us of our alliance with him and the oath we took; at one moment he asks us to stand alongside him, at the next he claims to be satisfied

6 ait se esse. nulline venit in mentem cur qui nondum socii
sunt plus petant quam socius? non fit hoc neque modestia

7 Philippi neque impudentia Romanorum, Achaei: fortuna
et dat fiduciam postulantibus et demit. Philippi praeter
legatum videmus nihil; Romana classis ad Cenchreas stat,
urbium Euboeae spolia prae se ferens, consulem legio-
nesque eius, exiguo maris spatio diiunctas, Phocidem ac

8 Locridem peruagantes videmus: miramini cur diffidenter
Cleomedon legatus Philippi ut pro rege arma caperemus

9 adversus Romanos modo egerit? qui, si ex eodem foedere
ac iure iurando cuius nobis religionem iniciebat rogemus
eum ut nos Philippus et ab Nabide ac Lacedaemoniis et
ab Romanis defendat, non modo praesidium quo tueatur
nos, sed ne quid respondeat quidem nobis sit inventurus,

10 non hercule magis quam ipse Philippus priore anno, qui
pollicendo se adversus Nabidem bellum gesturum cum
temptasset nostram iuventutem hinc in Euboeam extra-

11 here, postquam nos neque decernere id sibi praesidium
neque velle inligari Romano bello vidit, oblitus societatis
eius quam nunc iactat vastandos depopulandosque Nabidi
ac Lacedaemoniis reliquit.

12 "Ac mihi quidem minime conveniens inter se oratio
Cleomedontis visa est. elevabat Romanum bellum, eventumque eius eundem fore qui prioris belli quod cum Phi-

13 lippo gesserint dicebat. cur igitur nostrum ille auxilium
absens petit potius quam praesens nos, socios veteres, simul ab Nabide ac Romanis tueatur? nos dico? quid ita

---

84 Oddly, Cleomedon first appears here and is not known from
elsewhere.          85 Cf. 31.25.5–7.

86 After the First Macedonian War, Philip had retained possession of many of the places he had captured during that war.

if we do not join the fight. Does it not occur to any of you to wonder why men not yet our allies ask more of us than one who *is* our ally? It is not Philip's reserve or Roman brazenness that is responsible for this, men of Achaea— no, prevailing circumstances give or remove confidence when people are making a request. Of Philip we see nothing but his representative, whereas the Roman fleet lies off Cenchreae, with its spoils from the cities of Euboea on display, and we see the consul and his legions overrunning Phocis and Locris, a narrow stretch of sea away from us. Are we surprised at the hesitation with which Philip's representative, Cleomedon,[84] just now discussed our taking up arms against the Romans on Philip's behalf? Suppose we invite Cleomedon to comply with that same treaty and the oath that he kept trying to make us respect, and ask that Philip defend us against Nabis, the Spartans, and the Romans. Apart from finding no troops to protect us, he would not even find an answer for us—no more, for heaven's sake, than Philip did last year when he tried to draw away our fighting men from here to Euboea with an undertaking that he would prosecute a war against Nabis.[85] However, when he saw that we were unwilling to vote him this military assistance or become embroiled in a war with Rome, he forgot about that alliance, which he now plays up, and left us to be pillaged and plundered by Nabis and the Spartans.

"I for one find very little consistency in Cleomedon's address. He pooh-poohed the war with the Romans, and kept saying the result would be the same as in the last war they fought with Philip.[86] So why is Philip now absent, asking for our help, instead of being here giving us, his old allies, protection against both Nabis and the Romans? Do

passus est Eretriam Carystumque capi? quid ita tot Thes-
14  saliae urbes? quid ita Locridem Phocidemque? quid ita
nunc Elatiam oppugnari patitur? cur excessit faucibus
Epiri claustrisque illis inexpugnabilibus super Aoum amnem, relictoque quem insidebat saltu penitus in regnum
15  abiit? aut vi aut metu aut voluntate.[39] si sua voluntate tot
socios reliquit hostibus diripiendis, qui recusare potest
16  quin et socii sibi consulant? si metu, nobis quoque ignos-
cat timentibus; si victus armis cessit, Achaei Romana arma
sustinebimus, Cleomedon, quae vos Macedones non sus-
tinuistis?

"An tibi potius credamus Romanos non maioribus copiis nec viribus nunc bellum gerere quam antea gesserint,
17  potius quam res ipsas intueamur? Aetolos tum classe adiu-
verunt; nec duce consulari nec exercitu bellum gesserunt;
sociorum Philippi maritimae tum urbes in terrore ac tumultu erant; mediterranea adeo tuta ab armis Romanis
fuerunt ut Philippus Aetolos nequiquam opem Romano-
18  rum implorantes depopularetur: nunc autem defuncti
bello Punico Romani, quod per sedecim annos velut intra
uiscera Italiae toleraverunt, non praesidium Aetolis bel-
lantibus miserunt, sed ipsi duces belli arma terra marique
19  simul Macedoniae intulerunt. tertius iam consul summa vi
gerit bellum. Sulpicius in ipsa Macedonia congressus fudit

***

[39] aut . . . voluntate *hic Madvig*: *ante* relictoque χ: aut voluntate *ante* relictoque B: *del. Bekker*

I say 'Giving *us*' protection? Why did he allow Eretria and Carystus to be captured as he did? Why so many of the Thessalian cities? Why Locris and Phocis? Why is he now tolerating the siege of Elatia? Why did he retreat from the passes of Epirus and those unassailable barricades above the River Aous, and why did he abandon his hold on the gorge and withdraw deep into his kingdom? Either he was forced to, or he was afraid, or he did so voluntarily. If he did so voluntarily, leaving so many of his allies to be despoiled by his enemies, how can he object to his allies also looking after their own interests? If he was afraid, then he should pardon us if we are fearful, too. If he withdrew after military defeat, then, Cleomedon, are we Achaeans going to resist Roman arms, which you Macedonians failed to resist?

"Are we to believe your claim that the Romans are not prosecuting this war with more troops and greater resources than they did the last one, or should we rather face facts? On that occasion they assisted the Aetolians with their fleet; they did not fight the war with a leader who was a consul or with a consular army. At that time the coastal cities of Philip's allies were in a state of panic and disarray, but the regions of the interior were so safe from Roman arms that Philip plundered the Aetolians as they pleaded in vain for assistance from Rome. Now, however, the Romans have finished off the Punic War, which they endured for sixteen years within the guts of Italy and, instead of simply sending assistance to the Aetolian war effort, they have made themselves the leaders in the conflict, and mounted simultaneous attacks on Macedonia by land and sea. Already a third consul is devoting all his energies to the war. Engaging the king within Macedonia itself,

fugavitque regem, partem opulentissimam regni eius
20 depopulatus: nunc Quinctius tenentem claustra Epiri,
natura loci munimentis exercitu fretum, castris exuit, fu-
gientem in Thessaliam persecutus praesidia regia socias-
que urbes eius prope in conspectu regis ipsius expugnavit.
21 "Ne sint vera quae Atheniensis modo legatus de crudelitate avaritia libidine regis disseruit; nihil ad nos perti-
neant quae in terra Attica scelera in superos inferosque
22 deos sunt admissa, multo minus quae Ciani Abydenique,
qui procul ab nobis absunt, passi sunt; nostrorum ipsi
23 volnerum, si uoltis, obliviscamur, caedes direptionesque
bonorum Messenae in media Peloponneso factas, et hos-
pitem Cyparissiae Charitelen contra ius omne ac fas inter
epulas prope ipsas occisum, et Aratum patrem filiumque
Sicyonios, cum senem infelicem parentem etiam appel-
24 lare solitus esset, interfectos, filii etiam uxorem libidinis
causa in Macedoniam asportatam; cetera stupra virginum
25 matronarumque oblivioni dentur. ne sit cum Philippo res,
cuius crudelitatis metu obmutuistis omnes—nam quae
alia tacendi advocatis in concilium causa est?—: cum An-
tigono, mitissimo ac iustissimo rege et de nobis omnibus

---

[87] This incident is not recorded elsewhere.     [88] The elder
Aratus, a Sicyonian statesman, was initially on good terms with
Philip, according to Plutarch (*Arat.* 49–53), but when they be-
came estranged, the king, in 213, had him poisoned (in fact, Ara-
tus probably died of consumption). Plutarch also reports (54) that
Philip went on to poison the son.     [89] Polycrateia, who, taken
off to Macedon by Philip, became the mother of Philip's son
Perseus. (Book 27.31.8; cf. Walbank 1.589).     [90] Antigonus
III Doson, Philip's uncle and guardian, and predecessor on the
Macedonian throne (229–221), called "Doson" ("he who will
give") because he did not always immediately deliver on his
promises. He supported the Achaean League. Cf. *OCD* sv.

Sulpicius defeated him and put him to flight, and pillaged the richest part of his kingdom. Now Quinctius has driven him from his camp, although Philip held the key passes of Epirus and was confident in his geographical position, his fortifications and his army. He has pursued him in his flight into Thessaly and has stormed the royal garrisons and the cities allied to Philip virtually before the eyes of the king himself.

"Just suppose there is no truth in what the Athenian delegate said a moment ago about the king's brutality, greed, and lechery. Suppose that we are indifferent to crimes he has committed in Attic territory against the gods of the upper and lower worlds, and much less concerned about the sufferings of the people of Cios and Abydus, who are far removed from us. If you like, let us forget our own wounds and forget the murders and robberies he committed in Messene in the heart of the Peloponnese; the killing of his host Chariteles at Cyparissia,[87] virtually at the dinner table, in contravention of all law human and divine; the assassination of the Sicyonian father and son, both called Aratus[88] (although it had even been his custom to call the hapless old man 'father'); and his carting off to Macedonia the son's wife[89] to satisfy his lust. And let all the other instances of rape of young girls and matrons be consigned to oblivion. Let us pretend we are not dealing with Philip, through fear of whose brutality you have all been left speechless—for what other reason can there be for your silence after you have been summoned to this meeting? Let us suppose instead our debate is with Antigonus,[90] a most compassionate and fair-minded king

225

optime merito, existimemus disceptationem esse: num id
26 postularet facere nos quod fieri non posset? paeneinsula
est Peloponnesus, angustis Isthmi faucibus continenti
adhaerens, nulli apertior neque opportunior quam navali
27 bello. si centum tectae naves et quinquaginta leviores
apertae et triginta Issaei lembi maritimam oram vastare,
et expositas prope in ipsis litoribus urbes coeperint oppugnare, in mediterraneas scilicet nos urbes recipiemus,
tamquam non intestino et haerente in ipsis uisceribus ura-
28 mur bello? cum terra Nabis et Lacedaemonii mari classis
Romana urgebunt, unde regiam societatem et Macedonum praesidia imploremus?[40] an ipsi nostris armis ab
hoste Romano tutabimur urbes quae oppugnabuntur?
29 egregie enim Dymas priore bello sumus tutati! satis exem-
plorum nobis clades alienae praebent: ne quaeramus
quem ad modum ceteris exemplo simus.

30    "Nolite, quia ultro Romani petunt amicitiam, id quod
optandum vobis ac summa ope petendum[41] erat fastidire.
31 metu enim videlicet compulsi et deprensi in aliena terra,
quia sub umbra vestri auxilii latere volunt, in societatem
vestram confugiunt, ut portibus vestris recipiantur, ut
32 commeatibus utantur! mare in potestate habent; terras
quascumque adeunt extemplo dicionis suae faciunt; quod
rogant, cogere possunt; quia pepercisse vobis volunt, com-

[40] imploremus *Madvig*: implorem Bχ
[41] summa ope petendum χ: summa repetendum B

[91] Dymae (Dyme), an Achaean city on the west coast of the
Peloponnese (*Barr.* 58 B1), was captured and sacked by the Romans in 208 during the First Macedonian War (Paus. 7.17.5).

who has deserved well of us all. He would not demand of us what could not be done, would he? The Peloponnese is a peninsula, joined to the mainland by the narrow strip of the Isthmus, and it is above all exposed and vulnerable to naval attack. Suppose a hundred decked ships, fifty lighter open-decked vessels, and thirty Issaean cutters begin to conduct raids on our seacoast and attack the cities that are exposed to them, practically right on the shoreline. We shall retreat into our inland cities, shall we—as though we were not burning with an internal war, one clinging to our vitals? When Nabis and the Spartans put pressure on us by land, and the Roman fleet by sea, what will be the point of calling upon the king's treaty and Macedonian protection? Are we ourselves going to use our own arms against the Roman enemy to protect the cities that will be attacked? A fine job we did of protecting Dymae in the last war![91] The misfortunes of others offer enough in the way of object lessons for us; let us not search for a way for us to be a lesson to others!

"Because the Romans are taking the initiative in seeking your friendship do not spurn an offer you should have been wishing for and doing everything to gain. Of course it is because they are compelled by fear and because they are pinned down in a foreign land that they come running to you for the protection of your alliance, since they want to lurk in the shade of your assistance, have shelter in your harbors, and access to supplies. No! They have the sea in their power, and whatever lands they reach they immediately bring under their control. What they are asking of you they can take by force. Because they wish to spare you, they are not allowing you to commit a self-destructive act.

33 mittere vos cur pereatis non patiuntur. nam quod Cleomedon modo tamquam mediam et tutissimam vobis viam
consilii, ut quiesceretis abstineretisque armis, ostendebat,
34 ea non media sed nulla via est. etenim praeterquam quod
aut accipienda aut aspernanda[42] vobis Romana societas
est, quid aliud quam nusquam gratia stabili, velut qui
eventum exspectaverimus ut fortunae adplicaremus nostra consilia, praeda victoris erimus?
35     "Nolite, si quod omnibus votis petendum erat ultro
offertur, fastidire. non quemadmodum hodie utrumque
vobis licet, sic semper liciturum est: nec saepe nec diu
36 eadem occasio erit. liberare vos a Philippo iam diu magis
voltis quam audetis. sine vestro labore et periculo qui vos
in libertatem vindicarent cum magnis classibus exercitibus-
37 que mare traiecerunt. hos si socios aspernamini, vix mentis sanae estis; sed aut socios aut hostes habeatis oportet."
    22. Secundum orationem praetoris murmur ortum
aliorum cum adsensu, aliorum inclementer adsentientes
2 increpantium; et iam non singuli tantum sed populi universi inter se altercabantur. tum inter magistratus gentis—
damiurgos vocant, decem numero creantur—certamen
3 nihilo segnius quam inter multitudinem esse. quinque
relaturos de societate Romana se aiebant suffragiumque
daturos; quinque lege cautum testabantur ne quid quod
adversus Philippi societatem esset aut referre magistra-

---

[42] aspernanda φ: spernenda B: aspernanda ψ

---

[92] It seems that the "damiurges" (*damiurgi*) were magistrates
of each state who with the *strategos* functioned as the league's
government. They clearly prepared the materials for the general
assembly.

For what Cleomedon pointed to a moment ago as the middle course and the safest one for you, namely to remain neutral and avoid war, that is not the 'middle course'—it is a nonexistent course. Apart from the fact that you must either accept or reject an alliance with Rome, what else will accrue but failure to win goodwill in any quarter—we shall be seen as having awaited the outcome so that we could shape our policy in the light of events—and our becoming the prize of the victor?

"If you are actually being offered what you should be asking for in your every prayer, do not spurn it. You will not always have the choice of alternatives that is open to you today; an opportunity does not often return, and it does not last long. You have long wished to free yourselves from Philip but have not had the nerve to do so. Men have crossed the sea with powerful fleets and armies to champion your independence, with no suffering or risk for you. If you reject these men as your allies, you must be mad—but it is either as allies or as enemies that you must have them!"

22. Hubbub followed the praetor's address, some expressing approval and others sharply criticizing those who agreed; and soon the altercation involved not just individuals but entire member states. Then a dispute began among the national magistrates (they call them "damiurges," and they are elected officials, ten in number),[92] which was no less acrimonious than that among the general assembly. Five declared themselves ready to present the motion on the alliance with Rome and to put it to a vote; five claimed there was a legal provision against the magistrates presenting a motion or the council making a

tibus aut decernere concilio ius esset. is quoque dies iur-
giis est consumptus.

4     Supererat unus iusti concilii dies; tertio enim lex iube-
bat decretum fieri; in quem adeo exarsere studia ut vix
5 parentes ab liberis temperaverint. Pisias Pellenensis erat:
filium damiurgum nomine Memnonem habebat, partis
eius quae decretum recitari perrogarique sententias pro-
6 hibebat. is diu obtestatus filium ut consulere Achaeos
communi saluti pateretur, neu pertinacia sua gentem uni-
7 versam perditum iret, postquam parum proficiebant preces, iuratus se eum sua manu interempturum, nec pro filio
8 sed pro hoste habiturum, minis pervicit ut postero die
coniungeret iis se qui referebant. qui cum plures facti
referrent, omnibus fere populis haud dubie adprobantibus
relationem ac prae se ferentibus quid decreturi essent,
9 Dymaei ac Megalopolitani et quidam Argivorum, priusquam decretum fieret, consurrexerunt ac reliquerunt con-
10 cilium, neque mirante ullo nec improbante. nam Mega-
lopolitanos avorum memoria pulsos ab Lacedaemoniis
restituerat in patriam Antigonus, et Dymaeis captis nuper
direptisque ab exercitu Romano, cum redimi eos ubicum-
que servirent Philippus iussisset, non libertatem modo sed
11 etiam patriam reddiderat; iam Argivi, praeterquam quod

decision on any matter prejudicial to the alliance with
Philip. That day, too, was entirely taken up with internal
squabbling.

There remained a single day in the regular program of
the meeting, as the law stipulated that a decision must be
reached by the third day. Partisan feelings flared up so
much in anticipation of that day that parents had difficulty
in holding back from physical violence to their children.
There was one Pisias of Pellene. He had a son called Memnon who was a damiurge and a member of the group that
was against a motion being read and votes taken. He long
entreated his son to allow the Achaeans to take measures
for their collective protection and not destroy their nation
by his intransigence. But when his entreaties were of no
avail, he swore that he would kill Memnon with his own
hands and consider him an enemy of the people and not
as his son, and he finally brought him by his threats to join,
the following day, those who were for presenting a motion.
These were now in the majority, but when they put the
proposal forward, and nearly all the member states were
clearly in approval and openly demonstrating how they
would vote, the representatives from Dymae and Megalopolis and a number of the Argives rose and left the meeting before a decision was reached. Nobody was surprised
and nobody voiced disapproval. This was because when,
in the days of their grandfathers, the people of Megalopolis had been driven out by the Spartans, Antigonus had
restored them to their native land; and in the case of the
people of Dymae, recently captured and plundered by a
Roman army, Philip had ordered them ransomed wherever they were in servitude and restored to them not only
their freedom but their homeland. As for the Argives,

Macedonum reges ab se oriundos credunt, privatis etiam hospitiis familiarique amicitia plerique inligati Philippo
12 erant. ob haec concilio quod inclinaverat ad Romanam societatem iubendam excesserunt, veniaque iis huius secessionis fuit et magnis et recentibus obligati beneficiis.

23. Ceteri populi Achaeorum cum sententias perrogarentur, societatem cum Attalo[43] ac Rhodiis praesenti de-
2 creto confirmarunt: cum Romanis, quia iniussu populi non poterat rata esse, in id tempus quo Romam mitti legati
3 possent dilata est; in praesentia tres legatos ad L. Quinctium mitti placuit, et exercitum omnem Achaeorum ad Corinthum admoveri, captis Cenchreis iam urbem ipsam Quinctio oppugnante.
4 Et hi quidem e regione portae quae fert Sicyonem posuerunt castra. Romani Cenchreas[44] versam partem urbis, Attalus traducto per Isthmum exercitu ab Lechaeo, alterius maris portu, oppugnabant, primo segnius, sperantes seditionem intus fore inter oppidanos ac regium
5 praesidium. postquam uno animo omnes et Macedones tamquam communem patriam tuebantur et Corinthii ducem praesidii Androsthenen haud secus quam civem et
6 suffragio creatum suo imperio in se uti patiebantur, omnis

---

[43] Attalo *ed. Med. 1478*: Romanis $B\chi$
[44] Cenchreas $B\chi$: *ante add.* ad *ed. Rom.*, in *Herz*

---

[93] Corinth's port on the Saronic Gulf.

[94] On the Corinthian Gulf (cf. 17.3, above).

[95] Introduced here, he appears twice in Book 33 but is not known outside Livy.

apart from their belief that the Macedonian kings were descended from them, many were also attached to Philip by individual ties of hospitality and close personal friendships. For these reasons they took their leave from a meeting that had been disposed to sanction a treaty with Rome, and they were pardoned for this departure as being beholden for the important services they had received in the recent past.

23. When they were asked for their votes, all the other Achaean member states approved by immediate decree a treaty with Attalus and the Rhodians; the treaty with the Romans could not be ratified without authorization from the Roman people and so it was postponed until such time as envoys could be sent to Rome. For the moment it was decided that three envoys be dispatched to Lucius Quinctius and that the entire army of the Achaeans be taken to Corinth where Quinctius, who had now captured Cenchreae,[93] was already laying siege to the city itself.

The Achaean army pitched camp in the area of the gate on the Sicyon road. The Romans were concentrating their attack on the part of the city facing Cenchreae, and Attalus, who had brought his army across the Isthmus, was attacking from the direction of Lechaeum, the port on the other sea.[94] At first the offensive was somewhat halfhearted as the allies were hoping for internal conflict between the inhabitants and the king's garrison. It transpired, however, that the enemy were all in accord: the Macedonians were defending Corinth as though it were their common fatherland, and the Corinthians allowed the garrison commander, Androsthenes,[95] to exercise his authority over them just as if he were a Corinthian citizen elected by them. Thereafter all hope for the besieging

inde spes oppugnantibus[45] in vi et armis et operibus erat.
undique aggeres haud facili aditu ad moenia admove-
7  bantur. aries ex ea parte quam Romani oppugnabant aliquantum muri diruerat; in quem locum, quia nudatus
munimento erat, protegendum armis cum Macedones
concurrerent, atrox proelium inter eos ac Romanos ortum
8  est. ac primo multitudine facile expellebantur Romani;
adsumptis deinde Achaeorum Attalique auxiliis aequabant
certamen, nec dubium erat quin Macedonas Graecosque
9  facile loco pulsuri fuerint. transfugarum Italicorum magna
multitudo erat, pars ex Hannibalis exercitu metu poenae
a Romanis Philippum secuta, pars navales socii, relictis
nuper classibus ad spem honoratioris militiae transgressi:
hos desperata salus, si Romani vicissent, ad rabiem magis
quam audaciam accendebat.
10  Promunturium est adversus Sicyonem Iunonis quam
vocant Acraeam, in altum excurrens; traiectus inde Corin-
11  thum septem fere milium passuum. eo Philocles regius et
ipse praefectus mille et quingentos milites per Boeotiam
duxit; praesto fuere ab Corintho lembi qui praesidium id
12  acceptum Lechaeum traicerent. auctor erat Attalus incen-
sis operibus omittendae extemplo oppugnationis: pertina-

---

45 oppugnantibus *Gron.*: pugnantibus *B*χ

---

96 It is more likely that they were from the southern Italian
Greek states, which provided the Roman forces with ships and
sailors rather than soldiers, and that they were averse to fighting
for Rome against fellow Greeks.        97 "Acraea" (from ἄκρα,
"headland"/"peak") is a cult title of numerous goddesses worshipped on hills or headlands. For its position, cf. *Barr.* 58 D2
(Heraion).        98 On Philocles, cf. 31.16.2 and note.

parties lay in armed force and siege works. On every side the mounds were being advanced toward the walls, though access was difficult. The battering ram had demolished a section of the wall on the side that the Romans were attacking, and because it was denuded of protection the Macedonians hurriedly converged on that point to defend it with their arms, and a ferocious battle broke out between them and the Romans. Initially, the Romans were easily beaten off by superior numbers; but when they enlisted support from the Achaeans and Attalus they made it an even fight and, in fact, there was no doubt that they were easily going to drive back the Macedonians and Greeks from the position. There were, however, large numbers of Italian deserters present: some had been in Hannibal's army and had followed Philip from fear of retribution from the Romans; others had been ships' crews that had lately left their fleets and gone over to the enemy in the hope of finding more prestigious service.[96] These men had no hope of salvation in the event of a Roman victory, and this incited them to frenzy rather than bravado.

There is a promontory, sacred to Juno (whom they call "Acraean Juno"),[97] jutting out into the sea opposite Sicyon, and from there it is about seven miles' journey to Corinth. Philocles, who was also an officer of the king,[98] brought 1,500 men through Boeotia to this spot; there boats from Corinth were waiting to receive the troops and take them across to Lechaeum. Attalus advocated burning the allied siege works and immediately abandoning the siege,

cius Quinctius in incepto[46] perstabat. is quoque ut pro
omnibus portis disposita videt praesidia regia, nec facile
erumpentium impetus sustineri posse, in Attali senten-
13 tiam concessit. ita inrito incepto dimissis Achaeis reditum
ad naves est: Attalus Piraeum, Romani Corcyram petierunt.

24. Dum haec ab navali exercitu geruntur, consul in
Phocide, ad Elatiam castris positis, primo conloquiis rem
2 per principes Elatensium temptavit. postquam nihil esse
in manu sua, et plures validioresque esse regios quam
oppidanos respondebatur, tum simul ab omni parte operi-
3 bus armisque urbem est adgressus. ariete admoto cum[47]
quantum inter duas turres[48] muri erat prorutum cum ingenti fragore ac strepitu nudasset urbem, simul et cohors
4 Romana per apertum recenti strage iter invasit, et ex
omnibus oppidi partibus, relictis suis quisque stationibus,
in eum qui premebatur impetu hostium locum concurre-
5 runt. eodem tempore Romani et ruinas muri superuade-
bant et scalas ad stantia moenia inferebant; et dum in
unam partem oculos animosque hostium certamen aver-
terat, pluribus locis scalis capitur murus, armatique in
6 urbem transcenderunt. quo tumultu audito territi hostes,
relicto quem conferti tuebantur loco, in arcem omnes,
7 inermi quoque sequente turba, confugerunt. ita urbe poti-

[46] Quinctius in incepto *Gel.*: Romanus in incepto *Weiss.*: cum
intus Romanus in incepto *B*: Quintius anusi nineepio *(varie divisum)* χ
[47] admoto quum *Jacobs*: admotoque *B*: admoto χ
[48] duas turres *Madvig*: turres *B*χ: tres turres *Hertz*

but Quinctius persevered all the more stubbornly with the operation. When he saw the king's forces deployed before all the gates, however, and became aware that stemming their counterattacks would not be easy, he conceded that Attalus was right. And so, their enterprise aborted, the allies discharged the Achaeans and returned to their ships, Attalus made for Piraeus and the Romans for Corcyra.

24. During these operations by the navy, the consul established camp in Phocis near Elatia and at first tried to achieve his goal by negotiation through the leading Elatians. However, given the reply that any decision was out of their hands, and that the king's soldiers were more numerous and stronger than the townspeople, he assaulted the city from all directions at once with siege engines and weapons. When the battering ram was brought up, a section of the wall lying between two towers fell with a deafening crash and roar and laid bare the city. A Roman cohort then moved in through the gap opened up by the recent collapse, and at the same time the defenders all left their posts in every sector of the town and quickly converged on the spot that was under pressure from the enemy attack. Climbing over the ruins of the wall, the Romans were also simultaneously applying scaling ladders to the ramparts that were still standing; and while the fighting diverted the gaze and attention of the enemy to the one area, the wall was taken by means of the ladders at a number of points and soldiers climbed over into the city. Hearing the uproar, the enemy, terror-stricken, abandoned the spot they had been defending en masse, and all sought refuge in the citadel, with a crowd of unarmed civilians following them. Thus the consul occupied the city

tur consul; qua direpta, missis in arcem qui vitam regiis si
inermes abire vellent, libertatem Elatensibus pollicseren-
tur, fideque in haec data, post dies paucos arcem recipit.

25. Ceterum adventu in Achaiam Philoclis regii praefecti non Corinthus tantum liberata obsidione, sed Argivorum quoque civitas per quosdam principes Philocli
2 prodita est, temptatis prius animis plebis. mos erat comitiorum die primo velut ominis causa praetores pronun-
tiare Iovem Apollinemque et Herculem: additum lege
3 erat ut his Philippus rex adiceretur. cuius nomen post pactam cum Romanis societatem quia praeco non adiecit,
4 fremitus primo multitudinis ortus, deinde clamor sub-
icientium Philippi nomen iubentiumque legitimum honorem usurpare, donec cum ingenti adsensu nomen reci-
tatum est.

5 Huius fiducia favoris Philocles arcessitus nocte occupat
collem imminentem urbi—Larisam eam arcem vocant—,
positoque ibi praesidio cum lucis principio signis infestis
ad subiectum arci forum vaderet, instructa acies ex ad-
6 verso occurrit. praesidium erat Achaeorum, nuper impositum, quingenti fere iuvenes delecti omnium civitatium;
7 Aenesidemus Dymaeus praeerat. ad hos orator a praefecto
regio missus qui excedere urbe iuberet—neque enim

---

99 The Latin is *praetores*. These would be local Argive magistrates, if the reading is correct, but Briscoe notes that below it is
a *praeco* (herald) who omits Philip's name, perhaps suggesting
that we should read *praeconem* here rather than *praetores*.

100 It lay to the west. Argos had two citadels (cf. 34.25.5), the
other, the hill of Aspis, lying to the northeast.

and, after sacking it, sent men to the citadel to promise the king's soldiers their lives if they agreed to leave unarmed, and the citizens of Elatia their freedom. Guarantees were given on these terms and Flamininus took possession of the citadel a few days later.

25. However, the arrival in Achaea of the king's lieutenant Philocles not only raised the siege of Corinth but also led to the betrayal to Philocles of the city-state of Argos, through some prominent citizens who had first sounded out the feelings of the common people. It was an Argive custom for the magistrates,[99] on the day of an assembly, to call first of all upon Jupiter, Apollo, and Hercules, in order to avert evil omens, and by a legal rider King Philip had been appended to this list. After the commitment to a treaty with the Romans had been made, the herald omitted to add the king's name to the others, whereupon there was first of all muttering in the crowd, and then uproar as people supplied Philip's name and insisted that he be accorded the honor legally his, until finally the name was read out to deafening applause.

Drawn by confidence in the support Philip enjoyed, Philocles during the night seized a hill overlooking the city (a citadel that they call Larisa).[100] He left an armed detachment there and at dawn proceeded in formation to the forum that lay beneath the citadel, where he was met by a line of men drawn up for battle. This was the recently installed Achaean garrison, some 500 young soldiers handpicked from all the member states and commanded by Aenesidemus of Dymae. A spokesman was sent to these men by the king's officer to order them to leave the city as they were no match for the townspeople supporting the

239

pares eos oppidanis solis, qui idem quod Macedones sen-
tirent, nedum adiunctis Macedonibus esse, quos ne Romani quidem ad Corinthum sustinuissent—, primo nihil
8  nec ducem nec ipsos movit; post paulo, ut Argivos quoque
armatos ex parte altera venientes magno agmine viderunt,
certam perniciem cernentes, omnem tamen casum, si per-
9  tinacior dux fuisset, videbantur subituri. Aenesidemus, ne
flos Achaeorum iuventutis simul cum urbe amitteretur,
pactus a Philocle ut abire illis liceret, ipse quo loco steterat
10 armatus cum paucis clientibus non excessit. missus a Philocle qui quaereret quid sibi vellet: nihil statu moto,[49] cum
proiecto prae se clipeo staret, in praesidio creditae urbis
moriturum se armatum respondit. tum iussu praefecti a
11 Thracibus coniecta tela interfectique omnes. et post pactam inter Achaeos ac Romanos societatem duae nobilissi-
mae urbes, Argi et Corinthus, in potestate regis erant.
12 haec ea aestate ab Romanis in Graecia terra marique
gesta.

26. In Gallia nihil sane memorabile ab Sex. Aelio con-
2  sule gestum. cum duos exercitus in provincia habuisset,
unum retentum quem dimitti oportebat, cui L. Cornelius
proconsul praefuerat—ipse ei C. Helvium praetorem
3  praefecit—, alterum quem in provinciam adduxit, totum

---

[49] statu moto *Madvig*: statu modo *Bφ*: tantum modo *NLφMg*.

---

[101] Sex. Aelius Paetus Catus (105): cf. 7.12 and note, above.

Macedonian cause, even if these stood alone—and much
less so when they were joined by the Macedonians, whom
even the Romans had failed to withstand at Corinth. At
first the spokesman's words had no effect either on the
commander or his men; and a little later, when they observed the Argives, also under arms, approaching in a
large column from the opposite direction and they could
see that they were facing certain death, it still appeared
that they would have been ready to meet any eventuality,
had their leader been more resolute. Not to lose the pick
of Achaean soldiery along with the city, Aenesidemus
struck a bargain with Philocles that allowed the men to
leave; but then he himself, accompanied by a few clients,
refused to leave the spot where he had made his stand
under arms. A man was sent by Philocles to inquire what
the point of this was. Not budging an inch and standing
there with his shield held out before him, Aenesidemus
replied that he would die under arms defending the city
that had been put in his charge. Then, on an order from
the king's officer, the Thracians hurled their spears and the
Achaeans were killed to a man. And so, even after a treaty
was concluded between the Achaeans and the Romans,
those two most famous cities, Argos and Corinth, remained in the power of the king. Such were the land and
sea operations of the Romans in Greece that summer.

26. In Gaul nothing truly noteworthy was achieved by
the consul Sextus Aelius.[101] He had two armies in the
province. The first, which should have been demobilized,
he had kept—it had been under the command of the proconsul Lucius Cornelius—and put the praetor Gaius Helvius at its head; and the second he had brought with him

prope annum Cremonensibus Placentinisque cogendis redire in colonias, unde belli casibus dissipati erant, consumpsit.

4     Quemadmodum Gallia praeter spem quieta eo anno
fuit, ita circa urbem servilis prope tumultus est excitatus.
5 obsides Carthaginiensium Setiae custodiebantur: cum iis
6 ut principum liberis magna vis servorum erat; augebant
eorum numerum, ut ab recenti Africo bello, et ab ipsis
Setinis captiva aliquot nationis eius empta ex praeda man-
7 cipia. cum coniurationem[50] fecissent, missis ex eo numero
primum qui in Setino agro, deinde circa Norbam et Cerceios servitia sollicitarent, satis iam omnibus praeparatis,
ludis qui Setiae prope diem futuri erant spectaculo inten-
8 tum populum adgredi statuerant, Setia per caedem et
repentinum tumultum capta Norbam et Cerceios occupare . . . [51] servitia. huius rei tam foedae indicium Romam
ad L. Cornelium Lentulum praetorem urbanum delatum
9 est. serui duo ante lucem ad eum venerunt atque ordine
10 omnia quae acta[52] futuraque erant exposuerunt. quibus

[50] ex praeda mancipia cum coniurationem χ: *spat. B*: ex
praeda . . .‹. . .› cum coniurationem *sic lac. indicat Briscoe*

[51] *post* occupare *spat. AB*: . . . ut obsides captivosque
Carthaginiensium custodia solverent et sibi adiungerent ea quae
cum iis erant *suppl. McDonald*

[52] acta *Bχ*: facta *Lentz*

---

[102] See 31.10.2–7 and notes.

[103] Modern Sezze, southeast of Rome (*Barr.* 43 E3).

[104] No subject is identified in the Latin, leaving it unclear
whether the plot is hatched by the hostages or the slaves. Briscoe
therefore posits a lacuna (see textual note).

[105] There is a large lacuna here. McDonald, on the basis of

into the province. Even so, he spent almost the entire year forcing the peoples of Cremona and Placentia to return to their colonies, from which they had been scattered abroad by the vicissitudes of war.[102]

If Gaul was unexpectedly peaceful that year, in the environs of Rome there was almost a slave revolt. Carthaginian hostages were being kept under guard at Setia;[103] and with them, since they were the children of dignitaries, was a large body of slaves. (Their number was being further increased, as was to be expected in the aftermath of the recent African war, by prisoners of that race, bought as slaves from the booty by the people of Setia themselves.) These[104] hatched a plot and sent some of their number to incite to rebellion first the slaves in the territory of Setia, and later those around Norba and Cerceii. After all had been sufficiently prepared, they had decided to launch their attack during games soon to be held at Setia, while the people were engrossed in the spectacle. After Setia was captured in the bloody and unforeseen uproar, the slaves . . . to seize Norba and Cerceii.[105] Information about this appalling affair was brought to the urban praetor, Lucius Cornelius Lentulus,[106] in Rome. Two slaves came to him before dawn and gave him a full account of what had happened so far and what was likely to come.

*Per.* 32, postulates that an attempt to release the hostages has been lost (see textual note). Norba is about eight miles northwest of Setia (*Barr.* 44 C2), Cerceii about eighteen miles due south (D3). [106] The urban praetor is actually L. Cornelius Merula (7.13, and 8.5, above). Livy's error may have been occasioned by his mention of the proconsul L. Cornelius (Lentulus) at the start of the chapter.

domi custodiri iussis, praetor senatu vocato edoctoque
quae indices adferrent, proficisci ad eam coniurationem
11 quaerendam atque opprimendam iussus, cum quinque
legatis profectus obvios in agris sacramento rogatos arma
12 capere et sequi cogebat. hoc tumultuario dilectu, duobus
milibus ferme hominum armatis, Setiam omnibus quo
13 pergeret ignaris venit. ibi raptim principibus coniurationis
comprehensis, fuga servorum ex oppido facta est. dimissis
14 deinde per agros qui vestigarent . . . [53] egregia duorum
opera servorum indicum et unius liberi fuit. ei centum
milia gravis aeris dari patres iusserunt, servis vicena quina
milia aeris et libertatem: pretium eorum ex aerario solu-
tum est dominis.

15     Haud ita multo post ex eiusdem coniurationis reliquiis
16 nuntiatum est servitia Praeneste occupatura. eo L. Cornelius praetor profectus de quingentis fere hominibus qui in
ea noxa erant supplicium sumpsit. in timore civitas fuit
17 obsides captivosque Poenorum ea moliri. itaque et Romae
vigiliae per vicos servatae, iussique circumire eas minores
magistratus, et triumviri carceris lautumiarum intenti-
18 orem custodiam habere iussi; et circa nomen Latinum a
praetore litterae missae ut et obsides in privato servaren-

[53] qui vestigarent χ: *post lac. AEB*: fugivos . . . ipse praetor
quaestionem exercuit . . . de duobus ferme milibus hominum supplicium sumpsit . . . *suppl. McDonald, per. 32 conlato*

[107] There is another serious lacuna at this point. Mcdonald's
supplement (see textual note), again based on *Per.* 32, reads: "to
track down the fugitives . . . the praetor conducted the investigation in person . . . he executed some two thousand men."

[108] Stone quarries used as a prison, located on the northeast

The praetor ordered the slaves to be kept under guard at his home, convened the senate, and reported the information the informers brought. He was thereupon instructed to leave on a mission to investigate the conspiracy and crush it. Setting off with five legates, he compelled men whom he came across in the fields to swear the oath of allegiance, take up arms and follow him. With this make-shift force of some 2,000 armed men, he reached Setia without any of them aware of his destination. There he swiftly arrested the ringleaders of the conspiracy but the slaves fled the town. Lentulus then sent men through the countryside to track down ‹the fugitives›.[107] Sterling service had thus been provided by two slave informers and one free man. The senate ordered the latter be awarded 100,000 *asses,* and the slaves 25,000 *asses* each plus their freedom (their masters were reimbursed their price from the public purse).

Not much later it was reported that slaves still at large from the same conspiracy were going to seize Praeneste. The praetor Lucius Cornelius set off for the town and executed about 500 men who were guilty of involvement in the offense. The state now lived in fear that the Carthaginian hostages and captives were responsible for these events. Street patrols were therefore instituted at Rome, with the junior magistrates instructed to conduct inspections of them, and the triumvirs were ordered to keep a closer watch on the Lautumiae.[108] A letter was also circulated among the Latin allies by the praetor stipulating that

slope of the Capitoline and supposedly named after the quarries in Syracuse where the captured Athenians were imprisoned after the Sicilian expedition (Varr. 5.151). Cf. Richardson 234.

tur, neque in publicum prodeundi facultas daretur, et captivi ne minus decem pondo compedibus uincti in nulla alia quam in carceris publici custodia essent.

27. Eodem anno legati ab rege Attalo coronam auream ducentum quadraginta sex pondo in Capitolio posuerunt, gratiasque senatui egere quod Antiochus legatorum Romanorum auctoritate motus finibus Attali exercitum deduxisset.

2 Eadem aestate equites ducenti et elephanti decem et tritici modium ducenta milia ab rege Masinissa ad exercitum qui in Graecia erat peruenerunt. item ex Sicilia Sardiniaque magni commeatus et vestimenta exercitui missa.

3 Siciliam M. Marcellus, Sardiniam M. Porcius Cato obtinebat, sanctus et innocens, asperior tamen in faenore coer-

4 cendo habitus; fugatique ex insula faeneratores, et sumptus quos in cultum praetorum socii facere soliti erant circumcisi aut sublati.

5 Sex. Aelius consul ex Gallia comitiorum causa Romam cum redisset, creavit consules C. Cornelium Cethegum et

6 Q. Minucium Rufum. biduo post praetorum comitia habita. sex praetores illo anno primum creati, crescentibus

7 iam provinciis et latius patescente imperio; creati autem hi: L. Manlius Vulso, C. Sempronius Tuditanus, M. Sergius Silus, M. Helvius, M. Minucius Rufus, L. Atilius—

---

109 Not to be taken literally, as 246 pounds is an impossible weight for a crown. Latin *corona* (στέφανος) is often used of a gift of precious metal; cf. Walbank 3.86, Oakley 2.359–60.

110 C. Cornelius Cethegus: cf. 31.49.7 and note; Q. Minucius Rufus: plebeian aedile 201, praetor 200 (prorogued for 199).

111 Previously there were four. The increase of two for 197 was for the administration of the two new Spanish provinces.

the hostages should be confined in private houses and not permitted access to public places, while prisoners of war were to be shackled with chains weighing at least ten pounds and kept under guard in the public prisons and nowhere else.

27. That same year envoys from King Attalus placed a golden crown weighing 246 pounds on the Capitol[109] and gave thanks to the senate for the fact that Antiochus, persuaded by the authority of the Roman embassy, had withdrawn his army from Attalus' territory.

During the same summer 200 cavalry, 10 elephants, and 200,000 measures of wheat came from King Masinissa to the army campaigning in Greece. Large quantities of supplies and clothing for the army were likewise sent from Sicily and Sardinia. Sicily was under the governorship of Marcus Marcellus, and Sardinia under Marcus Porcius Cato. The latter was a man of high principles and integrity but was considered too severe in his suppression of usury. Moneylenders were driven from the island, and outlays that the allies had customarily made for the entertainment of the praetors were curtailed or discontinued.

On his return from Gaul for the elections, the consul Sextus Aelius pronounced Gaius Cornelius Cethegus and Quintus Minucius Rufus[110] as the elected consuls. Elections for the praetorship were held two days later. That year, for the first time, six praetors were elected, to meet the increase in the number of provinces and the expansion of the empire.[111] The following were elected: Lucius Manlius Vulso, Gaius Sempronius Tuditanus, Marcus Sergius Silus, Marcus Helvius, Marcus Minucius Rufus, and Lu-

8 Sempronius et Helvius ex iis aediles plebis erant, curules
aediles Q. Minucius Thermus et Ti. Sempronius Longus.
ludi Romani eo anno quater instaurati.

28. C. Cornelio et Q. Minucio consulibus omnium pri-
2 mum de provinciis consulum praetorumque actum. prius
de praetoribus transacta res quae transigi sorte poterat:
urbana Sergio, peregrina iurisdictio Minucio obtigit; Sardiniam Atilius, Siciliam Manlius, Hispanias Sempronius
3 citeriorem, Helvius ulteriorem est sortitus. consulibus Italiam Macedoniamque sortiri parantibus L. Oppius et Q.
Fulvius tribuni plebis impedimento erant, quod longinqua
4 provincia Macedonia esset, neque ulla alia res maius bello
impedimentum ad eam diem fuisset quam quod vixdum
incohatis rebus in ipso conatu gerendi belli prior consul
5 revocaretur: quartum iam annum esse ab decreto Macedonico bello; quaerendo regem et exercitum eius Sulpicium maiorem partem anni absumpsisse; Villium con-
6 gredientem cum hoste infecta re revocatum; Quinctium
rebus divinis Romae maiorem partem anni retentum ita
gessisse tamen res ut si aut maturius in provinciam venis-
7 set aut hiemps magis sera fuisset, potuerit debellare: nunc
prope in hiberna profectum ita comparare dici bellum ut

---

112 That is, they were plebeian aediles for that year (198), and
now became praetors for 197 (*MRR* 331).

113 Cf. 31.50.2 note (Roman Games) and 31.4.7 note (repetition [*instauratio*]).

114 L. Oppius Salinator (32): plebeian aedile in 193 and praetor in 191 (*MRR* 347).

115 Probably Q. Fulvius Flaccus (28), plebeian aedile in 189,
praetor 187, and consul suffect in 180 (*MRR* 362).

cius Atilius, of whom Sempronius and Helvius were plebeian aediles[112] (the curule aediles being Quintus Minucius
Thermus and Tiberius Sempronius Longus). The Roman
games were that year repeated four times.[113]

28. When Gaius Cornelius and Quintus Minucius assumed the consulship, the very first piece of business
transacted was that of the provinces for the consuls and
praetors. The matter of the praetors, which could be decided by sortition, was settled first. Jurisdiction of urban
affairs fell to Sergius, that of affairs of resident aliens to
Minucius; Atilius was allotted Sardinia, Manlius Sicily,
Sempronius Hither Spain and Helvius Farther Spain. As
the consuls were preparing to draw lots for Italy and
Macedonia, the plebeian tribunes Lucius Oppius[114] and
Quintus Fulvius[115] interposed an objection. Macedonia
was a distant province, they said, and to that day nothing
had proved a greater obstacle to the prosecution of a war
than the recall of a consul already in the field when hostilities had barely commenced and his conduct of the campaign was under way. It was already three years since war
had been declared on Macedon, they continued. During
that time Sulpicius had spent most of *his* year looking for
the king and his army; Villius had been recalled just when
he was coming to grips with the foe and before he had
achieved anything; Quinctius had been detained in Rome
most of his year for the conduct of religious ceremonies—
but had nevertheless achieved such success that he could
have finished off the war had he arrived earlier in his
province or had winter come later. Now, he had virtually
retired into winter quarters, but it was reported that his
preparations for the war were such that he seemed likely

nisi successor impediat, perfecturus aestate proxima videatur.

8 His orationibus pervicerunt ut consules in senatus auctoritate fore dicerent se, si idem tribuni plebis facerent. permittentibus utrisque liberam consultationem patres
9 consulibus ambobus Italiam provinciam decreverunt, T. Quinctio prorogarunt imperium donec successor ex senatus consulto venisset. consulibus binae legiones decretae et ut bellum cum Gallis Cisalpinis qui defecissent a populo Romano gererent.

10 Quinctio in Macedoniam supplementum decretum, sex milia peditum, trecenti equites, sociorum navalium
11 milia tria. praeesse eidem cui praeerat classi L. Quinctius Flamininus iussus. praetoribus in Hispanias octona milia peditum socium ac nominis Latini data et quadringeni equites, ut dimitterent veterem ex Hispaniis militem; et terminare iussi qua ulterior citeriorue provincia servare-
12 tur. Macedoniae legatos P. Sulpicium et P. Villium, qui consules in ea provincia fuerant, adiecerunt.

29. Priusquam consules praetoresque in provincias proficiscerentur, prodigia procurari placuit, quod aedes Volcani Summanique Romae et quod Fregenis murus et
2 porta de caelo tacta erant, et Frusinone inter noctem lux orta, et Aefulae agnus biceps cum quinque pedibus natus,

---

116 Cf. 31.10.1–7.      117 Cf. 31.5.4 note.

118 There had for some years been two commanders for Hither and Farther Spain, but their areas of command had not been demarcated until now.

119 "God of High Places," a cult title of Jupiter. His temple was in the Circus Maximus (Richardson 373–74), that of Vulcan in the Campus Martius (Richardson 432–33).

to bring it to an end the next season, if no successor got in his way.

With such arguments they brought the consuls to agree to abide by the authority of the senate if the tribunes did likewise. With the two sides now agreed on the senate having discretion in the matter, the senators decided that both consuls should have Italy as their province, and they prorogued Titus Quinctius' tenure of command until the arrival of a successor appointed by senatorial decree. The two consuls were each allocated two legions and given responsibility for conducting a war against the Cisalpine Gauls, who had defected from the Roman people.[116]

Quinctius was assigned a supplementary force for service in Macedonia, and this comprised 6,000 infantry, 300 cavalry, and 3,000 seamen. Lucius Quinctius Flamininus was instructed to continue as admiral of the fleet that he had been commanding. For the two Spains each of the praetors was granted 8,000 infantry, drawn from the allies and those with Latin rights,[117] and 400 cavalry, so that they could demobilize the veteran troops from the Spanish provinces. They were further instructed to define the administrative boundary between the farther and hither province.[118] The senate also appointed Publius Sulpicius and Publius Villius, former consuls in the province, as additional legates for Macedonia.

29. Before the consuls and praetors left for their provinces, it was decided that expiatory sacrifices should be held for the prodigies. At Rome the temples of Vulcan and Summanus[119] had been struck by lightning, as had a wall and a gate at Fregenae; and at Frusino daylight had appeared in the middle of the night. At Aefula a lamb had

et Formiis duo lupi oppidum ingressi obuios aliquot lania-
verant, Romae non in urbem solum sed in Capitolium
penetraverat lupus.

3    C. Atinius tribunus plebis tulit ut quinque coloniae in
oram maritimam deducerentur, duae ad ostia fluminum
Volturni Liternique, una Puteolos, una ad Castrum Sa-
4    lerni: his Buxentum adiectum; trecenae familiae in singulas colonias iubebantur mitti. triumviri deducendis iis, qui
per triennium magistratum haberent, creati M. Servilius
Geminus Q. Minucius Thermus Ti. Sempronius Longus.
5    Dilectu rebusque aliis divinis humanisque quae per
ipsos agenda erant perfectis, consules ambo in Galliam
profecti: Cornelius recta ad Insubres via, qui tum in armis
6    erant Cenomanis adsumptis; Q. Minucius in laeva Italiae
ad inferum mare flexit iter, Genuamque exercitu ducto ab
7    Liguribus orsus bellum est. oppida Clastidium et Litubium, utraque Ligurum, et duae gentis eiusdem civitates
Celeiates Cerdiciatesque sese dediderunt; et iam omnia
cis Padum praeter Gallorum Boios Iluates Ligurum sub
8    dicione erant: quindecim oppida hominum viginti milia
esse dicebantur quae se dediderant. inde in agrum Boiorum legiones duxit.

---

120 The places mentioned are close to Rome: *Barr.* 44 B2
(Fregenae), D2 (Frusino), E3 (Formiae), 43 D2 (Aefula).

121 The colonies were called Volturnum and Liternum.

122 At the center of today's Salerno.

123 In Lucania: *Barr.* 45 C4 (today Policastro Bussentino).

124 *Barr.* 39 D2 (Insubres), F3 (Cenomani).

125 Literally, "the lower sea" (*mare inferum*). The "upper sea"
(*mare superum*) is the Adriatic.

126 Clastidium (mod. Casteggio): *Barr.* 39 E3; Litubium: E4.

been born with two heads and five feet; at Formiae[120] two wolves had entered the town and mauled some people they chanced upon; and at Rome a wolf had made its way not just into the city but even into the Capitol.

The plebeian tribune Gaius Atinius proposed a bill for the establishment of five colonies on the coast—two at the mouths of the Rivers Volturnus and Liternus,[121] one at Puteoli, and one at Castrum Salerni,[122] with Buxentum[123] added to these as the fifth—and 300 families were to be dispatched to each of them. Marcus Servilius Geminus, Quintus Minucius Thermus, and Tiberius Sempronius Longus were elected triumvirs for a three-year term to found these colonies.

After completing the conscription and all the religious and secular duties for which they were responsible, the two consuls set off for Gaul. Cornelius took the direct route to the Insubres who, after making an alliance with the Cenomani,[124] were now up in arms. Quintus Minucius headed up the western flank of Italy to the Tyrrhenian sea[125] and, after bringing his army to Genua, chose the Ligurians as his first adversaries in the war. Clastidium and Litubium,[126] both Ligurian towns, and the Celeiates and the Cerdiciates, two communities of that same people, surrendered; and with that everything south of the Po was under Roman control, apart from the Gallic Boii and the Ligurian Ilvates.[127] Fifteen towns and 20,000 men were said to have surrendered. Minucius then led his legions into the territory of the Boii.

---

[127] The Ilvates, Celeiates, and Cerdiciates are not found outside Livy, and the latter two only here. The Ilvates: 31.10.2.

30. Boiorum exercitus haud ita multo ante traiecerat
2 Padum iunxeratque se Insubribus et Cenomanis, quod ita
acceperant coniunctis legionibus consules rem gesturos,
3 ut et ipsi conlatas in unum vires firmarent. postquam fama
accidit alterum consulem Boiorum urere agros, seditio
extemplo orta est: postulare Boii ut laborantibus opem
4 universi ferrent, Insubres negare se sua deserturos. ita
divisae copiae, Boiisque in agrum suum tutandum profec-
tis Insubres cum Cenomanis super amnis Minci ripam
consederunt.
5 Infra eum locum duo milia et consul Cornelius eidem
6 flumini castra adplicuit. inde mittendo in vicos Cenoma-
norum Brixiamque, quod caput gentis erat, ut satis comperit non ex auctoritate seniorum iuventutem in armis
esse, nec publico consilio Insubrum defectioni Cenoma-
7 nos sese adiunxisse, excitis ad se principibus id agere ac
moliri coepit ut desciscerent ab Insubribus Cenomani, et
sublatis signis aut domos redirent aut ad Romanos trans-
8 irent. et id quidem impetrari nequiit: in id fides data
consuli est ut in acie aut quiescerent, aut si qua etiam
9 occasio fuisset, adiuvarent Romanos. haec ita convenisse
Insubres ignorabant; suberat tamen quaedam suspicio
animis labare fidem sociorum. itaque cum in aciem edux-
issent, neutrum iis cornu committere ausi, ne si dolo ces-

---

128 Modern Mincio. It flows from Lake Garda and joins the
Po southeast of Mantova (*Barr.* 39 H3).
129 Modern Brescia (*Barr.* 39 G2).

30. Not long before this the army of the Boii had crossed the Po and joined up with the Insubres and the Cenomani. They had received news that the consuls had united their legions to launch their campaign, and so they also wanted to strengthen their forces by bringing them together. Then, when word came that one of the consuls was burning the lands of the Boii, dissension immediately arose. The Boii insisted that the combined forces bring aid to those in distress, but the Insubres refused to abandon their own property. Their troops therefore parted and the Boii left to protect their farmlands while the Insubres, along with the Cenomani, encamped on the bank of the River Mincius.[128]

Two miles downstream from that point the consul Cornelius also pitched camp on the same river. By sending scouts from there to the Cenoman villages and to Brixia,[129] which was the tribal capital, he gained reliable information that the armed uprising of their young men had not been sanctioned by the elders, and that the Cenomani had joined the Insubrian revolt without official consultation on the matter. Cornelius summoned their chieftains and proceeded to do all he could to make the Cenomi abandon the Insubres, break camp, and either go home or transfer their allegiance to the Romans. That end the consul did not achieve, but he was nevertheless given a solemn undertaking by the Cenomani that in the battle they would either remain inactive or, if an opportunity arose, help the Romans. The Insubres were ignorant of this, but in their minds lurked some suspicion that the loyalty of their allies was flagging. Accordingly, when they led out the troops to form the line, they did not dare entrust either of the wings to them from fear that they might compromise the entire

255

sissent, rem totam inclinarent, post signa in subsidiis eos
locaverunt.

10     Consul principio pugnae vovit aedem Sospitae Iunoni
si eo die hostes fusi fugatique fuissent: a militibus clamor
sublatus compotem voti consulem se facturos, et impetus
in hostes est factus. non tulerunt Insubres primum con-
11 cursum. quidam et a Cenomanis terga repente in ipso
certamine adgressis tumultum ancipitem iniectum auctores sunt, caesaque in medio quinque et triginta milia
12 hostium, quinque milia et ducentos vivos captos, in iis
Hamilcarem Poenorum imperatorem, qui belli causa fuisset; signa militaria centum triginta et carpenta supra
13 (. . . . . . oppida)[54] Gallorum, quae Insubrum defectionem
secuta erant, dediderunt se Romanis.

    31. Minucius consul primo effusis populationibus pera-
graverat fines Boiorum; deinde, ut relictis Insubribus ad
sua tuenda receperant sese, castris se tenuit, acie dimican-
2 dum cum hoste ratus. nec Boii detrectassent pugnam, ni
fama Insubres victos adlata animos fregisset; itaque relicto
duce castrisque dissipati per vicos sua quisque ut defen-
3 derent, rationem gerendi belli hosti mutarunt. omissa
enim spe per unam dimicationem rei decernendae rursus
populari agros et urere tecta vicosque expugnare coepit.
4 per eosdem dies Clastidium incensum.

---

[54] carpenta supra ‹. . . . . . .oppida› *McDonald*: *lac. BAE*: carpenta ‹. . .› Gallorumque *B*

---

[130] Earlier (31.21.18), he falls in battle, and later (33.23.5), he
turns up in Gaius Cornelius' triumphal procession. Livy has failed
to reconcile the versions in his sources: cf. 31.21.18 note.

[131] The text is lacunose and all suggested numbers for the
wagons and towns captured are conjectural.

engagement by treacherously giving ground. Instead they stationed them in reserve behind the standards.

At the start of the battle the consul made a vow of a temple to Juno Sospita should the enemy be defeated and routed on that day. A shout went up from his men, who declared that they would oblige him to discharge the vow, and the assault was then launched on the enemy. The Insubres failed to withstand the first onslaught. Some authorities claim that they were also suddenly attacked in the rear by the Cenomani when the battle was under way and were thrown into chaos on two fronts; that 35,000 of them were killed between the two lines, and 5,200 taken alive (including Hamilcar, the general of the Carthaginians,[130] who had been responsible for the war); and that 130 military standards and more than ‹. . .› wagons captured. . . . ‹towns›[131] of the Gauls, which had joined the uprising of the Insubrians, surrendered to the Romans.

31. The consul Minucius had at first swept through the lands of the Boii making widespread raids, but when the Boii left the Insubres and fell back to protect their own territory he stuck to his camp in the belief that he should meet his enemy in the field. The Boii, in fact, would not have refused battle had not the arrival of news of the Insubrian defeat broken their spirit. With that they abandoned their leader and their camp and dispersed through the towns, aiming to defend their own property; and thus they obliged their enemy to alter his plan of campaign. Minucius now abandoned hope of deciding the issue with a single confrontation and began once more to ravage farmlands, burn buildings, and storm towns. During this period Clastidium was put to the torch.

Inde in Ligustinos Ilvates, qui soli non parebant, le-
5 giones ductae. ea quoque gens ut Insubres acie victos,
Boios ita ut temptare spem certaminis non auderent ter-
6 ritos audivit, in dicionem venit. litterae consulum ambo-
rum de rebus in Gallia prospere gestis sub idem tempus
Romam adlatae. M. Sergius praetor urbanus in senatu eas,
deinde ex auctoritate patrum ad populum recitavit; supplicatio in quadriduum decreta.

32. Hiemps iam eo tempore erat, et cum T. Quinctius
capta Elatia in Phocide ac Locride hiberna disposita habe-
2 ret, Opunte seditio orta est. factio una Aetolos, qui pro-
3 piores erant, altera Romanos accersebat. Aetoli priores
venerunt; sed opulentior factio exclusis Aetolis missoque
ad imperatorem Romanum nuntio usque in adventum
4 eius tenuit urbem. arcem regium tenebat praesidium, neque ut decederent inde aut Opuntiorum minis aut auctoritate imperatoris Romani perpelli potuerunt.

5 Mora cur non extemplo oppugnarentur ea fuit quod
caduceator ab rege venerat locum ac tempus petens con-
6 loquio. id gravate regi concessum est, non quin cuperet
Quinctius per se partim armis partim condicionibus con-
7 fectum videri bellum: necdum enim sciebat utrum successor sibi alter ex novis consulibus mitteretur an, quod
summa vi ut tenderent amicis et propinquis mandaverat,

---

[132] Supplication: cf. 31.8.2 and note.
[133] Town east of Elatia (*Barr.* 55 D3 [Opous]).

From there Minucius led his legions against the Ligurian Ilvates, who alone refused compliance. But when they heard that the Insubres had been defeated in combat and that the Boii were so intimidated that they dared not pin their hopes on a battle, this tribe also submitted. Dispatches from the two consuls regarding their respective successes in Gaul were brought to Rome at about the same time. The urban praetor Marcus Sergius read them out in the senate and later, on the authority of the senate, to the people. Four days of supplication[132] were enjoined by decree.

32. It was winter by now and while, after the capture of Elatia, Titus Quinctius had his winter quarters established at various points in Phocis and Locris, civil discord broke out in Opus.[133] One faction called upon the Aetolians, who were closer, the other on the Romans. The Aetolians arrived first, but the wealthier faction shut them out and, after sending a message to the Roman commander, held the city until his arrival. The citadel was occupied by a garrison of the king, and it could be constrained to leave neither by the threats of the people of Opus nor by the authority of the Roman general.

A delay that forestalled an immediate attack occurred with the arrival of a herald from the king requesting a place and date for a meeting. This was granted to the king with some reluctance. It was not that Quinctius was disinclined to be seen as having terminated the war by a mixture of armed force and diplomacy; the fact was that he did not yet know whether one of the new consuls was being sent out to succeed him or whether his command would be prorogued, a goal that he had instructed his friends and relatives to do their utmost to attain. Still, he

8 imperium prorogaretur; aptum autem fore conloquium
credebat ut sibi liberum esset vel ad bellum manenti vel
9 ad pacem decedenti rem inclinare. in sinu Maliaco prope
Nicaeam litus elegere. eo rex ab Demetriade cum quinque
10 lembis et una nave rostrata venit: erant cum eo principes
Macedonum et Achaeorum exsul, vir insignis, Cycliadas.
11 cum imperatore Romano rex Amynander erat, et Dionysodorus Attali legatus, et Acesimbrotus[55] praefectus Rhodiae classis, et Phaeneas princeps Aetolorum, et Achaei
12 duo, Aristaenus et Xenophon. inter hos Romanus ad extremum litus progressus, cum rex in proram navis in ancoris
13 stantis processisset, "commodius" inquit, "si in terram
egrediaris, ex propinquo dicamus in vicem audiamusque."
cum rex facturum se id negaret, "quem tandem" inquit
14 Quinctius "times?" ad hoc ille superbo et regio animo:
"neminem equidem timeo praeter deos immortales: non
omnium autem credo fidei quos circa te video, atque om-
15 nium minime Aetolis." "istuc quidem" ait Romanus "par
omnibus periculum est qui cum hoste ad conloquium
16 congrediuntur, si nulla fides sit." "non tamen" inquit, "Tite
Quincti, par perfidiae praemium est, si fraude agatur, Philippus et Phaeneas; neque enim aeque difficulter Aetoli
praetorem alium ac Macedones regem in meum locum
substituant."

33. Secundum haec silentium fuit, cum Romanus eum

[55] Acesimbrotus *Niese*: Agesimbrotus *Bφ*: Hagesimbrotus *ψ*

---

[134] On the south coast of the Gulf (*Barr.* 55 D3).

[135] For Cycliadas cf. 31.25.3 and 19.2, above

[136] For Acesimbrotus cf. 31.46. 6 and 16.6, above.

felt the meeting would be convenient, giving him latitude
to incline toward war if he were to remain, or a peace
settlement if he were to leave. They chose as a site a beach
in the Malian Gulf near Nicaea,[134] and the king came there
from Demetrias with five cutters and a warship. With
him were some leading Macedonians and a distinguished
Achaean exile, Cycliadas.[135] With the Roman commander
were: King Amynander, Dionysodorus, a representative
of Attalus, Acesimbrotus, admiral of the Rhodian fleet,[136]
Phaeneas, chief of the Aetolians,[137] and two Achaeans,
Aristaenus and Xenophon. Surrounded by these the Roman went forward to the shoreline, and the king advanced
to the prow of his ship, which lay at anchor. "We could
more conveniently talk and listen to each other at close
quarters if you disembark," said the consul. When the king
refused to do so, Quinctius asked "Who are you afraid of,
then?" to which Philip replied with the pride of a king: "I
am afraid of no one but the immortal gods; however, I do
not have confidence in the integrity of all the men I see
around you, least of all the Aetolians." "Well, if reliability is lacking," said the Roman, "that's a danger that all
men face equally when meeting to parley with an enemy."
"But," replied the king "if treachery is afoot, Titus Quinctius, Philip and Phaeneas do not come as equal rewards
for duplicity—it would not be as difficult for the Aetolians
to find another magistrate as for the Macedonians to replace me as king."

33. After this silence fell, the Roman thinking it ap-

[137] He was *strategos* for 198/7 (and again in 192/1). He tried
to reach a settlement with Rome and commanded the Aetolian
troops supporting the Romans at Cynoscephalae (33.3.9).

aequum censeret priorem dicere qui petisset conloquium, rex eius esse priorem orationem qui daret pacis leges, non
2 qui acciperet; tum Romanus: simplicem suam orationem esse; ea enim se dicturum quae ni fiant nulla sit pacis
3 condicio. deducenda ex omnibus Graeciae civitatibus regi praesidia esse, captivos et transfugas sociis populi Romani reddendos, restituenda Romanis ea Illyrici loca quae post
4 pacem in Epiro factam occupasset, Ptolomaeo Aegypti regi reddendas urbes quas post Philopatoris Ptolomaei mortem occupavisset. suas populique Romani condiciones has esse; ceterum et socium audiri postulata verum esse.
5 Attali regis legatus naves captivosque quae ad Chium navali proelio capta essent, et Nicephorium Venerisque templum quae spoliasset evastassetque, pro incorruptis
6 restitui; Rhodii Peraean—regio est continentis adversus insulam, vetustae eorum dicionis—repetebant, postula-bantque praesidia deduci ab Iaso et a Bargyliis et Euro-
7 mensium urbe, et in Hellesponto Sesto atque Abydo, et Perinthum Byzantiis in antiqui formulam iuris restitui, et liberari omnia Asiae emporia portusque.

---

138 That is, Illyrian territory seized by Philip after the Peace of Phoenice in 205 (cf. Polyb. 18.1.14).

139 The father of the reigning king, Ptolemy v Epiphanes; he had died in 205.      140 In 201 (Polyb. 16.2–8).

141 Pergamene buildings. The Nicephorium was a shrine of Athene Nikephoros (Athena Victory-Bearer).

142 Peraea (περαίη), meaning "opposite," often refers to land controlled by an island facing it. Livy explains the term for his Roman readers.      143 *Barr.* 61 F3 for the three cities.

144 An important city on the northern coast of the Propontis (*Barr.* 52 B3), settled by the Samians in the sixth century (cf. *OCD* sv).

propriate for the man who had requested the meeting to speak first, and the king that the opening words belonged to the party dictating the terms of peace, not the one receiving them. The Roman then said that the statement he had to make was simple, that he would specify only those conditions without which there could be no peace accord. The king, he said, must withdraw his garrisons from all the city-states of Greece, return captives and deserters to the allies of the Roman people, restore to the Romans the regions of Illyricum that he had occupied subsequent to the peace treaty concluded in Epirus,[138] and return to King Ptolemy of Egypt the cities that he had seized after the death of Ptolemy Philopator.[139] Such, he said, were his conditions and those of Roman people, but it was right that the demands of the Roman allies should also be heard.

King Attalus' representative demanded the return of ships and prisoners taken in the naval battle off Chios[140] and the restoration to their original state of the Nicephorium and the temple of Venus, both of which Philip had pillaged and reduced to ruin.[141] The Rhodians sought the return of their Peraea (an area on the mainland, facing their island,[142] that had been under their sway since days of old) and also demanded the withdrawal of the garrisons from Iasus, Bargyliae, and the city of Euromus,[143] as well as from Sestus and Abydus in the Hellespont; the restitution of Perinthus[144] to the people of Byzantium, with restoration of their ancient rights; and the liberation of all the markets and ports of Asia.

8     Achaei Corinthum et Argos repetebant. praetor Aetolorum Phaeneas cum eadem fere quae Romani, ut Graecia
decederetur, postulasset, redderenturque Aetolis urbes
9 quae quondam iuris ac dicionis eorum fuissent, excepit
orationem eius princeps Aetolorum Alexander, vir ut inter
10 Aetolos facundus. iam dudum se reticere ait, non quo
quicquam agi putet eo conloquio, sed ne quem sociorum
dicentem interpellet: nec de pace cum fide Philippum
11 agere, nec bella vera virtute unquam gessisse. in conloquiis insidiari et captare; in bello non congredi aequo
campo neque signis conlatis dimicare, sed refugientem
incendere ac diripere urbes et vincentium praemia victum
12 corrumpere. at non antiquos Macedonum reges rem ita
gessisse,[56] sed acie bellare solitos, urbibus parcere quan-
13 tum possent, quo opulentius haberent imperium. nam de
quorum possessione dimicetur tollentem nihil sibi praeter
14 bellum relinquere, quod consilium esse? plures priore
anno sociorum urbes in Thessalia evastasse Philippum
15 quam omnes qui unquam hostes Thessaliae fuerint. ipsis
quoque Aetolis eum plura socium quam hostem ademisse;
Lysimachiam pulso praetore et praesidio Aetolorum oc-
16 cupasse eum; Cium, item suae dicionis urbem, funditus

---

[56] rem ita gessisse *suppl. M. Müller*: at non ita … reges *Weiss.*:
*post* reges *lac. indicat Briscoe*

---

[145] I.e., *strategos* (cf. 31.24.6 note)

[146] In Polybius (18.3.1) he is called Alexander Isios, presumably because Alexander was such a common name (cf. Walbank
2.554).

[147] *Barr.* 51 H3. Founded by Lysimachus in 309, it was an
important town in the Hellenistic period. Allied with the Aetolian

The Achaeans requested the return of Corinth and Argos. The Achaean praetor,[145] Phaeneas, made much the same demands as had the Romans, namely Philip's withdrawal from Greece and the restoration to the Aetolians of the cities formerly under their jurisdiction and control. Phaeneas' address was followed by an intervention from one of the leading Aetolians, Alexander, who, for an Aetolian, was unusually eloquent.[146] He had remained silent a long while, he said, not because he felt the meeting was serving any purpose, but so as not to interrupt any ally as he was speaking. Philip, he continued, did not conduct peace negotiations with honesty, nor had he ever fought wars with true courage. In discussion he was always laying traps and scheming; in war, instead of fighting in the open field and engaging his enemy in pitched battle, he would retreat, burning and sacking cities and, when conquered himself, ruining the prizes of the conquerors. This was not the way of the Macedonian kings of old. They would fight regular battles and do their best to spare the cities so as to have a richer empire. For what was the sense in destroying what one was fighting to possess, and leaving oneself nothing but the fighting? Philip had destroyed more cities of his allies in Thessaly in the course of the previous year than all the enemies of Thessaly had ever done in the past. From the Aetolians themselves he had taken more as an ally than as an enemy: he had seized Lysimachia[147] after driving out its praetor and the Aetolian garrison; he had reduced Cius, also a city under Aetolian control, to a state

League, it was captured by Philip in 202. Later, Antiochus would find it almost deserted after being sacked by the Thracians and would attempt a rebuilding program (33.38.10–14).

evertisse ac delesse; eadem fraude habere eum Thebas
Phthias[57] Echinum Larisam Pharsalum.

34. Motus oratione Alexandri, Philippus navem ut ex-
2 audiretur propius terram adplicuit. orsum eum dicere, in
Aetolos maxime, violenter Phaeneas interfatus non in verbis rem verti ait: aut bello vincendum aut melioribus pa-
3 rendum esse. "apparet id quidem" inquit Philippus "etiam
caeco," iocatus in valetudinem oculorum Phaeneae; et
erat dicacior natura quam regem decet, et ne inter seria
4 quidem risu satis temperans. indignari inde coepit Aetolos
tamquam Romanos decedi Graecia iubere, qui quibus finibus Graecia sit dicere non possent; ipsius enim Aetoliae
Agraeos Apodotosque et Amphilochos, quae permagna
eorum pars sit, Graeciam non esse.

5 "An quod a sociis eorum non abstinuerim iustam que-
rellam habent, cum ipsi pro lege hunc antiquitus morem
servent, ut adversus socios ipsi suos, publica tantum auctoritate dempta, iuventutem suam militare sinant, et con-
trariae persaepe acies in utraque parte Aetolica auxilia
6 habeant? neque ego Cium expugnavi, sed Prusiam socium
et amicum oppugnantem adiuvi; et Lysimachiam ab Thracibus vindicavi, sed quia[58] me necessitas ad hoc bellum a
7 custodia eius avertit, Thraces habent. et Aetolis haec; Attalo autem Rhodiisque nihil iure debeo: non enim a me

---

57 Phthias *Mog.*: Thias *B*: Phithias $\phi$: Pthias *ed. Med. 1478*
58 sed quia *Asc.*: et quia $B\chi$

---

148 *Barr.* 55 D2 (Phthiotic Thebes), D3 (Echinus and Larisa
[Cremaste]), C2 (Pharsalus). On Phthiotic Thebes, whose original population had been expelled by Philip, cf. 28.7.12, Polyb.
5.99–100.    149 On these "marginally Greek" peoples see Walbank 2.557.    150 King Prusias I of Bithynia, a relative of Philip
by marriage.

of total devastation and ruin; and by similar duplicity he now had in his power Phthiotic Thebes, Echinus, Larisa, and Pharsalus.[148]

34. Stung by Alexander's words, Philip brought his ship closer to shore so that he could be clearly heard. As he began to speak, aiming his remarks primarily at the Aetolians, Phaeneas cut him off abruptly, saying that it was not a matter of words—Philip either had to win in the field of battle or obey his superiors. "That, at least, is clear even to a blind man," said Philip, poking fun at Phaeneas' defective vision (Philip was, in fact, of a wittier disposition than was appropriate for a king, and he did not refrain from joking even in the midst of serious business). He then proceeded to wax indignant that the Aetolians, like the Romans, were calling for a withdrawal from Greece although they could not specify what the boundaries of Greece actually were. Even in Aetolia, he said, the Agraei, the Apodoti and the Amphilochi, though they represented a large section of the region, were not part of Greece.[149]

"Are the Aetolians justified in complaining that I have not kept my hands off their allies," he asked, "when they themselves have been observing as a rule, from days of old, the practice of allowing their men of military age —though without official sanction—to fight against their own allies (and it very often transpires that on both sides opposing armies have Aetolian auxiliaries)? And it was not I who captured Chios—I helped my ally and friend Prusias[150] when he was attacking it. I also championed Lysimachia against the Thracians, but the Thracians now hold it because my predicament diverted me from its defense to *this* war. So much for the Aetolians. To Attalus and the Rhodians I have no real obligation—the war began with

8   sed ab illis principium belli ortum est. Romanorum autem
honoris causa et Peraean[59] Rhodiis et naves Attalo cum
9   captivis qui comparebunt restituam. nam quod ad Nice-
10  phorium Venerisque templi restitutionem attinet, quid
restitui ea postulantibus respondeam, nisi quo uno modo
silvae lucique caesi restitui possunt, curam impensamque
sationis me praestaturum—quoniam haec inter se reges
postulare et respondere placet."
11       Extrema eius oratio adversus Achaeos fuit, in qua orsus
ab Antigoni[60] primum suis deinde erga gentem eam meritis, recitari decreta eorum iussit omnes divinos humanos-
12  que honores complexa, atque eis obiecit recens decretum
quo ab se descivissent; invectusque graviter in perfidiam
13  eorum, Argos tamen se iis redditurum dixit: de Corintho
cum imperatore Romano deliberaturum esse, quaesitu-
rumque ab eo simul utrum iisne urbibus decedere se aequum censeat quas ab se ipso captas iure belli habeat, an
iis etiam quas a maioribus suis accepisset.

      35. Parantibus Achaeis Aetolisque ad ea respondere,
cum prope occasum sol esset dilato in posterum diem
conloquio, Philippus in stationem ex qua profectus erat,
2  Romani sociique in castra redierunt. Quinctius postero
die ad Nicaeam—is enim locus placuerat—ad constitutum
tempus venit: Philippus nullus usquam, nec nuntius ab eo
per aliquot horas veniebat, et iam desperantibus ventu-

    [59] et Peraean *McDonald*: Epirean *Bψ*: Epiream *φ*: Peraeam
*Fr. 2*: et Peraeam *Kreyssig*
    [60] Antigoni *ed. Rom.*: Antigone *B*: Antigonis *χ*

them, not me. Out of respect for the Romans, however, I shall restore both the Peraea to the Rhodians and the ships to Attalus, along with such captives as come to light. As for the Nicophorium and renovations to the temple of Venus, all I can say to those demanding their restoration is this: I shall assume the responsibility for, and the costs of, replanting—the only way woods and groves that have been felled can be restored—since such are the requests and responses that kings like to make to each other."

The final part of his address was directed against the Achaeans. After listing the kindnesses shown to that people, first by Antigonus and then by himself, he had their decrees read out, which contained all manner of divine and human honors that had been paid to him, and he berated them for their recent decree with which they broke with him. After bitterly denouncing their perfidy he nonetheless said that he would restore Argos to them. As for Corinth, he would discuss the matter with the Roman commander and would at the same time ask him whether he thought it right that the king should leave the cities that he had captured himself and which he now occupied by the rules of war, or whether he should even withdraw from those that he had inherited from his ancestors.

35. The Achaeans and Aetolians were preparing to respond to his remarks, but since the sun was close to setting the meeting was adjourned to the following day. Philip returned to the naval base from which he had come, and the Romans and their allies to their camp. The next day Quinctius came to Nicaea—that was the agreed rendezvous location—at the appointed hour. Philip was nowhere to be seen and no messenger come from him for several hours, and it was only when they were all losing hope of his

3 rum repente apparuerunt naves. atque ipse quidem cum
tam gravia et indigna imperarentur inopem consilii diem
4 se[61] consumpsisse deliberando aiebat: volgo credebant de
industria rem in serum tractam, ne tempus dari posset
5 Achaeis Aetolisque ad respondendum; et eam opinionem
ipse adfirmavit petendo ut submotis aliis, ne tempus altercando tereretur et aliqui finis rei imponi posset, cum ipso
6 imperatore Romano liceret sibi conloqui. id primo non
7 acceptum, ne excludi conloquio viderentur socii; dein cum
haud absisteret petere, ex omnium consilio Romanus imperator cum Ap. Claudio tribuno militum, ceteris submo-
8 tis, ad extremum litus processit: rex cum duobus quos
pridie adhibuerat in terram est egressus.

Ibi cum aliquamdiu secreto locuti essent, quae acta
9 Philippus ad suos rettulerit minus compertum est; Quinctius haec rettulit ad socios: Romanis eum cedere tota Illy-
10 rici ora, perfugas remittere ac si qui sint captivi; Attalo
naves et cum iis captos navales socios, Rhodiis regionem
quam Peraean vocant reddere, Iaso et Bargyliis non ces-
11 surum; Aetolis Pharsalum Larisamque reddere, Thebas
non reddere; Achaeis non Argis modo sed etiam Corintho
12 cessurum. nulli omnium placere partium quibus cessurus

---

[61] se χ: *om. BE*

---

[151] Coastal towns south of Miletus: *Barr.* 61 F3.

coming that his ships suddenly appeared. Philip claimed that since the demands being made of him were so harsh and unreasonable, he had been at a loss what to think and had spent the whole day considering them. It was generally believed, however, that he had deliberately put the matter off until late in the day so the Achaeans and Aetolians could be given no time to make their reply to him; and he actually corroborated this view himself by requesting a discussion with the Roman commander with the others excluded, so that time would not be wasted in wrangling and some closure could be set on the business. At first, to avoid the impression that the allies were being barred from the debate, his request was not entertained. Philip, however, kept insisting, and so with everybody's approval the Roman commander, together with the military tribune Appius Claudius, advanced to the shoreline away from everyone else and the king disembarked with the two men he had had with him the previous day.

There they conversed in private for some time. What report Philip took back to his people is not known, but the account Quinctius gave to the allies was this: to the Romans Philip was ceding the entire coastline of Illyricum, and he was also releasing to them deserters and such prisoners as there were; to Attalus he was restoring the ships and the crews captured with them; to the Rhodians he ceded the region they call their Peraea, but he would not cede Iasus and Bargyliae;[151] to the Aetolians he returned Pharsalus and Larisa, but not Thebes; in the case of the Achaeans he was prepared to withdraw not only from Argos but also from Corinth. Absolutely nobody was satisfied with the areas designated by Philip as those that he would

13    aut non cessurus esset destinatio: plus enim amitti in iis
quam adquiri, nec unquam, nisi tota deduxisset Graecia
praesidia, causas certaminum defore.

   36. Cum haec toto ex concilio certatim omnes vocife-
rarentur, ad Philippum quoque procul stantem uox est
2    perlata. itaque a Quinctio petit ut rem totam in posterum
diem differret: profecto aut persuasurum se aut persua-
3    deri sibi passurum. litus ad Thronium conloquio destina-
tur. eo mature conventum est. ibi Philippus primum et
Quinctium et omnes qui aderant rogare ne spem pacis
4    turbare vellent, postremo petere tempus quo legatos mittere Romam ad senatum posset: aut iis condicionibus se
pacem impetraturum, aut quascumque senatus dedisset
5    leges pacis accepturum. id ceteris haudquaquam placebat:
nec enim aliud quam moram et dilationem ad conligendas
6    vires quaeri; Quinctius verum id futurum fuisse dicere si
aestas et tempus rerum gerendarum esset: nunc hieme
7    instante nihil amitti dato spatio ad legatos mittendos; nam
neque sine auctoritate senatus ratum quicquam eorum
fore quae cum rege ipsi pepigissent, et explorari dum bello
necessariam quietem ipsa hiemps daret senatus auctorita-
8    tem posse. in hanc sententiam et ceteri sociorum principes concesserunt; indutiisque datis in duos menses et ipsos mittere singulos legatos ad senatum edocendum, ne
9    fraude regis caperetur, placuit; additum indutiarum pacto

---

152 On the Malian Gulf: *Barr.* 55 D3.

or would not leave; they thought that more was being lost than gained in them and that unless the king withdrew his garrisons from all of Greece there would never be a shortage of causes for conflict.

36. While all present in the entire meeting were trying to outshout each other, the noise also carried to Philip although he stood some way off. He therefore asked Quinctius to postpone the whole question to the following day, saying that he would surely win over the delegates or allow himself to be won over by them. The coast at Thronium[152] was settled on as the venue. Here they assembled early in the day. There Philip began by asking Quinctius and all present not to incline toward upsetting their hopes of peace, and finally he requested time enough to able to send a deputation to the senate in Rome—either he would gain peace on the conditions already proposed, he said, or he would accept whatever peace terms the senate dictated. To this all were entirely opposed; what was being asked for was merely a delay and postponement in order to gather forces, they said. Quinctius, however, stated that this might have been true had it then been summer and the campaigning season; but, as it was, winter was coming on and nothing was lost by granting Philip time to send his deputation. For no item of any accord they made with the king could be ratified without senatorial authorization, and while winter imposed a necessary lull in the fighting the matter of the senate's authorization could be explored. All the other allied leaders supported this view; and so a two-month truce was granted, and it was decided that they, too, should each send one ambassador to brief the senate in case it were hoodwinked by the king's chicanery. A rider stipulating that the king's garrisons be immediately

ut regia praesidia Phocide ac Locride extemplo dedu-
10 cerentur. et ipse Quinctius cum sociorum legatis Amynandrum Athamanum regem, ut speciem legationi adiceret,
et Q. Fabium—uxoris Quincti sororis filius erat—et Q.
Fulvium et Ap. Claudium misit.

37. Vt ventum Romam est, prius sociorum legati quam
regis auditi sunt. cetera eorum oratio conuiciis regis con-
2 sumpta est: moverunt cum[62] maxime senatum demon-
3 strando maris terrarumque regionis eius situm, ut omnibus appareret si Demetriadem in Thessalia Chalcidem in
4 Euboea Corinthum in Achaia rex teneret, non posse liberam Graeciam esse, et ipsum Philippum non contumelio-
5 sius quam verius compedes eas Graeciae appellare. legati
deinde regis intromissi; quibus longiorem exorsis orationem brevis interrogatio, cessurusne iis tribus urbibus
esset sermonem incidit, cum mandati sibi de iis nominatim negarent quicquam. sic infecta pace regii dimissi:
6 Quinctio liberum arbitrium pacis ac belli permissum. cui[63]
ut satis apparuit non taedere belli senatum, et ipse victoriae quam pacis avidior neque conloquium postea Philippo dedit, neque legationem aliam quam quae omni
Graecia decedi nuntiaret admissurum dixit.

38. Philippus cum acie decernendum videret et undi-

[62] cum *Weiss.*: eo *B*: eum χ
[63] cui *Crév.*: quod *B*χ: qui *Holk. 345*: quo *Gron.*

---

[153] The military tribune mentioned above (35.7).
[154] Cf. note on 31.23.1.

withdrawn from Phocis and Locris was added to the agreement for the truce and, to give the deputation a higher profile, Quinctius himself also sent Amynander, king of the Athamanians, to accompany the allies' delegates, as well as Quintus Fabius, son of a sister of Quinctius' wife, plus Quintus Fulvius and Appius Claudius.[153]

37. When they reached Rome, the allies' ambassadors were heard before those of the king. Their presentation was essentially taken up with vituperation of the king, but they impressed the senate most by their elucidation of the geography of the region, both sea and land. This made it clear to everyone that if the king held Demetrias in Thessaly, Chalcis in Euboea, and Corinth in Achaea, Greece could not be free, and Philip himself, the ambassadors noted, used to refer to these cities as his "fetters of Greece,"[154] a term as accurate as it was insolent. Then the king's envoys were brought in. They had launched into a lengthy address when a curt question—would Philip withdraw from these three cities?—brought their presentation to a halt, since the representatives admitted that they had no specific instructions about them. And so the king's men were dismissed with no peace treaty concluded, and Quinctius was given a free hand to negotiate peace or make war. As it was now quite clear to him that the senate had not grown weary of the war and as he was personally more eager for victory than peace, he granted Philip no meeting after that and also said that he would entertain no deputation from him that did not announce his withdrawal from all of Greece.

38. Philip could see that the issue had to be decided in battle and that he needed to concentrate his forces from

que ad se contrahendas vires, maxime de Achaiae urbibus, regionis ab se diversae, et magis tamen de Argis quam de
2 Corintho sollicitus, optimum ratus Nabidi eam Lacedaemoniorum tyranno velut fiduciariam dare, ut victori sibi restitueret, si quid adversi accidisset ipse haberet, Philocli, qui Corintho Argisque praeerat, scribit ut tyrannum
3 ipse conveniret. Philocles, praeterquam quod iam veniebat cum munere, adicit, ad pignus futurae regi cum tyranno amicitiae, filias suas regem Nabidis filiis matrimonio coniungere velle.

4　　Tyrannus primo negare aliter urbem eam se accepturum nisi Argivorum ipsorum decreto accersitus ad auxi-
5 lium urbis esset, deinde, ut frequenti contione non aspernatos modo sed abominatos etiam nomen tyranni audivit, causam se spoliandi eos nactum ratus, tradere ubi vellet urbem Philoclen iussit.

6　　Nocte ignaris omnibus acceptus in urbem est tyrannus: prima luce occupata omnia superiora loca portaeque clau-
7 sae. paucis principum inter primum tumultum elapsis, eorum absentium direptae fortunae; praesentibus aurum atque argentum ablatum, pecuniae imperatae ingentes.
8 qui non cunctanter contulere, sine contumelia et laceratione corporum dimissi; quos occulere aut retrahere aliquid suspicio fuit, in servilem modum lacerati atque extorti.
9 contione inde advocata rogationes promulgavit, unam de

---

155 Whether such a marriage ever took place is unknown. For Philocles, Philip's "friend" and advisor, cf. 31.16.2 and note.

all quarters, and he was concerned above all about the cities of Achaea, an area far separated from him, and more about Argos than Corinth. Thinking that the best idea was to hand Argos over to Nabis, tyrant of Sparta, as a security, as it were—Nabis would restore the city to him if he were victorious, but retain it himself in the event of any mishap befalling him—he wrote to Philocles, who was in command of Corinth and Argos, instructing him to meet the tyrant in person. Philocles, in addition to coming to him now with what was a gift, also added the statement that the king wished to give his daughters in marriage to the sons of Nabis as a pledge of his friendship with the tyrant in future.[155]

At first, the tyrant claimed he would accept the city of Argos only if he were summoned to its aid by a decree of the Argives themselves. Later, however, on hearing that these had been uttering the term "tyrant" not only with disrespect but with venom in a crowded assembly, he thought he had now found a reason for plundering them and told Philocles to hand over the city whenever he wished.

The tyrant was let into the city at night without anyone knowing, and by dawn all its more elevated areas had been seized and the gates closed. A few of the most important citizens had slipped away in the initial turmoil, and their valuables were pillaged in their absence; those who remained found themselves despoiled of their gold and silver, and subjected to huge fines. Those bringing out their property with no hesitation were let off without verbal or physical abuse, but those suspected of hiding or holding back anything were thrashed and tortured like slaves. Nabis then called an assembly and proclaimed two mea-

tabulis novis, alteram de agro viritim dividendo, duas faces
novantibus res ad plebem in optimates accendendam.

39. Postquam in potestate Argivorum civitas erat, nihil
eius memor tyrannus a quo eam civitatem et in quam con-
2 dicionem accepisset, legatos Elatiam ad Quinctium et ad
Attalum[64] Aeginae hibernantem mittit, qui nuntiarent Argos in potestate sua esse: eo si veniret Quinctius ad conloquium, non diffidere sibi omnia cum eo conventura.
3 Quinctius, ut eo quoque praesidio Philippum nudaret,
cum adnuisset se venturum, mittit ad Attalum ut ab Ae-
4 gina Sicyonem sibi occurreret; ipse ab Anticyra decem
quinqueremibus, quas iis forte ipsis diebus L. Quinctius
frater eius adduxerat ex hibernis Corcyrae, Sicyonem tra-
misit.
5 Iam ibi Attalus erat; qui cum tyranno ad Romanum
imperatorem, non Romano ad tyrannum eundum diceret,
in sententiam suam Quinctium traduxit ne in urbem ipsam
6 Argos iret. haud procul urbe Mycenica vocatur: in eo loco
ut congrederentur convenit.
7 Quinctius cum fratre et tribunis militum paucis, Attа-
lus cum regio comitatu, Nicostratus Achaeorum praetor
8 cum auxiliaribus paucis venit. tyrannum ibi cum omnibus
copiis opperientem invenerunt. progressus armatus cum

---

[64] ad Attalum *Madvig*: Attalum *B*χ

---

[156] The standard inducements to revolution in Greece, but
also the two contentious issues in the struggle of the orders in
early Republican Rome.

[157] Anticyra is on the north coast of the Corinthian Gulf, Sicyon near the south coast (*Barr.* 57 A3). [158] This is clearly
Mycenae, but its rich history was apparently unknown to Livy.

sures, one on the cancellation of debts and the other on redistributing land to individuals[156]—thereby providing two torches for revolutionaries to inflame the proletariat against the nobles.

39. After the city of Argos was in his hands, the tyrant gave no thought whatsoever to the man from whom he had received it and the conditions on which he had done so. He sent envoys to Quinctius in Elatia and to Attalus, who was in winter quarters at Aegina, to report that Argos was now in his power. If Quinctius came to parley with him there, he said, he had no doubt that they would reach full agreement. In order to deprive Philip of this stronghold, too, Quinctius agreed to come, and he sent word to Attalus, asking him to proceed from Aegina to Sicyon to meet him. He then crossed from Anticyra to Sicyon[157] with ten quinqueremes, which his brother, Lucius Quinctius, had happened to bring with him from his winter quarters in Corcyra during those very days.

Attalus was already there. Declaring that the tyrant should come to the Roman commander, not the Roman to the tyrant, he won Quinctius over to his view that he should not go to the city of Argos itself. A place called Mycenica[158] lies not far from the city, and it was agreed that they would meet there.

Quinctius arrived with his brother and a few military tribunes, Attalus with his royal train of attendants, and Nicostratus, praetor of the Achaeans,[159] with a few auxiliary soldiers. They found the tyrant awaiting them with all his troops. Nabis, in armor himself and attended by

[159] Nicostratus, *strategos* in 198/7, advocated close relations with Rome.

satellitibus armatis est in medium fere interiacentis campi:
inermis Quinctius cum fratre et duobus tribunis militum,
inermi item regi praetor Achaeorum et unus ex purpuratis
9 latus cingebant. initium sermonis ab excusatione tyranni
ortum quod armatus ipse armatisque saeptus, cum inermes Romanum imperatorem regemque cerneret, in conloquium venisset: neque enim se illos timere dixit sed
10 exsules Argivorum. inde ubi de condicionibus amicitiae
11 coeptum agi est, Romanus duas postulare res, unam ut
bellum cum Achaeis finiret, alteram ut adversus Philippum mitteret secum auxilia. ea se missurum dixit; pro pace
cum Achaeis indutiae impetratae, donec bellum cum Philippo finiretur.

40. De Argis quoque disceptatio ab Attalo rege est
mota, cum fraude Philoclis proditam urbem vi ab eo teneri
2 argueret, ille ab ipsis Argivis se defenderet accitum. contionem rex Argivorum postulabat ut id sciri posset, nec
tyrannus adnuere; sed deductis ex urbe praesidiis liberam
contionem, non immixtis Lacedaemoniis, declaraturam
3 quid Argivi vellent praeberi debere dicebat rex: tyrannus
4 negavit deducturum. haec disceptatio sine exitu fuit. de
conloquio discessum, sescentis Cretensibus ab tyranno
datis Romano, indutiisque inter Nicostratum praetorem

armed bodyguards, advanced close to the midpoint of the field lying between them. Quinctius, accompanied by his brother and two of the military tribunes, was unarmed; and the king, with the praetor of the Achaeans and one of his courtiers at his side, was also unarmed. The conversation opened with an apology from the tyrant for coming to the meeting armed himself and encircled by armed men when he saw that the Roman commander and the king were unarmed. It was not they whom he feared, he said; it was the Argive exiles. Then discussion of the terms of alliance began, and the Roman demanded two things of Nabis: first, that he end his war with the Achaeans and, second, that he send auxiliary troops with him against Philip. The troops Nabis agreed to send, but instead of peace with the Achaeans Flamininus gained from him a truce until the war with Philip was finished.

40. The contentious issue of Argos was also raised by King Attalus. The city had been betrayed to Nabis through treachery on Philocles' part, he said, and was now being held by him under duress, while Nabis defended himself by saying that he had been called in by the Argives themselves. The king insisted upon a meeting of the Argive assembly so this could be established as a fact, and the tyrant did not object. However, the king added that Nabis' garrison should be withdrawn from the city, and the Argives given the opportunity of a free assembly—with no Spartans left among them—which would then reveal what the people of Argos wanted; but the tyrant refused to withdraw his men. Further discussion led nowhere. The meeting adjourned with the Roman granted 600 Cretan soldiers by the tyrant and a truce of four months' duration

Achaeorum et Lacedaemoniorum tyrannum in quattuor menses factis.

5    Inde Quinctius Corinthum est profectus, et ad portam cum Cretensium cohorte accessit, ut Philocli praefecto

6    urbis appareret tyrannum a Philippo descisse. Philocles et ipse ad imperatorem Romanum in conloquium venit, hortantique ut extemplo transiret urbemque traderet ita re-

7    spondit ut distulisse rem magis quam negasse videretur. a Corintho Quinctius Anticyram traiecit, inde fratrem ad temptandam Acarnanum gentem misit.

8    Attalus ab Argis Sicyonem est profectus. ibi et civitas novis honoribus veteres regis honores auxit, et rex ad id quod sanctum Apollinis agrum grandi quondam pecunia

9    redemerat iis, tum quoque ne sine aliqua munificentia praeteriret civitatem sociam atque amicam, decem talenta argenti dono dedit et decem milia medimnum frumenti; atque ita Cenchreas ad naves redit.

10    Et Nabis firmato praesidio Argis Lacedaemonem regressus, cum ipse viros spoliasset, ad feminas spoliandas

11    uxorem Argos remisit. ea, nunc singulas inlustres nunc simul plures genere inter se iunctas accersendo[65] blandiendoque ac minando, non aurum modo iis sed postremo vestem quoque mundumque omnem muliebrem ademit.

[65] accersendo *B*: domum arcessendo χ

arranged between Nicostratus, praetor of the Achaeans, and the Spartan tyrant.

Quinctius then set off for Corinth and came up to the gate with his Cretan cohort to make it clear to Philocles, who was in command of the city, that the tyrant had abandoned Philip. Philocles also came to confer with the Roman commander. When the Roman urged him to desert Philip immediately and deliver the city to him, Philocles so worded his reply as to appear to have postponed a decision rather than refused outright. Quinctius crossed from Corinth to Anticyra; from there he sent his brother to sound out the people of Acarnania.

Attalus left Sicyon for Argos. There the city augmented the former honors they had bestowed on the king with new ones; and the king, who had in the past paid an enormous sum of money to redeem the holy precinct of Apollo for the people of Sicyon, did not wish to lose a second occasion to show his generosity to a city-state that was an ally and friend. He made the city a gift of 10 talents of silver and 10,000 measures of grain. After this he returned to his fleet at Cenchreae.

As for Nabis, he strengthened the garrison at Argos and returned to Sparta. He had himself already despoiled the men of Argos, and he now sent his wife back to the city to despoil the women. She summoned the ladies of note, either individually or in family groups, and by a combination of flattery and menaces deprived them not only of their gold but eventually even of their clothing and all their female finery.

# LIBRI XXXII PERIOCHA

Complura prodigia ex diversis regionibus nuntiata referuntur, inter quae in Macedonia in puppe longae navis
lauream esse natam. T. Quinctius Flamininus cos. adversus Philippum feliciter pugnavit in faucibus Epiri fugatumque coegit in regnum reverti. ipse Thessaliam, quae
est vicina Macedoniae, sociis Aetolis et Athamanibus vexa-
vit, L. Quinctius Flamininus, frater consulis, navali proelio
Attalo rege et Rhodiis adiuvantibus Euboeam et maritimam oram. Achaei in amicitiam recepti sunt. praetorum
numerus ampliatus est, ut seni crearentur. coniuratio servorum facta de solvendis Carthaginiensium obsidibus
oppressa est, duo milia D necati. Cornelius Cethegus cos.
Gallos Insubres proelio fudit. cum Lacedaemoniis et tyranno eorum Nabide amicitia iuncta est. praeterea expug-
nationes urbium in Macedonia referuntur.

# SUMMARY OF BOOK XXXII

Many prodigies are recorded that were reported from various regions, including a laurel growing on the stern of a man o' war in Macedonia. The consul Titus Quinctius Flamininus fought with success against Philip in the gorges of Epirus, put him to flight and forced him to fall back to his kingdom. Flamininus himself, with the Aetolians and Athamanians as his allies, conducted raids on Thessaly, which abuts Macedonia, and the consul's brother, Lucius Quinctius Flamininus, aided by King Attalus and the Rhodians, did so on Euboea and the coast with naval operations. The Achaeans were accepted in an alliance. The number of praetors was increased, so that six were elected. A slave revolt, the aim of which was the release of the Carthaginian hostages, was put down and 2,500 were put to death. The consul Cornelius Cethegus put the Insubrian Gauls to flight in pitched battle. A treaty was made with the Lacedaemonians and Nabis their tyrant. In addition, there is an account of the storming of cities in Macedonia.

# LIBER XXXIII

1. Haec per hiemem gesta. initio autem veris Quinctius, Attalo Elatiam excito, Boeotorum gentem, incertis ad eam diem animis fluctuantem, dicionis suae facere cupiens, profectus per Phocidem quinque milia ab Thebis, quod
2 caput est Boeotiae, posuit castra. inde postero die cum[1] unius signi militibus et Attalo legationibusque, quae frequentes undique convenerant, pergit ire ad urbem, iussis legionis hastatis—ea duo milia militum erant—sequi se
3 mille passuum intervallo distantibus.[2] ad medium ferme viae Boeotorum praetor Antiphilus obvius fuit; cetera multitudo e muris adventum imperatoris Romani regisque
4 prospeculabatur. rara arma paucique milites circa eos apparebant; hastatos sequentes procul anfractus viarum vallesque interiectae occulebant.
5 Cum iam adpropinquaret urbi, velut obviam egre-

---

[1] cum *r*: *om. B*
[2] distantibus *Gron.*: distantis *B*

---

[1] For 33.1.1 to 17.6 the only surviving manuscript is the Bambergensis (*B*). The other source is the first edition (Rome, 1616) of Lusignanus (*r*) and its marginal additions (*rmg*). From 17.6 we also have the *codex Moguntinus* (*Mog.*).

[2] Literally, "spearmen," the first fighting line of the Roman legion. On the Roman army, see Introduction, lviii–lxv.

# BOOK XXXIII[1]

1. Such were the events of the winter. At the beginning of spring Quinctius summoned Attalus to Elatia and, wishing to bring under his control the Boeotians who to that point had been wavering in their sympathies, set off through Phocis and established camp five miles from Thebes, which is the capital of Boeotia. The next day he proceeded from there on his march to the city, taking with him the soldiers of a single maniple along with Attalus and the numerous deputations that had come to him from all parts, but having earlier ordered the *hastati*[2] of a legion, numbering 2,000 men, to follow him at a mile's distance. At about the halfway point of the journey Antiphilus,[3] praetor of the Boeotians, met them (the rest of the population were looking out for the arrival of the Roman commander and the king from the city walls). Around these two could be seen only the odd weapon and a few soldiers—the winding roads and valleys between them hid from view the *hastati* who were following at a distance.

When Quinctius was now approaching the city, he proceeded at a slower pace as if to greet the crowd coming

---

[3] Presumably the *strategos* of the Boeotian League, but not otherwise known.

dientem turbam salutaret, tardius incedebat: causa erat
6 morae ut hastati consequerentur. oppidani, ante lictorem
turba acta, insecutum confestim agmen armatorum non
ante quam ad hospitium imperatoris ventum est con-
7 spexere. tum velut prodita dolo Antiphili praetoris urbe
captaque obstipuerunt omnes; et apparebat nihil liberae
consultationis concilio quod in diem posterum indictum
8 erat Boeotis relictum esse. texerunt dolorem quem et
nequiquam et non sine periculo ostendissent.

2. In concilio Attalus primus verba fecit. orsus a maiorum suorum suisque et communibus in omnem Graeciam
2 et propriis in Boeotorum gentem meritis, senior iam et
infirmior quam ut contentionem dicendi sustineret, ob-
3 mutuit et concidit; et dum regem auferunt reficiuntque[3]
parte membrorum captum, paulisper contio intermissa
4 est. Aristaenus inde Achaeorum praetor eo cum maiore
auctoritate auditus quod non alia quam quae Achaeis
5 suaserat Boeotis suadebat. pauca ab ipso Quinctio adiecta,
fidem magis Romanam quam arma aut opes extollente
6 verbis, rogatio inde a Plataeensi Dicaearcho lata recita-

---

[3] reficiuntque *Gron.*: perfecuntque *B*: perferuntque *r*

---

[4] Lictors: cf. Introduction, lii. It is strange that only one is
mentioned, as a consul or a proconsul was attended by twelve, but
Livy may be referring to the one at the head of the group.

[5] Most likely from a stroke.

[6] In fact, the pro-Roman Aristaenus (cf. 32.19.2) was *strategos*
of the Achaean League in 199/8, and by now it was Nicostratus,
as Livy has already stated (32.39.7).

[7] Plataea was a member of the Boeotian League, but Dicaearchus is not known from elsewhere.

out to meet him, though the actual reason for the slow-
down was to allow the *hastati* to catch up. Since a crowd
of people had now gathered before the lictor,[4] the townspeople did not catch sight of the column of soldiers that
was speedily following until it reached the commander's
quarters. Then they were all taken aback, suspecting that
the city had been betrayed and captured through the
treachery of their praetor, Antiphilus, and the Boeotians
now seemed to be left with no opportunity for open discussion at the council, which was scheduled for the following day. They concealed their chagrin, which they would
have displayed to no purpose and not without risk to themselves.

2. At the council Attalus was the first to speak. He
opened with an account of the various services rendered
by his ancestors and by himself both to Greece as a whole
and to the people of Boeotia in particular. But, too old and
frail now to cope with the stress of public speaking, he fell
silent and collapsed; and the meeting was temporarily suspended while they carried the king out and tried to bring
him round (he had suffered a partial paralysis[5]). Thereupon Aristaenus, praetor of the Achaeans,[6] was given the
floor, and he made all the more impact because the advice
he had for the Boeotians was no different from what he
had given to the Achaeans. A few remarks were added
by Quinctius himself, who extolled the reliability of the
Romans rather than their military strength or material
resources. There followed a motion, proposed and read
aloud by Dicaearchus the Plataean,[7] about making a pact

taque de societate[4] cum Romanis iungenda, nullo contra dicere audente, omnium Boeotiae civitatium suffragiis
7 accipitur iubeturque. concilio dimisso Quinctius tantum
8 Thebis moratus quantum Attali repens casus coegit, post-quam non vitae praesens periculum vis morbi attulisse sed membrorum debilitatem visa est, relicto eo ad curationem necessariam corporis, Elatiam unde profectus erat redit,
9 Boeotis quoque sicut prius Achaeis ad societatem adscitis, et quoniam[5] tuta ea pacataque ab tergo relinquebantur, omnibus iam cogitationibus in Philippum et quod reli-quum belli erat conversis.

3. Philippus quoque primo vere, postquam legati ab Roma nihil pacati rettulerant, dilectum per omnia oppida
2 regni habere instituit in magna inopia iuniorum. absump-serant enim per multas iam aetates continua bella Mace-
3 donas; ipso quoque regnante et navalibus bellis adversus Rhodios Attalumque et terrestribus adversus Romanos
4 ceciderat magnus numerus. ita et tirones ab sedecim annis milites scribebat, et emeritis quidam stipendiis, quibus modo quicquam reliqui roboris erat, ad signa revocaban-
5 tur. ita suppleto exercitu secundum vernum aequinoctium omnes copias Dium contraxit, ibique stativis positis exer-cendo cotidie milite hostem opperiebatur.

6    Et Quinctius per eosdem ferme dies ab Elatia profec-tus praeter Thronium et Scarpheam ad Thermopylas per-

---

[4] de societate *rmg: om. B*     [5] quoniam *B:* quando *rmg*

---

[8] Greek Dion, just north of Mt. Olympus (*Barr.* 57 A1).

[9] Towns near the south shore of the Malian Gulf (*Barr.* 55 D3).

with the Romans; and since no one presumed to speak against it this was accepted and carried by the votes of all the city-states of Boeotia. When the council broke up Quinctius stayed on in Thebes only as long as Attalus' sudden affliction obliged him to do so. When it emerged that it had not been a life-threatening attack but that it had physically disabled him, the consul left him there to undergo the requisite treatment and returned to Elatia, from which he had set out for Thebes. He had now enlisted the Boeotians as allies, as he had earlier the Achaeans, and with territory to his rear left secure and pacified all his thoughts were focused on Philip and what remained of the war.

3. When his envoys brought no prospect of peace back from Rome, Philip, too, at the beginning of spring, proceeded with a muster of troops throughout all the towns of his realm since he faced a severe shortage of younger men. Ongoing warfare over many generations had taken its toll on the Macedonian population, and during his own reign, too, large numbers had fallen in wars fought at sea against the Rhodians and Attalus, and on land against the Romans. Accordingly he began to enroll recruits from the age of sixteen, and men whose service was over but who still possessed a modicum of vigor were also recalled to service. His army brought up to strength in this manner, he assembled all his troops at Dium[8] after the spring equinox and, establishing a base camp there, proceeded to await the enemy, drilling his men every day.

At about this time, too, Quinctius left Elatia and came to Thermopylae, by way of Thronium and Scarphea.[9] He

7 venit. ibi concilium Aetolorum Heracleam indictum tenuit
consultantium quantis auxiliis Romanum ad bellum se-
8 querentur. cognitis sociorum decretis tertio die ab Heraclea Xynias praegressus, in confinio Aenianum Thessalo-
9 rumque positis castris, Aetolica auxilia opperiebatur. nihil
morati Aetoli sunt: Phaenea duce sex milia peditum[6] cum
equitibus quadringentis venerunt. ne dubium esset quid
10 exspectasset, confestim Quinctius movit castra. trans-
gresso in Phthioticum[7] agrum quingenti Gortynii Cretensium, duce Cydante, et trecenti Apolloniatae haud dispari
armatu se coniunxere, nec ita multo post Amynander cum
Athamanum peditum ducentis et mille.
11 Philippus, cognita profectione ab Elatia Romanorum,
ut cui de summa rerum adesset certamen, adhortandos
12 milites ratus, multa iam saepe memorata de maiorum vir-
tutibus simul de militari laude Macedonum cum disseruis-
set, ad ea quae[8] tum maxime animos terrebant quibusque
erigi[9] ad aliquam spem poterant venit.
4. Acceptae ad Aoum flumen in angustiis cladi iterum
a[10] Macedonum phalange ad Atragem vi pulsos Romanos
2 opponebat; et illic tamen, ubi insessas fauces Epiri non
tenuissent, primam culpam fuisse eorum qui neglegenter

6 sex milia peditum *Drak.*: sescenti pedites *B*: ducenti pedites
r       7 Phthioticum *rmg*: Ptioticum *Briscoe*: Ptioticum *B*
8 ad ea quae *rmg*: de re *B*       9 erigi *rmg*: *spat. B*
10 <i>terum a *McDonald*: terra *B*: *obelo utitur Briscoe*

10 On Heraclea (*Barr.* 55 C3) cf. 31.46.2 note.
11 Aenis lay south of Thessaly and northeast of Aetolia (*Barr.*
55 C3) and was a member of the Aetolian League.
12 Phaeneas: cf. 32.32.11 and note.

was detained there by an assembly of the Aetolians, convened at Heraclea,[10] at which members were discussing the number of auxiliary forces they would take when they followed the Romans to war. Learning the decision of the allies, he advanced from Heraclea to Xyniae two days later, pitched camp on the border of the Ainianes[11] and the Thessalians, and waited there for the Aetolian auxiliaries. The Aetolians wasted no time, and 6,000 infantry and 400 cavalry arrived under the command of Phaeneas.[12] To leave no doubt about what he had been waiting for, Quinctius immediately struck camp. After he crossed over into Phthiotic territory, 500 Gortynians from Crete under the command of Cydas joined him, as did 300 similarly armed troops from Apollonia, and, not much later, Amynander with 1,200 Athamanian infantry.[13]

On learning of the Romans' departure from Elatia, and facing a decisive struggle as he was, Philip felt he should give encouragement to his men. After a long harangue on the hackneyed themes of their ancestors' glorious exploits and the military reputation of Macedon, he came to the items that were at that moment striking terror into them and those by which they could be inspired to some degree of hope.

4. Against the defeat suffered in the gorge at the River Aous, Philip set the twofold repulse inflicted on the Romans at Atrax by the Macedonian phalanx. And even at the Aous,[14] he said, when the Macedonians had failed to hold the passes of Epirus that they had seized, responsibility lay primarily with the men who had been negligent in their

[13] Amynander: cf. 31.28.1 and note.
[14] Atrax: 32.17.4–18.3; Aous: 32.10.2–12.10.

3 custodias servassent, secundam in ipso certamine levis armaturae mercennariorumque militum; Macedonum vero
phalangem et tunc stetisse et loco aequo iustaque pugna
semper mansuram invictam.

4 Decem et sex milia militum haec fuere, robur omne
virium eius regni; ad hoc duo milia caetratorum, quos peltastas appellant, Thracumque et Illyriorum—Tralles[11] est
5 nomen genti—par numerus, bina milia erant, et mixti ex
pluribus gentibus mercede conducti auxilia mille ferme
et quingenti et duo milia equitum. cum iis copiis rex hos-
6 tem opperiebatur. Romanis ferme par numerus erat; equitum[12] copiis tantum quod Aetoli accesserant superabant.[13]

5. Quinctius ad Thebas Phthioticas castra cum movis-
set, spem nactus per Timonem principem civitatis prodi
urbem, cum paucis equitum levisque armaturae ad muros
2 successit. ibi adeo frustrata spes est ut non certamen modo
cum erumpentibus sed periculum quoque atrox subiret,
ni castris exciti repente pedites equitesque in tempore
3 subvenissent. et postquam nihil conceptae temere spei
succedebat, urbis quidem amplius temptandae in praesentia conatu absistit; ceterum satis gnarus iam in Thessa-
4 lia regem esse, nondum comperto quam in regionem venisset, milites per agros dimissos vallum caedere et parare
iubet.
5 Vallo etiam[14] Macedones et Graeci usi sunt, sed usum

11 Tralles *McDonald*: Trailis *B*: Trallis *Gron.*
12 equitum *Gron.*: qui tum *B*    13 superabant *Horrion*:
superabat *B*    14 etiam *Tränkle*: et *B*

15 Cf. 31.36.1 and note.    16 Cf. 31.35.1 and note.
17 This section on the use of stakes follows Polyb. 18.18, which
Livy has abbreviated somewhat.

guard duty, and after that, in the battle itself, it lay with the light-armed and mercenary troops. The Macedonian phalanx, he claimed, had stood firm on that occasion, and would always remain invincible in pitched battle on level ground.

The phalanx comprised 16,000 men, and represented the kernel of the kingdom's strength. There were also 2,000 soldiers carrying the *caetra* (men they call "peltasts")[15] and an equal number—that is 2,000 from each nation—of Thracians and Illyrians, who came from a tribe called the Trallians.[16] There was also an assortment of some 1,500 mercenary auxiliaries of various nations and 2,000 cavalry. Such were the troops with which the king was awaiting his enemy. The Romans had roughly the same number; only in cavalry strength were they superior because of the Aetolian supplement.

5. After moving his camp to Phthiotic Thebes, Quinctius entertained the hope of the city being betrayed to him by Timon, a leading citizen of the community, and so he came up to the walls with only a few cavalry and light-armed infantry. This hope was fruitless, however, so much so that he faced not only a battle with counterattacking forces but also a dangerous situation that might have been critical had not his infantry and cavalry, suddenly called to action from the camp, arrived in the nick of time. When his incautiously conceived hope came to nothing, Quinctius for the moment halted his efforts to take the city. Well aware, however, that the king was already in Thessaly, but still without information on the area into which he had come, he sent his men through the fields with orders to cut and prepare palisade stakes.

The Macedonians and Greeks also used stakes,[17] but

6 nec ad commoditatem ferendi nec ad ipsius munitionis firmamentum aptaverunt; nam et maiores et magis ramosas arbores caedebant quam quas ferre cum armis miles posset, et cum castra his ante obiectis saepsissent, facilis

7 molitio eorum valli erat. nam et quia rari stipites magnarum arborum eminebant multique et validi rami praebebant

8 quod recte manu caperetur, duo aut summum tres iuvenes conixi arborem unam evellebant, qua evolsa portae instar extemplo patebat, nec in promptu erat quod obmolirentur.

9 tur. Romanus leves et bifurcos plerosque et trium aut cum plurimum quattuor ramorum vallos caedit, ut et suspensis

10 ab tergo armis ferat plures simul apte miles, et ita densos obfigunt implicantque ramos[15] ut neque ‹. . .›[16] quae cui-

11 usque stipitis palma sit pervideri possit; et adeo acuti aliusque per alium immissi rami locum ad inserendam manum non relinquunt ut neque prehendi quod trahatur

12 neque trahi, cum inter se innexi rami vinculum in vicem praebeant, possit; et si evolsus forte est unus, nec loci multum aperit et alium reponere perfacile est.

6. Quinctius postero die, vallum secum ferente milite

2 ut paratus omni loco castris ponendis esset, progressus modicum iter sex ferme milia a Pheris cum consedisset, speculatum in qua parte Thessaliae hostis esset quidue

[15] ramos *B*: ramis *Weiss.*
[16] ‹. . .› *lac. ind. Weiss.*: quis cuiusque palmae stipes neque *suppl. Crév.*

---

[18] There is clearly a lacuna here; see textual note. Crévier's supplement reads: "which trunk belongs to a particular branch."
[19] Thessalian town south of Lake Boebe: *Barr.* 55 D2.

they did not adapt their practice so as to make transporting them an easy matter or improve their defense capability. They would cut down trees that were too big and had too many branches for a soldier to be able to carry them together with his weapons, and when they had formed a circle of these around their camp breaking down the palisade made of them was easy. This was because the trunks of the large trees rose from the ground at wide intervals, and their numerous sturdy branches enabled one to get a firm hold of them with the hand. Thus two, or at most three, young men would with some effort pull up one of the trees, and when it was torn out an open space like a doorway was immediately created, with nothing readily available to block it. The Romans, however, cut stakes that are light and for the most part forked, bearing three or, at most, four branches, so that a soldier can easily carry a number at a time, his weapons hanging behind his back. Furthermore, they plant them so close together, and interlace the branches so well, that one can tell neither tell . . . [18] nor which branch belongs to a particular trunk; and the branches are so sharpened and so tightly intertwined as to leave no room for inserting a hand, with the result that nothing can be grasped for pulling out, and indeed nothing *can* be pulled out since the interlaced branches bond together to form a barrier. And if by chance one stake *is* pulled out, the space it leaves is small and it can be easily replaced.

6. The following day Quinctius advanced a short distance, his men carrying the palisade with them so as to be ready to pitch camp in any location. Halting about six miles from Pherae,[19] he sent out a scouting party to gather intelligence on where in Thessaly his enemy was located

3   pararet misit. circa Larisam erat rex. certior iam factus
Romanum ab Thebis Pheras movisse, defungi quam primum et ipse certamine cupiens, ducere ad hostem pergit,
4   et quattuor milia fere a Pheris posuit castra. inde postero
die cum expediti utrimque ad occupandos super urbem
tumulos processissent, pari ferme intervallo ab iugo quod
5   capiendum erat, cum inter se conspecti essent, constite-
runt, nuntios in castra remissos qui quid sibi, quoniam
praeter spem hostis occurrisset, faciendum esset con-
6   sulerent, quieti opperientes. et illo quidem die nullo inito
certamine in castra revocati sunt; postero die circa eosdem
tumulos equestre proelium fuit, in quo non minimum Aetolorum opera regii fugati atque in castra compulsi sunt.
7     Magnum utrisque impedimentum ad rem gerendam
fuit ager consitus crebris arboribus hortique, ut in subur-
banis locis, et coartata itinera maceriis et quibusdam locis
8   interclusa. itaque pariter ducibus consilium fuit excedendi
ea regione, et velut ex praedicto ambo Scotusam petierunt, Philippus spe frumentandi inde, Romanus ut prae-
9   gressus[17] corrumperet hosti frumenta. per diem totum,
quia colles perpetuo iugo intererant, nullo conspecta inter
10  se loco agmina ierunt. Romani ad Eretriam[18] Phthiotici[19]
11  agri, Philippus super amnem Onchestum posuit castra. ne
postero quidem die, cum Philippus ad Melambium quod

[17] praegressus *Gron.*: progressus *B*
[18] ad Eretriam *r*: Eretriam *B*
[19] Phthiotici *Horrion*: Pthiotici *Briscoe:* Ptiotici *B*

[20] About ten miles west of Pherae: for this and the other towns
mentioned here, cf. *Barr.* 55 D2.

and what he was doing. The king was in the neighborhood of Larisa. He had already been informed that the Romans had moved from Thebes to Pherae, and since he, too, wished to have done with the battle as soon as possible, he proceeded to march toward his enemy and pitched camp about four miles from Pherae. The next day light infantry from both sides went forward from there to seize the hills overlooking the city and caught sight of each other when they were about the same distance from the ridge that was their objective. They sent messengers back to camp to seek advice on what to do now that they had unexpectedly come across the enemy, and then they halted, quietly awaiting their return. That day they were called back to camp without engaging the enemy; but on the following day there was a cavalry battle in the area of those same hills, and in this the king's troops were routed and driven back to their camp, thanks not least to the Aetolians.

What seriously hindered both sides in their functioning was the fact that the countryside was covered with closely planted trees, that there were gardens, as was to be expected in suburban districts, and that the roads were restricted and, in places, completely blocked off by garden walls. The commanders therefore both decided to quit the area, and as if by prearrangement the two made for Scotusa,[20] Philip hoping to acquire provisions from the place, and the Roman intending to arrive ahead of his foe and destroy his grain supply. The two armies marched an entire day without catching sight of each other at any point because an unbroken chain of hills lay between them. The Romans encamped at Eretria, in Phthiotic territory, and Philip on the River Onchestus. The following day Philip pitched his camp at a place called Melambium in the area

299

vocant Scotusaei agri, Quinctius circa Thetideum Pharsa-
liae terrae posuisset castra, aut hi aut illi ubi hostis esset
12  satis compertum habuerunt. tertio die primo nimbus effu-
sus, dein caligo nocti[20] simillima Romanos metu insidiarum tenuit.

7. Philippus maturandi itineris causa, post imbrem
nubibus in terram demissis nihil deterritus, signa ferri ius-
2   sit; sed tam densa caligo occaecaverat diem ut neque signi-
feri viam nec signa milites cernerent, agmen ad incertos
3   clamores uagum velut errore nocturno turbaretur. super-
gressi tumulos qui Cynoscephalae vocantur, relicta ibi
statione firma peditum equitumque, posuerunt castra.
4   Romanus iisdem ad Thetideum castris cum se tenuisset,
exploratum tamen ubi hostis esset decem turmas equitum
et mille pedites misit, monitos ut ab insidiis, quas dies
obscurus apertis quoque locis tecturus esset, praecave-
5   rent. ubi ventum ad insessos tumulos est, pavore mutuo
iniecto velut torpentes quieverunt; dein nuntiis retro in
castra ad duces missis, ubi primus terror ab necopinato
visu consedit, non diutius certamine abstinuere.
6       Principio a paucis procurrentibus lacessita pugna est,
deinde subsidiis tuentium pulsos aucta. in qua cum haud-

----

[20] nocti *Kreyssig*: noctis *B*

----

[21] Literally, "dog's heads," named for their appearance (Plut.
*Flam.* 8.1). Lying west of Pherae, they had already seen battle, in
364 when Pelopidas there defeated Alexander of Pherae. Livy
follows a longer account in Polybius (18.19–27) but is wrong in
believing that Philip's army has already crossed the hills (in Polybius [18.20.9] he sends troops ahead only to occupy "the sum-

of Scotusa, while Quinctius pitched his in the neighborhood of Thetideum in Pharsalian territory, and even then neither side was certain of the location of its enemy. On the third day there was a downpour followed by a fog dark as night, and this pinned down the Romans, who were afraid of being ambushed.

7. To speed up his progress Philip, undaunted by the clouds that had come down to ground level after the rainstorm, ordered an advance. But the fog that had darkened the daylight was so thick that the standard-bearers could not see the road or the soldiers the standards; and the column, wandering about toward indistinct shouts as if lost in the night, was thrown into disarray. After crossing the hills called the Cynoscephalae[21] and leaving there a strong garrison of infantry and cavalry, the Macedonians pitched camp. The Roman commander had remained in the same encampment at Thetideum, but he did send out a scouting detachment of ten squadrons of cavalry and a thousand infantry to locate the enemy, warning them to beware of an ambush, which the poor daylight would hide even in the open. When the detachment reached the hills occupied by the enemy, each side struck panic into the other and both froze to a standstill. They then sent messengers back to their respective commanders in camp, and after the initial alarm from unexpectedly seeing each other had abated they no longer held back from the fray.

The fighting was first provoked by a handful of men who rushed ahead of the others, but it then escalated as support arrived for defeated comrades. The Romans, no

mits of the hills between him and the enemy"). On the site of the Battle of Cynoscephalae (with map), cf. Walbank 2.576–78.

quaquam pares Romani alios super alios nuntios ad ducem
7 mitterent premi sese, quingenti equites et duo milia peditum, maxime Aetolorum, cum duobus tribunis militum
8 propere missa rem inclinatam restituerunt, versaque fortuna Macedones laborantes opem regis per nuntios implo-
rabant. rex,[21] ut qui nihil minus illo die propter effusam
caliginem quam proelium exspectasset, magna parte hominum omnis generis pabulatum missa, aliquamdiu inops
9 consilii trepidavit; deinde, postquam nuntii instabant, et
iam iuga montium detexerat nebula, et in conspectu erant
Macedones in tumulum maxime editum inter alios com-
10 pulsi loco se magis quam armis tutantes, committendam
rerum summam in discrimen utcumque ratus, ne partis
11 indefensae iactura fieret, Athenagoram ducem mercede
militantium cum omnibus praeter Thracas auxiliis et equi-
12 tatu Macedonum ac Thessalorum mittit. eorum adventu
depulsi ab iugo Romani non ante restiterunt quam in pla-
13 niorem vallem perventum est. ne effusa detruderentur
fuga plurimum in Aetolis equitibus praesidii fuit. is longe
tum optimus eques in Graecia erat; pedite inter finitimos
vincebantur.

8. Laetior res quam pro successu pugnae nuntiata, cum
alii super alios recurrentes ex proelio clamarent fugere
2 pavidos Romanos, invitum et cunctabundum et dicentem

---

[21] rex *Jacobs*: sed *B*

[22] Cf. 31.27.6 and note.

match for the enemy, sent messenger after messenger back to their commander to inform him that they were under pressure. Then 500 cavalry and 2,000 infantry, Aetolians for the most part, were swiftly dispatched under two military tribunes, and they restored the flagging engagement. With the change of fortunes the hard-pressed Macedonians now proceeded to send messages to implore the king's assistance. After the widespread darkness that had fallen, however, the last thing the king expected on that day was a battle, and he had sent out a large section of his forces of every category on a foraging expedition. For a time he dithered, at a loss what to do. The messages, however, then became insistent; the cloud had now lifted to reveal the hilltops; and the Macedonians came into view massed together on a prominence higher than the others and defending themselves more by virtue of their position than their weapons. Concluding that, come what may, he had to throw everything into the fight so as not to sacrifice part of his army by leaving it unsupported, Philip sent out the leader of his mercenary troops, Athenagoras,[22] with all the auxiliaries (apart from the Thracians) along with the Macedonian and Thessalian cavalry. On their arrival the Romans were dislodged from the ridge and offered no resistance until they reached the more level part of the valley. It was mostly the support provided by the Aetolian cavalry that prevented a total rout. These were by far the best cavalry in Greece at the time, though in infantry the Aetolians were inferior to their neighbors.

8. The engagement was reported more positively than the Macedonian success warranted since men running back from the battle in waves called out that the Romans were fleeing in terror, and this made Philip bring all his

Philippum[22] temere fieri, non locum sibi placere non tem-
3 pus, perpulit ut educeret omnes copias in aciem. idem et
Romanus, magis necessitate quam occasione pugnae in-
ductus, fecit. dextrum cornu elephantis ante signa instruc-
4 tis in subsidiis reliquit; laevo cum omni levi armatura in
hostem vadit, simul admonens cum iisdem Macedonibus
pugnaturos quos ad Epiri fauces, montibus fluminibusque
saeptos, victa naturali difficultate locorum expulissent aci-
5 eque expugnassent, cum iis quos P. Sulpici prius ductu
obsidentes in Eordaeam aditum vicissent: fama stetisse
non viribus Macedoniae regnum; eam quoque famam tandem evanuisse.
6 Iam perventum ad suos in ima valle stantes erat, qui
adventu exercitus imperatorisque pugnam renovant, im-
7 petuque facto rursus avertunt hostem. Philippus cum caetratis et cornu dextro peditum, robore Macedonici exercitus, quam phalangem vocabant, prope[23] cursu ad hostem
8 vadit. Nicanori, ex purpuratis uni, ut cum reliquis copiis
9 confestim sequatur imperat. primo, ut in iugum evasit, et
iacentibus ibi paucis armis corporibusque hostium proelium eo loco fuisse, pulsosque inde Romanos et pugnari

[22] Philippum *suppl. Weiss.*: *spat. in fine versus* B: *lac. indicat*
*Briscoe*    [23] prope *Kreyssig*: propere B: propero *r*

---

[23] That is, the battle at the Aous gorge (32.11–12).

[24] The engagement at Eordea: 31.39.7–15.

[25] On peltasts cf. 31.36.1 and note.

[26] This is odd. Livy has already discussed the phalanx (4.3, above), making this explanation *de trop*, and furthermore neither the infantry right wing nor the army as a whole could be described as the phalanx (cf. Briscoe 1.262).

troops into action, reluctant and hesitant though he was—
it was a reckless maneuver, he declared, and he liked neither the locale nor the timing. The Roman general did the
same, prompted by necessity rather than because circumstances favored combat. He left his right wing in reserve,
with the elephants positioned before the standards; and
on the left he attacked the enemy with all his light infantry,
at the same time reminding the men that they would be
fighting the same Macedonians that they had dislodged
and defeated in battle at the gorges of Epirus[23] where,
though their enemies were shielded by mountains and
rivers, the Romans had surmounted all the obstacles of
nature. These were the men they had, under the leadership of Publius Sulpicius, defeated when they fought earlier as they held the pass into Eordaea,[24] he declared. It
was on reputation not real strength that the kingdom of
Macedon rested, and that reputation, too, had ultimately
faded.

By now the Romans had reached their comrades who
were making their stand in the lower reaches of the valley,
and, on the arrival of the army and their general, these
renewed the fight, went on the attack and again threw
back the enemy. With his peltasts[25] and the infantry right
wing that they called the "phalanx" (which constituted the
strength of the Macedonian army),[26] Philip now charged
his enemy almost at a run and ordered Nicanor, one of his
courtiers, to follow at a rapid pace with the rest of the
troops. On reaching the hilltop, Philip could first of all see
from the few weapons and enemy corpses lying around
there that the battle in that spot was finished and that the

10 prope castra hostium vidit, ingenti gaudio est elatus; mox
refugientibus suis et terrore verso paulisper incertus an in
11 castra reciperet copias trepidavit; deinde ut adpropinquabat hostis, et praeterquam quod caedebantur aversi nec
nisi defenderentur servari poterant, ne ipsi quidem in tuto
12 iam receptus erat, coactus nondum adsecuta parte suorum
periculum summae rerum facere, equites levemque arma-
13 turam qui in proelio fuerant dextro in cornu locat iuxta
caetratos[24] Macedonum phalangem hastis positis, quarum
14 longitudo impedimento erat, gladiis rem gerere iubet. simul ne facile perrumperetur acies, dimidium de fronte
demptum introrsus porrectis ordinibus duplicat, ut longa
potius quam lata acies esset; simul et densari ordines iussit, ut vir viro arma armis iungerentur.

9. Quinctius, iis qui in proelio fuerant inter signa et
2 ordines acceptis, tuba dat signum. raro alias tantus clamor
dicitur in principio pugnae exortus; nam forte utraque
acies simul conclamavere, nec solum qui pugnabant sed
subsidia etiam quique tum maxime in proelium veniebant.
3 dextro cornu rex loci plurimum auxilio, ex iugis altioribus

---

[24] locat iuxta caetratos *McDonald*: locatus caetratas *B*: locat,
caetratos et *rmg*: locat cum caetratis *Lachmann*: *obelo utitur*
*Briscoe*

---

[27] This is one of the most famous examples of Livy's misun-
derstanding of Polybius. Polybius (18.24.9) says Philip ordered
"the men of the phalanx to lower their spears and charge." Livy
takes "lower" ($\kappa\alpha\tau\alpha\beta\acute{\alpha}\lambda\lambda\epsilon\iota\nu$) to mean "lay down" and tries to
make sense of it by having the Macedonians drop their sarissas
(as being a hindrance) and resort to their swords.

[28] That is, by taking half of the phalanx's front and placing it
behind the other half.

Romans had been driven back, and he could also see fighting going on near his enemy's camp. His initial reaction was sheer delight. Soon, however, as his own men came running back and the terror changed sides, he panicked, unsure for the moment whether or not to take his troops back to their camp. Then, as the enemy kept approaching and, apart from his men being cut down when they turned to run and not able to be saved without support, there was no longer even any way for Philip himself to retire in safety. Thus, although a section of his force had not yet joined him, he was obliged to risk a decisive engagement. On the right wing, next to the peltasts, he positioned the cavalry and light infantry that had participated in the engagement, and he ordered the Macedonian phalanx to lay down their spears (the length of which was an encumbrance) and fight with their swords.[27] At the same, to prevent his line being easily penetrated, he took half of the front of the phalanx and with it doubled its depth,[28] narrowing the ranks, so that the battle line was deep rather than wide. He also ordered the ranks to be closed up so that men stood shoulder to shoulder and weapons were touching weapons.

9. After taking in between the ranks the men who had already been engaged in the battle, Quinctius gave the signal on the trumpet. Rarely, it is said, has there been so loud a war cry raised at the start of a battle; for as chance would have it both armies shouted at the same time, and not just those engaged in the fighting but also the reservists and those arriving for the battle at that very moment. On the right wing the king had the upper hand, mainly helped by his position, fighting as he was from a higher

pugnans, vincebat; sinistro, tum cum maxime adpropin-
quante phalangis parte quae novissimi agminis fuerat, sine
4 ullo ordine trepidabatur; media acies, quae propior dextrum cornu erat, stabat spectaculo velut nihil ad se perti-
5 nentis pugnae intenta. phalanx, quae venerat agmen magis
quam acies aptiorque itineri quam pugnae, vixdum in iu-
6 gum evaserat. in hos incompositos Quinctius, quamquam
pedem referentes in dextro cornu suos cernebat, elephantis prius in hostem actis impetum facit, ratus partem pro-
fligatam cetera tracturam.

7 Non dubia res fuit; extemplo terga vertere Macedones,
terrore primo bestiarum aversi. et ceteri quidem hos pul-
8 sos sequebantur; unus e tribunis militum ex tempore[25]
capto consilio cum viginti signorum militibus, relicta ea
parte suorum quae haud dubie vincebat, brevi circuitu
9 dextrum cornu hostium aversum invadit. nullam aciem ab
tergo adortus non turbasset; ceterum ad communem om-
10 nium in tali re trepidationem[26] accessit quod phalanx
Macedonum gravis atque immobilis nec circumagere se
poterat, nec hoc qui a fronte paulo ante pedem referentes
11 tunc ultro territis instabant patiebantur. ad hoc loco etiam
premebantur, quia iugum ex quo pugnaverant, dum per

[25] ex tempore *Duker*: extemplo *B*
[26] re trepidationem *r*: reparationem *B*: re desperationem
*Walter*

---

[29] For Livy's mistaken assumption here, see Introduction,
xxxiii.
[30] That is, maniples: Introduction, lxii–lxiii.

elevation. On the left, since the part of the phalanx that had formed the rear was just then coming up, there was confusion and turmoil. The center, positioned closer to the right wing, was stationary, the men engrossed in watching the battle as if they were not involved in it.[29] The phalanx, which had arrived as a column rather than a battle line and was more appropriately drawn up for marching than combat, had barely reached the brow of the hill. While these men were still in confusion Quinctius attacked (even though he could see his own men retreating on the right wing) after first driving the elephants against his enemy. He thought that if some of the enemy's forces were overwhelmed they would drag the rest along with them.

The outcome was not in doubt. The Macedonians immediately turned tail, sent running in terror at the first sight of the beasts. And the others did indeed follow these defeated comrades. Then one of the military tribunes made a snap decision. Leaving behind that section of his men that clearly had the upper hand, he took the soldiers of twenty companies[30] and with a short encircling maneuver attacked the rear of the enemy right wing. There is no battle line that an attack from the rear would not have thrown into disorder; but added to the universal panic normal in such circumstances there was the further problem that the Macedonian phalanx, cumbersome and unmaneuverable, was unable to wheel about, an operation that was also inhibited by those Romans who, though they had earlier been pulling back from the front, were at that moment bearing down on the terrified Macedonians. The Macedonians were, moreover, handicapped by their position: while chasing the defeated Romans down the slope,

proclive pulsos insequuntur, tradiderant hosti ad terga sua circumducto. paulisper in medio caesi, deinde omissis plerique armis capessunt fugam.

10. Philippus cum paucis peditum equitumque primo tumulum altiorem inter ceteros cepit unde[27] specularetur
2 quae in laeva parte suorum fortuna esset: deinde postquam fugam effusam animadvertit et omnia circa iuga sig-
3 nis atque armis fulgere, tum et ipse acie excessit. Quinctius cum institisset cedentibus, repente, quia erigentes hastas Macedonas conspexerat, quidnam pararent incer-
4 tus paulisper novitate rei constituit signa; deinde, ut accepit hunc morem esse Macedonum tradentium sese, par-
5 cere victis in animo habebat. ceterum ab ignaris militibus omissam ab hoste pugnam et quid imperator vellet impetus in eos est factus, et primis caesis ceteri in fugam dissipati sunt.

6 Rex effuso cursu Tempe petit. ibi ad Gonnos diem unum substitit ad excipiendos si qui proelio superessent. Romani victores in castra hostium spe praedae inrumpunt sed[28] ea magna iam ex parte[29] direpta ab Aetolis inveniunt.
7 caesa eo die octo milia hostium, quinque capta; ex victo-
8 ribus septingenti ferme ceciderunt. si Valerio qui credat

[27] unde *Horrion*: . . . *spat. B*: ut *r*: *lac. indicat Briscoe*
[28] inrumpunt sed *Rossbach*: irrumpunt *Grut.*: *spat. B*: irrumpentes *Weiss.*: *lac. indicat Briscoe*
[29] ex parte *rmg*: *spat. B*

[31] In Polybius (18.26.12) most of the enemy are killed, not just those at the front. Livy is evidently trying to put the Romans in a less unfavorable light.
[32] Tempe and Gonni (Gonnoi): *Barr.* 55 C–D 1.

they had ceded the higher ground from which they had been fighting to those of the enemy who had been brought around to their rear. For a short while they were cut down between two fronts; then most threw down their weapons and took to their heels.

10. Taking a few foot soldiers and cavalrymen, Philip at first seized a hillock higher than the others from which he could observe the fortunes of his men on the left flank. Then, when he saw them in disorderly flight and the hills all around glinting with standards and weapons, he also at that point quit the field. Quinctius had been putting pressure on the retreating Macedonians but then, because he saw them raise their spears and was unsure of their intentions, he was suddenly prompted by the strange move to halt his troops for a moment. Then, when he was told that this was the customary Macedonian signal for surrender, he had it mind to spare his defeated foes. However, they were attacked by his men, who did not know that the fight had been abandoned by the enemy and what their commander's wishes were; and after those at the front[31] were killed the others scattered in flight.

The king headed for Tempe at a headlong pace. There he halted at Gonni[32] for one day to gather up any who had survived the battle. The triumphant Romans, hoping for spoils, burst into the enemy camp, only to find that it had already been for the most part looted by the Aetolians. On that day 8,000 of the enemy were killed and 5,000 captured, while about 700 of the victors were lost. If one can believe Valerius,[33] who is guilty of gross exaggeration of

---

[33] For Valerius Antias and Claudius Quadrigarius (below), see Introduction, xxvii–xxix.

omnium rerum immodice numerum augenti, quadraginta
milia hostium eo die sunt caesa, capta—ibi modestius
mendacium est—quinque milia septingenti, signa milita-
9  ria ducenta undequinquaginta. Claudius quoque duo et
triginta milia hostium caesa scribit, capta quattuor milia et
10  trecentos. nos non minimo potissimum numero credidi-
mus sed Polybium secuti sumus, non incertum auctorem
cum omnium Romanarum rerum tum praecipue in Graecia gestarum.

11. Philippus, conlectis ex fuga qui variis casibus
pugnae dissipati vestigia eius secuti fuerant, missisque
Larisam ad commentarios regios comburendos ne in hostium venirent potestatem, in Macedoniam concessit.
2  Quinctius, captivis praedaque partim venundatis partim
militi concessis, Larisam est profectus, hauddum satis
3  gnarus quam regionem petisset rex quidve pararet. caduceator eo regius venit, specie ut induciae essent donec
tollerentur ad sepulturam qui in acie cecidissent, re vera
4  ad petendam veniam legatis mittendis. utrumque ab Romano impetratum. adiecta etiam illa uox, bono animo esse
regem ut iuberet, quae maxime Aetolos offendit, iam tu-
mentes querentesque mutatum victoria imperatorem:
5  ante pugnam omnia magna parvaque communicare cum
sociis solitum, nunc omnium expertes consiliorum esse,
suo ipsum arbitrio cuncta agere; cum Philippo iam gratiae
6  privatae locum quaerere, ut dura atque aspera belli Aetoli
exhauserint, pacis gratiam et fructum Romanus in se ver-

---

34 Polybius' figures (18.27.6) are, indeed, the same as Livy's,
except that the Macedonians captured are "not fewer than 5,000."
This is one of four places where Polybius is mentioned by name
(cf. also 34.50.6, 36.19.11, 39.52.1). See Introduction, xix–xxvi.

numbers of all kinds, 40,000 of the enemy were killed that day, and 5,700 taken prisoner (a more modest fabrication), with 249 military standards captured. Claudius, too, in his account gives the enemy dead as 32,000, with 4,300 taken captive. As for me, I have not simply accepted the lowest figures; rather, I have followed Polybius, no unreliable authority on Roman history in general, and particularly on events in Greece.[34]

11. Philip brought together the fugitives who had followed in his path after being dispersed by the various hazards of the battle, and he sent men to Larisa to burn the royal archives so they would not fall into enemy hands. He then withdrew to Macedonia. As for Quinctius, he sold some of the prisoners and booty and gave some to the men, and then set off for Larisa, though he did not yet know the area for which the king had headed or what his plans were. At Larisa a herald of the king came to him, ostensibly seeking a truce so that the casualties of the battle could be picked up for burial, but really to ask permission to send ambassadors. Both requests were granted by the Roman general. He added the comment that the herald should tell the king to take heart, which was particularly vexing for the Aetolians, already aggrieved and complaining that the commander had been changed by the victory: before the battle he used to involve his allies in everything, great or small, they said, but now they took no part in planning and he did everything on his own initiative. He was, they opined, seeking a way to make Philip personally grateful to him so that, while the Aetolians would have had their fill of the hardships and tribulations of the war, the Roman would be deflecting to himself the gratitude for the peace and the resulting profits. In fact, it

313

7 tat. et haud dubie decesserat iis aliquantum honoris; sed
cur neglegerentur ignorabant. donis regis imminere cre-
8 debant invicti ab ea cupiditate animi virum; sed et suscen-
sebat non immerito Aetolis ob insatiabilem aviditatem
praedae et adrogantiam eorum, victoriae gloriam in se
9 rapientium, quae vanitate sua omnium aures offendebat,
et Philippo sublato, fractis opibus Macedonici regni, Aeto-
10 los habendos Graeciae dominos cernebat. ob eas causas
multa sedulo ut viliores levioresque apud omnes essent et
viderentur faciebat.

12. Indutiae quindecim dierum datae hosti erant et
cum ipso rege constitutum conloquium; cuius priusquam
tempus veniret, in concilium[30] advocavit socios. rettulit
2 quas leges pacis placeret dici. Amynander Athamanum rex
paucis sententiam absolvit: ita componendam pacem esse
ut Graecia etiam absentibus Romanis satis potens tuendae
3 simul pacis libertatisque esset. Aetolorum asperior oratio
fuit, qui pauca praefati recte atque ordine imperatorem
Romanum facere quod, quos belli socios habuisset, cum
4 iis communicaret pacis consilia, falli aiunt[31] eum tota re si
aut Romanis pacem aut Graeciae libertatem satis firmam

[30] concilium *Briscoe*: consilium *B*
[31] aiunt *Madvig*: autem *B*

was clear that the Aetolians had lost a measure of their prestige; but they had no idea why they were being over-looked. They actually believed that a man whose character was not at all susceptible to such avarice had his eyes on the king's largesse; but in fact Quinctius was incensed with the Aetolians—and with good reason—because of their insatiable appetite for plunder and their arrogance in appropriating to themselves the credit for the victory, their boasts of which grated on everyone's ears. He could also see that, with Philip removed and the power of the Macedonian kingdom broken, it was the Aetolians who would have to be considered the masters of Greece. For these reasons he was methodically taking numerous measures to ensure that their standing and influence should be diminished, and seen to be diminished, in everyone's eyes.

12. The enemy had been granted a fifteen-day truce and a meeting had been scheduled with the king himself, but before the date of the meeting arrived Quinctius called the allies to a conference and brought up the matter of the peace terms they wished to see established. Amynander, king of the Athamanians, stated his position briefly: peace must be arranged on such terms as rendered Greece strong enough to preserve her independence as well as keep the peace even in the absence of the Romans. The speech of the Aetolians was harsher. After a few prefatory remarks, they said that the Roman commander was acting correctly and properly in consulting those who had been his allies in the war about plans for the peace settlement, but he was quite wrong if he thought that he would be putting peace for the Romans or independence for Greece on a secure footing without Philip being either

se credat relicturum nisi Philippo aut occiso aut regno pulso; quae utraque proclivia esse si fortuna uti vellet.

5     Ad haec Quinctius negare Aetolos aut moris Romanorum memorem[32] aut sibi ipsis convenientem sententiam

6 dixisse: et illos prioribus omnibus conciliis conloquiisque de condicionibus pacis semper, non[33] ut ad internecionem

7 bellaretur disservisse, et Romanos praeter vetustissimum morem victis parcendi praecipuum clementiae documentum dedisse pace Hannibali et Carthaginiensibus data.

8 omittere se Carthaginienses: cum Philippo ipso quotiens ventum in conloquium? nec unquam ut cederet regno actum esse. an quia victus proelio foret, inexpiabile bellum

9 factum? cum armato hoste infestis animis concurri debere: adversus victos mitissimum quemque animum maximum habere. libertati Graeciae videri graves Macedonum

10 reges: si regnum gensque tollatur, Thracas Illyrios Gallos deinde, gentes feras et indomitas, in Macedoniam se et in

11 Graeciam effusuras. ne proxima quaeque amoliendo maioribus gravioribusque aditum ad se facerent.

12     Interfanti deinde Phaeneae praetori Aetolorum, testificantique si elapsus[34] eo tempore Philippus foret mox

13 gravius eum rebellaturum, "desistite[35] tumultuari" inquit

---

32 memorem *Gron.*: memores *B*
33 non *Gron.*: om. *B*
34 elapsus *rmg*: lapsus *B*
35 desistite *rmg*: desistit et *B*

---

35 Cf. He was strategos 198/7. Cf. 32.32.11 and note.

killed or driven from his throne. Both these ends were easily attainable if he chose to follow up his success, they said.

In reply Quinctius observed that the statement of the Aetolians took no account of Roman practice and was also inconsistent with their earlier views. In all previous councils and meetings, he said, their discussions had concentrated on terms for peace, not fighting to the point of extermination; and the Romans, who had a long-established custom of sparing the defeated, had given a notable demonstration of their clemency in granting a peace treaty to Hannibal and the Carthaginians. But, to say nothing of the Carthaginians, on how many occasions had there been discussions with Philip himself? And there had never been any suggestion that he leave the throne. Or was it simply that war had become an unpardonable crime now that he had been defeated in battle? One should confront an armed foe with hostility, he said, but in the case of a defeated enemy it is the most humane victor who demonstrates the greatest character. Yes, the kings of Macedon seemed to pose a threat to the liberty of Greece; but if that kingdom and that people were eliminated, Thracians, Illyrians, and, after them, Gauls—barbarous and ferocious peoples—would come flooding into Macedonia and Greece. The Greeks, he concluded, should not leave themselves exposed to others more powerful and dangerous by tearing down everything nearest to them.

Phaeneas, praetor of the Aetolians,[35] then interrupted, and declared that if Philip gave them the slip on that occasion he would soon rise again with a more serious war. "Stop blustering when we have matters to discuss," replied

"ubi consultandum est: non iis condicionibus inligabitur rex[36] ut movere bellum possit."

13. Hoc dimisso concilio, postero die rex ad fauces quae ferunt in Tempe—is datus erat locus conloquio—ve-
2 nit; tertio die datur ei Romanorum ac sociorum frequens
3 concilium. ibi Philippus, perquam prudenter iis sine qui-bus pax impetrari non poterat sua potius voluntate omissis
4 quam altercando extorquerentur, quae priore conloquio aut imperata a Romanis aut postulata ab sociis essent om-nia se concedere, de ceteris senatui permissurum dixit.

5 Quamquam vel inimicissimis omnibus praeclusisse vo-cem videbatur, Phaeneas tamen Aetolus cunctis tacen-
6 tibus "quid? nobis" inquit, "Philippe, reddisne tandem Pharsalum et Larisam Cremasten et Echinum et Thebas
7 Phthias?" cum Philippus nihil morari diceret quo minus reciperent, disceptatio inter imperatorem Romanum et
8 Aetolos orta est de Thebis; nam eas populi Romani iure belli factas esse Quinctius dicebat, quod integris rebus exercitu ab se admoto vocati in amicitiam, cum potestas libera desciscendi ab rege esset, regiam societatem Roma-
9 nae praeposuissent; Phaeneas et pro societate belli quae ante bellum habuissent restitui Aetolis aequum censebat,
10 et ita in foedere primo cautum esse ut belli praeda rerum

---

[36] rex *Jacobs*: pax *B*

---

[36] Literally, "third" (i.e., by Roman inclusive counting).

[37] Livy here seems again to have misunderstood Polybius (see Briscoe 1.272).

Quinctius. "The conditions by which the king will be bound will not be such that he could possibly start a war."

13. The council was adjourned, and the next day the king arrived at the pass leading into Tempe, the venue set for their meeting; and on the day after that[36] he was introduced to a crowded assembly of Romans and their allies. Here Philip very wisely conceded of his own accord all items that were essential for negotiating peace rather than have them wrung out of him in argument; and he declared that he accepted all the terms laid down by the Romans or insisted upon by the allies at the previous meeting, and everything else he would leave to the discretion of the senate.

It seemed that he had now silenced all his critics, even the most hostile, but when everyone fell silent the Aetolian Phaeneas said: "So, Philip, are you finally returning to us Pharsalus, Larisa Cremaste, Echinus and Phthiotic Thebes?" When Philip said he saw no objection to their retrieving them, an argument broke out between the Roman commander and the Aetolians on the matter of Thebes.[37] Quinctius claimed that it had fallen to the Roman people by the rules of war. Before the conflict, he said, when he had brought the army to the city, the Thebans had been invited to form an alliance and, though they had the clear opportunity to break with the king, they had preferred a treaty with him over one with Rome. Phaeneas was of the opinion that, in the light of the alliance formed to prosecute the war, it was fair that the Aetolians be given back what they had held before the war, and he added that the terms of the original treaty had provided for spoils of the war, in the form of goods and chattels, going to the

quae ferri agique possent Romanos, ager urbesque captae
11 Aetolos sequerentur. "vos" inquit "ipsi" Quinctius "societatis istius leges rupistis quo tempore relictis nobis cum
12 Philippo pacem fecistis. quae si maneret, captarum tamen
urbium illa lex foret: Thessaliae civitates sua voluntate in
dicionem nostram venerunt."

13 Haec cum omnium sociorum adsensu dicta Aetolis non
in praesentia modo gravia auditu sed mox etiam belli
14 causa[37] magnarumque ex eo cladium iis fuerunt. cum Philippo ita convenit ut Demetrium filium et quosdam ex
amicorum numero obsides et ducenta talenta daret, de
ceteris Romam mitteret legatos: ad eam rem quattuor
15 mensum induciae essent. si pax non impetrata ab senatu
foret, obsides pecuniamque reddi Philippo receptum est.
causa Romano imperatori non alia maior fuisse dicitur
maturandae pacis quam quod Antiochum bellum trans-
itumque in Europam moliri constabat.

14. Eodem tempore atque, ut quidam tradidere, eodem die ad Corinthum Achaei ducem regium Androsthe-
2 nem iusto proelio fuderunt. eam urbem pro arce habiturus
Philippus adversus Graeciae civitates et principes inde
evocatos per speciem conloquendi quantum equitum dare
3 Corinthii ad bellum possent retinuerat pro obsidibus, et

[37] causa *Crév.*: causae B

---

[38] Disgruntled over this settlement, the Aetolians later incited
Philip, Nabis, and Antiochus against the Romans (Book 35.12).
Polybius (18.39.2) also states that this quarrel was "the spark from
which the [Romans'] war with the Aetolians and that with Antiochus were set alight."

Romans, and land and captured cities going to the Aetolians. "You yourselves broke the terms of that particular
treaty at the time when you deserted us and made peace
with Philip," replied Quinctius. "Even if it were still in
force, that clause would still apply only to cities that were
captured; the city-states of Thessaly came under our authority of their own free will."

These arguments met with applause from all the other
allies; but for the Aetolians, as well as being unpleasant to
hear at the time, they also later proved to be the cause of
a war that had disastrous consequences for them.[38] An
agreement was reached with Philip that he give his son
Demetrius and a number of his friends as hostages and
pay an indemnity of 200 talents, and that he send a delegation to Rome about the other items; for that he was granted
a truce of four months. Should peace not be granted by
the senate, an assurance was given that the hostages and
money would be returned to Philip. It is said that the
prime reason for the Roman commander's haste to make
peace was that it was now certain that Antiochus was making preparations for war and an invasion of Europe.

14. At this same time, and in some accounts on the very
same day,[39] the Achaeans defeated the king's general Androsthenes[40] in pitched battle at Corinth. Philip intended
using this city as a fortress against the city-states of Greece
and, after summoning the leading citizens on the pretext of discussing the number the cavalry the Corinthians
could supply for the war, he had detained them as hos-

[39] Such synchronisms were very popular in Greek and Roman
historiography and are not usually credible.

[40] Cf. 32.23.5 and note.

praeter quingentos Macedonas mixtosque ex omni genere
4   auxiliorum octingentos, quot iam ante ibi fuerant, mille
    Macedonum eo miserat et mille ac ducentos Illyrios Thra-
    casque et Cretenses, qui in utraque parte militabant,
5   octingentos. his additi Boeoti Thessalique et Acarnanes
    mille, scutati omnes, et septingenti ex[38] ipsorum Corin-
    thiorum iuuentute, impleta ut essent sex milia armatorum,
    fiduciam Androstheni fecerunt acie decernendi.
6       Nicostratus praetor Achaeorum Sicyone erat cum duo-
    bus milibus peditum, centum equitibus, sed imparem se
    et numero et genere militum cernens moenibus non ex-
7   cedebat. regiae copiae peditum equitumque uagae Pel-
    lenensem et Phliasium et Cleonaeum agrum depopu-
8   labantur; postremo exprobrantes metum hosti in fines
    Sicyoniorum transcendebant, navibus etiam circumvecti
9   omnem oram Achaiae vastabant. cum id effusius hostes et,
    ut fit ab nimia fiducia, neglegentius etiam facerent, Nico-
10  stratus, spem nactus necopinantes eos adgrediendi, circa
    finitimas civitates nuntium occultum mittit quo die et quot
    ex quaque civitate armati ad Apelaurum—Stymphaliae
11  terrae is locus est—convenirent. omnibus ad diem edic-
    tam paratis, profectus inde extemplo per Phliasiorum fines
    nocte Cleonas, insciis omnibus quid pararet, pervenit.
12  erant autem cum eo quinque milia peditum, ex quibus
    ⟨. . .⟩[39] armaturae levis, et trecenti equites. cum iis copiis,

---

[38] et septingenti ex *Walch*: et *B*
[39] . . . *lac. indicat Perizonius*

---

[41] Cf. 32.39.7 and note.
[42] *Barr.* 58 D1 (Pellene), D2 (Phlius and Cleonae).
[43] *Barr.* 58 C2.
[44] A number has here been clearly lost from the text.

tages. Furthermore, beside a contingent of 500 Macedonians and 800 auxiliaries of various nationalities that had already been stationed in the city, he had sent a further 1,000 Macedonians, 1,200 Illyrians and Thracians, and 800 Cretans (Cretans were to be found fighting on both sides). In addition to these there were a thousand Boeotians, Thessalians and Acarnanians, all shield-bearers, and 700 men of military age from among the Corinthians themselves, making total of 6,000 men under arms, which gave Androsthenes the confidence to decide matters in the field.

Nicostratus, praetor of the Achaeans,[41] was at Sicyon with 2,000 infantry and 100 cavalry, but since he could see he was at a disadvantage both in the numbers and the quality of his troops he would not venture beyond his fortifications. The king's infantry and cavalry troops were roaming around making raids on the countryside of Pallene, Phlius, and Cleonae.[42] Finally they passed over into the territory of Sicyon, taunting their enemy with cowardice, and they also used their ships to sail along the entire coast of Achaea, which they routinely plundered. Since the enemy was engaging in these operations in a sporadic and, as happens with overconfidence, even a remiss manner, Nicostratus conceived the hope of attacking them unawares. He surreptitiously sent a message around the neighboring states ordering armed men to assemble at Apelaurum,[43] an area in Stymphalian territory, and specifying the date and the numbers to come from each state. When preparations for the appointed day were complete, he forthwith set off by night through the land of Phlius and reached Cleonae with nobody aware of his plans. With him were 5,000 infantry, including . . . [44] light infantry and 300

dimissis qui specularentur quam in partem hostes effunderent sese, opperiebatur.

15. Androsthenes omnium ignarus Corintho profectus ad Nemeam—amnis est Corinthium et Sicyonium interfluens agrum—castra locat. ibi partem dimidiam exercitus dimissam, divisam trifariam,[40] et omnes equites discurrere ad depopulandos simul Pellenensem Sicyoniumque agros et Phliasium iubet. haec tria diversa agmina discessere. quod ubi Cleonas ad Nicostratum perlatum est, extemplo validam mercennariorum manum praemissam ad occupandum saltum per quem transitus in Corinthium est agrum, ante signa equitibus ut praegrederentur locatis, ipse confestim agmine duplici sequitur. parte una mercennarii milites ibant cum levi armatura, altera clipeati; id in illarum gentium exercitibus robur erat.

Iam haud procul castris aberant pedites equitesque, et Thracum quidam in vagos palatosque per agros hostes impetum fecerant, cum repens terror castris infertur. trepidare dux, ut qui hostes nusquam nisi raros[41] in collibus ante Sicyonem non audentes agmen demittere in campos vidisset, ad Cleonas[42] quidem accessuros nunquam credidisset. revocari tuba iubet vagos a castris dilapsos; ipse,

2

3

4
5

6

7

8

---

[40] partem dimidiam exercitus dimissam, divisam trifariam *Madvig*: parte dimidia exercitus dimissa dimidiam trifariam divisit (*corr. ex* dimsit) *B*    [41] raros *Duker*: raro *B*
[42] ad Cleonas *r*: ad Cleonis *B*: a Cleonis *Madvig*

---

[45] Shield-bearers (Lat. *clipeati*, Gk. ὑπασπισταί): elite troops developed on the pattern of the hypaspists of Alexander. In Hellenistic Macedonia there were units known as "Silver Shields" (ἀργυράσπιδες) and "Golden Shields" (χρυσάσπιδες).

cavalry. With these forces he began his wait, having dispatched scouts to observe the direction in which the enemy was spreading out.

15. Unaware of all this, Androsthenes set out from Corinth and encamped on the Nemea, which is a stream flowing between the lands of Corinth and those of Sicyon. There he disengaged half his army, divided it into three parts, and ordered these and all his cavalry to conduct simultaneous raids on the farmlands of Pellene, Sicyon, and Phlius. These three columns marched off in their various directions. When news of it reached Nicostratus at Cleonae, he immediately sent ahead a strong detachment of mercenaries to seize the pass that affords access to the territory of Corinth. Then, positioning the cavalry before the standards to lead the way, he himself swiftly followed the mercenaries with his army arranged in two columns. In one marched mercenary troops and light infantry, and in the other the shield-bearers (they were the main strength of the army for those nations).[45]

By now the infantry and cavalry were not far from the Macedonian camp, and a number of Thracians had attacked the enemy as they roamed in disorder through the countryside, when consternation suddenly struck the camp. The general panicked; he had not seen his enemy at any point, apart from an occasional glimpse in the hills before Sicyon—and then they would not venture to send their column down into the plains—and he had never believed they would reach Cleonae. He gave the command for those scattered in various places outside the camp to be recalled with a trumpet signal. Then, ordering his men

raptim capere arma iussis militibus, infrequenti agmine
9　porta egressus super flumen instruit aciem. ceterae copiae
vix conligi atque instrui cum potuissent, primum hostium
10　impetum non tulerunt. Macedones et maxime omnium
frequentes ad signa fuerant et diu ancipitem victoriae
11　spem fecerunt; postremo fuga ceterorum nudati, cum
duae iam acies hostium ex diverso, levis armatura ab latere, clipeati caetratique a fronte urgerent, et ipsi re incli-
12　nata primo rettulere pedem, deinde impulsi terga vertunt
et plerique abiectis armis, nulla spe castrorum tenendo-
rum relicta, Corinthum petierunt.
13　　　Nicostratus mercennariis militibus ad hos persequen-
dos, equitibus Thracumque auxiliis in populatores agri Si-
cyonii missis, magnam ubique[43] caedem edidit, maiorem
14　prope quam in proelio ipso. ex iis quoque qui Pellenen
Phliuntaque depopulati erant, incompositi[44] partim omniumque ignari[45] ad castra revertentes in hostium sta-
15　tiones tamquam in suas inlati sunt, partim ex discursu id
quod erat suspicati ita se in fugam passim sparserunt ut ab
16　ipsis agrestibus errantes circumvenirentur. ceciderunt eo
die mille et quingenti, capti trecenti. Achaia omnis magno
liberata metu.
　　　16. Priusquam dimicaretur ad Cynoscephalas, L.

[43] ubique *rmg:* ibique *B*: utrobique *Gron.*
[44] incompositi *rmg:* compositi *B*
[45] omniumque ignari *rmg:* omnium signari *B*

to take up arms at the double, he went out through the gate with a thinly manned column of soldiers and deployed his line of battle on the riverbank. All these troops, apart from the Macedonians, could only with difficulty be brought together and put into formation, and they failed to withstand the initial assault of their enemy. The Macedonians had assembled for the fight in by far the greatest numbers, and they long kept the prospect of victory for either side in doubt. Finally, left unprotected when the others fled, and with two enemy battle lines bearing down on them from different directions—the light infantry from the flank, the shield-bearers and peltasts from the front— they, too, the battle now lost, at first gave ground and then, coming under pressure, took to their heels. Most discarded their weapons and with no hope left of holding on to the camp headed for Corinth.

Sending his mercenaries in pursuit of them, Nicostratus dispatched his cavalry and Thracian auxiliaries against the troops ravaging the farmland of Sicyon and everywhere produced a great bloodbath, almost greater even than in the battle itself. Then there were the soldiers who had pillaged Pellene and Phlius. Returning to camp out of formation, and totally unaware of what had happened, some of them drifted into the outposts of their enemy, assuming that they were their own; others, surmising from the turmoil what had actually transpired, took flight and became so dispersed that they were waylaid even by the local peasants as they wandered here and there. On that day 15,000 men lost their lives, and 300 were captured. All Achaea was delivered from a terrible dread.

16. Before the battle at Cynoscephalae, Lucius Quinc-

Quinctius, Corcyram excitis Acarnanum principibus, quae
sola Graeciae gentium in societate Macedonum manserat,
2 initium quoddam ibi motus fecit. duae autem maxime causae eos tenuerant in amicitia regis, una fides insita genti,
3 altera metus odiumque Aetolorum. concilium Leucadem
indictum est. eo neque cuncti convenere Acarnanum populi nec iis qui convenerant idem placuit; sed[46] principes
et magistratus pervicerunt ut privatum decretum Roma-
4 nae societatis fieret. id omnes qui afuerant aegre passi; et
in hoc fremitu gentis a Philippo missi duo principes Acar-
5 nanum, Androcles et Echedemus, non ad tollendum modo
decretum Romanae societatis valuerunt, sed etiam ut
Archelaus et Bianor, principes gentis ambo, quod auctores
eius sententiae fuissent, proditionis in concilio damnaren-
tur, et Zeuxidae praetori, quod de ea re rettulisset, imperium abrogaretur.
6    Rem temerariam sed eventu prosperam damnati fecerunt. suadentibus namque amicis cederent tempori et
7 Corcyram ad Romanos abirent, statuerunt offerre se multitudini et aut eo ipso lenire iras aut pati quod casus tulis-
8 set. cum se frequenti concilio intulissent, primo murmur
ac fremitus admirantium, silentium mox a verecundia si-

---

[46] sed *Briscoe*: sed et *B*: sed duo *Madvig*

---

[46] The fear was understandable. In 211 M. Valerius Laevinus
had signed a treaty with the Aetolians that stipulated that the
Romans "would take steps to see that the Aetolians should have
possession of Acarnania" (26.24.11).          [47] Capital city of the
island of Leucas (also called Leucadia: cf. 17.6, below), off the
coast of Acarnania (*Barr.* 54 C4). The island's name derives from
the white (λευκός) cliffs on its west coast.

tius had summoned to Corcyra the leaders of the Acarnanians, the only people in Greece to have remained within the Macedonian alliance, and here he made a start on changing the situation. Two major factors in particular had kept the Acarnanians loyal to their treaty of friendship with the king: one, the inbred fidelity of their race, and the other their fear and hatred of the Aetolians.[46] An assembly was called at Leucas.[47] Not all the Acarnanian peoples came, however, and those who did attend were not in agreement. Nevertheless, their leading men and magistrates succeeded in getting a private decree passed authorizing an alliance with Rome. All who had not attended were enraged at this, and amid the national unrest two prominent Acarnanians, Androcles and Echedemus, sent to Leucas by Philip, were able not only to have the decree sanctioning the Roman alliance rescinded, but also to have Archelaus and Bianor, both notable members of their people, convicted of treason in the meeting for proposing the decree. They also had the praetor Zeuxis'[48] appointment annulled for having introduced the motion.

The condemned men followed a course of action that was impetuous but proved successful. Although their friends urged them to accept the situation and join the Romans on Corcyra, they decided instead to present themselves before the crowded assembly and either assuage its anger by this gesture or accept whatever might befall them. When they entered the packed meeting, there was at first a murmuring and buzz from the surprised audience, but silence soon fell, from respect for the men's

[48] All these men (Androcles, Echedemus, Archelaus, Bianor, and Zeuxis) are otherwise unknown.

mul pristinae dignitatis ac misericordia praesentis fortu-
9 nae ortum est. potestate quoque dicendi facta, principio
suppliciter, procedente autem oratione, ubi ad crimina
diluenda ventum est, cum tanta fiducia quantam innocen-
10 tia dabat disseruerunt; postremo ultro aliquid etiam queri
et castigare iniquitatem simul in se crudelitatemque ausi,
ita adfecerunt animos ut omnia quae in eos decreta erant
11 frequentes tollerent, neque eo minus redeundum in societatem Philippi abnuendamque Romanorum amicitiam
censerent.

17. Leucade haec sunt decreta. id caput Acarnaniae
2 erat, eoque in concilium omnes populi conveniebant. itaque cum haec repentina mutatio Corcyram ad legatum
Flamininum perlata esset, extemplo cum classe profectus
3 Leucadem ad Heraeum quod vocant naves adplicuit. inde
cum omni genere tormentorum machinarumque quibus
expugnantur urbes ad muros accessit, ad primum ter-
4 rorem ratus inclinari animos posse. postquam pacati nihil
ostendebatur, tum vineas turresque erigere et arietem
admovere muris coepit.

5 Acarnania universa inter Aetoliam atque Epirum po-
6 sita solem occidentem et mare Siculum spectat. Leucadia
nunc insula est, vadoso freto quod perfossum manu est ab
Acarnania divisa; tum paeninsula erat, occidentis regione
7 artis faucibus cohaerens Acarnaniae; quingentos ferme
passus longae eae fauces erant, latae haud amplius centum

former status as much as pity for their present misfortune. Given leave to speak, they began in suppliant tones; but as their speech progressed and they came to the point of defending themselves against the charges, they spoke with the confidence that their innocence gave them and finally went so far as to complain and protest about the unjust and cruel treatment meted out to them. Such was the impression they made that, with a large majority, the assembly reversed all the decisions that had been taken against them while nevertheless voting to return to the alliance with Philip and reject a pact of friendship with the Romans.

17. Such were the decisions taken at Leucas. This was the capital of Acarnania, and the place where all its peoples gathered for their assembly. So when news of this sudden change of heart was brought to the legate Flamininus on Corcyra he immediately set sail for Leucas with his fleet, and anchored off what they call the Heraeum.[49] From here he advanced to the city walls with all manner of artillery and siege engines used for storming towns, believing that the townspeople's outlook could change with the initial panic. When there was no sign of readiness for peace, he proceeded to erect siege sheds and towers and to move the battering ram up to the walls.

Situated in its entirety between Aetolia and Epirus, Acarnania faces west toward the Sicilian Sea. Leucadia is now an island, separated from Acarnania by a shallow, man-made strait, but at that time it was a peninsula, attached to Acarnania at its western end by a narrow isthmus, some 500 paces in length and no more than 120 in

[49] A temple of Hera, but its location is unknown

et viginti. in iis angustiis Leucas posita est, colli adplicata
8  verso in orientem et Acarnaniam; ima urbis plana sunt,
iacentia ad mare quo Leucadia ab Acarnania dividitur.
inde terra marique expugnabilis est; nam et vada sunt
stagno similiora quam mari, et campus terrenus omnis
9  operique facilis. itaque multis simul locis aut subruti aut
ariete decussi ruebant muri; sed quam urbs ipsa oppor-
10  tuna oppugnantibus erat, tam inexpugnabiles hostium
animi. die ac nocte[47] intenti reficere quassata muri, ob-
struere quae patefacta ruinis erant, proelia impigre inire
et armis magis muros quam se ipsos moenibus tutari;
11  diutiusque spe Romanorum obsidionem eam extraxissent
ni exsules quidam Italici generis Leucade habitantes ab
12  arce milites accepissent. eos tamen ex superiore loco
magno cum tumultu decurrentes, acie in foro instructa,
13  iusto proelio aliquamdiu Leucadii sustinuerunt. interim et
scalis capta multis locis moenia, et per stragem lapidum ac
14  ruinas transcensum in urbem; iamque ipse legatus magno
agmine circumvenerat pugnantes. tum pars in medio
15  caesi, pars armis abiectis dediderunt sese victori. et post
dies paucos, audito proelio quo ad Cynoscephalas pugnatum erat, omnes Acarnaniae populi in dicionem legati
venerunt.

[47] die ac nocte *Mog.*: diem ac noctem *B*

---

[50] According to tradition Leucas/Leucadia had been a peninsula, but its early (Corinthian) colonists severed the spit joining
it to the mainland. Livy is clearly wrong if he is saying that it was
a peninsula in 197 but an island in his day. He has probably been
careless in transmitting the traditional version, which he presumably found in Polybius.

width.[50] Leucas lies on the narrow isthmus, set on a hill that faces east toward Acarnania. The lower reaches of the city are flat, lying beside the sea by which Leucadia is divided from Acarnania. At this point it is vulnerable to attack both from land and sea as the shallow waters here resemble a pool more than a sea, while the plain is entirely made up of soft earth and is easy to dig. As a result the walls began to collapse at several points simultaneously, either undermined or else knocked down by the ram. But if the city itself was an easy proposition for its assailants, the spirit of the enemy was indomitable. Day and night they applied themselves to rebuilding the shattered portions of the wall, to blocking gaps left where it had collapsed, to joining battle with vigor, and to protecting their walls with their weapons rather than themselves with their ramparts. In fact, they would have drawn out the siege longer than the Romans expected had not some exiles of Italian stock who were living in Leucas come down from the citadel and admitted their soldiers. Even then the Leucadians, who had drawn up their battle line in the forum, held the Romans for some time in pitched battle, rushing down with a great commotion from their higher position. In the meantime the fortifications were taken by scaling ladders at several points, and the Romans clambered into the city over stones strewn on the ground and over the fallen walls, while by now the legate himself, at the head of a large column of men, had surrounded the still resisting Leucadians. Then some were cut down, encircled by their foes; others threw down their arms and surrendered to the victor. A few days later, on hearing of the battle that had been fought at Cynoscephalae, all the peoples of Acarnania capitulated to the legate.

18. Iisdem diebus, omnia simul inclinante fortuna, Rhodii quoque ad vindicandam a Philippo continentis regionem—Peraean vocant—possessam a maioribus suis,
2 Pausistratum praetorem cum octingentis Achaeis peditibus, mille et octingentis fere armatis ex vario genere auxi-
3 iliorum conlectis miserunt: Galli et Mniesutae[48] et Pisuetae et Tarmiani[49] et Theraei ex Peraea[50] et Laudiceni ex
4 Asia erant. cum iis copiis Pausistratus Tendeba[51] in Stratonicensi agro locum peropportunum ignaris regiis qui
5 Therae erant occupavit. in tempore et ad id[52] ipsum excitum auxilium, mille Achaei pedites cum centum equitibus
6 supervenerunt; Theoxenus iis praeerat. Dinocrates regius praefectus reciperandi castelli causa primo castra ad ipsa Tendeba movet, inde ad alterum castellum item Stratoni-
7 censis agri—Astragon vocant—; omnibusque eo[53] praesidiis, quae multifariam disiecta erant, devocatis et ab ipsa Stratonicea Thessalorum auxiliaribus, ad Alabanda, ubi
8 hostes erant, ducere pergit. nec Rhodii pugnam detractaverunt. ita castris in propinquo locatis extemplo in aciem descensum est.

48 Mniesutae *Holleaux*: et Nisuetae *Mog.*: *om. B*
49 Tarmiani *H.J.M.*: Tamiani *BMog.*
50 Theraei ex Peraea *Robert*: Trahi ex Africa *B*: Arei ex Africa *Mog.*
51 Tendeba *Freinsheim:* tenebat *B*: tendebat *Mog.*
52 id *Gel.*: *om. BMog.*
53 eo *Harant*: ex *BMog.*: *del. Madvig*

51 Cf. 32.33.6 and note.
52 Pausistratus here commands the Rhodian land forces but later is the Rhodian naval commander against Antiochus the

18. Philip's fortunes were waning everywhere simultaneously, and it was just at that time that the Rhodians also intended reclaiming from him an area of the mainland called the Peraea,[51] which had belonged to their forefathers. For that they sent out the praetor Pausistratus[52] in command of 800 Achaean infantry and some 1,800 auxiliary troops brought together from different races—Gauls, Mniesutae, Pisuetae, Tarmiani, and Theraei from the Peraea, and Laudiceni from Asia. With these troops Pausistratus seized Tendeba (which was very strategically situated in the territory of Stratonicea) without the knowledge of the king's forces stationed at Thera.[53] He was joined at the opportune moment by an auxiliary force raised for the operation: 1,000 Achaean infantry and 100 cavalry, all under the command of Theoxenus. To recover this fortified town, the king's prefect Dinocrates first moved his camp toward Tendeba itself, and from there to a second stronghold (they call it Astragon), also in Stratonicean territory. Then, after recalling to that place all the widely scattered Macedonian garrisons, as well as the Thessalian auxiliaries from Stratonicea itself, he proceeded to Alabanda,[54] where his enemy was located. The Rhodians did not refuse the fight. And so, with their camps established close to each other, the two sides immediately came forward for battle.

Great (36.45.6). For his death in 190 after being tricked by Antiochus' admiral Polyxenidas, cf. 37.9.5–11.12.

[53] Tendeba, Stratonicea, and Thera (and Astragon, below) lay in southern Caria: *Barr.* 61 G3.

[54] Alabanda: *Barr.* 61 F2.

9     Dinocrates quingentos Macedonas dextro cornu, laevo
Agrianas locat, in medium accipit contractos ex castellorum—Cares maxime erant—praesidiis, equites cornibus
10 circumdat et Cretensium auxiliares Thracumque. Rhodii
Achaeos dextro cornu, sinistro mercennarios[54] milites, lec-
tam peditum manum, habuere, medios mixta ex pluribus
11 gentibus auxilia, equites levisque armaturae quod erat
cornibus circumiectum.
12     Eo die steterunt tantum acies utraque super ripam torrentis qui tenui tum aqua interfluebat,[55] paucisque telis
13 emissis in castra receperunt sese. postero die eodem ordine instructi maius aliquanto proelium quam pro numero
edidere pugnantium. neque enim plus terna milia pedi-
14 tum fuere et centeni ferme equites; ceterum non numero
tantum nec armorum genere sed animis quoque paribus
15 et aequa spe pugnarunt. Achaei primi torrente superato in
Agrianas impetum fecerunt; deinde tota prope cursu
16 transgressa amnem acies est. diu anceps pugna stetit.
numero Achaei, mille ipsi, quadringentos loco pepulere;
inclinato deinde laevo cornu in dextrum omnes conisi.
17 Macedones usque dum ordines et veluti stipata phalanx
18 constabat moveri nequiverunt; postquam laevo latere
nudato circumagere hastas in venientem ex transverso

[54] dextro . . . mercennarios *Mog.*: *om. B*

[55] torrentis . . . interfluebat *H.J.M.*: qui tenui tum aqua interfluebat torrens *B*: quae tenui aqua interfluebat torrentis *Mog.*

---

[55] Light-armed Thracian troops (cf. *Barr.* 49 E1 for their territory). They figure prominently in Alexander the Great's army in
Arrian and Curtius Rufus.     [56] Presumably, given the previous two sentences, the Agrianes.

Dinocrates deployed 500 Macedonians on his right wing and the Agrianes[55] on the left; he brought into the center the men drawn from the garrisons of the fortified towns, Carians for the most part, and placed cavalry and Cretan and Thracian auxiliaries about the wings. The Rhodians had Achaeans on the right wing and an elite body of mercenary infantry on the left; the center comprised an assortment of auxiliaries drawn from several races; and the cavalry and such light infantry as they had covered the wings.

On that day the battle lines of each side merely took up a position on the banks of a torrent that flowed between them, at that time with low water level, and after hurling a few javelins they retired to camp. The following day, drawn up in the same formation, they fought a battle considerably more fierce than one would have expected given the numbers fighting. There were, in fact, no more than 3,000 infantry and about 100 cavalry on each side, but in the fight they were not just evenly matched in numbers and equipment but had equal fortitude and similar hopes of victory, as well. The Achaeans initiated the action by crossing the torrent and attacking the Agrianes; then the entire line crossed the stream almost at a run. For a long time it was an even fight. By virtue of their numbers the Achaeans, who totaled 1,000, forced their 400 adversaries[56] to give ground; then, when the left wing buckled, they all put pressure on the right. The Macedonians could not be budged for as long as the ranks and their compressed phalanx, as it were, held firm. But when their left flank was exposed, they attempted to bring their lances round to

hostem conati sunt, turbati extemplo tumultum primo
inter se fecerunt, terga deinde vertunt, postremo abiectis
armis in praecipitem fugam effunduntur. Bargylias petentes fugerunt; eodem et Dinocrates perfugit.

19 Rhodii, quantum diei superfuit secuti, receperunt sese
in castra. satis constat, si confestim victores Stratoniceam
20 petissent, recipi eam urbem sine certamine potuisse. prae-
termissa eius rei occasio est dum in castellis vicisque reci-
21 piendis Peraeae tempus teritur. interim animi eorum qui
Stratoniceam praesidio obtinebant confirmati sunt; mox et
Dinocrates cum iis quae proelio superfuerant copiis intra-
22 vit muros. nequiquam inde obsessa oppugnataque urbs
est, nec recipi nisi aliquanto post per Antiochum potuit.

Haec in Thessalia, haec in Achaia, haec in Asia per
eosdem dies ferme gesta.

19. Philippus cum audisset Dardanos transgressos fines
ab contemptu concussi tum regni superiora Macedoniae
2 evastare, quamquam toto prope orbe terrarum undique se
3 suosque exigente fortuna urgebatur, tamen morte tristius
ratus Macedoniae etiam possessione pelli, dilectu raptim
per urbes Macedonum habito cum sex milibus peditum et
quingentis equitibus circa Stobos Paeoniae improviso ho-
4 stes oppressit. magna multitudo hominum in proelio,
maior cupidine praedandi palata per agros caesa est. qui-

---

57 On the west coast of Caria (*Barr.* 61 F3).

58 On the historical problem posed by this statement, see
Briscoe 1.283.

59 This continues the narrative left at the end of chapter 14.

60 Stobi lay at the confluence of the rivers Axios and Erigon
(*Barr.* 50 A1).

face the enemy coming at them from the side, and were immediately disoriented. At first they produced chaos in their ranks; then they turned back; and finally they threw down their weapons and took off in headlong flight. They ran off heading for Bargyliae,[57] and Dinocrates fled in the same direction.

The Rhodians pursued them for what was left of the day and then retired to camp. It is widely accepted that, if the victors had immediately headed for Stratonicea, that city could have been taken without a struggle. The opportunity for that was lost while time was wasted on the recapture of fortified towns and villages of the Peraea. In the meantime those garrisoning Stratonicea regained their composure and soon Dinocrates also entered the town with the troops that had survived the battle. After that besieging and attacking the city proved fruitless, and it could not be taken until considerably later when it fell to Antiochus.[58]

Such were events in Thessaly, Achaea, and Asia, and they occurred at roughly the same time.

19. Philip[59] had heard that, from disdain for his now badly shaken kingdom, the Dardanians had crossed his frontiers and were devastating the upper stretches of Macedonia; and so he was under pressure almost the world over as fortune dogged him and his people at every turn. Nevertheless, feeling that being dispossessed of the throne of Macedonia was a fate worse than death, he conducted a hurried levy of troops throughout the cities of Macedonia and, at the head of 6,000 infantry and 500 cavalry, overpowered his enemy with a surprise attack in the area of Stobi in Paeonia.[60] Large numbers of men were killed in the action, even more as they roamed through the

bus fuga in expedito fuit, ne temptato quidem casu pugnae
5 in fines suos redierunt. ea una expeditione, non pro reli-
quo statu fortunae facta, refectis suorum animis Thessalo-
nicam sese recepit.

6     Non tam in tempore Punicum bellum terminatum erat,
ne simul et cum Philippo foret bellandum, quam opportune, iam Antiocho ex Syria moliente bellum, Philippus
7 est superatus: nam praeterquam quod facilius cum singulis quam si in unum ambo simul contulissent vires bellatum est, Hispania quoque sub idem tempus magno tumultu ad bellum consurrexit.

8     Antiochus, cum priore aestate omnibus quae in Coele
Syria sunt civitatibus ex Ptolomaei dicione in suam potestatem redactis in hiberna Antiochiam concessisset, ni-
9 hilo quietiora ea ipsis aestivis habuit. omnibus enim regni
viribus conixus cum ingentes copias terrestres maritimas-
que comparasset, principio veris praemissis terra cum exercitu filiis duobus Ardye ac Mithridate[56] iussisque Sardi-
bus se opperiri, ipse cum classe centum tectarum navium,
10 ad hoc levioribus navigiis cercurisque ac lembis ducentis
11 proficiscitur, simul per omnem oram Ciliciae Lyciaeque et
Cariae temptaturus urbes quae in dicione Ptolomaei essent, simul Philippum—necdum enim debellatum erat—
exercitu navibusque adiuturus.

---

[61] At this point Livy begins his account of the war with King
Antiochus (self-styled the Great) of Syria.     [62] Coele Syria
("Hollow Syria") was at this date the whole area south of Syria
down to the Nile delta.     [63] Antioch-on-the-Orontes, the
Syrian capital, founded by Alexander's general Seleucus (later,

fields, hungry for booty. Those who had the opportunity to flee returned to their own lands without even risking a fight. Philip retired to Thessalonica, the confidence of his people restored by that single campaign, so different from his fortunes elsewhere.

The timely ending of the war with the Carthaginians,[61] which saved the Romans from having to fight them and Philip at the same time, was not as opportune as Philip's defeat at a point when Antiochus was already fomenting war from his base in Syria. Apart from the fact that it was easier for Rome to fight these enemies separately than if the two had joined forces, there was also in that same period an armed uprising and great upheaval in Spain.

The previous summer, Antiochus had wrested from Ptolemy's control and brought into his own power all the city-states in Coele Syria,[62] and had then retired to Antioch[63] for the winter, which proved no less active a season for him than the summer had been. Exploiting all the resources of his kingdom, he had amassed huge land and sea forces; and at the beginning of spring[64] he sent ahead his two sons, Ardyes and Mithridates, overland with an army, ordering them to wait for him at Sardis. He then set out himself with a fleet of 100 ships with decks, plus 200 lighter vessels, Cyprian cutters and pinnaces. His aim was to strike at the cities under Ptolemy's control all along the coast of Cilicia, Lycia, and Caria, and at the same time to assist Philip (for the war against Philip was not yet finished) with his army and ships.

King Seleucus I). The modern Turkish town of Antakya (to which it gave its name) lies close to its ruins (*Barr.* 67 C4: Antiochia/Theoupolis).      [64] Spring of 197.

20. Multa egregie Rhodii pro fide erga populum Romanum proque universo nomine Graecorum terra marique
2 ausi sunt, nihil magnificentius quam quod ea tempestate,
non territi tanta mole imminentis belli, legatos ad regem
miserunt ne Chelidonias—promunturium Ciliciae est,
inclutum foedere antiquo Atheniensium cum regibus Per-
sarum—superaret: si eo fine non contineret classem co-
3 piasque suas, se obviam ituros, non ab odio ullo sed ne
coniungi eum Philippo paterentur, et impedimento esse
Romanis liberantibus Graeciam.
4 Coracesium eo tempore Antiochus operibus oppugnabat, Zephyrio et Solis et Aphrodisiade et Coryco et, superato Anemurio—promunturium id quoque Ciliciae est—,
5 Selinunte recepto. omnibus his aliisque eius orae castellis
aut metu aut voluntate sine certamine in dicionem acceptis, Coracesium praeter spem clausis portis tenebat eum.
6 ibi legati Rhodiorum auditi. et quamquam ea legatio erat
quae accendere regium animum posset, temperavit irae et
7 legatos se Rhodum missurum respondit, iisque mandaturum ut renovarent vetusta iura cum ea civitate sua maiorumque suorum, et vetarent eos pertimescere adventum
regis: nihil aut iis aut sociis eorum noxiae futurum frau-
8 dive; nam Romanorum amicitiam se non violaturum ar-

---

65 Chelidonian promontory: *Barr.* 65 D5. The treaty is the
"peace of Callias," made between Athens and Artaxerxes in the
mid-fifth century, which barred the Persian fleet from venturing
west of the Chelidonian islands. The historicity of such a treaty
is, however, much disputed (cf. *OCD* sv Callias, Peace of).

66 *Barr.* 65 G4 (Korakesion).

67 All towns on the coast of Cilicia (*Barr.* 66 B–F 3–4).

68 This is the only evidence for these "ancient bonds."

20. The people of Rhodes have performed many exceptional exploits on land and sea out of loyalty to the Roman people and on behalf of the entire Greek race, but none more glorious than their feat at this time. Undaunted by the magnitude of the war that threatened, they sent envoys to the king warning him not to pass beyond Chelidoniae, a promontory in Cilicia famous for the treaty concluded in days of old between Athens and the kings of Persia.[65] If Antiochus did not keep his fleet and land forces behind that line, they said, they would come to resist him, not from any animosity, but to prevent him from joining up with Philip and obstructing the Roman liberation of Greece.

At that time Antiochus was investing Coracesium[66] with siege works. He had already taken Zephyrium, Soli, Aphrodisias, Corycus and (after rounding Anemurium— also a promontory in Cilicia) Selinus.[67] However, while all these and other fortified towns on that coastline had submitted without a fight (either from fear or by choice), Coracesium had unexpectedly shut its gates on him and now had him bogged down there. Envoys from Rhodes were here granted an audience and, though the embassy's mission was such as might infuriate the king, he nonetheless controlled his anger and replied that he would send representatives to Rhodes. These he would instruct to renew the ancient bonds that he and his ancestors had with that state,[68] and tell the Rhodians not to feel apprehensive about the king's coming, that it would entail no harm or injury either for the Rhodians or for their allies. As proof that he would not violate his alliance with the

gumento et suam recentem ad eos legationem esse, et
9 senatus honorifica in se decreta responsaque. tum forte
legati redierant ab Roma comiter auditi dimissique, ut
tempus postulabat, incerto adhuc adversus Philippum
eventu belli.

10 Cum haec legati regis in contione Rhodiorum agerent,
nuntius venit debellatum ad Cynoscephalas esse. hoc nuntio accepto Rhodii, dempto metu a Philippo, omiserunt
11 consilium obviam eundi classe Antiocho: illam alteram
curam non omiserunt tuendae libertatis civitatium sociarum Ptolomaei quibus bellum ab Antiocho imminebat.
12 nam alias auxiliis iuverunt, alias providendo ac praemo-
nendo conatus hostis, causaque libertatis fuerunt Cauniis
13 Myndiis Halicarnassensibus Samiisque. non operae est
persequi ut quaeque acta in his locis sint, cum ad ea quae
propria Romani belli sunt vix sufficiam.

21. Eodem tempore Attalus rex, aeger ab Thebis Pergamum advectus, moritur altero et septuagesimo anno,
2 cum quattuor et quadraginta annos regnasset. huic viro
praeter divitias nihil ad spem regni fortuna dederat. iis
simul prudenter simul magnifice utendo effecit primum
3 ut sibi deinde ut aliis non indignus videretur regno. victis
deinde proelio uno Gallis, quae tum gens recenti adventu

---

69 This probably took place in the winter of 198/7 and would
have been in the context of the exchanges between Rome, Attalus, and Antiochus over Antiochus' attacks on Pergamene territory (cf. 32.8.9–16).

70 Caunus: *Barr.* 65 A4; Myndus and Halicarnassus: 61 E3.

71 Cf. 2.2–3, above.

Romans, he cited his recent delegation to them, and the decisions and answers given by the senate that did him honor. (As it happened, Antiochus' ambassadors had just returned from Rome, where they had been given a courteous hearing and then dismissed, as the situation demanded, since it was still uncertain how the war with Philip would turn out.)[69]

While the king's envoys were discussing these matters in the assembly of the Rhodians, news arrived that the war had been brought to an end at Cynoscephalae. On receiving this news, the Rhodians, who were now freed from fear of Philip, abandoned their plan of confronting Antiochus with their fleet, but they did not abandon their other concern, namely preserving the independence of the cities allied to Ptolemy, which were then threatened with war by Antiochus. Some of them they helped with military resources, others with advance warnings and intelligence on the enemy's movements, and they were responsible for maintaining the independence of the peoples of Caunus, Myndus, Halicarnassus[70] and Samos. A detailed report of military operations in these areas cannot really be justified when I am barely able to provide an account of those relevant to the war fought by the Romans.

21. In this same period King Attalus, who had been taken back to Pergamum after falling ill at Thebes,[71] died at the age of seventy-one after a rule of forty-four years. Fate had given this man nothing apart from wealth to foster any hope of his becoming a king. However, by a judicious and at the same time liberal use of his riches, he made himself appear not unfit for a throne, first in his own eyes, and subsequently in others'. He then, in a single battle, vanquished the Gauls, a race at the time all the

terribilior Asiae erat, regium adscivit nomen, cuius
4 magnitudini semper animum aequavit. summa iustitia
suos rexit, unicam fidem sociis praestitit, comis in uxorem
ac liberos[57]—quattuor superstites habuit—, mitis ac mu-
5 nificus amicis fuit; regnum adeo stabile ac firmum reliquit
ut ad tertiam stirpem possessio eius descenderit.
6 Cum hic status rerum in Asia Graeciaque et Macedonia
esset, vixdum terminato cum Philippo bello, pace certe
nondum perpetrata, ingens in Hispania ulteriore coortum
7 est bellum. M. Helvius eam provinciam obtinebat. is litteris senatum certiorem fecit Culcham et Luxinium regulos
8 in armis esse: cum Culcha decem et septem oppida, cum
Luxinio validas urbes Carmonem et Bardonem;[58] in maritima ora Malacinos Sexetanosque et Baeturiam omnem et
quae nondum animos nudaverant ad finitimorum motus
9 consurrectura. his litteris a M. Sergio praetore, cuius iurisdictio inter cives et peregrinos erat, recitatis, decreverunt
patres ut comitiis praetorum perfectis, cui praetori provincia Hispania obvenisset, is primo quoque tempore de
bello Hispaniae ad senatum referret.

---

[57] comis in uxorem ac liberos *Goeller*: comis uxor ac liberos    *B*: uxorem ac liberos *Mog.*: comis uxori ac liberis *Jacobs*
[58] Bardonem *Mog.*: Baldonem *B*

---

[72] Attalus was succeeded by his sons Eumenes II (197–159)
and Attalus II (159–138), and the kingdom ended when Attalus
III died in 133 and it became the Roman province of Asia.

[73] Carmo: *Barr.* 26 E4; TIR *J-30,* 125–27. Location of Bardo
or Baldo (see textual note) is unknown.

[74] Malaca (Malaga): *Barr.* 27 A5; TIR *J-30,* 227–29; Sexetani
(the people of Sexi Firmum Iulium, now Almuñécar): *Barr.* 27
B5; TIR *J-30,* 301; Baeturia: *Barr.* 26 D–E3; TIR *J-30,* 101.

more feared in Asia for having only just arrived; and after that he assumed the royal title and consistently revealed a disposition that matched the title's majesty. He ruled his subjects with consummate justice; he demonstrated a unique loyalty toward his allies; he was easygoing in his relationship with his wife and children (four of whom survived him); and he was tolerant and generous with his friends. He left his kingdom on such a firm and solid footing that his family's sovereignty over it lasted to the third generation.[72]

Such was the state of affairs in Asia, Greece, and Macedonia when the war with Philip was only just finished or when, at least, peace had not yet been concluded. Meanwhile a momentous war broke out in Farther Spain. Marcus Helvius was governor of the province. He informed the senate by letter that two minor kings, Culchas and Luxinius, were up in arms, that seventeen towns had joined Culchas, and the powerful cities of Carmo and Bardo[73] had joined Luxinius. On the coast, he said, the Malacini, the Sexetani, all Baeturia,[74] and the tribes that had not yet revealed their sympathies would join the uprising of their neighbors. This letter was read out by the praetor Marcus Sergius, who had jurisdiction in cases between citizens and foreigners,[75] and the senators then decreed that, after the elections for the praetorship, the praetor to whom the province of Spain was allotted should bring the question of the war in Spain before the senate at the earliest opportunity.

[75] Livy is mistaken: Marcus Sergius Silus (40) was urban praetor this year (cf. 32.28.2; *MRR* 333).

22. Sub idem tempus consules Romam venerunt; quibus in aede Bellonae senatum habentibus, postulantibus-
2 que triumphum ob res prospere bello gestas, C. Atinius
Labeo et C. Afranius tribuni plebis ut separatim de triumpho agerent consules postularunt: communem se relationem de ea re fieri non passuros, ne par honos in dispari
3 merito esset. cum Q. Minucius utrique Italiam provinciam
obtigisse diceret, communi animo consilioque se et colle-
4 gam res gessisse, et C. Cornelius adiceret Boios, adversus
se transgredientes Padum ut Insubribus Cenomanisque
auxilio essent, depopulante vicos eorum atque agros col-
5 lega ad sua tuenda aversos esse, tribuni res tantas bello
gessisse C. Cornelium fateri ut non magis de triumpho
eius quam de honore dis immortalibus habendo dubitari
6 possit: non tamen nec illum nec quemquam alium civem
tantum gratia atque opibus valuisse ut cum sibi meritum
triumphum impetrasset, collegae eundem honorem im-
7 meritum impudenter petenti daret. Q. Minucium in Liguribus levia proelia vix digna dictu fecisse, in Gallia
8 magnum numerum militum amisisse; nominabant etiam
tribunos militum T. Iuventium Cn. Ligurium legionis
quartae: adversa pugna cum multis aliis viris fortibus, civi-
9 bus ac sociis, cecidisse. oppidorum paucorum ac vicorum

---

76 Where the awarding of triumphs was often discussed (cf.
31.47.7 and note). On the consuls' campaigns in Gaul, the subject
of the following debate, cf. 32.29.5–31.6.

22. At about this same time the consuls reached Rome. They convened the senate in the temple of Bellona,[76] and requested a triumph in recognition of their military achievements, but they were faced with a demand from the plebeian tribunes, Gaius Atinius Labeo and Gaius Afranius, that the consuls hold separate debates on their triumphs. They would not, they said, allow a joint motion on the issue in case equal credit should be accorded when merit was not equal. Quintus Minucius made the point that both consuls had been allotted the province of Italy, and that he and his colleague had conducted the campaign with shared aims and strategy; and Gaius Cornelius added that when the Boii crossed the Po to confront him with the intention of aiding the Insubres and Cenomani, it was because of his colleague's plundering of their villages and fields that they turned away to protect their own property. The tribunes then acknowledged that Gaius Cornelius' achievements in the war were so significant that a triumph for him could no more be in doubt than could the honors to be paid to the immortal gods. Even so, they added, neither he nor any other citizen had so much influence or power that he could, after gaining a well-earned triumph for himself, bestow the same distinction, when it was *not* well earned, upon a colleague with the impertinence to request it. Quintus Minucius, they declared, had fought some inconsequential battles, barely worth the mention, among the Ligurians, and he had lost a large number of men in Gaul. They also mentioned by name the military tribunes of the fourth legion, Titus Iuventius and Gnaeus Ligurius. These had fallen in Minucius' defeat, they said, along with many other brave men, both citizens and allies. As for the capitulation of the few

falsas et in tempus simulatas sine ullo pignore deditiones factas esse.

10     Hae inter consules tribunosque altercationes biduum tenuerunt, victique perseverantia tribunorum consules separatim rettulerunt.

    23. C. Cornelio omnium consensu decretus triumphus; et Placentini Cremonensesque addiderunt favorem con-
2   suli, gratias agentes commemorantesque obsidione sese ab eo liberatos, plerique etiam, cum apud hostes essent,
3   servitute exemptos. Q. Minucius temptata tantum relatione, cum adversum omnem senatum videret, in monte Albano se triumphaturum et iure imperii consularis et multorum clarorum virorum exemplo dixit.

4     C. Cornelius de Insubribus Cenomanisque in magistratu triumphavit. multa signa militaria tulit, multa Gal-
5   lica spolia captivis carpentis transuexit, multi nobiles Galli ante currum ducti, inter quos quidam Hamilcarem ducem
6   Poenorum fuisse auctores sunt; ceterum magis in se convertit oculos Cremonensium Placentinorumque colono-
7   rum turba, pilleatorum currum sequentium. aeris tulit in triumpho ducenta triginta septem milia quingentos, ar-

---

77 On triumphs requested but refused, including that of Minucius Rufus, cf. Beard 206–14. Sage here suggests the "proof" may refer to hostages taken to corroborate the victory.

78 A few generals in the late third/early second centuries chose to celebrate a triumph on the Alban Mount (today Monte Cavo), some seventeen miles from Rome, when their application for a triumph within Rome was refused (cf. Beard 62–63).

79 See, however, 31.21.18 (and note), 32.30.12.

80 A soft cap (*pilleus*) was worn by slaves when granted their freedom. The colonists were thus signifying that Cornelius had delivered them from slavery. According to Suetonius (*Ner.* 57.1)

towns and villages, this was all lies made up for the occasion, with no proof given.[77]

This wrangling between the consuls and the tribunes took up two days, after which the consuls, frustrated by the doggedness of the tribunes, submitted their requests separately.

23. The decision to award Gaius Cornelius the triumph was unanimous. The people of Placentia and Cremona also lent their support to the consul, offering him their thanks and reminding the senate that it was Cornelius who had raised their siege; and many added that he had also delivered them from slavery when they were in the hands of the enemy. As for Quintus Minucius, he merely tried out his motion and then, seeing the senate entirely opposed to him, declared that he would celebrate a triumph on the Alban mount,[78] which was within the rights of his consular authority and also sanctioned by the precedent of many distinguished men.

Gaius Cornelius celebrated his triumph over the Insubres and Cenomani while still in office. He had many military standards put on display in the procession, large quantities of Gallic spoils transported on captured wagons, and many Gallic noblemen led before his chariot (and among them, some say, was the Carthaginian general, Hamilcar).[79] But what attracted most attention was the troop of colonists from Cremona and Placentia who followed the chariot with freedman caps[80] on their heads. Cornelius had 237,500 bronze *asses* carried along in his triumphal parade, and 79,000 silver coins stamped with

and Dio (63.29.1), some Romans donned caps "like freedmen" after Nero's downfall.

genti bigati undeoctoginta milia; septuageni aeris militibus divisi, duplex equiti centurionique.[59]

8    Q. Minucius consul de Liguribus Boiisque Gallis in
monte Albano triumphavit. is triumphus ut loco et fama
rerum gestarum et quod sumptum non erogatum ex aerario omnes sciebant inhonoratior fuit, ita signis carpentis-
9    que et spoliis ferme aequabat. pecuniae etiam prope par
summa fuit: aeris tralata ducenta quinquaginta quattuor
milia, argenti bigati quinquaginta tria milia et ducenti;
militibus centurionibusque et equitibus idem in singulos
datum quod dederat collega.

24. Secundum triumphum consularia comitia habita.
creati consules L. Furius Purpureo et M. Claudius Mar-
2    cellus. praetores postero die facti Q. Fabius Buteo, Ti.
Sempronius Longus, Q. Minucius Thermus, M'. Acilius
Glabrio, L. Apustius Fullo, C. Laelius.

3    Exitu ferme anni litterae a T. Quinctio venerunt se signis conlatis cum rege Philippo in Thessalia pugnasse, ho-
4    stium exercitum fusum fugatumque. hae litterae prius in
senatu a M. Sergio praetore, deinde ex auctoritate patrum

---

[59] duplex equiti centurionique *B*: duplex equiti triplex centurioni *Mog.*: duplex centurioni triplex equiti *Duker*

---

[81] A silver coin stamped with the two-horse chariot (*biga* or
*bigae*); cf. 31.49.2 note.

[82] L. Furius Purpureo (86): military tribune in 210, praetor in
200, had triumphed over the Gauls (31.47.6–49.3). M. Claudius
Marcellus (222): military tribune in 208, plebeian tribune in 204,
curule aedile in 200, praetor in 198.

[83] C. Laelius (2), a *novus homo* (cf. Introduction, lvi–lvii)
friend of Scipio Africanus, with whom he served in Spain (209–

the *biga*.[81] Seventy bronze *asses* were distributed to each
of the soldiers, twice that amount to each cavalryman and
centurion.

The consul Quintus Minucius celebrated his triumph
over the Ligurians and Gallic Boii on the Alban mount.
This triumph was a less exalted affair by virtue of its location, the reputation of the accomplishments involved, and
the fact that everyone knew the expenses for it were not
covered by the public purse. In terms of military standards, wagons and spoils, however, it almost rivaled the
other. Even the sums of money involved were roughly
equal: 254,000 bronze *asses* and 53,200 silver coins
stamped with the *biga* were carried in the procession, and
the common soldiers, centurions and cavalrymen were
each given the same amount as Minucius' colleague had
given to his men.

24. After the triumph, the consular elections were
held, and the consuls chosen were Lucius Furius Purpureo and Marcus Claudius Marcellus.[82] Those elected as
praetors the next day were: Quintus Fabius Buteo, Tiberius Sempronius Longus, Quintus Minucius Thermus,
Manius Acilius Glabrio, Lucius Apustius Fullo, and Gaius
Laelius.[83]

Toward the end of the year a dispatch arrived from
Titus Quinctius with the news that he had fought a pitched
battle with King Philip in Thessaly, and that the enemy
army had been vanquished and put to flight. The dispatch
was read out by the praetor Marcus Sergius, in the senate
first of all, and then, later, on the authorization of the sen-

206) and Africa (205–202); he rose through the offices to consul
in 190.

in contione sunt recitatae, et ob res prospere gestas in dies
5 quinque supplicationes decretae. brevi post legati et ab T.
Quinctio et ab rege Philippo venerunt. Macedones deducti extra urbem in villam publicam, ibique iis locus et
6 lautia praebita, et ad aedem Bellonae senatus datus. ibi
haud multa verba facta, cum Macedones quodcumque
7 senatus censuisset id regem facturum esse dicerent. decem legati more maiorum, quorum ex consilio T. Quinctius imperator leges pacis Philippo daret, decreti, adiec-
tumque ut in eo numero legatorum P. Sulpicius et P.
Villius essent, qui consules provinciam Macedoniam ob-
tinuissent.
8 Cosanis eodem anno[60] postulantibus ut sibi colonorum
9 numerus augeretur mille adscribi iussi, dum ne quis in eo
numero esset qui post P. Cornelium et Ti. Sempronium
consules hostis fuisset.

25. Ludi Romani eo anno in circo scaenaque ab aedilibus curulibus P. Cornelio Scipione et Cn. Manlio Vulsone
et magnificentius quam alias facti, et laetius propter res
2 bello bene gestas spectati, totique ter instaurati. plebeii

---

[60] eodem anno *H.J.M.*: eo die *BMog.*: eo anno *Weiss.*: obelo
utitur *Briscoe*

---

[84] On *supplicatio,* cf. 31.8.2 note.      [85] On the edge of the
Campus Martius, it was built in 435 as the censors' headquarters
(cf. Richardson 430–31) and was apparently later used also for
public functions, including the hosting of foreign ambassadors.

[86] Used also for receiving foreign dignitaries.

[87] P. Cornelius Scipio (330) and Ti. Sempronius Longus (66)
had been consuls in 218. The restriction was clearly aimed at any
who had defected to Hannibal in the Second Punic War.

ate, in a public assembly; and five days of supplication[84] were prescribed in thanks for the successful campaign. Shortly afterward envoys came from both Titus Quinctius and King Philip. The Macedonians were taken out of the city to the Public Villa[85] where they were housed and officially entertained, and they were granted a meeting with the senate at the temple of Bellona.[86] The proceedings here were not long since the Macedonians stated that the king would abide by any decision of the senate. In accordance with ancestral custom, a board of ten commissioners was appointed, in consultation with whom the general Titus Quinctius was to formulate peace terms for Philip; and a rider was added that Publius Sulpicius and Publius Villius, former consuls who had commanded Macedonia, be members of the board.

That same year the people of Cosa requested an increase in the number of their colonists. The enrollment of a thousand was authorized, with the condition that none be included who had been an enemy of Rome in the period following the consulship of Publius Cornelius and Tiberius Sempronius.[87]

25. The Roman Games were that year held in the circus and theater by the curule aediles,[88] Publius Cornelius Scipio and Gnaeus Manlius Vulso. The performances were more lavish than on other occasions, and were also watched with greater pleasure because of the military successes, and they were repeated three times in their en-

[88] Whose responsibility they were. On the Roman Games (*Ludi Romani*), cf. 31.50.2 note. Dramatic performances there go back to Livius Andronicus in 240 (cf. 31.12.10 note).

septiens instaurati; M'. Acilius Glabrio et C. Laelius eos
3  ludos fecerunt, et de argento multaticio tria signa aenea,
Cererem Liberumque et Liberam, posuerunt.

4      L. Furius et M. Claudius Marcellus consulatu inito,
cum de provinciis ageretur et Italiam utrique provinciam
senatus decerneret, ut Macedoniam cum Italia sortirentur
5  tendebant. Marcellus, provinciae cupidior, pacem simula-
tam ac fallacem dicendo, et rebellaturum si exercitus inde
deportatus esset regem, dubios sententiae patres fecerat;
6  et forsitan obtinuisset consul, ni Q. Marcius Ralla et C.
Atinius Labeo tribuni plebis se intercessuros dixissent ni
prius ipsi ad plebem tulissent vellent iuberentne cum rege
7  Philippo pacem esse. ea rogatio in Capitolio ad plebem
lata est: omnes quinque et triginta tribus "uti rogas" iusserunt.

8      Et quo magis pacem ratam esse in Macedonia volgo
9  laetarentur tristis ex Hispania adlatus nuntius effecit, vol-
gataeque litterae C. Sempronium Tuditanum proconsu-
lem in citeriore Hispania proelio victum, exercitum eius
fusum fugatum, multos inlustres viros in acie cecidisse,

---

89 On repetition (*instauratio*) and the Plebeian Games, cf.
31.4.7 note.      90 On fines used for public projects, cf. 31.50.2
and note. The temple of the three deities lay on the slope of the
Aventine near the west end of the Circus Maximus and was dedicated in 493 (Richardson 80–81).      91 This is the formula set
before the popular assembly, especially for declaring war or making peace: cf. 21.17.4, 30.43.3, 36.1.5, 45.21.4.      92 The Roman tribes (by this time there were four urban and thirty-one
rural tribes) were purportedly instituted by the king Servius Tul-
lus. Every citizen had to belong to one, and they were used as
voting units in voting assemblies (and also as the basis of the
census, taxation, and army recruitment). Cf. Introduction, l–li.

tirety. The Plebeian Games were repeated seven times.[89] Manius Acilius Glabrio and Gaius Laelius staged these games, and they erected three bronze statues—of Ceres, Liber, and Libera—from money taken in fines.[90]

When Lucius Furius and Marcus Claudius Marcellus began their consulship, and the question of their provinces arose, the senate was ready to assign Italy to both of them, but the consuls kept pressing for sortition for Macedonia along with Italy. Marcellus, who was the more eager to gain the province, declared that the peace accord was a specious bluff, that the king would go to war again if the army were removed from there, and this had made the senate think twice about their recommendation. The consul might possibly have had his way if the tribunes of the people, Quintus Marcius Ralla and Gaius Atinius Labeo, had not threatened to use their veto unless they themselves first brought before the people the question of whether it was their wish and command that there should be peace with Philip.[91] The motion was put to the people on the Capitol, and all thirty-five tribes[92] voted in favor of it.

In addition, the arrival of bad news from Spain actually served to increase public satisfaction with the conclusion of peace in Macedonia: a letter was made public[93] announcing the defeat of the proconsul Gaius Sempronius Tuditanus[94] in battle in Hither Spain. The letter stated that Tuditanus' army had been vanquished and put to

[93] Quite what this letter was is uncertain, but the expression "was made public" indicates that it was not the official dispatch.

[94] C. Sempronius Tuditanus (90); cf. 32.27.7. He was *praetor pro consule* in Spain.

Tuditanum cum gravi volnere relatum ex proelio haud ita
multo post exspirasse.

10     Consulibus ambobus Italia provincia cum iis legionibus quas superiores consules habuissent decreta, et ut
quattuor legiones novas scriberent, duas urbanas duas

11 quae quo senatus censuisset mitterentur; et T. Quinctius
Flamininus provinciam eodem exercitu obtinere iussus:
imperium ei prorogatum satis iam ante videri esse.

    26. Praetores deinde provincias sortiti, L. Apustius
Fullo urbanam iurisdictionem, M'. Acilius Glabrio inter

2 cives et peregrinos, Q. Fabius Buteo Hispaniam ulteriorem, Q. Minucius Thermus citeriorem, C. Laelius Sici-

3 liam, Ti. Sempronius Longus Sardiniam. Q. Fabio Buteoni
et Q. Minucio, quibus Hispaniae provinciae evenerant,
consules legiones singulas ex quattuor ab se scriptis quas

4 videretur ut darent decretum est, et socium ac Latini nominis quaterna milia peditum trecenos equites; iique

5 primo quoque tempore in provincias ire iussi. bellum in
Hispania quinto post anno motum est quam simul cum
Punico bello fuerat finitum.

6     Priusquam aut hi praetores ad bellum prope novum,
quia tum primum suo nomine sine ullo Punico exercitu aut
duce ad arma ierant, proficiscerentur aut ipsi consules ab
urbe moverent, procurare, ut adsolet, prodigia quae nun-

95 Cf. 32.28.9.
96 On allies/holders of Latin rights, cf. 31.5.4 note

flight, that many eminent men had fallen in the battle, and that Tuditanus had been carried from the fray with a serious wound and had died shortly afterward.

The two consuls were assigned Italy as their province with the legions that the previous consuls had commanded. They were also instructed to enroll four new legions, two for the city and two to be sent wherever the senate decided. Titus Quinctius Flamininus was also instructed to continue operations with the same army, and the earlier extension of his *imperium* was deemed sufficient.[95]

26. In the praetorian allotment of provinces that followed, Lucius Apustius Fullo gained the urban jurisdiction and Manius Acilius Glabrio citizen-foreigner affairs; Quintus Fabius Buteo received Farther Spain, Quintus Minucius Thermus Hither Spain, Gaius Laelius Sicily, and Tiberius Sempronius Longus Sardinia. It was decided that each of the consuls should transfer to Quintus Fabius Buteo and Quintus Minucius, to whom the Spanish provinces had fallen, one of the four legions that they had enrolled (the consuls selecting these legions), along with 4,000 infantry and 300 cavalry of the allies and those with Latin rights.[96] These praetors were instructed to leave for their provinces as soon as possible. War now broke out again in Spain four years after it had been last brought to an end along with the Punic War.

This was almost a new war because it was the first time the Spaniards had commenced hostilities on their own initiative without any Carthaginian forces or a Carthaginian leader; but before the two praetors could set out for it, or the consuls leave Rome themselves, they received orders to undertake the customary ritual of expiating prodi-

7  tiabantur iussi. P. Villius eques Romanus in Sabinos pro-
8  ficiscens fulmine ipse equusque exanimati fuerant; aedis
   Feroniae in Capenati de caelo tacta erat; ad Monetae dua-
9  rum hastarum spicula arserant; lupus Esquilina porta
   ingressus, frequentissima parte urbis cum in forum decur-
   risset, Tusco vico atque inde Cermalo per portam Cape-
   nam prope intactus evaserat. haec prodigia maioribus
   hostiis sunt procurata.

   27. Iisdem diebus Cn. Cornelius Blasio, qui ante C.
   Sempronium Tuditanum citeriorem Hispaniam obtinue-
2  rat, ovans ex senatus consulto urbem est ingressus. tulit
   prae se auri mille et quingenta quindecim pondo, argenti
   viginti milia, signati denarium triginta quattuor milia et
3  quingentos. L. Stertinius ex ulteriore Hispania, ne temptata quidem triumphi spe, quinquaginta milia pondo ar-
4  genti in aerarium intulit, et de manubiis duos fornices in
   foro bovario ante Fortunae aedem et matris Matutae,
   unum in maximo circo fecit, et his fornicibus signa aurata
5  imposuit. haec per hiemem ferme acta.

   Hibernabat eo tempore Elatiae T. Quinctius, a quo
   cum multa socii peterent, Boeoti petierunt impetrave-

---

97 Capena was just north of Rome, and Lucus Feroniae (a
grove sacred to the Sabine goddess Feronia) some four miles
southeast of it (*Barr.* 42 D4).      98 On the Capitoline (cf.
Richardson 215 sv Iuno Moneta, and fig. 19 [p. 69]). The origin
of the title Moneta is obscure but may have followed the establishment of the mint there in 273.      99 The Porta Esquilina
lay on the eastern side of the city, and the Porta Capena to the
southwest. The Vicus Tuscus was a busy shop-lined street (Richardson 429 sv).      100 For Cornelius Blasio and his colleague
in Spain Lucius Stertinius (below), cf. 31.50.11 and note.

gies that were being reported. A Roman knight, Publius Villius, had been killed by lightning, along with his horse, while setting off into Sabine territory; the temple of Feronia in the area of Capena[97] had been struck by lightning; the tips of two javelins had burst into flame near the temple of Moneta;[98] and a wolf had entered Rome by the Esquiline Gate, had run into the Forum through the most populous part of the city and made its way through the Vicus Tuscus and then the Cermalus before escaping almost untouched by way of the Porta Capena.[99] Expiation of these prodigies was performed with full-grown victims.

27. In this same period Gnaeus Cornelius Blasio,[100] governor of Hither Spain before Gaius Sempronius Tuditanus, entered the city in an ovation[101] authorized by senatorial decree. Carried before him were 1,515 pounds of gold, 20,000 pounds of silver, and 34,500 denarii in coin. Returning from Farther Spain, Lucius Stertinius did not even investigate the prospects of a triumph, but he deposited in the treasury 50,000 pounds of silver and from the proceeds of the spoils erected two arches in the Forum Boarium[102]—before the temples of Fortuna and Mater Matuta respectively—and one in the Circus Maximus. He set gilded statues on all three arches. Such, more or less, were the events of the winter.

During this time Titus Quinctius was wintering at Elatia. He received numerous petitions from the allies, including the Boeotians, who asked for (and were granted)

---

[101] On the ovation, cf. 31.20.5 note. We are not told why it was awarded here.     [102] The Roman cattle market, situated on the Tiber, occupied an area from the base of the Aventine to the Capitolinit (Richardson 162–64 [with diagram]).

runtque ut qui suae gentis militassent apud Philippum sibi
6  restituerentur. id a Quinctio facile impetratum, non quia
satis dignos eos credebat, sed quia Antiocho rege iam suspecto favor conciliandus nomini Romano apud civitates
7  erat. restitutis iis confestim apparuit quam nulla inita apud
Boeotos gratia esset; nam ad Philippum legatos gratias
agentes ei pro redditis hominibus, perinde atque ipsis et
8  non Quinctio et Romanis id datum esset, miserunt, et
comitiis proximis Boeotarchen ob nullam aliam causam
Brachyllem quendam quam quod praefectus Boeotorum
9  apud regem militantium fuisset fecerunt, praeteritis Zeuxippo et Pisistrato aliisque qui Romanae societatis auctores
10  fuerant. id aegre et in praesentia hi passi, et in futurum
etiam metum ceperunt: cum ad portas prope sedente exercitu Romano ea fierent, quidnam se futurum esse pro-
11  fectis in Italiam Romanis, Philippo ex propinquo socios
adiuvante et infesto iis qui partis adversae fuissent?

28. Dum Romana arma in propinquo haberent, tollere
2  Brachyllem principem fautorum regis statuerunt. et tempore ad eam rem capto, cum in publico epulatus reverte-
retur domum temulentus, prosequentibus mollibus viris
3  qui ioci causa convivio celebri interfuerant, ab sex armatis,
quorum tres Italici tres Aetoli erant, circumventus occidi-

---

103 "If the text is right . . . Livy implies that Quinctius transmit-
ted to Philip, with his approval, the request, and that the Boeotians ignored his intercession on their behalf" (Sage). Cf. also
Achard *ad loc.*

104 I.e., one of the seven Boeotian chief magistrates (cf. Walbank 2.608). Brachylles, one of repatriated Boeotians (Polyb.
18.43.1–4), had supported Philip at the conference at Nicaea
(Polyb. 18.1.2). What follows must have taken place in Thebes,
the Boeotian capital.

the repatriation of those of their people who had fought on Philip's side. This request was readily granted by Quinctius, not because he believed the Boeotians deserved it but because he was now suspicious of King Antiochus and needed to win support for the Roman cause among the city-states. When the men were returned it quickly became apparent how little appreciation there was among the Boeotians. It was to Philip that they sent a deputation to offer thanks for the return of the men, as if this had been a favor granted to them and not to Quinctius and the Romans.[103] They also elected a certain Brachylles as a Boeotarch[104] at the following elections, for the sole reason that he had been general of the Boeotians who fought on the king's side, and they passed over Zeuxippus, Pisistratus, and others who had advocated the alliance with Rome. These men took umbrage at this for the moment, and also harbored anxieties for the future. When such things happened with a Roman army sitting practically at their gates, they thought, what on earth would happen when the Romans had departed for Italy and Philip was still close at hand, helping his partisans and hostile to those who had been on the other side?

28. These men now decided to get rid of Brachylles, the king's leading supporter, while they still had Roman armed forces in the vicinity. The time they picked for the act was when he was returning home after a public banquet, drunk and in the company of some effeminate men who had been at the well-attended dinner to provide entertainment. Brachylles was waylaid by six armed men, three Italians and three Aetolians,[105] and assassinated. His

[105] Cf. Polyb. 18.43.8–12, who suggests that Flamininus, while not directly involved, was implicated in the assassination.

tur. fuga comitum et quiritatio facta, et tumultus per totam urbem discurrentium cum luminibus; percussores proxima porta evaserunt.

4     Luce prima contio frequens velut ex ante indicto aut
5 voce praeconis convocata in theatro erat. palam ab suo comitatu et obscenis illis viris fremebant interfectum, ani-
6 mis autem Zeuxippum auctorem destinabant caedis. in praesentia placuit comprehendi eos qui simul fuissent
7 quaestionemque ex iis haberi. qui dum quaeruntur, Zeuxippus, constanti animo avertendi ab se criminis causa in contionem progressus, errare ait homines qui tam atrocem
8 caedem pertinere ad illos semiviros crederent, multaque in eam partem probabiliter argumentatur;[61] quibus fidem apud quosdam fecit nunquam, si sibi conscius esset, oblaturum se multitudini mentionemve eius caedis nullo la-
9 cessente facturum fuisse; alii non dubitare impudenter obviam crimini eundo suspicionem averti.

Torti post paulo insontes, cum scirent ipsi nihil, opinione omnium pro indicio usi,[62] Zeuxippum et Pisistratum nominaverunt, nullo adiecto cur scire quicquam viderentur argumento. Zeuxippus tamen cum Stratonida quodam nocte perfugit Tanagram, suam magis conscientiam quam
11 indicium hominum nullius rei consciorum metuens; Pisistratus spretis indicibus Thebis mansit.

[61] argumentatur *J. Gron.*: argumentatus *BMog.*: argumentatus est *Weiss.*     [62] nihil . . . usi *Kreyssig*: *sic, sed om.* usi *B*: opinionem omnium, ea pro indicio usi *Mog.*

[106] Often a meeting place for assemblies in Greek cities.
[107] About fifteen miles east of Thebes.

companions fled, there was a hue and cry, and pandemonium broke out as men with torches ran to and fro throughout the city. The assassins slipped away through the nearest gate.

At dawn there was an assembly in the theater,[106] as well attended as if it had been convened by prior edict or called by a herald. In public, people angrily claimed that Brachylles had been killed by his retinue and the perverts in it, but in their hearts they had Zeuxippus singled out as the man responsible for the murder. For the moment they decided that those who had been with Brachylles should be arrested and interrogated. While the search for them was in progress, Zeuxippus coolly marched into the assembly to deflect incrimination from himself. People were wrong, he said, to believe such a heinous murder to be linked with these degenerates, and he produced many plausible arguments to support his case. With these he convinced some people that if he had a guilty conscience he would never have presented himself to the crowd or made mention of the murder when no one was pressing him to do so. Others, however, had no doubt that brazenly exposing himself to the charge was simply a way of averting suspicion.

Shortly afterward the innocent companions were tortured. They knew nothing but, taking as proof what everybody was thinking, they named Zeuxippus and Pisistratus but provided no further evidence to suggest they actually knew anything. Even so Zeuxippus fled by night to Tanagra[107] with a certain Stratonidas, more from fear of his own conscience than of the evidence supplied by men with no knowledge of the affair. Pisistratus remained in Thebes, with scant regard for the informers.

Servus erat Zeuxippi, totius internuntius et minister rei, quem indicem Pisistratus timens eo ipso timore ad indicium protraxit. litteras ad Zeuxippum mittit ut servum
12 conscium tolleret: non tam idoneum ad celandam rem eum videri sibi quam ad agendam fuerit. has qui tulerat
13 litteras iussus Zeuxippo dare quam primum, quia non statim conveniendi eius copia fuit, illi ipsi seruo, quem ex omnibus domino fidissimum credebat, tradit, et adicit a Pisistrato de re magno opere pertinente ad Zeuxippum
14 esse. conscientia ictus, cum extemplo traditurum eas adfirmasset, aperit perlectisque litteris pavidus Thebas refugit, et ad magistratus indicium defert. et Zeuxippus quidem, fuga servi motus, Anthedonem, tutiorem exsilio
15 locum ratus, concessit; de Pisistrato aliisque quaestiones tormentis habitae et sumptum supplicium est.

29. Efferavit ea caedes Thebanos Boeotosque omnes ad exsecrabile odium Romanorum, credentes non sine consilio imperatoris Romani Zeuxippum principem gentis id facinus conscisse. ad rebellandum neque vires neque
2 ducem habebant: proximum bello quod erat, in latrocinium versi, alios in hospitiis alios vagos per hiberna milites
3 ad varios commeantes usus excipiebant. quidam in ipsis itineribus ad notas latebras ab insidiantibus, pars in de-

---

108 About fifteen miles northeast of Thebes on the Gulf of Euboea (*Barr.* 55 E4).

Zeuxippus had a slave who had been a go-between and accomplice in the whole business. Pisistratus feared that the slave might denounce them, and it was because of that fear that he actually prompted the man to turn informant. He sent a letter to Zeuxippus advising him to get rid of the slave confederate; the man seemed less capable of keeping the affair secret than he had been of perpetrating it, he said. The bearer of the letter had been instructed to deliver it to Zeuxippus on the earliest possible occasion but, not having the opportunity to see him immediately, he passed it to that very slave, believing that of all Zeuxippus' slaves he was the one most faithful to his master. He added that it was a letter from Pisistratus on a matter of particular concern to Zeuxippus. Stricken by conscience, the slave swore to deliver it immediately but instead opened it and, after reading it, fled in panic to Thebes and laid his information before the magistrates. Troubled by the flight of his slave, Zeuxippus moved to Anthedon,[108] which he felt was a safer location for his exile. As for Pisistratus and the others, they were interrogated under torture and put to death.

29. The assassination aroused in all Thebans and Boeotians a venomous hatred of the Romans. They believed that, as a leader of their people, Zeuxippus could not have embarked on such a crime without consultation with the Roman commander. They were without the strength or a leader to mount a revolt and turned instead to the next best thing to war, terrorism. They surprised some Roman soldiers at inns, others as they moved around during the winter season on various everyday commissions. Some were killed by their assailants right on the highways, at spots notorious for ambushes, others after being treacher-

serta per fraudem deversoria deducti opprimebantur;
4 postremo non tantum ab odio sed etiam aviditate praedae
ea facinora fiebant, quia negotiandi ferme causa argentum
5 in zonis habentes in commeatibus erant. cum primo pauci,
deinde in dies plures desiderarentur, infamis esse Boeotia
omnis coepit, et timidius quam in hostico egredi castris
miles.
6    Tum Quinctius legatos ad quaerendum de latrociniis
per civitates mittit. plurimae caedes circa Copaidem paludem inventae: ibi ex limo eruta extractaque ex stagno ca-
davera saxis aut amphoris, ut pondere traherentur in profundum, adnexa; multa facinora Acraephiae et Coroneae
7 facta inveniebantur. Quinctius primo noxios tradi sibi
iussit et pro quingentis militibus—tot enim interempti
8 erant—quingenta talenta Boeotos conferre. quorum cum
fieret neutrum, verbis tantum civitates excusarent nihil
publico consilio factum esse, missis Athenas et in Achaiam
legatis qui testarentur socios iusto pioque se bello perse-
9 cuturum Boeotos, et cum parte copiarum Ap. Claudio
Acraephiam ire iusso, ipse cum parte Coroneam circum-
sidit, vastatis prius agris qua ab Elatia duo diversa agmina
10 iere. hac perculsi clade Boeoti, cum omnia terrore ac fuga
completa essent, legatos mittunt. qui cum in castra non

---

109 West of Thebes (*Barr.* 55 E4), but it was drained in the
late nineteenth century and is now the plain of Kopaida.
110 Towns on the shoreline of Lake Copais (*Barr.* 55 D–E).

ously lured into remote roadhouses. Eventually, such crimes were being committed not simply from enmity but also from greed for spoils, because the soldiers were usually on journeys to do business and had money in their belts. Initially, only a few were lost but as casualties mounted day by day all of Bocotia began to gain a bad reputation, with soldiers leaving the camp in greater fear than if they were in enemy territory.

At this point Quinctius sent envoys throughout the city-states to inquire into the terrorist activities. Most of the killings were found to have taken place in the area of Lake Copais[109]—here corpses, with rocks or amphoras attached to them to draw them into the depths with their weight, were pulled out of the slime and dragged from the marsh—and many of the crimes, it was discovered, had been perpetrated at Acraephia and Coronea.[110] At first, Quinctius issued orders for the guilty parties to be handed over to him and for the Boeotians to pay 500 talents for the 500 soldiers who had been murdered. When neither instruction was acted upon, and the states merely offered the verbal excuse that nothing that had taken place had official sanction, Quinctius sent envoys to Athens and Achaea to call upon his allies to witness the fact that the war he was going to fight with the Boeotians was just and righteous. He then ordered Appius Claudius to make for Acraephia with part of his forces and he himself besieged Coronea with the rest, having first laid waste the farmlands on the route followed from Elatia by the two separate columns. Taken aback by this catastrophic turn of events, and with panic and flight everywhere in evidence, the Boeotians dispatched ambassadors. These were being refused admission to the camp when the

admitterentur, Achaei Atheniensesque supervenerunt;
11 plus auctoritatis Achaei habuerunt deprecantes, quia ni
impetrassent pacem Boeotis, bellum simul gerere decre-
12 verant. per Achaeos et Boeotis copia adeundi adloquen-
dique Romanum facta est, iussisque tradere noxios et
multae nomine triginta conferre talenta, pax data et ab
oppugnatione recessum.

30. Paucos post dies decem legati ab Roma venerunt,
2 quorum ex consilio pax data Philippo in has leges est, ut
omnes Graecorum civitates quae in Europa quaeque in
Asia essent libertatem ac suas haberent leges; quae earum
sub dicione Philippi fuissent, praesidia ex iis Philippus
deduceret, vacuasque traderet Romanis ante Isthmiorum
3 tempus; deduceret et ex iis quae in Asia essent, Euromo
Pedasisque et Bargyliis et Iaso et Myrina et Abydo et
4 Thaso et Perintho: eas quoque enim placere liberas esse;
de Cianorum libertate Quinctium Prusiae Bithynorum
5 regi scribere quid senatui et decem legatis placuisset; captivos transfugasque reddere Philippum Romanis et naves
omnes tectas tradere praeter quinque et regiam unam
inhabilis prope magnitudinis, quam sedecim versus remo-

---

111 This is the probable meaning but the Latin is not clear; it
could possibly mean "alongside the Boeotians." See Achard *ad
loc.*     112 The terms mostly follow those in Polybius (18.44.2–
7), but Polybius has freedom being granted to all Greeks except
those then directly under Philip's control, who were to be handed
over to the Romans. Livy has *all* Greeks liberated, but he adds
that towns with Macedonian garrisons were to be handed over to
the Romans free of his troops, an obfuscation probably intended
to portray Flamininus as a true liberator.

113 A large ship with oars probably grouped in pairs and with
eight men to an oar. It remained in Macedonia until the war with

Achaeans and Athenians arrived on the scene. The intercession of the Achaeans carried more weight because they had already decided to fight alongside the Romans[111] should they fail to secure a peace for the Boeotians. It was through the Achaeans that the Boeotians were given the chance to meet and speak to the Roman commander, and they were ordered to hand over the guilty and pay a sum of thirty talents as a fine, after which they were granted peace and the siege was raised.

30. A few days later the ten commissioners arrived from Rome, and on their advice Philip was granted peace on the following terms:[112]

All Greek city-states, in Europe and Asia alike, were to have their independence and their own laws.

In the case of those states that had been under Philip's control, Philip was to withdraw his garrisons from them and hand them over to the Romans free of his troops before the time of the Isthmian Games.

Philip was also to withdraw his garrisons from the following cities in Asia: Euromus, Pedasa, Bargyliae, Iasus, Myrina, Abydus, Thasos and Perinthus, since it was decided that these, too, should be free. As for the freedom of the people of Cius, Quinctius was to write to Prusias, king of Bithynia, to communicate the decision of the senate and the ten commissioners.

Philip was to return prisoners of war and deserters to the Romans, and surrender all his decked ships apart from five and his one royal galley of almost unmaneuverable proportions, propelled by sixteen banks of oars.[113]

Perseus, but then it seems that Aemilius Paulus took it to Rome, where he sailed in it up the Tiber (45.35.3).

6 rum agebant; ne plus quinque milia armatorum haberet
neve elephantum ullum; bellum extra Macedoniae fines
7 ne iniussu senatus gereret; mille talentum daret populo
Romano, dimidium praesens dimidium pensionibus de-
8 cem annorum. Valerius Antias quaternum milium pondo
argenti vectigal in decem annos impositum regi tradit;
Claudius in annos triginta quaterna milia pondo et du-
9 cena, in praesens viginti milia pondo. idem nominatim
adiectum scribit ne cum Eumene Attali filio—novus is
tum rex erat—bellum gereret.
10     In haec obsides accepti, inter quos Demetrius Philippi
filius. adicit Antias Valerius Attalo absenti Aeginam insu-
11 lam elephantosque dono datos, et Rhodiis Stratoniceam
Cariaeque alias urbes quas Philippus tenuisset; Atheniensibus insulas datas Lemnum Imbrum Delum Scyrum.

31. Omnibus Graeciae civitatibus hanc pacem adprobantibus, soli Aetoli decretum decem legatorum clam
2 mussantes carpebant: litteras inanes vana specie libertatis
adumbratas esse. cur enim alias Romanis tradi urbes nec
nominari eas, alias nominari et sine traditione liberas iu-
3 beri esse, nisi quod quae in Asia sint liberentur, longinqui-
tate ipsa tutiores, quae in Graecia sint, ne nominatae quidem intercipiantur, Corinthus et Chalcis et Oreus cum
Eretria et Demetriade?

---

114 For the two historians Valerius Antias and Claudius
(Quadrigarius), see Introduction, xxvii–xxviii.     115 Eumenes
II had succeeded to the throne on his father's death (21.1 above).

116 Demetrius will appear in Flamininus' triumph (34.52.9).
He is represented as a tragic figure by Livy in Book 40.

117 Does Antias mean Philip's elephants? In any case, Attalus
was dead by this time.     118 Eretria, Demetrias: *Barr.* 55 D2;
Oreus: E3. Corinth, Chalcis, and Demetrias were, of course,
Philip's "fetters of Greece" (cf. 31.23.1, 32.37.4 and notes).

He was to keep no more than 5,000 soldiers and not one elephant.

He was not to wage war outside the confines of Macedonia without authorization from the senate.

He was to give the Roman people 1,000 talents, half immediately and half in installments over ten years. (Valerius Antias records that the king was subjected to an annual tribute of 4,000 pounds of silver for ten years, Claudius[114] that it was 4,200 pounds over thirty years, plus 20,000 payable immediately. Claudius also mentions a clause expressly forbidding him to go to war with Eumenes, son of Attalus, the new king of Pergamum at that time).[115]

Hostages were taken, including Philip's son Demetrius,[116] to ensure implementation of these conditions. Valerius Antias adds that the island of Aegina and some elephants were given to Attalus, in his absence, as a gift;[117] that the Rhodians were awarded Stratonicea and other cities in Caria that Philip had held; and that the Athenians were given the islands of Lemnos, Imbros, Delos and Scyros.

31. Although this peace treaty met with the approval of all the other city-states of Greece, the Aetolians alone secretly grumbled and criticized the decision of the ten commissioners as being just verbiage giving only the illusion of independence. Why, they asked, were some cities being passed over to the Romans without being specified by name when others were actually named and told to accept their independence without being handed over in this way? Obviously it was because the cities that lay in Asia, safer by virtue of their very remoteness, were to be liberated, while those in Greece were to be taken over without even being designated by name—Corinth, Chalcis, and Oreus, along with Eretria and Demetrias.[118]

373

4    Nec tota ex vano criminatio erat. dubitabatur enim de Corintho et Chalcide et Demetriade, quia in senatus consulto, quo missi decem legati ab urbe erant, ceterae Grae-
5  ciae atque Asiae urbes haud dubie liberabantur, de iis tribus urbibus legati quod tempora rei publicae postulassent id e re publica fideque sua facere ac statuere iussi
6  erant. Antiochus rex erat, quem transgressurum in Europam cum primum ei vires suae satis placuissent non dubitabant: ei tam opportunas ad occupandum patere urbes nolebant.
7    Ab Elatia profectus Quinctius Anticyram cum decem legatis, inde Corinthum traiecit. ibi consilia de libertate Graeciae dies prope totos in concilio decem legatorum
8  agitabantur: identidem Quinctius liberandam omnem Graeciam, si Aetolorum linguas retundere, si veram caritatem ac maiestatem apud omnes nominis Romani vellent
9  esse, si fidem facere ad liberandam Graeciam, non ad transferendum a Philippo ad se imperium sese mare traie-
10  cisse. nihil contra ea de libertate urbium alii dicebant: ceterum ipsis tutius esse manere paulisper sub tutela praesidii Romani quam pro Philippo Antiochum domi-
11  num accipere. postremo ita decretum est: Corinthus redderetur Achaeis ut in Acrocorintho tamen praesidium esset; Chalcidem ac Demetriadem retineri donec cura de Antiocho decessisset.

The charge was not entirely groundless as the status of Corinth, Chalcis, and Demetrias was not clear. In the senatorial decree under which the ten commissioners had been sent from Rome, all the other cities of Greece and Asia were clearly granted their freedom. In the case of these three, however, the commissioners' instructions had been to take such actions and decisions as were required by the situation in which the state was placed, being guided by the national interest and by their own integrity. And there was King Antiochus. As soon as he was satisfied that his forces were adequate, he would, they had no doubt, cross to Europe, and they did not want to leave strategically situated cities open for him to seize.

Along with the ten commissioners Quinctius left Elatia for Anticyra and then crossed to Corinth. There, in meetings of the ten, his days were almost entirely spent discussing the independence of Greece. Time and again Quinctius emphasized that they had to free Greece as a whole if they wished to make the Aetolians hold their tongues, inspire in everyone genuine affection and respect for the Roman race, and convince people that they had crossed the sea to liberate Greece rather than merely transfer power over it from Philip to themselves. The others did not oppose his arguments about the independence of the cities, but they argued that it was safer for the Greeks themselves to remain for a short period under the protection of a Roman garrison rather than accept Antiochus as their master in place of Philip. In the end the following decision was made: Corinth would be restored to the Achaeans, but with a garrison retained in the Acrocorinth; and Chalcis and Demetrias would remain occupied until the concern about Antiochus had passed.

32. Isthmiorum statum ludicrum aderat, semper quidem et alias frequens cum propter spectaculi studium
insitum genti, quo certamina omnis generis artium vi-

2  riumque et pernicitatis visuntur, tum quia propter oppor-
tunitatem loci, per duo diversa maria omnium rerum usus
ministrantis humano generi, concilium Asiae Graeciaeque

3  is mercatus erat. tum vero non ad solitos modo usus undique convenerant sed exspectatione erecti qui deinde status futurus Graeciae, quae sua fortuna esset. alii alia non
taciti solum opinabantur sed sermonibus etiam ferebant
Romanos facturos: vix cuiquam persuadebatur Graecia
omni cessuros.

4  Ad spectaculum consederant, et praeco cum tubicine,
ut mos est, in mediam aream, unde sollemni carmine ludicrum indici solet, processit, et tuba silentio facto ita pro-

5  nuntiat: "senatus Romanus et T. Quinctius imperator,
Philippo rege Macedonibusque devictis, liberos immunes
suis legibus esse iubet Corinthios Phocenses Locrensesque
omnes, et insulam Euboeam et Magnetas Thessalos Per-
rhaebos Achaeos Phthiotas."[63]

6  Percensuerat omnes gentes quae sub dicione Philippi
regis fuerant. audita voce praeconis maius gaudium fuit

[63] Phthiotas *Fr. 2*: Pthiotas *B*: Tietas *Mog.*

---

[119] This section has no parallel in Polybius (18.46.1ff.), and
Livy is perhaps drawing on his own knowledge of Greek festivals
(so Briscoe 1.310).

32. The date fixed for the Isthmian games was now approaching, always a well-attended event even on other occasions because of the enthusiasm inbred in that race for spectacles involving all manner of competitions in the arts, as well as in physical strength and fleetness of foot, and also because of its favorable location: thanks to its two different seas, by which it provided all manner of goods for mankind, this commercial center was a gathering place for Asia and Greece.[119] But on this occasion people had assembled from all over not just for the usual purposes; they were also eager to find out the future status of Greece and their own destiny. Not only did they have their various private thoughts on what the Romans would do, but they would bring the topic up in their conversations; and hardly anyone could be persuaded that they would withdraw from all of Greece.

They had now taken their seats for the pageant and, as usual, a herald came forward with a trumpeter to the middle of the site, where the games are customarily opened with a ceremonial hymn. When silence fell after the trumpet call, the herald made the following announcement: "The senate of Rome and the commander Titus Quinctius, having defeated King Philip and the Macedonians, declare that the following peoples are to be free, exempt from taxes and living under their own laws: the Corinthians, the Phocians, all the Locrians, the island of Euboea, the Magnesians, the Thessalians, the Perrhaebians, and the Phthiotic Achaeans."

The herald had listed all the peoples that had been under King Philip's rule, and when his announcement had been heard the elation was too great for people to take it

7   quam quod universum homines acciperent: vix satis credere se quisque audisse et alii alios intueri mirabundi
velut ad somni uanam speciem; quod ad quemque perti-
nebat, suarum aurium fidei minimum credentes, proximos
8   interrogabant. revocatus praeco, cum unusquisque non
audire modo sed videre libertatis suae nuntium averet,
9   iterum pronuntiavit eadem. tum ab certo iam gaudio tantus cum clamore plausus est ortus, totiensque repetitus, ut
facile appareret nihil omnium bonorum multitudini gra-
10  tius quam libertatem esse. ludicrum deinde ita raptim
peractum est ut nullius nec animi nec oculi spectaculo
intenti essent: adeo unum gaudium praeoccupaverat omnium aliarum sensum voluptatium.

     33. Ludis vero dimissis cursu prope omnes tendere ad
2   imperatorem Romanum, ut ruente turba in unum adire
contingere dextram cupientium, coronas lemniscosque
iacientium, haud procul periculo fuerit. sed erat trium
3   ferme et triginta annorum, et cum robur iuventae tum
gaudium ex tam insigni gloriae fructu vires suppeditabat.
4   nec praesens tantummodo effusa est laetitia, sed per multos dies gratis et cogitationibus et sermonibus renovata:
5   esse aliquam in terris gentem quae sua impensa suo labore
6   ac periculo bella gerat pro libertate aliorum, nec hoc finitimis aut propinquae vicinitatis hominibus aut terris conti-
7   nentibus iunctis praestet, sed maria traiciat, ne quod toto
orbe terrarum iniustum imperium sit, ubique ius fas lex
potentissima sint; una voce praeconis liberatas omnes

all in at once. They could all scarcely believe their ears, and they looked at each other in amazement, as though witnessing a fleeting dream. They kept questioning those next to them about how each of them was affected, very unwilling to accept the evidence of their own ears. The herald was called back—everyone was eager not just to hear but to see the harbinger of their liberty—and he re peated the announcement. At this, the reason for their rejoicing now confirmed, such applause and cheering went up, and was so often repeated, that it was readily apparent that of all possible blessings none is more welcome to the masses than freedom. The games were then put on, so hastily that nobody's mind or eyes were focused on the spectacle—so far had this one delight preempted the awareness of all other pleasures.

33. The games over, nearly everybody swiftly headed for the Roman commander. As the crowd rushed forward, eagerly wishing to approach this one man and shake his hand and showering him with garlands and ribbons, he was almost in danger; but he was about thirty-three years of age and the vigor of his youth and the pleasure he derived from such remarkable celebrity gave him strength. Nor was their outpouring of joy just a thing of the moment; it was revived over many days, as people's thoughts and conversations centered on their gratitude. There was, then, some nation on earth that waged war for the freedom of others, at its own expense and itself assuming the hardship and danger; and it did so not just for its neighbors or for people geographically close or on the same landmass, but it actually crossed seas to prevent an unjust empire existing anywhere in the world and to ensure that right, divine justice, and law should be paramount everywhere.

8    Graeciae atque Asiae urbes: hoc spe concipere audacis animi fuisse, ad effectum adducere et virtutis et fortunae ingentis.

    34. Secundum Isthmia Quinctius et decem legati lega-
2  tiones regum gentium civitatiumque[64] audivere. primi omnium regis Antiochi vocati legati sunt. iis eadem fere quae Romae egerant verba sine fide rerum iactantibus,
3  nihil iam perplexe ut ante, cum dubiae res incolumi Philippo erant, sed aperte denuntiatum ut excederet Asiae urbibus quae Philippi aut Ptolomaei regum fuissent, abstineret liberis civitatibus, neu quam lacesseret armis: et in pace et in libertate esse debere omnes ubique Graecas
4  urbes;[65] ante omnia denuntiatum ne in Europam aut ipse transiret aut copias traiceret.
5    Dimissis regis legatis conventus civitatium gentiumque est haberi coeptus, eoque maturius peragebatur quod decreta decem legatorum in[66] civitates nominatim pro-
6  nuntiabantur. Orestis—Macedonum ea gens est—, quod primi ab rege defecissent, suae leges redditae. Magnetes
7  et Perrhaebi et Dolopes liberi quoque pronuntiati. Thessalorum genti praeter libertatem concessam Achaei Phthiotae[67] dati, Thebis Phthioticis[68] et Pharsalo excepta. Aeto-

---

[64] gentium civitatiumque *Mog.*: gentiumque *B*: *fort.* civitatium gentiumque *Briscoe*    [65] abstineret ... urbes *Madvig: sic, sed* ne umquam *B*: abstinerent liberas omnesque Graecas *Mog.*
[66] in *Crév.*: *om. BMog.*    [67] Phthiotae *Mog.*: Pthiotae *B*
[68] Phthioticis *Mog.*: Pthioticis *B*

---

[120] They are Lysias and Hegesianax in Polybius (18.47.4): for Hegesianax, cf. 34.57.6. On their careers, cf. Walbank 2.615–16.
[121] For this area of Macedonia: *Barr.* 49 D3 (Orestis).

With a single announcement from a herald, all the cities of Greece and Asia had been set free; it took an intrepid soul to formulate such an ambitious project, and phenomenal valor and fortune to bring it to fruition.

34. After the Isthmian Games, Quinctius and the ten commissioners granted audiences to deputations from monarchs, peoples and city-states. The first to be called were the envoys of King Antiochus.[120] They made more or less the same blustering declarations as they had at Rome, mere verbiage with no substance to inspire confidence, but this time there was no imprecision about the response they were given as there had been earlier when the situation was fluid and Philip's position still intact. They were explicitly told that Antiochus was to withdraw from the cities of Asia that had belonged to King Philip or King Ptolemy, and not touch the city-states that were free or employ armed aggression against any city—all Greek cities everywhere were to have both peace and independence. Above all Antiochus was forbidden either to cross to Europe himself or to send troops there.

When the king's envoys were dismissed, a meeting of cities and peoples got under way, and business there proceeded all the more briskly because the decrees of the commissioners were delivered to each of the states by name. The Orestae, a people of Macedonia,[121] had their autonomy restored for having been the first to defect from the king. The Magnesians, Perrhaebians, and Dolopians were also pronounced free. Apart from being awarded their independence, the people of Thessaly were further granted the Phthiotic Achaeans, with the exception of Phthiotic Thebes and Pharsalus. The Aetolians claimed

los de Pharsalo et Leucade postulantes ut ex foedere sibi
8 restituerentur ad senatum reiecerunt; Phocenses Locrensesque, sicut ante fuerant, adiecta decreti auctoritate iis
9 contribuerunt. Corinthus et Triphylia et Heraea—Pelo-
10 ponnesi et ipsa urbs est—redditae[69] Achaeis. Oreum et
Eretriam decem legati Eumeni regi, Attali filio, dabant
dissentiente Quinctio: ea una res in arbitrium senatus
reiecta est; senatus libertatem iis civitatibus dedit Carysto
11 adiecta. Pleurato Lychnidus et Parthini dati: Illyriorum
utraque gens sub dicione Philippi fuerant. Amynandrum
tenere iusserunt castella quae per belli tempus Philippo
capta ademisset.

35. Dimisso conventu decem legati, partiti munia inter
se, ad liberandas suae quisque regionis civitates discesse-
2 runt, P. Lentulus Bargylias, L. Stertinius Hephaestiam et
Thasum et Thraciae urbes, P. Villius et L. Terentius ad
3 regem Antiochum, Cn. Cornelius ad Philippum. qui, de
minoribus rebus editis mandatis, percunctatus si consilium non utile solum sed etiam salutare admittere auribus
4 posset, cum rex gratias quoque se acturum diceret si quid
5 quod in rem suam esset expromeret, magno opere ei sua-
sit, quoniam pacem impetrasset, ad societatem amici-
6 tiamque petendam mitteret Romam legatos, ne si quid
Antiochus moveret, exspectasse et temporum opportuni-

---

[69] redditae *F*: reddita *BMog*.

---

[122] Triphylia (region) and Heraea (town): *Barr.* 58 B2.

[123] Oreus (Oreos) and Eretria: *Barr.* 55 E3, D2.

[124] *Barr.* 58 G1 (Karystos).       [125] *Barr.* 49 C2 (Lychni-
dos), B2 (Parthini).       [126] Bargylia: *Barr.* 61 F3; Hephaestia,
a town on Lemnos: 57 D2.

that Pharsalus and Leucas should be restored to them
under the terms of their treaty, and the commissioners
referred their claim to the senate. They did, however, keep
the Phocians and Locrians annexed to the Aetolians as
before, but with the authority of a decree now added.
Corinth, Triphylia, and Heraca (this, too, is a city in the
Peloponnese)[122] were restored to the Achaeans. The ten
commissioners were for giving Oreus and Eretria[123] to
King Eumenes, son of Attalus, but Quinctius disagreed;
and this one issue was referred to the senate for a decision.
The senate granted these states their independence, along
with Carystus.[124] Pleuratus was given Lychnidus and the
Parthini[125] (both these Illyrian peoples had been under
Philip's control). Amynander they directed to retain the
strongholds he had captured from Philip during the time
of the war with him.

35. When the meeting was adjourned, the ten commissioners divided their responsibilities and each went off
to liberate the city-states in his region. Publius Lentulus went to Bargyliae, Lucius Stertinius to Hephaestia,[126]
Thasos, and the cities of Thrace; Publius Villius and Lucius Terentius to King Antiochus; and Gnaeus Cornelius
to Philip. After delivering to the king such instructions as
he had been given for him on less important matters, Cornelius asked Philip if he could bear to listen to advice that
was not just sound but truly salutary. When the king replied that he would even demonstrate his gratitude if the
Roman furnished any advice to improve his position, Cornelius strongly urged him, now that he had gained his
peace accord, to send a deputation to Rome to ask for an
alliance and a treaty of friendship. Otherwise, he said,
should Antiochus make a move, Philip could be thought

383

7 tates captasse ad rebellandum videri posset. ad Tempe
8 Thessalica Philippus est conventus. qui cum se missurum
extemplo legatos respondisset, Cornelius Thermopylas,
ubi frequens Graeciae statis diebus esse solet conventus—
Pylaicum appellant—, venit.

9 Aetolos praecipue monuit ut[70] constanter et fideliter in
10 amicitia populi Romani permanerent. Aetolorum principes alii leniter questi sunt quod non idem erga suam gentem Romanorum animus esset post victoriam qui in bello
11 fuisset; alii ferocius incusarunt, exprobraruntque non
modo vinci sine Aetolis Philippum sed ne transire quidem
12 in Graeciam Romanos potuisse. adversus ea respondere,
ne in altercationem excederet[71] res, cum supersedisset
Romanus, omnia eos aequa impetraturos si Romam mi-
sissent dixit. itaque ex auctoritate eius decreti legati sunt.
hunc finem bellum cum Philippo habuit.

36. Cum haec in Graecia Macedoniaque et Asia ge-
rerentur, Etruriam infestam prope coniuratio servorum
2 fecit. ad quaerendam opprimendamque eam M'. Acilius
Glabrio praetor, cui inter cives peregrinosque iurisdictio
obtigerat, cum una ex duabus legione urbana est missus.
3 alios . . . [72] alios iam congregatos pugnando vicit: ex his
multi occisi multi capti; alios verberatos crucibus adfixit,
qui principes coniurationis fuerant, alios dominis restituit.

[70] ut *FMog.*: *om.* B    [71] excederet *Mog.*: c . . . *F²*: cresceret B
[72] . . . *lac. indicat Madvig*

[127] This is the second time that Livy has confused Thermum
with Thermopylae (see also 31.32.3 and note). On the Aetolian
autumn and spring meetings, cf. 31.29.1 note.
[128] M'. Acilius Glabrio (35). For his appointment: 26.1, above.
[129] There is clearly a lacuna in the text at this point.

to have been simply biding his time, on the lookout for suitable occasions to resume the war. The meeting with Philip took place at Tempe in Thessaly. When the king replied that he would send a deputation immediately, Cornelius moved on to Thermopylae where, at fixed dates, there is a plenary council meeting of the Greek peoples called the Pylaic Council.[127]

Here Cornelius advised the Aetolians in particular to remain scrupulously loyal to their alliance with the Roman people. Some of the leading Aetolians meekly complained that the attitude of the Romans toward their people was not the same since the victory as during the war. Others were more outspoken in their criticisms and reproaches, saying that without Aetolian help not only could Philip not have been defeated but the Romans could not even have crossed to Greece. The Roman refrained from responding to this in order to avoid a quarrel, and merely observed that the Aetolians would obtain complete satisfaction if they sent a delegation to Rome. And so, on Cornelius' advice, envoys were selected. Such was the conclusion of the war with Philip.

36. In the course of these events in Greece, Macedonia and Asia, a slave revolt almost turned Etruria into hostile territory. The praetor Manius Acilius Glabrio, to whom jurisdiction over citizen-foreigner affairs had fallen,[128] was dispatched with one of the two city legions to investigate it and put it down. Some . . . [129] others he defeated in battle when they had already assembled. Of these many were killed and many taken prisoner. Some—those who had been ringleaders in the conspiracy—he flogged and crucified, others he returned to their masters.

4      Consules in provincias profecti sunt. Marcellum Boiorum ingressum fines, fatigato per diem totum milite via facienda, castra in tumulo quodam ponentem Corolamus quidam, regulus Boiorum, cum magna manu adortus ad
5  tria milia hominum occidit; et inlustres viri aliquot in illo tumultuario proelio ceciderunt, inter quos praefecti socium Ti.[73] Sempronius Gracchus et M. Iunius Silanus et tribuni militum de legione secunda M. Ogulnius et P.
6  Claudius. castra tamen ab Romanis impigre permunita retentaque, cum hostes prospera pugna elati nequiquam
7  oppugnassent. stativis deinde iisdem per dies aliquot sese tenuit, dum et saucios curaret et e[74] tanto terrore animos
8  militum reficeret. Boii, ut est gens minime ad morae taedium ferendum patiens, in castella sua vicosque passim dilapsi sunt.
9      Marcellus, Pado confestim traiecto, in agrum Comensem, ubi Insubres, Comensibus ad arma excitis, castra habebant, legiones ducit. Galli, feroces Boiorum ante dies paucos pugna, in ipso itinere proelium committunt; et primo adeo acriter invaserunt ut antesignanos impulerint.
10  quod ubi Marcellus animadvertit, veritus ne moti semel pellerentur, cohortem Marsorum cum opposuisset, equi-
11  tum Latinorum omnes turmas in hostem emisit. quorum cum primus secundusque impetus rettudisset inferentem se ferociter hostem, confirmata et reliqua acies Romana
12  restitit primo, deinde signa acriter intulit; nec ultra susti-

[73] Ti. *Sig.*: T. *BMog.*
[74] e *Briscoe*: *om. BMog.*: a *Gron.*

---

[130] The Marsi, renowned for their bravery, lived in the mountains of central Italy (*Barr.* 44 E2).

The consuls then left for their provinces. Marcellus entered the territory of the Boii but as he was pitching camp on a hill, his soldiers exhausted after a whole day on the march, a certain Corolamus, a chieftain of the Boii, attacked him with a large force and killed up to 3,000 of his men. A number of distinguished men also fell in the melée, including the allied commanders Tiberius Sempronius Gracchus and Marcus Iunius Silanus, as well as Marcus Ogulnius and Publius Claudius, military tribunes from the second legion. Even so the camp was established and held with determination by the Romans, and an attack from the enemy, elated by their successful encounter earlier, came to nothing. Marcellus remained within his encampment for a number of days, giving himself the time both to tend to his wounded and restore the men's confidence after such a daunting episode. The Boii, a people with little patience for delays, slipped away in all directions to their strongholds and villages.

Marcellus swiftly crossed the Po and took his legions into the area of Comum where the Insubres, who had called the people of Comum to arms, had their encampment. Ebullient after the fight put up by the Boii a few days earlier, the Gauls joined battle while still in marching formation, and their initial attack was fierce enough to throw back the Roman front ranks. Seeing this, Marcellus feared that his men might be driven back in defeat by this first shock, and he set a Marsian cohort[130] in the enemy's path and then unleashed all his squadrons of Latin cavalry against them. Their first and second cavalry charge blunted the foe's spirited advance, and this gave confidence to the rest of the Roman line, which first held its ground and then made a fierce attack. The Gauls were no

387

nuere certamen Galli quin terga verterent atque effuse
fugerent.

13      In eo proelio supra quadraginta milia hominum caesa
Valerius Antias scribit, octoginta[75] septem signa militaria
capta, et carpenta septingenta triginta duo et aureos torques multos, ex quibus unum magni ponderis Claudius in
14  Capitolio Iovi donum in aede positum scribit. castra eo die
Gallorum expugnata direptaque, et Comum oppidum post
dies paucos captum; castella inde duodetriginta ad con-
15  sulem defecerunt. id quoque inter scriptores ambigitur
utrum in Boios prius an Insubres consul exercitum duxerit
adversamque prospera pugna oblitteraverit, an victoria ad
Comum parta deformata clade in Boiis accepta sit.

37. Sub haec tam varia fortuna gesta L. Furius Pur-
2  pureo alter consul per tribum Sapiniam in Boios venit. iam
castro Mutilo adpropinquabat, cum veritus ne interclude-
retur simul a Boiis Liguribusque exercitum eadem via qua
adduxerat reduxit, et magno circuitu per aperta eoque tuta
3  loca ad collegam pervenit. inde iunctis exercitibus primum
Boiorum agrum usque ad Felsinam oppidum populantes
4  peragraverunt. ea urbs ceteraque circa castella et Boii fere
omnes praeter iuventutem, quae praedandi causa in armis
erat,—tunc in devias silvas recesserat—in deditionem venerunt.

[75] octoginta *Kreyssig*: octingenta *B*: et quingenta *Mog.*: et
quinquaginta *Gron.*

---

131 For Valerius Antias and Claudius (Quadrigarius), see Introduction, xxvii–xxviii.
132 For the Tribus Sapinia and Mutilum, cf. 31.2.6 and note.
133 Later renamed Bononia, it is now Bologna.

longer able to keep up the struggle, and they turned and scattered in flight.

In the battle, according to Valerius Antias' account, more than 40,000 men lost their lives, and 87 military standards were captured, along with 732 wagons and many gold torques, including a very heavy one that Claudius[131] states was placed in the temple on the Capitoline as a gift to Jupiter. The camp of the Gauls was taken and sacked that day, and the town of Comum was captured a few days later. After this, twenty-eight fortified towns went over to the consul. A matter of dispute among historians is whether the consul led his army in the first place against the Boii or against the Insubres—whether by the successful engagement he obliterated the memory of the earlier reverse, or whether the victory gained at Comum was then sullied by defeat among the Boii.

37. Soon after these operations of mixed success, the other consul, Lucius Furius Purpureo, advanced on the Boii through the Tribus Sapinia. He was already approaching the stronghold of Mutilum[132] when, fearful of being cut off simultaneously by the Boii and the Ligurians, he led his army back along the same route by which he had brought it, and reached his colleague by a long detour through open, and therefore safe, terrain. Their armies united, the consuls first moved through the lands of the Boii, plundering as they went, as far the town of Felsina.[133] That city and all the other strongholds in the neighborhood surrendered to him, as did almost all the Boii, apart from their men of military age, who had taken up arms in order to plunder and had at that point fallen back deep into the woods.

5 In Ligures inde traductus exercitus. Boii, neglegentius coactum agmen Romanorum, quia ipsi procul abesse viderentur, improviso adgressuros se rati, per occultos saltus
6 secuti sunt. quos non adepti, Pado repente navibus traiecto Laevos Libuosque cum pervastassent, redeuntes inde per Ligurum extremos fines cum agresti praeda in agmen inci-
7 dunt Romanum. proelium celerius acriusque commissum quam si tempore locoque ad certamen destinato praepa-
8 ratis animis concurrissent. ibi quantam vim ad stimulandos animos ira haberet apparuit; nam ita caedis magis quam victoriae avidi pugnarunt Romani ut vix nuntium cladis hosti relinquerent.

9 Ob has res gestas, consulum litteris Romam adlatis, supplicatio in triduum decreta est. brevi post Marcellus consul Romam venit, triumphusque ei magno consensu
10 patrum est decretus. triumphavit in magistratu de Insubribus Comensibusque; Boiorum triumphi spem collegae reliquit, quia ipsi proprie adversa pugna in ea gente eve-
11 nerat, cum collega secunda. multa spolia hostium captivis carpentis travecta, multa militaria signa; aeris lata trecenta viginti milia, argenti bigati ducenta triginta quattuor milia;
12 in pedites singulos dati octogeni aeris, triplex equiti centurionique.

---

[134] The former are a Ligurian tribe (*Barr.* 39 D3), the latter very probably the Libicii (C3), a Gallic tribe living between the Po and Ticino rivers.

[135] Cf. 31.8.2 note.

[136] Cf. 31.49.2 and note.

The Ligurians were the army's next objective. The Boii now followed the Roman column, taking pathways hidden from view with the idea of making a surprise attack—the column would be carelessly organized, they assumed, because they themselves would be thought to be a long way off. Failing to overtake the Romans, they suddenly crossed the Po in boats and conducted raids on the Laevi and Libui,[134] and as they were returning along the borders of Ligurian territory, carrying their spoils from the fields, they ran into the Roman column. The battle that ensued was more spirited and ferocious than if the two sides had been prepared for the confrontation with time and place for the engagement arranged. Here the potency of anger as a stimulant to courage was made apparent: the Romans craved bloodshed more than victory, and fought so aggressively that they scarcely left the enemy any survivor to report the debacle.

When the consuls' dispatch reached Rome, a three-day period of supplication[135] was decreed in thanks for this success. Shortly afterward the consul Marcellus arrived in Rome and was awarded a triumph by a large majority in the senate. During his term of office, Marcellus celebrated a triumph over the Insubres and Comenses, but left to his colleague the prospect of a triumph over the Boii since he personally had suffered defeat against that people but had gained victory cooperating with the colleague. Large quantities of enemy spoils and many military standards were carried along on captured wagons. In the procession, 320,000 bronze coins were transported, and 234,000 pieces of silver stamped with the *biga*.[136] Infantrymen were granted eighty bronze *asses* apiece, a cavalryman and a centurion three times that amount.

38. Eodem anno Antiochus rex, cum hibernasset Ephesi, omnes Asiae civitates in antiquam imperii formu-
2 lam redigere est conatus. et ceteras quidem, aut quia locis planis positae erant, aut quia parum moenibus armisque ac iuventuti fidebant, haud difficulter videbat iugum ac-
3 cepturas: Zmyrna et Lampsacus libertatem usurpabant, periculumque erat ne si concessum iis foret quod inten-derent, Zmyrnam in Aeolide Ioniaque, Lampsacum in
4 Hellesponto aliae urbes sequerentur. igitur et ipse ab Epheso ad Zmyrnam obsidendam misit, et quae Abydi copiae erant, praesidio tantum modico relicto, duci ad
5 Lampsacum oppugnandam iussit. nec vi tantum terrebat, sed per legatos leniter adloquendo, castigandoque teme-ritatem ac pertinaciam, spem conabatur facere brevi quod
6 peterent habituros, sed cum satis et ipsis et omnibus aliis appareret ab rege impetratam eos libertatem, non per
7 occasionem raptam habere. adversus quae respondebatur nihil neque mirari neque suscensere Antiochum debere si spem libertatis differri non satis aequo animo paterentur.
8 Ipse initio veris navibus ab Epheso profectus Helles-pontum petit, terrestres copias traici ab Abydo Chersone-sum iussit. cum ad Madytum, Chersonesi urbem, terrestri
9 navalem exercitum iunxisset, quia clauserant portas, cir-cumdedit moenia armatis; et iam opera admoventi deditio

---

137 Smyrna (*Barr.* 56 E5) lay on the Ionian coast close to mod-ern Izmir, to which it gave its name. Lampsacus (*Barr.* 51 H4) was on the eastern coast of the Hellespont near the modern Lapseki.
138 *Barr.* 51 G4.

38. In that same year, after spending the winter at Ephesus, King Antiochus attempted to reduce all the states of Asia to their former state of subjection to him. He could see that all of them, Smyrna and Lampsacus[137] apart, would readily accept the yoke, either because of their location in the plains or because they had little confidence in their fortifications, arms and fighting men. Smyrna and Lampsacus, however, were asserting their independence and if their demands were met there was a risk of other cities in Aeolis and Ionia following the lead of Smyrna and those in the Hellespont following Lampsacus. Antiochus therefore sent a force directly from Ephesus to besiege Smyrna and also instructed his troops in Abydus to leave a small garrison in place and advance to attack Lampsacus. Nor did he simply try to intimidate the cities by force; he also made mild overtures to them through envoys, gently reproving them for their foolhardiness and obstinacy, and tried to raise their hopes that they would soon have what they were seeking—but only when it was evident, to everybody else as well as themselves, that their freedom had been granted by the king and not seized through opportunism. Their reply was that Antiochus should be neither surprised nor angry if they could not calmly accept their hopes of freedom being postponed.

Setting off from Ephesus with his fleet at the beginning of spring, Antiochus himself made for the Hellespont and ordered his land forces to be taken across from Abydus to the Chersonese. After bringing his navy and army together at Madytus, a city on the Chersonese,[138] he surrounded the walls with his soldiers because the people had shut their gates against him. He was already moving up siege engines when the town capitulated. Fear of similar treat-

facta est. idem metus Sestum incolentes aliasque Cher-
10 sonesi urbes in deditionem dedit. Lysimachiam inde omnibus simul navalibus terrestribus copiis venit. quam cum
11 desertam ac stratam prope omnem ruinis invenisset—ce-
perant autem direptamque incenderant Thraces paucis
ante annis—cupido eum restituendi nobilem urbem et
12 loco sitam opportuno cepit. itaque omni cura[76] simul est
adgressus et tecta muros restituere, et partim redimere
servientes Lysimachenses, partim fuga sparsos per Helles-
13 pontum Chersonesumque conquirere et contrahere, partim novos colonos spe commodorum proposita adscribere
14 et omni modo frequentare; simul, ut Thracum submove-
retur metus, ipse parte dimidia terrestrium copiarum ad
depopulanda proxima Thraciae est profectus, partem navalesque omnes socios reliquit in operibus reficiendae
urbis.

39. Sub hoc tempus et L. Cornelius, missus ab senatu
ad dirimenda inter Antiochum Ptolomaeumque reges cer-
2 tamina, Selymbriae substitit, et decem legatorum P. Lentulus a Bargyliis P. Villius et L. Terentius ab Thaso Lysimachiam petierunt. eodem et ab Selymbria L. Cornelius
et ex Thracia paucos post dies Antiochus convenerunt.
3 primus congressus cum legatis et deinceps invitatio benigna et hospitalis fuit; ut de mandatis statuque praesenti
4 Asiae agi coeptum est, animi exasperati sunt. Romani omnia acta eius ex quo tempore ab Syria classem solvisset

---

[76] omni cura *Mog.*: omnia *B*: omnia cum cura *M. Müller*

[139] *Barr.* 51 H3; cf. also 32.33.15 and note.
[140] L. Cornelius Lentulus (188). Cf. 31.20.1 and note.
[141] On the north coast of the Propontis: *Barr.* 52 C2.

ment prompted the inhabitants of Sestus and other cities of the Chersonese to surrender. From there Antiochus came to Lysimachia[139] with all his naval and land forces together. Finding the place deserted and almost completely in ruins—the Thracians had captured it a few years earlier and had looted it and burned it—he was overtaken by a desire to reestablish the famous city that was also strategically located. And so, with the utmost care, he proceeded with everything at the same time: restoring buildings and walls; ransoming citizens of Lysimachia who were in slavery; searching out and bringing together refugees scattered throughout the Hellespont and Chersonese; enrolling new colonists with the prospect of betterment; and doing everything possible to repopulate the city. At the same time, to remove the threat of the Thracians, he personally set off with half his land forces to plunder the closest regions of Thrace, and left the other half and all his naval crews to work on rebuilding the city.

39. It was at about this time that Lucius Cornelius,[140] who had been sent by the senate to settle the differences between the kings Antiochus and Ptolemy, halted at Selymbria,[141] and certain members of the ten-man commission made for Lysimachia, Publius Lentulus, coming from Bargyliae, and Publius Villius and Lucius Terentius coming from Thasos. Lucius Cornelius also arrived there from Selymbria and Antiochus from Thrace a few days later. Antiochus' first meeting with the commissioners and the reception that followed it were genial and affable, but when discussion began of the commissioners' assignments and the current situation in Asia tempers flared. The Romans made no secret of the senate's displeasure with all of Antiochus' activities since he had set sail from Syria, and

displicere senatui non dissimulabant, restituique et Ptolomaeo omnes civitates quae dicionis eius fuissent aequum
5 censebant: nam quod ad eas civitates attineret quas a Philippo possessas Antiochus per occasionem, averso Phi-
6 lippo in Romanum bellum, intercepisset, id vero ferendum non esse Romanos per tot annos terra marique tanta
pericula ac labores exhausisse, Antiochum belli praemia
7 habere. sed ut in Asiam adventus eius dissimulari ab Romanis tamquam nihil ad eos pertinens potuerit, quod[77]
iam etiam in Europam omnibus navalibus terrestribusque
copiis transierit, quantum a bello aperte Romanis indicto
abesse? illum quidem, etiam si in Italiam traiciat, negatu-
rum; Romanos autem non exspectaturos ut id posset facere.

40. Adversus ea Antiochus mirari se dixit Romanos tam
diligenter inquirere quid regi Antiocho faciendum aut
2 quousque terra marique progrediendum fuerit, ipsos non
cogitare Asiam nihil ad se pertinere, nec magis illis in-
quirendum esse quid Antiochus in Asia quam Antiocho
3 quid in Italia populus Romanus faciat. quod ad Ptolomaeum attineat, cui ademptas civitates querantur, sibi
cum Ptolomaeo et amicitiam esse et id agere ut brevi
4 etiam adfinitas iungatur. nec[78] ex Philippi quidem adversa
fortuna spolia ulla se petisse, aut adversus Romanos in
Europam traiecisse, sed qua Lysimachi quondam regnum

---

[77] quod *Mog.*: quid quod *B*: quid? quod *Goeller*
[78] nec *B Mog.*: ne *Bekker*

---

[142] That is, of course, to Ptolemy.
[143] By betrothing his daughter Cleopatra to Ptolemy (cf.
Polyb. 18.51.10, Walbank 2.623).

they opined that all the states formerly under Ptolemy's control should by rights be restored to him.[142] Then, they said, there were the cities that had belonged to Philip, which Antiochus had filched from him by a stroke of opportunism when Philip's attention was distracted by his war with Rome. It was quite unacceptable that the Romans should have experienced such perils and hardships over all those years only to see Antiochus reaping the profits of the war. Even if the Romans could overlook his arrival in Asia as being of no concern to them, there was the fact that he had now also crossed to Europe with all his naval and land forces—how far did that fall short of an open declaration of war on Rome? Of course, Antiochus would deny this even if he should sail to Italy; but the Romans were not going to wait for him to have the capability to do that.

40. In reply Antiochus said he was amazed that the Romans were making such a thorough investigation into what King Antiochus ought to have done or how far he should have advanced by land and sea. He was surprised, he said, at their failure to see that Asia was none of their business and that they should no more be inquiring into the activities of Antiochus in Asia than Antiochus should into the activities of the Roman people in Italy. As for Ptolemy, he continued, the Romans protested that city-states had been taken from him, but Antiochus actually had an alliance with him and, moreover, was taking measures for that to be strengthened shortly by a family tie.[143] He had not, in fact, sought to profit from Philip's misfortunes, and it was not to challenge the Romans that he had crossed into Europe. Rather, he thought that all the lands

fuerit, quo victo omnia quae illius fuissent iure belli Se-
5 leuci facta sint, existimare suae dicionis esse. occupatis
maioribus suis rerum aliarum cura primo quaedam ex iis
Ptolomaeum, inde et Philippum usurpandae alienae pos-
6 sessionis causa tenuisse.[79] Chersonesus quidem et proxima Thraciae quae circa Lysimachiam sint, quem dubitare
quin Lysimachi fuerint? ad ea recipienda in antiquum ius
venisse et Lysimachiam deletam Thracum impetu de integro condere, ut Seleucus filius eam sedem regni habeat.

41. His disceptationibus per dies aliquot habitis, rumor
sine ullo satis certo auctore adlatus de morte Ptolomaei
2 regis ut nullus exitus imponeretur sermonibus effecit. nam
et dissimulabat pars utraque se audisse, et L. Cornelius,
cui legatio ad duos reges Antiochum Ptolomaeumque
mandata erat, spatium modici temporis ad conveniendum
3 Ptolomaeum petebat, ut priusquam moveretur aliquid in
nova possessione regni praeveniret in Aegyptum, et Antiochus suam fore Aegyptum, si tum occupasset, censebat.
4 itaque dimissis Romanis, relictoque Seleuco filio cum
terrestribus copiis ad restituendam ut instituerat Lysi-
5 machiam, ipse omni classe navigat Ephesum, legatis ad

---

[79] usurpandae alienae possessionis causa tenuisse *B*: sic, *sed
om.* causa tenuisse *Mog.*: usurpanda aliena possessionis causa
tenuisse *Madvig*

---

[144] Alexander's general who, after Alexander's death, became
the first *strategos* of Thrace, where he established a kingdom, and
later occupied Macedonia. In 281 he was defeated by Seleucus I
Nicator at Corupedium in Asia Minor.

[145] He became Seleucus IV Philopater.

that formerly constituted the kingdom of Lysimachus[144] were under his rule, since on Lysimachus' defeat all his possessions passed into the hands of Seleucus by the rules of war. When his ancestors had been preoccupied with concerns elsewhere, some of these lands had been taken over first by Ptolemy, and then by Philip, from a simple wish to appropriate another's possessions. Who could doubt that the Chersonese and the closest parts of Thrace in the neighborhood of Lysimachia had belonged to Lysimachus? It was to reestablish his former authority over these that he had come, and also to refound Lysimachia (which had been destroyed by a Thracian attack), so that his son Seleucus[145] might have it as the capital of his realm.

41. This wrangling had lasted a number of days when a rumor was reported (though it could not be verified) that King Ptolemy had died, and this resulted in the discussions reaching no conclusion. Both sides, in fact, pretended not to have heard the rumor and Lucius Cornelius, who had been charged with the mission to the two kings, Antiochus and Ptolemy, requested a short adjournment in order to meet Ptolemy (his intention being to reach Egypt before there could be any upheaval at the time of the new king's succession). Antiochus for his part thought that Egypt would be his if he overran it then. He therefore dismissed the Romans, left his son Seleucus with the land forces to continue his planned reconstruction of Lysimachia, and himself sailed to Ephesus with his entire fleet, having first sent envoys to Quinctius to discuss their alli-

Quinctium missis qui ad fidem faciendam nihil novaturum regem de societate agerent.

Oram Asiae legens pervenit in Lyciam, Patarisque cognito vivere Ptolomaeum navigandi quidem in Aegyptum
6    omissum consilium est. Cyprum nihilo minus petens, cum Chelidoniarum promunturium superasset, paulisper seditione remigum est retentus in Pamphylia circa Euryme-
7    dontem amnem. inde profectum eum ad capita quae vocant Sari fluminis foeda tempestas adorta prope cum omni classe demersit: multae fractae, multae naves eiectae,
8    multae ita haustae mari ut nemo in terram enarit.[80] magna vis hominum ibi interiit, non remigum modo militumque
9    ignotae turbae, sed etiam insignium regis amicorum. conlectis reliquiis naufragii, cum res non in eo essent ut Cyprum temptaret, minus opulento agmine quam profectus erat Seleuciam rediit. ibi subduci navibus iussis—iam enim et hiemps instabat—, ipse in hiberna Antiochiam concessit. in hoc statu regum erant res.

42. Romae eo primum anno triumviri epulones facti C. Licinius Lucullus tribunus plebis, qui legem de creandis his tulerat, et P. Manlius et P. Porcius Laeca; iis triumviris

---

[80] terram enarit *Kreyssig*: terram enaverit *Mog.*: terra menaret *B*

---

[146] A major Lycian city, near the mouth of the River Xanthus: *Barr.* 65 B5.

[147] Chelidonian Promontory: *Barr.* 65 D5; Eurymedon: F3.

[148] What "heads" means is unclear (mouths?); the Sarus (now Ceyhan) reaches the Mediterranean southeast of Tarsus: *Barr.* 66 G3.

ance and thereby give him assurance that the king would do nothing to change it.

Skirting the coast of Asia, Antiochus reached Lycia, and on learning at Patara[146] that Ptolemy was still alive he abandoned his plan of sailing to Egypt. He nevertheless still made for Cyprus, but after rounding the promontory of Chelidoniae he was held up for a short time in the area of the Eurymedon River[147] in Pamphylia by a mutiny of his oarsmen. When he had moved forward from there, a terrible storm arose around what they call "the heads" of the River Sarus,[148] and this almost sunk him and his entire fleet. Many of his ships were disabled and many driven ashore; many were so completely swallowed up by the sea that no one managed to swim to land. Large numbers of men perished in this incident, and not just a nameless herd of rowers and common soldiers, either, but some illustrious friends of the king as well. After he brought together what remained after the wreck, Antiochus was in no position to launch an expedition to Cyprus, and so he returned to Seleucia with a retinue less grand than at his departure. There he ordered the ships to be drawn up on land, since winter was already coming on, and he himself withdrew to winter quarters in Antioch. This was how matters stood with the kings.

42. In Rome, this was the first year that the *triumviri epulones*[149] were elected, and the appointees were Gaius Licinius Lucullus (the plebeian tribune who had proposed the law authorizing the election), Publius Manlius and Publius Porcius Laeca. These triumvirs were given the

---

[149] A priestly college (later called the *septemviri epulones,* when their number was raised to seven), whose main function was organizing the great feast (*epulum*) of Jupiter at the games.

item ut pontificibus lege datum est togae praetextae ha-
2 bendae ius. sed magnum certamen cum omnibus sacerdotibus eo anno fuit quaestoribus urbanis Q. Fabio Labeoni
3 et L. Aurelio. pecunia opus erat, quod ultimam pensionem
pecuniae in bellum conlatae persolvi placuerat privatis.
4 quaestores ab auguribus pontificibusque quod stipendium
per bellum non contulissent petebant. ab sacerdotibus tribuni plebis nequiquam appellati, omniumque annorum
per quos non dederant exactum est.
5 Eodem anno duo mortui pontifices novique in eorum
locum suffecti, M. Marcellus consul in locum C. Semproni
Tuditani, qui praetor in Hispania decesserat, et L. Valerius
6 Flaccus in locum M. Corneli Cethegi. et Q. Fabius Maximus augur mortuus est admodum adulescens, priusquam
ullum magistratum caperet; nec eo anno augur in eius
locum est suffectus.
7 Comitia inde consularia habita a M. Marcello consule.
creati consules L. Valerius Flaccus et M. Porcius Cato.
praetores inde facti Cn. Manlius Vulso, Ap. Claudius
Nero, P. Porcius Laeca, C. Fabricius Luscinus, C. Atinius
Labeo,[81] P. Manlius.
8 Eo anno aediles curules M. Fulvius Nobilior et C. Flaminius tritici deciens centena milia binis aeris populo dis-

[81] C. Fabricius . . . Labeo *hic Weiss., ante* C. Manlius *Fr. 2:* C.
Fabricius Labeo *hic B: om. Mog.*

---

150 Cf. 31.11.12 note.

151 Cf. 31.13.2–9 and note.

152 L. Valerius Flaccus (173): legatus in Gaul (200) and praetor in 199, he was the patron of the elder Cato, whose partner in
the consulship he was now to be. Cato had been military tribune
in 214 and quaestor in 204. The two would be censors in 184.

legal right, also accorded the pontiffs, to wear the *toga praetexta*.[150] That year, however, the city quaestors, Quintus Fabius Labeo and Lucius Aurelius, were involved in a bitter struggle with all the priests. Money was needed because it had been decided that private individuals should be paid the last installment of the moneys they had contributed toward the war, and the quaestors were dunning the augurs and pontiffs for taxes they had not paid during the period of the war.[151] An appeal made by the priests to the tribunes of the people was ineffective, and an amount was collected to cover all the years of nonpayment.

In the same year two pontiffs died and were replaced by new ones: the consul Marcus Marcellus succeeded Gaius Sempronius Tuditanus, who had died while holding the praetorship in Spain, and Lucius Valerius Flaccus succeeded Marcus Cornelius Cethegus. The augur Quintus Fabius Maximus also died while still very young and before he could hold any magistracy, but no augur was chosen to replace him that year.

The consular elections were then conducted by the consul Marcus Marcellus, and Lucius Valerius Flaccus and Marcus Porcius Cato were elected as consuls.[152] The following were chosen as praetors: Gnaeus Manlius Vulso, Appius Claudius Nero, Publius Porcius Laeca, Gaius Fabricius Luscinus, Gaius Atinius Labeo, and Publius Manlius.

During that year the curule aediles, Marcus Fulvius Nobilior[153] and Gaius Flaminius,[154] distributed a million

---

[153] M. Fulvius Nobilior (190), later a consul (189) and censor (179), was an enemy of the Scipios.   [154] C. Flaminius (3), quaestor in 209, would later be praetor (193) and consul (187).

cripserunt. id C. Flamini honoris causa ipsius patrisque
9 aduexerant Siculi Romam: Flaminius gratiam eius com-
municaverat cum collega. ludi Romani et apparati mag-
10 nifice sunt et ter toti instaurati. aediles plebis Cn. Domitius Ahenobarbus et C. Scribonius Curio multos pecuarios
ad populi iudicium adduxerunt: tres ex his condemnati
sunt; ex eorum multaticia pecunia aedem in insula Fauni
11 fecerunt. ludi plebeii per biduum instaurati, et epulum
fuit ludorum causa.

43. L. Valerius Flaccus et M. Porcius Cato consules
idibus Martiis, quo die magistratum inierunt, de provin-
2 ciis cum ad senatum rettulissent, patres censuerunt, quoniam in Hispania tantum glisceret bellum ut iam consulari
et duce et exercitu opus esset, placere consules Hispaniam
citeriorem Italiamque provincias aut comparare inter se
3 aut sortiri: utri Hispania provincia evenisset, eum duas
legiones et quindecim milia socium Latini nominis et octingentos equites secum portare, et naves longas viginti
4 ducere; alter consul duas scriberet legiones: iis Galliam
obtineri provinciam satis esse fractis proximo anno Insubrum Boiorumque animis.
5 Cato Hispaniam Valerius Italiam est sortitus. praetores
deinde provincias sortiti, C. Fabricius Luscinus urbanam,

---

155 The father, C. Flaminius (2), had been the first governor
of Sicily after it became a province (227). He was consul in 223
and again in 217, when he lost his life, and his reputation, at
Trasimene, and so this is a "striking tribute" (Briscoe, 1.330).

156 Cf. 31.4.5 note.        157 The island in the Tiber. For this,
the only known temple of Faunus in Rome, cf. Richardson 148.
For fines used for public projects, cf. 31.50.2 and note.

158 Cf. 31.4.7 and note.

measures of grain to the people at a price of two *asses* per measure. The people of Sicily had brought the grain to Rome as a mark of respect for Gaius Flaminius and his father,[155] and Flaminius had shared the credit for it with his colleague. The Roman Games were celebrated with great ceremony, and were repeated three times in their entirety.[156] The plebeian aediles, Gnaeus Domitius Ahenobarbus and Gaius Scribonius Curio, arraigned a large number of cattle breeders before the people. Three were found guilty, and from the fines exacted from them the aediles built a temple of Faunus on the Island.[157] The Plebeian Games[158] were repeated over a second two-day period, and a banquet was held in honor of the games.

43. On the Ides of March, the day of their entry into office, the consuls Lucius Valerius Flaccus and Marcus Porcius Cato referred to the senate the matter of their provinces. The senators decided that, since the war in Spain was escalating at such a rate as to require both a consular general and a consular army, the consuls should have as their provinces Hither Spain and Italy respectively, the choice being left to mutual agreement or sortition. The one who received Spain as his province was to transport with him two legions, 15,000 infantry of the allies and those with Latin rights, and 800 cavalry, and also take with him 20 warships. The other consul was to enroll two legions; these were deemed sufficient to hold the province of Gaul as the spirit of the Insubres and Boii had been broken in the previous year.

Cato drew Spain as his province and Valerius Italy. The praetorian sortition then went as follows: Gaius Fabricius Luscinus received the City Jurisdiction, and Gaius Atinius

C. Atinius Labeo peregrinam, Cn. Manlius Vulso Siciliam, Ap. Claudius Nero Hispaniam ulteriorem, P. Porcius Laeca Pisas, ut ab tergo Liguribus esset; P. Manlius in Hispaniam citeriorem adiutor consuli datus.

6     T. Quinctio, suspectis non solum Antiocho et Aetolis sed iam etiam Nabide Lacedaemoniorum tyranno, prorogatum in annum imperium est, duas legiones ut haberet: in eas si quid supplementi opus esset, consules scribere et 7 mittere in Macedoniam iussi. Ap. Claudio praeter legionem quam Q. Fabius habuerat, duo milia peditum[82] et 8 ducentos equites novos ut scriberet permissum. par numerus peditum equitumque novorum et P. Manlio in citeriorem Hispaniam decretus, et legio eadem quae fuerat 9 sub Q. Minucio praetore data. et P. Porcio Laecae circa[83] Pisas decem milia peditum et quingenti equites ex Gallico exercitu decreti. in Sardinia prorogatum imperium Ti. Sempronio Longo.

44. Provinciis ita distributis, consules priusquam ab urbe proficiscerentur ver sacrum ex decreto pontificum 2 iussi facere, quod A. Cornelius Mammula praetor voverat de senatus sententia populique iussu Cn. Servilio C. Fla- 3 minio consulibus. annis post uno et viginti factum est quam votum. per eosdem dies C. Claudius Appi filius Pul-

---

[82] peditum *Fr. 1*: *om. BMog.*
[83] circa *Madvig*: ad Etruriam circa *BMog.*

---

[159] This was in 217 (cf. 22.10.2–6). The Sacred Spring (*ver sacrum*) was an ancient Italic practice in times of disaster. An oath was made to sacrifice all living things born in the coming spring, but children who were born then were not killed; rather, on reaching maturity, they were sent off to settle new lands.

Labeo the Jurisdiction of Foreigners; Gnaeus Manlius Vulso drew Sicily, and Appius Claudius Nero Farther Spain, while Publius Porcius Laeca drew Pisae (so he would be to the rear of the Ligures), and Publius Manlius was to be a consular aide for Hither Spain.

Since there were now concerns not only about Antiochus and the Aetolians but also about the Spartan tyrant Nabis, Titus Quinctius had his *imperium* prorogued for a year, with the command of two legions; and the consuls were authorized to enroll and dispatch to Macedonia any forces that might be needed to supplement them. As well as receiving the legion formerly under Quintus Fabius, Appius Claudius was permitted to enlist 2,000 infantry and 200 new cavalry. The same number of new infantry and cavalry was also assigned to Publius Manlius for service in Hither Spain, and he was further given the legion that had been under the command of the praetor Quintus Minucius. Publius Porcius Laeca was also officially allocated 10,000 infantry and 5,000 cavalry from the army in Gaul for service around Pisae. In Sardinia Tiberius Sempronius Longus had his *imperium* prorogued.

44. Such was the allocation of provinces. Before the consuls left the city, they were instructed, in accordance with a decision of the pontiffs, to carry out the "Sacred Spring" that the praetor Aulus Cornelius Mammula had promised in a vow that he had made by senatorial decree and a vote of the people during the consulship of Gnaeus Servilius and Gaius Flaminius.[159] The rite was performed twenty-one years after the vow was made. In the same period Gaius Claudius Pulcher, son of Appius, was elected

cher augur in Q. Fabi Maximi locum, qui priore anno
mortuus erat, lectus inauguratusque est.

4    Mirantibus iam volgo hominibus quod Hispania movis-
set bellum neglegi, litterae a Q. Minucio adlatae sunt se
ad Turdam oppidum cum Budare et Baesadine imperato-
ribus Hispanis signis conlatis prospere pugnasse: duodecim milia hostium caesa, Budarem imperatorem captum,
5    ceteros fusos fugatosque. his litteris lectis minus terroris
ab Hispanis erat, unde ingens bellum exspectatum fuerat.
omnes curae utique post adventum decem legatorum in
6    Antiochum regem conversae. hi, expositis prius quae cum
Philippo acta essent et quibus legibus data pax, non mi-
7    norem belli molem instare ab Antiocho docuerunt: ingenti
classe egregio terrestri exercitu in Europam eum traiecisse, et nisi avertisset vana spes ex vaniore rumore orta
Aegypti invadendae, mox bello Graeciam arsuram fuisse;
neque enim ne Aetolos quidem quieturos, cum ingenio
8    inquietam tum iratam Romanis gentem. haerere et aliud
in visceribus Graeciae ingens malum, Nabim, nunc Lacedaemoniorum, mox si liceat universae Graeciae futurum
tyrannum, avaritia et crudelitate omnes fama celebratos
9    tyrannos aequantem; cui si Argos velut arcem Peloponn-
neso impositam tenere liceat, deportatis in Italiam Romanis exercitibus nequiquam liberatam a Philippo Graeciam

---

160 Mentioned only here, its location is unknown, and it is not
even known whether it is Turdetanian: cf. TIR *J-30,* 325–26.

and installed as augur to replace Quintus Fabius Maximus, who had died the previous year.

While people now generally felt surprised at the indifference being shown toward the war that Spain had started, a dispatch arrived from Quintus Minucius with the news that he had fought a successful pitched battle with the Spanish commanders Budares and Baesadines near the town of Turda.[160] Twelve thousand of the enemy had been killed, Minucius said, the commander Budares had been taken prisoner, and the others had been defeated and put to flight. After the dispatch was read out, there was less alarm regarding Spain, where a momentous war had been expected. All concern was now focused instead on King Antiochus, especially after the arrival of the ten commissioners. After first reporting on their dealings with Philip and the terms on which he had been granted peace, these explained that they were threatened with a war no less serious with Antiochus. The king had crossed to Europe with a mighty fleet and a first-rate land army, they said, and if he had not been distracted by a groundless hope, arising from an even more groundless rumor, of invading Egypt, Greece would soon have been engulfed in the flames of war. The Aetolians would not remain inactive, either—they were by nature an unruly people who also bore a grudge against the Romans. There was, too, another great cancer fixed in the entrails of Greece— Nabis, currently tyrant of the Spartans, but soon to be tyrant of all Greece if given the chance, a man who rivaled all the notorious tyrants in greed and brutality. Should he be allowed to hold Argos—which dominates the Peloponnese like a citadel—after the Roman armies were withdrawn to Italy, then the liberation of Greece from Philip

fore, pro rege, si nihil aliud, longinquo, vicinum tyrannum
dominum habituram.

45. Haec cum ab tam gravibus auctoribus, ut qui[84] om-
2 nia per se ipsos explorata adferrent, audirentur, maior res
quod ad Antiochum attineret, maturanda magis, quoniam
rex quacumque de causa in Syriam concessisset, de ty-
3 ranno consultatio visa est. cum diu disceptatum esset
utrum satis iam causae videretur cur decerneretur bellum,
an permitterent T. Quinctio, quod ad Nabim Lacedaemonium attineret, faceret quod e re publica censeret esse,
4 permiserunt, eam rem esse rati quae maturata dilatave
non ita magni momenti ad summam rem publicam esset:
5 magis id animadvertendum esse quid Hannibal et Carthaginienses, si cum Antiocho bellum motum foret, acturi
essent.
6   Adversae Hannibali factionis homines principibus Romanis, hospitibus quisque suis, identidem scribebant nuntios litterasque ab Hannibale ad Antiochum missas, et ab
7 rege ad eum clam legatos venisse: ut feras quasdam nulla
mitescere arte, sic immitem et implacabilem eius viri animum esse; marcescere otii situ queri civitatem et inertia
8 sopiri, nec sine armorum sonitu excitari posse. haec pro-
babilia memoria prioris belli per unum illum non magis
gesti quam moti faciebat. inritaverat etiam recenti facto
multorum potentium animos.

[84] ut qui *Wesenberg*: tum qui *B Fr. 2*: tum quia *Mog.*: *obelo utitur Briscoe*

---

[161] On Livy's characterization of Hannibal, see Introduction,
xlv–xlvi.

would have been for nothing. Instead of a king—who was, if nothing else, at least far removed—Greece would have as its master a tyrant who was close at hand.

45. When they heard this from the lips of such reliable witnesses—men bringing reports entirely based on their own inquiries—it seemed to them that, while the major problem was that of Antiochus, discussion focused on the tyrant was now more urgent since the king had, for whatever reason, withdrawn into Syria. There was a long debate on whether there appeared to be sufficient grounds for declaring war or whether they should simply give Titus Quinctius leave to do what he felt was in the national interest with regard to the Spartan Nabis. They did give Quinctius such leave, thinking it of slight importance to the best interests of the state whether they acted quickly or left things till later. Of greater concern was what the reaction of Hannibal and the Carthaginians would be to war breaking out with Antiochus.[161]

Members of the faction opposed to Hannibal had been writing time and again to their friends among the leading Romans to say that messengers and letters had been sent to Antiochus by Hannibal, and that envoys had come secretly to him from the king. Just as some wild animals could not be tamed by any means, they said, so this man's disposition was, just like that, fierce and recalcitrant. He would complain that his city-state was atrophying in idleness and inactivity, was drowsing in inertia, and could be roused only by the clash of weapons. What gave plausibility to these statements was the recollection of the last war, which Hannibal had fomented as well as conducted. In addition, he had ruffled the feelings of many of the important people of Carthage by his recent conduct.

46. Iudicum ordo Carthagine ea tempestate dominaba-
2 tur, eo maxime quod iidem perpetui iudices erant. res
fama vitaque omnium in illorum potestate erat; qui unum
eius ordinis offendisset, omnes adversos habebat, nec ac-
3 cusator apud infensos iudices deerat. horum in tam impotenti regno—neque enim civiliter nimiis opibus uteban-
tur—praetor factus Hannibal vocari ad se quaestorem
4 iussit. quaestor id pro nihilo habuit; nam et adversae factionis erat, et quia ex quaestura in iudices, potentissimum
ordinem, referebatur, iam pro futuris mox opibus animos
5 gerebat. enimvero indignum id ratus, Hannibal viatorem
ad prendendum quaestorem misit, subductumque in contionem non ipsum magis quam ordinem iudicum, prae
quorum superbia atque opibus nec leges quicquam essent
6 nec magistratus, accusavit. et ut secundis auribus accipi
orationem animadvertit, et infimorum quoque libertati
7 gravem esse superbiam eorum, legem extemplo promulgavit pertulitque ut in singulos annos iudices legerentur,
neu quis biennium continuum iudex esset. ceterum quantam eo facto ad plebem inierat gratiam, tantum magnae
8 partis principum offenderat animos. adiecit et aliud quo[85]
bono publico sibi proprias simultates inritavit. vectigalia

[85] quo *Heinsius*: quod *BMog.*

[162] The body, comprising 104 members, had evidently acquired considerable power, like the Areopagus at Athens before
Ephialtes' reforms in the late 460s. Aristotle (*Pol.* 2.8.2) compares
it with the ephorate at Sparta.

[163] As Livy uses "praetor" for the chief magistrates of foreign
states (cf. 31.24.6 and note) and in Carthage these were the two
*sufetes,* Hannibal must have been elected as one of the two.

46. At that time power in Carthage lay with the order of judges, mainly because the same judges had lifetime tenure of office.[162] Everybody's property, reputation, and life rested in these men's hands. Anyone falling foul of a single member of that order had them all against him, and there was never an accuser lacking before such unsympathetic judges. While these men were enjoying their autocratic rule—for they did not exercise their exceptional powers as citizens should—Hannibal, who had been elected praetor,[163] ordered a quaestor[164] to be summoned to him. The quaestor completely ignored the summons; not only was he a member of the faction opposed to Hannibal but he was also in the process of being promoted from the quaestorship to the supreme order, that of the judges, and was already displaying an arrogance in keeping with the power soon to be his. Finding such conduct unacceptable, Hannibal sent an officer to arrest the quaestor. He then brought the man before the assembly, where he attacked not so much the individual concerned as the order of judges—before their arrogant manipulation of power, he said, neither the laws nor the magistrates counted for anything. Observing that his speech was falling on willing ears and that the judges' arrogance threatened the liberty of the lower orders as well, he immediately promulgated and carried a law that judges be elected for one year only and which barred anyone from being a judge for two consecutive years. The appreciation that this move won for him with the masses was on a par with the offense he gave to most of the nobility. Another action that he took for the public good also stirred up personal ani-

---

[164] Evidently, a lesser official, perhaps a financial officer.

publica partim neglegentia dilabebantur, partim praedae
ac divisui et principum quibusdam et magistratibus erant,
9  et[86] pecunia quae in stipendium Romanis suo quoque
anno penderetur deerat tributumque grave privatis imminere videbatur.

47. Hannibal postquam vectigalia quanta terrestria
maritimaque essent, et in quas res erogarentur animadvertit, et quid eorum ordinarii rei publicae usus con-
2  sumerent, quantum peculatus averteret, omnibus residuis
pecuniis exactis, tributo privatis remisso, satis locupletem
rem publicam fore ad vectigal praestandum Romanis pronuntiavit in contione, et praestitit promissum.
3  Tum vero ii quos paverat per aliquot annos publicus
peculatus, velut bonis ereptis, non furtorum manubiis
extortis, infensi et irati Romanos in Hannibalem et ipsos
4  causam odii quaerentes instigabant. ita diu repugnante P.
Scipione Africano, qui parum ex dignitate populi Romani
esse ducebat subscribere odiis accusatorum Hannibalis, et
factionibus Carthaginiensium inserere publicam auctori-
5  tatem, nec satis habere bello vicisse Hannibalem nisi velut
accusatores calumniam in eum iurarent ac nomen de-
6  ferrent, tandem pervicerunt ut legati Carthaginem mitterentur, qui ad senatum eorum arguerent Hannibalem cum
Antiocho rege consilia belli faciendi inire.

[86] et *B*: quin et *Mog.*

mosities against him. The public revenues were trickling away, partly through poor administration and partly because they were divided up as spoils among certain noblemen and the magistrates. There was, accordingly, a shortage of money to pay the annual indemnity to the Romans, and private citizens seemed to be faced with heavy taxation.

47. Hannibal turned his attention to the amount of taxes collected on goods transported by land and sea and the items on which these taxes were disbursed, noting what portion the regular expenses of state consumed and how much was diverted by embezzlement. He then announced before the assembly that, if all outstanding monies were collected, the state would be sufficiently solvent to pay the tribute to the Romans without levying a tax on private citizens, and he made good his assurance of this.

At this point the men whom embezzlement of public funds had fattened over a number of years became furiously angry, as if they were being deprived of their own property rather than relieved of loot gained by theft, and they began to incite the Romans—who were themselves looking for an excuse to vent their hatred on him—to take action against Hannibal. Publius Scipio Africanus long opposed this. He thought it ill suited the dignity of the Roman people to countenance the antipathies of Hannibal's accusers, to lend official support to the factions of Carthage and, not content with having defeated Hannibal in war, to act now as his prosecutors, swearing to the legitimacy of the allegations and bringing charges against him. Eventually, however, Hannibal's accusers convinced the senate to send a delegation to Carthage to lay before the Carthaginian senate allegations that Hannibal was plotting war in league with King Antiochus.

7    Legati tres missi, Cn. Servilius M. Claudius Marcellus
Q. Terentius Culleo. qui cum Carthaginem venissent, ex
8  consilio inimicorum Hannibalis quaerentibus causam adventus dici iusserunt venisse se ad controversias quae cum
Masinissa rege Numidarum Carthaginiensibus essent diri-
9  mendas. id creditum volgo: unum Hannibalem se peti ab
Romanis non fallebat, et ita pacem Carthaginiensibus
datam esse ut inexpiabile bellum adversus se unum mane-
10  ret. itaque cedere tempori et fortunae statuit; et praeparatis iam ante omnibus ad fugam, obversatus eo die in foro
avertendae suspicionis causa, primis tenebris vestitu fo-
rensi ad portam cum duobus comitibus ignaris consilii est
egressus.

48. Cum equi quo in loco iusserat praesto fuissent,
nocte Byzacium—ita regionem quandam agri vocant—
transgressus, postero die ad mare inter Acyllam et Thap-
2  sum ad suam turrim pervenit; ibi eum parata instructaque
remigio excepit navis. ita Africa Hannibal excessit, saepius
3  patriae quam suum eventum miseratus. eodem die in Cer-
cinam insulam traiecit. ubi cum in portu naves aliquot
Phoenicum onerarias cum mercibus invenisset, et ad
egressum eum e nave concursus salutantium esset factus,
percunctantibus legatum se Tyrum missum dici iussit.
4  veritus tamen ne qua earum navis nocte profecta Thap-
sum aut Hadrumetum nuntiaret se Cercinae visum, sacri-

---

165 A plausible pretext as boundary quarrels between Car-
thage and Numidia were interminable and led eventually to the
Third Punic War in 149 BC.        166 Byzacium: *Barr.* 33 G1–3;
Acylla (Acholla): H2; Thapsus: H1.

167 An island southeast of Acholla (*Barr.* 33 H3).

168 Modern Sousse: *Barr.* 33 G1.

Three envoys were sent: Cnaeus Servilius, Marcus Claudius Marcellus, and Quintus Terentius Culleo. Arriving in Carthage, they followed the advice of Hannibal's enemies and when people asked the reason for their visit ordered the answer given that they had come to settle disputes that the Carthaginians were having with Masinissa, king of Numidia.[165] This was generally accepted. Only Hannibal was not fooled—he could see that he was the real target of the Romans and that the peace granted to the Carthaginians was dependent on an implacable war continuing against him alone. He decided therefore to yield to circumstances and fortune. Having already prepared everything in advance for his escape, he spent the day in the forum to avert suspicion; and then, at dusk, he proceeded to one of the gates, dressed in his city clothes, with two companions who had no idea what his intentions were.

48. Horses were at the ready where he had ordered them to be, and during the night he crossed Byzacium (the name of some open country) arriving the following day at his castle on the sea between Acylla and Thapsus.[166] There a ship was awaiting him, fitted out and manned with a crew. So it was that Hannibal left Africa, bemoaning his country's fate more often than his own. That same day he crossed to the island of Cercina.[167] Here he found in port a number of Phoenician merchant vessels loaded with cargo, and as he disembarked a crowd gathered as people came to greet him. When they asked about him, he ordered the answer given that he was on a diplomatic mission to Tyre. Even so, fearing that one of these ships might set off at night and take the news to Thapsus or Hadrumetum[168] that he had been spotted on Cercina, he gave in-

ficio apparari iusso magistros navium mercatoresque invi-
5 tari iussit, et uela cum antemnis ex navibus corrogari ut
umbraclum—media aestas forte erat—cenantibus in li-
6 tore fieret. quanto res et tempus patiebatur apparatu cele-
bratae eius diei epulae sunt, multoque vino in serum noc-
7 tis convivium productum. Hannibal cum primum fallendi
8 eos qui in portu erant tempus habuit, navem soluit. ceteri
sopiti cum postero die tandem ex somno pleni crapulae
surrexissent, ad id quod serum erat, aliquot horas referen-
dis in naves conlocandisque[87] et aptandis armamentis
absumpserunt.

9 Carthagine ut multitudinis adsuetae domum Hannibalis frequentare concursus ad vestibulum aedium est factus,
10 et[88] non comparere eum uolgatum est, in forum turba
convenit principem civitatis quaerentium; et alii fugam
11 conscisse, id quod erat, alii fraude Romanorum interfectum idque magis volgo fremebant, variosque voltus cer-
neres ut in civitate aliorum alias partes foventium et factionibus discordi; visum deinde Cercinae eum tandem
adlatum est.

49. Et Romani legati cum in senatu exposuissent compertum patribus Romanis esse et Philippum regem ante
ab Hannibale maxime accensum bellum populo Romano
2 fecisse, et nunc litteras nuntiosque ab eo ad Antiochum et
Aetolos missos, consiliaque inita impellendae ad defec-

---

[87] conlocandisque et aptandis *Kreyssig*: collocandis *B*: collocandis et aptandis *Mog.*

[88] ut multitudinis . . . et *Drak.*: et multitudinis . . . ut *BMog.*

structions for a sacrifice to be prepared and the ship captains and traders invited to it. He also issued orders for the sails and spars to be gathered from the ships to form a sunshade for his guests (it happened to be midsummer), who would be dining on the shore. On that day the banquet was as elaborate as the circumstances and time permitted and the party was drawn out till late at night with heavy drinking. As soon as Hannibal found the occasion to give those in the port the slip, he set sail. The other diners were asleep, and when they finally awoke from their slumber the next day, severely hungover, not only was it late but they spent several hours carrying the rigging back to the ships and then setting it up and adjusting it.

In Carthage the large numbers of people who usually visited Hannibal's house were gathered at the entrance to the building, and when word spread that he was nowhere to be found a crowd converged on the forum demanding their leading citizen. Some loudly proclaimed that he had escaped, which was the case, but others that he had been treacherously murdered by the Romans. This was what the majority were angrily claiming, and one could see the various expressions to be expected in a community with loyalties divided between different parties and split by factions. Then finally word was brought that Hannibal had been sighted on Cercina.

49. The Roman envoys declared in the Carthaginian senate that the Roman senators had learned that Philip had earlier made war on the Roman people mainly at Hannibal's instigation, and also that dispatches and messages had of late been sent by Hannibal to Antiochus and the Aetolians. He had formed plans for provoking Carthage to rebellion, they said, and the destination of his

tionem Carthaginis, nec alio eum quam ad Antiochum
regem profectum—haud quieturum antequam bellum
3 toto orbe terrarum concisset; id ei non debere impune
esse, si satisfacere Carthaginienses populo Romano vellent
nihil eorum sua voluntate nec publico consilio factum
4 esse—, Carthaginienses responderunt quidquid aequum
censuissent Romani facturos esse.
5     Hannibal prospero cursu Tyrum pervenit, exceptusque
a conditoribus Carthaginis ut ab altera patria, vir tam cla-
rus omni genere honorum, paucos moratus dies Antio-
6 chiam navigat. ibi profectum iam regem in Asiam cum
audisset, filiumque eius sollemne ludorum ad Daphnen
celebrantem convenisset, comiter ab eo exceptus nullam
7 moram navigandi fecit. Ephesi regem est consecutus, fluctuantem adhuc animo incertumque de Romano bello; sed
haud parvum momentum ad animum eius moliendum
8 adventus Hannibalis fecit. Aetolorum quoque eodem tempore alienati ab societate Romana animi sunt, quorum
legatos Pharsalum et Leucadem et quasdam alias civitates
ex primo foedere repetentes senatus ad T. Quinctium re-
iecit.

present journey was undoubtedly King Antiochus' court—
he would not rest until he had fomented war the world
over. He should not remain unpunished for that, they
added, if the Carthaginians wished to satisfy the Roman
people that none of his activities had their approval or had
been officially sanctioned. The Carthaginians replied that
they would do whatever the Romans thought right.

Hannibal arrived in Tyre after a good journey, and
there was welcomed by the founders of Carthage as one
coming from their second fatherland,[169] a man of distinction laden with all manner of honors. He remained a few
days and then sailed on to Antioch.[170] There he was told
that the king had already left for Asia, and he met Antiochus' son, who was engaged in the seasonal celebration of
the games at Daphne.[171] Hannibal was given a warm welcome by him but did not delay his voyage. At Ephesus he
overtook the king, who was still vacillating and ambivalent
about war with Rome, but Hannibal's arrival had no little
influence in bringing him to make up his mind. At this
same time the Aetolians were also inclined to abandon
their alliance with Rome: their envoys had been asking for
the return of Pharsalus, Leucas, and certain other states
in accordance with the terms of their original treaty, only
to be referred by the senate to Titus Quinctius.

[169] Carthage was a Tyrian settlement, founded about 800.

[170] This is Antioch-on-the-Orontes, the Syrian capital (cf. 19.8
and note, above).

[171] Village close to Antioch: *Barr.* 67 C4.

# LIBRI XXXIII PERIOCHA

T. Quintius Flamininus procos. cum Philippo ad Cy-
no‹s›cephalas in Thessalia acie victo debellavit. L. Quinctius Flamininus, ille frater procos., Acarnanas, Leucade
urbe, quod caput est Acarnanum, expugnata, in deditionem accepit. pax petenti Philippo Graecia liberata data
est. Attalus ab Thebis ob subitam valetudinem Pergamum
translatus decessit. C. Sempronius Tuditanus praetor ab
Celtiberis cum exercitu caesus est. L. Furius Purpurio et
Claudius Marcellus coss. Boios et Insubres Gallos subege-
runt. Marcellus triumphavit. Hannibal frustra in Africa
bellum molitus et ob hoc Romanis per epistulas ab adversae factionis principibus delatus propter metum Romanorum, qui legatos ad senatum Carthaginiensium de eo mi-
serant, profugus ad Antiochum, Syriae regem, se contulit
bellum adversus Romanos parantem.

# SUMMARY OF BOOK XXXIII

As proconsul Titus Quinctius Flamininus brought the war with Philip to an end when he defeated him in pitched battle at Cynoscephalae in Thessaly. The proconsul's brother, Lucius Quinctius Flamininus, accepted the surrender of the Acarnanians after capturing the city of Leucas, which is the capital of the Acarnanians. Peace was given to Philip at his request after Greece was liberated. Attalus was transported from Thebes to Pergamum because of his sudden illness and died there. The praetor Gaius Sempronius Tuditanus was killed by the Celtiberians along with his army. The consuls Lucius Furius Purpurio and Claudius Marcellus crushed the Boii and the Insubrian Gauls. Marcellus celebrated a triumph. Hannibal had tried in vain to foment war and for this was betrayed to the Romans in letters sent by the leaders of a faction opposed to him. Out of fear of the Romans, who had sent delegates to the senate of Carthage about him, he fled and came to Antiochus, the king of Syria, who was preparing for war with the Romans.

# LIBER XXXIV

1. Inter bellorum magnorum aut vixdum finitorum aut imminentium curas intercessit res parva dictu sed quae
2 studiis in magnum certamen excesserit. M. Fundanius et L. Valerius tribuni plebi ad plebem tulerunt de Oppia lege
3 abroganda. tulerat eam C. Oppius tribunus plebi Q. Fabio Ti. Sempronio consulibus in medio ardore Punici belli, ne qua mulier plus semunciam auri haberet, neu vestimento versicolori uteretur, neu iuncto vehiculo in urbe oppidove aut propius inde mille passus nisi sacrorum publicorum
4 causa veheretur. M. et P. Iunii Bruti tribuni plebi legem Oppiam tuebantur, nec eam se abrogari passuros aiebant; ad suadendum dissuadendumque multi nobiles prodibant; Capitolium turba hominum faventium adversantiumque legi complebatur.

---

[1] Probably L. Valerius Tappo (350), praetor in 192. It is he who rises to defend their bill in chapters 5 to 7. Fundanius is otherwise unknown.       [2] The first eight and a half chapters of Book 24 concern what Livy himself calls an "insignificant event," the debate over and repeal of the *Lex Oppia,* a sumptuary law on women's expenses, carried by the plebeian tribune Gaius Oppius in 215. Apart from the law and his tribuneship, nothing more is known of Oppius. The speech of Cato (chaps. 2–4) is generally agreed to be Livy's invention.       [3] Q. Fabius Maximus (116), the famous Cunctator ("Delayer") and Ti. Sempronius Gracchus (51), great-uncle of the Gracchi brothers.

# BOOK XXXIV

1. Amid concerns over serious wars that were either barely terminated or else looming on the horizon there occurred an event that was insignificant for the record but which led to acrimonious debate with the passions it aroused. The plebeian tribunes Marcus Fundanius and Lucius Valerius[1] brought before the popular assembly a proposal to annul the Oppian law.[2] The law had been enacted by the plebeian tribune Gaius Oppius in the consulship of Quintus Fabius and Tiberius Sempronius,[3] when the flames of the Punic War were burning fiercely; and its provisions were that no woman was to own more than a half-ounce of gold, wear colored clothes,[4] or ride a horse and carriage in the city or a town, or within a mile of a town, except to attend public religious rites.[5] The plebeian tribunes Marcus and Publius Iunius Brutus defended the Oppian law and said they would not permit its repeal; many eminent men came forward to speak for or against its annulment; and the Capitol was filled with hordes of the law's supporters and opponents.

[4] This probably means purple clothes, the only color mentioned by Cato and Lucius Valerius in the debate.

[5] Levene (83) notes that although religious rites figure here as an exception to the sumptuary restrictions, "religious material is almost entirely absent" in the following debate on the law.

5 Matronae nulla nec auctoritate nec verecundia nec imperio virorum contineri limine poterant, omnes vias urbis aditusque in forum obsidebant, viros descendentes ad forum orantes ut florente re publica, crescente in dies privata omnium fortuna, matronis quoque pristinum orna-
6 tum reddi paterentur. augebatur haec frequentia mulierum in dies; nam etiam ex oppidis conciliabulisque conve-
7 niebant. iam et consules praetoresque et alios magistratus adire et rogare audebant; ceterum minime exorabilem alterum utique consulem M. Porcium Catonem habebant, qui pro lege quae abrogabatur ita disseruit:

2. "Si in sua quisque nostrum matre familiae, Quirites, ius et maiestatem viri retinere instituisset, minus cum uni-
2 versis feminis negotii haberemus: nunc domi victa libertas nostra impotentia muliebri hic quoque in foro obteritur et calcatur, et quia singulas sustinere non potuimus[1] universas horremus. equidem fabulam et fictam rem ducebam
3 esse virorum omne genus in aliqua insula coniuratione
4 muliebri ab stirpe sublatum esse; ab nullo genere non summum periculum est si coetus et concilia et secretas

---

[1] sustinere non potuimus χ: non potuimus B: non domuimus *vel* compescuimus *Madvig*: non continuimus *Hertz*

---

[6] Marcus Porcius Cato (9) ("Cato the Censor"). Consul this year, he had been quaestor in 204 (serving under Scipio Africanus in Sicily and Africa), plebeian aedile in 199, and praetor in 198 (*MRR* 339). A champion of traditional Roman morality, he was much concerned about the creeping philhellenism of the time. Cf. *OLD* sv Porcius Cato, Marcus (1).

[7] The Lemnian women, who (with the exception of Hypsipyle) murdered their husbands (cf. Hyg. *Fab.* 15).

As for married women, they could be kept indoors by no authority, no feelings of modesty, and no command from their husbands. They blocked all the roads in the city and all approaches to the Forum and made earnest entreaties to their husbands when they went down to the Forum. As the Republic was prospering and everybody's private fortune was increasing day by day, they said, they should also allow married women to have the finery they once enjoyed restored to them. This large gathering of women kept growing every day as they were even starting to come in from the towns and market centers. They were already presuming to accost consuls, praetors and other magistrates with their appeals; but they continued to find one of the consuls, at least, adamantly opposed to them. This was Marcus Porcius Cato,[6] who spoke as follows about the law whose repeal was under consideration:

2. "My fellow citizens: had each of us, individually, resolved to preserve his rights and standing as a husband with his own wife, we should now be having less of a problem with our women as a whole. As it is, our autonomy, broken in our homes, is also being crushed and trodden under foot here in the Forum by female indiscipline; and because we have been unable to keep them under control individually, we are now frightened of them as body. Frankly, I used to think that the notion of the entire male sex on some island being utterly wiped out by a female cabal was merely a fable and just a piece of fiction;[7] but there is extreme danger with any group of people if you allow them to hold gatherings, meetings, and clandestine

consultationes esse sinas. atque ego vix statuere apud animum meum possum utrum peior ipsa res an peiore exem-
5 plo agatur; quorum alterum ad nos consules reliquosque
magistratus, alterum ad vos, Quirites, magis pertinet. nam
utrum e re publica sit necne id quod ad vos fertur, vestra
6 existimatio est qui in suffragium ituri estis. haec conster-
natio muliebris, sive sua sponte sive auctoribus vobis, M.
Fundani et L. Valeri, facta est, haud dubie ad culpam
magistratuum pertinens, nescio vobis, tribuni, an consuli-
7 bus magis sit deformis: vobis, si feminas ad concitandas
tribunicias seditiones iam adduxistis; nobis, si ut plebis
quondam sic nunc mulierum secessione leges accipiendae
sunt.

8    "Equidem non sine rubore quodam paulo ante per
medium agmen mulierum in forum perveni. quod nisi me
verecundia singularum magis maiestatis et pudoris quam
universarum tenuisset, ne compellatae a consule videren-
9 tur, dixissem: 'qui hic mos est in publicum procurrendi et
obsidendi vias et viros alienos appellandi? istud ipsum
10 suos quaeque domi rogare non potuistis? an blandiores in
publico quam in privato et alienis quam vestris estis?
quamquam ne domi quidem vos, si sui iuris finibus matronas contineret pudor, quae leges hic rogarentur abroga-
renturve curare decuit.'

11    "Maiores nostri nullam, ne privatam quidem, rem

---

8 The precedent is the magistrates' concern, the actual affair
and its repercussions that of the citizens as a whole.

9 The famous secession of the plebs to the sacred mount in
494, which won them the right to their tribunes (Book 2.31–33),
a curious example of which the plebeian Cato might have been
expected to approve.

discussions. I personally have difficulty in deciding in my own mind which is worse, the affair itself or the precedent it may set—one of which is more a concern for us consuls and other magistrates, while the other[8] pertains more to you, my fellow citizens. For whether what is being proposed to you is or is not in the interests of the state is for you to judge—you who will be voting on the matter. But this disorderly conduct of the women, whether it is spontaneous or occasioned by you, Marcus Fundanius and Lucius Valerius, must certainly be blamed on the magistrates, and I do not know whether it brings more disgrace on you, the tribunes, or on the consuls. It brings more on *you* if you have drawn the women into your tribunician revolts, and more on *us* if laws must be accepted because of a secession of women, as formerly because of a secession of the plebs.[9]

"Frankly, I was blushing somewhat a moment ago when I came into the Forum through the midst of a crowd of women. Had I not been held back by respect for the status and modesty of some of the individuals present rather than of the group as a whole—I feared they might appear to have been rebuked by a consul—I would have said: 'What sort of conduct is this, all this running out into public places, blocking streets and accosting other women's husbands? Couldn't you all have asked your own husbands the very same thing at home? Are your charms more seductive in public than in private and to other women's spouses more than your own? And yet not even at home should the proposing or repealing of laws in this place have been any concern of yours, not if modesty kept married women within their proper limits.'

"Our ancestors did not want women conducting busi-

agere feminas sine tutore auctore voluerunt, in manu esse
parentium, fratrum, virorum: nos, si dis placet, iam etiam
rem publicam capessere eas patimur et foro prope[2] et
12 contionibus et comitiis immisceri. quid enim nunc aliud
per vias et compita faciunt quam rogationem tribunorum
13 plebi suadent, quam legem abrogandam censent? date
frenos impotenti naturae et indomito animali et sperate
14 ipsas modum licentiae facturas: nisi vos facietis, minimum
hoc eorum est quae iniquo animo feminae sibi aut moribus
aut legibus iniuncta patiuntur. omnium rerum libertatem,
immo licentiam, si vere dicere volumus, desiderant. quid
enim, si hoc expugnaverint, non temptabunt?

3. "Recensete omnia muliebria iura quibus licentiam
earum adligaverint maiores vestri per quaeque[3] subiece-
rint viris; quibus omnibus constrictas vix tamen continere
2 potestis. quid? si carpere singula et extorquere et exae-
quari ad extremum viris patiemini, tolerabiles vobis eas
3 fore creditis? extemplo, simul pares esse coeperint, superiores erunt.

"At hercule ne quid novum in eas rogetur recusant, non
4 ius sed iniuriam deprecantur: immo ut quam accepistis
iussistis suffragiis vestris legem, quam usu tot annorum et
experiendo comprobastis, hanc ut abrogetis, id est, ut
5 unam tollendo legem ceteras infirmetis. nulla lex satis

---

[2] prope *Mg*: quoque *B*χ
[3] per quaeque *A*[2] *Gel.*: per quae *B*: perquamque χ: per quaeque eas *Wulsch*

---

[10] Theoretically true, and a woman who did not have a male
relative exercising *potestas* over her was assigned a *tutor* (guardian), but this often became a mere formality.

ness, even private business, without a guardian acting as her spokesman; they were to remain under the protection of fathers, brothers or husbands.[10] But we, for God's sake, are now allowing them even to engage in affairs of state and almost to involve themselves in the Forum, in our meetings and in our assemblies. For what else are they doing at this moment in the streets and at the crossroads but urging acceptance of a bill of the plebeian tribunes and voting for repealing a law? Give free rein to their wild nature, to this unbroken beast, and then hope that they themselves will impose a curb on their license! If *you* do not impose it, this curb on them is merely the least of the restraints that women resent having imposed upon them by convention or the law. What they want is freedom—no, complete license, if we are willing to speak the truth,—in everything. If they win on this point, what then will they not try?

3. "Consider all the laws pertaining to women that the ancients employed to curb their license and make them subject to their husbands; though they are restricted by all of these you are still barely able to keep them in order. Suppose you allow them to pick away at these laws one by one, to tear them from you, and finally to put themselves on a par with their husbands. Do you believe you will find them bearable? As soon as they begin to be your equals they will immediately be your superiors.

"But, you may say, they are protesting so that no new measures should be taken against them; it is not the law they object to but injustice. Not true! What they want is for you to rescind a law that you have accepted and passed with your votes, a law that has met with your approval after many years of experience of living with it; which is to say, they want you to weaken all the other laws by remov-

431

commoda omnibus est: id modo quaeritur, si maiori parti
et in summam prodest. si quod cuique privatim officiet
ius, id destruet ac demolietur, quid attinebit universos rogare leges quas mox abrogare in quos latae sunt possint?

6 "Volo tamen audire quid sit propter quod matronae
consternatae procucurrerint in publicum ac vix foro se et
7 contione abstineant; ut captivi ab Hannibale redimantur
parentes viri liberi fratres earum? procul abest absitque
semper talis fortuna rei publicae; sed tamen, cum fuit,
8 negastis hoc piis precibus earum. at non pietas nec solicci-
tudo pro suis sed religio congregavit eas: matrem Idaeam
a Pessinunte ex Phrygia venientem accepturae sunt. quid
honestum dictu saltem seditioni praetenditur muliebri?
9 'ut auro et purpura fulgeamus,' inquit, 'ut carpentis festis
profestisque diebus, velut triumphantes de lege victa et
abrogata et captis et ereptis suffragiis vestris, per urbem
vectemur: ne ullus modus sumptibus, ne luxuriae sit.'

4. "Saepe me querentem de feminarum, saepe de virorum, nec de privatorum modo sed etiam magistratuum
2 sumptibus audistis, diversisque duobus vitiis, avaritia et
luxuria, civitatem laborare, quae pestes omnia magna im-
3 peria everterunt. haec ego, quo melior laetiorque in dies

---

11 This refers to the refusal to redeem Roman captives in 216
after Cannae (cf. 22.61.1–4).

12 A sarcastic reference to the Magna Mater brought from
Pessinus to Rome in 205 and the Roman matrons receiving her
(29.10.4–8, 14.10–14).

ing this one. No law satisfies everybody; all one asks is that it satisfies the majority and is of general benefit. If a person is to shred and overthrow any law that inconveniences him as an individual, what point will there be in society enacting laws that can shortly afterward be rescinded by those against whom they are directed?

"I should like to hear, by the way, what it is that has brought these married ladies to run in an uproar into the streets and why they barely hold themselves back from the Forum and public assemblies. Is it so that their fathers, husbands, children, and brothers in captivity might be ransomed from Hannibal? Such dire fortune is far removed from our state, and may it ever be! And yet, when that misfortune *was* ours, you refused to accede to the dutiful entreaties of the women.[11] Well, then, it was not family duty or concern for their dear ones that brought the women together—it was religion. They are going to welcome the Idaean Mother, coming from Pessinus in Phrygia![12] And what reason that might at least *sound* respectable is offered for this female revolt? 'So that we can shine in gold and purple,' she says. 'So we can ride our carriages through the city on holidays and ordinary days alike, in triumph, as it were, after the defeat and annulment of the law, and after the capture and seizure of your ballots. And so there may be no limit to our expenditure, no limit to our extravagance.'

4. "You have often heard me complain about the lavish spending of women, and of men, and not just of private citizens but magistrates, too. You have heard me complain that our state is plagued with two contrary vices, greed and extravagance, afflictions that have been the downfall of all great empires. The more the fortunes of our Republic

fortuna rei publicae est, quo magis imperium crescit—et iam in Graeciam Asiamque transcendimus omnibus libidinum inlecebris repletas, et regias etiam attrectamus gazas—, eo plus horreo, ne illae magis res nos ceperint

4 quam nos illas. infesta, mihi crede, signa ab Syracusis inlata sunt huic urbi. iam nimis multos audio Corinthi et Athenarum ornamenta laudantes mirantesque, et antefixa

5 fictilia deorum Romanorum ridentes. ego hos malo propitios deos, et ita spero futuros si in suis manere sedibus patiemur.

6 "Patrum nostrorum memoria per legatum Cineam Pyrrhus non virorum modo sed etiam mulierum animos donis temptavit. nondum lex Oppia ad coercendam luxuriam

7 muliebrem lata erat; tamen nulla accepit. quam causam fuisse censetis? eadem fuit quae maioribus nostris[4] nihil de hac re lege sanciundi: nulla erat luxuria quae coerceretur.

8 sicut ante morbos necesse est cognitos esse quam remedia eorum, sic cupiditates prius natae sunt quam leges quae iis modum facerent. quid legem Liciniam excitavit de quingentis iugeribus nisi ingens cupido agros conti-

9 nuandi? quid legem Cinciam de donis et muneribus nisi

---

[4] nostris *L*: vestris *B*χ

---

[13] Cf. 25.40.1–3, where Livy claims that Marcellus' removal to Rome of the treasures of Syracuse "first started the appreciation for Greek works of art and the license we now see in the looting of things sacred and profane."

[14] *antefixa* were statues of gods placed on the pediments of Etruscan and Roman temples. They were, indeed, often terracotta, but the statues within the temple were not necessarily so.

[15] Cineas was Pyrrhus' minister and friend, known for his

grow and prosper with every passing day and the more our empire expands—we are now crossing into Greece and Asia, which are replete with all manner of seductive pleasures, and we are even laying hands on the treasures of kings—the more I shudder at the thought that these things may have captured us rather than we them. Those statues from Syracuse were enemy standards brought against the city, believe me.[13] Already I hear all too many people praising and admiring the artifacts of Corinth and Athens, and ridiculing the earthenware antefixes of the Roman gods.[14] But I prefer to have these gods smiling on us, and I hope they will, if we allow them to remain in their abodes.

"In our fathers' day Pyrrhus used his envoy Cineas[15] to solicit the support not only of our men, but of our women, too, with gifts. The Oppian law had not yet been enacted to curtail female extravagance and even so no woman accepted the gifts. Why do you think that was? For the same reason that our ancestors had no need for legal sanctions in such matters—there was no extravagance to be curtailed. Just as diseases must be diagnosed before cures are found, so desires appear before the laws to curb them. What brought about the Licinian law of the 500 iugera[16] but the unconscionable greed for extending one's lands? What gave rise to the Cincian law regarding emoluments and honoraria but the fact that the commons had

oratory (Plut. Pyrrh. 14.1), who tried (unsuccessfully) to bribe the Romans (Pyrrh. 18.2–4).

[16] Of uncertain date, the law restricted the holding of ager publicus to a maximum of five hundred iugera (iugerum = two-thirds of an acre).

quia vectigalis iam et stipendiaria plebs esse senatui coe-
10  perat? itaque minime mirum est nec Oppiam nec aliam
ullam tum legem desideratam esse quae modum sumptibus mulierum faceret, cum aurum et purpuram data et
11  oblata ultro non accipiebant. si nunc cum illis donis Cineas
urbem circumiret, stantes in publico invenisset quae acciperent.

"Atque ego nonnullarum cupiditatium ne causam qui-
12  dem aut rationem inire possum. nam ut quod alii liceat tibi
non licere aliquid fortasse naturalis aut pudoris aut indig-
nationis habeat, sic aequato omnium cultu quid unaquae-
13  que vestrum veretur ne in se conspiciatur? pessimus
quidem pudor est vel parsimoniae vel paupertatis; sed
utrumque lex vobis demit cum id quod habere non licet
14  non habetis. 'hanc' inquit 'ipsam exaequationem non fero'
illa locuples. 'cur non insignis auro et purpura conspicior?
cur paupertas aliarum sub hac legis specie latet, ut quod
habere non possunt, habiturae, si liceret, fuisse videan-
tur?'

15  "Voltis hoc certamen uxoribus vestris inicere, Quirites,
ut divites id habere velint quod nulla alia possit, pauperes,
ne ob hoc ipsum contemnantur, supra vires se extendant?
16  ne simul pudere quod non oportet coeperit, quod oportet

---

17 Passed probably in 204 by the plebeian tribune M. Cincius
Alimentus (5), the law prohibited payment to advocates (cf. Tac.
*Ann.* 11.5.3), but its provisions may have been much wider.

started to become tribute-paying subjects of the senate?[17] Little wonder then that neither the Oppian nor any other law was required to limit expenditure by women at a time when women of their own accord would not accept gold and purple offered to them as gifts. If it were today that Cineas was doing the rounds of the city with those gifts, he would have found women standing in the streets to receive them.

"And yet in the case of some appetites I, personally, cannot fathom the rhyme or reason for them. Your not being allowed something that another is allowed might cause some understandable shame or annoyance; but if everybody's level of personal adornment is standardized, what is it that each of you fears may make her, in particular, stand out? The deepest embarrassment arises over penny-pinching or lack of means, but the law removes that from you in both cases when you do not have precisely what you are not allowed to have. 'It is just this kind of leveling that I cannot tolerate,' says the rich woman. 'Why can I not be admired for the splendor of my gold and purple? Why is other women's lack of means hidden and excused by this law, which makes it appear that they would have had, if it were lawful, just what they are unable to have?'

"My fellow citizens, do you want to inspire this kind of competitiveness in your wives, with rich women wanting to possess what no other woman can, and poorer women extending themselves beyond their means in order not to be looked down upon for not possessing it? Indeed, let them begin to be embarrassed about the things that should not embarrass them and they will stop being embarrassed about the things that should. The woman able

non pudebit. quae de suo poterit, parabit: quae non pote-
17 rit, virum rogabit. miserum illum virum, et qui exoratus et
qui non exoratus erit, cum quod ipse non dederit datum
18 ab alio videbit. nunc volgo alienos viros rogant et, quod
maius est, legem et suffragia rogant, et a quibusdam impe-
trant. adversus te et rem tuam et liberos tuos exorabilis es:
simul lex modum sumptibus uxoris tuae facere desierit, tu
nunquam facies.
19    "Nolite eodem loco existimare[5] futuram rem quo fuit
20 antequam lex de hoc ferretur. et hominem improbum non
accusari tutius est quam absolui, et luxuria non mota tole-
rabilior esset quam erit nunc, ipsis vinculis sicut ferae
21 bestiae inritata, deinde emissa. ego nullo modo abrogandam legem Oppiam censeo: vos quod faxitis, deos omnes
fortunare velim."
5. Post haec tribuni quoque plebei qui se intercessuros
professi erant, cum pauca in eandem sententiam adie-
cissent, tum L. Valerius pro rogatione ab se promulgata ita
disseruit:
"Si privati tantummodo ad suadendum dissuadendumque id quod ab nobis rogatur processissent, ego quoque,
cum satis dictum pro utraque parte existimarem, tacitus
2 suffragia vestra exspectassem: nunc cum vir clarissimus,[6]
consul M. Porcius, non auctoritate solum, quae tacita satis
momenti habuisset, sed oratione etiam longa et accurata

[5] existimare *Bχ*: *post add.* Quirites *ed. Rom.*
[6] clarissimus *Mg*: gravissimus *Bχ*

to buy from her own means will buy; the one who cannot will ask her husband. And what a sorry man that husband is—whether he accedes to her wishes or whether he does not (in which case he will see what he has not given himself given to her by another man)! At the moment they are petitioning other women's husbands in public and, what is worse, petitioning them for a law and for their votes, in some cases with success. By acceding you are, as an individual, working against yourself, your own interests and your children: once the law ceases to curb your wife's expenditure, you will never curb it yourself.

"Do not think that matters will stand where they did before the law on this was passed. It is safer for a criminal not to be charged than to be acquitted, and extravagance left unchallenged would have been easier to bear than it will be now after it has, like a wild beast, been provoked by its shackles and then set free. In my opinion the Oppian law should not be repealed under any circumstances, but whatever your decision I would wish for it the blessing of all the gods."

5. After this the plebeian tribunes who had declared that they would interpose their veto added a few words in the same vein. Then Lucius Valerius spoke as follows on the motion that he had proposed:

"Had it been only private citizens who had come forward to speak for and against the proposal tabled by us, I too should have awaited your votes on the matter in silence, believing (as I would have) that enough had been said on both sides. As it is, a most eminent man, the consul Marcus Porcius, has attacked our proposal, using not merely his authority, which itself would have carried enough weight even without a word being spoken, but also

insectatus sit rogationem nostram, necesse est paucis re-
3 spondere. qui tamen plura verba in castigandis matronis
quam in rogatione nostra dissuadenda consumpsit, et quidem ut in dubio poneret utrum id quod reprenderet ma-
4 tronae sua sponte an nobis auctoribus fecissent. rem de-
fendam, non nos, in quos iecit magis hoc consul verbo
tenus quam ut re insimularet.

5 "Coetum et seditionem et interdum secessionem muliebrem appellavit, quod matronae in publico vos rogassent
ut legem in se latam per bellum temporibus duris in pace
6 et florenti ac beata re publica abrogaretis. verba magna
quae rei augendae causa conquirantur et haec et alia esse
scio, et M. Catonem oratorem non solum gravem sed
interdum etiam trucem esse scimus omnes, cum ingenio
7 sit mitis. nam quid tandem novi matronae fecerunt, quod
frequentes in causa ad se pertinente in publicum proces-
serunt? nunquam ante hoc tempus in publico apparue-
8 runt? tuas adversus te Origines revolvam. accipe quotiens
id fecerint, et quidem semper bono publico.

"Iam a principio, regnante Romulo, cum Capitolio ab
Sabinis capto medio in foro signis conlatis dimicaretur,
nonne intercursu matronarum inter acies duas proelium
9 sedatum est? quid? regibus exactis cum Coriolano Marcio duce legiones Volscorum castra ad quintum lapidem
posuissem, nonne id agmen quo obruta haec urbs esset

---

18 Cato's *Origines*, which did not survive antiquity, was the
first Roman history written in Latin (see Introduction, xxvi). Not
begun until 168, it was unfinished at his death; so this is another
anachronism on Livy's part.

a long, carefully composed oration. I must therefore make a brief response. The consul, however, has spent more words on criticizing married women than he has on rebutting our proposal, to the point of making it unclear whether the behavior for which he was reproaching the women came naturally or was motivated by us. I shall defend the proposal, not ourselves, since the consul directed at us only a verbal attack rather than an accusation based on facts.

"Cato has used the words 'gathering,' 'revolt,' and sometimes 'secession of women,' because married women had asked you in public to rescind at a time of peace, when the Republic was flourishing and prosperous, a law passed against them in the hard times of war. I know the emotive expressions that are raked up to exaggerate a case—those he has used and others—and we all know Marcus Cato to be not only severe but sometimes even brutal in his oratory, though he is by nature compassionate. Now, what is so strange about the women's action in coming into the streets in large numbers over a matter that concerns them? Have they never appeared in public before? I shall open your own *Origins*[18] to contradict you. Listen to how often they have done it, and always, you will see, for the common good.

"Right in the beginning, in the reign of Romulus, when the Capitol had been captured by the Sabines and a pitched battle was being fought in the middle of the Forum, was not the fighting stopped by married women running between the two lines? Why, after the expulsion of the kings, when the legions of the Volsci, led by Marcius Coriolanus, had encamped at a point five miles from Rome, was it not the women who turned back the army

441

matronae averterunt? iam capta a Gallis quo redempta
urbs est? nempe aurum[7] matronae consensu omnium in
10  publicum contulerunt. proximo bello, ne antiqua repetam,
nonne et, cum pecunia opus fuit, viduarum pecuniae adiu-
verunt aerarium, et cum di quoque novi ad opem feren-
dam dubiis rebus accerserentur, matronae universae ad
mare profectae sunt ad matrem Idaeam accipiendam?
11  dissimiles, inquis, causae sunt. nec mihi causas aequare
12  propositum est: nihil novi factum purgare satis est. ceterum quod in rebus ad omnes pariter viros feminas perti-
nentibus fecisse eas nemo miratus est, in causa proprie ad
13  ipsas pertinente miramur fecisse? quid autem fecerunt?
superbas, me dius fidius, aures habemus, si cum domini
servorum non fastidiant preces, nos rogari ab honestis
feminis indignamur!

    6. "Venio nunc ad id de quo agitur. in quo duplex
consulis oratio fuit; nam et legem ullam omnino abrogari
est indignatus, et eam praecipue legem quae luxuriae
2  muliebris coercendae causa lata esset. et illa communis
pro legibus visa consularis oratio est, et haec adversus
3  luxuriam severissimis moribus conveniebat; itaque periculum est, nisi quid in utraque re vani sit docuerimus, ne
quis error vobis offundatur.

    [7] iam capta a Gallis quo redempta urbs est? nempe aurum
*Madvig*: *sic, sed* iam urbe capta *Mg*: iam urbe capta a Gallis au-
rum quo redempta urbs est nempe *Bχ*: *sic, sed* nonne *pro* nempe
*Duker*

---

[19] These are famous stories of early Rome in Livy's first books:
Sabine women (1.9.1–13.5); Coriolanus (2.33.3–40.12); matrons'
gold contribution for the ransom (5.50.7).

by which this city would have been overwhelmed? When the city had been taken by the Gauls, by whom was it ransomed? The women, as we all know, with everybody's consent, gathered together their gold for public use.[19] In the most recent war—not to go back to ancient history— was it not the widows' money that assisted the treasury when money was needed?[20] And when new gods were also brought in to help us at a critical moment, did not all the married women go the sea to welcome the Idaean mother?[21] Ah, you say, these cases are different. But it is not my intention to put the cases in the same category— showing that this is nothing new is a sufficient defense. Nobody was surprised at actions they took in matters pertinent to the whole population, to men and women alike, so are we surprised that they took action in an affair specifically pertaining to them? But what have they actually done? Considering that masters do not spurn the entreaties of slaves, then (my god!) we have proud ears if we are indignant over requests made of us by respectable ladies!

6. "I come now to the matter at issue. On this the consul had two positions in his oration. He was indignant at the repeal of any law whatsoever and also, and especially, at the repeal of the particular law that had been enacted to curb women's extravagance. The first position, the defense of the laws in general, seemed fitting for a consul, while the second, the attack on extravagance, was in keeping with the man's very strict principles. There is therefore some danger that unless I demonstrate the speciousness of both lines of argument you may be led into error.

[20] Livy means the Second Punic War; cf. 24.18.14–15.
[21] Cf. 3.8, above, and note.

4    "Ego enim quemadmodum ex iis legibus quae non in
tempus aliquod sed perpetuae utilitatis causa in aeternum
latae sunt nullam abrogari debere fateor, nisi quam aut
usus coarguit aut status aliquis rei publicae inutilem fecit,
5    sic quas tempora aliqua desiderarunt leges, mortales, ut
6    ita dicam, et temporibus ipsis mutabiles esse video. quae
in pace lata sunt, plerumque bellum abrogat, quae in bello
pax, ut in navis administratione alia in secunda alia in adversa tempestate usui sunt.

7    "Haec cum ita natura distincta sint, ex utro tandem
8    genere ea lex esse videtur quam abrogamus? regia[8] lex
simul cum ipsa urbe nata, aut, quod secundum est, ab decemviris ad condenda iura creatis in duodecim tabulis
scripta? sine qua cum maiores nostri non existimarint
decus matronale servari posse, nobis quoque verendum sit
ne cum ea pudorem sanctitatemque feminarum abroge-
9    mus. quis igitur nescit novam istam legem esse Q. Fabio
et Ti. Sempronio consulibus viginti ante annis latam? sine
qua cum per tot annos matronae optimis moribus vixerint,
quod tandem ne abrogata ea effundantur ad luxuriam
10   periculum est? nam si ista lex[9] ideo lata esset ut finiret libidinem muliebrem, verendum foret ne abrogata incitaret:
cur sit autem lata, ipsum indicabit[10] tempus.

8 regia *Damsté*: quae uetus regia *B*: quia uetus regia χ: quid
uetus regia *Asc.*: numquae uetus? regia *McDonald*
9 lex *Pmg*: lex aut *B*χ: lex aut antiqua aut *Madvig*: lex vetus aut
*Mayerhoefer*    10 indicabit *Gron.*: indicavit *B*χ

22 Tradition had it that two successive boards of ten in 451–
450 drafted legislation that became the Laws of the Twelve Tables, inscribed on bronze and set up in public (cf. *OCD* sv).

"There are indeed laws that are not temporary measures but enacted to stand for ever because of their continued practicality. I myself grant that none of these should be repealed, unless experience demonstrates it to be ineffective or some political situation renders it impractical. But I also see that there are some laws that have been required by temporary emergencies, mortal laws, as it were, which can change as circumstances themselves change. Measures passed in peacetime are often annulled in time of war, and those passed in war are often annulled in peace. It is like steering a ship, for which some maneuvers are useful in fair weather, others in foul.

"Legal measures falling by nature into two categories, to which class then does this law that we wish to repeal seem to belong? Is it a law of the kings, born when the city itself was born, or (next to that) was it inscribed on the Twelve Tables by the decemvirs appointed to establish our legal code?[22] In that case it was a law without which our forefathers thought the dignity of married women could not be protected, and we should also be concerned that in annulling it we might be annulling the modesty and purity of womanhood. But who does not know that the law is a new one, passed twenty years ago in the consulship of Quintus Fabius and Tiberius Sempronius? Since our married women lived without it for many years with the highest morals, what danger is there that they will lapse into extravagant living if it is repealed? If the purpose of that legislation had been specifically to repress female passions, then we ought to fear that its annulment would actually kindle them; but its very date will reveal why it was passed.

11     "Hannibal in Italia erat, victor ad Cannas; iam Tarentum iam Arpos iam Capuam habebat; ad urbem Romam
12 admoturus exercitum videbatur; defecerant socii; non
milites in supplementum, non socios navales ad classem
tuendam, non pecuniam in aerario habebamus; servi quibus arma darentur ita ut pretium pro iis bello perfecto
13 dominis solveretur emebantur; in eandem diem pecuniae
frumentum et cetera quae belli usus postulabant prae-
benda publicani se conducturos professi erant; servos ad
remum numero ex censu constituto cum stipendio nostro
14 dabamus; aurum et argentum omne, ab senatoribus eius
rei initio orto, in publicum conferebamus; viduae et pupilli
pecunias suas in aerarium deferebant; cautum erat quo ne
plus auri et argenti facti, quo ne plus signati argenti et
15 aeris domi haberemus. tali tempore in luxuria et ornatu
matronae occupatae erant, ut ad eam coercendam Oppia
lex desiderata sit, cum quia Cereris sacrificium lugentibus
omnibus matronis intermissum erat, senatus finiri luctum
16 triginta diebus iussit? cui non apparet inopiam et mise-
riam civitatis, quia omnium privatorum pecuniae in usum
publicum vertendae erant, istam legem scripsisse tam diu
mansuram quam diu causa scribendae legis mansisset?
17 nam si quae tunc temporis causa aut decrevit senatus aut
populus iussit in perpetuum servari oportet, cur pecunias

---

23 Capua defected to Hannibal in 216, Arpi (in Apulia) surrendered in 215, but Tarentum did not surrender until 212.

24 Italian *socii navales;* cf. 31.17.3 note.

"Hannibal was in Italy, the victor at Cannae. He now held Tarentum, Arpi, and Capua.[23] It looked as if he was going to move his army up to the city of Rome; the allies had deserted us; we had no soldiers in reserve, no sailors[24] to maintain the fleet, and no money in the treasury. Slaves were being bought up to be put under arms on the understanding that their masters would be paid for them when the war was finished. With that same date fixed also for their payment, contractors offered to provide wheat and the other things needed for the conduct of the war. At our own expense we supplied slaves to act as oarsmen, their number being dependent on our tax assessment. We, following the lead of the senators, contributed all our gold and silver to the public weal, and widows and orphans contributed their money to the treasury. There was a provision against our having at home more than a fixed quantity of wrought gold and silver, and of silver and bronze coin. At a time like that were married women so preoccupied with extravagant living and clothing that an Oppian law was needed to repress this tendency—a time when the ceremonies in honor of Ceres were suspended because all the married women were in mourning, and the senate decreed that the period of mourning be limited to thirty days? No, who cannot see that it was financial exigency and the miseries suffered by our state that drafted that law—because the moneys of all private individuals had to be diverted to public use—and that the law was intended to last only as long as the reason for its drafting remained with us? If measures that were at that point decreed by the senate or dictated by the people to meet a temporary crisis must be kept in force for ever, then why do we repay loans to private citizens? Why do we tender public con-

447

18 reddimus privatis? cur publica praesenti pecunia loca-
mus? cur servi qui militent non emuntur? cur privati non
damus remiges sicut tunc dedimus?

7. "Omnes alii ordines, omnes homines mutationem in
meliorem statum rei publicae sentient: ad coniuges tantum vestras pacis et tranquillitatis publicae fructus non
2 perveniet? purpura viri utemur, praetextati in magistratibus in sacerdotiis; liberi nostri praetextis purpura togis
utentur; magistratibus in coloniis municipiisque, hic Romae infimo generi, magistris vicorum, togae praetextae
3 habendae ius permittemus, nec id ut vivi habeant tantum[11] insigne sed etiam ut cum eo crementur mortui:
feminis dumtaxat purpurae usu interdicemus? et cum tibi
viro liceat purpura in vestem stragulam uti, matrem familiae tuam purpureum amiculum habere non sines, et
4 equus tuus speciosius instratus erit quam uxor vestita? sed
in purpura, quae teritur absumitur, iniustam quidem sed
aliquam tamen causam tenacitatis video; in auro vero, in
quo praeter manupretium nihil intertrimenti fit, quae
malignitas est? praesidium potius in eo est et ad privatos
et ad publicos usus, sicut experti estis.

5 "Nullam aemulationem inter se singularum, quoniam
nulla haberet, esse aiebat. at hercule universis dolor et
indignatio est, cum sociorum Latini nominis uxoribus vi-

---

[11] vivi . . . tantum *Madvig*: vivi solum habeant (habent χ) tantum Bχ: *sic, sed del.* tantum *H.J.M.*

---

[25] Cf. 31.11.12 and note.

[26] The "street masters" (*vicorum magistri*) were given charge
of the city's streets by Augustus in 7 (Dio 55.8.6–7), but as Livy

tracts on the basis of cash payments? Why are slaves not purchased to serve as soldiers? Why do we not, as private citizens, supply oarsmen as we did in those days?

7. "Are all social classes and all men to feel that the Republic's condition has changed for the better, and is it only your wives that the rewards of the common peace and tranquility will not reach? Shall we men wear the purple? Shall we wear the *praetexta*[25] in our magistracies and priesthoods? Will our sons wear the purple-fringed *praetexta*? Are we going to grant the right to wear the *toga praetexta* to magistrates in the colonies and municipal towns, along with even the lowest category of administrators here in Rome, the 'street masters'?[26] And not only allow them to have this mark of distinction in their lifetime but even to be cremated with it when they die? Is it only to women that we shall forbid the wearing of purple? While you, as a husband, are permitted to use purple as an outer garment, are you going to refuse your wife a purple cloak, and will your horse have trappings more impressive than your spouse's clothing? And yet in the case of purple, which deteriorates and wears out, I suppose I can see some sort of justification for inflexibility, unfair though it be. But in the case of gold, where there is no loss except in the workmanship, what kind of stinginess is this? In gold we have, rather, security for both private and public needs, as you know from experience.

"Cato kept saying that there was no rivalry between individual women because each woman had nothing. But, heavens above, they all as a class feel hurt and angry when

cannot have been writing Book 34 as late as that, this is either a later addition to an earlier draft or an interpolation.

6 deant ea concessa ornamenta quae sibi adempta sint, cum
insignes eas esse auro et purpura, cum illas uehi per urbem, se pedibus sequi, tamquam in illarum civitatibus,
7 non in sua, imperium sit. virorum hoc animos volnerare
posset: quid muliercularum censetis, quas etiam parva
8 movent? non magistratus nec sacerdotia nec triumphi nec
insignia nec dona aut spolia bellica iis contingere possunt:
9 munditiae et ornatus et cultus, haec feminarum insignia
sunt, his gaudent et gloriantur, hunc mundum muliebrem
10 appellarunt maiores vestri.[12] quid aliud in luctu quam
purpuram atque aurum deponunt? quid cum eluxerunt
sumunt? quid in gratulationibus supplicationibusque nisi
excellentiorem ornatum adiciunt?

11 "Scilicet, si legem Oppiam abrogaritis, non vestri arbi-
trii erit si quid eius vetare volueritis quod nunc lex vetat:
minus filiae uxores sorores etiam quibusdam in manu
12 erunt. nunquam salvis suis exuitur servitus muliebris, et
ipsae libertatem quam viduitas et orbitas facit detestantur.
13 in vestro arbitrio suum ornatum quam in legis malunt esse;
et vos in manu et tutela, non in servitio debetis habere eas,
14 et malle patres vos aut viros quam dominos dici. invidiosis
nominibus utebatur modo consul, seditionem muliebrem
et secessionem appellando. id enim periculum est ne Sacrum montem, sicut quondam irata plebs, aut Aventinum

---

[12] vestri $B\chi$: nostri $a$

---

[27] For *supplicatio* cf. 31.8.2 and note.
[28] That is, even if the law is repealed a woman will still be
subject to her father or another male relative, or to her husband.
[29] A hill just north of the Anio (*Barr.* 43 C2 *sacer mons*).

they see the wives of our allies with Latin rights granted
the accessories that have been taken from *them,* when
they see those women resplendent in gold and purple,
when they see them riding through the city while they
themselves follow on foot—just as if empire lay in those
women's towns, not in their own! This could wound the
sensibilities of *men;* how do you think it affects those of
our little women, whom even trivial things disturb? Magistracies, priesthoods, triumphs, insignia, prizes or spoils
of war are not accessible to them. Elegance, grooming, a
fine appearance—these are women's insignia. These are
their pride and joy. This is what your ancestors called
'woman's embellishment.' In time of mourning what do
they put aside but their purple and gold? What do they
take up again when the mourning is finished? In periods
of public thanksgiving and supplication[27] what do they add
if not more elegant finery?

"If you do repeal the Oppian law, then naturally you
will have no authority if you wish to disallow anything that
the law currently disallows! For some of you daughters,
wives, and even sisters will be less under your control! No,
never can the subservience of women be removed while
their kinsmen still live[28]—and yet they themselves hate
the independence they are granted by the loss of husbands
or fathers. They prefer to have their refinements under
your control rather than under the law's; and you for your
part should keep them under your care and protection, not
in servitude, and you should prefer to be called fathers and
husbands rather than masters. The consul used pejorative
terms just now when he referred to a 'female revolt' and
'secession.' There is a danger, he thinks, of their seizing
the Sacred Mount,[29] as the plebs once did in their anger,

451

15   capiant! patiendum huic infirmitati est, quodcumque vos
censueritis. quo plus potestis, eo moderatius imperio uti
debetis."

8. Haec cum contra legem proque lege dicta essent,
aliquanto maior frequentia mulierum postero die sese in
2   publicum effudit, unoque agmine omnes Brutorum ianuas
obsederunt, qui collegarum rogationi intercedebant, nec
ante abstiterunt quam remissa intercessio ab tribunis est.
3   nulla deinde dubitatio fuit quin omnes tribus legem abro-
garent. viginti annis post abrogata est quam lata.
4   M. Porcius consul, postquam abrogata lex Oppia est,
extemplo viginti quinque navibus longis, quarum quinque
sociorum erant, ad Lunae portum profectus est, eodem
5   exercitu convenire iusso, et edicto per oram maritimam
misso navibus omnis generis contractis, ab Luna proficiscens edixit ut ad portum Pyrenaei sequerentur: inde se
6   frequenti classe ad hostes iturum. praetervecti Ligustinos
montes sinumque Gallicum ad diem quam dixerat convenerunt. inde Rhodam ventum et praesidium Hispanorum
7   quod in castello erat vi deiectum. ab Rhoda secundo vento
Emporias perventum: ibi copiae omnes praeter socios navales in terram expositae.

---

30 On the Roman tribes cf. 33.25.7 note, and Introduction,
l–li.        31 Today Luni, it lay at the mouth of the River Makra
(*Barr.* 41 C1) and was a base for operations against the Ligures.

32 Perhaps to be identified with Portus Veneris (mod. Port
Vendres) in southwest France: *Barr.* 25 I3.

33 The Golfe du Lion.

34 Modern Rosas in Catalonia (*Barr.* 25 I3).

35 Now Empúries (*Barr.* 25 I3; TIR *K/J-31,* 71–75). Livy's

or the Aventine. No! As the weaker sex they must abide by whatever you decide. And the greater your power, the more lenient you should be in exercising it."

8. On the day after these speeches for and against the law were delivered a considerably larger crowd of women flooded into the streets. En masse they all blockaded the doors of the Bruti, who were for vetoing the proposal of their colleagues, and they did not give up until the veto they had threatened was withdrawn by the tribunes. After that there was no question but that all the tribes[30] would repeal the law. And twenty years after it was passed, the law was repealed.

After the repeal of the Oppian law, the consul Marcus Porcius immediately left for the port of Luna[31] with twenty-five warships, five of them belonging to the allies. He had earlier ordered the army to muster at the same place and by an edict relayed along the coastline had also assembled here ships of all kinds. Setting out from Luna he issued instructions for these ships to attend him to the port of Pyrenaeus,[32] saying that he would proceed against the enemy from there with his fleet united. They sailed past the Ligurian mountains and the Gallic Gulf,[33] and met up on the day he had fixed. From Pyrenaeus they moved on to Rhoda[34] where a Spanish garrison installed in the stronghold was forcibly ejected. From Rhoda they came with a favorable wind to Emporiae,[35] and there the entire force, with the exception of the crews, was set ashore.

claim below that it was "inhabited by Greeks from Phocaea" (cf. also 26.19.11) is incorrect; it was actually a Massiliot colony. Cf. *OCD* sv Emporion.

9. Iam tunc Emporiae duo oppida erant muro divisa.
unum Graeci habebant, a Phocaea, unde et Massilienses,
2 oriundi, alterum Hispani; sed Graecum oppidum in mare
expositum totum orbem muri minus quadringentos passus
patentem habebat, Hispanis retractior a mari trium mi-
3 lium passuum in circuitu murus erat. tertium genus Romani coloni ab divo Caesare post devictos Pompei liberos
adiecti. nunc in corpus unum confusi omnes, Hispanis
prius postremo et Graecis in civitatem Romanam adscitis.
4 miraretur qui tum cerneret, aperto mari ab altera parte,
ab altera Hispanis tam fera et bellicosa gente obiectis,
quae res eos tutaretur.

Disciplina erat custos infirmitatis, quam inter validio-
5 res optime timor continet. partem muri versam in agros
egregie munitam habebant, una tantum in eam regionem
porta imposita, cuius adsiduus custos semper aliquis ex
6 magistratibus erat. nocte pars tertia civium in muris excu-
babat; neque moris causa tantum aut legis sed quanta si
hostis ad portas esset et servabant vigilias et circumibant
7 cura. Hispanum neminem in urbem recipiebant: ne ipsi
quidem temere urbe excedebant. ad mare patebat omni-
8 bus exitus. porta ad Hispanorum oppidum versa nunquam
nisi frequentes, pars tertia fere cuius proxima nocte vigi-
9 liae in muris fuerant, egrediebantur. causa exeundi haec
erat: commercio eorum Hispani imprudentes maris gau-

---

36 Massilia (Marseille) was founded ca. 600 by settlers from
Phocaea (now Phoça) on the Aegean coast of northern Turkey.
For a romanticized account, cf. Just. *Epit.* 43.3. 5–13.

37 No other evidence exists for this. Pompey's sons, Gnaeus
and Sextus, were defeated by Caesar in 45 at the battle of Munda
in Spain, where Gnaeus was killed but Sextus escaped.

9. Even in those days Emporiae comprised two towns separated by a wall. One was inhabited by Greeks from Phocaea (mother country also of the Massiliots),[36] the other by Spaniards. The Greek town, however, was exposed to the sea and had a wall whose entire compass was less than 400 yards, while the Spaniards' wall, lying further back from the sea, had a circumference of three miles. A third category of inhabitants, Roman settlers, was added by the deified Caesar after the defeat of the sons of Pompey.[37] These days they are all integrated into a single body, with first the Spaniards and then the Greeks admitted to Roman citizenship. Anyone who saw them in those days— open sea facing them on one side, the barbarous and aggressive race of Spaniards on the other—would have wondered just where their protection lay.

What safeguarded them in their weak position was discipline, which fear very effectively preserves when one is surrounded by stronger peoples. The landward part of the wall they would keep well defended, with only a single gate located in this sector, which was constantly guarded by one of the magistrates. During the night a third of the citizen body kept watch on the walls, and this was not just a matter of routine or law—they posted guards and also did the rounds of them with as much care as if an enemy were at the gates. They allowed no Spaniard into the city and would not even go out of town themselves without good reason. All had freedom of exit on the side facing the sea; but they would leave only in large numbers from the gate facing the Spanish town, that usually meaning the third of the citizens who had provided the watch on the walls the previous night. And their reason for going out was the fact that the Spaniards, who had no experience of

debant, mercarique et ipsi ea quae externa navibus in-
veherentur, et agrorum exigere fructus volebant. huius
mutui usus desiderium ut Hispana urbs Graecis pateret
faciebat.

10    Erant etiam eo tutiores quod sub umbra Romanae
amicitiae latebant, quam sicut minoribus viribus quam
Massilienses pari colebant fide. tum quoque consulem
11  exercitumque comiter ac benigne acceperunt. paucos ibi
moratus dies Cato, dum exploraret ubi et quantae hostium
copiae essent, ut ne mora quidem segnis esset, omne id
12  tempus exercendis militibus consumpsit. id erat forte tempus anni ut frumentum in areis Hispani haberent; itaque
redemptoribus uetitis frumentum parare ac Romam di-
13  missis, "bellum" inquit "se ipsum alet." profectus ab Emporiis agros hostium urit vastatque, omnia fuga et terrore
complet.

10. Eodem tempore M. Helvio decedenti ulteriore
Hispania cum praesidio sex milium dato ab Ap. Claudio
praetore Celtiberi agmine ingenti ad oppidum Iliturgi
2   occurrunt. viginti milia armatorum fuisse Valerius scribit,
duodecim milia ex iis caesa, oppidum Iliturgi receptum et
3   puberes omnes interfectos. inde ad castra Catonis Helvius

---

38 The people who provided the army with supplies. Cato was
thus cutting out the "middle men."

39 For his election and provincial sortition, cf. 32.27.7, 28.2.

40 *Barr.* 25 C4, TIR *K-30,* 91–93. They comprised several different tribes, but the Celtic character of their culture differenti-
ated them from their neighbors.

41 Since Helvius fought the battle "in another man's province"
(below) this is perhaps not the Iliturgi in Farther Spain noted by
*Barr.* and TIR *J-30,* 202, but another somewhere in Hither Spain.

the sea, enjoyed trading with them—they wanted to purchase the foreign goods imported by ship and at the same time to export the produce of their lands. Desire for such reciprocal advantages opened up the Spanish city to the Greeks.

The Greeks were also more secure from the fact that they lived under the shelter of an alliance with Rome, which they preserved with a loyalty equal to that of the Massiliots, though with resources lesser than theirs. On this occasion, too, they gave the consul and his army a courteous and warm welcome. Cato waited there a few days until he could gather intelligence on the location and size of the enemy forces and, so as not to be idle even in a period of enforced delay, he spent the whole time drilling his soldiers. It happened to be the season of year when the Spaniards had their wheat on the threshing floor, and Cato therefore forbade the contractors[38] to buy the wheat, sending them back to Rome with the words: "The war will be self-supporting." After setting off from Emporiae, he burned and razed the fields of the enemy, and spread flight and panic throughout the area.

10. At this same time, as Marcus Helvius[39] was withdrawing from Farther Spain with a detachment of 6,000 men given to him by the praetor Appius Claudius, the Celtiberians[40] confronted him with a massive column at the town of Iliturgi.[41] Valerius[42] records that they numbered 20,000 under arms and that 12,000 were killed, the town of Iliturgi captured, and all adult males put to death. Helvius then came to Cato's camp and, because the area

---

[42] On Valerius Antias, see Introduction, xxv–xxvii. Livy usually cites him to discredit him, but here he may have had no better authority.

pervenit et quia tuta iam ab hostibus regio erat, praesidio in ulteriorem Hispaniam remisso Romam est profectus, et
4 ob rem feliciter gestam ovans urbem est ingressus. argenti infecti tulit in aerarium quattuordecim milia pondo septingenta triginta duo, et signati bigatorum septemdecim milia viginti tres, et Oscensis argenti centum undeviginti
5 milia quadringentos undequadraginta. causa triumphi negandi senatui fuit quod alieno auspicio et in aliena provincia pugnasset; ceterum biennio post redierat, cum provincia successori Q. Minucio tradita annum insequentem
6 retentus ibi longo et gravi fuisset morbo. itaque duobus modo mensibus ante Helvius ovans urbem est ingressus
7 quam successor eius Q. Minucius triumpharet. hic quoque tulit argenti pondo triginta quattuor milia octingenta, et bigatorum septuaginta tria milia, et Oscensis argenti ducenta septuaginta octo milia.

11. In Hispania interim consul haud procul Emporiis
2 castra habebat. eo legati tres ab Ilergetum regulo Bilistage, in quibus unus filius eius erat, venerunt querentes castella sua oppugnari nec spem ullam esse resistendi nisi
3 praesidium Romanus misisset: tria milia militum satis esse, nec hostes, si tanta manus venisset, mansuros. ad ea consul moveri quidem se vel periculo eorum vel metu
4 dicere, sed sibi nequaquam tantum copiarum esse ut cum magna vis hostium haud procul absit, et quam mox signis

---

43 Cf. 31.49.2 note.

44 Osca (mod. Huesca) lay north of Ilerda (*Barr.* 25 E3; TIR *K-30*, 168). Coins were evidently minted there.

45 On auspices (= authority), cf. 31.4.1 note.

46 Q. Minucius Thermus (65), later consul (in 193), was actually governor of *Hither* Spain (33.26.2).

was now out of danger from the enemy, sent his detachment back to Farther Spain, set off for Rome and, because of his successful operation, entered the city in ovation. He brought to the treasury 14,732 pounds of unwrought silver, 17,023 pieces of silver stamped with the *biga*,[43] and 119,439 silver Osca-minted coins.[44] The reason for the senate's refusal to award him the triumph was that he had fought the battle under another man's auspices[45] and in another man's province. But he had in fact come home two years later than scheduled; after handing over his province to his successor Quintus Minucius,[46] he had been detained there during the following year by a long and severe illness. It thus transpired that Helvius entered the city in ovation a mere two months before his successor Quintus Minucius celebrated his triumph. Minucius also brought to Rome 34,800 pounds of silver, 73,000 pieces stamped with the *biga*, and 278,000 Osca-minted silver coins.

11. In Spain, meanwhile, the consul had his camp pitched not far from Emporiae. Here three envoys came to him from Bilistages, chieftain of the Ilergetes,[47] including one of Bilistages' sons, with a complaint that their fortresses were under attack and that they had no hope of holding out unless the Roman commander sent help. Three thousand men would suffice, they said, and if such a force arrived the enemy would not stay to fight. The consul replied that he was moved by their predicament and their fears but he had nowhere near enough forces to enable him to diminish his strength without risk by dividing his army, not while large numbers of the enemy were

[47] They lived near Ilerda (*Barr.* 25 F4, TIR *K-30,* 131).

conlatis dimicandum sit in dies exspectet, dividendo exer-
5 citum minuere tuto vires possit. legati, ubi haec audierunt,
flentes ad genua consulis provolvuntur, orant ne se in rebus tam trepidis deserat: quo enim se, repulsos ab Roma-
6 nis, ituros? nullos se socios, nihil usquam in terris aliud
7 spei habere. potuisse se extra id periculum esse, si decedere fide, si coniurare cum ceteris voluissent. nullis minis
nullis terriculis se motos, sperantes satis opis et auxilii sibi
8 in Romanis esse. id si nullum sit, si sibi a consule negetur,
deos hominesque se testes facere invitos et coactos se, ne
eadem quae Saguntini passi sint patiantur, defecturos et
cum ceteris potius Hispanis quam solos perituros esse.

12. Et illo quidem die sine[13] responso dimissi. con-
2 sulem nocte quae insecuta est anceps cura agitare: nolle
deserere socios, nolle minuere exercitum, quod aut moram sibi ad dimicandum aut in dimicando periculum ad-
3 ferre posset. stat sententia non minuere copias, ne quid
interim hostes inferant ignominiae; sociis spem pro re
4 ostentandam censet: saepe vana pro veris, maxime in
bello, valuisse, et credentem se aliquid auxilii habere, perinde atque haberet, ipsa fiducia et sperando atque au-
dendo servatum.
5    Postero die legatis respondit, quamquam vereatur ne

[13] sine *B*: sic sine χ

in the vicinity and he was each day waiting to see how soon he would be forced into pitched battle. On hearing this, the envoys flung themselves at the consul's feet in tears and begged him not to abandon them when they were in such dire straits. Where were they to turn if they were rebuffed by the Romans? They had no allies, they said, and no other hope anywhere in the world. They could have avoided this danger had they decided to abandon their loyalty and join the other tribes in their plots, but they had been swayed by no threats and no intimidation as they expected to find sufficient support and assistance with the Romans. If that expectation proved futile and they were refused help by the consul, then they called on gods and men to witness that they would be joining the uprising unwillingly and under compulsion in order to avoid what the people of Saguntum suffered, and that they would perish along with the other Spanish tribes rather than do so alone.

12. The envoys were dismissed that day with no answer given. During the night that followed a dilemma plagued the consul: he was unwilling to abandon the allies, but also unwilling to weaken his army as this could delay a decisive encounter with the enemy or add danger to that encounter. He remained determined not to reduce his troops, fearing that the enemy might meanwhile inflict some ignominious defeat on him. The allies, he thought, should be given hope of aid rather than actual aid—often, especially in warfare, appearances have been as effective as reality, and a man believing he had support has often been saved as effectively as if he actually had it, because the assurance he feels gives him hope and spirit.

The next day he gave the envoys his answer. Although

suas vires aliis eas commodando minuat, tamen se illorum temporis ac periculi magis quam sui rationem habere.
6 denuntiari militum parti tertiae ex omnibus cohortibus iubet ut cibum quem in naves imponant mature coquant,
7 navesque in diem tertium expediri. duos ex legatis Bilistagi atque Ilergetibus nuntiare ea iubet; filium reguli
8 comiter habendo et muneribus apud se retinet. legati non ante profecti quam impositos in naves milites viderunt; id pro haud dubio iam nuntiantes, non suos modo sed etiam hostes fama Romani auxilii adventantis impleverunt.

13. Consul ubi satis quod in speciem fuit ostentatum
2 est, revocari ex navibus milites iubet: ipse, cum iam id tempus anni appeteret quo geri res possent, castra hiberna tria milia passuum ab Emporiis posuit. inde per occasiones nunc hac parte nunc illa, modico praesidio castris
3 relicto, praedatum milites in hostium agros ducebat; nocte ferme proficiscebantur, ut et quam longissime a castris procederent et inopinantes opprimerent. et exercebat ea res novos milites et hostium magna vis excipiebatur, nec iam egredi extra munimenta castellorum audebant.

4 Vbi admodum[14] et suorum et hostium animos est expertus, convocari tribunos praefectosque et equites om-
5 nes et centuriones iussit. "tempus" inquit "quod saepe optastis venit, quo vobis potestas fieret virtutem vestram ostendendi. adhuc praedonum magis quam bellantium

---

[14] admodum *B*: satis admodum χ: satis ad hunc modum *Duker*: ad hunc modum *Madvig*

---

[48] Which probably suggests that Cato arrived in Spain in late summer 195 (see Briscoe 2.63–66).

he feared that he would weaken his forces by lending some of them to others, he said, he nevertheless took more account of his allies' parlous situation than his own. He then issued orders for one third of each cohort to be instructed to cook food swiftly to put aboard the ships, which were to be made ready for sailing in two days. He commanded two of the envoys to report this to Bilistages and the Ilergetes, but kept with him the chieftain's son, entertaining him and plying him with gifts. The envoys set out only after seeing the soldiers embarked on the ships, and when they reported this as a certainty they saturated the enemy as well as their own people with rumors of forthcoming Roman aid.

13. When enough of a show had been put on to be convincing, the consul had the men recalled from the ships and, as the time was approaching when campaigning was possible, established winter quarters three miles from Emporiae.[48] From here he led the men into enemy territory on raiding parties, varying the direction according to circumstances and leaving a small detachment in the camp. They usually set off at night so they could advance as far as possible from camp and also fall upon the enemy unawares. This practice provided training for his raw recruits, and large numbers of the enemy were also taken prisoner (in fact, the enemy would no longer venture beyond the fortifications of their strongholds).

When the consul had fully tested the mettle both of his men and the enemy, he had the tribunes, prefects, and all the cavalrymen and centurions called to a meeting. "The time that you have often longed for has arrived," he told them, "the time when you might have the opportunity to demonstrate your courage. So far you have been fighting

463

6   militastis more: nunc iusta pugna hostes cum hostibus
    conferetis manus; non agros inde populari sed urbium
7   opes exhaurire licebit. patres nostri, cum in Hispania
    Carthaginiensium et imperatores[15] et exercitus essent, ipsi
    nullum in ea militem haberent, tamen addi hoc in foedere
8   voluerunt ut imperii sui Hiberus fluvius esset finis. nunc
    cum duo praetores, cum consul, cum tres exercitus Ro-
    mani Hispaniam obtineant, Carthaginiensium decem iam
    prope annis nemo in his provinciis sit, imperium nobis
9   citra Hiberum amissum est. hoc armis et virtute recipere-
    tis oportet, et nationem rebellantem magis temere quam
    constanter bellantem iugum quo se exuit accipere rursus
    cogatis."

10      In hunc modum maxime adhortatus, pronuntiat se
    nocte ad castra hostium ducturum. ita ad corpora curanda
    dimissi.

        14. Nocte media, cum auspicio operam dedisset, pro-
    fectus ut locum quem vellet priusquam hostes sentirent
    caperet, praeter castra hostium circumducit, et prima luce
2   acie instructa sub ipsum vallum tres cohortes mittit. mi-
    rantes barbari ab tergo apparuisse Romanum, discurrere
3   et ipsi[16] ad arma. interim consul apud suos "nusquam nisi
    in virtute spes est, milites," inquit "et ego sedulo ne esset
4   feci. inter castra nostra et nos medii hostes, et ab tergo
    hostium ager est. quod pulcherrimum idem tutissimum:
    in virtute spem positam habere."

    [15] in Hispania . . . imperatores *Gron.*: Hispania . . . impera-
    tores ibi *B*χ
    [16] et ipsi *Duker*: ipse *B*: ipsi χ

    _____

    [49] On Saguntum as the boundary, see 31.7.3 note.

more like robbers than warriors, but now you will meet in regular battle, one enemy against another—and then, instead of raiding fields, you will have leave to drain the wealth of cities. When the Carthaginians had both generals and armies in Spain and they themselves had not a single soldier there, our fathers nevertheless wanted a clause added to the treaty stating that the River Ebro should be the boundary of their empire.[49] Today, when we have two praetors, a consul, and three Roman armies in Spain, and no Carthaginian has set foot in these provinces for almost ten years, our empire north of the Ebro is lost to us. This you must recover by your courage in arms; and you must compel a race of people that is engaged in a headstrong revolt rather than a determined struggle to accept once more the yoke it has thrown off."

After exhorting them very much in this manner, Cato announced that he would lead them against the enemy camp that night. With that he sent them off to take food and rest.

14. After attending to the auspices, Cato set off at midnight. In order to take up a position in a place of his choosing and before the enemy became aware of it, he made a detour to a point beyond the enemy camp; and at first light he drew up his line and sent three cohorts right up to the enemy rampart. The barbarians, shocked to see the Romans to their rear, also rushed to arms. Meanwhile the consul addressed his men, saying: "Men! Your hope lies in your courage and nowhere else, and my actions have been deliberately taken to ensure this. The enemy sits between our camp and ourselves, and to our rear lies enemy territory. The noblest plan is also the safest, namely to have your hopes residing in your valor."

Sub haec cohortes recipi iubet, ut barbaros simulatione
5 fugae eliceret. id quod crediderat evenit. pertimuisse et
cedere rati Romanos, porta erumpunt et quantum inter
castra sua et aciem hostium relictum erat loci armatis com-
6 plent. dum trepidant acie instruenda, consul iam paratis
ordinatisque omnibus incompositos adgreditur. equites
primos ab utroque cornu in pugnam induxit; sed in dextro
extemplo pulsi cedentesque trepidi etiam pediti terrorem
7 intulere. quod ubi consul vidit, duas cohortes delectas ab
dextro latere hostium circumduci iubet, et ab tergo se
8 ostendere priusquam concurrerent peditum acies. is terror obiectus hosti rem metu Romanorum equitum inclinatam aequavit; tamen adeo turbati erant dextrae alae
pedites equitesque ut quosdam consul manu ipse repren-
9 derit et aversos in hostem verterit.[17] ita et quamdiu missilibus pugnatum est anceps pugna erat, et iam ab dextra
parte, unde terror et fuga coeperat, aegre Romanus resta-
10 bat; ab sinistro cornu et a fronte urgebantur barbari, et
11 cohortes a tergo instantes pavidi respiciebant. ut emissis
soliferreis falaricisque gladios strinxerunt, tum velut re-
dintegrata est pugna: non caecis ictibus procul ex improviso volnerabantur, sed pede conlato tota in virtute ac viribus spes erat.

[17] et aversos in hostem verterit *Gron.*: *sic, sed* adversos *Mg*:
verteritque in hostem *Bχ*

---

[50] Latin *falarica,* a heavy projectile covered with pitch that
was set alight and thrown by hand or launched from a catapult.

With that he ordered the cohorts to retreat so as to draw the barbarians out with a simulated flight. It turned out as he had anticipated. Thinking the Romans had lost their nerve and were in retreat, the Spaniards burst forth from their gate and filled the area between their camp and their enemy's battle line with armed men. As they scrambled to deploy their formation, the consul, who had everything ready and in order, attacked them while they in disarray. He first of all led the cavalry into the fight on both wings. On the right, however, they were immediately repulsed, and giving ground in alarm they struck fear into the infantry as well. Seeing this, the consul issued orders for two elite cohorts to be taken around the right flank of the enemy and for them to let themselves be seen at the rear before the infantry lines engaged. The terror that this struck into the enemy redressed the balance of the fight, which had been upset by the panic in the Roman cavalry. But the infantry and cavalry on the right wing were thrown into such disorder that the consul grabbed a few of them with his own hands and turned them back toward the enemy. Thus, as long as the battle was being fought with projectiles, the contest was even and, in addition, on the right flank, where the panic and flight had started, the Romans were now finding it difficult to hold their ground. On the left and in the center it was the barbarians who were under pressure, and they looked back with anxiety at the cohorts bearing down on their rear. When the javelins and incendiary spears[50] had been thrown, however, and the combatants drew their swords, the battle was virtually renewed; for now they were not being dealt unforeseen wounds randomly delivered from afar but, with foot set against foot, their hopes all lay in their courage and their physical strength.

15. Fessos iam suos consul ex secunda acie subsidiariis
2 cohortibus in pugnam inductis accendit. nova acies facta.
integri recentibus telis fatigatos adorti hostes primum acri
impetu velut cuneo perculerunt, deinde dissipatos in fugam averterunt; effuso per agros cursu castra repeteban-
3 tur. ubi omnia fuga completa vidit Cato, ipse ad secundam
legionem, quae in subsidio posita erat, revehitur, et signa
prae se ferri plenoque gradu ad castra hostium oppug-
4 nanda succedere iubet. si quis extra ordinem avidius pro-
currit, et ipse interequitans sparo percutit et tribunos
centurionesque castigare iubet.

5 Iam castra oppugnabantur, saxisque et sudibus et omni
genere telorum submovebantur a vallo Romani. ubi recens admota legio est, tum et oppugnantibus animus cre-
6 vit et infensius hostes pro vallo pugnabant. consul omnia
oculis perlustrat ut qua minima vi resistatur ea parte in-
rumpat. ad sinistram portam infrequentes videt: eo secun-
7 dae legionis principes hastatosque inducit. non sustinuit
impetum eorum statio quae portae apposita erat; et ceteri,
postquam intra vallum hostem vident, ipsi castris exuti
8 signa armaque abiciunt. caeduntur in portis, suomet ipsi
agmine in arto haerentes. secundani terga hostium cae-
9 dunt, ceteri castra diripiunt. Valerius Antias supra quadra-

---

[51] See Introduction, lx–lxiii.

15. His men now fatigued, the consul revitalized them by bringing into the battle reserve cohorts from the second line. A new battle line was thus constituted. Fresh troops now attacked a weary enemy with weapons as yet unused, at first pushing them back with a spirited charge in wedge formation, and then scattering them and driving them off in flight. The enemy ran in confusion through the fields and headed back to camp. When Cato saw them fleeing in every quarter, he himself rode back to the second legion, which had been kept in reserve, and ordered it to move up and advance at a brisk pace to attack the enemy camp. If any man ran forward and broke ranks from an excess of enthusiasm, he personally struck him with his short spear as he rode between the lines and also ordered the tribunes and centurions to punish him.

The camp was by now under attack, and the Romans were being driven back from the palisade with stones, stakes, and all manner of projectiles. Then, with the arrival of the fresh legion, the spirits of the attacking force were raised, while the enemy also fought more aggressively to defend their palisade. The consul surveyed the entire field, intending to burst through at the point of least resistance. He spotted a shortage of defenders at the left gate and led the *principes* and *hastati*[51] of the second legion to that point. The sentinels stationed at the gate could not fend off their charge, and the rest of the Spaniards, when they saw the enemy inside their palisade, proceeded to throw down their standards and their arms, the camp being now lost to them. They were massacred in the gateways, wedged in the limited space by their own numbers; and the men of the second legion cut them down from the rear while the rest pillaged the camp. Valerius An-

ginta milia hostium caesa eo die scribit; Cato ipse, haud
sane detractator laudum suarum, multos caesos ait, numerum non adscribit.

16. [Tria eo die laudabilia fecisse putatur: unum, quod
circumducto exercitu procul navibus suis castrisque, ubi
spem nisi in virtute haberent, inter medios hostes proelium commisit; alterum, quod cohortes ab tergo hostibus
2 obiecit; tertium, quod secundam legionem ceteris omnibus effusis ad sequendos hostes pleno gradu sub signis
compositam instructamque subire ad portam castrorum
3 iussit.][18] nihil deinde a victoria cessatum. cum receptui
signo dato suos spoliis onustos in castra reduxisset, paucis
horis noctis ad quietem datis ad praedandum in agros
4 duxit: effusius, ut sparsis hostibus fuga, praedati sunt.
quae res non minus quam pugna pridie adversa Empori-
tanos Hispanos accolasque eorum in deditionem compu-
5 lit. multi et aliarum civitatium, qui Emporias perfugerant,
dediderunt se; quos omnes appellatos benigne, uinoque
et cibo curatos,[19] domos dimisit.
6     Confestim inde castra movit; et quacumque incedebat
agmen legati dedentium civitates suas occurrebant, et
cum Tarraconem venit iam omnis cis Hiberum Hispania
7 perdomita erat, captivique et Romani et socium ac Latini

[18] 16.1–2 *Mg*: *om. B*χ
[19] vinoque . . . curatos *Mg*: *om. B*χ

---

[52] See Introduction, xxv–xxviii.

[53] On Cato as historian, see Introduction, xxvi.

[54] These lines, found in the codex Moguntinus but absent
from the main manuscript tradition, may be spurious: see Briscoe
2.78.

tias[52] reports enemy dead that day to be more than 40,000. Cato himself, certainly not one to underestimate his own achievements, says that many were killed, but does not specify a number.[53]

16. [Cato is reckoned to have performed three commendable acts that day. In the first place he led his army around the enemy far from his own ships and camp, and proceeded to fight in the midst of the foe, where his men's hope lay entirely in their valor. Secondly, he brought in the cohorts to the enemy's rear. And, thirdly, when all the others had broken ranks to pursue the enemy, he ordered the second legion to move forward to the camp gate at full speed, but in proper formation under the standards].[54] There was no cessation of activity after the victory. When the signal to retire had been given, Cato brought his men back to camp laden with spoils, gave them a few hours of the night to sleep, and then led them out to conduct raids on the countryside. The raids were more wide-ranging now that the enemy was scattered in flight. This, no less than their defeat the day before, forced the Spaniards of Emporiae and their neighbors to capitulate. Many inhabitants of other states who had sought refuge in Emporiae also surrendered. Cato addressed them politely and sent them off to their homes after entertaining them with wine and food.

He then swiftly moved camp, and wherever his army advanced delegates from various states met him, offering submission. When he reached Tarraco,[55] all Spain north of the Ebro had been completely vanquished, and prisoners of war, Romans as well as allies and men with Latin

---

[55] Modern Terragona (*Barr.* 25 G4). It had been the main Roman base during the Hannibalic War.

nominis variis casibus in Hispania oppressi donum consuli
8 a barbaris reducebantur. fama deinde volgatur consulem
in Turdetaniam exercitum ducturum, et ad devios monta-
9 nos profectum etiam falso perlatum est. ad hunc vanum et
sine auctore ullo rumorem Bergistanorum civitatis septem castella defecerunt: eo deducto[20] exercitu consul sine
10 memorando proelio in potestatem redegit. haud ita multo
post eidem, regresso Tarraconem consule, priusquam
inde quoquam procederet, defecerunt. iterum subacti;
sed non eadem venia victis fuit: sub corona veniere omnes,
ne saepius pacem sollicitarent.

17. Interim P. Manlius praetor, exercitu vetere a Q.
Minucio, cui successerat, accepto, adiuncto et Ap. Claudi
Neronis ex ulteriore Hispania vetere item exercitu, in Tur-
2 detaniam proficiscitur. omnium Hispanorum maxime im-
belles habentur Turdetani; freti tamen multitudine sua
3 obviam ierunt agmini Romano. eques immissus turbavit
extemplo aciem eorum. pedestre proelium nullius ferme
certaminis fuit: milites veteres, periti hostium bellique,
4 haud dubiam pugnam fecerunt. nec tamen ea pugna debellatum est: decem milia Celtiberum mercede Turduli

---

[20] eo deducto *Mg*: eos deducto *Bχ*: eos educto *Gron.*

---

[56] Cf. 31.5.4 note.     [57] The lands of the Turdetani were
extensive (*Barr.* 26 D–F 4; TIR J-30, 325–26). Livy's geography
may be confused, however, as the Bergistani (below) were far to
the north in Hispania Citerior (*Barr.* 25 G4; TIR K/J-31, 48).

[58] Literally, "sold under the wreath/chaplet," because slaves
wore a garland of flowers when put up for sale.

[59] A "mere variant for Turdetani" (Briscoe 2.80). In fact, the
Turduli (*Barr.* 26 C4, D4; TIR J-30, 326–27) seem to have lived
north and west of the Turdetani (*Barr.* 26 E4; TIR J-30, 325–26),

rights[56]—people who had fallen victim to various mischances in Spain—were brought back to the consul by the barbarians as a gift. Then word spread abroad that the consul was going to lead his army into Turdetania,[57] and there was even a false report that he had already begun to march against the remote mountain peoples. In response to this empty and groundless rumor seven fortified towns in the state of the Bergistani rebelled. The consul brought his army to the area and subdued them once more without a fight of any note. Not much later there was a second revolt of the same peoples, after the consul's return to Tarraco and before he left again. Once more they were subdued, only this time the conquered were not shown the same mercy as before. All were auctioned off[58] to put an end to their frequent breaking of the peace.

17. In the meantime the praetor Publius Manlius set off for Turdetania with the veteran army that he had taken over from Quintus Minucius (whom he had succeeded) and to which he had added the army of Appius Claudius Nero from Farther Spain, which was also a veteran force. Of all the Spanish peoples the Turdetani are considered the least warlike but they confronted the Roman column from reliance on their numbers. The cavalry were unleashed against them and this immediately threw the Spanish line into disarray. The infantry engagement was almost no contest: the Roman veteran troops, well acquainted with the enemy as well as the art of war, left the outcome of the battle in no doubt. And yet the war did not end with that battle. The Turduli[59] hired 10,000 Cel-

but Briscoe may be right that for Livy they were the same (cf. Strabo 3.1.6: "some believe that they are the same people, others different").

5 conducunt, alienisque armis parabant bellum. consul interim rebellione Bergistanorum ictus, ceteras quoque civitates ratus per occasionem idem facturas, arma omnibus
6 cis Hiberum Hispanis adimit; quam rem adeo aegre passi
ut multi mortem sibimet ipsi conscicerent, ferox genus,
7 nullam vitam rati sine armis esse. quod ubi consuli renun-
tiatum est, senatores omnium civitatium ad se vocari iussit, atque iis "non nostra" inquit "magis quam vestra refert
8 vos non rebellare, siquidem id maiore Hispanorum malo
quam exercitus Romani labore semper adhuc factum est.
id ut ne fiat, uno modo arbitror caveri posse, si effectum
9 erit ne possitis rebellare. volo id quam mollissima via
consequi. vos quoque in ea re consilio me adiuvate: nullum libentius sequar quam quod vosmet ipsi attuleritis."
10 tacentibus spatium se ad deliberandum dierum paucorum
11 dare dixit. cum revocati secundo quoque consilio tacuis-
sent, uno die muris omnium dirutis, ad eos qui nondum
parebant profectus, ut in quamque regionem venerat, omnes qui circa incolebant populos in dicionem[21] accepit.
12 Segesticam tantum, gravem atque opulentam civitatem,
vineis et pluteis cepit.

18. Eo maiorem habebat difficultatem in subigendis
hostibus quam qui primi venerant in Hispaniam, quod ad
illos taedio imperii Carthaginiensium Hispani deficiebant,
2 huic ex usurpata libertate in servitutem velut adserendi

---

[21] dicionem *Bχ*: deditionem *Holk. 345*

---

[60] For the Celtiberians cf. 10.1, above, and note.
[61] Its location is nevertheless unknown (TIR *J-30,* 296).

tiberians,[60] and were preparing to continue the war with the weapons of others. Meanwhile the consul, shocked by the uprising of the Bergistani and thinking the other communities would seize the opportunity to do the same, disarmed all the Spaniards north of the Ebro. The Spaniards were so humiliated by this measure that many took their own lives—they are a headstrong people who feel life is nothing without weapons. When news of this was brought to the consul, he had the senators of all the communities summoned to him and said: "Not to rebel is as much in your interest as it is ours, for up to now this course has proved more of a disaster for the Spaniards than it has a hardship for the Roman army. I think there is only one way of safeguarding against it and that is to see that the opportunity for rebellion is removed from you. I want to attain this end in the smoothest possible way. You, too, must help me in the matter with your advice. There is no suggestion I would more willingly follow than the one you bring to me yourselves." The Spaniards remained silent, and Cato said he would give them a few days to think it over. When they were called back and remained silent also at this second meeting, Cato in one day tore down all their city walls, set out against those still refusing to submit, and brought under his control all the neighboring peoples in each area through which he passed. Only for the capture of Segestica, an important and wealthy city,[61] did he use siege sheds and mantlets.

18. Cato had greater difficulty subduing his enemies than did the Romans who had originally arrived in Spain, and for the following reason. The Spaniards defected to those Romans because they were tired of Carthaginian rule, but Cato virtually had to reclaim mastery over the

erant; et ita mota omnia accepit ut alii in armis essent, alii
obsidione ad defectionem cogerentur, nec nisi in tempore
3  subventum foret, ultra sustentaturi fuerint. sed in consule
ea vis animi atque ingenii fuit ut omnia maxima mini-
maque per se adiret atque ageret, nec cogitaret modo
4  imperaretque quae in rem essent, sed pleraque ipse per
se transigeret, nec in quemquam omnium gravius severius-
5  que quam in semet ipsum imperium exerceret, parsimonia
et vigiliis et labore cum ultimis militum certaret, nec quicquam in exercitu suo praecipui praeter honorem atque
imperium haberet.

19. Difficilius bellum in Turdetania praetori P. Manlio
Celtiberi mercede exciti ab hostibus, sicut ante dictum
est, faciebant; itaque eo consul accersitus litteris praetoris
2  legiones duxit. ubi eo venit, castra separatim Celtiberi et
Turdetani habebant. cum Turdetanis extemplo levia proelia incursantes in stationes eorum Romani facere, semperque victores ex quamvis temere coepto certamine abire.
3  ad Celtiberos in conloquium tribunos militum ire consul
4  atque iis trium condicionum electionem ferre iubet: primam, si transire ad Romanos velint, et duplex[22] stipendium accipere quam quantum a Turdetanis pepigissent;
5  alteram, si domos abire, publica fide accepta nihil eam
rem noxiae futuram quod hostibus se Romanorum iunxis-
6  sent; tertiam, si utique bellum placeat, diem locumque

---

[22] et duplex χ: duplex *B*

natives after they had already seized their freedom; and he inherited a situation so turbulent that some were already up in arms while others were being forced into rebellion by siege, and these would not have held out any longer had not timely assistance been brought to them. But there was so much forcefulness of mind and character in the consul that he would personally approach and undertake all manner of operations, great or small, not simply formulating and presiding over measures appropriate to the situation but for the most part seeing them through in person. Nor did he bring the rigor and severity of his authority to bear on anyone in the entire army more than he did on himself; and in frugal living, vigilance, and industry he rivaled his lowest ranking men—indeed, in his army he enjoyed no special privilege apart from his rank and *imperium.*

19. The Celtiberian mercenaries hired by the enemy (as noted above) were making the war in Turdetania more difficult for the praetor Publius Manlius. Accordingly the consul, whom the praetor sent for by letter, led his legions to the area. When he arrived, the Celtiberians and Turdetani had two separate camps. The Romans immediately had some minor skirmishes with the Turdetani, attacking their outposts, and they always departed victors no matter how imprudent their engagement. As for the Celtiberians, the consul ordered the military tribunes to go to parley with them and offer them a choice of three options. First, they could go over to the Romans and receive twice the pay that they had agreed upon with the Turdetani; secondly, they could go home with an official guarantee that they would not be punished for having joined the enemies of Rome; or, thirdly, if they wanted war at all costs, they

7 constituant ubi secum armis decernant. a Celtiberis dies
ad consultandum petita. concilium immixtis Turdetanis
habitum magno cum tumultu; eo minus decerni quicquam
8 potuit. cum incerta bellum an pax cum Celtiberis essent,
commeatus tamen haud secus quam in pace ex agris cas-
tellisque hostium Romani portabant, deni saepe munimenta eorum, velut communi pacto commercio, privatis
indutiis ingredientes.

9 Consul ubi hostes ad pugnam elicere nequit, primum
praedatum sub signis aliquot expeditas cohortes in agrum
10 integrae regionis ducit, deinde audito Saguntiae[23] Celtiberum omnes sarcinas impedimentaque relicta, eo pergit
11 ducere ad oppugnandum. postquam nulla moventur re,
persoluto stipendio non suis modo sed etiam praetoris
militibus, relictoque omni exercitu in castris praetoris,
ipse cum septem cohortibus ad Hiberum est regressus.

20. Ea tam exigua manu oppida aliquot cepit. defecere
2 ad eum Sedetani Ausetani Suessetani. Lacetanos, deviam
et silvestrem gentem, cum insita feritas continebat in armis, tum conscientia, dum consul exercitusque Turdulo
bello est occupatus, depopulatorum subitis incursionibus
3 sociorum. igitur ad oppidum eorum oppugnandum consul
ducit non Romanas modo cohortes, sed iuventutem etiam

---

[23] Seguntiae *McDonald*: Saguntiae *BVoss.*: Secuntiae *APNL*:
Secultiae *E*; Secuirtiae *V*

---

[62] Almost certainly Seguntia, today Sigüenza (*Barr.* 25 D4;
TIR *K-30,* 208).   [63] Sedetani: *Barr.* 25 E4; TIR *K-30,* 206;
Ausetani: *Barr.* 25 H4; TIR *K/J-31,* 39; Suessetani: *Barr.* 25 E3;
TIR *K-30,* 215.   [64] Lacetani: In northeast Spain: *Barr.* 25 G4;
TIR *K/J-31,* 96–97, but see also Briscoe 2.83.

could fix a day and a location to decide the issue with him in the field. The Celtiberians requested a day to consider the matter. A meeting was then held, which the Turdetani attended and at which there was great disorder; and so reaching any decision was impossible. It was now unclear whether a state of war or peace existed with the Celtiberians, but the Romans kept transporting provisions from the farms and strongholds of the enemy as in peacetime, frequently entering their fortifications in groups of ten under private truces, as if mutual trading relations had been formally sanctioned.

When the consul failed to entice his enemy out to fight, he first of all led out in formation a number of light-armed cohorts to raid some countryside that was as yet untouched. Then, hearing that all the baggage and accouterments of the Celtiberians had been left at Seguntia,[62] he proceeded to take them in that direction in order to attack the town. When the enemy could be moved by no provocation, he paid off not only his own men but the praetor's troops as well, and then, leaving all the other forces in the praetor's camp, returned to the Ebro with seven cohorts.

20. With this force, so small as it was, Cato captured a number of towns. The Sedetani, Ausetani, and Suessetani[63] went over to him. The Lacetani,[64] an isolated tribe living in the woods, were kept in arms both by their natural belligerence and by pangs of guilt over having plundered the Roman allies with sudden raids while the consul and his army were preoccupied with the war against the Turdetani. The consul therefore brought against their town not only his Roman cohorts but also men of military

4   merito infensorum iis sociorum. oppidum longum, in lati-
tudinem haudquaquam tantundem patens habebant. qua-
5   dringentos inde ferme passus constituit signa. ibi delecta-
rum cohortium stationem relinquens praecepit iis ne se ex
eo loco ante moverent quam ipse ad eos venisset; ceteras
copias ad ulteriorem partem urbis circumducit.

     Maximum ex omnibus auxiliis numerum Suessetanae
iuventutis habebat: eos ad murum oppugnandum subire
6   iubet. quorum ubi arma signaque Lacetani cognovere,
memores quam saepe in agro eorum impune persultas-
sent, quotiens ipsos signis conlatis fudissent fugassentque,
7   patefacta repente porta universi in eos erumpunt. vix clamorem eorum, nedum impetum Suessetani tulere. quod
postquam sicut futurum ratus erat consul fieri etiam vidit,
8   equo citato subter murum hostium ad cohortes avehitur,
atque eas arreptas, effusis omnibus ad sequendos Suesse-
tanos, qua silentium ac solitudo erat in urbem inducit,
9   priusque omnia cepit quam se reciperent Lacetani. mox
ipsos nihil praeter arma habentes in deditionem accepit.

     21. Confestim inde victor ad Bergium castrum ducit.
receptaculum id maxime praedonum erat, et inde incur-
2   siones in agros pacatos provinciae eius fiebant. transfugit
inde ad consulem princeps Bergistanus et purgare se ac
populares coepit: non esse in manu ipsis rem publicam;

---

65 About seven hundred yards.

66 Unidentified, but probably the main town of the Bergistani,
and so somewhere within *Barr.* 25 G4. Cf. TIR *K-30*, 63: Bergi-
dum (Ptol. *Geog.* 2.6.67, Βέργιδον).

age from among the allies, who had good reason to be hostile to them. The Lacetani lived in a town that was long but not correspondingly wide. Cato halted some 400 paces[65] from it. Leaving some elite cohorts on guard at this point, he instructed them not to move from the spot until he came back to them in person, and then he took the rest of his troops around to the other side of the town.

The largest contingent among all his auxiliary detachments were the soldiers of the Suessetani, and these Cato ordered to move up to attack the wall. When the Lacetani recognized their armor and standards, they recalled how often they had roamed around this people's territory with impunity and the many occasions on which they had beaten and routed them in pitched battle; and suddenly they threw open their gate and burst forth in a body against them. The Suessetani barely withstood their battle cry, much less their charge. When the consul saw things progressing as he had predicted, he rode off at a gallop beneath the enemy wall to rejoin his cohorts. Taking charge of them he led them into the city, where silence and solitude now reigned, the townspeople having all poured out in pursuit of the Suessetani, and before they could return he took it over completely. Soon afterward Cato accepted their surrender, since they now had nothing left but their weapons.

21. The victor then swiftly led his army to the fortress of Bergium.[66] This was for the most part a hideaway for robbers and from it raids were being conducted on the pacified country areas of the province. The chieftain of the Bergistani slipped away from there to see the consul and proceeded to plead innocence on the part of himself and his fellow townspeople. Their government, he said,

praedones receptos totum suae potestatis id castrum fe-
3 cisse. consul eum domum redire, conficta aliqua probabili
4 cur afuisset causa, iussit: cum se muros subisse cerneret
intentosque praedones ad tuenda moenia esse, tum uti
cum suae factionis hominibus meminisset arcem occupare.

5    Id uti praeceperat factum; repente anceps terror, hinc
muros ascendentibus Romanis illinc arce capta, barbaros
circumuasit. huius potitus loci consul eos qui arcem tenue-
6 rant liberos esse cum cognatis suaque habere iussit, Ber-
gistanos ceteros quaestori ut venderet imperavit, de prae-
7 donibus supplicium sumpsit. pacata provincia vectigalia
magna instituit ex ferrariis argentariisque, quibus tum
8 institutis locupletior in dies provincia fuit. ob has res gestas in Hispania supplicationem in triduum patres decreverunt.

22. Eadem aestate alter consul L. Valerius Flaccus in
Gallia cum Boiorum manu propter Litanam silvam signis
2 conlatis secundo proelio conflixit. octo milia Gallorum
caesa traduntur; ceteri omisso bello in vicos suos atque
3 agros dilapsi. consul reliquum aestatis circa Padum Pla-
centiae et Cremonae exercitum habuit, restituitque quae
in iis oppidis bello diruta fuerant.
4    Cum hic status rerum in Italia Hispaniaque esset, T.
Quinctio in Graecia, ita hibernis actis ut exceptis Aetolis,

---

[67] Location uncertain but probably in Boian territory near
Mutina (*Barr.* 39 H4). There had been a Roman defeat there in
216 (23.24.7–13).

was not under their control—the robbers whom they had taken in had brought the fortress entirely into their power. The consul told him to invent some plausible reason for his absence and go home; when he saw Cato approaching the walls and the robbers preoccupied with defending their battlements, he, along with the men belonging to his party, was to see to capturing the citadel.

This order was put into effect, and a twofold fear suddenly overtook the barbarians when the Romans were climbing the walls on one side and the citadel had already been lost on the other. Taking charge of the place, the consul issued orders that the men who had occupied the citadel should be set free together with their relatives and be granted continued possession of their property. The rest of the Bergistani he ordered the quaestor to sell into slavery, and he executed the robbers. With peace restored to the province, he imposed heavy taxes on the iron and silver mines, and through them the province grew richer every day. The senators decreed three days of supplication in thanks for these achievements in Spain.

22. That same summer the other consul, Lucius Valerius Flaccus, fought a successful pitched battle against a contingent of the Boii near the Litana forest[67] in Gaul. Eight thousand Gauls are reported to have been killed; the others abandoned the fight and slipped away to their villages and farms. The consul kept his army at Placentia and Cremona, close to the Po, for the rest of the summer, and rebuilt the sections of the towns that had been destroyed in the war.

Such was the state of affairs in Italy and Spain. In Greece, meanwhile, Titus Quinctius had ensured by his activities over the winter that the whole country, the Ae-

quibus nec pro spe victoriae praemia contigerant nec diu
quies placere poterat, universa Graecia simul pacis liber-
5 tatisque perfruens bonis egregie statu suo gauderet, nec
magis in bello virtutem Romani ducis quam in victoria
temperantiam iustitiamque et moderationem miraretur,
senatus consultum quo bellum adversus Nabim Lacedae-
6 monium decretum erat adfertur. quo lecto Quinctius conventum Corinthum omnium sociarum civitatium legationibus in diem certam edicit; ad quam ubi frequentes
undique principes convenerunt, ita uti ne Aetoli quidem
abessent, tali oratione est usus:

7 "Bellum adversus Philippum non magis communi
animo consilioque Romani et Graeci gesserunt quam
8 utrique suas causas belli habuerunt. nam et Romanorum
amicitiam nunc Carthaginienses hostes eorum iuvando,
9 nunc hic sociis nostris oppugnandis violaverat, et in vos
talis fuit ut nobis, etiamsi nostrarum oblivisceremur iniu-
10 riarum, vestrae iniuriae satis digna causa belli fuerit. ho-
dierna consultatio tota ex vobis pendet. refero enim ad vos
utrum Argos, sicut scitis ipsi, ab Nabide occupatos pati
11 velitis sub dicione eius esse, an aequum censeatis nobilis-
simam vetustissimamque civitatem, in media Graecia sitam, repeti in libertatem et eodem statu quo ceteras urbes
12 Peloponnesi et Graeciae esse. haec consultatio, ut videtis,
tota de re pertinente ad vos est: Romanos nihil contingit,

---

68 Cf. 31.1.10 and note.

tolians apart, was simultaneously enjoying the fruits of peace and independence, and relishing its new status—as full of admiration for the Roman commander's restraint, fairness and moderation in victory as it had been for his courage in war. For the Aetolians, however, the rewards of victory had not been as great as they had hoped and protracted inactivity could not be to their liking, either. Such were circumstances when Flamininus was brought the senatorial decree by which war was declared on Nabis the Lacedaemonian. After reading it, Quinctius called for a meeting of delegations from all the allied states to be held at Corinth on a specified date. On this day the leading citizens came together in large numbers from all over Greece, with not even the Aetolians failing to appear, and the commander made the following address:

"The Romans and Greeks fought against Philip with a unified spirit and policy, though their motives for the war were very different. Philip had violated his treaty with the Romans by at one time aiding our enemies the Carthaginians[68] and at another by attacking our allies here; and his conduct toward you was such that, even were we to overlook the wrongs done to us, those done to you would have been sufficient grounds for war. But today's decision rests with you and you alone. I am bringing before you the issue of whether you want Argos which, as you yourselves well know, is occupied by Nabis, to remain under that man's control, or whether you think it fair that this famous and ancient state, situated in the heart of Greece, should have its liberty restored and enjoy the same status as the other cities of the Peloponnese and Greece. This discussion, as you can see, is entirely focused on a matter that is your concern—it has nothing to do with the Romans, except

485

nisi quatenus liberatae Graeciae unius civitatis servitus
13 non plenam nec integram gloriam esse sinit. ceterum si
vos nec cura eius civitatis nec exemplum nec periculum
movet, ne serpat latius contagio eius mali, nos aequi bo-
nique facimus. de hac re vos consulo, staturus eo quod
plures censueritis."

23. Post orationem Romani imperatoris percenseri
2 aliorum sententiae coeptae sunt. cum legatus Atheniensium quantum poterat gratiis agendis Romanorum in
Graeciam merita extulisset—imploratos adversus Philip-
3 pum tulisse opem, non rogatos ultro adversus tyrannum
Nabim offerre auxilium—, indignatusque esset haec tanta
merita sermonibus tamen aliquorum carpi futura calum-
4 niantium, cum fateri potius praeteritorum gratiam de-
5 berent, apparebat incessi Aetolos. igitur Alexander princeps gentis, invectus primum in Athenienses, libertatis
quondam duces et auctores, adsentationis propriae gratia
communem causam prodentes, questus deinde Achaeos,
6 Philippi quondam milites, ad postremum inclinata fortuna
eius transfugas, et Corinthum recepisse et id agere ut
7 Argos habeant, Aetolos, primos hostes Philippi semper
socios Romanorum, pactos in foedere suas urbes agrosque
8 fore devicto Philippo, fraudari Echino et Pharsalo, insi-
mulavit fraudis Romanos quod vano titulo libertatis osten-

---

69 On Alexander (Isios), cf. 32.33.9 and note.

inasmuch as the servitude of a single city does not allow the glory of Greece's liberation to be full and complete. However, if concern neither for this city nor the precedent set nor the danger that contamination from this foul disease may spread further does not bother you, then we are quite satisfied. I am consulting you on this matter and shall abide by the majority decision."

23. After the Roman commander's address a review began of the opinions of the others present. The Athenian representative, in his vote of thanks to the Romans, was as fulsome as he could be in extolling their services to Greece—they had provided assistance against Philip when called upon, he said, and now they were freely offering help against the tyrant Nabis without being asked. He expressed indignation that such great services were nevertheless criticized in the talk of certain people who were misrepresenting what the future held when they should be expressing gratitude for the past. He was clearly attacking the Aetolians. Accordingly, Alexander, the leading Aetolian,[69] first launched into an attack on the Athenians—once the leading advocates and champions of independence, these were now traitors to the common cause by virtue of their self-serving obsequiousness, he said. He then complained about the Achaeans' recovery of Corinth and their efforts to take possession of Argos—the Achaeans who, he said, had earlier been soldiers of Philip, and had finally deserted him only when his fortunes turned. The Aetolians, by contrast, had been the earliest opponents of Philip, and had always been allies of the Romans, and yet they were being cheated out of Echinus and Pharsalus despite the commitment the Romans had made in their treaty that these towns and lands would be

487

tato Chalcidem et Demetriadem praesidiis tenerent, qui
9  Philippo cunctanti deducere inde praesidia obicere semper soliti sint nunquam donec Demetrias Chalcis et Co-
10  rinthus tenerentur liberam Graeciam fore, postremo quia
manendi in Graecia retinendique exercitus Argos et Na-
11  bim causam facerent. deportarent legiones in Italiam: Aetolos polliceri aut condicionibus et voluntate sua Nabim
praesidium Argis deducturum, aut vi atque armis coactu-
ros in potestate consentientis Graeciae esse.

24. Haec uaniloquentia primum Aristaenum praetorem Achaeorum excitavit.
2  "Ne istuc" inquit "Iuppiter optimus maximus sirit Iu-
noque regina cuius in tutela Argi sunt, ut illa civitas inter
tyrannum Lacedaemonium et latrones Aetolos praemium
sit, posita in eo discrimine ut miserius a vobis recipiatur
3  quam ab illo capta est. mare interiectum ab istis praedo-
nibus non tuetur nos, T. Quincti: quid si in media Peloponneso arcem sibi fecerint futurum nobis est? linguam
tantum Graecorum habent sicut speciem hominum: mori-
4  bus ritibusque efferatioribus quam ulli barbari, immo
quam immanes beluae uivunt. itaque vos rogamus, Romani, ut et ab Nabide Argos reciperetis, et ita res Graeciae
constituatis ut ab latrocinio quoque Aetolorum satis pacata
haec relinquatis."

---

70 Philip V's "fetters of Greece"; cf. 31.23.1, 32.37.3 and notes.
71 Pro-Roman league *strategos* in 199–98: cf. 32.19.2.

theirs on Philip's defeat. Alexander further accused the Romans of duplicity. They were occupying Chalcis and Demetrias with their garrisons after bandying about the empty term "freedom"—and it was they who had persistently criticized Philip when he hesitated to withdraw his garrisons from those towns, saying that Greece would never be free as long as Demetrias, Chalcis, and Corinth[70] were occupied. And finally, he said, they were making Argos and Nabis a pretext for staying in Greece and keeping their armies there. Let them take their legions back to Italy, he concluded—the Aetolians guaranteed that Nabis would either withdraw his garrison from Argos on their terms and according to their wishes or they would oblige him by force of arms to accept the authority of a united Greece.

24. This blustering prompted a response first of all from Aristaenus, praetor of the Achaeans.[71]

"May Jupiter Optimus Maximus not permit it to come to pass," he said, "nor Queen Juno in whose protection Argos lies, that the city should become a prize set between a Spartan tyrant and Aetolian bandits, in danger of suffering more from being recovered by you than it did from its capture by Nabis! A sea lies between us but it does not protect us from those marauders, Titus Quinctius. What will become of us if they establish a citadel for themselves in the heart of the Peloponnese? The only Greek feature they possess is the language, just as their only human one is their shape! They live with customs and practices more barbaric than those of any foreigners—no, more barbaric than those of beasts of the wild. We therefore ask you, Romans, to recover Argos from Nabis and also to settle matters in Greece in such a fashion as to leave these areas untroubled by the depredations of the Aetolians, as well."

5    Romanus, cunctis undique increpantibus Aetolos, responsurum se fuisse iis dixit, nisi ita infensos omnes in eos
6  videret ut sedandi potius quam inritandi essent. contentum itaque opinione ea quae de Romanis Aetolisque esset
referre se dixit quid de Nabidis bello placeret, nisi redde-
7  ret Achaeis Argos. cum omnes bellum decressent, auxilia
ut pro viribus suis quaeque civitates mitterent est horta-
tus. ad Aetolos legatum etiam misit, magis ut nudaret animos, id quod evenit, quam spe impetrari posse.

25. Tribunis militum ut exercitum ab Elatia arcesserent
2  imperavit. per eosdem dies et Antiochi legatis de societate agentibus respondit nihil se absentibus decem legatis
sententiae habere: Romam eundum ad senatum iis esse.
3  ipse copias adductas ab Elatia ducere Argos pergit; atque
ei circa Cleonas Aristaenus praetor cum decem milibus
Achaeorum equitibus mille occurrit, et haud procul inde
4  iunctis exercitibus posuerunt castra. postero die in campum Argivorum descenderunt et quattuor ferme milia ab
5  Argis locum castris capiunt. praefectus praesidii Laconum
erat Pythagoras, gener idem tyranni et uxoris eius frater,
qui sub adventum Romanorum et utrasque arces—nam
duas habent Argi—et loca alia quae aut opportuna aut
6  suspecta erant validis praesidiis firmavit; sed inter haec
agenda pavorem iniectum adventu Romanorum dissimu-
lare haudquaquam poterat.

---

[72] The Roman winter quarters in 198/7 and 197/6 (32.39.2,
33.27.5).

[73] Apega according to Polybius (13.7.6), or possibly Apia,
daughter of Aristippus, tyrant of Argos (cf. Walbank 2.421).

On all sides there was unanimous criticism of the Aetolians, and the Roman commander declared that he would have given them a reply had he not seen all the delegates so opposed to them that they needed to be mollified rather than provoked. He was, he said, content with the opinions expressed about the Romans and the Aetolians, and he was now laying before them the question of what their pleasure would be with regard to a war with Nabis if he refused to return Argos to the Achaeans. When they all voted for war, Flamininus urged them to send him auxiliary forces, each state according to its resources. He even sent an envoy to the Aetolians, more in order to bring their intentions into the open—which is what happened—than from any hope that his request could be granted.

25. Flamininus then ordered the military tribunes to summon the army from Elatia.[72] At about this same time he also responded to an embassy from Antiochus, which had come to discuss an alliance, saying that in the absence of the ten commissioners he could not express an opinion and they would have to approach the senate in Rome. He then proceeded to lead toward Argos the forces that had been brought from Elatia, and the praetor Aristaenus met him near Cleonae with 10,000 Achaean infantry and 1,000 cavalry. The two joined forces and pitched camp not far from there. The next day they went down into the Argive plain and chose a site for their camp about four miles from Argos. In command of the Spartan garrison was Pythagoras, who was a son-in-law of the tyrant and also the brother of his wife.[73] At the approach of the Romans, Pythagoras reinforced both citadels (Argos has two) and other points of vantage or weakness with strong detachments of guards. But even as he did this he was totally unable to hide the panic inspired by the arrival of the Romans.

LIVY

Et ad externum terrorem intestina etiam seditio acces-
7 sit. Damocles erat Argivus adulescens maioris animi quam
consilii, qui primo iure iurando interposito de praesidio
expellendo cum idoneis conlocutus, dum vires adicere
8 coniurationi studet incautior fidei aestimator fuit. conlo-
quentem eum cum suis satelles a praefecto missus cum
accerseret, sensit proditum consilium esse, hortatusque
coniuratos qui aderant ut potius quam extorti morerentur
9 arma secum caperent. atque ita cum paucis in forum pergit ire, clamitans ut qui salvam rem publicam vellent auc-
10 torem et ducem se libertatis sequerentur. haud sane movit
quemquam, quia nihil usquam spei propinquae, nedum
11 satis firmi praesidii cernebant. haec vociferantem eum
Lacedaemonii circumventum cum suis interfecerunt.
12 comprensi deinde quidam et alii; ex iis occisi plures, pauci
in custodiam coniecti[24] proxima nocte funibus per murum
demissi ad Romanos perfugerunt.

26. Quinctius, adfirmantibus iis si ad portas exercitus
2 Romanus fuisset, non sine effectu motum eum futurum
fuisse, et si propius castra admoverentur, non quieturos
Argivos, misit expeditos pedites equitesque, qui circa Cy-
larabim—gymnasium id est minus trecentos passus ab
3 urbe—cum erumpentibus a porta Lacedaemoniis proelium commiserunt, atque eos haud magno certamine
compulerunt in urbem. et castra eo ipso loco ubi pugna-

[24] coniecti *B*χ: *post add.* multi *Asc.*, alii *McDonald*

---

[74] Lying to the south of the city and, according to Pausanias (2.18.5, 22.8), named after Cylarabes, a legendary king of Argos.

In addition to the threat from without there was also sedition within the town. There was an Argive, Damocles, a young man who, having more courage than prudence, initiated discussions with some likely individuals, after an exchange of oaths, about driving out the garrison, and in his eagerness to strengthen the plot he was a rather poor judge of reliability. When an attendant sent by the garrison commander summoned him as he was conversing with his accomplices, he realized that the plan had been betrayed, and he encouraged his confederates there present to take up arms with him rather than die under torture. So it was that, with a few supporters, he proceeded into the forum crying out for all wishing to save the state to follow him as the champion and leader of their freedom. He persuaded hardly anyone as people saw no hope anywhere of immediate success and much less any robust support for the conspiracy. Damocles was still shouting out his appeals when the Spartans surrounded him and killed him along with his men. A number of the other conspirators were then also arrested. Most were executed, but a few who were thrown into prison let themselves down the wall with ropes the following night and made good their escape to the Romans.

26. When the fugitives insisted that the uprising would not have been abortive had the Roman army been at the gates and that the Argives would not sit idly by if his camp were moved closer to the city, Flamininus sent forward his light infantry and cavalry. These fought a battle near Cylarabis (a gymnasium not 300 paces from the city)[74] with some Spartans who sallied forth from the gate, and drove them back into the city with no great effort. The Roman commander pitched his camp in the very spot where the

tum erat imperator Romanus posuit; diem inde unum in
4 speculis fuit, si quid novi motus oreretur. postquam op-
pressam metu civitatem vidit, advocat consilium de op-
5 pugnandis Argis. omnium principum Graeciae praeter
Aristaenum eadem sententia erat, cum causa belli non alia
6 esset, inde potissimum ordiendum bellum. Quinctio id
nequaquam placebat, et Aristaenum contra omnium consensum disserentem cum haud dubia adprobatione audi-
7 vit; et ipse adiecit, cum pro Argivis adversus tyrannum
bellum susceptum sit, quid minus conveniens esse quam
8 omisso hoste Argos oppugnari? se vero caput belli Lacedaemonem et tyrannum petiturum. et dimisso consilio
frumentatum expeditas cohortes misit. quod maturi erat
circa, demessum et convectum est: viride, ne hostes mox
haberent, protritum et corruptum.
9 Castra deinde movit, et Parthenio superato monte
praeter Tegeam tertio die ad Caryas posuit castra. ibi
priusquam hostium intraret agrum, sociorum auxilia ex-
10 spectavit. venerunt Macedones a Philippo mille et quingenti et Thessalorum equites quadringenti. nec iam auxilia, quorum adfatim erat, sed commeatus finitimis urbibus
11 imperati morabantur Romanum. navales quoque magnae
copiae conveniebant: iam ab Leucade L. Quinctius quadraginta navibus venerat, iam Rhodiae duodeviginti tectae
naves, iam Eumenes rex circa Cycladas insulas erat cum
decem tectis navibus, triginta lembis mixtisque aliis mino-

---

75 In northern Laconia, but location uncertain (possibly *Barr.*
58 D3 [Karyai]).

battle had been fought. He then spent one day watching for any fresh developments; but when he saw the city paralyzed with fear he called a meeting to discuss an assault on Argos. All the Greek leaders apart from Aristaenus were of one opinion: since this city was the sole reason for the campaign, the campaign should start right there. Quinctius was not at all happy with this, and he listened with evident approval to Aristaenus when he expressed a view at variance with the general consensus. He added the further point that, since the war had been undertaken on behalf of Argos and against the tyrant, nothing could make less sense than that Argos should be attacked and the enemy left alone. *He* was going to march on Sparta, the source of the war, and on the tyrant, he said. The meeting was then adjourned and Quinctius sent his light-armed cohorts on a foraging expedition. All ripe grain in the area was harvested and brought in, and the unripe was trampled underfoot and spoiled so the enemy could not use it later.

Flamininus then struck camp and two days later, after crossing Mt Parthenium and passing by Tegea, he encamped at Caryae.[75] Here he awaited auxiliaries from the allies before entering his enemy's territory. Fifteen hundred Macedonians came from Philip along with 400 Thessalian cavalry. It was no longer lack of auxiliaries that held the Roman commander back—with these he was abundantly supplied—but the provisions that had been requisitioned from nearby cities. In addition, large naval forces were beginning to assemble there: Lucius Quinctius had already arrived from Leucas with forty ships; there were eighteen decked vessels from Rhodes; and King Eumenes was now off the Cyclades with ten decked ships, thirty

12 ris formae navigiis. ipsorum quoque Lacedaemoniorum
exsules permulti, tyrannorum iniuria pulsi, spe reciperan-
13 dae patriae in castra Romana convenerunt: multi autem
erant iam per aliquot aetates ex quo tyranni tenebant
14 Lacedaemonem, alii ab aliis expulsi. princeps erat exsulum Agesipolis, cuius iure gentis regnum Lacedaemone
erat, pulsus infans ab Lycurgo tyranno post mortem Cleo-
menis, qui primus tyrannus Lacedaemone fuit.

27. Cum terra marique tantum belli circumstaret tyrannum, et prope nulla spes esset vere vires suas ho-
2 stiumque aestimanti, non tamen omisit bellum, sed et a
Creta mille delectos iuventutis eorum excivit, cum mille
iam haberet, et tria milia mercennariorum militum, decem milia popularium cum castellanis agrestibus in armis
3 habuit, et fossa valloque urbem communivit; et ne quid
intestini motus oreretur, metu et acerbitate poenarum
tenebat animos, quoniam ut salvum vellent tyrannum sperare non poterat.

4 Cum suspectos quosdam civium haberet, eductis in
5 campum omnibus copiis—Dromon ipsi vocant—positis
armis ad contionem vocari iubet Lacedaemonios, atque

---

76 Clearly an exaggeration: the tyranny started only with
Cleomenes III seizing quasi-autocratic power in late 227: cf. Briscoe 2.92; *OCD* sv Cleomenes III.

77 Agesipolis had as a child succeeded Cleomenes III as Agiad
king in 219 but was expelled (though this passage is the only evidence for it) by the Eurypontid king Lycurgus, who was not a
direct descendant of the Eurypontid line.

78 The meaning of *castellani* is unclear; Briscoe (2.92) argues
that they were only country dwellers and not, as one might expect,
"occupants of a fortress" (*OLD* sv *castellanus*). They are called

cutters, and an assortment of other craft of smaller dimensions. Large numbers of exiles from among the Spartans themselves, men who had been driven out by the injustice of the tyrants, also converged on the Roman camp in the hope of being restored to their native land. There were many of them; they had been driven out by one tyrant or another over the several generations[76] that the tyrants had held sway in Sparta. The leader of the exiles was Agesipolis, to whose family the throne of Sparta rightly belonged; he had been expelled in his infancy by the tyrant Lycurgus after the death of Cleomenes, who was the first tyrant of Sparta.[77]

27. Although such a great war on land and sea faced the tyrant on all sides, and although a realistic appraisal of his own and his enemy's forces showed that he had practically no hope of victory, he nevertheless did not abandon the fight. He sent for 1,000 elite warriors from Crete (he already had 1,000) and he also had under arms 3,000 mercenaries and 10,000 of his own countrymen, along with a number of the inhabitants of the rural towns;[78] and he also fortified the town with a ditch and a rampart. To prevent any internal upheaval, he cowed people's spirits by intimidation and callous punishments as he could not expect them to wish a tyrant well.

Since he harbored suspicions about some of his compatriots, Nabis led all his troops out into the plain (local people call it the Dromos)[79] and, ordering the Spartan citizens to be summoned to a meeting after laying down

helots below (*Ilotarum:* §9), but helots in the classical period were not armed, as these clearly were.

[79] Greek Δρόμος (running course).

6 eorum contioni satellites armatos circumdedit. et pauca
praefatus cur sibi omnia timenti caventique ignoscendum
in tali tempore foret, et ipsorum referre, si quos suspectos
status praesens rerum faceret, prohiberi potius ne quid
7 moliri possint quam puniri molientes; itaque quosdam se
in custodia habiturum donec ea quae instet tempestas
praetereat; hostibus repulsis—a quibus, si modo proditio
intestina satis caveatur, minus periculi esse—extemplo eos
emissurum.

8    Sub haec citari nomina octoginta ferme principum
iuventutis iussit, atque eos, ut quisque ad nomen re-
sponderat, in custodiam tradidit: nocte insequenti omnes
9 interfecti. Ilotarum deinde quidam—hi sunt iam inde
antiquitus castellani, agreste genus,—transfugere voluisse
insimulati, per omnes vicos sub verberibus acti necantur.
hoc terrore obstipuerant multitudinis animi ab omni
10 conatu novorum consiliorum. intra munitiones copias continebat, nec parem se ratus, si dimicare acie vellet, et urbem relinquere tam suspensis et incertis omnium animis
metuens.

   28. Quinctius, satis iam omnibus paratis profectus ab
stativis, die altero ad Sellasiam super Oenunta fluvium
pervenit, quo in loco Antigonus Macedonum rex cum

----

80 Helots appear in Latin only here and in Cornelius Nepos
(*Paus.* 3.6). Livy clearly knows little about them as serfs in Laconia and Messenia in the classical period. Whether they still
existed as such in Nabis' time is uncertain (Livy seems to be suggesting that they did in his own time).

their weapons, he threw a cordon of armed attendants around their gathering. He then made a few prefatory remarks, explaining why in the circumstances he should be pardoned for fearing everything and taking all manner of precautions—it was in their own best interests, he said, that any people whom the present crisis rendered suspect should be prevented from mutinous activity rather than punished later for engaging in it. He was therefore going to hold a number of people in custody until the storm that threatened them passed; when their enemies were repelled—and these would pose less of a threat if only sufficient precaution could be taken against internal treachery—he would immediately release them.

With that the tyrant ordered the names of about eighty prominent young Spartans to be read aloud and as each answered to his name had him put under lock and key. During the oncoming night they were all put to death. Next a number of the Ilotae (these are a rustic people, living in the country from early times)[80] were accused of planning to desert and were executed after being driven through all the streets with lashes. Through intimidation of this kind Nabis had paralyzed the spirit of the masses, effectively deterring them from any attempt at revolution. He also kept his forces confined to their fortifications: he thought himself no match for the enemy if he wished to decide the issue in the field, and he was also afraid to leave the city when the general mood was so volatile and unstable.

28. When all was now satisfactorily prepared Quinctius set out from his base camp and the following day reached Sellasia on the River Oenus, the place where the Macedonian king Antigonus was said to have fought a pitched

Cleomene Lacedaemoniorum tyranno signis conlatis di-
2 micasse dicebatur. inde cum audisset descensum difficilis
et artae viae esse, brevi per montes circuitu praemissis qui
munirent viam, lato satis et patenti limite ad Eurotam
3 amnem, sub ipsis prope fluentem moenibus, pervenit. ubi
castra metantes Romanos Quinctiumque ipsum cum equitibus atque expeditis praegressum auxiliares tyranni adorti
in terrorem ac tumultum coniecerunt, nihil tale exspectantes quia nemo iis obvius toto itinere fuerat ac veluti
4 pacato agro transierant. aliquamdiu peditibus equites
equitibus pedites vocantibus, cum in se cuique minimum
fiduciae esset, trepidatum est; tandem signa legionum
5 supervenerunt, et cum primi agminis cohortes inductae in
proelium essent, qui modo terrori fuerant trepidantes in
6 urbem compulsi sunt. Romani cum tantum a muro reces-
sissent ut extra ictum teli essent, acie derecta paulisper
steterunt; postquam nemo hostium contra exibat, redierunt in castra.

7 Postero die Quinctius prope flumen praeter urbem sub
ipsas Menelai montis radices ducere copias instructas pergit: primae legionariae cohortes ibant, levis armatura et
8 equites agmen cogebant. Nabis intra murum instructos
paratosque sub signis habebat mercenarios milites, in
quibus omnis fiducia erat, ut ab tergo hostem adgredere-
9 tur. postquam extremum[25] agmen praeteriit, tum ab op-

---

[25] extremum χ: postremum B

---

[81] Sellasia, R. Oinous: *Barr.* 58 C3. Cleomenes III was defeated here by Antigonos III Doson in 222.

battle with the Spartan tyrant Cleomenes.[81] Told that the way down from here was by a difficult and narrow path, he sent men ahead by a short detour through the mountains to construct a road and arrived, now by way of a quite broad and open route, at the River Eurotas, which flows practically at the foot of the city walls. When the Romans were laying out the camp and Quinctius had himself gone ahead with the cavalry and light-armed troops, the tyrant's auxiliary forces attacked them, throwing them into panic and consternation (they had not been expecting any such thing since, for the whole length of the march, they had come across no one and had passed through what seemed like peaceful countryside). For some time there was confusion as infantry appealed for help from cavalry and cavalry from infantry, neither having much confidence in its own capabilities. Eventually the legionary standards came on the scene, and when the cohorts at the head of the column were brought into the fray the men who moments earlier had been causing the alarm were driven back in terror into the city. The Romans moved back from the wall far enough to be out of javelin range and for a short while stood there in a properly ordered line. When no enemy ventured forth against them they returned to camp.

The following day Quinctius proceeded to lead his troops, drawn up in battle order, along the river and past the city toward the foot of Mount Menelaus; the legionary cohorts were at the front and the light armed and cavalry brought up the rear of the column. Nabis kept his mercenaries—in whom all his confidence lay—within the wall, drawn up and ready for action under their standards, his intention being to make an attack on the enemy from the rear. After the end of the column had passed, these burst

pido eodem quo pridie eruperant tumultu pluribus simul
10 locis erumpunt. Ap. Claudius agmen cogebat; qui ad id
quod futurum erat, ne necopinatum accideret, praeparatis
suorum animis, signa extemplo convertit totumque in hos-
11 tem agmen circumegit. itaque, velut rectae acies concurrissent, iustum aliquamdiu proelium fuit. tandem Nabidis
milites in fugam inclinarunt; quae minus trepida[26] fuisset
ni Achaei locorum prudentes institissent. ii et caedem ingentem ediderunt, et dispersos passim fuga plerosque
12 armis exuerunt. Quinctius prope Amyclas posuit castra;
unde cum perpopulatus omnia circumiecta urbi frequen-
tis et amoeni agri loca esset, nullo iam hostium porta ex-
cedente castra movit ad fluvium Eurotam. inde vallem
Taygeto subiectam agrosque ad mare pertinentes evastat.

29. Eodem fere tempore L. Quinctius maritimae orae
2 oppida partim voluntate partim metu aut vi recepit. certior deinde factus Gytheum oppidum omnium maritima-
rum rerum Lacedaemoniis receptaculum esse, nec procul
a mari castra Romana abesse, omnibus id copiis adgredi
3 constituit. erat eo tempore valida urbs, et multitudine ci-
4 vium incolarumque et omni bellico apparatu instructa. in
tempore Quinctio rem haud facilem adgredienti rex Eu-
5 menes et classis Rhodiorum supervenerunt. ingens multi-

---

[26] trepida *B*χ: infesta ac trepida *M. Müller*: *alii alia*

---

[82] Ap. Claudius Pulcher (294). He was later praetor (188 or
187: cf. *MRR* 367, n. 1) and consul (185).

[83] South of Sparta and west of the Eurotas: *Barr.* 58 C3.

[84] Gytheion, in the Mani: *Barr.* 58 D4.

forth from the town at several points simultaneously and with the same frenzy as they had the previous day. Appius Claudius[82] was bringing up the rear; and he had his men mentally prepared for what was likely to happen so it would not catch them unawares, and now he immediately wheeled around, bringing his entire column to face the enemy. Thus, for a time, there was a regular engagement, just as if two lines in battle formation had clashed, but finally Nabis' men turned to flee, which might have involved less panic had not the Achaeans, who knew the ground, maintained pressure on them. The Achaeans inflicted enormous casualties, and also deprived most of the enemy of their weapons as they scattered in flight in every direction. Quinctius pitched camp close to Amyclae,[83] from which point he conducted devastating raids on all the well-populated and attractive country areas around the city, and when none of the enemy now ventured forth from the gate he moved camp to the River Eurotas. He then laid waste the valley below Taygetus and the fields stretching down to the sea.

29. At about the same time Lucius Quinctius accepted the surrender of towns along the coastline, some of whom capitulated voluntarily, others after intimidation or under duress. Then, being informed that the town of Gytheum[84] served the Spartans as a depot for all their naval supplies, and that the Roman camp lay not far from the sea, he decided to attack the town with all his forces. At that time Gytheum was a powerful city, home to a large population of citizens and resident foreigners, and well furnished with all manner of military equipment. Quinctius was embarking on this difficult venture when King Eumenes and the Rhodian fleet made a timely arrival on the scene. A huge

tudo navalium sociorum, e tribus contracta classibus, intra
paucos dies omnia quae ad oppugnationem urbis terra
6  marique munitae facienda opera erant effecit, iam testudinibus admotis murus subruebatur, iam arietibus quatie-
batur. itaque una crebris ictibus eversa est turris, quodque
7  circa muri erat casu eius prostratum; et Romani simul a
portu, unde aditus planior erat, ut distenderent ab aper-
tiore loco hostes, simul per patefactum ruina iter inrum-
8  pere conabantur. nec multum afuit quin qua intenderant
penetrarent; sed tardavit impetum eorum spes obiecta
dedendae urbis, mox deinde eadem turbata.

Dexagoridas et Gorgopas pari imperio praeerant urbi.
9  Dexagoridas miserat ad legatum Romanum traditurum se
urbem; et cum ad eam rem tempus et ratio convenisset, a
Gorgopa proditor interficitur, intentiusque ab uno urbs
10  defendebatur. et difficilior facta oppugnatio erat ni T.
Quinctius cum quattuor milibus delectorum militum su-
11  pervenisset. is cum supercilio haud procul distantis tumuli
ab urbe instructam aciem ostendisset, et ex altera parte L.
12  Quinctius ab operibus suis terra marique instaret, tum
vero desperatio Gorgopan quoque cogit id consilii quod in
13  altero morte vindicaverat capere, et pactus ut abducere
inde milites quos praesidii causa habebat liceret, tradit[27]

---

[27] tradit $B\chi$: tradidit $a$

[85] Cf. 31.39.14 and note.

force of sailors drawn from three fleets completed in a matter of days all the preparations that had to be made for an assault upon a city defended by land and sea. The tortoise formations[85] were brought up, and soon a start was made on undermining the wall, which was also pounded by the battering rams. One of the towers was demolished by the repeated blows and by its collapse the adjacent section of the wall was also brought down. The Romans thereupon attempted to break through from the direction of the harbor (from which access lay along more even ground) in order to divert the enemy from more vulnerable spots and at the same time to burst in where a path had been opened up by the breach. They were not far from gaining entry at the designated point, but their momentum was slowed when they were offered hope of the city's surrender, a hope that was soon frustrated.

Dexagoridas and Gorgopas had joint command of the city. Dexagoridas had sent word to the Roman legate that he would deliver the town. Then, after the timing and procedure for this had been settled, the traitor was killed by Gorgopas and the city was defended with greater energy by the one commander. In fact, the assault on Gytheum would have been more difficult had not Titus Quinctius appeared with 4,000 elite troops. When he had exposed his battle line to view drawn up on the brow of a hill not far distant from the city, while on the other side Lucius Quinctius was piling on the pressure from his siege works on land and sea, desperation then obliged Gorgopas also to adopt the strategy for which he had actually punished the other commander with death. After striking a bargain to be allowed to take away the soldiers he had there serving as a garrison, he delivered the city to Quinc-

14  Quinctio urbem. priusquam Gytheum traderetur, Pythagoras praefectus Argis relictus, tradita custodia urbis Ti-
mocrati Pellenensi, cum mille mercennariis militibus et
duobus milibus Argivorum Lacedaemonem ad Nabim venit.

30. Nabis sicut primo adventu Romanae classis et traditione oppidorum maritimae orae conterritus erat, sic
2  parva spe cum acquievisset Gytheo ab suis retento, postquam id quoque traditum Romanis audivit esse, et[28] cum
ab terra omnibus circa hostilibus[29] nihil spei esset, a mari
3  quoque toto se interclusum, cedendum fortunae ratus,
caduceatorem primum in castra misit ad explorandum si
4  paterentur legatos ad se mitti. qua impetrata re Pythagoras
ad imperatorem venit nullis cum aliis mandatis quam ut
5  tyranno conloqui cum imperatore liceret. consilio advo-
cato cum omnes dandum conloquium censuissent, dies
6  locusque constituitur. in mediae regionis tumulos modicis
copiis sequentibus cum venissent, relictis ibi in statione
7  conspecta utrimque cohortibus, Nabis cum delectis custodibus corporis, Quinctius cum fratre et Eumene rege et
Sosila Rhodio et Aristaeno Achaeo[30] tribunisque militum
paucis descendit.

31. Ibi permisso seu dicere prius seu audire mallet, ita
coepit tyrannus: "si ipse per me, T. Quincti vosque qui
adestis, causam excogitare cur mihi aut indixissetis bellum

[28] esse et *Drak.*: esse *B*χ

[29] hostilibus *Gron.*: hostibus *B*χ

[30] Achaeo *BNL*: Achaeo tribunis *V*: Achaeorum tribunis φ:
Achaeorum praetore *Holk. 353*

---

[86] Nabis' son-in-law: cf. 25.5, above.

tius. Before the surrender of Gytheum, Pythagoras,[86] who had been left as commander in Argos, consigned safekeeping of the city to Timocrates of Pellene and came to Nabis in Sparta at the head of 1,000 mercenaries and 2,000 Argives.

30. While Nabis had been panic-stricken by the first arrival of the Roman fleet and the capitulation of the towns along the coast, he could still feel some slight reassurance as long as Gytheum had remained in the hands of his troops. When he heard that this, too, had been delivered to the Romans and that, in addition to having no hope on land (everything around him being under enemy occupation), he had also been entirely cut off from the sea, he, thinking he should yield to fortune, first sent a message to the Roman camp to explore the possibility of his enemies allowing a delegation to be sent to them. When this was granted, Pythagoras came to the commander with no other instructions than to gain permission for the tyrant to parley with the commander. A meeting was called and, as there was unanimous agreement that Nabis be allowed to parley, a date and venue were arranged. The two leaders came to some hills in the country that lay between them with a few troops in attendance. Here they left their cohorts on guard in plain sight of each other and came down to the meeting. Nabis was accompanied by a select group of bodyguards, Quinctius by his brother and by King Eumenes, Sosilas the Rhodian, Aristaenus the Achaean and a few military tribunes.

31. Given the choice there of speaking first or listening, the tyrant opened the proceedings as follows:

"Titus Quinctius and all here present: If I could on my own work out the reason for your having declared war on

aut inferretis possem, tacitus eventum fortunae meae ex-
2 spectassem: nunc imperare animo nequivi quin prius-
3 quam perirem, cur periturus essem scirem. et hercules, si
tales essetis quales esse Carthaginienses fama est, apud
quos nihil societatis fides sancti haberet, in me quoque
4 vobis quid faceretis minus pensi esse non mirarer. nunc
cum vos intueor, Romanos esse video, qui rerum divina-
rum foedera, humanarum fidem socialem sanctissimam
5 habeatis; cum me ipse respexi, eum me[31] esse spero cui et
publice, sicut ceteris Lacedaemoniis, vobiscum vetustissimum foedus sit, et meo nomine privatim amicitia ac societas, nuper Philippi bello renovata.

6    "At enim ego eam violavi et everti, quod Argivorum
7 civitatem teneo. quomodo hoc tuear? re an tempore? res
mihi duplicem defensionem praebet; nam et ipsis vocantibus ac tradentibus urbem eam accepi, non occupavi, et
accepi urbem cum Philippi partium non in vestra societate
8 esset. tempus autem eo me liberat, quod cum iam Argos
haberem, societas mihi vobiscum convenit, et ut vobis mit-
terem ad bellum auxilia, non ut Argis praesidium dedu-
9 cerem pepigistis. at hercule in ea controversia quae de

---

[31] eum me *Siesbye*: eum *B*χ: me eum *Madvig*

---

[87] The standard Roman assumption of Punic treachery and
dishonesty (proverbially, *Punica fides,* "Punic fidelity") is here
made by a Spartan. Whether it occurred in Polybius, missing at
this point, we cannot tell. See further Walbank 1.412.

[88] On the sanctity of treaties for Romans and the impiety involved in the breaking of them, cf. Levene 7.

[89] Flamininus denies this at the start of the next chapter, but
Nabis' claim has some merit; for details cf. Briscoe 2.98–99.

me or for your waging it now, then I should have quietly waited to see what fate had in store for me. As it is, I have been unable to suppress a longing to know before being destroyed just why I am to be destroyed. Why, if you were the sort of people the Carthaginians are reputed to be, a people for whom there is nothing sacred about an oath of alliance,[87] then I should not be surprised at lack of concern on your part about how you deal with me, too. As it is, when I look at you, I see that you are Romans, men who reportedly hold treaties as the most inviolable of things in the divine sphere, and good faith with one's allies as the most inviolable in the human.[88] When I look at myself, I hope I see a man who has enjoyed, along with all other Lacedaemonians, a treaty of great antiquity with you on the public level, and who on the private level has also enjoyed a personal relationship of friendship and alliance with you, which was recently renewed in the war with Philip.[89]

"But, you will say, I have violated and destroyed this relationship by holding on to the state of Argos. How am I to defend myself against this charge? By appealing to the facts of the case or to the timing? The facts offer me two lines of defense. It was a matter of my accepting the city, not seizing it—the inhabitants actually appealed to me and offered it to me—and I accepted it when it was on Philip's side and not in alliance with you. The timing also exonerates me because my alliance with you was forged at a point when I was still in possession of Argos, and your stipulation was that I should send you auxiliary forces for your campaign, not remove my garrison from Argos. Why, as far as the Argive question goes, I have the edge both from

Argis est superior sum et aequitate rei, quod non vestram
10 urbem sed hostium, quod volentem non vi coactam accepi, et vestra confessione, quod in condicionibus societatis Argos mihi reliquistis.

11 "Ceterum nomen tyranni et facta me premunt, quod
servos ad libertatem uoco, quod in agros inopem plebem
12 deduco. de nomine hoc respondere possum, me, qualis-
cumque sum, eundem esse qui fui cum tu ipse mecum, T.
13 Quincti, societatem pepigisti. tum me regem appellari a
vobis memini: nunc tyrannum vocari video. itaque si ego
nomen imperii mutassem, mihi meae inconstantiae, cum
14 vos mutetis, vobis vestrae reddenda ratio est. quod ad multitudinem servis liberandis auctam et egentibus divisum
agrum attinet, possum quidem et in hoc me iure temporis
15 tutari: iam feceram haec, qualiacumque sunt, cum societatem mecum pepigistis et auxilia in bello adversus Philip-
16 pum accepistis; sed si nunc ea fecissem, non dico 'quid in
eo vos laesissem aut vestram amicitiam violassem?' sed
17 illud, me more atque instituto maiorum fecisse. nolite ad
vestras leges atque instituta exigere ea quae Lacedaemone
fiunt. nihil comparare singula necesse est. vos a censu
equitem a censu peditem legitis, et paucos excellere opi-
18 bus, plebem subiectam esse illis voltis: noster legum lator

---

90 The history of Roman political institutions is obscure. Many
were attributed to Servius Tullius, the penultimate king (traditionally, 578–535), though most probably belong to the fourth
century. But the argument here is specious in any case, as the
Spartan (Lycurgan) system, to which Nabis refers, rested on suppression of the helots and Messenians.

the equity of the case—I accepted a city that was in the enemy's hands, not yours, one that came to me of its own volition, not under duress—and also from your own admission, in that you left Argos to me in the terms of our treaty.

"But what weighs against me is the title 'tyrant' and my record of summoning slaves to freedom and settling destitute common people on the land. Regarding the title, I can make this point in response: whatever my qualities, I am the same man that I was, Titus Quinctius, when you yourself concluded the treaty with me. At that time, as I remember, I was addressed as 'king' by you, and now I see I am called 'tyrant.' In fact, had I myself altered the title that gives me power, I should have been obliged to account for my inconsistency; since it is you who are changing it, you must account for yours. As for my increasing the numbers of the proletariat by freeing slaves and distributing land to the impoverished, I can in fact use the plea of timing to defend myself on that score, too. These measures, whatever one thinks of them, I had already taken by the time you concluded the treaty with me and accepted my assistance in the war against Philip. But if I had taken them only recently, I would not be saying to you 'How could I have harmed you or violated the treaty with you by that?' but rather I should be arguing that I acted in accordance with the ways and institutions of our ancestors. Do not gauge what happens in Lacedaemon by the measure of your own laws and institutions.[90] There is no need for a detailed comparison between the two. You choose your cavalry and your infantry by assessment of wealth, and you want a few to be preeminent for their riches, and the common people to be subject to these. Our

511

non in paucorum manu rem publicam esse voluit, quem vos senatum appellatis, nec excellere unum aut alterum ordinem in civitate, sed per aequationem fortunae ac dignitatis fore credidit ut multi essent qui arma pro patria ferrent.

19     "Pluribus memet ipse egisse quam pro patria sermonis brevitate fateor; et breviter peroratum esse potuit nihil me, postquam vobiscum institui amicitiam, cur eius vos paeniteret commisisse."

32. Ad haec imperator Romanus: "amicitia et societas nobis nulla tecum, sed cum Pelope, rege Lacedaemonio-
2  rum iusto ac legitimo, facta est, cuius ius tyranni quoque, qui postea per vim tenuerunt Lacedaemone imperium, quia nos bella nunc Punica nunc Gallica nunc alia ex aliis occupaverant, usurparunt, sicut tu quoque hoc Macedo-
3  nico bello fecisti. nam quid minus conveniret quam eos qui pro libertate Graeciae adversus Philippum gereremus bellum cum tyranno instituere amicitiam? et tyranno si qui unquam fuit[32] saevissimo et violentissimo in suos?
4  nobis vero, etiamsi Argos nec cepisses per fraudem nec teneres, liberantibus omnem Graeciam Lacedaemon quoque vindicanda in antiquam libertatem erat, atque in leges

---

[32] si qui unquam fuit *Briscoe*: quam qui unquam fuit *B*: *sic, sed om.* fuit χ: qui unquam fuit *Madvig*

---

[91] Lycurgus, the (possibly legendary) figure to whom the Spartans ascribed their laws and constitution.

[92] The famous Spartan "laconicism."

[93] Son of the tyrant Lycurgus (cf. 26.14, above), Pelops could not be called a "rightful and legitimate king." As Briscoe (2.101) notes, this could hardly have stood in Polybius.

lawgiver[91] did not want the state to rest in the hands of a few—in a body you call the senate—and he did not want one or another class to be preeminent within the community. Instead he believed that a leveling of affluence and rank would result in many men bearing arms for the fatherland.

"I have, I confess, spoken at greater length than is in keeping with our native brevity,[92] and a brief summing-up could have gone as follows: since entering my compact of friendship with you, I have done nothing to make you regret it."

32. To this the Roman general replied: "Our treaty of friendship and alliance was made not with you but with Pelops, rightful and legitimate king of the Spartans,[93] whose title to the throne the tyrants usurped. These men went on to hold power in Lacedaemon by force because we were preoccupied with wars—with Carthage at one time, with Gaul at another, and then with a succession of other nations just as you, too, have held on to your power because of this recent war with Macedon. What, I ask you, could be more incongruous than that we, a people who fought a war against Philip for the freedom of Greece, should enter into a compact of friendship with a tyrant? And with a tyrant who has been the most ruthless and violent ever toward his own people? Even if you had not taken Argos by duplicity and were not now occupying it, we should still have been obliged as liberators of all of Greece to restore Sparta, too, to her ancient liberty and to her own laws—the laws that you mentioned a moment ago

suas, quarum modo tamquam aemulus Lycurgi menti-
5  onem fecisti. an ut ab Iaso et Bargyliis praesidia Philippi
deducantur curae erit nobis, Argos et Lacedaemonem,
duas clarissimas urbes, lumina quondam Graeciae, sub
pedibus tuis relinquemus, quae titulum nobis liberatae
6  Graeciae servientes deforment? at enim cum Philippo
Argivi senserunt. remittimus hoc tibi, ne nostram vicem
irascaris. satis compertum habemus duorum aut summum
7  trium in ea re, non civitatis culpam esse, tam hercule
quam in te tuoque praesidio arcessendo accipiendoque in
8  arcem nihil esse[33] publico consilio actum. Thessalos et
Phocenses et Locrenses consensu omnium scimus partium Philippi fuisse, tamen cum cetera liberavimus Graecia: quid tandem censes in Argivis, qui insontes publici
consilii sint, facturos?

9     "Servorum ad libertatem vocatorum et egentibus hominibus agri divisi crimina tibi obici dicebas, non quidem
nec ipsa mediocria; sed quid ista sunt prae iis quae a te
10  tuisque cotidie alia super alia facinora eduntur? exhibe
liberam contionem vel Argis vel Lacedaemone, si audire
11  iuvat vera dominationis impotentissimae crimina. ut alia
omnia vetustiora omittam, quam caedem Argis Pythagoras
iste, gener tuus, paene in oculis meis edidit? quam tu ipse,
12  cum iam prope in finibus Lacedaemoniorum essem? age-
dum, quos in contione comprehensos omnibus audienti-
bus civibus tuis te in custodia habiturum esse pronuntiasti,

---

[33] esse *Asc.*: sit χ: si in *B*: est *Hertz*

---

[94] The lawgiver, of course, not the tyrant.
[95] Cf. 25.11–12, above.
[96] Cf. 27.8–9, above.

as if you were trying to rival Lycurgus![94] Are we going
to see that Philip's garrisons are withdrawn from Iasus
and Bargyliae and then leave under your feet Argos and
Sparta, two illustrious cities that were once the shining
lights of Greece, so that by their subjugation they may
sully our reputation as liberators of Greece? But the Argives sympathized with Philip, you will say. We release you
from the obligation to be angry with them on our behalf!
We have it on good authority that two or at most three
people were to blame in this affair, not the whole city—in
the same way (for God's sake!) that in the case of inviting
and welcoming you and your garrison into the citadel no
action was officially sanctioned. We know that the Thessalians, Phocians, and Locrians sided with Philip with the
agreement of all their respective peoples, and yet we have
liberated them along with the rest of Greece. So what on
earth do you think we are going to do in the case of the
Argives, who are innocent of giving public authorization
in this matter?

"You said that you were accused of summoning slaves
to liberty and distributing land to the poor, which are of
themselves not inconsequential charges; but what are they
compared with the crimes committed one after the other,
day after day, by you and your supporters? Convene a free
assembly in either Argos or Sparta if you want to hear
genuine charges made against a brutal dictatorship. To
pass over all the other, older, atrocities, think of the blood
bath that the infamous Pythagoras, your son-in-law, created at Argos, almost before my own eyes.[95] Or the one for
which you yourself were responsible when I was almost on
the borders of Lacedaemon.[96] Come on, have those prisoners brought out—the ones you arrested at the assembly
when, in the hearing of all your fellow citizens, you pro-

515

iube vinctos produci: miseri parentes quos falso lugent
13  vivere sciant. at enim, ut iam ita sint haec, quid ad vos,
Romani? hoc tu dicas liberantibus Graeciam? hoc iis qui
ut liberare possent mare traiecerunt, terra marique gesserunt bellum?

14      "'Vos tamen' inquis 'vestramque amicitiam ac societatem proprie non violavi.' quotiens vis te id arguam fecisse?
15  sed nolo pluribus: summam rem complectar. quibus igitur
rebus amicitia violatur? nempe his maxime duabus, si socios meos pro hostibus habeas, si cum hostibus te coniun-
16  gas. utrumque a te factum est; nam et Messenen, uno
atque eodem iure foederis quo et Lacedaemonem in amicitiam nostram acceptam, socius ipse sociam nobis urbem
17  vi atque armis cepisti, et cum Philippo, hoste nostro, non
societatem solum sed, si dis placet, adfinitatem etiam per
18  Philoclen praefectum eius pepigisti, et ut bellum adversus
nos gerens, mare circa Maleum infestum navibus piraticis
fecisti, et plures prope cives Romanos quam Philippus
19  cepisti atque occidisti, tutiorque Macedoniae ora quam
promunturium Maleae commeatus ad exercitus nostros
portantibus navibus fuit.

20      "Proinde parce, sis, fidem ac iura societatis iactare, et
omissa populari oratione tamquam tyrannus et hostis lo-
quere."

33. Sub haec Aristaenus nunc monere Nabim nunc

---

97 Both Nabis and the Messenians were listed as Roman allies
in the Peace of Phoenice (29.12.14).

98 For Philocles and the "family bond" alluded to here, cf.
32.38.3, but whether any such bond was actually forged by marriage is not known.

claimed that you would keep them in custody. Let their poor parents know that the sons for whom they mistakenly grieve are still alive! But, you will say, supposing that all this is true, what business is it of yours, Romans? Can you say such a thing to the people who are liberating Greece? Would you say such a thing to men who have crossed the sea achieve this liberation, men who have waged war on land and sea?

"'But,' you say, 'strictly speaking, I have been guilty of no violation in your case or in my pact of friendship and my alliance with you.' How many instances do you want me to cite where you *have* been guilty? But I do not wish to go on at length. Let me sum up the whole thing. What are instances of violation of friendship? Surely there are these two above all: if you treat my allies as enemies and if you join my enemies. Both of these things you have done. Messene was welcomed into an alliance with us with exactly the same treaty rights as Sparta, and you, an ally yourself, captured by force of arms this city that was allied to us.[97] Moreover, you not only concluded a treaty with our enemy Philip but—for heaven's sake!—you even established a family bond with him through his prefect Philocles.[98] As though you were waging war on us, you made the waters off Maleum a dangerous area for us with your pirate vessels and you captured and killed almost more Roman citizens than Philip did; and the shoreline of Macedonia was actually safer than the Malean promontory for ships transporting supplies to our armies!

"So please refrain from bandying about the words 'loyalty' and 'treaty rights.' Cut out this demagogic speechifying and talk like a tyrant and our enemy."

33. Immediately after this Aristaenus proceeded to al-

etiam orare, ut dum liceret dum occasio esset, sibi ac for-
2 tunis suis consuleret; referre deinde nominatim tyrannos
civitatium finitimarum coepit, qui deposito imperio resti-
tutaque libertate suis non tutam modo sed etiam honora-
3 tam inter cives senectutem egissent. his dictis in vicem
auditisque nox prope diremit conloquium.

Postero die Nabis Argis se cedere ac deducere praesidium, quando ita Romanis placeret, et captivos et perfugas
4 redditurum dixit; aliud si quid postularent, scriptum ut
5 ederent petiit, ut deliberare cum amicis posset. ita et tyranno tempus datum ad consultandum est, et Quinctius,
sociorum etiam principibus adhibitis, habuit consilium.
6 maximae partis sententia erat perseverandum in bello esse
et tollendum tyrannum: nunquam aliter tutam libertatem
7 Graeciae fore; satius multo fuisse non moveri bellum ad-
8 versus eum quam omitti motum; et ipsum velut compro-
bata dominatione firmiorem futurum, auctore iniusti imperii adsumpto populo Romano, et exemplo multos in aliis
civitatibus ad insidiandum libertati civium suorum incita-
turum.

9 Ipsius imperatoris animus ad pacem inclinatior erat.
videbat enim compulso intra moenia hoste nihil praeter
10 obsidionem restare, eam autem fore[34] diuturnam; non
enim Gytheum, quod ipsum tamen traditum non expug-
natum esset, sed Lacedaemonem, validissimam urbem

[34] fore *Par. 5741*: fore et *B*χ: lentam fore et *Weiss.*: ancipitem
fore et *M. Müller*

ternate warnings and pleas to Nabis to take thought for his position and his circumstances while it was still possible and he had the opportunity. He next began to list by name tyrants of neighboring city-states who had laid down their power and restored liberty to their people, and then gone on to spend their old age among their fellow citizens not just in security but with honor. After this interchange of speeches, the discussion broke off just before nightfall.

The following day Nabis said that he was leaving Argos and withdrawing his garrison, since such was the Romans' pleasure, and that he would return prisoners and deserters. He requested that they give him in writing any further demands they had so that he could discuss them with his friends. Thus the tyrant was granted time to think things over and Quinctius held a meeting to which the leaders of the allies were also invited. The majority opinion was that they should press ahead with the war and remove the tyrant. In no other way would the freedom of Greece be assured, they said, and not to have started a war against him in the first place would have been far preferable to abandoning it once it had begun. With his tyranny virtually given approval, Nabis would be in a stronger position through having gained the support of the Roman people for his lawless rule; and by the precedent set he would incite many in other city-states to scheme against the liberty of their fellow citizens.

The Roman commander's feelings inclined rather toward peace. He could see that after the enemy was driven back within his walls there was no alternative to a siege, and that would take a long time as it would not be Gytheum that they would be besieging—and even this had been delivered to them, not captured—but Sparta, which

11   viris armisque, oppugnaturos. unam spem fuisse si qua
admoventibus exercitum dissensio inter ipsos ac seditio
excitari posset: cum signa portis prope inferri cernerent,
12   neminem se movisse. adiciebat et cum Antiocho infidam
pacem Villium legatum inde redeuntem nuntiare: multo
maioribus quam ante terrestribus navalibusque copiis in
13   Europam eum transisse. si occupasset obsidio Lacedaemonis exercitum, quibus aliis copiis adversus regem tam
14   validum ac potentem bellum gesturos? haec propalam
dicebat: illa tacita suberat cura ne novus consul Graeciam
provinciam sortiretur, et incohata belli victoria successori
tradenda esset.

     34. Cum adversus tendendo nihil moveret socios, si-
mulando se transire in eorum sententiam omnes in adsen-
sum consilii sui traduxit.

2    "Bene vertat" inquit, "obsideamus Lacedaemonem,
quando ita placet. ceterum[35] cum res tam lenta quam ipsi
scitis oppugnatio urbium sit, et obsidentibus prius saepe
quam obsessis taedium adferat, iam nunc hoc ita propo-
nere vos animis oportet, hibernandum circa Lacedaemo-
3   nis moenia esse. quae mora si laborem tantum ac periculum haberet, ut et animis et corporibus ad sustinenda ea
4   parati essetis hortarer vos; nunc impensa quoque magna
eget in opera, in machinationes et tormenta quibus tanta
urbs oppugnanda est, in commeatus vobis nobisque in hie-

---

[35] ceterum *Bχ*: illud modo ne fallat ceterum *Mg*: illud modo
ne fallat *Madvig*

had great strength in manpower and weaponry. There had been one hope, he said, and that was the possibility of internal conflict and dispute being stirred up among the Spartans as the Romans brought up their forces; but when they saw the standards brought up almost to their gates, no one had reacted. He added that Villius, returning from an embassy to the king, reported that the peace with Antiochus was precarious—the king had crossed to Europe with larger land and sea forces than before. If a blockade of Sparta tied up his army, what other troops would Flamininus use for a war against so great and powerful a king? Such were the arguments he used openly; but there also lurked in his mind a secret concern, namely that the new consul might receive the province of Greece by sortition and he, Flamininus, would be obliged to pass on to his successor a military victory on which he had made a start.

34. When he made no impression on the allies with the opposing case, Flamininus brought them to accept his strategy by pretending to go over to their view.

"May it turn out well," he said. "Let us lay siege to Sparta, since this is your decision. But blockading cities is a long process, as you yourselves know, and one that often exasperates the besiegers before the besieged. You should therefore get this into your minds right now: you have to spend the winter around the walls of Sparta. If spending that interval here involved only hardship and danger, I would be giving you encouragement to prepare yourselves mentally and physically to bear them. As it is, though, considerable expense is required for siege works, for engines and catapults needed for an assault on a city of such a size, and for acquiring provisions for the winter

5   mem expediendos. itaque, ne aut repente trepidetis aut
rem incohatam turpiter destituatis, scribendum ante vestris civitatibus censeo, explorandumque quid quaeque
6   animi quid virium habeat. auxiliorum satis superque ha-
beo; sed quo plures sumus, pluribus rebus egebimus. nihil
iam praeter nudum solum ager hostium habet: ad hoc
hiemps accedet ad comportandum ex longinquo difficilis."
7      Haec oratio primum animos omnium ad respicienda
sua cuiusque[36] domestica mala convertit, segnitiam invi-
diam et obtrectationem domi manentium adversus mili-
8   tantes, libertatem difficilem ad consensum, inopiam pu-
9   blicam, malignitatem conferendi ex privato. versis itaque
subito voluntatibus, faceret quod e re publica populi Romani sociorumque esse crederet imperatori permiserunt.

     35. Inde Quinctius, adhibitis legatis tantum tribunis-
que militum, condiciones in quas pax cum tyranno fieret
2   has conscripsit: sex mensium indutiae ut essent Nabidi
Romanisque et Eumeni regi et Rhodiis; legatos extemplo
mitterent Romam T. Quinctius et Nabis, ut pax[37] auctori-
3   tate senatus confirmaretur; et qua die scriptae condiciones
pacis editae Nabidi forent, ea dies ut indutiarum principium esset, et ut ex ea die intra decimum diem ab Argis
ceterisque oppidis quae in Argivorum agro essent praesi-

[36] sua cuiusque *H.J.M.*: cuique *Bχ*: cuiusque *Briscoe*
[37] pax *Duker*: pax ex *Bχ*

for you and for us. So, to avoid any sudden anxieties on your part or the humiliating abandonment of an operation already started, I feel you should first write to your respective city-states and investigate each one's inclinations and strength. Of auxiliary forces I have enough and more than enough. But the greater our numbers, the more the provisions we shall need. Already, the countryside of the enemy has nothing to offer us but bare soil, and in addition winter will be coming on to make long-distance transportation difficult."

It was this speech that first turned everybody's attention to the problems each had in his own state: apathy, the jealousy and malice of those remaining at home toward men serving in the field, the individual liberty that made consensus difficult, lack of public funds, and the niggardliness of contributions from the private sector. And so, suddenly experiencing a change of heart, they allowed the Roman general to take whatever action he thought to be in the interests of the Roman people and their allies.

35. Then, convening a meeting limited to his officers and military tribunes, Quinctius drafted the following terms on which peace was to be made with the tyrant:

There was to be a six-month truce between Nabis on the one hand and the Romans, King Eumenes, and the Rhodians on the other.

Titus Quinctius and Nabis were both to send envoys immediately to Rome so that the peace could be ratified by senatorial authority.

The day marking the start of the truce was to be the day on which the drafted peace terms were issued to Nabis, and all garrisons were to be withdrawn from Argos and the other towns in Argive territory within ten days from that

4    dia omnia deducerentur, vacuaque et libera traderentur
Romanis, et ne quod inde mancipium regium publicumue
aut privatum educeretur: si qua ante educta forent, domi-
5    nis recte restituerentur;[38] naves quas civitatibus maritimis
ademisset redderet, neve ipse navem ullam praeter duos
lembos, qui non plus quam sedecim remis agerentur, ha-
6    beret; perfugas et captivos omnibus sociis populi Romani
civitatibus redderet, et Messeniis omnia quae compare-
7    rent quaeque domini cognossent; exsulibus quoque Lacedaemoniis liberos coniuges restitueret quae earum viros
8    sequi voluissent, inuita ne qua exsulis comes esset; mercennariorum militum Nabidis qui aut in civitates suas aut
ad Romanos transissent, iis res suae omnes recte redde-
9    rentur; in Creta insula ne quam urbem haberet, quas habuisset redderet Romanis; ne quam societatem cum ullo
Cretensium aut quoquam alio institueret neu bellum ge-
10   reret; civitatibus omnibus, quasque ipse restituisset quaeque se suaque in fidem ac dicionem populi Romani tradi-
dissent, omnia praesidia deduceret, seque ipse suosque ab

---

[38] si . . . restituerentur *M. Müller*: regium . . . educeretur si (et
si χ) qua ante educta forent dominis recte restituerentur *B*χ: si
qua publice aut privatim ante educta forent, dominis recte restituerentur *Mg*

---

[99] Not to Eumenes, as Sage has it, but to Nabis, to whom
Flamininus now refers as "king" rather than "tyrant."

day. These towns were to be handed over to the Romans free of troops and under no constraint, and with no slave removed, whether he belonged to the king,[99] the state, or an individual (and with any slaves formerly removed being duly restored to their owners).

Nabis was to return the vessels that he had appropriated from the coastal communities and himself retain no ship apart from two cutters that were propelled by no more than sixteen oars.

He was to restore deserters and prisoners of war to all city-states allied to the Roman people, and also give back to the Messenians any property that was found and its owners recognized.

He was also to return to exiled Spartans their children and wives, but only those wives willing to follow their husbands, with no woman involuntarily accompanying an exile.

All possessions were to be duly returned to mercenaries of Nabis who had deserted either to their own city-states or to the Romans.

Nabis was to hold no city on the island of Crete and was to hand over to the Romans those that he had occupied.

He was to enter into no alliance and wage no war with any of the peoples of Crete or any other people at all.

With respect to all the city-states that he himself had surrendered or had delivered themselves and their possessions to the protection and authority of the Roman people, Nabis was to withdraw all his garrisons from them, and keep his own hands, and those of his allies, off them in future.

11 iis abstineret; ne quod oppidum neu quod castellum in suo
alienove agro conderet; obsides ea ita futura daret quinque quos imperatori Romano placuisset, et filium in iis
suum, et talenta centum argenti in praesentia, quinquaginta talenta in singulos annos per annos octo.

36. Haec conscripta, castris propius urbem motis, Lacedaemonem mittuntur. nec sane quicquam eorum satis
2 placebat tyranno, nisi quod praeter spem reducendorum
exsulum mentio nulla facta erat; maxime autem omnium
ea res offendebat quod et naves et maritimae civitates
3 ademptae erant. fuerat autem ei magno fructui mare omnem oram a Maleo praedatoriis navibus infestam habenti;
iuventutem praeterea civitatium earum ad supplementum
longe optimi generis militum habebat.

4 Has condiciones quamquam ipse in secreto volutaverat
cum amicis, volgo tamen omnes fama ferebant, vanis ut ad
ceteram fidem sic ad secreta tegenda satellitum regiorum
5 ingeniis. non tam omnia universi quam ea quae ad quemque pertinerent singuli carpebant. qui exsulum coniuges
in matrimonio habebant aut ex bonis eorum aliquid pos-
sederant, tamquam amissuri non reddituri indignabantur.
6 servis liberatis a tyranno non inrita modo futura libertas,
sed multo foedior quam fuisset ante servitus redeuntibus
in iratorum dominorum potestatem ante oculos obversa-
7 batur. mercennarii milites et pretia militiae casura in pace
aegre ferebant, et reditum sibi nullum esse in civitates

---

100 His name was Armenes (cf. 52.9, below).
101 That is, his advisers.

He was to establish no town and no fortress on his own or other people's territory.

To guarantee implementation of these conditions, he was to supply five hostages of the Roman general's choosing, including his own son,[100] plus 100 talents of silver immediately and 50 talents every year for eight years.

36. These terms were drafted and delivered to Sparta after the camp had been moved closer to the city. Nothing in them pleased the tyrant very much apart from the fact that, contrary to his expectations, no mention was made of repatriating the exiles. But most galling of all was that his ships as well as his coastal cities had been taken from him. The sea had proved very lucrative for him: he had the entire coastline from Cape Malea at the mercy of his pirate vessels and, in addition, the men of military age from these city-states furnished him with supplementary troops of the highest quality.

Although he had discussed the terms with his friends[101] in secret, they nevertheless became the subject of general gossip, royal courtiers being by nature as unreliable in keeping secrets as they are in other areas of trust. But it was not so much that people as a whole criticized everything as that individuals criticized any that affected them personally. Those who had married the wives of exiles or appropriated some assets of exiles were resentful, as if they were going to lose property rather than return it. Slaves who had been freed by the tyrant pictured to themselves not only a forthcoming cancellation of their liberation but enslavement far more oppressive than it had been before since they would be returning to the authority of indignant masters. The mercenary troops were displeased that payment for their services would fall off in peacetime, and they also saw no chance of returning to their own city-

videbant, infensas non tyrannis magis quam satellitibus eorum.

37. Haec inter se primo circulos[39] serentes fremere;
2 deinde subito ad arma discurrerunt. quo tumultu cum per se satis inritatam multitudinem cerneret tyrannus, con-
3 tionem advocari iussit. ubi cum ea quae imperarentur ab Romanis exposuisset, et graviora atque indigniora quae- dam falso adfinxisset, et ad singula nunc ab universis nunc a partibus contionis acclamaretur, interrogavit quid se re-
4 spondere ad ea aut quid facere vellent. prope una voce omnes nihil responderi et bellum geri iusserunt; et pro se quisque, qualia multitudo solet, bonum animum habere et bene sperare iubentes, fortes fortunam adiuvare aiebant.
5 his vocibus incitatus tyrannus et Antiochum Aetolosque adiuturos pronuntiat, et sibi ad obsidionem sustinendam copiarum adfatim esse.
6 Exciderat pacis mentio ex omnium animis, et in sta- tiones non ultra quieturi discurrunt. paucorum excursio lacessentium et emissa iacula extemplo et Romanis dubi-
7 tationem quin bellandum esset exemerunt. levia inde proelia per quadriduum primum sine ullo satis certo
8 eventu commissa. quinto die prope iusta pugna adeo pa- ventes in oppidum Lacedaemonii compulsi sunt ut qui- dam milites Romani terga fugientium caedentes per inter- missa, ut tunc erant, moenia urbem intrarint.

---

[39] circulos *RBχ*: in circulis *ed. Rom.*: per circulos *Weiss.*

states, which were no more hostile to the tyrants themselves than they were to their minions.

37. At first they formed small groups and aired these
grievances among themselves; then they suddenly rushed
to arms. When the tyrant saw from the unrest that the
common people were sufficiently exasperated on their
own account, he ordered an assembly to be called. He
then presented the demands made by the Romans, and
falsely represented a number of them as being harsher and
more demeaning than they really were. Each item was
met with cries of disapproval from the whole assembly or
from parts of it, and Nabis then asked what response they
wanted him to make to the terms or what action they
wished him to take. With almost one voice they all told
him that no answer should be given and the war should go
on. And, as usual with crowds, everyone urged him to take
heart and have confidence and said that fortune favored
the brave. Stirred by these exclamations, the tyrant declared that both Antiochus and the Aetolians would help
and that he had more than sufficient troops to withstand
a siege.

Any idea of peace had now vanished from the minds of
all and, unwilling to remain inactive any longer, they ran
off to their various stations. When a few ran out to harry
the enemy and immediately hurled their javelins, this also
removed from the Romans any doubt about their having
to continue the war. For the first four days there was only
light skirmishing with no clear result. On the fifth there
was something approaching a regular battle in which the
Spartans were driven back into their town in such panic
that some Roman soldiers, still hacking at the backs of the
retreating enemy, entered the city through the gaps that
existed in the wall at that time.

38. Et tunc quidem Quinctius, satis eo terrore coercitis excursionibus hostium nihil praeter ipsius oppugnationem urbis superesse ratus, missis qui omnes navales socios a Gytheo accerserent, ipse interim cum tribunis militum ad

2 visendum urbis situm moenia circumvehitur. fuerat quondam sine muro Sparta; tyranni nuper locis patentibus planisque obiecerant murum: altiora loca et difficilia[40] aditu stationibus armatorum pro munimento obiectis tutabantur.

3 Vbi satis omnia inspexit, corona oppugnandum ratus, omnibus copiis—erant autem Romanorum sociorumque, simul peditum equitumque, simul terrestrium ac navalium copiarum, ad quinquaginta milia hominum—urbem

4 cinxit. alii scalas, alii ignem, alii alia quibus non oppugnarent modo sed etiam terrerent, portabant. iussi clamore sublato subire undique omnes, ut qua primum occurrerent quave opem ferrent ad omnia simul paventes Lacedaemonii ignorarent.

5 Quod roboris in exercitu erat trifariam divisum: parte una a Phoebeo, altera a Dictynnaeo, tertia ab eo loco quem Heptagonias appellant—omnia autem haec aperta

6 sine muro loca sunt—adgredi iubet. cum tantus undique terror urbem circumvasisset, primo tyrannus et ad cla-

---

[40] difficilia $B^1$ (difficia $B$)χ: difficiliora $R$

---

[102] Sparta had famously remained without a defensive wall until the late fourth century.     [103] Latin *corona:* a ring of troops set around an enemy position.

[104] The Phoebeum was a temple of Apollo, south of Sparta, and the Dictynnaeum was a shrine of the Cretan goddess Dictynna; what the Heptagoniae was is unknown.

38. By the fright he had given them on that occasion Quinctius at least arrested the counterattacks of the enemy and now thought he had no option but to blockade the city. He sent men to bring all the marines from Gytheum and in the meantime rode around the walls himself with the military tribunes to take stock of the city's position. Sparta had once been without a wall; only recently had the tyrants erected a defensive wall in the exposed and flat areas,[102] while spots that were higher and difficult to reach they continued to protect with outposts of armed sentinels rather than a rampart.

After a thorough inspection of the whole site, Flamininus thought he should attack by means of a military cordon[103] and he surrounded the city with all his troops— there were Romans and allies, infantry and cavalry, land and naval forces, about 50,000 men in all. Some carried ladders, some torches, and some various other implements for intimidating as well as attacking the enemy. They were all ordered to raise a shout and advance on all sides so that the Spartans, in total panic everywhere, should have no idea where first to confront the enemy or where to bring assistance.

The main strength of the Roman army was divided into three parts. Flamininus ordered the attack mounted with one division at the Phoebeum, a second at the Dictynneum, and the third in the area they call Heptagoniae[104]— all these areas were open and without walls. As the city was now facing such terrifying danger from every direction, the tyrant at first reacted to the sudden outbursts of

mores repentinos et ad nuntios trepidos motus, ut quisque maxime laboraret locus, aut ipse occurrebat aut aliquos
7 mittebat; deinde circumfuso undique pavore, ita obtorpuit ut nec dicere quod in rem esset nec audire posset, nec inops modo consilii sed vix mentis compos esset.

39. Romanos primo sustinebant in angustiis Lacedaemonii, ternaeque acies tempore uno locis diversis pugnabant; deinde crescente certamine nequaquam erat proe-
2 lium par. missilibus enim Lacedaemonii pugnabant, a quibus se et magnitudine scuti perfacile Romanus tuebatur miles, et quod alii vani alii leves admodum ictus erant.
3 nam propter angustias loci confertamque turbam non modo ad emittenda cum procursu, quo plurimum concitantur, tela spatium habebant, sed ne ut de gradu quidem
4 libero ac stabili conarentur. itaque ex adverso missa tela nulla in corporibus rara in scutis haerebant; ab circum-
5 stantibus ex superioribus locis volnerati quidam sunt; mox progressos iam etiam ex tectis non tela modo sed tegulae
6 quoque inopinantes perculerunt. sublatis deinde supra capita scutis, continuatisque ita inter se ut non modo ad caecos ictus sed ne ad inserendum quidem ex propinquo telum loci quicquam esset, testudine facta subibant.
7 Et primae angustiae paulisper sua hostiumque refertae turba tenuerunt: postquam in patentiorem viam urbis

---

105 What these are is unclear, especially in the light of "The first narrow streets" (*primae angustiae*) below (7).

106 The famous *testudo* (cf. 31.39.14 note).

shouting and panic-stricken reports by going in person, or sending men, to the points most under pressure. Then, as the panic spread everywhere, he was so paralyzed as to be unable to offer or listen to any useful information, and was not only incapable of formulating strategy but was almost out of his mind.

39. At first, the Spartans kept the Romans at bay in the narrow passages,[105] and the three battle lines were in combat at the same time in different locations. Then, as the conflict became more intense, the battle was not at all even. The Spartans were fighting with javelins and the Roman soldier very easily kept himself protected from them by the size of his shield and also because some were off target while others fell with very little impact. For, because of the cramped space and the large numbers in it, the Spartans not only lacked room for hurling their weapons on the run—which gives them the most momentum— but even for attempting their throw with an unimpeded and firm footing. Thus none of the spears dispatched from directly opposite became embedded in bodies, and only a few in shields. A number were wounded by Spartans who were standing about them on higher ground and presently, as they advanced, they also began to sustain unexpected injuries not only from spears but also from tiles thrown from the roofs of buildings. They then advanced in tortoise formation,[106] raising their shields above their heads and interlocking them so tightly as to remove any chance of success not only for random throwing but even for thrusting in a javelin from close at hand.

The first narrow streets that they encountered briefly checked their progress as they were filled with crowds of their own men and the enemy's; but then by putting grad-

paulatim urgentes hostem processere, non ultra vis eorum
8 atque impetus sustineri poterant. cum terga vertissent
Lacedaemonii et fuga effusa superiora peterent loca, Nabis quidem ut capta urbe trepidans quanam ipse evaderet
9 circumspectabat: Pythagoras cum ad cetera animo offi-
cioque ducis fungebatur, tum vero unus ne caperetur urbs
causa fuit; succendi enim aedificia proxima muro iussit.
10 quae cum momento temporis arsissent, ut adiuvantibus
ignem qui alias ad exstinguendum opem ferre solent,
11 ruere in Romanos tecta, nec tegularum modo fragmenta
sed etiam ambusta tigna ad armatos pervenire et flamma
late fundi, fumus terrorem etiam maiorem quam pericu-
12 lum facere. itaque et qui extra urbem erant Romanorum,
tum maxime impetum facientes, recessere a muro, et qui
iam intraverant, ne incendio ab tergo oriente interclude-
13 rentur ab suis, receperunt sese; et Quinctius postquam
quid rei esset vidit, receptui canere iussit. ita iam capta
prope urbe revocati redierunt in castra.

40. Quinctius, plus ex timore hostium quam ex re ipsa
spei nactus, per triduum insequens territavit eos nunc
proeliis lacessendo nunc operibus, intersaepiendoque[41]
2 quaedam ne exitus ad fugam esset. his comminationibus
compulsus tyrannus Pythagoran rursus oratorem misit:
quem Quinctius primo aspernatus excedere castris iussit,
dein suppliciter orantem advolutumque genibus tandem

---

[41] intersaepiendoque *Rχ*: intersaepiendo *BHolk.Voss*

ual pressure on the enemy they reached one of the city's wider roads, and the force of their onslaught could no longer be resisted. When the Spartans had turned tail and were heading for higher ground in disordered flight, Nabis panicked as though the city was already lost and cast about for an escape route for himself. It was Pythagoras, valiantly carrying out the duties of a general in all respects, who was also single-handedly responsible for the city not being taken, since he gave the order for the buildings next to the wall to be set on fire. They flared up in an instant, the flames being stoked by men who on other occasions usually bring help to put them out. The structures collapsed on the Romans; charred beams and not just pieces of tile fell on the soldiers; flames spread far and wide; and the smoke generated even greater terror than it did danger. The result was that the Romans outside the city, who were at that very moment making their assault, fell back from the wall and those who had entered it also retired, afraid of being cut off from their comrades by the fire springing up to their rear; and Quinctius, seeing what was happening, ordered the retreat to be sounded. With that the men, recalled when the city was almost taken, returned to camp.

40. Quinctius saw more reason for hope in the enemy's panic than in the operation itself. For the next three days he intimidated them, provoking them at one moment with attacks, at another with siege engines, and also, at points, sealing off escape routes. Cowed by these threats, the tyrant once more sent Pythagoras as his spokesman. At first, Quinctius rejected Pythagoras' petition and ordered him from the camp, but when he resorted to abject entreaties and fell at Quinctius' knees, he finally granted him a hear-

3 audivit. prima oratio fuit omnia permittentis arbitrio Ro-
4 manorum; dein cum ea velut vana et sine effectu nihil
proficeret, eo deducta est res ut iis condicionibus quae ex
scripto paucis ante diebus editae erant indutiae fierent,
pecuniaque et obsides accepti.

5     Dum oppugnatur tyrannus, Argivi nuntiis aliis super
alios adferentibus tantum non iam captam Lacedaemo-
6 nem esse erecti et ipsi, simul eo quod Pythagoras cum
parte validissima praesidii excesserat, contempta paucitate eorum qui in arce erant, duce Archippo quodam
7 praesidium expulerunt; Timocratem Pellenensem, quia
clementer praefuerat, vivum fide data emiserunt. huic laetitiae Quinctius supervenit, pace data tyranno dimissisque
ab Lacedaemone Eumene et Rhodiis et L. Quinctio fratre
ad classem.

    41. Laeta civitas celeberrimum festorum dierum ac
nobile ludicrum Nemeorum, die stata propter belli mala
praetermissum, in adventum Romani exercitus ducisque
indixerunt, praefeceruntque ludis ipsum imperatorem.
2 multa erant quae gaudium cumularent: reducti cives ab
Lacedaemone erant quos nuper Pythagoras quosque ante
3 Nabis abduxerat; redierant qui post compertam a Pytha-
gora coniurationem et caede iam coepta effugerant; libertatem ex longo intervallo libertatisque auctores Romanos,

---

107 Timocrates of Pallene: cf. 29.14, above.

108 The games were held biennially at the sanctuary of Zeus
in Nemea in the Argolid, at a date in July, in the first and third
years of every Olympiad.

ing. The start of his address was a declaration of complete submission to the will of the Romans, and although that made no headway, being considered an empty and useless offer, the point was nevertheless reached where a truce was concluded on the terms that had been given in writing a few days earlier, and the money and hostages were received.

While the tyrant was under attack, the Argives felt encouraged themselves, first because messenger after messenger brought news that Sparta was all but captured and then also because Pythagoras had quit the town with the strongest part of the garrison. With disdain for the slight numbers left in the citadel, and led by a certain Archippus, they drove out the garrison. Timocrates of Pellene they let go alive with a guarantee of safe conduct because his regime had been easygoing.[107] During the ensuing jubilation Quinctius arrived; he had now granted peace to the tyrant and sent Eumenes, the Rhodians, and his brother Lucius Quinctius back to the fleet from Lacedaemon.

41. The most popular of Argive feast days, the famous Nemean Games, had not been observed on the regular date[108] because of the difficulties of the war. The joyful city now announced that the celebration was to coincide with the arrival of the Roman army and its commander, and they appointed the general himself president of the games. A number of factors combined to increase the Argives' elation: their fellow citizens who had recently been seized by Pythagoras, and earlier by Nabis, had been brought home from Sparta; those men had now returned who had fled after the conspiracy had discovered by Pythagoras and the bloody reprisals had already started; and after a long interval the citizens could see their freedom restored and set eyes on those responsible for it—the Ro-

quibus causa bellandi cum tyranno ipsi fuissent, cernebant. testata quoque ipso Nemeorum die voce praeconis
libertas est Argivorum.

4     Achaeis quantum restituti Argi in commune Achaiae
concilium laetitiae adferebant, tantum serva Lacedaemon
relicta et lateri adhaerens tyrannus non sincerum gaudium
5 praebebant. Aetoli vero eam rem omnibus conciliis lace-
rare: cum Philippo non ante desitum bellari quam omnibus excederet Graeciae urbibus, tyranno relictam La-
6 cedaemonem; regem autem legitimum, qui in Romanis
fuerit castris, ceterosque nobilissimos cives in exsilio vic-
turos; Nabidis dominationis satellitem factum populum
Romanum.

7     Quinctius ab Argis Elatiam, unde ad bellum Sparta-
num profectus erat, copias reduxit.

8     Sunt qui non ex oppido proficiscentem bellum gessisse
tyrannum tradant, sed castris adversus Romana positis
9 castra diuque cunctatum, quia Aetolorum auxilia exspectasset, coactum ad extremum acie confligere impetu in
10 pabulatores suos a Romanis facto: eo proelio victum
castrisque exutum pacem petisse, cum cecidissent quattuordecim milia militum, capta plus quattuor milia essent.

42. Eodem fere tempore et a T. Quinctio de rebus ad
Lacedaemonem gestis et a M. Porcio consule ex Hispania
litterae adlatae. utriusque nomine in dies ternos supplicatio ab senatu decreta est.

---

109 Livy is very likely reporting a variant version of the battle
that he found in his annalistic sources: see Introduction, xxvi–
xxxiv.

110 *supplicatio*: cf. 31.8.2 note.

mans, whose reason for war with the tyrant had been the Argives themselves! On the very day of the Nemean Games the freedom of Argos was also proclaimed out loud by a herald.

Much as the return of Argos to the common council of Achaea brought joy to the Achaeans, the fact that Sparta was still in bondage and that they still had a tyrant constantly at their side would not allow their happiness to be complete. The Aetolians for their part excoriated the arrangement at all their council meetings. The war with Philip was not brought to an end, they said, until he withdrew from *all* the cities of Greece; and Sparta had been left to a tyrant while its rightful king, who was in the Roman camp, and other Spartan citizens of the highest rank were to live in exile. The Roman people had become a tool of Nabis' oppression, they said.

Quinctius then led his troops back from Argos to Elatia, the point from which he had set out for the war with Sparta.

There are some who claim that the tyrant did not fight the war by counterattacking from the city.[109] Rather, they say, he pitched his camp opposite the Roman camp, delayed a long while because he had been waiting for support from the Aetolians, and was finally obliged to commit himself to battle when an attack was made on his foragers by the Romans. Defeated in that engagement, and driven from his camp, he sued for peace after 14,000 of his men had fallen and more than 4,000 had been taken prisoner.

42. At about the same time dispatches arrived from Titus Quinctius concerning his Spartan campaign and also from the consul Marcius Porcius in Spain. Three days of supplication[110] were decreed by the senate in recognition of both men's success.

2     L. Valerius consul, cum post fusos circa Litanam silvam
Boios quietam provinciam habuisset, comitiorum causa
3   Romam rediit, et creavit consules P. Cornelium Scipionem
Africanum iterum et Ti. Sempronium Longum. horum
patres primo anno secundi Punici belli consules fuerant.
4     Praetoria inde comitia habita: creati P. Cornelius Scipio
et duo Cn. Cornelii, Merenda et Blasio, et Cn. Domitius
5   Ahenobarbus et Sex. Digitius et T. Iuventius Thalna. comitiis perfectis consul in provinciam rediit.

Novum ius eo anno a Ferentinatibus temptatum, ut
Latini qui in coloniam Romanam nomina dedissent cives
6   Romani essent: Puteolos Salernumque et Buxentum ad-
scripti coloni qui nomina dederant, et cum ob id se pro
civibus Romanis ferrent, senatus iudicavit non esse eos
cives Romanos.

43. Principio anni quo P. Scipio Africanus iterum et Ti.
Sempronius Longus consules fuerunt legati Nabidis ty-
2   ranni Romam venerunt. iis extra urbem in aede Apollinis
senatus datus est. pax quae cum T. Quinctio convenisset
ut rata esset petierunt impetraruntque.

---

111 Cf. 22.1–3, above.

112 Ti. Sempronius Longus (67). Scipio's first consulship had
been in 205.

113 These were P. Cornelius Scipio (330) and Ti. Sempronius
Longus (66).

114 The decision to found them was taken in 197 (32.29.3), but
not implemented until 194 (45.2, below). Cf. also Vell. 1.15.3.

115 The senate's ruling now clarified the situation: a Latin
became a citizen only when he became a resident in a Roman
colony; simple enrollment as a colonist was insufficient.

116 Dating from 431, it was the only temple of Apollo before

After the defeat of the Boii near the forest of Litana,[111] the consul Lucius Valerius had peace in his province. He returned to Rome for the elections and declared Publius Cornelius Scipio Africanus and Titus Sempronius Longus elected consuls (Scipio for the second time).[112] The fathers of these men had been consuls in the first year of the Second Punic War.[113]

The praetorian elections were then held; those elected were Publius Cornelius Scipio, the two Gnaei Cornelii (Merenda and Blasio), Gnaeus Domitius Ahenobarbus, Sextus Digitius, and Titus Iuventius Thalna. At the end of the elections the consul returned to his province.

That year the people of Ferentinum attempted to secure a new legal prerogative: that Latins who had merely submitted their names for membership in a Roman colony should become Roman citizens. Those who had submitted their names for Puteoli, Salernum, and Buxentum[114] were enrolled as colonists, and because of this they comported themselves as if they were Roman citizens. The senate adjudged that they were not Roman citizens.[115]

43. At the beginning of the year when Publius Scipio Africanus and Tiberius Sempronius Longus were consuls (Scipio for the second time) envoys came to Rome from the tyrant Nabis. They were given an audience with the senate outside the city in the temple of Apollo.[116] They asked for ratification of the peace treaty that had been concluded with Titus Quinctius, and their request was granted.

the Temple of Apollo Palatinus built by Augustus (cf. Richardson 12–13). It lay outside the *pomerium,* which representatives of states at war with Rome could not cross.

3    De provinciis cum relatum esset, senatus frequens in eam sententiam ibat ut quoniam in Hispania et Macedonia debellatum foret, consulibus ambobus Italia provincia esset.
4    Scipio satis esse Italiae unum consulem censebat, alteri Macedoniam decernendam esse: bellum grave ab Antiocho imminere, iam ipsum sua sponte in Europam
5    transgressum. quid deinde facturum censerent, cum hinc Aetoli, haud dubii[42] hostes, vocarent ad bellum, illinc Hannibal, Romanis cladibus insignis imperator, stimula-
6    ret? dum de provinciis consulum disceptatur, praetores
7    sortiti sunt: Cn. Domitio urbana iurisdictio T. Iuventio peregrina evenit, P. Cornelio Hispania ulterior Sex. Digitio citerior, duobus Cn. Corneliis, Blasioni Sicilia Merendae Sardinia.
8    In Macedoniam novum exercitum transportari non placuit, eum qui esset ibi reduci in Italiam a Quinctio ac dimitti; item eum exercitum dimitti qui cum M. Porcio
9    Catone in Hispania esset; consulibus ambobus Italiam provinciam esse et duas urbanas scribere eos legiones, ut dimissis quos senatus censuisset exercitibus octo omnino Romanae legiones essent.

    44. Ver sacrum factum erat priore anno, M. Porcio et
2    L. Valerio consulibus. id cum P. Licinius pontifex non esse recte factum collegio primum, deinde ex auctoritate col-

---

[42] dubii *Gron.*: dubie *B$\chi$*

[117] In 195; on the *ver sacrum* cf. 33.44.1–2 and note.
[118] On the college, cf. 31.9.8 and note.

When the matter of the provinces was raised, a full house of the senate decided that the two consuls should have Italy as theirs since the wars in Spain and Macedonia were now finished. Scipio expressed the opinion that one consul was sufficient for Italy and that Macedonia should be officially mandated to the other. A momentous war with Antiochus was impending, he said, and Antiochus had already himself crossed to Europe on his own initiative. What did the senators think the king was going to do when he had the Aetolians, indubitably enemies of Rome, calling him to war on the one side, and Hannibal, a general famous for his crushing Roman conquests, inciting him on the other? While the consular provinces were still being discussed, the praetorian sortition went as follows: the city jurisdiction fell to Gnaeus Domitius and foreigners' jurisdiction to Titus Iuventius; Farther Spain fell to Publius Cornelius, Nearer Spain to Sextus Digitius, Sicily to Gnaeus Cornelius Blasio and Sardinia to Gnaeus Cornelius Merenda.

It was decided that no new army should be transported to Macedonia, and that the army already there should be brought back to Italy by Quinctius and demobilized. The army that had been with Marcus Porcius Cato in Spain was likewise to be demobilized. The two consuls were to have Italy as their province and were authorized to enroll two city legions so that, after the demobilization of the legions decreed by the senate, there should be a total of eight Roman legions.

44. A "Sacred Spring" had been conducted the previous year in the consulship of Marcus Porcius and Lucius Valerius.[117] The pontiff Publius Licinius reported, first to the college of pontiffs,[118] and afterward—on the college's authorization—to the senators, that the correct procedure

legii patribus renuntiasset, de integro faciendum arbitratu
pontificum censuerunt, ludosque magnos qui una voti
3 essent tanta pecunia quanta adsoleret faciendos: ver sacrum videri pecus quod natum esset inter kalendas Martias et pridie kalendas Maias P. Cornelio et Ti. Sempronio
consulibus.

4 Censorum inde comitia sunt habita. creati censores
Sex. Aelius Paetus et C. Cornelius Cethegus principem[43]
senatus P. Scipionem consulem, quem et priores censores
legerant, legerunt. tres omnino senatores, neminem curuli
5 honore usum, praeterierunt. gratiam quoque ingentem
apud eum ordinem pepererunt, quod ludis Romanis aedilibus curulibus imperarunt ut loca senatoria secernerent a
populo; nam antea in promiscuo spectarant. equitibus
quoque perpaucis adempti equi, nec in ullum ordinem
saevitum. atrium Libertatis et villa publica ab iisdem re-
fecta amplificataque.

6 Ver sacrum ludique votivi[44] quos voverat Ser. Sulpicius

---

[43] Cethegus principem *Bχ*: Cethegus ii principem *vel* Cethegus. principem *H.J.M.*
[44] votivi *Bχ*: Romani votivi *Mg*

---

[119] For the vow, made in 217, cf. 22.10.7, and on the problems
of date raised by it, Briscoe 2.22–23.
[120] I.e., this year (194).
[121] "Leader of the senate." He had his name entered first on
the list of senators compiled by the censors and gave his opinion
first on any matter under discussion. The position was held for
life, and the holder was invariably from one of the great families
(*gentes maiores*). All known holders came from one of six *gentes:*
the Aemilii, Claudii, Cornelii, Fabii, Manlii, and Valerii.

had not been followed, and the senators accordingly voted that the ceremony be repeated under the direction of the pontiffs. They also voted that the Great Games, which had been promised in a vow at the same time as the Sacred Spring,[119] be celebrated with the usual level of expenditure. It was further decided that the Sacred Spring applied to all animals born between March 1st and April 30th in the consulship of Publius Cornelius and Tiberius Sempronius.[120]

The election of the censors came next. Elected were Sextus Aelius Paetus and Gaius Cornelius Cethegus, and these chose as *princeps senatus*[121] the consul Publius Scipio (who had also been the choice of the previous censors). They rejected, in all, three senators, none of whom had held a curule office. They won enormous gratitude from the senatorial class by ordering the curule aediles to separate senatorial seating from the public at the Roman Games;[122] before that there had been mixed seating for spectators. Very few equestrians had their horses confiscated, and no class was severely treated. The Hall of Freedom and the Public Villa[123] were restored and extended by these same censors.

The "Sacred Spring" and the games that Servius Sulpicius Galba[124] had vowed as consul were both celebrated.

[122] The curule aediles were responsible for the major public games. On the *Ludi Romani,* cf. 31.50.2 note.

[123] Both buildings were used by the censors, the former for their offices, the latter (cf. also 33.24.5 note) for the census (atrium Libertatis: Richardson 41; villa publica: 430–31).

[124] Livy has the *praenomen* incorrect; it is Publius, not Sulpicius (cf. 31.4.4).

Galba consul facti. cum spectaculo eorum occupati animi hominum essent, Q. Pleminius, qui propter multa in deos hominesque scelera Locris admissa in carcerem coniectus
7 fuerat, comparaverat homines qui pluribus simul locis urbis nocte incendia facerent, ut in consternata nocturno
8 tumultu civitate refringi carcer posset. ea res indicio consciorum palam facta delataque ad senatum est. Pleminius in inferiorem demissus carcerem est necatusque.

45. Coloniae civium Romanorum eo anno deductae sunt Puteolos Volturnum Liternum, treceni homines in
2 singulas. item Salernum Buxentumque coloniae civium Romanorum deductae sunt. deduxere triumviri Ti. Sempronius Longus, qui tum consul erat, M. Servilius Q. Mi-
3 nucius Thermus. ager divisus est qui Campanorum fuerat. Sipontum item in agrum qui Arpinorum fuerat coloniam civium Romanorum alii triumviri D. Iunius Brutus M.
4 Baebius Tamphilus M. Helvius deduxerunt. Tempsam item et Crotonem coloniae civium Romanorum deductae. Tempsanus ager de Bruttiis captus erat: Bruttii Graecos
5 expulerant; Crotonem Graeci habebant. triumviri Cn. Octavius L. Aemilius Paullus C. Laetorius Crotonem, Tempsam L. Cornelius Merula Q. ⟨. . .⟩[45] C. Salonius deduxerunt.

---

[45] Merula Q. ⟨. . .⟩ C. Salonius *Weiss.*: Merulaq. *B*: Merula χ

---

[125] For the Pleminius affair, cf. 29.6.9—22.10.

[126] The Tullianum, where executions took place: cf. Richardson 71 sv *Carcer*.     [127] See 42.6 and note, above. Apart from Buxentum, all are founded on Campanian land confiscated, as is clear below, for the Campanian defection to Hannibal.

[128] *Barr.* 45 C1.     [129] *Barr.* 46 D3 (Tempsa), F3 (Croton).

While people's attention was focused on the games, Quintus Pleminius, a man who had been thrown in prison for many crimes against the gods and men at Locri,[125] had gathered together men to set fires simultaneously at numerous points in the city. His plan was that the prison could be broken open while the whole community was panic-stricken by the commotion during the night. The scheme came to light and was reported to the senate when Pleminius' associates denounced him. Pleminius was sent down to the lower prison[126] and executed.

45. Colonies of Roman citizens were that year founded at Puteoli, Volternum, and Liternum, with three hundred assigned to each. Colonies of Roman citizens were likewise established at Salernum and Buxentum.[127] The triumvirs establishing the colonies were Tiberius Sempronius Longus, who was consul at the time, Marcus Servilius, and Quintus Minucius Thermus. Land that had belonged to the Campanians was divided among the colonists. A second board of triumvirs, comprising Decimus Iunius Brutus, Marcus Baebius Tamphilus, and Marcus Helvius, also founded a colony of Roman citizens at Sipontum,[128] on land that had belonged to the Arpini. At Tempsa, too, and at Croton[129] colonies of Roman citizens were founded. The land at Tempsa had been captured from the Bruttii—the Bruttii had driven out the Greeks—and Croton had been inhabited by Greeks. The founding triumvirs for Croton were Gnaeus Octavius, Lucius Aemilius Paullus and Gaius Laetorius; for Tempsa they were Lucius Cornelius Merula, Quintus . . . ,[130] and Gaius Salonius.

---

[130] The third triumvir's *nomen* must have appeared in the lacuna.

6 Prodigia quoque alia visa eo anno Romae sunt, alia nuntiata. in foro et comitio et Capitolio sanguinis guttae visae sunt; et terra aliquotiens pluvit et caput Volcani arsit.

7 nuntiatum est Nare amni lac fluxisse, pueros ingenuos Arimini sine oculis ac naso, et in Piceno agro non pedes non manus habentem natum. ea prodigia ex pontificum de-

8 creto procurata. et sacrificium novendiale factum est, quod Hadriani nuntiaverant in agro suo lapidibus pluvisse.

46. In Gallia L. Valerius Flaccus proconsul circa Mediolanium cum Gallis Insubribus et Boiis, qui Dorulato duce ad concitandos Insubres Padum transgressi erant, signis conlatis depugnavit; decem milia hostium sunt caesa.

2 Per eos dies collega eius M. Porcius Cato ex Hispania triumphavit. tulit in eo triumpho argenti infecti viginti quinque milia pondo, bigati centum viginti tria milia, Oscensis quingenta quadraginta, auri pondo mille qua-

3 dringenta. militibus ex praeda divisit in singulos ducenos septuagenos aeris, triplex equiti.

4 Ti. Sempronius consul, in provinciam profectus, in Boiorum primum agrum legiones duxit. Boiorix tum regulus eorum cum duobus fratribus tota gente concitata ad

---

131 A frequently reported prodigy (e.g., 24.7.10, 42.20.5; Cic. *Div.* 2.58). The phenomenon still occurs; it results from the red Sahara dust being blown over to Italy by the Scirocco wind.

132 In his temple on the Campus Martius (Richardson 432–33).

133 The river joins the Tiber north of Rome (*Barr.* 42 C4).

134 The nine-day sacrifice was the normal expiation for celestial prodigies. The shower of stones was probably meteorites.

135 Capital town of the Insubres, today Milan.

There were also prodigies that year, some observed at Rome and some reported from elsewhere. Droplets of blood were observed in the Forum, in the comitium and on the Capitol.[131] There were occasional showers of earth, and the head of Vulcan[132] caught fire. There was a report that milk had been flowing in the River Nar;[133] and that freeborn children had been born in Ariminum without ears and noses, and one in the district of Picenum without feet and hands. These prodigies were expiated by decree of the pontiffs. In addition, there was a nine-day sacrifice because the people of Hadria had reported that stones had fallen as rain in their territory.[134]

46. In Gaul the proconsul Lucius Valerius Flaccus fought a decisive pitched battle close to Mediolanium[135] against the Insubrian Gauls and the Boii who, led by Dorulatus, had crossed the Po to incite the Insubres to rebellion. Ten thousand of the enemy were killed.

In the same period, Flaccus' colleague, Marcus Porcius Cato, celebrated a triumph for his Spanish campaign. He had 25,000 pounds of unwrought silver, 123,000 silver coins stamped with the *biga*,[136] 540 Osca-minted coins,[137] and 1,400 pounds of gold carried along in the procession. From the booty Cato distributed 270 *asses* to each of his infantrymen and three times that amount to each cavalryman.

Setting off for his province, the consul Tiberius Sempronius first led his legions into the territory of the Boii. Their chieftain at that time was Boiorix who, along with his two brothers, had incited the entire tribe to rebellion.

---

[136] Cf. note on 31.49.2.
[137] Cf. note on 10.4, above.

rebellandum castra locis apertis posuit, ut appareret dimi-
5 caturos si hostis fines intrasset. consul ubi quantae copiae
quanta fiducia esset hosti sensit, nuntium ad collegam
mittit, ut si videretur ei maturaret venire: se tergiversando
6 in adventum eius rem extracturum. quae causa consuli
cunctandi, eadem Gallis, praeterquam quod cunctatio hostium animos faciebat, rei maturandae erat, ut priusquam
7 coniungerentur consulum copiae rem transigerent. per
biduum tamen nihil aliud quam steterunt parati ad pugnandum, si quis contra egrederetur; tertio subiere ad val-
8 lum castraque simul ab omni parte adgressi sunt. consul
arma extemplo capere milites iussit; armatos inde paulisper continuit, ut et stolidam fiduciam hosti augeret, et
disponeret copias quibus quaeque portis erumperent.
9    Duae legiones duabus principalibus portis signa ef-
ferre iussae. sed in ipso exitu ita conferti obstitere Galli ut
10 clauderent viam. diu in angustiis pugnatum est; nec dex-
tris magis gladiisque gerebatur res quam scutis corpori-
11 busque ipsis obnixi urgebant, Romani ut signa foras ef-
ferrent, Galli ut aut in castra ipsi penetrarent aut exire
12 Romanos prohiberent. nec ante in hanc aut illam partem
moveri acies potuerunt quam Q. Victorius primi pili centurio et C. Atinius tribunus militum, quartae hic ille se-

---

138 The gates at each end of the *via principalis,* the chief
thoroughfare of a Roman camp.

Boiorix pitched camp in an open area to make it clear that he would resist an enemy incursion into his lands. When the consul perceived how strong his enemy's forces were and how great his confidence, he sent word to his colleague to ask him to come quickly, if he saw fit—Sempronius would take evasive action to draw matters out until his arrival. Apart from the fact that their enemy's hesitation encouraged the Gauls, they had the same reason for bringing on the action as the consul did for delaying, namely to finish the business before the two consuls' forces could be combined. Nevertheless, for two days they did no more than stand ready for action should anyone come out to face them. On the third day, however, they moved up to the Roman fortifications and assaulted the camp on all sides at once. The consul immediately ordered his men to take up their weapons but held them back under arms for a short while in order to boost the enemy's dimwitted confidence and also to marshal his troops at the gates through which the various units would make the counterattack.

Two legions were ordered to advance from the camp through the two main gates,[138] but the Gauls stood before them right at the exits, so densely packed as to block their way. There was fighting in the confined spaces for a long while; but the issue now depended less on the strength of the arm and the sword than on the use of the shield and pure bodily force as both sides surged forward, the Romans trying to break out, and the Gauls trying either to enter the camp themselves or to prevent the Romans from getting out. The battle lines could not move in one direction or the other until a senior centurion, Quintus Victorius, and a military tribune, Gaius Atinius, who belonged

cundae legionis, rem in asperis proeliis saepe temptatam,
13 signa adempta signiferis in hostes iniecerunt. dum repetunt enixe signum, priores secundani se porta eiecerunt.

47. Iam hi extra vallum pugnabant, quarta legione in
porta haerente, cum alius tumultus ex aversa parte cas-
2 trorum est exortus. in portam quaestoriam inruperant
Galli, resistentesque pertinacius occiderant L. Postumium
quaestorem, cui Tympano fuit cognomen, et M. Atinium
et P. Sempronium praefectos socium, et ducentos ferme
3 milites. capta ab ea parte castra erant, donec cohors ex-
traordinaria, missa a consule ad tuendam quaestoriam
portam, et eos qui intra vallum erant partim occidit partim
4 expulit castris, et inrumpentibus obstitit. eodem fere tempore et quarta legio cum duabus extraordinariis cohortibus porta erupit. ita simul tria proelia circa castra locis
distantibus erant, clamoresque dissoni ad incertos suorum
eventus a praesenti certamine animos pugnantium averte-
5 bant. usque ad meridiem aequis viribus ac prope pari spe
pugnatum est. labor et aestus mollia et fluida corpora Gallorum et minime patientia sitis cum decedere pugna coegisset, in paucos restantes impetum Romani fecerunt,
6 fusosque compulerunt in castra. signum inde receptui ab

---

139 The loss of a standard was a great disgrace. For the tactic
see especially Frontin. *Str.* 2.8.1–4.

140 The rear gate of the Roman camp, more commonly known
as the decuman gate (*porta decumana*).

141 A typical Livian comment on the Gauls' lack of endurance:
cf. 10.28.3–4, 22.2.4, 27.48.16, etc.

respectively to the fourth and second legions, resorted to a
tactic often attempted in critical moments of battle: they
took the standards from the bearers and hurled them into
the enemy ranks.[139] As they frantically attempted to re-
trieve the standards, the legionaries of the second were
the first to force their way through the gate.

47. These soldiers were now engaged outside the palisade while the fourth legion was still bogged down inside the gate, when another commotion arose on the other
side of the camp. The Gauls had broken in through the
quaestorian gate[140] and, in the teeth of furious resistance,
had managed to kill the quaestor Lucius Postumius (whose
*cognomen* was Tympanus) and the allied commanders
Marcus Atinius and Publius Sempronius, along with some
two hundred regular soldiers. In that sector the camp was
in enemy hands until an elite cohort, sent by the consul to
defend the quaestorian gate, killed some of the Gauls
within the palisade, drove the others from the camp, and
then blocked further attacks on it. At about the same time
the fourth legion also burst out through the gate with two
elite cohorts. The result was that there were at the same
time three battles in progress around the camp in three
different locations, and the confused shouting began to
draw the attention of the combatants away from the battle
in hand to the unclear fortunes of their comrades in the
others. The conflict continued until midday, with both
sides displaying similar energy and almost the same opti-
mism. Then fatigue and the heat forced the Gauls, who
are physically weak and flabby, with little tolerance of
thirst,[141] to quit the field, and the Romans mounted an
attack on the few who remained, routed them and drove
them back into their camp. The signal for retreat was now

consule datum est; ad quod pars maior receperunt sese,
pars certaminis studio et spe potiundi castris hostium
7 perstitit ad vallum. eorum paucitate contempta Galli universi ex castris eruperunt: fusi inde Romani quae imperio
consulis noluerant suo pavore ac terrore castra repetunt.
ita varia hinc atque illinc nunc fuga nunc victoria fuit;
8 Gallorum tamen ad undecim milia, Romanorum quinque
milia sunt occisa. Galli recepere in intima finium sese,
consul Placentiam legiones duxit.

48. Scipionem alii coniuncto exercitu cum collega per
Boiorum Ligurumque agros populantem isse, quoad progredi silvae paludesque passae sint, scribunt, alii nulla
memorabili re gesta Romam comitiorum causa redisse.
2 Eodem hoc anno T. Quinctius Elatiae, quo in hiberna
reduxerat copias, totum hiemis tempus iure dicendo
consumpsit, mutandisque iis quae aut ipsius Philippi aut
praefectorum eius licentia in civitatibus facta erant, cum
suae factionis hominum vires augendo ius ac libertatem
3 aliorum deprimerent. veris initio Corinthum conventu
edicto venit. ibi omnium civitatium legationes in contionis
4 modum circumfusas est adlocutus, orsus ab inita primum
Romanis amicitia cum Graecorum gente, et imperatorum
qui ante se in Macedonia fuissent suisque rebus gestis.
5 omnia cum adprobatione ingenti sunt audita, praeterquam

given by the consul; in response most of his men fell back, but some, in their ardor for the fight and in the hope of seizing the enemy camp, forged ahead to the rampart. With contempt for their small numbers the Gauls burst forth en masse from their camp. The Romans were put to flight, and driven by their own panic and terror they headed back to the camp to which they had refused to retire on the consul's order. Thus on both sides there was alternation of flight and victory, but up to 11,000 Gauls were killed, and 5,000 Romans. The Gauls withdrew to the interior of their lands and the consul led his legions to Placentia.

48. Some sources claim that Scipio united his army with that of his colleague and proceeded on a raiding expedition through the territory of the Boii and Ligurians, as far as the forests and marshes would allow him to advance; others say that he returned to Rome for the elections without achieving anything of note.

This same year Titus Quinctius spent all winter dispensing justice at Elatia, to which he had withdrawn his troops to pass the winter. He also used that time to repeal the capricious measures taken in the city-states by Philip himself or by his lieutenants, measures that infringed the rights and freedoms of others by bolstering the strength of the men of their own party. At the beginning of spring Quinctius called a meeting and came to Corinth. There he addressed delegations from all the city states, who were positioned around him as in a public assembly. He began with the time when the Roman treaty of friendship with the Greek people first started, and continued with the achievements of the generals who had preceded him in Macedonia and with his own exploits. Everything was received with wholehearted approval, except when it came

cum ad mentionem Nabidis ventum esset: id minime
6 conveniens liberanti Graeciam videbatur, tyrannum reli-
quisse non suae solum patriae gravem, sed omnibus circa
civitatibus metuendum, haerentem visceribus nobilissi-
mae civitatis.

49. Nec ignarus huius habitus animorum Quinctius, si
sine excidio Lacedaemonis fieri potuisset, fatebatur pacis
cum tyranno mentionem admittendam auribus non fuisse:
2 nunc, cum aliter quam ruina gravissimae civitatis opprimi
non posset, satius visum esse tyrannum debilitatum ac totis prope viribus ad nocendum cuiquam ademptis relin-
3 qui, quam intermori vehementioribus quam quae pati
possit remediis civitatem sinere, in ipsa vindicta libertatis
peritura.

4 Praeteritorum commemorationi subiecit proficisci sibi
in Italiam atque omnem exercitum deportare in animo
5 esse: Demetriadis Chalcidisque praesidia intra decimum
diem audituros deducta, Acrocorinthum ipsis extemplo
6 videntibus vacuam Achaeis traditurum, ut omnes scirent
utrum Romanis an Aetolis mentiri mos esset, qui male
commissam libertatem populo Romano sermonibus distu-
lerint, et mutatos pro Macedonibus Romanos dominos.
7 sed illis nec quid dicerent nec quid facerent quicquam
unquam pensi fuisse; reliquas civitates monere ut ex factis,[46] non ex dictis amicos pensent intellegantque quibus
8 credendum et a quibus cavendum sit. libertate modice

---

[46] ex factis *ed. Med. 1505*: factis *B*χ

to the mention of Nabis—it seemed to make very little sense for the liberator of Greece to have left a tyrant sticking in the vital organs of a city of great renown when the man was not only a burden to his own land but a threat to all states in the area.

49. Quinctius, not unaware that such was their thinking, declared that he would have been duty bound not to entertain any suggestion of peace with the tyrant had that been possible without the destruction of Sparta. As it was, he said, Nabis could not be crushed without the ruin of a very important city-state, and it therefore seemed better for the tyrant to be left in place, crippled and with almost all his power to harm anyone wrested from him. Rather that than to allow the state to die from remedies too drastic for her to bear, and see it destroyed in the very act of claiming its freedom.

He added to his account of past events the comment that he intended to leave for Italy and take all of his army with him. Within ten days they would hear of the withdrawal of the garrisons of Demetrias and Chalcis, and he would immediately, and before their very eyes, hand Acrocorinth over to the Achaeans free of troops. Thus all would know whether lying was a practice of the Romans or of the Aetolians, who had spread rumors to the effect that it had been a mistake to entrust the independence of Greece to the Roman people and that it meant only a change of masters, Roman instead of Macedonian. But the Aetolians had never been much concerned about what they said or did, and he advised all the other states to appraise their friends on the basis of actions not words and use their judgment about whom to trust and whom to treat with caution. Liberty they should use judiciously, he said.

utantur: temperatam eam salubrem et singulis et civitatibus esse, nimiam et aliis gravem et ipsis qui habeant prae-
9  cipitem et effrenatam esse. concordiae in civitatibus principes et ordines inter se et in commune omnes civitates
consulerent. adversus consentientes nec regem quem-
10  quam satis validum nec tyrannum fore: discordiam et seditionem omnia opportuna insidiantibus facere, cum pars
quae domestico certamine inferior sit externo potius se
11  adplicet quam civi cedat. alienis armis partam externa fide
redditam libertatem sua cura custodirent servarentque,
ut populus Romanus dignis datam libertatem ac munus
suum bene positum sciret.

50. Has velut parentis voces cum audirent, manare
omnibus gaudio lacrimae, adeo ut ipsum quoque confun-
2  derent dicentem. paulisper fremitus adprobantium dicta
fuit, monentiumque aliorum alios ut eas voces velut ora-
3  culo missas in pectora animosque demitterent. silentio
deinde facto petiit ab iis ut cives Romanos, si qui apud eos
in servitute essent, conquisitos intra duos menses mitterent ad se in Thessaliam: ne ipsis quidem honestum esse
4  in liberata terra liberatores eius servire. omnes acclama-
runt gratias se inter cetera etiam ob hoc agere, quod ad-
moniti essent ut tam pio tam necessario officio fungeren-
5  tur. ingens numerus erat bello Punico captorum, quos

Kept in control, it was salutary both for individuals and for communities as a whole; unchecked, it was an affliction for others and led those possessing it to reckless and unruly behavior. He urged leading citizens and the various classes in the states to direct their policies toward concord, and all the states as a whole to consider their common welfare. Facing a united front, no king and no tyrant would have the strength to challenge them; but disharmony and internal dissension furnished all manner of opportunities for fifth-columnists since the loser in a domestic conflict preferred to support an outsider rather than yield to a fellow citizen. Their liberty, concluded Flamininus, had been won by the arms of others and restored to them through the loyal support of foreigners; they should now protect and preserve it by their own efforts in order to make the Roman people aware that they had bestowed that liberty on men who deserved it and that their gift was well placed.

50. When the Greeks heard these words, as though from a father, tears of joy streamed from every eye, to the point of even causing the consul himself distress as he spoke. There was a brief murmuring as they expressed approval for his address and urged each other to let his words, which seemed to have been sent from an oracle, sink into their hearts and minds. Then, when silence fell, Flamininus asked them to seek out any Roman citizens that were in slavery among them and send them to him in Thessaly within two months. Even for them, he said, it was a disgrace for liberators of their country to be slaves in the land they had liberated. All the delegates loudly proclaimed their gratitude to him for, among other things, reminding them to discharge such a solemn and urgent duty. (In the Punic war there had been an enormous num-

Hannibal, cum ab suis non redimerentur, venum dederat.
6 multitudinis eorum argumentum sit quod Polybius scribit
centum talentis eam rem Achaeis stetisse, cum quingenos
denarios pretium in capita quod redderetur dominis sta-
7 tuissent. mille enim ducentos ea ratione Achaia habuit:
adice nunc pro portione quot verisimile sit Graeciam totam habuisse.

8     Nondum conventus dimissus erat, cum respiciunt
praesidium ab Acrocorintho descendens protinus duci ad
9 portam atque abire. quorum agmen imperator secutus
prosequentibus cunctis, servatorem liberatoremque accla-
mantibus, salutatis dimissisque iis eadem qua venerat via
10 Elatiam rediit. inde cum omnibus copiis Ap. Claudium
legatum dimittit; per Thessaliam atque Epirum ducere
11 Oricum iubet atque ibi se opperiri: inde namque in animo
esse exercitum in Italiam traicere. et L. Quinctio fratri,
legato et praefecto classis, scribit ut onerarias ex omni
Graeciae ora eodem contraheret.

    51. Ipse Chalcidem profectus, deductis non a Chalcide
solum sed etiam ab Oreo atque Eretria praesidiis, conven-
2 tum ibi Euboicarum habuit civitatium, admonitosque in
quo statu rerum accepisset eos et in quo relinqueret dimi-
3 sit. Demetriadem inde proficiscitur deductoque praesidio, prosequentibus cunctis sicut Corinthi et Chalcide,

---

142 Valerius Maximus (5.2.6) talks of two thousand Roman
citizens "wearing the cap of freedom" in attendance at Flamininus' triumph, but the figure is unverifiable.

143 A port in northern Epirus convenient for the crossing to
Brundisium: *Barr.* 49 B3 (Orikon).

ber of Roman captives whom Hannibal had sold off when they were not ransomed by their families. An estimate of the total figure could be made from Polybius' comment that the transaction cost the Achaeans 100 talents after they had fixed the amount of compensation for the masters at 500 denarii per head. On that reckoning Achaea contained 1,200. On the basis of that ratio now calculate the number the whole of Greece probably held.)[142]

The assembly had not yet been adjourned when the delegates caught sight of the garrison coming down from Acrocorinth, heading straight for the gate and leaving. The commander followed the column, all the delegates streaming after him and hailing him as their savior and liberator. He then saluted them and took his leave, and returned to Elatia by the same road by which he had come. From there he sent off his legate Appius Claudius with all his troops, instructing him to march through Thessaly and Epirus to Oricum[143] and wait for him there; it was from there that he intended to take his army across to Italy. He also wrote to his brother, Lucius Quinctius, who was his legate and navy commander, ordering him to bring together in that same location transport vessels from all along the Greek coastline.

51. Flamininus then set off for Chalcis, where, after removing the garrisons not only from Chalcis but also from Oreus and Eretria, he convened a meeting of the Euboean states. There he pointed out to the representatives the circumstances in which he had found them and those in which he was now leaving them, and after that adjourned the meeting. He then made for Demetrias. Here he removed the garrison and, with all the citizens escorting him (as had happened at Corinth and Chalcis),

4  pergit ire in Thessaliam, ubi non liberandae modo civitates erant sed ex omni conluvione et confusione in ali-
5  quam tolerabilem formam redigendae. nec enim temporum modo uitiis ac violentia et licentia regia turbati erant,
sed inquieto etiam ingenio gentis, nec comitia nec conventum nec concilium ullum non per seditionem ac tumultum
iam inde a principio ad nostram usque aetatem traducen-
6  tis. a censu maxime et senatum et iudices legit, poten-
tioremque eam partem civitatium fecit cui salua et tran-
quilla omnia esse magis expediebat.

52. Ita cum percensuisset Thessaliam, per Epirum Ori-
2  cum, unde erat traiecturus, venit. ab Orico copiae omnes
Brundisium transportatae; inde per totam Italiam ad urbem prope triumphantes non minore agmine rerum cap-
3  tarum quam suo prae se acto venerunt. postquam Romam
ventum est, senatus extra urbem Quinctio ad res gestas
edisserendas datus est, triumphusque meritus ab lubenti-
bus decretus.

4  Triduum triumphavit. die primo arma tela signaque
aerea et marmorea transtulit, plura Philippo adempta
quam quae ex civitatibus ceperat; secundo aurum argen-
5  tumque factum infectumque et signatum. infecti argenti
quadraginta tria[47] milia pondo et ducenta septuaginta,
facti vasa multa omnis generis, caelata pleraque, quaedam
eximiae artis; ex aere multa fabrefacta; ad hoc clipea ar-

---

[47] quadraginta tria *Madvig (conl. Plut. Flam. 14.2)*: decem et
octo $B\chi$

---

[144] Outside the *pomerium:* cf. 31.47.7 and note.
[145] On the booty and value of the materials carried in Flamininus' procession, see Briscoe 2.128–29.

carried on to Thessaly, where his task was not only to liberate the states but also restore them to some acceptable order from the whole chaotic mess they were in. For the Thessalians were in turmoil not just because of the problems of the day and the king's violent and wayward behavior, but also because of the turbulent character of their race—from their very beginnings down to our own times they have been able to hold no elections, no meeting and no assembly without dissension and mayhem. Flamininus selected both a senate and judges for them, primarily on the basis of property, and gave greater power to that constituency in the city-states more interested in maintaining overall stability and tranquility.

52. After he had conducted his review of Thessaly, Flamininus came through Epirus to Oricum, the point from which he was to make his crossing. From Oricum all his troops were transported to Brundisium. Then they came through the whole of Italy to the city in what was virtually a triumphal procession, the line of captured goods before the general being no shorter than his own column of men. Arriving in Rome, Quinctius was granted an audience with the senate outside the city[144] so he could give an account of his achievements, and after that he was readily accorded a truly deserved triumph by the well-pleased senators.

His triumph lasted three days. On the first, he put armor, weaponry, and statues of bronze and marble on display in the procession, most of which he had confiscated from Philip rather than captured from the states. On the second he displayed gold and silver, wrought, unwrought and coined.[145] There were 43,270 pounds of unwrought silver, and in wrought silver many vessels of every shape and size, most with carvings in relief, and some of superla-

6 gentea decem. signati argenti octoginta quattuor milia
fuere Atticorum: tetrachma vocant, trium fere denario-
7 rum in singulis argenti est pondus. auri pondo fuit tria
milia septingenta quattuordecim, et clipeum unum ex
auro totum, et Philippi nummi aurei quattuordecim milia
8 quingenti quattuordecim. tertio die coronae aureae, dona
9 civitatium, tralatae centum quattuordecim; et hostiae ductae, et ante currum multi nobiles captivi obsidesque, inter
quos Demetrius regis Philippi filius fuit et Armenes Nabi-
10 dis tyranni filius, Lacedaemonius. ipse deinde Quinctius
in urbem est invectus. secuti currum milites frequentes,
11 ut exercitu omni ex provincia deportato. his duceni quin-
quageni aeris in pedites divisi, duplex centurioni, triplex
12 equiti. praebuerunt speciem triumpho capitibus rasis secuti qui servitute exempti fuerant.

53. Exitu anni huius Q. Aelius Tubero tribunus plebis
ex senatus consulto tulit ad plebem plebesque scivit uti
duae Latinae coloniae, una in Bruttios altera in Thurinum
2 agrum, deducerentur. his deducendis triumviri creati,
quibus in triennium imperium esset, in Bruttios Q. Naevius M. Minucius Rufus M. Furius Crassipes, in Thurinum agrum A. Manlius Q. Aelius L. Apustius. ea bina
comitia Cn. Domitius praetor urbanus in Capitolio habuit.
3 Aedes eo anno aliquot dedicatae sunt. una Iunonis

---

[146] Gold coins first minted by Philip II, Alexander's father.
Such coins with the names of Philip and Alexander continued to
be minted by the Successors in the third century and later.

[147] *corona* (στέφανος) is often not used literally but refers to
a gift of precious metal (cf. 32.27.1 and note).

[148] Slaves wore long hair, so a shaved head was an indication
of release from slavery.

tive workmanship. There were also many vessels made of bronze, as well as ten silver shields. In coined silver there were 84,000 "Attic" coins (they call these "tetrachms," and in each there is a weight of silver equivalent to about three denarii). There were 3,714 pounds of gold, a single shield made of solid gold, and 14,514 gold Philippics.[146] On the third day 114 golden crowns[147]—gifts from the city-states—were carried in the procession; sacrificial animals were paraded; and before the triumphal chariot there were many prisoners and hostages of noble birth, including Demetrius, son of King Philip, and the Spartan Armenes, son of the tyrant Nabis. Then Quinctius himself entered the city and a large crowd of soldiers followed his chariot since the entire army had been brought back from the province. The moneys distributed to these men were: 250 *asses* per infantryman, double that for each centurion, and triple for each cavalryman. A spectacular sight in the triumph was provided by the men who had been released from slavery marching along with their heads shaved.[148]

53. At the end of this year the plebeian tribune Quintus Aelius Tubero, following a decision of the senate, proposed to the plebs the establishment of two Latin colonies, one in Bruttium and a second in the territory of Thurii, and the plebs ratified the proposal. Triumvirs were elected, with a three-year mandate, to establish the colonies and these men were: Quintus Naevius, Marcus Minucius Rufus, and Marcus Furius Crassipes for the Bruttium colony; and Aulus Manlius, Quintus Aelius, and Lucius Apustius for that in the territory of Thurii. The two elections were held on the Capitol by Gnaeus Domitius, the urban praetor.

A number of temples were consecrated that year. One

Matutae in foro holitorio, vota locataque quadriennio ante
4 a C. Cornelio consule Gallico bello: censor idem dedicavit. altera Fauni: aediles eam biennio ante ex multaticio
argento faciendam locarant C. Scribonius et Cn. Domi-
5 tius, qui praetor urbanus eam dedicavit. et aedem Fortunae Primigeniae in colle Quirinali dedicavit Q. Marcius
6 Ralla, duumvir ad id ipsum creatus: voverat eam decem
annis ante Punico bello P. Sempronius Sophus consul,
7 locaverat idem censor. et in insula Iovis aedem C. Servilius
duumvir dedicavit: vota erat sex annis ante Gallico bello
ab L. Furio Purpureone praetore, ab eodem postea consule locata. haec eo anno acta.

54. P. Scipio ex provincia Gallia ad consules subrogan-
dos venit. comitia consulum fuere quibus creati sunt L.
2 Cornelius Merula et Q. Minucius Thermus. postero die
creati sunt praetores L. Cornelius Scipio, M. Fulvius Nobilior, C. Scribonius, M. Valerius Messalla, L. Porcius
3 Licinus et C. Flaminius. Megalesia ludos scaenicos A. Atilius Serranus L. Scribonius Libo aediles curules primi

---

149 It was actually a temple of Juno Sospita (cf. 32.30.10). The
Vegetable Market (Forum Olitorium) lay outside the Porta Car-
mentalis (cf. Richardson 164–65, with fig. 38).

150 For fines used for public projects, cf. 31.50.2 and note.

151 This must be P. Sempronius Tuditanus (96), who promised
a temple to this goddess in 204 (29.36.8). There was no Sempronius Sophus in office during the Punic War.

152 A doublet of this appears at 35.41.8.

153 However, the following chapter also deals with the year
194, suggesting that this sentence has somehow been misplaced.

154 L. Cornelius Scipio Asiagenes (337) was the brother of
Africanus, with whom he served as legate from 207 to 202. He
was consul in 190 (cf. MRR 356, where he appears as Asiaticus).

was the temple of Juno Matuta in the vegetable market,[149] which had been vowed and its building contracted out four years earlier during the Gallic War by the consul Gaius Cornelius, who also now had it consecrated in his position as censor. A second was the temple of Faunus, the construction of which, financed by money from fines,[150] had been contracted out two years earlier by the aediles Gaius Scribonius and Gnaeus Domitius, the latter of whom now saw to its consecration in his position as urban praetor. A temple to Fortuna Primigenia was also consecrated on the Quirinal hill by Quintus Marcius Ralla, a duumvir elected for that purpose, and this had been vowed ten years previously during the Punic war by the consul Publius Sempronius Sophus, who had also, as censor, contracted out its construction.[151] Furthermore, the duumvir Gaius Servilius saw to the consecration on the island of a temple of Jupiter,[152] which had been vowed six years earlier during the Gallic War by the praetor Lucius Furius Purpureo, who had subsequently, as consul, also contracted out its construction. Such were the events of the year.[153]

54. Publius Scipio came from his province of Gaul to appoint the next consuls. In the consular elections Lucius Cornelius Merula and Quintus Minucius Thermus were chosen. The next day the following praetors were elected: Lucius Cornelius Scipio,[154] Marcus Fulvius Nobilior, Gaius Scribonius, Marcus Valerius Messalla, Lucius Porcius Licinus, and Gaius Flaminius. The curule aediles for that year, Aulus Atilius Serranus and Lucius Scribonius Libo, were the first to stage dramatic performances at the

4 fecerunt. horum aedilium ludos Romanos primum senatus a populo secretus spectavit, praebuitque sermones,
sicut omnis novitas solet, aliis tandem quod multo ante
5 debuerit tributum existimantibus amplissimo ordini, aliis
demptum ex dignitate populi quidquid maiestati patrum
adiectum esset interpretantibus, et omnia discrimina talia
quibus ordines discernerentur et concordiae et libertatis
6 aequae minuendae esse: ad quingentesimum quinquagesimum[48] octavum annum in promiscuo spectatum esse;
quid repente factum cur immisceri sibi in cavea patres
7 plebem nollent? cur dives pauperem consessorem fastidi-
ret? novam superbam libidinem, ab nullius ante gentis
8 senatu neque desideratam neque institutam. postremo
ipsum quoque Africanum quod consul auctor eius rei fuisset paenituisse ferunt; adeo nihil motum ex antiquo pro-
babile est: veteribus, nisi quae usus evidenter arguit, stari
malunt.

55. Principio anni quo L. Cornelius Q. Minucius consules fuerunt terrae motus ita crebri nuntiabantur ut non
rei tantum ipsius sed feriarum quoque ob id indictarum
2 homines taederet; nam neque senatus haberi neque res
publica administrari poterat sacrificando expiandoque oc-

[48] quinquagesimum *Glar.*: om. Bχ

---

[155] The first time at the *Megalesia,* but not at any games. The
first dramatic performance at the games is believed to be that of
Livius Andronicus at the *Ludi Romani* in 240 (cf. 31.12.10 note).

[156] Latin *cavea,* the area where the spectators were seated.

[157] Livy earlier claims (44.5, above) that the censors first proposed segregation at the *Ludi Romani,* but it is elsewhere attributed to Scipio (Cic. *Har.* 24; cf. also Val. Max. 4.5.1).

*Megalesia.*[155] It was at the Roman Games presided over by these aediles that the senate was for the first time segregated from the public as spectators and this, as usually happens with any innovation, made people talk. Some thought that the distinguished order had now been accorded a privilege long overdue; others surmised that anything adding to the prestige of the senators detracted from the standing of the common people, and that any such divisions separating the classes must entail a weakening of the harmony and balance of freedoms within the community. For 558 years they had had mixed seating to watch the games, they said—what had suddenly happened to make the senators reluctant to have the common people rub shoulders with them in the audience?[156] Or to make a rich man now disdain the poor man seated next to him? This was a strange and arrogant whim, they said, neither wished for nor set in place by the senate of any people in the past. In the end, they say, even Africanus himself regretted having been the consul to propose the idea.[157] So true it is that no change in time-honored practice wins approval; people prefer to stick with the old ways unless practice clearly finds them wanting.

55. At the start of the year in which Lucius Cornelius and Quintus Minucius were consuls, earthquakes were reported so often that people grew tired not just of the phenomenon itself but also of the holidays declared because of it. Meetings of the senate could not be held and no public business conducted because the consuls were busy with sacrifices and expiatory rites. Eventually, the

3 cupatis consulibus. postremo decemviris adire libros ius-
4 sis, ex responso eorum supplicatio per triduum fuit. coro-
nati ad omnia pulvinaria supplicaverunt, edictumque est
ut omnes qui ex una familia essent supplicarent pariter.
item ex auctoritate senatus consules edixerunt ne quis,
quo die terrae motu nuntiato feriae indictae essent, eo die
alium terrae motum nuntiaret.

5     Provincias deinde consules prius, tum praetores sortiti.
6 Cornelio Gallia Minucio Ligures evenerunt; sortiti praetores C. Scribonius urbanam, M. Valerius peregrinam, L.
Cornelius Siciliam, L. Porcius Sardiniam, C. Flaminius
Hispaniam citeriorem, M. Fulvius Hispaniam ulteriorem.

    56. Nihil eo anno belli exspectantibus consulibus litte-
2 rae M. Cinci—praefectus is Pisis erat—adlatae: Ligurum
viginti milia armatorum, coniuratione per omnia concilia-
bula universae gentis facta, Lunensem primum agrum de-
populatos, Pisanum deinde finem transgressos, omnem
3 oram maris peragrasse. itaque Minucius consul, cui Ligures provincia evenerat, ex auctoritate patrum[49] in rostra
4 escendit, et edixit ut legiones duae urbanae quae superiore anno conscriptae essent post diem decimum Arretii
adessent: in earum locum se duas legiones urbanas scrip-
5 turum. item sociis et Latino nomini, magistratibus lega-
tisque eorum qui milites dare debebant, edixit ut in Capi-

---

[49] patrum *Mg*: senatus *B*χ

---

[158] The Sibylline Books: cf. 31.12.9 and note.
[159] Luna: cf. 8.4, above, and note.
[160] Arretium (Arezzo): cf. 31.21.1 and note.

decemvirs were ordered to have recourse to the Books,[158] and on their ruling a three day period of supplication was held. People made supplication at the gods' couches with garlands on their heads, and a proclamation was issued that all members of the same household should worship together. Furthermore, on the authorization of the senate, the consuls made a declaration forbidding anyone to report another earthquake on a day on which a holiday had been proclaimed because of a previously reported earthquake.

There followed the provincial sortitions, the consular first, then the praetorian. Gaul fell to Cornelius and the Ligures to Minucius, and of the praetors Gaius Scribonius drew the City Jurisdiction and Marcus Valerius the Foreigners' Jurisdiction; Lucius Cornelius drew Sicily and Lucius Porcius Sardinia; and Gaius Flaminius drew Hither Spain and Marcus Fulvius Farther Spain.

56. The consuls were expecting no hostilities that year but a dispatch arrived from Marcus Cincius—he was prefect at Pisae—with the news that 20,000 Ligurians were up in arms after fomenting a conspiracy throughout the hamlets of the whole tribe. They had ravaged the countryside around Luna[159] first of all, said Cincius, and then passed through the lands of Pisae and overrun the whole coastline. The consul Minucius, to whom the province of Liguria had fallen, therefore mounted the *rostra* with the authorization of the senators and ordered the two urban legions enrolled the previous year to present themselves at Arretium[160] in nine days. He added that he would raise two urban legions to replace them. He also ordered the allies and those with Latin rights (that is, the magistrates and representatives of those under obligation to furnish

6 tolio se adirent. iis quindecim milia peditum et quingentos
7 equites pro numero cuiusque iuniorum discripsit, et inde
ex Capitolio protinus ire ad portam, et ut maturaretur res,
8 proficisci ad dilectum iussit. Fulvio Flaminioque terna milia Romanorum peditum centeni equites in supplementum, et quina milia socium Latini nominis et duceni
equites decreti, mandatumque praetoribus ut veteres dimitterent milites cum in provinciam venissent.

9 Cum milites qui in legionibus urbanis erant frequentes
tribunos plebei adissent, uti causas cognoscerent eorum
quibus aut emerita stipendia aut morbus causae essent
10 quo minus militarent, eam rem litterae Ti. Semproni dis-
cusserunt, in quibus scriptum erat Ligurum decem milia
in agrum Placentinum venisse, et eum usque ad ipsa coloniae moenia et Padi ripas cum caedibus et incendiis per-
populatos esse; Boiorum quoque gentem ad rebellionem
11 spectare. ob eas res tumultum esse decrevit senatus: tribunos plebei non placere causas militares cognoscere quo
12 minus ad edictum conveniretur. adiecerunt etiam ut socii
nominis Latini qui in exercitu P. Corneli Ti. Semproni
fuissent et dimissi ab iis consulibus essent, ut ad quam
diem L. Cornelius consul edixisset et in quem locum
13 edixisset Etruriae convenirent, et uti L. Cornelius consul
in provinciam proficiscens in oppidis agrisque qua iturus
esset, si quos ei videretur, milites scriberet armaretque et

fighting men) to come to him at the Capitol. From them he requisitioned a total of 15,000 infantry and 5,000 cavalry, according to the number of military-aged men each possessed, and instructed them to leave the Capitol, go straight to the city gate and, in order to speed things along, proceed with the conscription. Fulvius and Flaminius were each assigned a supplementary force of 3,000 Roman infantry and 100 cavalry as well as 5,000 infantry and 200 cavalry of the allies and those with Latin rights, and the praetors were given orders to demobilize the veterans when they reached their provinces.

The men in the urban legions approached the plebeian tribunes in large numbers requesting that they examine the cases of those who had either completed their service or had poor health as grounds for exemption. The issue, however, was forestalled by a letter from Tiberius Sempronius in which it was reported that 10,000 Ligurians had invaded the lands of Placentia and had plundered them as far as the very walls of the colony and the banks of the Po, slaughtering and burning as they went; and that the tribe of the Boii was also contemplating rebellion. In view of this, the senate declared a state of emergency and announced that it was not their wish that the plebeian tribunes consider the soldiers' grounds for disregarding the edict to mobilize. They also added orders that allies and holders of Latin rights who had served in the army of Publius Cornelius and Tiberius Sempronius and had been discharged by these consuls were to muster in Etruria on the day and at the location announced by the consul Lucius Cornelius. Further, the consul Lucius Cornelius, who was leaving for his province, was to enroll any men he thought fit in the towns and countryside that he would pass

573

duceret secum, dimittendique ei quos eorum quandoque vellet ius esset.

57. Postquam consules dilectu habito profecti in provincias sunt, tum T. Quinctius postulavit ut de iis quae cum decem legatis ipse statuisset senatus audiret, eaque,

2 si videretur, auctoritate sua confirmaret: id eos facilius facturos si legatorum verba qui ex universa Graecia et magna parte Asiae quique ab regibus venissent audissent.

3 eae legationes a C. Scribonio praetore urbano in senatum introductae sunt, benigneque omnibus responsum.

4 Cum Antiocho quia longior disceptatio erat, decem legatis, quorum pars aut in Asia aut Lysimachiae apud

5 regem fuerant, delegata est. T. Quinctio mandatum ut adhibitis iis legatorum regis verba audiret, responderetque iis quae ex dignitate atque utilitate populi Romani responderi possent.

6 Menippus et Hegesianax principes regiae legationis erant. ex iis Menippus ignorare se dixit quidnam perplexi sua legatio haberet, cum simpliciter ad amicitiam pe-

7 tendam iungendamque societatem venissent.[50] esse autem tria genera foederum quibus inter se pasciscerentur amicitias civitates regesque: unum, cum bello victis dicerentur leges; ubi enim omnia ei qui armis plus posset dedita essent, quae ex iis habere victos quibus multari eos

---

[50] venissent *Ald.*: venisset *Bχ*

---

[161] Menippus was a Macedonian (cf. 36.11.6) who would draw the Aetolians into war with Rome (35.32.2–33.11) and bring about a massacre of a Roman force at Delium (35.51.1–5). Hegesianax was an emissary of Antiochus who had met the Roman commissioners to settle matters in Greece (33.34.2 note).

through on his way; he was to arm them and take them with him, and would have the right to discharge any of them whenever he pleased.

57. After conducting the levy of their troops, the consuls left for their provinces. At this point Titus Quinctius requested that the senate listen to the settlement that he and the ten commissioners had put together and ratify it by their authority if they saw fit. He added that they would the more readily do this if they heard statements from the ambassadors who had arrived from all over Greece, from most of Asia and from the kings. These delegations were ushered into the senate by the urban praetor, Gaius Scribonius and were given courteous replies.

Since the dispute with Antiochus was a longer affair, it was referred to the ten commissioners, a number of whom had met the king in Asia or in Lysimachia. Titus Quinctius was instructed to listen, along with the commissioners, to what the king's ambassadors had to say and give whatever response he could that befitted the dignity of the Roman people and served their interests.

Leading the king's embassy were Menippus and Hegesianax.[161] One of them—Menippus—declared that he could not fathom what was complicated about their mission, since they had come simply to ask for the Romans' friendship and to conclude an alliance with them. There were, he said, three types of treaty by which city-states and kings cemented alliances among themselves. The first was when terms were dictated to those defeated in war: when everything has been surrendered to the party who was superior in the field, it was the victor's right and privilege

8 velit, ipsius ius atque arbitrium esse; alterum, cum pares
bello aequo foedere in pacem atque amicitiam venirent;
tunc enim repeti reddique per conventionem res, et si
quarum turbata bello possessio sit, eas aut ex formula iuris

9 antiqui aut ex partis utriusque commodo componi; tertium esse genus cum qui nunquam hostes fuerint ad amicitiam sociali foedere inter se iungendam coeant; eos neque dicere nec accipere leges; id enim victoris et victi esse.

10 ex eo genere cum Antiochus esset, mirari se quod Romani
aequum censeant leges ei dicere quas Asiae urbium liberas et immunes quas stipendiarias esse velint, quas intrare
praesidia regia regemque uetent; cum Philippo enim

11 hoste pacem, non cum Antiocho amico societatis foedus
ita sanciendum esse.

58. Ad ea Quinctius: "quoniam vobis distincte agere
libet et genera iungendarum amicitiarum enumerare, ego
quoque duas condiciones ponam, extra quas nullam esse
regi nuntietis amicitiae cum populo Romano iungendae:

2 unam, si nos nihil quod ad urbes Asiae attinet curare velit,

3 ut et ipse omni Europa abstineat; alteram, si se ille Asiae
finibus non contineat et in Europam transcendat, ut et
Romanis ius sit Asiae civitatium amicitias et tueri quas
habeant et novas complecti."

to decide what property the vanquished may retain, and what they are to lose to confiscation. The second was when the two parties, evenly balanced militarily, entered a pact of nonaggression and friendship on equal terms. In this case requests for restitution of property and the actual restitution are a matter of mutual agreement, and in cases where possession of property is rendered indeterminate by the war the matters are settled by time-honored legal prescriptions or by the mutual convenience of the parties. The third type was when parties who had never been enemies came together to forge an alliance of friendship on equal terms, and in such cases there was no imposition or acceptance of terms, as that belongs in the context of victorious and defeated parties. Since Antiochus was in the last category, said Menippus, he was surprised that the Romans thought it reasonable to dictate terms to him, specifying which cities of Asia they wanted left free and nontributary, which they wanted to be tribute-paying, and which they forbade the king and the king's troops to enter. This, he said, was how peace should be concluded with Philip, an enemy, but not how a treaty of alliance should be struck with Antiochus, their friend.

58. Quinctius replied as follows: "Since you wish to be precise and to list different ways of contracting alliances, I shall for my part set down two conditions without which (you can report to your king) there can be no alliance contracted with the Roman people. First: if he wants us to pay no attention to the affairs of the cities of Asia, he must keep his hands off Europe completely. Second: should he not stay within the boundaries of Asia but crosses into Europe, then the Romans would also have the right both to safeguard the alliances that they currently have with the Asian states and to contract new ones."

4     Enimvero id auditu etiam dicere indignum esse Hegesianax Thraciae et Chersonesi urbibus arceri Antiochum,
5 cum quae Seleucus, proavus eius, Lysimacho rege bello
victo et in acie caeso per summum decus parta reliquerit,
pari cum laude eadem, ab Thracibus possessa, partim armis receperit Antiochus, partim deserta, sicut ipsam Lysimachiam, et revocatis cultoribus frequentaverit, et quae
strata ruinis atque incendiis erant, ingentibus impensis
6 aedificaverit: quid igitur simile esse ex ea possessione, ita
parta ita reciperata, deduci Antiochum, et Romanos abs-
7 tinere Asia, quae nunquam eorum fuerit? amicitiam expe-
tere Romanorum Antiochum, sed quae impetrata gloriae
sibi non pudori sit.

8     Ad haec Quinctius "quandoquidem" inquit "honesta
pensamus, sicut aut sola aut prima certe pensari decet
principi orbis terrarum populo et tanto regi, utrum tan-
9 dem videtur honestius, liberas velle omnes quae ubique
10 sunt Graeciae urbes, an servas et vectigales facere? si sibi
Antiochus pulchrum esse censet quas urbes proavus belli
iure habuerit, avus paterque nunquam usurpaverint pro
11 suis, eas repetere in servitutem, et populus Romanus susceptum patrocinium libertatis Graecorum non deserere
12 fidei constantiaeque suae ducit esse. sicut a Philippo Grae-

---

[162] Lysimachia had been destroyed by the Thracians in 197,
and Antiochus had adopted a scheme of rebuilding and repopu-
lating it (33.38.10–14).

At this point Hegesianax retorted that this was indeed an insulting proposition for them to listen to—Antiochus was being excluded from the cities of Thrace and the Chersonese! These were areas that his great-grandfather, Seleucus, had won most honorably —defeating King Lysimachus in war and killing him in the field—and then bequeathed to his descendants. When the lands were later occupied by the Thracians, Antiochus had matched his great-grandfather's glorious achievement by recovering some of them with armed force. To others that were deserted, like Lysimachia itself, he had restored their inhabitants, and had also rebuilt at enormous expense what had been ruined and burned.[162] What parallel was there, then, he asked, between Antiochus being deprived of possessions that he had won and retrieved in such a manner, and the Romans keeping out of Asia, which had never been theirs anyway? Antiochus was seeking a treaty of friendship with the Romans, but only one that brought that him honor if he obtained it, not disgrace.

Responding to this, Quinctius said: "Since we are weighing up honor—which should be the only, or at least the prime, consideration for the leading people of the world and for so great a king—which, I ask you, seems more honorable, to want all Greek cities everywhere to be free, or to make them tribute-paying slaves? If Antiochus thinks the noble course for him is to reduce to slavery the cities held by his great-grandfather by the rules of war—but which his grandfather and father never treated as their possessions—then the Roman people also feel that duty and consistency of policy oblige them not to abandon the cause Greek independence that they have taken in hand. As they freed Greece from Philip, so they intend to free

ciam liberavit, ita et ab Antiocho Asiae urbes quae Graii
13 nominis sint liberare in animo habet. neque enim in Aeo-
lidem Ioniamque coloniae in servitutem regiam missae
sunt, sed stirpis augendae causa gentisque vetustissimae
per orbem terrarum propagandae."

59. Cum haesitaret Hegesianax, nec infitiari posset ho-
nestiorem causam libertatis quam servitutis praetexi titulo, "quin mittimus ambages?" inquit P. Sulpicius, qui
2 maximus natu ex decem legatis erat, "alteram ex duabus
condicionibus quae modo diserte a Quinctio latae sunt
3 legite, aut supersedete de amicitia agere." "nos vero" inquit Menippus "nec volumus nec possumus pacisci quicquam quo regnum Antiochi minuatur."

4 Postero die Quinctius legationes universas Graeciae
Asiaeque cum in senatum introduxisset, ut scirent quali
animo populus Romanus quali Antiochus erga civitates
5 Graeciae essent, postulata et regis et sua exposuit: renun-
tiarent civitatibus suis populum Romanum, qua virtute
quaque fide libertatem eorum a Philippo vindicaverit,
eadem ab Antiocho, nisi decedat Europa, vindicaturum.
6 tum Menippus deprecari et Quinctium et patres institit ne
festinarent decernere, quo decreto turbaturi orbem terrarum essent: tempus et sibi sumerent et regi ad cogitandum
7 darent: cogitaturum cum renuntiatae condiciones essent,
8 et impetraturum aliquid aut pacis causa concessurum. ita
integra dilata res est. legatos mitti ad regem eosdem qui
Lysimachiae apud eum fuerant placuit, P. Sulpicium P.
Villium P. Aelium.

---

163 In fact, neither Sulpicius nor Aelius is mentioned as meeting Antiochus in Lysimachia in 196 (cf. 33.39.2 and 33.12, above,
with Briscoe's note [2.105] and Walbank 2.621).

from Antiochus the cities of Asia that are of Greek stock. For colonies were not sent out to Aeolis and Ionia to be slaves of a king but rather to increase the Greek race and spread this ancient people throughout the world."

59. Hegesianax was in a quandary; he could not deny that a more honorable front was provided by the label "freedom" than "slavery." "Enough of all this beating about the bush," said Publius Sulpicius, who was the eldest of the ten commissioners. "Choose one of the two conditions eloquently laid down by Quinctius just now, or else stop talking about a treaty of friendship." "In fact," replied Menippus, "we have neither the wish nor the power to make any agreement by which Antiochus' regal power may be diminished."

The next day Quinctius brought before the senate all the deputations from Greece and Asia so they could see the attitude of the Roman people and that of Antiochus toward the city-states of Greece, and he presented the demands of the king as well as his own. The envoys were to report back to their governments that if Antiochus did not quit Europe the Roman people would champion their states' liberty from him with the same courage and loyalty as they had from Philip. At this Menippus proceeded to entreat both Quinctius and the senators not to rush into a decision by which they would shake the entire world. He should allow both himself and the king time to reflect, he said; the king would reflect when the conditions were reported to him and would either gain some concessions or else make some for the sake of peace. And so the whole question was shelved. It was decided that the envoys to be sent to the king would be those who had been with him at Lysimachia: Publius Sulpicius, Publius Villius, and Publius Aelius.[163]

60. Vixdum hi profecti erant, cum a Carthagine legati bellum haud dubie parare Antiochum Hannibale ministro attulerunt, inieceruntque curam ne simul et Punicum ex-
2 citaretur bellum. Hannibal patria profugus pervenerat ad Antiochum, sicut ante dictum est, et erat apud regem in magno honore, nulla alia arte nisi quod volutanti diu consilia de Romano bello nemo aptior super tali re particeps
3 esse sermonis poterat. sententia eius una atque eadem semper erat, ut in Italia bellum gereretur: Italiam et com-
4 meatus et militem praebituram externo hosti; si nihil ibi moveatur liceatque populo Romano viribus et copiis Italiae extra Italiam bellum gerere, neque regem neque gen-
5 tem ullam parem Romanis esse. sibi centum tectas naves et decem milia peditum mille equites deposcebat: ea se classe primum Africam petiturum; magno opere confidere et Carthaginienses ad rebellandum ab se compelli posse;
6 si illi cunctentur, se aliqua parte Italiae excitaturum Romanis bellum. regem cum ceteris omnibus transire in Europam debere, et in aliqua parte Graeciae copias continere, neque traicientem, et—quod in speciem famamque belli satis sit—paratum traicere.

61. In hanc sententiam cum adduxisset regem, praeparandos sibi ad id popularium animos ratus, litteras, ne quo casu interceptae palam facerent conata, scribere non est

---

164 Hannibal had caught up with him at Ephesus (33.49.7).

60. Barely had these envoys started their journey when ambassadors brought word from Carthage that Antiochus was clearly making preparations for war with the assistance of Hannibal, and they gave rise to anxiety about a Punic war being stirred up at the same time. Fleeing his country, Hannibal had come to Antiochus, as noted above,[164] and was held in great honor by the king for no other reason than that Antiochus had long been considering plans for a war with Rome and nobody could be more fit than Hannibal to participate in discussions on this topic. Hannibal had always had the same unwavering opinion on the subject, namely that the war should be fought in Italy. Italy, he claimed, would furnish both provisions and men for an enemy from abroad; but if no initiative were taken there, and the Roman people were allowed to wage war outside Italy with Italian manpower and troops, neither the king nor any nation would be a match for the Romans. He requested for himself 100 decked ships, 10,000 infantry, and 1,000 cavalry. With the fleet he would head first for Africa, where, he said, he had every confidence that the Carthaginians could also be pushed into revolt by him; and if the Carthaginians held back, he would foment war against the Romans somewhere in Italy. The king should set sail for Europe with the rest of his forces and keep his troops based somewhere in Greece, not making the crossing but being ready to cross, which would suffice to create the impression and start a rumor that war was imminent.

61. After bringing the king around to this point of view, Hannibal felt he should prepare his countrymen's minds for what was to come, but he dared not write a letter in case, intercepted somehow, it gave his project away. He

583

2    ausus. Aristonem quendam Tyrium nanctus Ephesi, expertusque[51] sollertiam levioribus ministeriis, partim donis
partim spe praemiorum oneratum, quibus etiam ipse rex

3    adnuerat, Carthaginem cum mandatis mittit. edit nomina
eorum quibus conventis opus esset; instruit etiam secretis
notis, per quas haud dubie agnoscerent sua mandata esse.

4    Hunc Aristonem Carthagine obversantem non prius
amici quam inimici Hannibalis qua de causa venisset cog-

5    noverunt. et primo in circulis conviviisque celebrata ser-

6    monibus res est; deinde in senatu quidam nihil actum esse
dicere exsilio Hannibalis si absens quoque novas moliri
res, et sollicitando animos hominum turbare statum civi-

7    tatis posset: Aristonem quendam, Tyrium advenam, in-
structum mandatis ab Hannibale et rege Antiocho venisse;
certos homines cotidie cum eo secreta conloquia serere;
in occulto concoqui[52] quod mox in omnium perniciem
erupturum esset.

8    Conclamare omnes vocari Aristonem debere et quaeri
quid venisset, et nisi expromeret, cum legatis Romam
mitti: satis pro temeritate unius hominis suppliciorum

9    pensum esse; privatos suo periculo peccaturos, rem publicam non extra noxam modo sed etiam extra famam noxae
conservandam esse.

10    Vocatus Ariston[53] purgare sese, et firmissimo propug-
naculo uti quod litterarum nihil ad quemquam attulisset;

---

[51] expertusque $\psi$: expertumque $\phi$: exercitusque *B*
[52] concoqui *Tafel*: conloqui *B$\chi$Mg\**: coqui *Crév.*
[53] Ariston *B$\chi$*: Aristo *Mg*

had come across a certain Tyrian, Ariston, at Ephesus, and
had put the man's ingenuity to the test by sending him on
some minor errands. Now he showered him with gifts as
well as promises of rewards, which the king himself had
also approved, and then sent him to Carthage with a set of
instructions. He supplied Ariston with the names of people to meet and also provided him with secret codes from
which the people would clearly recognize that it was from
him that the instructions came.

When this Ariston appeared in Carthage, Hannibal's
enemies found out the reason for his coming as quickly as
did his friends. At first it was a popular topic of conversation in social gatherings and dinner parties, but then some
people declared in the senate that Hannibal's exile had
served no purpose if he could orchestrate revolution in his
absence and cause civil unrest by inciting men to intrigue.
A Tyrian stranger, one Ariston, had arrived in town with
instructions from Hannibal and King Antiochus, they said,
and certain individuals had been engaging in clandestine
discussions with him on a daily basis. Some scheme was
being concocted in secret that would soon erupt to destroy
them all.

There was a general outcry that Ariston should be
brought in and asked why he had come, and that he should
be sent to Rome with a deputation if he had no explanation. They had been punished enough for the reckless
conduct of one man, they said; private citizens could transgress at their own risk but the state must be kept free not
only from guilt but from any whisper of guilt.

When summoned, Ariston protested his innocence and
resorted to his strongest line of defense, that he had
brought no letter to anyone. But his explanation of why he

11 ceterum nec causam adventus satis expediebat, et in eo
maxime haesitabat quod cum Barcinae solum factionis
12 hominibus conlocutum eum arguebant. orta inde alter-
catio est, aliis pro speculatore comprehendi iam et custodiri iubentibus, aliis negantibus tumultuandi causam esse:
13 mali rem exempli esse de nihilo hospites corripi; idem
Carthaginiensibus et Tyri et in aliis emporiis quo[54] fre-
14 quenter commeent eventurum. dilata eo die res est.

Ariston, Punico ingenio inter Poenos usus, tabellas
conscriptas celeberrimo loco super sedem cotidianam magistratuum prima vespera suspendit, ipse de tertia vigilia
15 navem conscendit et profugit. postero die cum sufetes ad
ius dicendum consedissent, conspectae tabellae demptae-
que et lectae. scriptum erat Aristonem privatim ad neminem, publice ad seniores—ita senatum vocabant—
16 mandata habuisse. publicato crimine minus intenta de
paucis quaestio erat; mitti tamen legatos Romam qui rem
ad consules et senatum deferrent placuit, simul qui de
iniuriis Masinissae quererentur.

62. Masinissa postquam et infames Carthaginienses et
inter se ipsos discordes sensit, principibus propter conloquia Aristonis senatui, senatu propter indicium eiusdem
2 Aristonis populo suspecto,[55] locum iniuriae esse ratus,

[54] quo *Holk. 356*: quae *B*χ
[55] sensit, principibus . . . senatui, senatu . . . suspecto *Gel.*:
principibus . . . senatui senatum . . . suspectum *B*χ: principes . . .
sensit, senatum . . . suspectum *Mog.*

[165] That is, the Barca clan, to which Hannibal belonged.
[166] The Carthaginians' notorious *Punica fides* (cf. 31.3 note,
above, and, for the most famous instance of it, 62.12, below).

had come was unsatisfactory and he was particularly disconcerted by their allegation that he had been in conversation only with members of the Barca faction.[165] A dispute then broke out, with some demanding that Ariston be arrested as a spy and imprisoned and others saying that there was no cause for alarm. Arresting visitors for no reason set a bad precedent, these people said; the same thing would happen to Carthaginians both in Tyre and in other mercantile centers that they frequently visited. On that day the issue was left in abeyance.

Ariston now employed some Carthaginian ingenuity[166] on the Carthaginians. As evening fell, he hung a written tablet above the spot where the magistrates sat each day, in the most crowded part of the city, and then, at the third watch, boarded his ship and fled. The next day, when the suffetes took their seats to dispense justice, the tablet was noticed, taken down and read. It said that Ariston had not been carrying private instructions to any one individual but public ones to the elders (which was what they called their senate). Since the charge was now made general, the inquiry into the few suspects lost its intensity. Even so, the decision was made that a deputation be dispatched to Rome to report the matter to the consuls and the senate and, at the same time, to lodge a protest about the wrongs they were suffering at Masinissa's hands.

62. Masinissa was aware that the Carthaginians had been discredited at Rome and were also at each other's throats, the leading citizens distrusted by their senate because of their discussions with Ariston and the senate distrusted by the people because of the information supplied by the same Ariston. Thinking he had an opportunity

agrum maritimum eorum et depopulatus est, et quasdam urbes vectigales Carthaginiensium sibi coegit stipendium

3 pendere. Emporia vocant eam regionem: ora est minoris Syrtis et agri uberis; una civitas eius Lepcis: ea singula in

4 dies talenta vectigal Carthaginiensibus dedit. hanc tum regionem et totam infestam Masinissa et ex quadam parte dubiae possessionis, sui regni an Carthaginiensium esset,

5 effecerat. et quia simul ad purganda crimina et questum de se Romam eos ituros comperit, qui et illa onerarent suspicionibus et de iure vectigalium disceptarent legatos et ipse Romam mittit.

6 Auditi de Tyrio advena primum Carthaginienses curam iniecere patribus ne cum Antiocho simul et Poenis bellan-

7 dum esset. maxime ea suspicio crimen urgebat quod quem comprensum Romam mitti placuisset nec ipsum nec navem eius custodissent.

8 De agro deinde cum regis legatis disceptari coeptum.

9 Carthaginienses iure finium causam tutabantur, quod intra eos terminos esset quibus P. Scipio victor agrum qui iuris esset Carthaginiensium finisset, et confessione regis,

10 qui cum Apthirem[56] profugum ex regno suo cum parte

---

[56] Apthirem *Briscoe*: Amphirem *B*: Aphirem *χ*: Anthirem *Mg*: Aphthirem *Weiss*.

---

[167] Greek Ἐμπόρια (Markets). If Leptis (Lepcis) Magna (below) is included among the "Markets," then the area must have stretched from the Lesser Syrtes (*Barr.* 35 C1) to Leptis Magna (G2), a distance of well over two hundred miles.

to hurt them, he raided their coastal farmlands and also forced a number of cities that paid tribute to the Carthaginians to remit their taxes to him. The area in question they call The Emporia;[167] it is on the coastline of the lesser Syrtes and is a fertile area. One of the city-states here is Lepcis, which paid taxes to the Carthaginians at a rate of a talent a day. Masinissa had at this time brought disorder into the whole region and also raised doubts about territorial rights to part of it, creating uncertainty over whether it belonged to his kingdom or to the Carthaginians. He also discovered that the Carthaginians were about to go to Rome to clear themselves of the charges against them and at the same time to complain about him; and so he himself also sent a deputation to Rome to lend weight to the charges against them by fostering suspicion and to raise arguments about the tribute rights.

The Carthaginians were granted a hearing first, and their account of the stranger from Tyre fired the senators with anxiety that they might have to fight wars simultaneously with Antiochus and the Carthaginians. The suspicious circumstances particularly told against the Carthaginians: having decided that the man should be arrested and sent to Rome, they had nevertheless kept guard neither on him nor his vessel.

Then the territorial dispute began with the envoys of the king. The Carthaginians defended their position by reference to their boundary rights—the area in question, they said, lay within the limits defined by their conqueror Publius Scipio for lands under Carthaginian jurisdiction—and by reference to the king's own words. For when Masinissa was pursuing Apthir, a fugitive from his kingdom who was at large in the area of Cyrene with a group of

589

Numidarum vagantem circa Cyrenas persequeretur, precario ab se iter per eum ipsum agrum tamquam haud
dubie Carthaginiensium iuris petisset.

11      Numidae et de terminatione Scipionis mentiri eos arguebant, et si quis veram originem iuris exigere vellet,
quem proprium agrum Carthaginiensium in Africa esse?
12  advenis, quantum secto bovis tergo amplecti loci potuerint, tantum ad urbem communiendam precario datum:
quidquid Bursam, sedem suam, excesserint, vi atque iniu-
13  ria partum habere. neque eum de quo agatur probare eos
posse non modo semper ex quo ceperint[57] sed ne diu quidem possedisse. per opportunitates nunc illos nunc reges
Numidarum usurpasse ius, semperque penes eum posses-
14  sionem fuisse qui plus armis potuisset. cuius condicionis
res fuerit priusquam hostes Romanis Carthaginienses,
socius atque amicus rex Numidarum esset, eius sinerent
esse, nec se interponerent quo minus qui posset teneret.
15      Responderi legatis utriusque partis placuit missuros se
in Africam qui inter populum Carthaginiensem et regem
16  in re praesenti disceptarent. missi P. Scipio Africanus et

[57] ceperint χ: coeperint B

---

[168] This episode is misplaced. In Polybius it comes much later
(31.21.7): see Walbank 3.489–91.

[169] "Bursa" (according to Strabo [17.3.14] the Phoenician for
"citadel," or "their citadel), was associated by the Greeks with
their word "bursa" (hide), whence, the famous story, adumbrated
here, of the Phoenician settlers being granted only as much land
as could be covered by a single ox hide. Using "typically Punic"
cunning, they cut the hide into strips so that it would enclose
more ground (cf. Verg. *Aen.* 1.365–68).

Numidians, he had asked the Carthaginians, as a favor, for permission to pass through the very land in question, thus indicating that it was quite clearly under Carthaginian jurisdiction.[168]

The Numidians claimed that the Carthaginians were lying about the Scipionic boundary, and added the question of what territory in Africa was genuinely Carthaginian, anyway, if one wished to examine the true beginnings of property rights there. As new immigrants, they said, the Carthaginians had, in order to build a city, been granted as a kindness as much ground as they could encompass with a bull's hide cut in strips. Whatever they now possessed beyond their original settlement, the Bursa,[169] they had acquired unlawfully by force. As for the territory in question, the Carthaginians could not even prove long-term possession of it since the time they captured it, and certainly not timeless possession of it. The Carthaginians and the kings of Numidia had alternated claim to it as the opportunity arose and possession had always rested in the hands of the one who was militarily the stronger. The Numidians therefore asked the Romans to leave matters stand as they were before the Carthaginians had become Rome's enemy and the king of the Numidians had become her ally and friend, and not obstruct possession of the territory by whoever was capable of holding it.

It was decided that the embassies of both sides be given the answer that the senate would send a commission to Africa to arbitrate on the spot between the people of Carthage and the king. The commissioners sent were Publius

C. Cornelius Cethegus et M. Minucius Rufus, audita inspectaque re, suspensa omnia neutro inclinatis sententiis
17 reliquere. id utrum sua sponte fecerint, an quia mandatum ita fuerit, non tam certum est quam videtur tempori
18 aptum fuisse integro certamine eos relinqui; nam ni ita esset, unus Scipio vel notitia rei vel auctoritate, ita de utrisque meritus, finire nutu disceptationem potuisset.

Scipio Africanus, Gaius Cornelius Cethegus, and Marcus Minucius Rufus. After hearing both sides and making an inspection, they decided in favor of neither party and left everything up in the air. Whether they reacted spontaneously or under orders is not clear; but it *is* clear that leaving the parties with the dispute unresolved suited the needs of the moment. Otherwise, from his expertise in the matter or through the authority he had acquired by his services to both parties, Scipio could have brought closure to the dispute on his own with a nod of his head.

# LIBRI XXXIV PERIOCHA

Lex Oppia, quam C. Oppius trib. pl. bello Punico de fi-
niendis matronarum cultibus tulerat, cum magna conten-
tione abrogata est, cum Porcius Cato auctor fuisset ne ea
lex aboleretur. is in Hispaniam profectus bello, quod Emporiis orsus est, citeriorem Hispaniam pacavit. T. Quinctius Flamininus bellum adversus Lacedaemonios et tyrannum eorum, Nabidem, prospere gestum data his pace,
qualem ipse volebat, liberatisque Argis, qui sub dicione
tyranni erant, finiit. res praeterea in Hispania et adversus
Boios et Insubres Gallos feliciter gestae referuntur. senatus tunc primum secretus a populo ludos spectavit. id ut
fieret, Sextus Aelius Paetus et C. Cornelius Cethegus
censores intervenerunt cum indignatione plebis. coloniae
plures deductae sunt. M. Porcius Cato ex Hispania triumphavit. T. Quinctius Flamininus, qui Philippum, Macedonum regem, et Nabidem, Lacedaemoniorum tyrannum,
vicerat Graeciamque omnem liberaverat, ob hoc [rerum
factarum multitudinem][58] triduo triumphavit. legati Car-

[58] rerum . . . multitudinem *secl. Rossbach*

# SUMMARY OF BOOK XXXIV

The Oppian Law, which the plebeian tribune Gaius Oppius had brought in during the Punic War and which was aimed at suppressing ladies' extravagance was repealed after heated debate, although Porcius Cato had advocated against rescinding the law. Cato set off to Spain and brought peace to Hither Spain in a war that he embarked on at Emporiae. Titus Quintius Flamininus brought to an end the war that he had successfully fought against the Lacedaemonians and their tyrant Nabis, giving them a peace that accorded with his own wishes and liberating Argos, which was in the tyrant's power. There is in addition an account of the successful campaigns in Spain and also against the Boii and the Insubrian Gauls. The senate then for the first time watched the games in an area separated from the general public. This happened through an intervention by the censors Sextus Aelius Paetus and Gaius Cornelius Cethegus and was received with anger by the common people. Several colonies were established. Marcus Porcius Cato held a triumph over Spain. Titus Quinctius Flamininus, who had conquered Philip, king of Macedon, and Nabis, tyrant of the Lacedaemonians, celebrated a triumph lasting three days for this achievement. Ambassadors of the Carthaginians brought word that Hannibal,

thaginiensium nuntiaverunt Hannibalem, qui ad Antiochum confugerat, bellum cum eo moliri. temptaverat autem Hannibal per Aristonem Tyrium sine litteris Carthaginem missum ad bellandum Poenos concitare.

who had sought refuge with Antiochus, was assisting him in fomenting war. In addition to that, Hannibal had, through the agency of the Tyrian Aristo, whom he had sent to Carthage without documentation, tried to instigate the Carthaginians to war.

# INDEX

The Index follows Briscoe's Teubner in citing book and chapter numbers rather than page numbers (as does the former Loeb edition).

611

# INDEX